EUROPEAN POLITICAL PARTIES

EUROPEAN
POLITICAL PARTIES

edited by
Stanley Henig and John Pinder

PEP
Political and Economic Planning
12 Upper Belgrave Street
London

London
GEORGE ALLEN & UNWIN LTD
RUSKIN HOUSE   MUSEUM STREET

PRINTED IN GREAT BRITAIN
in 10 *on* 12 *pt Times type*
BY UNWIN BROTHERS LIMITED
WOKING AND LONDON

CONTENTS

LIST OF AUTHORS

Dr P. Allum, *Department of Politics, University of Reading.*

Professor N. Andren, *Professor of Political Science, University of Copenhagen.*

Dr P. Baehr, *Lecturer in International Relations, University of Amsterdam*

Professor B. Chubb, *Department of Political Science, Trinity College, Dublin.*

M. Forsyth, *Department of Politics, University of Leicester.*

S. Henig, MP, *Political and Economic Planning.*

K. Hill, *Department of Politics, University of Leicester.*

Professor C. J. Hughes, *Department of Politics, University of Leicester.*

Dr R. Morgan, *Assistant Director of Studies, Royal Institute of International Affairs.*

Dr P. G. J. Pulzer, *Christ Church, Oxford.*

M. Steed, *Department of Government, University of Manchester.*

FOREWORD

Our object in this study has not been simply a collection of essays on each European nation's political parties. As far as possible we wanted to produce a genuinely comparative study with certain common themes running through all the national chapters. To this end there were two contributors' seminars and a continuous exchange of ideas and information between authors and editors. Responsibility for individual chapters was allocated as follows:

Austria—Dr P. Pulzer
Belgium—Mr K. Hill
France—Mr M. Steed
Germany—Dr R. Morgan
Ireland—Professor B. Chubb
Italy—Dr P. Allum
Netherlands—Dr P. Baehr

Scandinavia—Professor N. Andren
Switzerland—Professor C. J. Hughes
United Kingdom—Mr S. Henig
European Assemblies—Mr M. Forsyth

Mr Henig was also responsible for the Introductory and Concluding chapters. Bibliographical information was compiled by Miss S. Knopp. Information on the Christian Democratic international movement was supplied by Dr K. J. Hahn. In addition, many other people, far too numerous to acknowledge individually, helped in a variety of important ways, particularly by reading manuscripts and supplying information and ideas. Above all, the editors owe a great debt of thanks to Mrs M. Rees for an inordinate amount of secretarial work without which this book would never have appeared. Finally, the whole project was made possible by a grant to PEP from the Ford Foundation.

S.H./J.P.

CHAPTER 1

INTRODUCTION

The concept of party is now generally recognized in political science as a universal phenomenon. Essentially the party is a group of people acting together for political purposes, with objectives defined in terms of the relations between different sections of society and the appropriate role of government. It is not necessary for a party to possess a strict and total ideology: on the other hand, common ideas and policies are an essential bond. The party may also be the political embodiment of certain sectional interests. The characteristic aim is to control, or otherwise influence, governmental machinery in accordance with the ideas and/or interests of the party.

Virtually every country has or has had political parties operating. Once they have appeared, their repression is difficult. They are not limited to democratic countries. Most modern oligarchies find it hard to carry out the functions of government without the aid of a party. Parties nominally suppressed by a regime are frequently able to continue with a clandestine existence. On the other hand, parties in essence and concept seem to be relatively modern. Whilst the historian and political scientist can go back into the annals of time in search of organizations resembling the party, the species, strictly defined, does not appear to date back more than a couple of hundred years. La Palombara and Weiner[1] have attempted to delineate the origins of parties. Drawing on their work we can postulate a number of operational factors. A fairly sharp growth in the amount and complexity of the work needed to run a society places the task beyond the competence of a single man to organize. There is a growing need to employ specialists and other advisers. There will also be the beginnings of the clash and confrontation of economic interests likely to be affected by government decisions. Different

[1] La Palombara and Weiner (ed.), *Political Parties and Political Development*, OUP, London, 1966.

11

views on the running of society become possible and the advantages of influence over the government apparent. Finally, the mass public become more involved in the processes which shape their lives. Parties seek to canalize and give expression to different feelings amongst the governed. One theory links the development of parties to the extension of the suffrage. In its widest sense this has a good deal of truth. Universal suffrage gives an indispensable role to the parties as the link between government and governed. On the other hand, the quest for extension of the suffrage in pre-democratic countries plays an equally formative role in party development.

Perhaps the most useful operational device for the recognition of political parties is that employed by Leon Epstein.[1] He considers a party in any Western democracy to be a 'group, however loosely organized, seeking to elect governmental office-holders under a given label'. Perhaps, though, this ought not to be considered in isolation. At the beginning of the century in Britain, there were Miners' candidates for parliament, yet one could hardly have talked of the Miners as a political party. They ought to be considered an interest group pursuing ends through various means, including the political. It would be appropriate to add to the Epstein definition that the group's primary aim is to seek political power. Since the latter should not be considered indivisible this covers also the case of the party with no aspiration to anything other than minority status.

La Palombara and Weiner differentiate between internally and externally created parties. The former are groups of people, already involved in government and normally on the legislative side, who organize into parties and only later seek a mass base. On the other hand, externally created parties emerge independently of the government processes. They may define their goals in terms of working through the established system, or by trying to overthrow it. In Britain, the Conservative and Liberal parties can be considered as internally created and Labour as externally created. However, differences in origin do not necessarily imply variations in contemporary structure. This leads naturally to a consideration of party typology where much of the pioneering work has been done

[1] Leon Epstein, *Political Parties in Western Democracies*, Pall Mall, London, 1967.

by Duverger.[1] In classifying party organization, he differentiates four types of basic unit: the caucus, the branch, the cell and the militia.

The caucus is the favoured form for a cadre party. These are notables or groups of *élites* who do not seek party strength through mass membership, but rather through family links, traditional influence and governmental manœuvre. Originally, all internally created parties operated through the caucus, but increasingly today they use other forms of organization as well. Most major, modern parties in West European countries cater for a mass membership and are organized through branches. This does not necessarily imply that the members have complete democratic control over the party: it does, however, indicate a function expressed in terms of gaining popular support. The cell too may be a feature of mass membership parties although it resembles the caucus in exclusiveness and secrecy. Specifically, it is an invention of the Communist movement and each cell operates as the chosen instrument of the central party organization in electoral contests and in efforts to penetrate other organizations. Finally, the militia is a regular weapon of parties designed, in fact as well as in theory, for the rapid revolutionary overthrow of existing government. The party becomes a kind of private army and its co-existence on a long-term basis with parties organized in alternative ways seems improbable.

Considerations of party structure throw out a number of possible courses for analysis which will be considered in this book. Perhaps the most interesting, and one which has attracted political scientists and sociologists ever since the work of Michels,[2] is the question of the distribution of power inside political parties. At one extreme is the party which seeks members simply to strengthen its machine. The members are like soldiers, expected to take orders from those in control and to implement policies in the formulation of which they have virtually no influence. This typifies the single party in one-party countries where there is a complete monopoly of political power. It is also an aspiration, but one less easily fulfilled, of totalitarian parties operating in pluralist or democratic countries.

[1] M. Duverger, *Political Parties* (2nd English Edition), Methuen, London, 1959.

[2] Michels, *Political Parties* available in various editions, particularly Dover, London, 1962.

Opposed to this is a theoretical model giving each member of the organization a full and equal share in the elaboration of policy. That this model is theoretical is clear from the fact that the operation of these rights by the first members of a party must prejudice their exercise by subsequent recruits. In any case, political power can no more be equally divided inside a party than it can be inside society as a whole. Nonetheless, the degree of rank and file control over the leadership of a party will be a major theme in this book.

A major, perhaps the major, determinant of the structure and function of political parties is the nature of the society within which they are operating. A three-fold classification may be suggested: one-party states where a single political party is tolerated and organizes through itself political society; other forms of dictatorship in which all political parties are outlawed and thus may become the foci for opposition; and democratic countries in which various parties organize and co-ordinate the struggle for political power. An essential difference is between those parties enjoying a political monopoly inside their society and those which can, at best, only share power. In a country like the Soviet Union or Communist China, one party controls the regime and thus defines the conditions under which it operates. In a democratic country, by way of contrast, the regime is rather more than the sum of all the parties for it determines the rules under which they operate. The state, in its widest sense, is not simply the instrument of party. In establishing the essential character of democratic countries, parties play a prime role. Three vital characteristics of democracy are the existence of established rules and procedures regulating the government, the guarantee of existence and organization for minorities and an ordered process by which one group may hope to gain control over the government from another. Clearly, this accords a very special role to political parties.

In this book, the countries to be considered are all democratic, despite differing histories. The countries are also all in Western Europe, so that the study may make some small contribution to 'European' literature. As will be shown later in this chapter, parties stand in a very special position towards the movement for European integration. A chapter on European assemblies will have a look at the first rudimentary steps towards the organizing of parties on a European basis. Otherwise the bulk of the book will be taken up with country-by-country chapters in which there will be an analysis

14

of the party system and a structural-functional consideration of each major party. In considering the overall system, special interests will be the number of parties, their role in, and effect on, government, and interrelation with the electoral system. In examining the parties individually, major areas of interest will be sources of membership, finance and electoral support and the internal distribution of power. It is to place these endeavours in an appropriate framework that the rest of this chapter will consider in general terms the functions fulfilled by parties in democratic countries, and also the role they can play in integrating societies.

The first function of the party in a democratic country is normally the recruitment of personnel for government, particularly on the legislative and administrative side. A good many Western systems have tried to preclude the intrusion of this onto the administrative side. The bureaucracy is, thus, given the power of recruitment for itself. Even then, promotion may be not unconnected with party patronage, as in France. In Austria and Italy, political placing in the administration is more normal. For the fourteen countries considered in this book, recruitment of legislators is a universal party function; recruitment of the executive is a party function everywhere save perhaps in Fifth Republic France; recruitment of administrators is a function of parties in certain systems. One might conclude tentatively that it is a 'natural' function of parties to try to recruit for all these positions, but the political systems operating in certain countries are deliberately designed to prevent them fulfilling this.

As mentioned, recruitment of legislators is a universal function, and, in fact, it is virtually impossible for a citizen to aspire to this kind of service without party membership. Where the executive is drawn from the ranks of parliament—which is the case in a majority of Western democracies—party membership is obviously a major qualification. Where the head of the executive is directly elected himself, he is likely to need party support to gain his position. However, he may not be constrained to fill all ministerial positions from party ranks. This is illustrated by the United States and also Fifth Republic France.

It can be suggested that recruitment through party is not the ideal method of achieving the best management of society. A successful party politician may not be a good legislator or a good member of

15

the executive. On the other hand, a government of philosopher-kings is not a very practicable proposition. In any case, parties add to their recruitment function a second task which is quite essential to the ordered workings of government.

Parties ensure that members of a government at different levels are bound together by certain common theories and policies. Whilst it might be purely a matter of good administrative expertize as to which economic policies will best produce which goals, the selection of the latter can be only a question of values. For example, the economist can tell us that the equal distribution of income is likely to mean less individual saving in total than a very unequal distribution. He can go on to argue that a country needs more savings at a particular time. What he cannot do is to contrast the relative values of equality in income with more savings and make a choice. On the other hand, if confronted with a decision that equal distribution is preferable, the economist may again produce a scheme for avoiding the harmful effects of inadequate saving. This gives a perspective to the ideal relationship between parties and bureaucracies. Politicians determine goals and civil servants find the best means of fulfilling them. It is then the job of the parties to work out ideas on the best uses of government and desirable policies to follow. On the other hand, the desirable pattern is frequently not the actual. Under the spoils system, amateur politicians may become imitation experts with disastrous consequencies. The reverse of the coin is the tendency of the professional civil servants to use their own expertize to impose different goals on the amateur politician.

In working out ideas on government, parties fulfil a further useful function in acting as the catalyst for political discussion. This takes place both between parties and inside them, and is likely to play an important role in the evolution of political thought. Moreover, this involves a large number of people at some level or other in helping to determine the direction of society. This involvement is perhaps a separate function, for it is the parties which make it possible for a large number of people in many walks of life to play a part in politics. This can be through joining in discussions inside the party, the result of which may be changes in political philosophy, or participating in the electoral drive of the party and thus determining who will be the legislators and the executive.

The fifth function of parties follows naturally: to act as a link between public opinion and government. They help to ensure that the government keeps in touch with the desires of the public, especially those sections which initially supported them. The party has the task of trying to explain, or explain away, government policies to the public. This is a crucial role for party activists. The latter may not control what is being done by their leaders in their name. However, the leaders are likely to use the activists as a sounding board for what is likely to be generally acceptable to public opinion.

The exact relationship between party and public opinion makes a fascinating study. Any system distorts in a variety of ways the expression of public opinion, which is only indirectly responsible for the particular system in which it manifests itself. President de Gaulle argued that the multifarious parties of the Fourth Repulic represented France as in a cracked mirror: they emphasized the points of disunity. He claimed in his own person to embody the real, united France. In practice, public opinion in France was clearly more complicated than this simple description, manifesting itself in support for both de Gaulle and the historical parties. The 'real' France, though, may be no more accurately revealed by a Presidential than by a legislative election. The British and American systems produce a dual polarization on practically every major issue of the day. Clearly, reality is more complicated. Yet as well as reflecting the public, parties also help to create mass opinion and this introduces a sixth function.

Through their political discourse, the parties have an educative effect on the public who become versed in the great controversies of the day. In a democratic country, the distortions which the parties might give to an issue are alleviated by their own competition. John Stuart Mill justified democracy by, amongst other things, the suggestion that the involvement of all people in the governmental process at some level or another has an educative effect. The competition by the parties for general support enables them to take over this role for the democracy in which they operate.

Emerging from this functional analysis is the central role of party in interest aggregation: the bringing about of sufficient consensus in society on political questions for stable government by consent to be possible. It is worth noting that in the one-party state, this function is fulfilled by one monololithic if heterogeneous party.

On the other hand, in countries with more than one party, a useful distinction can be made between those with just two *majoritaire*[1] parties alternating in power and those operating a multiparty system where coalition between two or more groups is the norm. In the two-party system much interest aggregation takes place inside each major group. However, in the multiparty system, a great deal of the aggregation takes place through the act of coalition. In either case, though, the parties in their role as the forum for political discourse concentrate on themselves society's discussions on the desirable ends of government. The parties making up the government should ensure that decisions reflect the wishes and desires of at least a large part of society. In turn, when governmental decisions have been made, party machinery may help in making them acceptable to the public. In old and traditionally established societies, parties are likely to reflect the degree of homogeneity that it has been possible to establish. In newer societies, the parties are required to undertake a more positive role in creating consensus through interest aggregation. This is particularly true in nascent federations, where at the outset factors making for unity may be only fractionally stronger than more fissiparous tendencies. The historic example is the United States of America.

Despite the fact that American political parties are themselves loosely articulated at the national level, their existence has been necessary for building a stable political system in a heterogeneous continent. Significantly, there has been only one occasion in US history when the national political parties all broke down and when all consensus gave way to pure sectionalism; this was in the period just preceding the Civil War. Another interesting case-study concerns the incipient West Indies Federation. This was always controversial, but in its brief history no genuinely federal political parties emerged. Alignments were little more than electoral coalitions. The failure to produce federal parties may not have caused the breakdown, but the lack of political consensus which this illustrated certainly paralleled and reflected it. Switzerland is Western Europe's only country with a genuinely federal tradition. The existence of political parties cutting across cantonal, ethnic and religious boundaries

[1] This Anglo-French term designates parties which can aspire to a majority. Majoritaire party is the logical opposite of a minority party.

18

has been a crucial stabilizing factor since the Civil War in the 1840s. Facing similar problems, the very survival of Belgium as one country must be bound up with the continued existence of some national political parties.

This is the additional reason for focusing this study on Western Europe. Here are the beginnings of an attempt to bring about greater unity, perhaps even a federal state, through the process of integration—the assimilation of the differing ends and procedures of government of a number of European countries. Now the parties can be looked on as an object of this process, in the same kind of way as the legislature and bureaucracy can be. However, the parties' role must be active as well as passive. If the object of the integration process is the creation of a new community, then diverse interests must be aggregated and a degree of consensus established. This is a function that in West European society must fall heavily on political parties. The closer Europe moves towards unity, the greater the need for parties to establish close and institutionalized links with their equivalents in other countries. As decisions taken at the centre of the nascent community begin to impinge on the lives of all citizens in the different member countries, the role of the parties will become more crucial.

In these circumstances, different developments by Western Europe's political parties are possible. One can assume that some links will exist between different parties on a transnational basis. If the consensus does not exist for even the loosest links, it is hard to imagine any further progress towards the 'European' idea. That this degree of consensus exists inside the European Community, resulting in trans-national party groups, will be shown in the chapter on Parties in the European Assemblies. However, the links can ultimately take different forms: European-wide parties may emerge into which existing national groups will merge their identity, or progress may be limited to loose alliances and electoral coalitions. The nature of the organization chosen by the parties will reflect existing progress towards integration, but it will also affect the future. Given the importance of Europe's decision and the vital role the parties must play in it, there is ready justification for this book to consider the international links and attitudes of parties operating in a national framework, in an attempt to ascertain how far the conditions for co-operation can be said to exist.

In conclusion, this book has two functions. First, it sets out to supply the essential material for any comparative considerations relating to West European political parties. Second, it tries to estimate the degree to which national parties seem likely to be able to adjust their activities to help fulfil essential roles in the process of European integration.

CHAPTER 2

THE FEDERAL REPUBLIC OF GERMANY

'I see no parties any more: I see only Germans.' The Kaiser's triumphant expression of satisfaction in August 1914, after the quasi-unanimous approval of his government's war credits by the Reichstag, also reflected his feeling that the political system had returned to normal. 'Parties', indeed, have been regarded by many Germans, both before and since the Kaiser, as something unhealthy and abnormal. Perceived as representatives either of particular ideological commitments such as socialism or Catholicism, or of the sectional economic interests of manual workers, farmers or industrialist, political parties were condemned (both verbally and legally) by Bismarck and later by Hitler. In neither case did this condemnation arouse significant protests from the majority of the German people.

Against such a background, special significance attaches to Article 21, Para 1 of the West German Basic Law of 1949, which states quite explicitly 'Parties contribute to the development of the political will of the people. They may be freely founded'.[1] This was not only the first occasion when the role of political parties was written into a constitution; it also affirmed a norm which was by no means central to German political culture.

The century of German political history which separated the collapse of the 1848–49 Revolution from the adoption of the Basic Law in 1949 was on the whole disastrous for the development of political parties. After the quiescent period of the 1850s political parties, committed variously to democracy, liberalism, political Catholicism and socialism, emerged painfully during the 1860s, only to come, each in its turn, into unsuccessful conflict with the Prussian State, then with the German Reich led by Bismarck. When this Reich had been established, its political system—both under Bismarck and under Kaiser Wilhelm II—allotted only a small place

---

1 *Grundgesetz*, Art. 21, Para 1, Edition of C. H. Beck, Munich/Berlin, 1954.

to parties and to the *Reichstag* in which they were represented. Parties, instead of being the recognized channels to political power, remained the representatives of ideological and/or economic interests. After the collapse of the Empire in 1918, its unprepared and stunted political parties found power suddenly thrust on them, and not surprisingly they failed to exercise it effectively, so that their repeated crises and clashes led in 1933 to their brutal suppression from the political scene by Hitler's Third Reich. After twelve years of one-party tyranny, ending in the total political void of 1945, the party leaders who undertook the task of rebuilding Germany's political life were uncomfortably aware that their predecessors had left them more precedents for disaster than for success.

Each of these successive periods in the history of the German party system will be examined later from the point of view of the development of individual parties. Each period should, however, first be examined from the point of view of the salient characteristics which it imprinted on the German party system as a whole.

THE BISMARCKIAN AND WILHELMINE REICH

Three features of the political structure built by Bismarck were of particular importance for the development of political parties. In the first place, the introduction of universal suffrage impelled the representatives of the main shades of political opinion to build more or less highly-structured parties, based on mass membership, for purposes of electoral propaganda and inter-election organization. Secondly, the electoral system introduced by Bismarck, which remained unchanged until 1918, was one in which, although the use of single-member constituencies did something to limit the number of political parties, the institution of a double ballot encouraged each of them to make a pronouncedly ideological appeal to the electorate on the first. Thirdly, Bismarck's careful exclusion of the democratically-elected *Reichstag* from any share in the control of the executive, and its members from any prospect of ministerial responsibility, set sharp upper limits to the ambitions of party leaders, so that despite their mass support and apparent power, they confronted one another, and the government, in the strictest sense as irresponsible representatives of ideological commitments or economic interests.

22

Bismarck, when he gave Germany two successive political structures—the North German Confederation after the war of 1866 against Austria, and the unified Reich after the war of 1870 against France—included in both of them the feature that the *Reichstag* or parliament should be elected by the suffrage of all male Germans over 25. Bismarck's motive in this was to mobilize the force of popular nationalism against the Prussian Liberals who objected to his absolutism and militarism, and against the particularist princes and other political leaders of the non-Prussian states. As well as being influenced by his contact with left wing survivors of 1848, such as Lothar Bucher and Ferdinand Lassalle, Bismarck may also have hoped to attach the German people to his new Empire by making them feel that, through the ballot box, it was theirs also—just as he was later to try to convince them that it could deliver such goods as sickness insurance and old age pensions. To some extent these calculations proved justified, and in the first few all-German elections of the 1870s the majority of votes went to parties wholly committed to Bismarck's new order: Conservatives and National Liberals. The results of Bismarck's decision, however, included the unforeseen one that not just these, but all political parties, faced with the challenge of enlisting and keeping the support of a new mass electorate, had to adopt suitable organizational structures. The German electorate, which numbered just under eight million in 1871, rose to nearly 14·5 million by the eve of the first world war, and the political parties, in their growing ideological sophistication and organizational complexity, more than kept pace with it. The challenge of how to 'encadre' the newly enfranchized masses produced the response of the trained and bureaucratically organized party cadres, especially (as in most countries) in the parties on the left and centre, but also to some extent on the right.

A second salient feature of Imperial Germany's constitutional structure was its electoral system, by which 397 deputies were elected in single-member constituencies on a double ballot. In a constituency where the leading candidate obtained more than 50 per cent of the votes on the first ballot, he was elected outright, but in most cases a run-off second ballot was necessary. This situation, combined with the need to make the maximum appeal to a mass electorate before the vote, and the unhappy certainty that even considerable success in it would not greatly increase their political responsibilities, induced most parties to sharpen their differences with one another to the maximum in presenting their pre-election case. The parties which knew from the beginning that they faced a strong probability of coming together in the second ballot—such as Conservatives and National Liberals who would normally coalesce against the left, or in some cases the various branches of liberalism between themselves—would see no objection to staking out extreme positions before the first ballot, so as to improve their position in the subsequent bargaining. At the other extreme, parties which had great difficulties in concluding electoral alliances—notably, for most of this period, the Social Democrats—found nothing in the system to deter them from adopting the intransigent positions to which they were in any case inclined.

Party politics at Reich level, strongly influenced by universal suffrage of the kind here described, came to bear marked differences from that within some of the Reich's constituent states, where electoral systems and other factors varied considerably. In Prussia —where attempts to introduce universal suffrage were frustrated until the very end of the Empire, and the electoral law was the so-called 'three-class system' which grossly favoured the wealthier classes—both conservatism and Social Democracy were much more extreme than their respective counterparts in the Reich as a whole, and the Kingdom of Saxony produced an even more extreme left-wing form of social democracy for essentially similar reasons. On the other hand, in the South German states of Bavaria and Baden, where universal suffrage was combined with the granting of real political power to the State Parliament or *Landtag*, electoral coalitions between Social Democrats and various brands of Liberals or even the Catholic Centre Party were both possible and fruitful. These contrasts between the conditions prevailing among Germany's various states, and between state level and Reich level, help to explain the divergences within each of the main political viewpoints—conservatism, liberalism, socialism, and political catholicism—which will be discussed later.

The last and most important of Bismarck's three legacies was the deliberately ensured impotence of the parliamentary assembly. The sovereign power in the German Reich was vested in the Emperor, in other words the King of Prussia, who still claimed to rule by

Divine Right. The Imperial *Reichstag* was a direct descendant, via the *Reichstag* of the North German Confederation (1867–71), of the *Landtag* of the Kingdom of Prussia, whose claims to control the King's ministers had been decisively smashed by Bismarck as Minister-President in the early 1860s. Insofar as the Imperial Chancellor (almost invariably the Minister-President of Prussia) was responsible to any assembly at all, it was to the upper house, or *Bundesrat*, a successor of the old federal assembly (*Bundestag*) of the medieval empire, composed of representatives of the state governments and without any vestige of popular representativeness. Even the *Bundesrat*, however, was merely a facade for Prussian supremacy, since Prussia held 17 seats out of a total of 58, ensuring an automatic right of veto against constitutional changes—which could be blocked by 14 negative votes.[1] This provision, combined with the absence of a cabinet system—the Chancellor being the only federal minister, to whom the others, essentially civil servants, were responsible—made any sort of parliamentary control of the executive impossible. The federal bureaucracy soon emerged as simply that of the old Prussian Monarchy writ large (or in some ways not so large: up to 1913 the total revenue and national debt of the Reich were less than those of the State of Prussia), and parliamentary institutions remained an ill-fitting and barely tolerated adjunct to the quasi-absolutist *Obrigkeitsstaat*. In this 'artfully constructed chaos'[2], the *Reichstag*—though it was consulted by the government on matters requiring legislation—was constantly aware of the limitations of its powers. Party leaders with no prospect of bringing down a government by a vote of no confidence, and even less of taking power themselves as a result of an electoral victory, were reduced to sterile confrontation with the government, rather than any sort of interaction or transaction. The civil service remained the road to ministerial office, and so the parliamentary benches were deprived of men of top-rate ability. This in turn made party leaders more prone than ever to regard themselves, on basic issues,

[1] Koppel S. Pinson, *Modern Germany*, Macmillan, N.Y. 1954. For a perceptive general analysis, cf. Herbert J. Spiro, 'The German Political System' in *Patterns of Government* (ed. S. Beer and A. Ulam), Random House, New York, 2nd ed., 1962, pp. 463–592.

[2] Gerhard Loewenberg, *Parliament in the German Political System*, Cornell University Press, 1967, p. 10.

as essentially spokesmen for the economic or ideological interests they represented; they failed on the whole to take a balanced and responsible view of the great questions of Germany's political destiny.

These three characteristics of the Bismarckian and Wilhelmine Reich—universal suffrage, the two-ballot electoral procedure and the impotence of the *Reichstag*—produced a party system characterised by wide ideological differences, sectarian leadership, and almost total inexperience in the responsibilities of government. The party leaders produced by this system were to be forced, after a brief and quite inadequate period of apprenticeship in the last months of the doomed Empire, to take over total responsibility for Germany's political destiny in the stormy beginnings of the Weimar Republic.

THE WEIMAR REPUBLIC

The Weimar Republic, like the regime it succeeded, left a triple legacy to German political party life. The essential characteristics of the situation from 1919 to 1933 were a deeply divided society, with substantial sections of opinion right across the spectrum from extreme right to extreme left; the concentration of sovereignty in an assembly (*Reichstag*) elected by an extreme form of proportional representation allowing every sector of opinion its due parliamentary weight, and encouraging most to proceed along the lines of ideological intransigence and organizational bureaucratization marked out by their predecessors under the Empire; and the existence in the background (looming into the foreground under Hindenburg) of a quasi-monarchical president, endowed with the full prestige of election by universal suffrage and empowered to suspend parliamentary government in an emergency. The presidential institution suggested that government by parties need not be taken too seriously, since an all-wise national father-figure was waiting in the background to clear up the mess if they went wrong.

The deep rifts in German society after the defeat and revolution of 1918, and the party-political rifts which reflected them, are best illustrated by the fact that substantial sections of political opinion rejected the Republic from the beginning. On the Right, the German Nationalist Party won nearly 15 per cent of the votes in 1920 and nearly 9 per cent in November 1932 (together with the 33 per cent won by the Nazis, this produced a victorious coalition), and on the extreme Left, the Communist Party rose from small electoral beginnings in 1920 to just under 17 per cent of the votes in November 1932. Between these two extremes, a wide variety of political parties governed in a series of shifting coalitions: the Social Democrats, the Catholic Centre Party, and the two rival branches of liberalism represented by the Democratic Party and the German People's Party, were the largest groups, but there were others, including a Bavarian separatist party with a steady score of 3 or 4 per cent of the national vote, so that the total number of parties was at times as high as 30.[1] In this situation, it is not surprising that the word 'parties' retained the connotations of 'trouble-making, divisive' implied in the Kaiser's celebrated remark of 1914, nor that German party leaders since 1945 have tried hard to protect themselves against any accusations of similar factiousness.

Secondly, there was the Weimar Republic's electoral system of mathematically exact proportional representation. This was achieved by abandoning the single-member constituencies of the old Empire in favour of a system of 35 very large ones, from which half the members of the *Reichstag* were elected directly, while the remaining seats were distributed to the national lists of the respective parties, in proportion to the votes cast for each of them. The effects of this system included the multiplication of parties represented in the *Reichstag*, and also the organizational strengthening and ideological ossification of nationally-organized political parties. Prevented by their divided state from effectively exercising the supreme power entrusted to the parties by the constitution, leaders reverted to the patterns of behaviour they had developed in their political apprenticeship under the Empire. Instead of seeing themselves as national leaders, they were content to strengthen their authority over their respective party machines, building up their bureaucracy and mass membership and, if anything, sharpening the doctrinaire approach they had learned before 1918. The situation of deadlock in parliament, combined with the persistence of the tradition by which men of real

[1] The election results for the Weimar Republic are conveniently analysed in S. Neumann, *Modern Political Parties*, University of Chicago Press, 2nd ed. 1965. See also on this period S. Neumann, *Die Parteien der Weimarer Republik*, Kohlhammer, Munich, 1965; originally published in 1932.

talent did not on the whole enter party politics, led to a general decline in the authority of parliamentary leaders. The real centres of power in some parties were to be found in national executive committees or occasionally even in party congresses.[1] Thus the ultra-democratic institution of unmodified proportional representation helped to bring about permanent deadlock, in which incessant negotiations between the parties produced ever smaller results in terms of effective government. In March 1930 the break-down of the Great Coalition led by the last Social Democratic Chancellor, Hermann Müller, marked the effective end of this experiment with parliamentary government.

There remained, as a third main feature of the Weimar system, the institution of the powerful President. When the National Assembly was debating the new constitution at Weimar in the early part of 1919, in an atmosphere dominated by menacing external insecurity and incipient domestic revolution from Left and Right, the granting of substantial powers to the President went unquestioned. Apart from the immediate situation, this can be explained by the fear of giving too much power to an elected assembly (as the Third French Republic had clearly suffered from doing), a certain respect for the English type of constitutional monarchy, and the surviving influence of Germany's own recent monarchical past. For several years the powers granted to the President remained in reserve, but after the acute deadlock of parliamentary government early in 1930, and the general election of September of that year (which produced a barely workable assembly, including 107 Nazis and 77 Communists, against a previous strength of 12 and 54 respectively), the transfer of power to the President came almost automatically. The party leaders themselves seemed glad to abdicate to President Hindenburg and to successive Chancellors—Brüning, Papen, and Schleicher—who ruled by virtue of his special powers. The role of the political parties in this system reverted essentially to the inglorious one they had occupied before 1918. Papen's deposition of the Social Democratic government of Prussia in July 1932, and Hitler's abolition of the political parties themselves in the months after he reached power in January 1933, came almost as epilogues. The parties had been unable to cope with the over-dose of power

[1] Loewenberg, *op. cit.*, p. 21.

thrust on them in 1919, and had themselves begun the process of their abasement.

THE FEDERAL REPUBLIC

The makers of the Basic Law or provisional constitution of the West German Federal Republic, in their discussions between the collapse of the Third Reich in 1945 and the Republic's establishment in 1949, were guided by a determination to avoid the weaknesses of the two regimes analysed above. They rejected both previous electoral systems—the double ballot of the Empire and the pure proportional representation of Weimar—and adopted instead one designed to avoid both the fragmentation and the doctrinaire intransigence of political parties. They wanted political power to be in the hands of a Chancellor who would be fully responsible to a democratically elected parliament, and who would normally be the head of the largest party within it; and they took special care to limit the powers of the Federal President to guard against repetition of the accumulation of power by Hindenburg.

This realization that political parties had not on the whole made a very successful contribution to German public life—even though this was partly for reasons beyond their own control—explains why the drafters of the Basic Law took such care to insert the specific description of the role of political parties quoted at the beginning of this chapter. It also explains the prominence given to this description. Article 21, which contains it, appears almost at the beginning of the Constitution, separated from Articles 1 to 19 (a comprehensive statement of the Rights of Man) only by Article 20 which describes the fundamental characteristics of the Federal Republic as 'a democratic and social federal state', in which 'all authority emanates from the people'.[1]

In an attempt to eliminate the fundamental obstacles to the effective working of political parties which had been characteristic of the Bismarckian Empire and the Weimar Republic, the founding fathers of the Federal Republic made several specific provisions.

First, in the electoral system: the Parliamentary Council which elaborated the Basic Law in 1948–49 contained a majority of sup-

[1] *Grundgesetz, op. cit.,* Art. 20, para. 2.

porters of pure proportional representation, but it also contained a large minority—the Christian Democratic Union—who supported the adoption of the British system of single-member constituencies to be won by the candidate obtaining the plurality of votes in a single ballot. The argument between these two tendencies followed classic lines, the former side arguing for mathematical justice for minority groups, and the latter arguing for the greater governmental stability and closer relations with the electorate said to be characteristic of single-member constituencies. In the end, however, a compromise was adopted. Under this system, by which it was hoped to combine the advantages of both proposals, 60 per cent of the members of the *Bundestag* were to be elected as representatives of single-member constituencies, and the remaining 40 per cent by proportional representation. Under this electoral law, which was in force for the first *Bundestag* elections in August 1949, 242 of the 402 members were elected by plurality vote in single-member constituencies, while the other 160 were the first in order on their respective party lists (drawn up on a *Land* basis), on the basis of proportional representation. (This division of MPs into two classes might be expected to make those elected in their own constituencies less amenable to party discipline than those dependent on election through the *Land* list, but, despite their undeniably higher average prestige, there is little evidence that this has happened.) For subsequent elections, from 1953 onwards, the details were varied: the number of members of the *Bundestag* was increased to 497 when the Saar became a *Land* of the Federal Republic, and the percentage of seats filled by proportional representation was increased to 50, but the essentials remained unchanged. A voter is asked, on election day, to give two votes, of which the first is for a specific candidate in his own constituency, and the second for the party list of the elector's choice. This system has encouraged the German electors to give their votes, much more markedly than under any previous political system, to a small number of large, nationally organized parties. As a further inducement to do so, the Electoral Law of 1949 ordained that no party should be represented in the *Bundestag* which did not either secure 5 per cent of the vote in a given *Land*, or obtain a seat by direct election in any constitutency. (This penalty against smaller parties was made more stringent in 1953, when a share of the seats distributed by proportional representation was denied to all parties

30

winning less than 5 per cent of the 'second votes' for the whole Federal Republic, or alternatively one seat—and even this was later changed to three—in the constituency elections.)[1]

Secondly, the power of the Federal Chancellor: the Parliamentary Council of 1948–49, having established an electoral law which was expected to produce a workable governmental majority—both Christian Democrats and Social Democrats voted for the final draft, each expecting to gain a majority—took further steps to make certain that the Chancellor would be in a position to govern effectively. The Basic Law explicitly provides that the Chancellor shall have the support of the majority of votes in the *Bundestag* (which in practice means that he must be the leader of the largest party). In the event of a candidate for the Chancellorship failing to obtain the majority of one half of the votes plus one, the one obtaining the largest number of votes (plurality) is still elected. In the event of such a candidate failing to obtain a majority the Federal President is constitutionally required either to appoint him all the same, or to dissolve the *Bundestag*. These provisions clearly strengthen the power of the Chancellor against any rebellious groups in parliament, including those within his own party. His greatest strength under the Basic Law, however, lies in the innovation of the so-called 'constructive vote of no confidence', by which a Chancellor may only be removed from office if the *Bundestag* majority, by the same vote, can agree on his successor. This provision, designed to protect the Federal Chancellor against the unhappy fate of his predecessors of Weimar (or the heads of governments of the Third and Fourth French Republics) effectively prevents the overthrow of a government by a parliamentary majority which can agree only on a negative vote of no confidence and on nothing else.

Thirdly, the powers of the Federal President: mindful of the abuse of power by Hindenburg the makers of the Basic Law were careful to restrict the powers of the Federal President to the symbolic and representative ones of Head of State, as distinguished from the Head of Government. It is true that in 1959 Chancellor Adenauer considered taking over the office of Federal President with the idea that, in his hands, it might come to resemble the presidency of the

---

[1] The electoral law is conveniently summarized by A. Grosser, *The Federal Republic of Germany*, Praeger, New York, 1964, Chapter IV; see also A. Grosser, *Die Bundesrepublik Deutschland*, Wunderlich Verlag, Tübingen, 1967.

Fifth French Republic, but his realization that there were well-designed constitutional obstacles to this, together with other reasons, made him abandon the idea. The constitution, indeed, while it specifies that the President's signature is required for such public documents as laws, the appointment of federal judges, etc. makes it clear that this is normally only a formality. The President is explicitly prevented from appointing or dismissing a Chancellor on his own authority, selecting cabinet ministers, dissolving parliament, or declaring a state of emergency. For each of these decisions the Basic Law firmly allocates the responsibility to the Federal Chancellor and Federal Government.

As well as these fundamental provisions, designed to ensure the smooth functioning of a parliamentary democracy in which political parties could play a central and constructive role, two further stipulations of the Basic Law are important.

Firstly, there is the rule contained in Article 21, para. 2 of the Basic Law, that 'parties, which according to their objectives or according to the behaviour of their members aim to threaten or to abolish the free democratic basic order, or to endanger the substance of the German Federal Republic, are unconstitutional'. On the basis of this, the Federal Constitutional Court decided in 1952 that a neo-Nazi party, the *Sozialistische Reichspartei* (SRP) was illegal, and this was followed in August 1956 by the banning of the German Communist Party.

Secondly, as provided in Article 21 of the Basic Law, attempts have been made to spell out in more detail the precise constitutional functions of political parties indicated in general terms in that Article, in a so-called 'party law'. Draft legislation to this effect, which attempted to provide legal guarantees of a democratic distribution of power in the interior of political parties, was prepared by the Ministry of the Interior and presented to the Cabinet as early as June 1951, but although it has been discussed in the *Bundestag*, this legislation has not yet been passed. The main reason for this is the unwillingness of two of the major parties, the CDU and the FDP, to agree to the full publication of their sources of financial support, to which political parties had been committed in principle by the Basic Law of 1949, and which the proposed legislation attempted to make them do in practice.[1] Even though the

[1] Günter Olzog, *Die Politischen Parteien*, Olzog Verlag, Munich, 1965, pp. 77–82.

proposed law on political parties has not yet been approved, its conception and discussion, together with the other provisions of Article 21 and a series of decisions of the Federal Constitutional Court, have contributed to establishing in German political life the notion that parties are, in the words of one of these Court decisions (of July 20, 1954), 'necessary elements of the constitutional construction', which, by their contribution to the development of political opinion, 'carry out the functions of an organ of the constitution'.[1]

The legal provisions and proposals of postwar West Germany have thus placed the political parties of the Federal Republic in a stronger position than their predecessors. The electoral laws and other measures have resulted in a steady reduction of the number of parties represented in each successive *Bundestag*: ten in 1949, five in 1953, four in 1957, and three in 1961 and 1965. The share of the votes going to the three largest parties—CDU-CSU, SPD, FDP— has risen steadily at every federal election: 72·1 per cent in 1949, 83·5 per cent in 1953, 89·7 per cent in 1957, 94·1 per cent in 1961, and 95·9 per cent in 1965.[2]

This immense simplification of the German party system has had important effects on the distribution of power within each party. For each of the three main parties, the combination of sizeable representation in the *Bundestag* with either the reality or the good prospect of ministerial office for parliamentary leaders (the reality, for the CDU-CSU, continuously since 1949; for the FDP, intermittently from 1949 until 1966; for the SPD, since 1966 only) have strengthened the position of the latter in relation to back-benchers and the rank and file outside. This reality or prospect of ministerial office, in Germany as elsewhere, has added those factors conducive to oligarchic leadership analysed by Robert McKenzie to those which Robert Michels noted at an earlier stage of German party development.[3] These factors, along with others, now have to be

---

[1] Olzog, *ibid.*, p. 14. See also Ulrich Dübber, *Parteifinanzierung in Deutschland*, Westdeutscher Verlag, Cologne, 1962.

[2] Grosser, *op. cit.* See also *Revue Française de Science Politique*, Vol. XVI, April 21, 1966, p. 280.

[3] Robert McKenzie, *British Political Parties*, 2nd ed., Heinemann, London, 1963. Robert Michels, *Political Parties*, English translation, Dover Books, New York, 1959; London, 1962.

examined in relation to each of the main West German political parties.

THE SOCIAL DEMOCRATIC PARTY OF GERMANY (SPD)

The SPD has had a continuous history among the longest of any political party in the world. In 1963 the party celebrated the centenary of its foundation, under the name of General Association of German Workers, by Ferdinand Lassalle, a flamboyant lawyer and man of letters, a Prussian nationalist and an acquaintance of Bismarck's. His Association merged in 1875 with the Social Democratic Labour Party (otherwise known as the Eisenach Party, from its foundation at a Congress in Eisenach in 1869), led by the anti-Prussian democratic socialists Wilhelm Liebknecht and August Bebel, who were associated with Marx and to some extent influenced by Marxism. From the Unity Congress held at Gotha in 1875 emerged the Socialist Labour Party, and the Gotha Programme was a mixture of the ideas of Lassalle and Marx, which earned the deep scorn of the latter. At its Congress in Erfurt in 1891, the party adopted its present title of Social Democratic Party of Germany (SPD), and a programme of strict Marxist orthodoxy drafted, in the main, by the 'Pope' of German Marxism, Karl Kautsky. In 1921, after the collapse of the Empire had left the SPD, as Germany's biggest party, with the unexpected responsibilities of government, the Erfurt Programme was replaced by a much more moderate and reformist document drawn up at a Congress in Görlitz. After the membership of the SPD was swollen in 1922 by the influx of part of the Independent Social Democratic Party (USPD), the Heidelberg Programme of 1925 was adopted, combining the general commitment to Marxism contained in the Erfurt Programme with the strong emphasis on practical reformist policies contained in the document of 1921. This Heidelberg Programme, with its incongruous juxtaposition of a Marxist *Weltanschauung* and essentially reformist concerns, was retained until the party's reconstruction after 1945. It was replaced by a brief sixteen-point programme at the time of the first federal election in 1949, and then by the much more detailed party programme adopted at the Dortmund Congress in September 1952, which played down the Marxist, and indeed the Socialist element altogether, and concentrated on practical reform proposals and questions of foreign and defence policy. This in turn was replaced, at the Bad Godesberg Congress of November 1959 by an outspokenly revisionist programme, which proclaimed the party's attachment to Christianity, the profit motive, and a programme of moderate social reform. This programme, which was followed in 1960 by the SPD's acceptance, through the mouth of Herbert Wehner, of a bipartisan foreign policy, contributed considerably to the electoral successes of the SPD in 1961 and 1965. There is no doubt that the Bad Godesberg programme represented an outspoken 'revision' of the SPD's traditional socialist objectives—a parallel in the British Labour Party would perhaps only have occurred if Gaitskell had succeeded in obtaining the revision of Clause 4 of the party constitution—but it is open to debate whether the SPD's governmental policies, at *Land* level and since 1966 at Federal level, have in fact been less 'socialist' than those of the British Labour Party.[1]

Where does power lie in the SPD? As the foregoing survey of successive programmes has suggested, the highest policy-making body (this is confirmed in the party's organizational statutes) is the party congress. In the years since 1945, however, real power has lain more clearly than ever in the hands of the leadership, partly because congresses—in contrast to the practice before 1933—have met only every two years. The two other bodies with formal responsibility for determining policy are the parliamentary group in the *Bundestag* (known as the *Fraktion*), and the Executive or *Vorstand*. The parliamentary group consists of all the SPD members of the *Bundestag* (202 after the election of September 1965); it elects its own committee of 23 members including a Chairman—a post held successively by Schumacher, Ollenhauer, Erler, and since 1965 by Helmut Schmidt—and also a Chief Whip, who has since 1949 been Karl Mommer. The group, like that of other parties, is responsible for deciding on parliamentary tactics, presenting Bills in the name of the party, formulating policy on the Bills presented by other parties, and questioning the government in the house. A large part of the work of the *Bundestag* takes place in specialist committees, and the choice of SPD representatives in these committees is the responsibility

[1] On the recent history of the SPD, cf. (despite their bias) David Childs, *From Schumacher to Brandt*, Pergamon Press, Oxford, 1966, and Theo Pirker, *Die SPD nach Hitler*, Rütten and Loening, Munich, 1965.

of the leadership of the parliamentary group. It also decides who shall represent the party in the formal public sessions of the *Bundestag*.

As for the party Executive, this 'has the responsibility for the leadership of the party' in the words of the party organization statute. For much of the postwar period 'organization' has been very widely interpreted so that strictly policy-making functions have also been exercised by this body, which includes the paid officials of the SPD Headquarters, as well as representatives of the parliamentary leadership. Until 1958, the executive, elected by the party congress, was composed of 25 members, seven places being reserved for paid members of the party bureaucracy (these included the Chairman, Ollenhauer). After the electoral defeat of 1957, a high-level committee was established for the purpose of reorganizing the structure of the leadership. On the one hand, the Executive's membership was enlarged to 33 (it still meets roughly once a month, since its members are scattered throughout the Federal Republic), but a new group of nine members, known as the Party Presidium, has been established consisting entirely of people active in Bonn, and able therefore to meet at least once a week. Although the functions of the parliamentary group and those of the Executive and Presidium are formally different, the fact of a very considerable overlapping membership (the leadership of the parliamentary group being almost identical with that of the Presidium) makes the latter organ supreme both in laying down parliamentary tactics and in running the party organization. The effects of this concentration of power will be discussed later.[1]

The national organization of the SPD consists of about 20 regions (*Bezirke*)—the largest of the 10 *Länder* such as Lower Saxony and North Rhine-Westphalia being divided into several *Bezirke*—in which the party membership of about 650,000 is organized and served by a full-time staff of about 300. The smallest units of local organization in the SPD are the Town Groups (*Ortsvereinen*) whose relations with the party at the national level are conducted through the *Bezirk* organization. Whether or not the *Bezirk* organization covers the whole of a *Land*, the importance of political life at that level ensures a well-developed organization which expresses also

---

[1] On the SPD's organization, see Olzog, *op. cit.*, Chapter 4.

the traditional particularism of some of the German States (the Social Democrats of Bavaria have successfully insisted on a special organization of their own ever since the days of their great leader Georg von Vollmar in the 1890s).

The *Bezirk* organization forms the basis for the election of delegates to the congress (*Parteitag*), officially the highest policy-making body in the party, which consists of three hundred delegates elected in proportion to the paid-up membership of each *Bezirk*. As mentioned above, the congress exercises less influence in policy-making than it did before 1914, partly because it meets biennially instead of annually, and partly because of the power and prestige which the leaders derive from their positions of power in national or local government, but the debates still exercise some influence. The functions of congress are officially described as: consideration of reports on the activities of the party Executive, the parliamentary group, and other national organs; the determination of where the seat of the Executive shall be; election of the Executive and another national body, the Control Commission (to be described later); decisions on organization and all questions affecting the life of the party; and voting on policy resolutions submitted by the latter— a traditional and still important channel through which the membership can attempt to influence the leadership. It should be noted, however, that the ritual formalities of the congress—speeches by the party leaders, addresses from visiting trade union, governmental or foreign visitors, and the like—usually allow little time for full debate on policy resolutions, and the leadership has shown itself increasingly adept at warding off critical or embarrassing debates on these occasions. (It should also be noted that the leadership has confirmed its authority by refusing urgent requests for the convocation of an emergency congress to discuss a difficult question of policy; notably on the occasion when the party entered a coalition with the Christian Democrats in November 1966.)

For the sake of completeness, two other elements of the SPD organization should be mentioned. The Control Commission, referred to above, is a body whose origins go back to the statutes of the Eisenach Party of 1869, which did its best to introduce safeguards against any autocratic rule like that of the President and founder of the rival party, Lassalle. The Control Commission consists of nine members of the party, who may not be its full-time employees, and who are elected by the congress for the purpose of considering any complaints from party members against the Executive. The Control Commission is required to meet at least quarterly, but it has not played a particularly important role on any occasion in the post-war history of the SPD.

More important is the Party Council (*Parteirat*), a consultative body consisting of the Chairmen and up to three representatives from each *Bezirk* according to membership. The council also includes the chairmen of *Land* committees, when these are separate from the *Bezirk* committees; the leaders of SPD parliamentary groups in the various *Landtage* (or State Parliaments); and the Prime Ministers or Deputy Prime Ministers of State Governments, provided of course that they are SPD members. The Party Council has the right to express an opinion before any decision of the Executive on questions of domestic and foreign policy, basic party organization, and the preparation of election campaigns. Its main importance has been in achieving some measure of co-ordination between SPD policies at national and at state level, though its post-war history offers numerous occasions when this has failed. The European policy of Schumacher was strenuously opposed by the SPD both in Berlin (under Ernst Reuter) and in Bremen (under Wilhelm Kaisen); the party in Hessen was responsible in 1965 for initiating the judicial process by which State subsidies to political parties were declared illegal in July 1966; and there have also been numerous occasions when the SPD in one *Land* or another has been in a governing coalition with a party opposed to the SPD in Bonn, leading to strains between the regional and national organizations.

The financial situation of the SPD is different from that of other German parties in one radical respect. As the table shows (see p. 67) the income of the SPD is provided overwhelmingly (60 per cent in 1962) from membership dues paid by a large and well organized membership. This figure of 60 per cent of the SPD's income is in striking contrast to the figure for the CDU (12 per cent) and for the FDP (18 per cent). The historical reasons for this difference go right back in the SPD's history as a mass party, which was always forced to rely on its members for its main income. To this should be added other factors such as allowing local party collectors to keep 5 per cent of the membership dues as an incentive to efficiency; and the tradition by which the salaries paid to SPD parliamentarians from public funds, since such payments began in the late Wilhelmine period under the title of expenses, have been regularly taxed by the party. Today, for instance, an SPD member of the *Bundestag* has to hand over 20 per cent of his parliamentary salary to the party, whereas the FDP fixes the smaller amount of DM 50 (£1 = 9·6 DM) a month, and the CDU leaves the size of contributions from its parliamentarians up to them.

The difference is most strikingly illustrated by the fact that in the SPD's income, membership dues are easily the largest source of income (DM 14 million in 1963, compared with a contribution from public funds of DM 10·2 million). The total income of the CDU is similar to that of the SPD but it receives only DM 3 million from membership dues, against DM 11·5 million from public subsidies. Figures for the FDP are DM 1·4 million and DM 4·5 million respectively. This situation means that the SPD can accept the July 1966 judgement of the Federal Constitutional Court, that the public subsidies paid to political parties since 1959 are unconstitutional, with relative equanimity. Unlike the other parties, it can certainly live in its present style, in between election campaigns at least, from membership-dues income alone. In any event, at the time of writing it appears that expenses for election campaigns will continue to be paid largely from public funds, officially for the purpose of 'political education'. Subsidies from *Land* funds, based on the strength of parties in the local *Landtag*, including the NPD (see below), will also continue to be paid.

The fact that the SPD machine is financed so largely from member's dues also contributes to the authority of the party leadership. (In the CDU and FDP, the relative affluence of certain members of the *Bundestag*, or local party leaders, sometimes resulting from their personal backing by industrial or other interest groups, tends to give them a greater degree of independence from a party leadership which finds that the direct control of large parts of the party funds escapes it.) This seems to reinforce the view that power in the SPD lies in the hands of the parliamentary leadership in Bonn, of which the party machine outside forms a distinctly subordinate ally. This is an over-simplification in that the SPD contains several other sizeable concentrations of power. There has always been the so-called 'Bürgermeister-Wing' of the party, composed of powerful leaders like Reuter in Berlin, Kaisen in Bremen, Brauer in Hamburg,

Zinn in Lower Saxony, and Kopf in Hessen, not to mention the Bavarian SPD under Hoegner or von Knoeringen; there are also the experts, mainly economists such as Professor Karl Schiller (the present Finance Minister) and Dr Heinrich Deist, who set the SPD's economic policy firmly on a reformist course by the late 1950s; and the SPD's 'businessmen group' consisting of the managers of the large-scale municipal and co-operative enterprises which have played a considerable part in West Germany's 'economic miracle'. This latter group has been strengthened by the trade unionists and SPD members who have gained experience of industrial management under the provisions of the co-determination laws enacted since 1949. Finally, it should not be forgotten that despite all tendencies to oligarchy, the formal organizations within the SPD, such as the Party Congress, the Young Socialist Movement, the Socialist Women's Organizations, retain considerable degrees of autonomy, and real possibilities of influencing the party leadership. These groups probably exert more influence on long-term party policy than the DGB (the German TUC) which is not formally linked with the SPD and has disagreed with it on numerous important issues, from German rearmament to the 1968 emergency legislation.[1]

Despite this fairly considerable dispersal of power there is no doubt that the last word in SPD policy-making rests with the parliamentary leadership. Under Schumacher, the SPD was ruled in an openly authoritarian way, and even though a period of relative anarchy ensued under the mild-mannered Erich Ollenhauer, the reins of control were firmly drawn together again in the later 1950s by the new leadership team consisting of Willy Brandt, Fritz Erler, and Herbert Wehner. This team guided the SPD through the radical changes whose main landmarks were the adoption of the totally reformist Godesberg Programme in 1959, the acceptance of a bipartisan foreign policy in 1960, and the situation in which a coalition government with the CDU became possible at the end of 1966. (The role of Herbert Wehner in bringing the SPD into the coalition has been exaggerated in many accounts. He is credited with manœuvring this almost single-handed, whereas in reality the majority of the parliamentary group—and even of the local party

[1] Childs, *op. cit.*

groups—appear to have become genuinely convinced by the time the coalition was formed that this was the right policy for the party.)[1]

There have of course been movements of revolt against the policies pursued by the party leadership, particularly at times when the leadership showed lack of conviction or toughness, as under Ollenhauer. More recently, there were the violent protests against the MLF proposal by the Hamburg veteran Max Brauer at the Karlsruhe Congress of November 1964. The Congress endorsed the MLF—ironically, a month before President Johnson dropped it— and voted Brauer off the Executive.[2] At the Dortmund Congress in June 1966 there were protests against Brandt's reformist policies but he reaffirmed his leadership; his young radical opponents criticized him from a position 'based altogether on the Godesberg programme'.[3] Thus the distribution of power in the SPD remains in essentials the oligarchic one described by Robert Michels. The tradition of discipline built up during decades of quasi-permanent opposition and frequent persecution has been reinforced by occasional periods of governmental power in the Weimar Republic (Hermann Müller was the SPD Chancellor in 1920; therefore without question he had to become Chancellor again after the party's electoral success in 1928, instead of the more gifted but 'junior' Otto Braun), and by the authoritarian leadership of Schumacher. The renewed taste of ministerial office since November 1966 will also accentuate this trend, particularly if the SPD is able in 1969 to consolidate its electoral gains of 1965. These were considerable in rural and Catholic areas as well as in the party's traditional industrial and Protestant strongholds, and they confirmed the broad public appeal of the party leadership. It is true that the SPD's set-back in the land election in Baden-Württemberg (April 1968) has led to renewed criticism of the leaders, but the long-term trend appears

[oligarchy]

[1] Gerhard E. Grundler, 'Die Grosse Koalition—eine Zwangshandlung', in *Frankfurter Hefte*, Vol. XXII, No. 1, January 1967, pp. 3–5.

[2] *Parteitag der Sozialdemokratischen Partei Deutschlands, Karlsruhe 1964. Protokoll der Verhandlingen.*

[3] Hans Langerhans, 'Repolitisierung der SPD' in *Frankfurter Hefte*, Vol. XXI, No. 7, July 1966, pp. 443–5. See also the reports on the SPD's Nuremburg Congress of April 1968, notably in *Die Zeit*.

to be the strengthening of their authority, partly due to their increased electoral appeal.[1]

THE CHRISTIAN DEMOCRATIC UNION (CDU)

The organization of the CDU is more difficult to describe in formal terms than that of the SPD, for at least three reasons. Firstly, unlike the SPD, the CDU has had no long history of opposition and relative impotence, during which an elaborate party bureaucracy was likely to develop. Secondly, the CDU has been heavily influenced for most of its existence by the dominating figure of Konrad Adenauer, whose chancellorship lasted from 1949 to 1963; longer than the entire life span of the Weimar Republic. And thirdly, since the CDU has held a large share of the ministerial posts in every cabinet of the Federal Republic (8 out of 13 in 1949; 11 out of 18 in 1953; 16 out of 18 in 1957; 15 out of 20 in 1961; and 11 out of 21 in the Great Coalition of 1966),[2] the party has always possessed centres of political influence and administrative facilities in the form of the state bureaucracy. Indeed, this has often been accused by the opposition of becoming a CDU party bureaucracy, thus making a formal organizational structure for the party less necessary than for the SPD.

Despite these peculiarities, and the fact that the CDU must therefore be described as a party of notables or 'a voters' party' rather than 'a membership party', a certain organizational development of the party can of course be traced. Its main antecedent in the Bismarckian as in the Weimar period was the Centre Party (*Zentrum*), whose ideological, tactical and organizational legacy to the CDU has been considerable.

The Centre Party, founded by Ludwig Windthorst in 1870, represented a development at the national level of the Catholic groups

[1] For a detailed analysis of the 1965 election, see *Revue Française de Science Politique*, *loc. cit.*, pp. 286–305. It should be added that one result of the SPD's accession to governmental office is the placing of its party members in high civil service posts, e.g. Egon Bahr, a former Berlin associate of Willy Brandt, at present head of the Policy Planning Staff in the Foreign Ministry. It appears likely that such appointments help to increase ministerial control over the strong German Civil Service, though probably only to a limited degree.

[2] Grosser, *Die Bundesrepublik Deutschland*, Wunderlich Verlag, Tübingen, 1967, pp. 86–7.

which had played a more or less organized role in the politics of several of the German States since before the 1848 revolution. The Centre Party, like the Social Democratic Party (with which it was to share power for much of the Weimar Republic, and with which it is now, in its new incarnation as the CDU, in coalition again) stood in a posture of fundamental hostility to the Bismarckian empire. Bismarck himself regarded the Catholics, whom he persecuted in his *Kulturkampf* of the 1870s as he persecuted the Social Democrats during the period of the Exceptional Law in 1878 to 1890, as dangerous enemies. Both Catholics and Socialists owed allegiance to ideals and even organizations outside the nation state, and they condemned the shortcomings of the Empire Bismarck had created in terms of values to which they and their followers gave priority.

The resemblance between the *Zentrum* and the SPD was, however, superficial. Whereas social democracy meant a rigorously organized and well-drilled army, united by at least the profession of belief in a detailed socialist programme derived from its philosophical creed, the party of political Catholicism was altogether looser. The basic programme of the *Zentrum*, the so-called Soest Programme of October 1870, was a deliberately vague document, and, perhaps for this reason, it remained a successful basis for the party's political activities for several decades. After four paragraphs insisting on the importance of Christianity, the rights of the Church, and support for Catholic schools, the programme calls for political and administrative decentralization in the 'federal state of the German Fatherland' and the limitation of taxes and public expenditure, and concludes with a statement of social principles limited to the pious hope of 'reconciliation of the interests of capital and landed property, as well as of capital and landed property on one side and labour on the other, through the support and development of a powerful middle class', and legislation to remove extreme manifestations of social injustice.[1]

The programme was general enough to appeal to Catholics in every region of Germany; the anti-Bismarckian separatists of Bavaria and of the South West, as well as the Catholics of the Prussian Rhineland, always mistrustful of the rule of Protestant Berlin. It

[1] W. Mommsen, *Deutsche Parteiprogramme*, Isar Verlag, Munich, 1954, pp. 71–2.

also appealed to a very wide variety of social groups: priests, aristocrats, peasants, workers, some representatives of heavy industry, and many tradesmen, artisans, and white-collar employees.

Thanks to consistent support from the Catholic Church, the Centre Party managed for 40 years to exist very successfully without any formal organization, which was only set up in 1911. After successfully withstanding Bismarck's persecution in the 1870s, the party won on average 18 per cent of the votes at every general election from 1871 to 1912, and played a major part in the parliamentary life, such as it was, of Wilhelmine Germany. Thanks to its central position in the parliamentary spectrum, and its relatively undoctrinaire approach to political problems (except those directly touching the Church), the Centre, though it was often denounced from both right and left as unprincipled and unscrupulous, played a consistently important role.

Its leaders, from the founder Windthorst down to his successors during the First World War such as Matthias Erzberger (a parliamentarian who played a prominent role in developing the nucleus of the future Weimar coalition, around the famous Reichstag peace resolution of July 1917) or Adam Stegerwald (a leader of the Christian Trade Union movement who was also an active member of the Reichstag), developed their political skill in somewhat the same way as Social Democratic leaders, such as August Bebel or Friedrich Ebert. They were able to fulfil an important role as leaders of a party representing a diversity of economic and regional interests, as well as divergent ideological viewpoints.

During Weimar the Centre Party like the 'SPD' was called on to administer the legacy of a revolution it had only indirectly contributed to bringing about. The Centre, despite the loss it suffered by the tragic assassination of Erzberger, played a leading role from the beginning to the end of the Republic. Its Chancellors ranged from Joseph Wirth, a left-wing leader in the early 1920s, to Heinrich Brüning, much further to the Right, who was Chancellor from 1930 to 1932. The Centre Party operated successfully as a partner in the most varied governments (frequently, it was in coalition with the SPD in the state of Prussia, while in a right-wing alignment at the Reich level). Like the SPD, it succeeded in retaining the support of most of its voters right up to the collapse of democracy in 1933. (The SPD vote declined from 21·7 per cent in 1920 to 18·3 per cent

44

in March 1933; the Centre Party vote from 18·1 per cent to 14 per cent in the same period—a striking contrast to the decimation of the smaller parties of the centre and right, whose voters went over *en masse* to the Nazis.)[1]

After 1945, a minority of Catholics in the Rhineland re-established the Centre Party under its old name as a purely Catholic organization, and it even had some electoral success in the early years of the Federal Republic. The majority of German Catholics, however, followed the lead given by a prominent Centre politician, Adenauer (which in fact followed the lines already suggested by Stegerwald as long ago as 1920), and widened the party to include Protestants. The party, known as the Christian Democratic Union (in Bavaria, out of deference to traditional separatist feeling, it was called the Christian Social Union, and was essentially a descendent of the pre-1933 Bavarian People's Party) could thus count on wide support in post-1945 Germany, a society reacting against the pagan excesses of the Third Reich, and anxious to build on all the traditional pillars of stability, Protestant as well as Catholic.

The old Centre Party tradition of comprehensiveness, therefore, was not so much rejected as subsumed into an even wider synthesis in which a record number of divergent interests appeared to be reconciled. Some of Adenauer's colleagues in the CDU leadership in the early years were men of pronounced left-wing views: for instance, Karl Arnold, a Catholic trade unionist from the Rhineland, for several years Minister President of North Rhine-Westphalia; Jakob Kaiser, originally the leader of Christian Democracy in the Soviet Zone and later Adenauer's Minister for all-German affairs; and Gustav Heinemann, a Protestant pastor and Minister of the Interior until his resignation in September 1950 in opposition to West German rearmament and Adenauer's authoritarian methods of executing it (Heinemann later joined the SPD and in March 1969 was elected President of the Federal Republic).

Under the influence of such men, particularly of Arnold, the CDU's first programme took a markedly left-wing line on social and economic questions. This programme was adopted at a conference at Ahlen in the British Zone, in February 1947, when at least some of the influence of the occupation authorities pointed in a left

[1] S. Neumann, *op. cit.* and S. M. Lipset, *Political Man*, Heinemann, London, 1963.

wing direction, and when the CDU faced an apparently overwhelming superiority of the SPD under Schumacher. The Ahlen programme announced the CDU's attachment both to political freedom and to economic emancipation (political and social democracy being regarded as equally indispensable); it proclaimed that capitalism had failed and that monopoly was intolerable; and it committed the party to a policy of a planned economy directed by councils operating under the control of parliament. This left-wing direction, however, did not remain dominant in the CDU for long. The industrialists of the Rhineland and such prophets of economic liberalism as Professor Erhard of Frankfurt, who became prominent in the party's affairs under the guidance of Adenauer, won a clear victory at the CDU's congress at Dusseldorf in July 1949, which rejected all state planning, whether of economic production, labour matters, or domestic or foreign trade, and allowed the government no more than the traditional liberal role of deciding fiscal policy and carrying out minimal regulation of imports from abroad. This uncompromising programme, the first blue-print for the policy of the 'social market economy' to be pursued with such acclaim by Professor Erhard as Minister responsible for the German economy from 1949 to 1963, was in fact somewhat modified the following year, when a full party policy was issued.

This 1950 programme of the CDU was a statement of classical economic liberalism mixed with commitments to 'a reorganization of social insurance and of public welfare institutions', and 'the putting into practice of the right of the workers to consultation, co-operation and co-determination'. It included one sentence which points sharply to the dilemmas which in the long run—a very successful run—were to give the party serious trouble: 'The "social market economy" can only be put into practice if it wins the confidence of all sections of the people, that means if industrialists, workers, employees and consumers actively participate in carrying it out'.[1]

As will be seen, the CDU was to find it increasingly difficult by the mid-1960s, faced with a new shortage of economic resources and a consciousness in Germany of growing pressures from outside, to maintain the degree of public confidence which the 1950 programme

[1] Mommsen, *op. cit.*, p. 152.

so rightly identified as an essential prerequisite for success. For several years, however, the very general statement of principles which it contained, supplemented by slightly more detailed statements adopted during the election campaigns of 1953 and 1957, and by a general policy restatement approved at a congress in Dortmund in 1962, formed the basis for a phenomenally successful political consensus.

The CDU–CSU, in fact, has beaten all records in German political history by winning the largest share of the votes cast at each one of the five federal elections (31 per cent in 1949; 45·2 per cent in 1953; 50·2 per cent in 1957; 45·4 per cent in 1961; and, even at the moment when it was exposed to internal dissension and opposition pressure, 47·6 per cent in 1965).[1] One way of interpreting the popularity of the CDU would be to say that it combined something of the support won by the British Labour Party for developing the Welfare State with the support given to the Conservative Party for 'setting industry free'. This means that the CDU is in many ways similar to the British Conservative Party, though it might be said to be more 'right-wing' in economic policy, and more 'left-wing' in social policy. Because of the balance between Catholic and Protestant influences, and the more advanced economic and social climate of Germany, it is very different from Italian Christian Democracy.

The CDU, like the Centre Party, is a much less formally organized party than the SPD. It only adopted a formal structure at a Congress in Goslar in October 1950, after having won the first federal election of August 1949 without the help of any national party organization. Before we return to the reasons why the formal constitutional structure of the CDU has not played an important role in practice, this structure should at least be described.

On paper, the organization of the CDU is not unlike that of the SPD. The highest policy-making body is formally the Federal Congress, consisting of delegates of the *Land* federations, representation being based on an interesting mixture of electoral success, in that one delegate is allowed for every 75,000 CDU votes at the last federal election; and of actual membership, in that a further delegate is allowed for every thousand members. The party congress (which is

1 Grosser, *Revue Française de Science Politique*, Vol. XVI, April 1966.

required to meet at least annually, and which also includes 75 representatives of Christian Democrats in the Soviet zone, and 20 delegates representing the exile organizations of CDU—Germans from East of the Oder–Neisse line) is entrusted with the task of electing the party's Federal Executive, and approving reports by it and by the group in the *Bundestag*, and taking decisions on basic policy.

The CDU is directed between congresses, on paper at least, by the Federal Committee (*Bundesausschuss*) and the Federal Executive Committee (*Bundesvorstand*). The former is the larger, including all members of the Executive and also delegates of the *Land* organizations and other groups (such as women members), the presidents of the CDU groups in the *Land* parliaments, the chairmen of the federal committees of expert advisors of the party, and the full-time secretaries of the CDU *Land* organizations. This committee is responsible for all political and organizational questions, except the basic matters which the Federal Congress in theory handles. It elects the federal treasurer and 15 further members of the Federal Executive for two years, and also an 'election campaign committee' (*Wahlkommission*), which expresses the national party's point of view in the choice of election candidates, in conjunction with the *Land* organizations.

The more important and smaller group is the Federal Executive Committee, which consists of a presidium (Federal Chairman, managing chairman, one or two deputies for the latter and four further members), as well as the federal treasurer, the general secretary, the chairman and deputy chairman of the group in the *Bundestag*, the chairman of the *Land* organizations and other specialized sections of the party, CDU leaders of *Land* governments, the president of the *Bundestag*, Federal Ministers belonging to the CDU, 15 further members elected by the Federal Committee and a further three co-opted members. The functions of this second body are officially described as 'the leadership of the Federal party, and the carrying out of decisions of the Federal congress and the Federal Committee'. The presidium, which can in theory be called together at short notice, represents the party for legal purposes.[1]

These constitutional arrangements appear at first sight to provide for a reasonably democratic distribution of power within the CDU,

[1] Olzog, *op. cit.*

but any chance they might have had of achieving this was foiled from the beginning by the dominant personality of Dr Adenauer, the chairman of the party from immediately after the war until the Congress of 1966, three years after he gave up the Chancellorship.[1]

Adenauer ruthlessly exerted his authority, and got his way on a series of key issues which had to be settled even before the Federal Republic came into existence, such as the nature of the Basic Law which was worked out in 1948–49, and the question of whether the capital of the Federal Republic should be in Bonn or in Frankfurt am Main. After the 1949 election, when a number of important CDU leaders favoured a coalition with the SPD (for instance, Karl Arnold, who led a CDU–SPD coalition in the important state of North Rhine–Westphalia), Adenauer over-ruled them, and forced the CDU leaders in North Rhine–Westphalia and in Hessen to break off their coalitions with the SPD. When the formal organizational structure was being established at the Goslar Congress in October 1950, the leaders at *Land* level tried to counter-attack by insuring for themselves positions of power on the federal committees. The large membership of both the *Ausschuss* and the *Vorstand*, however (respectively about 100 and 50), makes them unwieldy as vehicles of any serious opposition to the party leadership and Adenauer was able to manipulate them without much difficulty.

This remained true even after a reform of the party organization, carried out—against the Chancellor's opposition—at the Sixth Party Congress held in Bonn in 1956. On this occasion, Karl Arnold (who had lost his post as Minister President of North Rhine–Westphalia, thanks to his obedience to Adenauer's dictates), led the move to increase the number of vice-chairmen from two to four with the idea of strengthening the presidium against the Federal Chairman. The move was successful—an up-and-coming CDU leader from the Rhineland, Dufhues, made the point in proposing the reform that the Federal Chancellor and party leader should henceforth submit to more discussion with his colleagues—and the two newly created vice-chairmanships were filled by Arnold and by Gerstenmaier, the President of the *Bundestag*.

Adenauer, however, circumvented this by making flagrant use of

---

[1] On Adenauer as party leader, see Arnold J. Heidenheimer, *Adenauer and the CDU*, The Hague, Nijhoff, 1960.

his right as party chairman not to convene either the Federal Committee or the Executive. The result was the farcical situation in which, during the acute crisis caused by Adenauer's toying with the idea of moving from the Chancellorship to the Presidency (which opened up the basic question of who was to succeed him as party leader and Chancellor), the CDU Executive met only once, and the Federal Committee not at all between September 1958 and September 1959. The party's organizational statute actually provides for the Federal Committee to meet quarterly, but it also confirms the right of the Chairman to convene the meetings—or by implication, not to convene them.

Dr Erhard, towards the end of his unhappy three-year spell as Chancellor, succeeded Adenauer as party Chairman at the Congress of March 1966. However, Adenauer's removal led to a situation in which real debate was possible on who was to succeed the unfortunate Chancellor himself. At last, the chairmen of the CDU *Land* parties, and the other members of the Federal Executive, who for years had been excluded from any say in the policies or affairs of the national party, were able to participate in decisions of some importance. The outcome of the crisis was that one of the CDU '*Land* Princes', Minister President Kiesinger from Stuttgart, himself became the Federal Chancellor; he duly succeeded Erhard in the party chairmanship at the Brunswick Congress of May 1967, but within two years his rule over the party appeared to resemble the relative anarchy prevailing under Erhard, rather than the autocracy of Adenauer.

The finances of the CDU, as mentioned earlier, differ radically from those of the SPD (see table on p. 67). The small share of the CDU's income which comes from membership dues (12 per cent in contrast to 60 per cent for the SPD) can be explained partly by the much lower total of the membership—in 1964–65 the CDU–CSU membership totalled 377,379, compared with 648,415 for the SPD— and also by the much lower average rate of dues. Whereas the SPD succeeds in obtaining from its members a very high level of contributions, based on their respective incomes, and which goes as high as DM 40 or just under £4 per month for a member earning above DM 2,500, the CDU until quite recently charged a flat rate of only DM 1 per month for membership. In March 1964 a new scale was introduced, somewhat like that of the SPD, and this attempt to

50

increase the party's income from membership dues is likely to be pursued further as a result of the court decision that the contributions to political parties paid since 1959 from federal and state funds are at least potentially illegal.

As can be seen from the table, the CDU in 1963 is estimated to have received about half its total income of DM 11·5 million from public funds, as against DM 3 million produced by membership dues. The decision of the Federal Constitutional Court therefore poses a grave threat to the CDU's finances, particularly as industrialists who have generously supported it in the past are now less willing to do so; either because of lack of resources in a period of mild recession or because of a feeling that the threat of nationalization or other anti-capitalist policies by the SPD is now less acute than it was, or even because some of them now support the NPD instead.

The dominant position of the CDU in the political life of the Federal Republic has been well summarized by a German observer: 'to analyse the CDU is to describe the Federal Republic . . . the Union has not only always provided the Chancellor, provided most of the ministers, and tamed the Bonn parliament for its purposes. It has done much more: in fact it has created the climate of this state, and brought into existence its—partly strong, partly jagged and partly painful—consciousness of itself.'[1] The secret of this success, the writer goes on, is that the CDU has reflected views of a wide variety of Germans: 'it has not so much provided leadership as kept itself open for the political needs of as many groups, social orders, and classes as possible', providing a simple addition of the national 'emotional reactions and categories of thinking' of Germany. 'To vote CDU,' at least after 1953, when the CDU toned down the strongly ideological tone of its anti-socialist campaign of 1949, 'was to vote like one's neighbour: but this did not by any means allow the neighbour to claim that one shared his views', since the CDU throve on 'feelings of community (*Gemeinsamkeiten*) without definite public commitment'.[2]

In foreign policy, unity could always be preserved, thanks to the pressures of the Cold War which limited West Germany's range of

1 Günter Gaus, 'Der weite Mantel. Die CDU auf dem Weg zum Zweiparteiensystem', *Der Monat*, No. 220, January 1967, pp. 5–8.
2 *ibid.*, p. 6.

options so drastically. In domestic politics, the difficult decisions were postponed during the long years of CDU rule, since the 'economic miracle' allowed subsidies to be paid to whichever groups, such as farmers or pensioners, appeared to be most in need, and might otherwise split the artificial concensus.

The CDU has always reflected, in the composition of its leading committees, the diversity of the social groups to which it seeks to appeal.[1] The presidium of the party has always included at least one representative of its trade union wing—Kaiser, Arnold, or Theodor Blank. The party has always taken particular care to balance Catholics and Protestants (the two groups with the widest coverage and appeal; CDU parliamentary candidates must belong actively to one confession or the other) in its leadership. The seven-man presidium has normally included four Catholics and three Protestants and even though it was almost automatic that Erhard, as Chancellor, should succeed Adenauer in the party chairmanship when the latter finally consented to retire in March 1966, the fact that Erhard was a Protestant—as well as a weak Chancellor—appeared to give the Catholic Rainer Barzel a serious chance of defeating him for the party chairmanship, on the grounds that the Chancellorship and the party chairmanship should now be held by members of different denominations, even though Adenauer had held both posts.

The outstanding feature of the CDU leadership, under the conditions of the Federal Republic, is certainly that the leader in parliament (and, hence, normally Federal Chancellor) automatically possesses the lion's share of power within the party. This was indisputably the case during the long and autocratic reign of Adenauer, and indeed his prestige as a successful politician was such that, even after he resigned the Chancellorship in 1963 (and even to some extent after he relinquished the party chairmanship in 1966) his long shadow was still cast over the affairs of the party. His successor, Erhard, despite his apparent promise as a vote-winner and party leader (illustrated, for instance, in the parliamentary group's solid support for him in 1959, or in his prominence alongside Adenauer in the party's election posters of 1961, and confirmed in the CDU's increase in votes under his leadership in 1965), failed to establish

[1] Heidenheimer, *op. cit.*

52

his authority as Chancellor, partly for reasons of international politics which were outside his control. His leadership of the party remained, as a result, disputed. As already noted, he did not automatically inherit the party chairmanship from Adenauer at the same time as the Chancellorship, or later, and his three years in office were marked by bitter dissension between different groups in the CDU–CSU, notably in foreign policy between the 'Atlanticist' wing represented by Erhard, Schroeder, and Hassel, and the misleadingly named 'Gaullist' wing under Strauss, Guttenberg, and Adenauer.[1]

When the economic and political situation of West Germany during 1966 had declined so far that Erhard's authority was rejected by a large section of his own party, as well as by its coalition partner the FDP, a situation arose where for once the CDU members of the *Bundestag*, and the chairmen of the party at the *Land* level (though not the more humble party members) were given real power to make a choice. They were able to elect the successor to Erhard from a number of possible candidates: the President of the *Bundestag*, Gerstenmaier; the retiring President of the European Economic Community's Commission, Professor Hallstein; the Federal Foreign Minister, Gerhard Schroeder; the ambitious chairman of the CDU parliamentary group, Rainer Barzel; and, the ultimately successful candidate, Kurt-Georg Kiesinger, the Minister-President of Baden-Württemberg and a former star of the *Bundestag's* debates on foreign and defence policy.

Once the choice was made, however, the mantle of governmental authority was assumed with quiet firmness by the new Chancellor and after six months' apparently successful conduct of the affairs of state (more successful than the six months that followed) his party rewarded him, as noted above, by electing him its chairman by 423 votes out of a total of 449 at the CDU Congress in Brunswick at the end of May 1967. The CDU, by granting to Kiesinger the dual role of Chancellor and chairman which Adenauer's tenacity had denied for over two years to Erhard, thus confirmed that the combination of these two offices under Adenauer was not merely a reflection of the latter's authoritarian personality, but was the normal situation for a major party in the Federal Republic. Parlia-

---

[1] See the present writer's study, 'The Scope of German Foreign Policy', in *Year Book of World Affairs*, Vol. 20, London, Stevens, 1966, pp. 78–105.

mentary and governmental power confer an almost automatic right to the exercise of supreme control within the party, in Germany as elsewhere.

It should be noted that Franz-Josef Strauss has similarly been constantly re-elected to the chairmanship of the CSU, even at times when his standing in Bonn has been damaged as it was by the *Spiegel* affair of November 1962. His past and potential future authority as a Federal Minister and national political figure made him an automatic choice for CSU party chairman. The SPD, similarly, has made a practice in the last ten years of allocating the leading party positions to those—led by Willy Brandt—who formed its 'government team' or shadow cabinet, i.e. men with a standing in national politics, who indeed since 1966 have been ministers.

THE FREE DEMOCRATIC PARTY (FDP)

The electoral appeal of the FDP, and its political weight, has always been considerably smaller than that of its two great rivals; in 1965, it won 11·9 per cent of the votes. Despite the broad spectrum of political views which it represents, it failed to win over the supporters of the other small parties of post-war Germany—the German Party and the Refugee Party—when these collapsed at the end of the 1950s (their votes, like their leaders, mainly went to the CDU at that stage). It has also failed to elect any members to the *Bundestag* on a constituency vote, so that its parliamentary representation, due entirely to the proportional part of the electoral system, would be annihilated by the adoption of straight majority voting, proposed by the CDU at intervals from 1949 to the present. Despite its apparent weakness, the FDP has often been in a position, thanks particularly to the delicate balance of parliamentary strength between the two larger parties after the elections of 1953 and 1961, to claim a sizeable share of government posts and influence on policy.

Even though the FDP appears for the moment excluded from any serious political influence, partly through its own miscalculation in provoking the government crisis of October–November 1966, the ideas it represents are nevertheless important. The FDP attempts to reconcile two contradictory strands of German liberalism, which split into enmity a century ago over the question of whether or not to support Bismarck. On the one hand, there remains the South

German, profoundly democratic and anti-militaristic tradition represented by the German People's Party of the 1860s and 1870s, the Free Thought Party of the Wilhelmine period, and the German Democratic Party of the Weimar Republic, culminating in the views of Theodore Heuss, the first President of the Federal Republic. In opposition to this left-wing Liberal tradition, there has always been the more authoritarian and nationalistic trend represented by the National Liberal Party (which broke away from the older branch in 1867 and strongly supported Bismarck), by Stresemann's German People's Party in the Weimar Republic (though this had at least the outward appearance of the softer form of liberalism), and by such post-1945 leaders, well to the right of Heuss, as Thomas Dehler, Erich Mende and the 'Young Turks' of North Rhine-Westphalia, for instance, Willy Weyer.

The party programmes of the FDP since 1945 have proclaimed liberalism in both the political sense, democracy and personal freedom, and the economic one, freedom from any form of state control of the economy. Its electoral appeal has been mainly to the Protestant or free-thinking middle classes, in particular to business circles.

The membership of the FDP is small (70,000) both in absolute terms and in relation to its vote (3,136,506 in 1965). The members, however, are in a position to pay fairly high membership dues of DM 20 per month, which produced 1,400,000 in 1963, or about one fifth of the party's total estimated income of DM 7·7 million. The FDP, like the CDU, depends heavily on subsidies from public funds, which amounted to DM 4·5 million in 1963 (see Table p. 67).

The organization of the FDP, like that of its two large rivals, comprises a party Congress, a National Committee, and an executive, but again, in practice, power lies with the parliamentary leadership in Bonn. There have been periodic revolts against the leadership by the FDP organizations in the *Länder*, particularly in North Rhine–Westphalia, but the tenure of national ministerial office by successive leaders—Blucher, Dehler, and Mende—has helped to ensure their control of the party, for most of its history.[1]

At the elections of 1965, the FDP lost heavily in some areas to

---

1 On the FDP's organization structure, see Olzog, *op. cit.*

the CDU (partly because of the increased Protestant representation in the top level of the latter under Erhard, Schroeder, and Hassel), and its strength in the *Bundestag* was reduced to 49, which since November 1966 has formed a weak opposition to the combined strength of the government parties CDU–CSU and SPD, which total 449. The FDP, as the only opposition party in the *Bundestag*, has picked up some protest votes in *Land* elections, but it lost two of its outstanding leaders during 1967 by the death of Dehler in July and the resignation of Mende in September. The party's most prominent leaders now include its chairman, Walter Scheel (a former minister) and the eminent young sociologist Ralf Dahrendorf. It has been deeply divided on the problems of relations with Eastern Europe and the Oder–Neisse line (notably at its Hanover Congress in April 1967), and it is again threatened with parliamentary extinction if the proposed introduction of simple majority voting comes about after the 1969 election.

THE NATIONAL DEMOCRATIC PARTY OF GERMANY (NPD)

Founded in Hanover in November 1964, the NPD is the latest in a series of neo-Nazi parties and organizations which have made their appearance throughout the history of the Federal Republic. As many as 92 such parties and groups have been identified, of which the best known before the NPD was the Socialist Reichs Party (SRP), founded by Major Otto Remer in 1949 and declared illegal in 1952, but of these the NPD has been easily the most successful.[1]

In the *Bundestag* elections of September 1965, less than a year after the NPD's foundation, it won 2·1 per cent of the votes (but no seats); it has followed this up by securing between 7·4 per cent and 9·8 per cent of the votes, and a corresponding number of seats, in six *Landtag* elections, starting in November 1966 with scores of 7·9 per cent in Hessen and 7·4 per cent in Bavaria, and culminating after 8·8 per cent, and eight seats in Bremen (October 1967), with 9·8 per cent and 12 seats in Baden–Württemberg in April 1968.

In November 1967, at a national congress in Hanover, the party's

---

[1] On the NPD, see Ivor Montague, *Germany's New Nazis*, Panther Books, London, 1967, and several German studies reviewed in *Die Zeit* in early 1968.

leader, Adolf von Thadden, was elected as its chairman by an over-whelming vote of 1,293 delegates against 32, with 48 abstentions. Von Thadden (a member of the *Bundestag* from 1949 to 1953, when he belonged to the *Deutsche Reichspartei*) had in fact been the NPD's guiding spirit from the beginning, and emerged decisively as the victor in a conflict with the original chairman, Fritz Thielen, who was forced to resign from the party in May 1967 and founded a splinter group. Thadden was shortly afterwards elected to the *Landtag* of Lower Saxony, while Thielen failed to be elected in his home town of Bremen in October.

The original manifesto of the NPD, adopted in 1964, was marked by a crude nationalism—demanding an end of foreign aid payments by Germany, an assertion of her national interests against her domination by 'territorially alien powers', and the restoration of her lost Eastern territories—and by several other echoes of Nazi pro-grammes. The NPD's emblem, also, is clearly a deliberate revival of the Nazi one. At the Hanover Congress of November 1967 some of these more extreme passages were toned down in a redrafted party programme, but this still includes the demand for the restoration of the Sudetenland and other 'German' territories, including Austria and South Tyrol, and is couched in generally nationalistic and authoritarian terms.

The party officially claims to seek the support of 'peasantry, middle class, skilled workers and independent, enterprising em-ployers',[1] but the available evidence suggests that its main voting strength so far has been limited to small sections of the population —small tradesmen and white-collar employees feeling the pressures of big business and organized labour. It should, however, be added that these groups, the normal clientele of any right-wing authori-tarian party, appear to have been joined in the Bremen poll of October 1967 by disillusioned SPD voters (the SPD lost 8·7 per cent of the total vote, and the NPD gained 8·8 per cent), who were dis-appointed by the fruits of 12 months of Great Coalition Govern-ment, and voted for the most outspoken opposition party, the KPD of course being illegal. The same trend appeared in Baden–Württemberg in April 1968.

1 Quoted by Reinhard Kühnl, 'Die NPD: Analyse Rechtsradikaler Entwick-lungen in der Bundesrepublik', in *Frankfurter Hefte*, Vol. 22, No. 1, January 1967, pp. 22–30.

The scale of the NPD's propaganda activities is such that the party must have considerable financial resources, probably from industrialists, in addition to the dues paid by its membership (now about 35,000), but their exact amounts and sources remain unclear. Not being represented in the *Bundestag* the NPD receives no subsidies from public funds, and it has emphatically condemned this form of party financing. It does, however, get funds from *Land* resources in those *Länder* where it has local parliamentary representation.

The organizational structure of the party is uncomplicated. The national chairmen (since 1967 Von Thadden) is assisted by three vice-chairman: Siegfried Pohlmann, leader of the 15-man NPD group in the Bavarian *Landtag*; Wilhelm Gutmann, leader of the NPD in Baden–Württemberg; and Karl Lamker, its leader in North Rhine–Westphalia—a *Land* where the NPD did not put up candidates in the *Landtag* election of July 1966, but has subsequently won some support among the victims of structural unemployment in the mining industry. A national committee (*Bundesvorstand*) of 42 members conducts the affairs of the party, whose regional structure is divided into organizations for each *Land* (*Landsverbände*) and about 500 local groups (*Ortsvereine*).

The NPD's voters are somewhat above the average age of those in other parties: for example, their strongest support in Bavaria and Hessen came from the 45–60 group. The party's appeal, however, appears likely to grow, at least to a small extent partly because of a degree of inevitable disappointment with the Great Coalition, and partly because of a general rise in German national sentiment. On its present showing the NPD might win 40 to 50 seats in the *Bundestag* election of 1969; this might have been prevented by a proposed reform of the electoral law (the adoption of majority voting in single-member constituencies), on which the Federal Government was expected to make a decision early in 1968, but which now appears to have been shelved indefinitely.

PARTICIPATION IN EUROPEAN ASSEMBLIES

The post-1945 movement towards Western European unity was strongly supported in Germany from the beginning—partly because of a reaction against the Third Reich's extreme nationalism in favour of a development in which Germany's reacquired sovereignty might be merged on an equal basis with that of other states—and the Basic Law makes a point of providing that West Germany 'can hand over sovereign rights to international organizations', and 'will agree to limitations on its sovereign rights which bring about a peaceful and stable order in Europe'.[1]

Despite concern felt by the SPD and some members of the FDP during the 1950s that an excessive degree of integration with the West would harm the prospects of German reunification (this meant that the SPD opposed the Schuman Plan and EDC, and for a time boycotted the NATO Parliamentarians Conference), German parties have taken their role in European assemblies very seriously.

The Federal Republic was not yet in existence when the Council of Europe was set up in May 1949, but it has been a member of the Council since 1950, and has been represented since then in the Consultative Assembly, as well as in the Common Assembly of ECSC, the European Parliament, the WEU Assembly and the NATO Parliamentarians Conference.

The most striking feature of German representation, at least in the Consultative Assembly, the Common Assembly, and now the European Parliament, is its continuity. The German delegations to these bodies have tended to remain virtually identical for periods of several years, in striking contrast, for instance, to British representation in the Consultative Assembly or the Assembly of WEU. One reason for this continuity lies in the legislation under which delegates are selected, which provides that they shall serve, like members of *Bundestag* committees (to which, as will be seen, European Assemblies are for some purposes officially likened) for the whole four years between *Bundestag* elections. A further reason is that the main parties, particularly the SPD, have preferred to reappoint most members of their existing delegations after each *Bundestag* election, provided of course that they were still available.

The number of seats allocated to Germany is the same as for France and Italy: 18 delegates and 18 substitutes to the Consultative Assembly, and 36 delegates to the European Parliament. In Bonn, the allocation of these seats between the parties is carried out by

Grundgesetz, Art. 24, Arts. 1 and 2.

the d'Hondt system of proportional representation, which gives, for the *Bundestag* elected in 1965, a total of 18 representatives in each assembly to the CDU–CSU, 16 to the SPD, and 2 to the FDP. The nomination of members by the *Bundestag* must take place within six weeks of its first sitting after the election, and is invariably the subject of an understanding between the three parties; the leaders of the three groups table a joint resolution asking for approval of the nominations made by each party, and this is normally granted without debate.

The composition of each party's team is in practice decided essentially by its leaders in parliament. It should, however, be noted that the *Bundestag* has a special staff of three civil servants, led by a *Regierungsdirektor*, whose special function is to serve and advise German delegations to the European assemblies, and that this secretariat itself may occasionally suggest to the parties that their delegation ought to include, for instance, more experts on agricultural or welfare problems.

The most striking change in German attitudes towards European integration has certainly been the development of the SPD's attitude, from one of hostility to the Schuman Plan in 1950, to one of enthusiasm for the Common Market later in the decade: this change has brought the SPD into line with the other socialist parties of the Six.

The SPD, in composing its delegations to European assemblies (despite its initial reserve toward the Schuman Plan, it attended the Common Assembly from the beginning), has been favoured by the fact that it was in opposition, at the federal level, for the whole period up to the end of 1966, and could, therefore, spare its top leadership more easily than the governing parties. Ollenhauer, Wehner, Metzger, Birkelbach, Deist, Kalbitzer, Schone, Kurt Conrad, Käte Strobel and Fritz Erler, have been among those to serve for long periods in the Common Assembly and/or European Parliament, while the SPD delegation to the Consultative Assembly has included (as well as Ollenhauer, Metzger, Birkelbach, Kalbitzer and Erler of those in the other Assembly), Willi Eichler, Carlo Schmidt, Helmut Schmidt, Louise Schroeder, Karl Mommer, and Ernst Wilhelm Meyer.

As might have been expected, the SPD's representatives have concentrated to some extent on the economic and social welfare activities of the European assemblies; Deist and Kalbitzer were prominent in economic debates, the latter being also *rapporteur* of the Consultative Assembly's Economic Committee, and Louise Schroeder, Käte Strobel and Willi Birkelbach were prominent in social welfare matters. Professor Carlo Schmidt played a leading part in the Political Committee of the Consultative Assembly, and Dr Karl Mommer was the first chairman of the Assembly's important Working Party for liaison with National Parliaments, created to ensure a systematic follow-up of Council of Europe matters in national politics. In the Common Assembly and European Parliament SPD delegates, besides presenting the workers' viewpoint in the economic and social development of ECSC and EEC, have in recent years pressed for the development of economic and political integration among the Six, the extension of the Communities to include the United Kingdom and other new members, and the strengthening of the role of the European Parliament, combined with its election by direct suffrage.

The SPD delegations to European assemblies have from time to time been depleted as their more prominent members took on more important political responsibilities at home; as when Willi Birkelbach took on a ministerial post in Hessen, when Dr Mommer became the SPD's whip in the *Bundestag*, or when Professor Schmidt and Frau Strobel joined the coalition government in 1966. However, as Uwe Kitzinger has pointed out,[1] the experience at Strasbourg of such prominent party leaders has almost certainly influenced the development of a more favourable attitude towards European integration on the part of the SPD; with the party's participation in government, it has more important potential consequences than before.

The CDU's representation at Strasbourg has suffered for longer than that of the SPD from the tendency for members to be called away to more important tasks in Germany. The CDU has also, in composing its delegations, been constantly obliged to take careful account of the need for a balance between the various groups—denominational, regional, and professional—of which it is composed. This is done for the Strasbourg delegations, as it is for committee

---

[1] Uwe Kitzinger, 'West German Republic' in *European Assemblies: The Experimental Period, 1949–1959* (ed. Kenneth Lindsay), London, Stevens, 1960, pp. 171–89.

membership in the *Bundestag* itself, by a very careful selection process which begins after each election with every member of the party being asked to complete a questionnaire indicating his preferences among the various committees. The process continues with a choice made by a 'committee on committees'—itself carefully chosen to be as representative as possible—whose nominations are then submitted to a full meeting of the group. Care is taken to see that CDU members who are delegates to Strasbourg, particularly to the European Parliament, are not overburdened with other committee work in Bonn. The post of delegate to Strasbourg in the CDU, as indeed in the SPD, is in considerable demand among parliamentarians. There is said to be as much demand to go to the European Parliament, though no longer to the Consultative Assembly, as to join the *Bundestag's* Foreign Affairs Committee.

Prominent CDU 'European parliamentarians' have included Chancellor Kiesinger, who was Vice-President of the Consultative Assembly until he left Bonn in 1957 to become Minister-President of Baden–Württemberg; Eugen Gerstenmaier and Heinrich von Brentano, who in the mid-1950s became respectively President of the *Bundestag* and Foreign Minister; Dr Hermann Kopf, Chairman of the *Bundestag* Foreign Affairs Committee since 1960, and still a member of the Consultative Assembly; Dr Fritz Hellwig and Dr Paul Leverkuhn, active members of the Consultative Assembly's Economic Committee; and Professor Hans Furler, almost a full-time 'European parliamentarian', who for several years was simultaneously an active and important President of the European Parliament and a member of the Consultative Assembly.

The few representatives of the FDP in European assemblies, normally no more than two or three at a time, have included such distinguished Bonn parliamentarians as Dr Max Becker, Karl Pfleiderer and Dr Erich Mende (before his assumption of the party leadership). The party's present representatives, Rutschke and Hellige in the Consultative Assembly and Achenbach in the European Parliament, have been active both in the assemblies and committees, and in the respective Liberal groups.

The German Government, as has been noted, has less need than others ơi a parliamentary stimulus to pursue 'European' policies, but a number of institutions and procedures exist to make quite sure both that the *Bundestag* is fully informed about the activities of European assemblies, and that suitable pressure is put on the Federal Government whenever this is necessary.

The permanent secretariat of the *Bundestag's* delegations to the assemblies plays a key role on the parliamentary side of these processes. The staff of this secretariat, whose permanent office is in an annexe of the *Bundestag*, deals with the administrative and secretarial arrangements of German delegations to the assemblies, but also advises them on political tactics, and in particular helps them with the task of feeding the results of their European parliamentary activity back into the *Bundestag*. After every session of a European assembly, for instance, the secretariat distributes a full report of the proceedings to every member of the *Bundestag* and these proceedings are debated on each occasion by the *Bundestag's* Foreign Affairs Committee.

More specialized than the Foreign Affairs Committee is the *Bundestag's* so-called *Integrations-Aeltestenrat*, or 'Council of Elders on Integration'. This body, constituted in 1963, consists of senior members of all parties, and its function is to receive reports from the Federal Government on the progress of European integration, and to arrange for their substance to be debated in the *Bundestag*. This device has its origins in the *Bundestag* debates on the Rome Treaty in 1957 when the SPD opposition, concerned about the possibly excessive powers of the EEC Council of Ministers, got the *Bundestag* to include a provision (Article 2 of the *Einfuhrungsgesetz*, or introduction to the relevant Act) which requires the government to inform the *Bundestag* regularly of the progress of the European Communities.

The Federal Government has, on the whole, been unwilling to go into details on these occasions (even the confidential proceedings of the *Integrations-Aeltestenrat* are said to be disliked by the Bonn Foreign Office, and the government has on occasion declined to give information on the grounds that this would be a breach of the Treaty of Rome), so that members of the *Bundestag* interested in EEC affairs are often forced to get information directly from Brussels through their own channels. These are now often very effective, so that *Bundestag* committees whose responsibilities are affected by developments in the EEC are able to act on quite accurate and up-to-date information.

The *Bundestag* keeps up to date with the general position of the

EEC by debating regular inter-party motions at roughly six monthly intervals, calling on the government to explain its European policy and to report on its progress. In April and October 1967, for instance the *Bundestag* members active in the European assemblies pressed the government—in October using material contained in the June proclamation of the Action Committee for the United States of Europe —to take a more active stand in favour of the strengthening and enlargement of the European committees.

As far as Council of Europe recommendations and conventions are concerned, a well-established machinery exists by which these are automatically forwarded to the *Bundestag* from the Consultative Assembly's Working Party on Liaison with National Parliaments, aided by the German delegation's secretariat, one member of which is responsible for following their progress through the *Bundestag*.

In conclusion, there seems to be general agreement that membership of European assemblies is important from the average German parliamentarian's own point of view, and from that of developing a coherent German policy on these important matters. What is not so clear is whether this is fully understood by the average voter. The careers of a few parliamentarians are said to have suffered because of their concern with European affairs, though, on the other hand, the voters of someone like Professor Furler (in a very safe CDU seat) appear to be proud of his European eminence.

RELATIONS WITH PARTIES IN OTHER COUNTRIES

All three of West Germany's main parties belong to 'Internationals' representing their respective ideological commitments. Membership of these Internationals is, of course, by no means the only channel through which political parties make contacts abroad. International parliamentarians' meetings such as the Anglo-German Königswinter Conferences, for instance, may be of more importance in influencing the views of party members and potential leaders.

Nominal commitment to a common ideology is by no means a guarantee of co-operation or even good relations between parties or their leaders in different countries. In the 1950s, despite all the talk of a Christian Democratic 'Black International' promoting

Western European integration, it was no secret that Chancellor Adenauer was closer in his views to the French Socialist leader Guy Mollet (or to Paul-Henri Spaak) than to his French Christian Democrat opposite number Georges Bidault. The Liberal International, in particular, has always been deeply divided about its political objectives. Despite these complications, however, the official international links of the various German parties—SPD, CDU, and FDP—have considerable importance.

For the SPD, the tradition of international links is a century old. Its early pioneers, especially Wilhelm Liebknecht and August Bebel, were in close contact with the First Workers' International founded in 1864. Parties representing the workers were less integrated into their national political systems than others and they naturally laid great verbal stress on their commitment to international proletarian solidarity. Although this ideal suffered a disastrous set-back in 1914 —and with it the Second International set up in 1889, in which the SPD had played a predominant role—the International was recreated in 1919, and SPD leaders such as Otto Wels and Rudolph Breitscheid were prominent in its activities.

After the Second World War had again swept away the fragile structure of the international labour movement, the new Socialist and Labour International was formally established in March 1951, in Frankfurt am Main, confirming the importance of the SPD, which had in fact already been accepted, thanks partly to the insistence of the French socialist Salomon Grumbach, at a preliminary conference in Antwerp in November – December 1947.

At the full congresses of the Socialist International, the SPD has been well represented. Its leaders Ollenhauer and Brandt have been successively Vice-Presidents of the International and Hans-Eberhard Dingels, the head of the SPD's international department, has played an important role, for instance, in representing the International in a dispute concerning the Labour Party of Malaya in 1966.

The SPD has also been strongly represented at congresses organized through the 'Liaison Office of the Social-Democratic Parties of the European Community and of the Socialist group in the European Parliament' (Herbert Wehner holds the post of Deputy President of the Liaison Committee), and the importance of these contacts is obviously considerable. A last point of importance, in connection with the SPD, is that the party's group in the *Bundestag* has a research staff of its own (independently of the staff at party headquarters); one member of this staff is responsible for European questions, including links with other European Socialist parties.

The Christian Democrats, despite their supranational ideological commitment, have never organized their international links to the same extent as have the Socialists. German participation in the 'Nouvelles Equipes Internationales' (Christian Democrat International) took place as early as the Second Congress, held in Luxemburg in January 1948, with the presence of 'le docteur Adenauer, ancien bourgmestre de Cologne'.

The annual congresses of NEI during the early 1950s, in which the CDU continued to be well represented, were mainly devoted to the problems of European integration. Congresses and study sessions of this the European Christian Democratic Union (as the NEI is now called) have provided the CDU with close contacts at the European level, symbolized by the fact that Dr Franz Meyers, the CDU Minister-President of North Rhine-Westphalia from 1958 to 1966, is one of the Vice-Presidents.

FDP participation in the Liberal International has been uneven. The highly respected publisher Hans-Albert Klüthe has been active in the International for several years, and is now its Vice-President. The FDP's interest in the International cooled under the leadership of Reinhold Maier in the mid-1950s; but current FDP leaders, including Walter Scheel, the International's Treasurer, have taken an active interest in its affairs. At the European level, the Liberal Movement for a United States of Europe, established at Zurich in 1952 and reorganized at Brussels in 1961, has provided a forum for contacts; the FDP is again represented by Hans-Albert Klüthe, the Movement's Vice-President. Recent FDP activities in the Liberal International have tended to be marked by a preoccupation with the party's domestic problems. For instance Dr Mende, at a meeting of European Liberal leaders in Paris in July 1967, was mainly concerned to win support for the FDP's opposition to possible electoral reform in Germany. Under new leadership, the FDP may take a more active part in the Liberal International's affairs.

BUNDESTAG ELECTIONS, 1948–65

(each column gives the percentage of votes cast and number of seats)

	1949		1953		1957		1961		1965	
CDU–CSU	31	139	45·2	243	50·2	270	45·4	242	47·5	245
SPD	29·2	131	28·8	151	31·8	169	36·2	190	39·3	202
FDP	11·9	52	9·5	48	7·7	41	12·8	67	9·5	49
Deutsche Partei	4·0	17	3·2	15	3·4	17			—	—
GB–BHE							2·8	—		
(Refugee Party)	—		5·9	27	4·6	—			—	—
DRP, 1949–61 NPD 1965	1·8	5	1·1	—	1·0	—	0·8	—	2·1	—
Others	22·1	58	6·3	3	1·3	—	1·9	—	1·5	—
Total Seats		402		487		497		499		496

INCOME AND EXPENDITURE OF THREE MAIN PARTIES, 1963

(DM '000)*

	CDU–CSU	SPD	FDP
Income			
Membership dues	3,000	14,000	1,400
From parliamentarians	500	2,700 (2)	200
Donations	9,000 (1)	—	1,600
Federal subsidies	8,000	7,200	3,100
Land subsidies	3,500	3,000	1,400
Total	24,000	26,900	7,700
Expenditure			
Administrative costs (rent, stationery, post, etc.)	2,500	3,000	1,050
Staff salaries (3)	6,000	6,700	1,750
Regular publicity, etc.	8,000	12,200 (4)	1,750
Landtag and local elections	7,000	4,500	2,400
Total	23,500	26,400	6,950

Notes

* £1 = 9·6 DM

(1) Half already paid, half promised.

(2) Including a small amount from other donations.

(3) Full-time staff, approximately: CDU–CSU 650; SPD 700; FDP 200.

(4) Including 5,200 for 'political education'.

Source: '*Capital*', reprinted in *Tatsachen-Argumente*, No. 93, April 1964.

CHAPTER 3

BELGIUM

THE BELGIAN PREDICAMENT: THE POLITICS OF MULTIPLE CONFLICT

The Belgian revolution of 1830 was made by one class, speaking one language, in the name of one faith. The unitary constitution, which naturally succeeded, enfranchised 1 per cent of the population, made French the language of government, and accorded the Catholic Church a privileged and independent position in the state. The religious consensus soon vanished with the growth of nineteenth-century secularism. As early as 1846, anti-clerical opinion coalesced into a loosely structured Liberal Party. The Liberal assault in the 1870s on clerical education and catholic practice provoked the formation of an organised Catholic party which, for 30 years from 1884, provided Belgium with homogeneous governments. Until the 1880s, the political game was fought within the intensely narrow limits of the *régime censitaire* (property-owners franchise). But, in 1885, a working-class party with a socialist programme was founded. From the start, the Parti Ouvrier Belge (POB)[1] espoused constitutionalism. Its campaign for universal suffrage, pressed paradoxically enough by means of three general strikes, was partly conceded in 1894 in the form of a male franchise with plural voting. In that year, 28 deputies entered the Chamber of Representatives: a number which rose to 70 on the withdrawal of the plural vote in 1919. The constitution of 1830 has remained otherwise substantially intact.[2] Moreover, the three parties which had consolidated by the end of the nineteenth century have remained dominant in Belgian political life. At that period, they embodied almost concisely the conflicting elements in

[1] Since French is likely to be the more familiar of the two official languages of Belgium to the British reader, French forms of titles will be used wherever appropriate.
[2] Female suffrage was introduced in 1945.

the Belgian situation: the Parti Libéral—anti-clerical, laissez-faire, and middle-class; the Parti Catholique—designated defender of the Church, sharing, overwhelmingly as yet, Liberal economic doctrine, and, despite the accession of the newly enfranchised Flemish electorate, directed by the same social elements as those which composed the Liberal camp; the POB—socialist, working-class, and, in the face of the antagonism of the Church, anti-clerical.

The internal unity of the three parties was maintained by more than philosophical and class factors. French remained the language of political intercourse although Dutch[1] was, and has always been, spoken by the majority of Belgians. (Between 55 and 60 per cent of the population are now normally Dutch-speaking.) For a century after the creation of Belgium, French was the language of social control. It was, of course, native to the Walloon professional and entrepreneurial class. But, the cultural influence of France, the value of French as a lingua franca and its monopoly in government turned the middle class of Flanders into a predominantly francophone group. At the same time, French was the language of the working-class movement. It was in the Borinage, centred on Mons, and in the Sambre-Meuse valley, between Charleroi and Liège, that the first Belgian industrial revolution took place. Industrialization did spill over into Flanders, notably into Ghent and Antwerp, and the 1890s saw the exploitation of the coal deposits of the Limburg Campine. Even so, the POB made little electoral headway in a catholic and agrarian Flanders. At the beginning of the First World War, only six of the 40 socialist deputies in the lower house represented Flemish constituencies; the POB was a Walloon party.

In the General Election of March, 1968, the POB's successor, the Parti Socialiste Belge (PSB) received more of its votes from Flanders than from Wallonia;[2] 48 per cent as against 40 per cent. The same

---

[1] It would, however, be more accurate to say that, until the growth of mass education and mass literacy, the Flemish population spoke a variety of Dutch dialects. In any case, Dutch is now the language of the greater number of Belgians.

[2] Throughout this chapter, Wallonia means the provinces of Liège, Hainault, Luxembourg, Namur and also the arrondissement of Nivelles (province of Brabant). Flanders means the provinces of Western Flanders, Eastern Flanders, Antwerp, Limbourg and the arrondissement of Louvain (province of Brabant). The exclusion of Brussels avoids the problem of the linguistic dispersal of votes amongst the parties in the Brussels arrondissement (province of Brabant) which is, of course, a bilingual region. There is a lack of solid evidence on this score; but, it is a relatively minor lacuna in this context.

is true of the other major 'traditional' party, the catholic Parti Social Chrétien (PSC), which received 63 per cent of its vote from Flemish constituencies (with just over 20 per cent from Wallonia). The Liberal Party, Parti de la Liberté et du Progrès, received 40 per cent as against 41 per cent. In the first two parties, the Flemish wings enjoy a clear political ascendancy over the francophone wings. The hegemony of French in the nineteenth century has found its anti-thesis in the triumph of Flemish nationalism in this century. The Flemish nationalist movement, which emerged as a major political force both within and outside the traditional parties in the interwar period, was of a largely defensive character, aiming to remove the disabilities experienced by the non-French speaking community in a number of areas. Now that the Flemish community has achieved its demands for equality with French in the legal, administrative and educational spheres, the movement has developed from first-stage defensive nationalism to second-stage aggressive nationalism. If the edge of Flemish consciousness continues to be sharpened by concrete grievances such as the encroachment of French into the dormitory (and, originally, Flemish) communes around Brussels, the need for a redistribution of parliamentary seats in favour of Flanders, and continued francophone control at the highest levels of capitalism, the new motivating force of the movement appears to be a desire to assert that political domination which would correspond to the increasing demographic preponderance of the Flemish popu-lation within Belgium. The potency of the Flemish movement may be seen in the rise of the Flemish federalist party (Volksunie) which, in ten years from 1958, has increased its number of deputies in the lower house from two to 20 and replaced the liberals as the third party in Flanders. Inevitably, the Flemish sections of the traditional parties (and, especially, the PSC) find themselves under increasing pressure from both the Volksunie itself and the Flemish activists amongst their own electoral clienteles. Meanwhile, the economic ascendancy of Wallonia has been replaced by that of Flanders. With obsolescent plant and high-cost coal mining weakening the Walloon economy, increased capital investment has taken place in Flanders since the end of the war. By the mid-1950s, less than 17 per cent of the Flemish working population was engaged in agriculture.

Since 1945, a succession of political crises concerning the

monarchy, education and economic policy, which has ranged a majority of the Flemish population against a majority of the Walloon population, has forced a painful recognition of its minority position on the francophone community. This sense of 'minorization' has been fed by economic depression in Wallonia. The result has been the development of a movement both inside and outside all three major parties, asserting the claims of the French language and of Wallonia within the Belgian state. The linguistic crisis is now the central issue in Belgian politics. The factors of class, religion and language which had united the makers of Belgium have become the elements of conflict. However divisive and potentially centrifugal, they are as yet accommodated within the country's traditional political structure. This structure, in the shapes of the traditional parties and the unitary constitution, is still struggling to contain them. But, the difficulty in trying to subsume subcultural, potentially ultimately divisive, elements within single parties was illuminated in the electoral campaign of March, 1968. As a result of critical divergences within the two major parties (PSC and PSB) over the future administrative character of the Brussels dormitory communes and the fate of the French section of the University of Louvain, separate electoral lists (one pro-Flemish, the other pro-francophone) for these two parties were presented in the arrondissement of Brussels.

An analysis in terms of language, socio-economic doctrine, and adherence or non-adherence to the Catholic Church reveals the diversity of political tendency in Belgium. Four tendencies, at least, are current within each linguistic community: catholic-conservative; catholic-progressive; secularist-conservative; secularist-progressive. Even these eight sub-groups fail to comprehend the total diversity of Belgian politics. (They do not include the nationalist strands in each community.) Moreover, the interests of the francophone population of the Brussels region, for example, are not identical with those of the inhabitants of the four Walloon provinces. The linguistic struggle is at its harshest in the bilingual administrative region of Brussels. In the General Election of 1965, the Front Démocratique des Francophones (FDF), created mainly by Brussels socialists in revolt against the imputed failure of the PSB to offer an adequate resistance to Flemish demands, returned three deputies and one senator to the Belgian Parliament. The FDF polled only 1·33 per cent of the total valid vote for the Chamber of Representatives. This FDF achievement was of more than passing interest, for it demonstrated the potential for party-atomization in the Belgian electoral system: a d'Hondt system of proportional representation with redistribution at the provincial level. Yet, the eight sub-groups indicated represent larger segments of the electorate than do the adherents of the FDF, and all eight have some form of institutional expression: at random, the Flemish catholic middle-class association (Nationaal Christelijk Middenstandverbond), the Liberal Flemish Union (Liberaal Vlaams Verbond), or the Walloon federations of the PSB. They would all have sufficient cohesion to form separate political parties. This 'reductio ad absurdum' at once illuminates the remarkable ascendancy of the three traditional parties in the political system and the causes of the divisions which reign within them, for all eight sub-groups are variously contained by the three main parties.

There were 12 general elections between 1919, when equal male suffrage was introduced, and 1958. The average percentage of the total number of valid votes cast in these elections for the Liberal, Catholic and Socialist parties together was 88·05 per cent. In 1961, they received 90·59 per cent of the vote; in 1965, 84·34 per cent; and, in March 1968, 80·59 per cent. Rather more significant than the continuing three-party domination of the political system is the stability of their electoral, and thus parliamentary, relationship. The six elections of the interwar period gave the Catholic Party a slight superiority over the POB in votes and seats on all but two occasions. A comparison of the average percentages acquired by the two parties in these elections reveals a marginal preponderance for the socialists, viz. 35·2 per cent against 34·9 per cent. But, this calculation includes the freak result of 1936, when, as a result of a radicalization of Belgian politics around anti-parliamentary parties of left and right, which was not sustained in the 1939 election, the catholics lost 11 per cent of their 1932 vote and the socialists 5 per cent. If both unparalleled losses are excluded, the average percentages for the other five elections are 36·1 per cent for the catholics and 35·7 per cent for the POB. The average proportion of the vote for the Parti Libéral stands at 15·8 per cent.

The postwar period saw the clear emergence of the Catholic Party (PSC) as the dominant party in the system. There were two reasons for the sharp improvement in the PSC's electoral fortunes: it benefited from the heightened tendency towards catholicism and conservatism produced by the introduction of the female suffrage, but, far more important, it inherited the electoral clientele of the prewar Flemish nationalist party, discredited by collaboration during the occupation and, subsequently, denuded of its leadership by the imposition of civil disabilities. The PSC's average percentage in the five elections from 1946 to 1958 was 44·3, while the socialist average declined fractionally to 34·7. The Parti Libéral's average vote registered a fall to 12·3 per cent. In 1961, the Parti Social Chrétien received 41·5 per cent of the vote, the Parti Socialiste Belge, 36·7 per cent, and the Parti Libéral, 12·4 per cent. However, in 1965, an almost revolutionary upheaval, at least in terms of Belgian voting patterns, occurred when the Parti Libéral's successor, Parti de la Liberté et du Progrès (PLP), received no less than 21·6 per cent of the total valid vote, and the PSC and PSB percentages were reduced to 34·4 per cent and 28·5 per cent respectively. In the short term, at least, the PLP has consolidated its electoral revolution, as it showed in the General Election of March, 1968, when (under considerable pressure from the francophone party (FDF) in its traditional stronghold in Brussels) it suffered an electoral loss of less than 1 per cent. In global electoral terms, the PSB retained exactly the same percentage of the vote in March, 1968, that it had acquired in 1965. Even so, a marginal increase in its vote in Flanders did not compensate for strategic losses to the francophone parties in Wallonia and Brussels, with the result that the party's representation in the Chamber of Representatives declined by five seats to 59. The continued growth of subcultural, rather than national, allegiance led to a further loss of electoral strength for the PSC, whose share of the vote fell to 31·7 per cent.

The picture of three-party dominance is impressive at the governmental level. The three traditional parties are essentially governmental rather than oppositional in disposition. Since 1919, Belgium has been ruled almost exclusively by bi- or tripartite coalitions. The only exception of significant duration was the four-year rule of the PSC, after it received a majority in both Chamber and Senate on a 48 per cent vote at the 1950 General Election. From 1919 to 1940, the catholics and liberals were virtually permanent incumbents in ministerial office, while the POB was in office for 48 per cent of the time. From the Liberation, in 1944, to the replacement of the

C* 73

PSC-PLP coalition by the PSC-PSB coalition in June 1968, the PSC governed for 76 per cent, the PSB for 59 per cent and the Parti Libéral for 52 per cent of the period. Until 1947, various forms of National Union governments were in power. Since then—with the PSC exception mentioned above—bipartites have constituted the norm. The PSC has shared power with the PSB for rather more than nine years *in toto*; and with the liberals, for rather more than five years. From 1954 to 1958, there was a PSB–Liberal coalition.

Two strands have acquired established positions on the periphery of Belgian politics: Flemish nationalism and communism. The Flemish nationalist parties have usually advocated federalist solutions to Flemish grievances. Although the emergence of Flemish consciousness, and the demands of the Flemish community for equal status in the Belgian state, lay at the heart of political controversy in the interwar period, Flemish nationalism never achieved a popular electoral base. The catholic and socialist parties had already pre-empted the loyalties of the Flemish working class. The prewar Flemish nationalist party (Vlaamsch Nationaal Verbond), whose political orientation, therefore, became catholic and conservative, reached its high-water mark in 1939, when it received 8·3 per cent of the vote. Its postwar successor, Volksunie, has consciously adopted a more progressive social programme, which has enabled it to act as a pressure group on the PSC in the Flemish interest: for 55 per cent of the PSC's vote in Flanders comes from the wage-earning and employé class. The social radicalism of the Volksunie is further strengthened by the nature of the nearest objects of its ethnic resentment. There remains in Flanders a residual French speaking middle class (of about 200,000) which is not only commercially powerful, but has also arrogated a caste position *vis-à-vis* the Flemish population. At the same time, the expansion of the Brussels conurbation is seen as an invasion of the Flemish patrimony by the francophone *bourgeoisie*. In 1965, the Volksunie secured the largest postwar vote for Flemish separatism when it nearly doubled its 1961 percentage to gain 6·85 per cent of the total valid vote; a reflection of the extent to which relations between the communities worsened in the early 1960s. In March 1968, with 9·79 of the total valid vote, the party surpassed the prewar electoral achievement of Flemish separatism.

In 1965, the Parti Communiste received nearly 5 per cent of the total valid vote; its largest vote in a general election since 1949. This result, too, owed more than a little to the linguistic crisis. The Parti Communiste's electoral base has always been almost wholly Walloon. In 1965, the party came to terms with its limited territorial and linguistic base and aligned itself with the emergent francophone federalist movement. The most potent separatist movement had emerged in the francophone wings of the PSB and the socialist trade union organization, the Fédération Générale du Travail de Belgique (FGTB). In espousing the federalist cause, the Parti Communiste's evident intention has been to drive a wedge between the PSB and the FGTB. In the short term, it does not appear to have succeeded. No rift has opened up between the political and trade union arms of the socialist movement, and, indeed, in March 1968, the Parti Communiste's electoral base (at 3·30 per cent) narrowed to little more than its 1961 share of the vote.

Although the communists had reaped a limited electoral advantage in 1965, by identifying with Walloon federalism, by no means all the Walloon socialists to defect from the PSB had embraced the Parti Communiste. Instead they had adhered to a number of dissident federalist parties which sprang up at the 1965 General Election. Of these parties, which together received rather less than 4 per cent of the vote in Wallonia (1·03 per cent of the total valid vote), two gained a seat each in the lower house. Insofar as these federalist parties were explicitly socialist in composition and aims, they reflected the consistent support lent to the principle of federalism by the Walloon federations of the PSB in the postwar period. If the francophone movement only emerged as a distinct political force in 1965, the francophone tendency had, nonetheless, acquired an obliquely established position in Belgian politics since 1944. The Walloon sections of the three traditional parties all contained organized federalist elements. As these elements have become activated by the mounting communal crisis, the specifically socialist character of Walloon federalism (such as it appeared in 1965) has all but disappeared. The new Walloon federalist party, the Rassemblement Wallon, created to fight the March 1968 elections, projects itself as a non-partisan political formation, informed solely by a nationalist ideology. In this capacity, it achieved a notable electoral coup by gaining 10·5 per cent of the Walloon vote. The success of the Rassemblement Wallon was matched by that of its political

75

ally, the Front Démocratique des Francophones, which doubled its share of the vote in the Brussels arrondissement. The francophone parties together received 5·90 per cent of the total valid vote (as compared with 2·52 per cent in 1965). Given the inevitable political dominance of the Flemish within the unitary state and the immanent economic distress of Wallonia, a further growth in the appeal of Walloon separatism would seem a fairly sure expectation. In short, the General Election of March 1968, with the continued success of the Volksunie and the striking emergence of the francophone parties, may well have signalled the failure of the traditional parties to keep the nationalist impulses of this century within the nineteenth century framework of Belgium.

SPIRITUAL FAMILIES AND SOCIO-ECONOMIC WORLDS

Belgians describe their political system in terms of three 'spiritual families', sustained by three 'worlds'. The description covers a predictable reluctance to speak of 'the nation' and indicates the compartmentalism of Belgian society. Yet, the political institutions of Belgium are still not primarily compartmentalized into national units. The compartments are, instead, the social and economic institutions which surround the major parties. Just as parties include both communities, so do their economic and social auxiliaries: their trade unions, co-operative, friendly societies, and educational and leisure organizations. The advantages for the parties are obvious. Daily identification with the socio-economic interests of a large section of a party's electoral clientele is a fair guarantee of political loyalty. The Parti Socialiste Belge and the Parti Social Chrétien are so placed; the Parti de la Liberté et du Progrès to a less extent, for trade union and co-operative organization has never been relevant to the professional and commercial class, which has historically provided its electoral support. Yet, even the liberals have acquired their own trade unions, grouped together in the Centrale Générale des Syndicats Libéraux de Belgique.

The socialist 'world' was the first to emerge, not as a propagandist device, but as a means of self-protection. Socialist co-operatives pre-dated the POB. It was their members and funds which created the party; and, it was the party which proceeded to the creation of a trade union movement. Until 1945, the movement formed an integral component of the Socialist Party: membership of a trade union constituted automatic membership of the party, and the direction of the Socialist trade union movement was under its political control. If party membership is not based on individual affiliation, and the statutes of the Fédération Générale du Travail de Belgique precludes its officials from holding political posts, effective co-ordination between the PSB and its trade union arm remains at both local and national level. As an organization capable of taking independent, politically significant action, the FGTB, with a membership around 700,000 in 1963, represents the most important political element outside the party in the Socialist 'world'. Probably more important in shaping the ethos of Belgian socialism are the friendly societies, which have replaced the co-operatives as the infra-structure of the socialist movement. With their considerable funds, commercially invested and administered by a professional bureaucracy, they have a vested interest in the financial and economic *status quo*. At the same time, they are a major source of income and trained managers for the party itself. Party, trade unions, co-operatives and friendly societies compose the citadel of the socialist 'world'. It is buttressed by ancillary social and cultural organizations, which range from socialist youth organizations to socialist holiday camps.

The catholic 'world' contains a corresponding socio-economic complex, which grew up under the joint impulse of the social catholicism of 'Rerum Novarum' and 'Quadragesimo Anno' and the determination of the Catholic Church in Belgium to insulate the catholic proletariat and peasantry from atheistic socialism. By the time that universal suffrage was conceded, the Walloon working class was considered lost to the Church, which, therefore, concentrated its mission on Flanders. In one respect, this was a miscalculation: in the long run, Catholicism has retained the adherence of the Walloon agrarian community and of a limited section of the Walloon urban working class, some 25 per cent of which normally votes for the Catholic party. Catholic peasants' leagues and Catholic trade unions were founded by the church in the last decade of the nineteenth century. The membership of the peasants' leagues is now over a hundred thousand. Four-fifths of these members belong to the Flemish organization, the *Boerenbond*. In 1964 the Christian trade union organization, the Confédération des Syndicats Chrétiens

(CSC), claimed a membership of more than 800,000; almost 30 per cent of the total working population. Like the other Catholic social and economic groups, its majority membership lies in the Flemish community; in a ratio of three to one. The CSC is linked to the Catholic co-operatives and 'friendly societies' through the Mouvement Ouvrier Chrétien (MOC), whose semi-Federal structure disguises a practical unity of action on the part of the social organs of Catholicism in both communities.

This unity is *political*. It is demanded by the character of the catholic 'world', which, in contrast to its socialist counterpart, displays the heterogeneity of occupational and class interest of Belgian society at large. The Catholic lower middle-class is represented in the Flemish Nationaal Christelijk Middenstandverbond (with 60,000 members in 1961). It has no equivalent in Wallonia, because the PSC's wing is dominated by precisely this class. The Catholic financial and entrepreneurial elements are organised in the Fédération des Patrons Catholiques. The Catholic 'world' consists of interest groups competing within the framework of the Catholic party. All three 'traditional' parties have adopted the system of electoral polls—akin to American primaries—to determine the composition of arrondissemental lists in elections. But, the system has most significance in the PSC: for each competing organization is geared to ensuring its representation at parliamentary level. Shifts in PSC policy can usually be traced to the performance of the different groups at the electoral polls. Historically, these diverse Catholic groups have found their unity in the defence of the Church's interests, specifically in the field of education. There is some indication that this unity is weakening in the face of the solution of the education conflict in the all-party School Pact of 1958 and the hastening depoliticization of the Catholic Church. The religious cleavage in Belgian society remains institutionalized in the PSC. Nevertheless, the process of 'desacralization' and the emergence of a Walloon consciousness have modified the structure of political relationships both between the parties and within them.

THE TRADITIONAL PARTIES

Parti Social Chrétien

When the PSC was constituted in 1945, it proclaimed itself 'a new party, with a new programme and a young cadre'. Its new unitary structure, based on individual affiliation, was designed to provide the cohesion at parliamentary and local levels which the diversification of political loyalties between the component organizations of the Catholic 'world' had prevented during the inter-war period. The Catholic party had been an 'organization of estates' (in the concise Dutch form *standsorganisatie*). Its electoral candidates and the members of its councils were nominees of the various affiliated *standen*. The Parti Social Chrétien has eschewed the *standen* as formal components of its organization. It also created a highly centralized structure, which has achieved an unprecedented, if by no means complete, degree of cohesion at all levels of the party. Yet, the PSC is still a *standsorganisatie*, and it has been the informal recognition of this fact which has preserved the unity of the party. The formal structure of the PSC, like the new programme of 1945, in which it attempted to deconfessionalize its electoral appeal, merely disguises the political structure—and the electoral clientele—of the earlier period.

The PSC, whose membership in June 1967 was almost 100,000, combines two parties: the Parti Social Chrétien in the francophone community and the Christelijke Volkspartij in the Flemish community. The two wings are administered separately from the party's National Committee, but have until recently enjoyed no autonomous decision-making power.[1] They meet as separate entities only for the purpose of electing their representatives to that committee; and, these meetings are simultaneous with, and composed of delegates from, the appropriate arrondissements to the party's national Congress. Their existence results from the PSC's somewhat elaborate machinery for maintaining formal parity between the communities

[1] In the General Election of March 1968, the francophone section of the National Committee took the decision to present a separate PSC list in the Brussels arrondissement. This list competed with a Catholic list headed by the retiring Prime Minister, Vanden Boeynants, which was composed mainly of Flemish candidates. Nevertheless, the full National Committee continued to meet, although the effect of this novel display of independence must be to weaken the authority of that body yet further.

Moreover, with the continuation of the linguistic crisis since March 1968, the formal unitary bonds of the PSC have been undermined by the first separate congresses of the two wings of the party; and as the crisis has developed, the relations between the two wings of the PSC have become increasingly those of a working alliance rather than those of a unitarist party.

in the National Committee. Within the committee, the linguistic groups have specific responsibility for maintaining the party machinery and for apprising the committee as a whole of political developments in the communities. In this sense, central control is strengthened by the system of separate administration. Parity of representation has also proved a stabilizing factor in the relations between the communities in the PSC, in that it has accorded the francophone wing a means of political influence which it would lack in a fully unitary party organization. In the latter case, the francophone wing, dominated by a middle-class conservative establishment, would have found itself subjected more directly to the political control of the larger Flemish wing, in which the progressive social organizations preponderate.

The PSC's organizational structure is encased in a familiar quasi-democratic mould, in which the exercise of authority delegated from the base is the decisive element in the conduct of power relationships within the party. According to the statutes, the party's Congress retains 'supreme authority'. While it is true that substantive policy decisions and organizational changes must be approved by Congress, such generalities have little bearing on the day-by-day exercise of power. Since the PSC is normally in office, short-term tactics and the negotiated compromises dictated by coalition government comprise the most significant decisions which the party has to take. The statutes place short-term decision-making in the hands of the National Committee. Moreover, the National Committee is responsible for preparing the agenda of the Congress and choosing the date for its annual meeting. Between the echelons of Congress and National Committee there is interposed a body composed of delegates from the Congress and the members of the National Committee. This is the Conseil Général, whose function is to provide soundings for the party leadership and to disseminate through arrondissemental, cantonal and local organisations the decisions taken by that leadership. Its role is purely consultative: like most of the organs of the PSC, the Conseil Général is geared to approval rather than to opposition. Even the Congress, which may censure the leadership, has no statutory power to dismiss it. In this respect, its means of influence are distinctly weaker than those of the PSB Congress.

Control over the selection of candidates assumes central importance in a party such as the PSC with its disparate composition. This requirement, symptomatic of the leadership's perennial concern to create a balance between the dichotomous elements in its electorate, explains the strong articulation between the National Committee and the arrondissemental organizations, which draw up the electoral lists for parliamentary elections. The National Committee disposes of three statutory instruments for asserting its influence in the arrondissemental parties. All candidates for the Presidency of the arrondissemental organization are subject to the preliminary approval of the National Committee. The direction of the party in the arrondissement is carried out by a council of delegates chosen by the cantonal and local sections of the party, which in turn elects a committee headed by the President. This committee contains *ex officio* the parliamentary representative of the arrondissement, and a number of co-opted members equivalent to half the number of elected delegates. The presence of the parliamentarians and the co-opted members is designed to dilute the militancy of the local membership. Finally, the list of candidates for the preliminary electoral poll is automatically submitted to the appropriate wing of the National Committee, which has the right to modify the order of candidates on the list and even to remove certain candidatures.

The gulf between the formal and real structure of the PSC is embodied in the party's executive organs. Its statutes may grant the National Committee executive direction of the party and the authority to take decisions on its short-term governmental or oppositional role in the Belgian Parliament, but two factors have combined to undermine its theoretical dominance. One is its un-representative character. The National Committee is composed of 31 members: the President, elected by the whole Congress; seven delegates from each linguistic wing of the mass-party; three parliamentary representatives from each linguistic group in the Chamber and Senate; and four co-opted members. The statutory provision of parity at this level between the communities stands in marked contrast to the fact that the PSC has always drawn its electoral support overwhelmingly from Flanders. Indeed, the exacerbation of relations between the communities in the past few years has only served to emphasize the disparity. The 1965 elections gave the PSC 54 Flemish and 23 francophone deputies. Although the PSC received fewer votes in both communities in 1968, the loss of francophone votes was greater, thus strengthening the Flemish strand in the party. PSC representation in the Chamber now stands at 51 Flemish and only 18 francophone deputies. The same disparity is observed in the Senate. The National Committee lacks representatives not only in the linguistic sphere. The francophone wing of the party contributes a disproportionate weight in the committee to the PSC's conservative membership. As a result, the committee has been replaced as the *de facto* decision-making body by a non-statutory committee, whose members better reflect the interest-groups in the PSC. This is the Agenda Committee, around which there prevails an aura of mystery and disapprobation, no doubt because of its non-elective character. It meets through the PSC's Study Centre and functions as the effective organ for the formulation of policy. Information about its precise composition is not easy to come by, but the following list of members for the period 1956–58 has been published:[1] two members each from the catholic employers' federation, the Catholic trade unions, the Mouvement Ouvrier Chrétien, and the peasants' leagues; one representative from the Flemish middle-class association; and six representatives from the PSC itself, notably the President and the two Vice-Presidents. The National Committee is, therefore, best seen as an executive instrument. But, the fact that official decision-making must take place there gives some weight to its role in this sphere.

Nevertheless, its influence as a body has become subordinate to that of the President of the party. The President is, after all, the only official elected by the whole Congress. He is the co-ordinator of the activities of the formal and informal directive organs of the party. The permanent party apparatus is centred on him. Above all, whether the PSC is in government or opposition, the President embodies the will of the party against that of the government, for the statutes of the PSC forbid the joint tenure of office in government and party executive. The most obvious explanation of this prohibition is that the party has wished to preserve itself as an institution from too close an identification with the compromises in policy terms inherent in coalition government and also, as the quasi-permanent party, to leave an opening towards the other possible partner. The consequence has been that presidents have felt able to

---

[1] Annexe No. 1 of the Courrier Hebdomadaire No. 83, November 11, 1960, produced by the Centre de Recherche et d'Information Socio-Politiques, Brussels.

express their opposition—in the name of the party—to the policies of a coalition in which the PSC has been participating. In 1960, the President of the PSC, Théo Lefèvre, hastened the demise of the PSC–Parti Libéral coalition by attacking the inadequacy of its social programme. In this way, he was reflecting the pressure from the MOC and the catholic trade unions for a *travailliste* coalition with the PSB. Similarly, his successor, Paul Vanden Boeynants, interpreting a swelling current of antagonism in the PSC to its coalition with the PSB after the 1965 General Election, publicized his preference for a coalition with the Liberals. It is an indication of the status of the presidency that both Lefèvre and Vanden Boeynants became Prime Minister after the collapse of the objects of their attack.

The PSC's 1945 programme represented an attempt to trace a new *personalist* socio-economic programme between collectivism and unrestrained capitalism. Both alternatives were condemned, but a distinctive PSC programme has failed to emerge. One reason for this is that the PSC has fought most of its electoral campaigns on specific short-term issues: the defence of the monarchy in the late 1940s, the defence of clerical education in the 1950s, resistance to trade union agitation in 1961, and the linguistic crisis in 1965. The other reason is that PSC social and economic policy is no fixed quantity, but a response to the shifts in influence within the party of its progressive and conservative aims. The success of the MOC in the electoral polls in 1961 took the party into coalition with the PSB; in 1966, the strength of the conservative reaction against this experience and the PSC's electoral rebuff took it into coalition with the PLP. From 1961 to 1966, the PSC pursued a policy of moderate reformism; when it went into coalition with the liberals in March 1966, it embarked on a programme of stringent governmental retrenchment.

Parti Socialiste Belge

The Parti Socialiste Belge—the POB was renamed in 1945—has historically presented a far more monolithic face than the PSC. A belief in the indivisibility of the class interests of the Walloon and Flemish working class has meant that, until quite recently, its structure has made little formal concession to the dual ethnic character of the country. At the parliamentary level, its representatives have exhibited a discipline unparalled by their Catholic and Liberal counterparts. However, in the last decade, an ideological crisis in Belgian social democracy has become identified with the linguistic crisis, and this development has produced stresses on the unity of the party.

The duality of the population is recognized in three articles of the party's statutes. Firstly, the President and Vice-President represent two communities, but each arrondissemental federation must propose two candidates, one francophone, the other Flemish, who are then voted upon by the whole Congress. Secondly, the PSB Bureau, in many respects the formal equivalent of the PSC's National Committee, shares with it a stipulated regional composition. Before 1963, it contained eight representatives from each community, who were elected by the whole Congress. But, the statutory revision of that year strengthened its regional character by providing for the election (the Flemish, Walloon and Brussels federations voting separately) of twelve members: five from the Walloon federations, five from the Flemish federations, and two from the Brussels federation. This is a fairly accurate reflection of the regional composition of the party's membership; the PSB Congress of December 1965 indicated a Walloon membership of 79,000, a Flemish membership of 67,000, and a Brussels membership of 23,000. The other members of the Bureau comprise twelve delegates elected by the whole Congress, the President and the party secretaries. Thirdly, in one significant provision, the statutes of the PSB exceed those of the PSC in permitting an element of horizontal connection between the arrondissemental organizations of the linguistic regions. The Walloon and Flemish federations may meet separately in regional congresses. The initiative for these meetings must come from five arrondissemental federations; and the party Bureau exercises a close supervision over what takes place in them. While there have been only two Flemish Congresses, in 1937 and 1951, it is revelatory of the growth of francophone consciousness that, although the first Walloon Congress was not held until 1947, there have been five since then. They have unquestionably fostered the distinctive role of the Walloon federations within the PSB.

The mass organization of the PSB is similar to that of the PSC. Indeed, it provided the model when the Catholic party was restructured after the Liberation. It shares an organization based on local sections and arrondissemental federations, which correspond to electoral divisions. Its Congress is vested with ultimate authority in the fields of policy-making and party administration. There is the same statutory division between party leadership and government. Yet, the PSB's structure manifests two important differences, both of which have been germane to its recent difficulties. The first characteristic of the PSB is that its formal structure provides a broader dispersal of power. Its Bureau, while exercising executive and disciplinary powers, defers in decisions on tactics and the formulation of electoral programmes to the Conseil Général. This body is composed of the Bureau and arrondissemental delegates, one for every 500 party members. The Bureau is obliged to resign on a censure vote by the Congress, and, Vice-President included, to seek re-election every two years. Unlike the PSC National Committee, the PSB Bureau does not have the authority to arrange electoral lists. The final decision here rests with the arrondissemental federations, whose influence over their parliamentary representatives is thereby increased. Of course, the prestige of the leadership and a loyalist tradition have meant that these democratic provisions have normally constituted a potential, rather than actual, restraint on the leadership; and it has its own means of control. The Bureau selects the permanent arrondissemental officials. Moreover, the higher echelons of the PSB structure are dominated by the parliamentary party and the party bureaucracy. The Bureau itself is wholly composed of these elements, and the Conseil Général in a large majority. The second major characteristic of the PSB is the close relationship between the leadership of the party organization and the party's ministerial representatives. It is a relationship which finds institutional expression in the fact that ministers join the Bureau in a consultative capacity, and are thus consultative members of the Conseil Général. PSB ministers or ministerial candidates are assured a far more effective voice in party decisions than their PSC counterparts, who are not only excluded from the Agenda and National Committees, but are also only allowed a consultative role in the PSC Conseil Général on the invitation of the National Committee.

In the last decade, the moderate reformism of the PSB leadership has become the centre of a dissension which has undermined the party's traditional unity. The official doctrine of the PSB, reaffirmed in its first postwar Congress in 1945, remains the principles embodied in the 1894 Quaregnon programme. These include collective ownership of resources and the means of production, the elimination of the class system, and the Saint-Simonian formula of the transformation of the state into an 'administration of things'. The doctrine, like the reaffirmation, has proved a formality in the light of the party's permanent failure to achieve a parliamentary majority and the determination of the party leadership to exercise constitutional power—as the exigencies of the electoral system demand—through coalitions with non-socialist parties.

The party leadership's accommodation to the inevitability of administering a capitalist regime has produced a pragmatism aimed at ensuring its electoral clientele an increased share of the national income: by raising or, at least, maintaining wage-levels; by increased welfare benefits; by proportional and progressive taxation; and by the struggle against inflation and unemployment. The pragmatic zeal of the PSB has cast it, on occasion, in a more overtly conservative role than the PSC. When both parties propounded schemes for a national planning agency in their 1961 electoral programmes, the PSC's 'programmation bureau', designed to evolve a development programme to be executed by a number of subsiding organs, promised greater centralization than the PSB's 'planning commissariat', which was envisaged rather as the co-ordinator of proposals from the lower echelons of the planning structure. The PSB had no proposals for the nationalization of the energy sectors. Its programme, like the PSC's, aimed at compensating for the inadequacies of capitalism.

The PSB's 1961 programme marked the extent to which the party leadership had overriden a growth of militancy in the mass movement. In 1956, the congress of the socialist Fédération Générale du Travail adopted a programme of mid-term structural reform, involving planning, nationalization of key sectors of the economy and a national health service, which was in turn taken up by the PSB Congress in 1959. The new radical trend in both organizations emanated overwhelmingly from their Walloon wings; a trend which received further impetus from the month-long strike from mid-December 1960, directed against the economies in government social expenditure proposed by the PSC–Parti Libéral coalition. In response to an appeal from the Catholic hierarchy, the Catholic trade unions withdrew their initial support from the strike; and the FGTB's national leadership, with its Flemish secretary-general, reflecting the slight preponderance of its Flemish wing, refused to make it official. When the strike was called off, the strike movement had become almost entirely a Walloon phenomenon. The result was an immediate agitation for federalism amongst Walloon socialists, who see the socialist plurality, if not majority, which would emerge in a federal Walloon state, as the only means of achieving the structural changes essential to the Walloon economy. Socialist pressure for federation was carried on outside the PSB through the Mouvement Populaire Wallon (MPW). The MPW, which was founded a fortnight after the end of the strike, less than a year later had a membership, composed largely of trade unionists, of about 100,000. It derived its greatest support from the Liège area. But, the dynamism of this socialist federalist movement has become dissipated. The MPW's reluctance to undermine the PSB by leading a secession from the party removed a unity from the federalist elements in the Walloon socialist movement, with a resulting fragmentation into a number of marginal political parties.

Within the PSB, the leadership has been able to control Walloon militancy, but not without difficulty. In 1963, opposition from the Walloon federations to the legislative projects for strengthening the powers of government against a general strike, which had been drawn up by the PSB in coalition with the PSC, was great enough to force the PSB leadership to renegotiate the projects. The modified proposals were then presented to the second national Congress, where they were opposed by 30 per cent of the delegates. The opposition came largely from the Walloon federations, 58 per cent of whose delegates voted against their acceptance. The leadership derived huge support, however, from the Flemish delegation, which voted over 97 per cent in favour; and from the Brussels federation which voted 88 per cent in favour. Opposition in the Congress was followed by opposition in Parliament, chiefly from the eight deputies and six senators of the Liège Federation, who were instructed by the Liège organization to abstain in the vote.

The only precedent for such large-scale indiscipline in the Socialist ranks was the refusal, in 1938, of 18 deputies to vote for the establishment of diplomatic relations with the National Government in Spain. The recent case was met by temporary suspension of the offending parliamentarians, and the indiscipline has not recurred since 1963. The analysis of voting patterns in the second 1963 Congress provides the key to the leadership's means of control over the Congress. It can count upon the solid support of the Flemish and Brussels federations, neither of which share the militant tradition or the regional economic problems of the Walloon federations. Between them, the Flemish and Brussels delegations dispose of almost 55 per cent of the votes at Congress. The same pro-leadership support is forthcoming on the federalist issue. The Flemish socialists, with less than a third of the popular vote in Flanders, fear that any federalist solution would place them in a permanent exclusion from power. The PSB has been able in this way to maintain its adherence to the unitary state, while demanding certain constitutional guarantees to prevent Wallonia's political subjection. In any case, the problem presented by Walloon federalists within the party has been solved by the defection of the more extreme federalists to the dissident autonomist parties.

Parti de la Liberté et du Progrés
After the General Election of 1961, the Parti Libéral acquired a new President and with him a new organization, programme and name. The party also embarked on an effort at expansion; from 44,000 members in 1962, its membership had reached 77,000 less than a year later. The novelties did not end there, for the PLP's electoral success in 1965 provides the exception to the general stability of the Belgian political system.

It was said of the old Parti Libéral, in explanation of a certain lack of concreteness in its electoral and governmental policies, that the party stood for a spirit of tolerance and individualism rather than a programme. Be that as it may, the party's organization certainly justified the description. The Parti Libéral's structure exhibited the same pyramidal mould as the organizations of the other traditional parties. Local sections delegated representatives to the assemblies and directive committees of the arrondissemental federations which, in turn, sent their delegates to the party's General Assembly, which was endorsed with the supreme authority in political and organizational matters. Emanating from the General Assembly came the Permanent Committee (the counterpart of the PSB's Conseil Général in short-term decision-making), the Bureau, the executive and disciplinary organ of the party, and the President. But, the edifice of direction and control proved somewhat illusory in the face of the practical independence of parliamentarians and federations. On more than one occasion, the party found itself losing votes to dissident liberal lists, which resulted from a failure of the arrondissemental federations to agree on common lists.

The revised statutes of 1961 are aimed at strengthening central control in the new party. Although the selection of candidate-lists remains in the hands of the federations, the President is empowered to intervene and settle disputes, either on his own initiative or at the request of the federation in question. Sanctions against parliamentary indiscipline are available under the new system. The PLP has been called a 'presidential regime', and there is some evidence in the statutory innovations to support this view.

The President, for instance, designates the majority of members in the PLP's executive organ, the Bureau Permanent. Certainly, the party's first President, Omer Vanaudenhove, has provided it with forceful leadership, which the Parti Libérale had lacked since the interwar period. It was his policy of complete opposition to the *travailliste* PSC–PSB coalition, which contrived to create a large measure of unity amongst the PLP parliamentarians from 1961 to 1966.

There is, nevertheless, room for suspicion that the unity and centralization of the party may still be more apparent than real. The PLP, like its predecessor, is an alliance of three powerful regional organizations, each of which unites, more or less, the party's membership in their respective regions: the Liberaal Vlaams Verbond (Flemish Liberal Union), the Entente Libérale Wallonne, and the Brussels Liberal Federation. The Entente Libérale Wallonne and the Brussels Federation have perpetuated the Liberal Party's interwar policy of defending francophone interests: indeed, in 1965, the francophone Liberals conducted a fiercely anti-Flemish campaign aimed at prising the francophone Catholic middle class from the PSC, in which the numerically preponderant Flemish progressive forces were presented as incorporating not only the threat of a permanent *travailliste* alliance in government but also the threat of the complete submergence of the francophone element in the PSC. On the other hand, the Liberaal Vlaams Verbond has vociferously championed Flemish demands. In the linguistic conflict, the francophone and Flemish wings of the party converge only in recognizing that none of them stands to gain from federalism. That makes the PLP the most unitarist of the three major parties.

In 1961, Vanaudenhove declared that 'the new party of the future will be progressive'. But the PLP's new economic policies are very much the mixture as before: an emphasis on financial measures, such as economies in the budgetary deficit, and thus social, sectors of government activity, designed to lighten direct taxation; controls on the development of governmental agencies; opposition to nationalization; fewer restrictions on banking and investment corporations; an increase in the powers of government against trade union agitation. If the PLP has retained the mantle acquired by the Parti Libéral in 1945 as the protagonist of *laissez-faire*, it *has* transformed itself by casting off the mantle of anti-clericalism. The 1958 School Pact, by guaranteeing both lay and clerical systems of education, removed the chief issue between secularists and catholics. Since then, the Liberals have sought to wean from their alliegance to the PSC, the Catholic counterparts of the small entrepreneurs, civil servants and professional class, which have traditionally provided the Liberal clientele. Already, in 1961, the Parti Libéral included prominent Catholics in its electoral lists, and, in the Flemish province of Limburg, formed joint-lists with dissident Catholics. The PLP has intensified the policy and reaped its fruits. In 1965, the party's vote in Flanders increased by half. In the Walloon arrondissements, its total vote more than doubled; and that vote came overwhelmingly from the PSC: in part, no doubt, the result of the Entente Libérale Wallonne's anti-Flemish campaign, but also, as in Flanders, a reflection of the realignment of the Catholic middle class in Belgium behind a party which seemed to represent more accurately its social and economic aspirations.

THE PARTIES AND THE INTERNATIONAL ASSEMBLIES

Three factors might create the expectation that Belgian political parties have been influenced by their contacts with foreign political parties. Belgium has a broad experience of European assemblies. It participates in the Benelux Inter-Parliamentary Council, as well as in the three major Western European assemblies. It has also sent parliamentarians of considerable status within their own parties to these gatherings. P. H. Spaak, PSB ex-Prime Minister, J. Duvieusart, PSC ex-Prime Minister, and R. Motz, Parti Libéral ex-President and ex-Minister, are the most notable examples, but, even its most recent representatives at the European Parliament have included two PSB ex-cabinet ministers, F. Dehousse and L. E. Troclet, and R. Pêtre, who is a member of the PSC National Committee. Finally, the Chamber of Representatives contains a Committee on European Affairs,[1] established in 1962, which hears the annual reports of the delegations to the various assemblies and uses the information thus acquired, and on occasion the reports of individual delegates, in its dual function as parliamentary supervisor of the European activities of the Ministry of Foreign Affairs and as a device for ensuring the conformity of domestic legislation to EEC norms. Yet, there is no evidence that these possible means of influence have effected any concrete change in the political practice or philosophy of the Belgian parties.

The selection of delegates to the European assemblies takes place after each general election and is proportionate to the parliamentary representation of the parties. Between 1965 and 1968, Belgium sent three PSC, two PSB and two PLP delegates to the Council of Europe, and six PSC, four PSB and four PLP delegates to the European Parliament. Each party delegation includes senators and deputies in as nearly equal numbers as possible, and they mirror the linguistic and regional composition of the party's parliamentary composition. Moreover, in the PSC, an attempt is made to reflect the balance of progressive and conservative elements in the parliamentary party.

Methods of selection for the European Parliament are the same in the three parties. Normally, the candidates (who propose themselves) are equal in numbers to the number of places available. The decision on the delegates appears to be made by the party acting as a committee, not by any leadership group. The candidates present themselves to a party meeting and are elected by acclaim. If there is a choice, a secret ballot takes place, but this rarely occurs. A rule of the Belgian Parliament requires that the party lists should be promulgated, but their approval is only a formality.

There is no discussion of the 'party-line' of the delegates at the European Parliament in the parliamentary party, if only because the European Parliament usually deals with matters which are too technical to be worth discussion or decision-taking at Brussels. The

[1] On the work of the European Affairs Committee, see the article by Dr Moreels (Beschouwingen betreffende de Commissie voor de Europese Zaken in de Belgische Kamer van Volksvertegenswoordigers) in *Tijdschrift voor Bestuurswetenschappen en Publiekrecht*, March–April 1966.

delegates, therefore, act primarily as members of the groups at the Parliament rather than as delegates of their national parties. Within the Christian Democrat group, the PSC tends to divide along progressive and conservative lines. But, the PSB delegation appears to be the consistent protagonist of radical solutions in the Social Democrat group. The chief reason for this is the incipient depression of the Belgian, and specifically the Walloon, economy. It has no regular allies in the group, but takes its allies as the occasion affords, for example, the SPD on the treatment of coal-mining within the EEC. Although the Belgians are amongst the keenest supporters of Western European political and economic unity, there is no suggestion that they act as a group in the European Parliament. The role of the Belgian secretariat at the Parliament is purely administrative. Such instruction as there is comes from the political groups.

REGIONAL DISTRIBUTION OF SEATS IN THE CHAMBER OF REPRESENTATIVES, BY PARTY, 1965 AND 1968

| Parties | Flemish | | | | | | Francophones | | | | | | General Total | |
| | Flanders | | Brussels | | Total | | Wallonia | | Brussels | | Total | | | |
	1968	1965	1968	1965	1968	1965	1968	1965	1968	1965	1968	1965	1968	1965
PSC	45	(51)	6	(3)	51	(54)	14	(18)	4	(5)	18	(23)	69	(77)
PSB	27	(27)	2	(2)	29	(29)	25	(28)	5	(7)	30	(35)	59	(64)
PLP	17	(18)	2	(2)	19	(20)	22	(19)	6	(9)	28	(28)	47	(48)
Communists	—	(—)	—	(—)	—	(—)	4	(5)	1	(1)	5	(6)	5	(6)
Volksunie	18	(11)	2	(1)	20	(12)	—	(—)	—	(—)	—	(—)	20	(12)
FDF	—	(—)	—	(—)	—	(—)	—	(—)	5	(3)	5	(3)	5	(3)
Rassemblement Wallon	—	(—)	—	(—)	—	(—)	7	(2)	—	(—)	7	(2)	7	(2)
Total	107	(107)	12	(8)	119	(115)	72	(72)	21	(25)	93	(97)	212	(212)

SEATS IN THE CHAMBER OF REPRESENTATIVES, BY PARTY, IN THE POSTWAR PERIOD

Year	Social-ists	Social-Christ-ians	Liberals	Com-munists	Volk-sunie	Union Démo-crat-ique Belge	Rassemble-ment Social-Chrétien de la Liberté	Indé-pen-dents	Rassemble-ment National	Front des Franco-phones	Walloon Federal-lists	Rassemble-ment Wal-loon	Num-ber of seats
1946	69	92	17	23	—	1	—	—	—	—	—	—	202
1949	66	105	29	12	—	—	—	—	—	—	—	—	212
1950	77	108	20	7	—	—	—	—	—	—	—	—	212
1954	86	95	25	4	1	—	1	—	—	—	—	—	212
1958	84	104	21	2	1	—	—	—	—	—	—	—	212
1961	84	96	20	5	5	—	—	1	1	—	—	—	212
1965	64	77	48	6	12	—	—	—	—	3	2	—	212
1968	59	69	47	5	20	—	—	—	—	5	—	6	212

VOTES FOR THE CHAMBER OF REPRESENTATIVES, BY PARTY, IN THE POSTWAR PERIOD

(as percentages of total number of valid ballots)

40% 30% 20% 10%

PSC
42·53 43·55 47·68 41·15 46·50 41·46 34·48 31·73

PSB
31·59 29·75 34·51 37·34 35·79 36·73 28·28 27·99

PCB
12·68 15·25 11·25 12·15 11·05 12·33 21·61 20·87

UB|PLP
8·92 7·49 4·75 2·20 3·57 1·89 1·98 3·08 3·56 2·52 3·30 FRANCOPHONES

VOLKSUNIE
6·69 9·79

FDF/RW
4·56 5·90

1946 1949 1950 1954 1958 1961 1965 1968

The Grand Duchy of Luxembourg has a smaller population than several dozen of Western Europe's larger cities. Despite this it has played a role of some importance in the creation of the European Communities. The right of veto for once became more real than apparent when Luxembourg delayed the merger of the executives of the three communities until she received adequate compensation for the loss of the High Authority of the Coal and Steel Community. Luxembourg's political parties gain in importance from the allocation to her of an entirely disproportionate number of seats in the European Parliament—six out of 142.[1]

Two political parties are dominant—the Christian Social and the Socialist. Together they always win about three quarters of the seats in the Chamber of Deputies and a rather smaller share of the popular vote.[2] The Christian Social Party has always been the largest parliamentary force, although the Socialists won more votes in 1964. With the Liberals placed to the far right of the political spectrum, there have, in practice, been only two possible governmental alignments—Christian Social/Socialist and Christian Social/Liberal. Since 1947, the grand coalition has been preferred for twelve years as against ten. Elections have played some role in the changes—four since 1947. In 1951 and 1964 the Socialists made considerable gains and promptly re-entered the government. The same happened to the Liberals in 1959 and 1968. There is thus a fairly ordered system of political change to be offset against the general picture of stability. The Christian Socials have been the dominant government party and they have supplied all the Prime Ministers since the war, of whom there have only been four.

The two larger parties have their strength spread fairly evenly across the country. The Liberals do disproportionately well in the centre constituency, including Luxembourg City, whilst the traditional Communist bastion is in the southern mining areas. The Communists are now probably the most obscurantist in Western Europe: certainly they were the only party to support the invasion of Czechoslovakia.

Election Results to Chamber of Deputies
(seats won by each party)

	1946	1948*	1951*	1954	1959	1964	1968	% share of popular vote in 1968
Christian Social	25	22	21	26	21	22	21	35·3
Socialist	11	14	18	17	17	21	18	32·3
Liberal	9	9	8	6	11	6	11	16·6
Communist	5	5	4	3	3	5	6	15·5
Others	1	1	1			2		

* Only half the seats were up for election in 1948 and 1951, under the electoral law subsequently modified in 1956.

[1] Compared to three out of 147 in the Consultative Assembly.

[2] There are four multi-member constituencies within which seats are allocated by proportional representation. Voting is compulsory.

CHAPTER 4

FRANCE

A study of French political parties at the present moment presents both special interest and peculiar difficulties, for the surface pattern has changed completely since 1962. How far is this a superficial change and how far a fundamental transformation? At the June 1968 Election, three major groups shared between them 80 per cent of the vote, whilst only three other groups were able individually to exceed 1 per cent. This is in striking contrast to the final election in the Fourth Republic in 1956 when the three largest parties mustered only 50 per cent of the total vote between them, and at least six and possibly nine (according to classification) other groups won individually 1 per cent of the poll or more.

Hence both the fascination of the French party scene and the difficulty of dealing with it objectively. The regrouping of the existing parties, the creation of new parties, the question of where the divisions of opinion lie, the problem of how many parties are needed, indeed the very role of political parties: all these have been the major part of the political debate in France since the end of the Algerian war. Inextricably linked have been institutional controversies: the relative roles of President, Executive and Parliament. In the background has been the work of French political scientists on parties, and this means that any transformation has been conscious. France has convinced itself that its party system is rotten but has left its politicians free to adapt themselves and reclaim their country's allegiance. In no other case have major changes in the party system been attended by so much academic analysis. France deserves, perhaps, an intensive study of the effect of political science on politicians.

Yet this is about the worst time to undertake any durable analysis of the French political scene. The changes are so far advanced that it would be absurd, and seriously misleading, to examine the party system as it was until five or six years ago with a supplementary discussion of recent developments. Yet to treat the four-party system of 1967–68 as fundamental, with older parties and systems treated in the past tense, would be to make a gigantic assumption about the future. However, either treatment would be easier, certainly to write and probably to read, than the one adopted here, which is a mixture of the systematic and the chronological, with the former covering both the parties and certain of their characteristics. This poses real problems of distinguishing the possible ephemeral present from the very recent past. The structural character of French parties is grouped with the section dealing with the party system 1945–62, whilst the ideological and socio-economic characteristics are dealt with mainly in the concluding section on the significance of these developments.

BACKGROUND

France is a nation rather than a country. All political forces relate themselves to a certain concept of the French nation state and to a particular attitude to French history. All political parties like to claim for themselves some strand of French tradition. Yet French politics has a curious combination of the intensely parochial with the essentially national. There is very little in between: none of the sectionalism of North American politics and, despite both physical and electoral geography, less regional flavour than in most West European countries. Most French politicians like to have strong local roots: most of them are, or would like to be, mayor of their home town or village (home may be natal or constituency). Yet most regard themselves as thinking in essentially national or ideological terms. The traditional parties have tended to be structured round departments, essentially administrative divisions which rarely bear any relationship to cultural ties or economic realities. This is related to the electoral system but it also reflects an attitude: the department is a division of the French nation state, not a historic unit to which personal or political loyalties could be given which might rival loyalty to France. So Alsace, Provence or Normandy hardly exist for French political organisations. Yet at a general election the local strength of a personality can easily outweigh any national movement of opinion while the difference in voting behaviour between local and national elections, although the same labels are normally worn, can be greater than in any other major European country.

The French state includes odd islands and territories scattered round the world. In Europe it includes one island, Corsica, which although conventionally regarded as part of metropolitan France has a quite different national background and utterly different political behaviour from the mainland.

Mainland France is not homogenous. There are three national minorities (Alsacian, Basque and Breton), Jewish and Moslem communities in the larger cities and several pockets of Protestants, mainly in Alsace or the South. There is also a substantial population of *rapatriés*, those who left the Maghreb rather than live under independent governments. From the political point of view only the Protestant and *rapatrié* minorities are of any significance. Traditionally Protestants have voted on the Left and, although there are some signs that this is breaking down, the Protestant villages of the Cevennes which survived Louis XIV's persecution seemed to regard President de Gaulle as his lineal successor. The *rapatriés* became numerically significant only after 1962 and there has been some speculation about whether they might not become a political force and the basis of a new extreme right-wing party. There is very little doubt that their votes were a large part of those received by Jean-Louis Tixier-Vignancour in the 1965 presidential election but, this apart, there has been no sign that they are cohesive or concentrated enough to become politically significant.

There is, however, one deep cultural divide in France: that between devout and lapsed Catholics. Roughly one third of the nation are devout Catholics, one third are totally detached from the Church and one third in intermediate categories. The former are dominant in North-western and North-eastern France, including Alsace-Lorraine, and in mountainous pockets of the Jura, Savoy, the South-east of the Massif Central and the West Pyrenees. The second are dominant in the rural areas of the South-west, the North-eastern part of the Massif Central (Limousin) and a zone to the South-east of Paris. This pattern was laid down during the eighteenth century—though in part it reflects older patterns of heresy and huguenotism—and crystallized in 1789. Detailed research on voting in neighbouring villages has thrown up cases of the boundaries of the eighteenth-century dioceses showing through; the

French Revolution was welcomed or rejected in much of provincial France according to the local character of the Church and the memory has stuck.

In terms of economic geography, France is also two nations. France of the industrial revolution is the Paris area, a pocket round Lyon and St Etienne and a broad belt along the North-eastern frontier as far as the Jura. France west of a line from the mouth of the Seine to the mouth of the Rhone was, until almost yesterday, essentially pre-industrial revolution: an agricultural country with market towns and small enterprises. Recently, however, this has changed dramatically. New industrial centres such as Grenoble or Le Mans have expanded rapidly and the proportion of the working population engaged in agriculture has fallen from 27·5 per cent (1954 Census) to 15·3 per cent in 1968.

The division into social classes overlies these patterns irregularly. In Paris the vote is divided between Communist and the Right (Conservative or Gaullist) essentially in terms of social class; but for the rest of France, Paris would long since probably have become a two-party system based as much on social class as in Britain. Some other industrial areas follow suit to a lesser degree. However, others take little or no notice of a social class divide and vote by their local traditions: in March 1967 Lyon returned five Gaullists for its five seats while Marseille, no more industrial, returned four Communists and four SFIO.[1] These social and cultural divisions operate through strong historical memories. Because men fought and died in the clashes between Catholic Reaction and Rationalist Progress at the Revolution, between Monarchy and Republic in 1848 and in the Paris Commune, the ideas for which they died—or the ideas which later generations have placed in their heads—are the stronger.

Leaving aside memory and myth for the historical record, three of the existing parties date back to the Third Republic, the Radicals (founded 1901), the SFIO (1905) and the Communists (1920). Of these, the SFIO had very little and the Communists no responsibility for governing the country until the Fourth Republic. But the Radicals came to dominate the Third Republic through shifting

[1] Most French parties are known by their initials and this practice is followed here. A glossary of initials is appended. However, the Communist and Radical parties are referred to as such. The terms Centre-Left, Conservative and Gaullist are used as defined on pp. 113, 119 and 121.

alliances based on nuances of Centre-Left or Centre-Right. Possessing a strong distrust of executive power they never submerged their intense individualism for the common good of party or country. The result was unstable and short-lived cabinets, despite an underlying continuity of methods of government. The Third Republic collapsed on July 10, 1940, when a joint sitting of the Chamber of Deputies and of the Senate effectively voted suicide by 569 to 80[1] handing the powers of the Republic to Pétain.

A provisional government under de Gaulle took over with the Liberation and France expressed its overwhelming desire for a fresh start by voting more than 15·5 million to under 600,000 for a constituent assembly to draw up a new constitution, rather than a reconstitution of the Third Republic. Only the Radicals fought for the latter and little more than half their voters supported their Party's advice. Consensus about the political system broke up immediately and never returned until in another referendum in 1958 France turned its back decisively on the Fourth Republic. The first draft of the constitution was defeated by a million votes in May 1946; in the third referendum within twelve months, the second draft was agreed by a million votes in October 1946. However, it received fewer actual votes than the first draft, and was passed with 64 per cent of the electorate voting against or abstaining.

The essential characteristic of the socialist and communist inspired Constitution was the dominance of the Assembly and the corresponding weakness of the Executive, let alone the Council of the Republic (Senate) or President. Throughout, it was dogged by all the ills of the Third Republic and worse. Ministries were short-lived and grew shorter as time went on. The abandonment in the Assembly of an alignment presented to the electorate for approval—a fault of the Third Republic—became a characteristic of the Fourth. This betrayal of faith with the electorate was possibly as responsible as the notorious instability for France's loss of faith in the Fourth Republic and its politicians. What made it worse was that whereas in the Third Republic the dominant party had believed it a virtue to chasten the Executive by bringing it down from time to time, this provincial Radical philosophy was held by fewer and fewer—even

---

[1] The 80 were 36 SFIO, 35 Radical and Centre-Left, 3 ex-Communist (the party had been banned) and 6 others.

101

in the Radical party—in the Fourth Republic. The politicians themselves steadily lost faith in the system which a few years before they had vigorously defended from Gaullist and Communist attacks. The Fourth Republic committed suicide almost as easily as the Third when on June 2, 1958, the Assembly voted by 350 to 161 (of whom 148 were Communist) to allow de Gaulle to write, and submit directly to referendum, a new Constitution.

Fact and myth about the Fourth Republic will always take much sorting out. The four dominant groups (SFIO, Centre-Left, Conservatives and MRP) together with the Communists received the blame; in the eyes of many it extended to political parties as such. There can be much debate about how much blame there is (the first major steps towards European unity, the important stages of decolonisation and the reinvigoration of the French economy were three substantial achievements of its twelve years) and to whom it should attach. But the important thing is the myth and the memory of it, however unfair the judgements involved. In the autumn of 1958 the electorate expressed its views in no uncertain terms. All the major non-Communist groups accepted the new constitution, however much it stuck in their gullet; minorities in the SFIO and Centre-Left (in the name of the *Union des Forces Démocratiques*) joined the Communists to campaign for the *Non* but they took care to explain that they wanted a new constituent assembly to draw up a new constitution, not a return to the Fourth Republic. The votes cast in 1956 for those groups advocating *Non* in 1958 had been nearly a third of the total; only a fifth voted *Non* in September 1958.

The replacement of the Fourth Republic by the Fifth was an act of faith in two senses: in de Gaulle's ability to solve the Algerian problem; and in a new set of institutions to solve the problems of the Fourth Republic. Confusion between these two acts of faith dominated the four-and-a-half year period from May 1958 to November 1962: a period which is best seen as an interregnum between the two regimes. Technically de Gaulle ruled as the last Prime Minister of the Fourth Republic up to January 1959 and thence as the first President of the Fifth. But formal changeover from the Fourth to the Fifth is of much less significance than the changes of May-June 1958, when the Fourth Republic politicians handed over the Algerian problem to de Gaulle and September-November 1962 when they tried to wrest power back and were defeated. Throughout the interregnum, the parties thought in terms of the first act of faith (Algeria) and forgot the second (the institutions). Whether de Gaulle ruled constitutionally as a Fourth Republic Prime Minister, constitutionally by taking emergency powers as he did for a period in 1961 or unconstitutionally by directing the policy of the nation while President (a function clearly given to the Prime Minister and his government by the constitution), his rule was overwhelmingly acceptable to the people and parties alike during this interregnum. For the Fourth Republic parties, who had a majority in the Assembly over the strict Gaullists, this was a price of the Algerian war.

THE PARTIES AND THE SYSTEM: 1944–62
THE STATUS OF PARTIES

Politicial parties go largely unrecognized in French constitutional texts. At the beginning of the Fourth Republic the SFIO and MRP had both wanted to include a basic law on parties which would recognize their role in the state, regulate their internal life to ensure both reasonable discipline and democracy and safeguard abuses by external inspection of finances. Both the SFIO and MRP conceived of strong, honest and democratic parties as fundamental to democracy. The Conservatives, however, did not believe in political parties at all; the Radicals did after a fashion but did not want their traditional ways interfered with; and the Communists wanted neither discipline for their opponents nor internal democracy and inspection of finances for themselves. Thus an unholy alliance defeated the proposal for a *statut des Partis* and the constitution pretended not to notice them much.[1] Paradoxically the constitution of the Fifth Republic, conceived in loathing of political parties, gave them some of their due: 'Political parties and groups play a part in the exercise of the right to vote. The right to form parties and their freedom of action are unrestricted. They must respect the principles of national sovereignty and of democracy' (Art. 4).

Parliamentary groups had been recognized for limited purposes since 1910 and were referred to in the Fourth Republic constitution.

---

[1] See P. Williams, *Crisis and Compromise*, Longmans, London, 1964, pp. 387–8, and P. Arrighi, *Le Statut des partis politiques*, 1948.

Their role in the National Assembly has been fully recognized in standing orders. Assembly groups need not be indentical to the parties or even to the Senate (or Council of the Republic) groups. However, for most of the time there is a close correspondence. During the Fourth Republic the Conservative deputies were brought together by the CNIP in the country; meanwhile the fissiparity of the Radicals and their allies brought the total number of Assembly groups up to 15 in 1957. A few months before its fall the Assembly decided to counteract this proliferation by doubling the minimum membership of a group to 28 as from the following session. In the Fifth Republic the minimum went up to 30 and only five or six groups have been able to function. The five of the 1958–62 Assembly (a sixth for a time was based mainly on Algerian deputies) together with the Communists (who, having only ten deputies, could not form a group) correspond almost exactly with the six parties or groups of related parties of the Fourth Republic.

Some recognition of parties also comes from the electoral system. Throughout the Fourth Republic a list system was in use, although only in 1945–46 was proportional representation fully used.[1] Although most votes were cast for lists nominated by and consisting solely of members of one party, there were enough composite or unclear lists to cause nightmares to any electoral statisticians unused to French politics. For the Fifth Republic, Assembly elections were with single-member seats (two-ballot) with candidates nominated as individuals and bearing a misleading multiplicity of labels on their ballot papers. Even where the party identity of the candidate can be clearly identified, that of his running-mate—the person who will replace him if he dies or becomes a minister—may be different. In practice again most votes are cast for the candidates whose single-party allegiance is quite clear but enough votes are cast for ones with double or murky party allegiance—very few claim none at all —to blur the lines considerably. The list system is still in use for some other elections.

---

[1] The 1951–56 electoral system is perhaps best summed up by Williams as 'bastard proportional representation'. It worked proportionately in certain circumstances (as in 1956) but involved in other circumstances a heavy preference for certain types of majority (as in 1951). To take advantage of its rules, parties were encouraged to form *apparentement* with each other. See Williams, pp. 310–16 and 504–6 or P. Campbell, *French Electoral Systems and Elections since 1789*, Faber, London, (revised ed. 1965).

The Ministry of the Interior does issue official election returns in which all candidates are duly classified, usually without any escape to a miscellaneous category, and these form the basis of most election statistics.

It is traditional in France to list the parties in the order of a left-right spectrum: Communist, Extreme-Left or PSU, SFIO, Radical, Centre-Left, MRP, Conservative groups, Gaullist party, Extreme-Right or Poujadist. It is based on the traditional order in which the Assembly groups seated themselves around the half-circle of the chamber and seems firmly fixed in the minds of political commentators and probably of the public as well. The position of the Gaullists in this order causes some difficulty and sometimes they are placed between the MRP and the Conservative groups. However, in 1962 the Gaullist *Union pour la nouvelle République-Union démocratique de Travail* (UNR-UDT) tried to repudiate the notion that it had a place on the right of the political spectrum by annexing the whole of the front of the semi-circle and seating itself from extreme-left to extreme-right.

Finally some form of official recognition comes at election time in the allocation of the right to broadcast. In 1951 and 1956 'national' parties were allowed time; the law defined them as parties with lists in at least thirty departments. However this definition encouraged the creation of satellite or imaginary parties and there were 11 national parties in 1951 and 18 in 1956. More recently the right has been restricted to parties with distinct groups in the Assembly together with any other parties with at least seventy-five candidates, bringing recognition to seven parties in 1967 and a slightly differently composed seven in 1968.

Despite all this complexity, the party system of 1944-62 can be readily simplified into six formations. With two ephemeral exceptions, every party or group of any significance either belonged to, or later joined, or split off from, sometimes rejoining, one of the following:

The Communist Party
The Socialist SFIO
The Radical-Centre-Left Alliance, loosely linked in the RGR and
    later in the *Entente démocratique* (ED)
The MRP

Conservative groups who came together in the CNIP

The Gaullist *Rassemblement du Peuple Français* (RPF) and its lineal successor, the UNR-UDT

The only party which lay completely outside all six of these groups was the Poujadist *Union de Défense des Commerçants et des Artisans* (UDCA) formed in 1953 as a campaign for the small shop-keeper but without, then, any obvious political connotations or ambitions. It was rapidly successful and acquired a set of peculiar, largely right-wing extremist political aims. It shocked everyone, and itself, by polling over 2·5 million votes in 1956; these votes seem to have been acquired across the political spectrum but most probably from Gaullists in the North-west and from the traditional Left in the South. It had not the slightest idea as to what to do with its group in the Assembly and, as the absurdity of Pierre Poujade's political views became apparent, it broke up (his ablest deputies, all ultra-nationalists, left over his instructions to oppose the Suez war on the grounds that it involved fighting for the Queen of England) and lost almost all its voters at the 1958 general election. However, in 1958 more than half a million votes were cast for various candidates and groups of the Extreme-Right. They formed a parliamentary group *Unité de la République* based mainly on Algerian deputies, most of whom had claimed Gaullist colours in 1958. At the 1962 Election, almost all its deputies were defeated very badly and the threat of an Extreme-Right-wing Party passed. It was revived by Tixier-Vignancour's vote at the Presidential elections in 1965 but failed to materialize at the March 1967 elections. From time to time, between 5 and 7 per cent of the French voters seem prepared to give a temporary boost to that strand of political tradition involving a type of native fascism which flowered under the Vichy regime, but which has practically no sizeable permanent following.

The Communist Party

The French Communist Party is the largest, best organized, most consistently popular but, from the point of view of winning government office, the least successful of French parties. It was born out of a split in the 1920 Congress of the SFIO at Tours and started by annexing a good part of the traditional Left-wing vote and the majority of the party's membership. For a period, it set out to defeat the SFIO and failed utterly, declining to a small extremist group so opposed to democratic socialism and parliamentary democracy that it could work with Fascists. In 1934 the line changed abruptly and led to the Popular Front election of 1936 when, in alliance with the SFIO and Radicals, the Communists won 1·5 million votes and 70 seats. Another somersault in 1939, when they denounced the war with Hitler, led to the suppression of the party, although a clandestine organization continued and was able to denounce the Free French movement and to offer help to the Vichy government against their former comrades of the Popular Front. After Hitler's attack on the Soviet Union in June 1941, the party joined the Resistance and in many parts of France was soon leading it. After the Liberation, the Communist Party's reputation stood high and membership topped a million. De Gaulle accepted its leaders into his provisional government rather than the traditional Radical or Conservative politicians of the Third Republic and, after his departure, the party of the devout Catholics, the MRP, was willing to try governing in the coalition with it and the SFIO. Its vote amounted to nearly 5·5 million (28 per cent) in November 1946.

However, its record over the previous 20 years was not forgotten by the other parties. All those with any loyalty to France, whether the nationalist Conservatives and Gaullists or the Socialist and Radical inheritors of an essentially native revolutionary tradition, could neither understand nor tolerate the Communist Party's obvious subservience to Moscow. The MRP was more internationalist but was soon the most affected by the anti-Communism of the Cold War period. When the break came, in May 1947, with the dismissal of the Communist ministers from the Government, it was a bitter one and made worse by the Communists' attempts to reply by organizing strikes. The Communist Party, with its popular support, was placed permanently out of government office. Perhaps the most significant aspect of this political outlawry pronounced by the rest of France was that the Socialist Party joined fully in passing sentence; there was practically no fellow-travelling Socialist left. One small group did link its fortunes with the Communist Party as the *Union Progressiste*. It was based on former left-wing Radicals, of whom Pierre Cot was the most outstanding, and acted as a reminder that the French Communist Party drew a good deal of its support from a tradition sprung from the French Revolution.

Outlawry lasted the length of the Fourth Republic; there were signs of a thaw in anti-Communist attitudes in the mid-1950s (in one department the local SFIO, later expelled for doing so, ran a joint list with the Communists in 1956), but the reminder of where the Party's first loyalty lay at the time of the Hungarian uprising in 1956 postponed any change. After May 1958, the *Union des Forces Démocratiques* (UFD) and then the PSU found themselves in lonely opposition with the Communists and began the process of the non-Communist French Left thinking of the Communist Party as an ally again. A few popular front alliances turned up at the 1959 Municipal Elections. But the Communist Party was isolated by its virtual exclusion from Parliament, where the SFIO and the Radicals were still able to operate, and by its refusal to recognize the legitimacy of the Fifth Republic constitution. In the September 1962 Senate Elections, there was no popular front alliance at the second ballot although, significantly, the Communist Party reproached itself publicly afterwards for having thereby allowed reactionary candidates to defeat the Socialists.

The most remarkable aspect of this exile was that practically all Communist voters struck to the party; its vote in both 1951 and in 1956 was 26 per cent, exactly as in the first post-war election. Only in the confrontation with the Fifth Republic in the November 1958 Election did one quarter of the Communist voters desert their party. However, the intensive commitment of the 1944–47 period among its voters did wane rapidly; within ten years claimed membership was reduced by more than half and the circulation of the Communist Press was cut by more than two-thirds. If the vote had fallen in the same way, the Communist Party might still be in isolation. But as the voters remained loyal, the rest of the Left became aware that in pretending that the Communist Party did not exist (thus both Pierre Mendès-France and Guy Mollet, the only two Prime Ministers who were invested with Communist support during this period, undertook to disregard their votes in calculating whether they had the requisite majority), they were turning their backs on the bulk of those working-class votes which were politically class conscious.

The SFIO

The *Section Française de l'Internationale Ouvrière* was founded as it was named. The 1904 Congress of the Socialist International, under German leadership, demanded that two Socialist groups in France amalgamate, which they did. During the rest of the Third Republic, the SFIO participated in the electoral and parliamentary process, but was in government only in 1936. It suffered several crises and splits over the question of whether it was a revolutionary cadre working to take over government in due course or should pursue short term ends in conjunction with the Radicals. Despite its commitment to the international Socialist movement, it had an intense involvement with the French Left-wing traditions. Membership reached two peaks during the Third Republic: 180,000 in 1920 (to fall to 50,000 following the split with the Communists) and 287,000 in 1937. At the end it did not know whether to react to Hitler with pacifism or with military resistance and three-quarters of its parliamentarians voted for the installation of the Vichy regime. However, it came out of the Resistance creditably and found that Socialism was more popular than ever before or since: 355,000 members in 1946 and a vote of 24 per cent in 1945.

Some of its leaders, notably Blum and the Secretary-General Daniel Mayer, hoped to harness the new formations coming out of the Resistance to the old SFIO to create a broadly-based party akin to the British Labour or Scandinavian Social Democratic parties. But those militants who had accepted Vichy were purged while the remainder set out their Marxist goals clearly in the declaration of principle adopted in February 1946 (and still in force):

'The distinctive character of the Socialist Party is to make the freedom of the individual dependent on the abolition of the system of capitalist property which has divided society into necessarily antagonistic classes. . . . The Socialist Party is essentially a revolutionary Party; its aims are to bring about the replacement of the system of capitalist property by a system in which natural wealth such as the means of production and exchange will become collective property and in which, as a result, classes will be abolished. . . . The Socialist Party has always been and been known to be a Party of the class struggle. . . .'

The declaration puts the first emphasis on personal freedom in the French Revolutionary and Radical tradition. But the Marxist note of the central part of the declaration epitomized the attitude which the SFIO combined with its wider concern. Also in 1946 Mollet, then claiming to be an ardent Marxist, ousted Mayer from his post and brought into the direction of the party organization a team of similar convictions. The ascendancy of party over parliamentary group was reaffirmed and made more effective. The victory of Mollet, a state school teacher in the purest SFIO tradition, also marked a re-emphasis on *laicité*[1] which, while shared by the Radicals, was of little interest to many resistance elements and guaranteed to kill any chance of a link with progressive Catholics.

Having emphasized its ideological purity, the SFIO was forced to become a party of government for most of the Fourth Republic. It found itself continually defending the parliamentary system from Communist, Gaullist and Poujadist attacks while it tended to receive coldly proposals for reform from Conservatives and Radicals. The Fourth Republic constitution, after all, belonged to the SFIO more than to any other single party. The SFIO vote dropped considerably in 1951 (to 14½ per cent) and barely rose again after four and a half years of opposition in 1956 (15 per cent), although the *Front Républicain* gained ground. Membership sank to little more than 100,000 from 1952 onwards; more serious for the SFIO was the fact that it was an ageing membership, a dwindling band of erstwhile revolutionaries whose actions belied their words. Yet they stuck together and odd groups and candidates on the Extreme-Left failed to get any alternative off the ground in both 1951 and 1956. What little support such groups got owed more to left-wing Catholics

---

[1] *Laicité* cannot be translated into English without losing much of its sense. Components of rationalism, humanism, anti-clericalism and secularism are included but these do not convey the intensity of the feeling. Two quotations, from proponents of two sides of the *laique* coin, show this attitude. First, from René Billères (a practising Catholic whose main political interest lies in the field where *laicité* matters most, education; president of the Radical party since 1965) 'What is *laique* is French humanism par excellence. In a country like ours, where ideas are so full of nuances, so diverse and so vigorous, *l'idéal laique* the ideal of respect for one's neighbour, of understanding for one's neighbour is a vital national necessity.' (Radical Congress, 1959.) In contrast, a woman delegate at the 1946 Radical General Assembly explaining why the party did not attract women: 'If the women are not with you it is your fault, why? It is because you do not have *la foi laique*. How many of you have I seen who have sent their wives to mass, who have had their children baptised and who were married in church? If you do not fight against the Church it will fight against you. . . . I have had in my hands a history book used in Church schools; it treated the French Revolution as ignominious.'

disillusioned with MRP than to dissatisfied SFIO adherents. Even the repressive policy of the Mollet Government in Algeria failed to shake the firm loyalty of his internal opponents to their party.

When the Fourth Republic fell, the SFIO was still united, still ruled by Mollet and still committed to its declaration of principles, but in government it had almost totally failed the hopes of its supporters[1] and was irrevocably associated with the Fourth Republic system. Many of the small groups and individuals wandering unhappily between it and the Communists had come together to form a new party, *Union de la Gauche socialiste* (UGS), in December 1957. The issue over which the SFIO could no longer bear the strain was nothing to do with Socialism but rather concerned constitutional change. The SFIO deputies split half and half in May 1958 on whether to accept de Gaulle. Between then and September the party debated bitterly its attitude to the new regime and to its constitution. At the Congress in September the proponents of a *Oui* vote at the referendum won by 2,687 to 1,176; the following day the leaders of the dissidents announced the creation of the *Parti socialiste autonome* (PSA).

To campaign against the constitution, the PSA, the UGS and a number of Radicals and other Centre-Left politicians formed a cartel, the UFD, which they carried forward to the November General Election. It polled poorly but that did not discourage its members. The PSA attracted several former SFIO ministers and several of its local sections. By its first Congress in May 1959, it claimed federations in 69 departments and 8,000 members. In September 1959, Mendès-France and most of the Radicals in the UFD joined the PSA. The following year the PSA, the UGS and a very small group of ex-Communists who had left their party over Hungary, *Tribune Communiste*, agreed to fuse into the *Parti Socialiste Unifié*. Although the PSA was much larger than the UGS, the merger (which was immediate and complete) was arranged on a basis of a 5–5–1 split on the new 11-member bureau and 55-member political bureau. This was not without misgivings; the UGS doubted the socialist credentials of the Mendèsist Radicals in the PSA while

---

1 To be fair the enlightened outline law on colonial development passed in 1956 must rank as one of the major achievements of the Fourth Republic; without it de Gaulle would almost certainly not have been able to arrange the peaceful transition to independence of the colonial empire in 1960.

the latter was suspicious of whether the UGS was fully committed to *laicité*. The PSU started with some 20,000 members and for a time seemed set to make a serious bid to replace the SFIO. But soon the SFIO moved to a position of clearer opposition to the Gaullist regime while the PSU discredited itself with internal dissension.

The Radical Party

The Radical Party was formed, to quote its statutes (Article 1), 'between the militants, the *élus* (deputies, senators and local councillors) and newspapers' to combat the Right at the time of the Dreyfus affair. The militants have always been only one section of the party; it has never sought mass-membership or an ideologically closely knit cadre. The *élus* have always been the main focus of what has frequently seemed to be little more than a cartel to protect the electoral interests of a shifting group of deputies. The Radicals have always preferred the single-member seat electoral system to list-voting because of the advantage this gives to the locally known deputy. It has long had a mass of local councillors. The newspapers which radiated its influence were central to its role in the Third Republic; most of them were expropriated for compromising with the Vichy regime after the Liberation and with them the Radical Party lost much of its former support. One exception, *La Depêche du Midi*, of Toulouse, has remained a strong influence within the party. Even after the 1968 Election, more than one-third of Radical deputies came from its circulation area although this covers less than a twelfth of the population.

The springs of Radicalism in France run deep. Its attitudes—a rationalist and tolerant humanism, an intense individualism, a strong distrust of centralized power and therefore of both the capital city and of the Executive, a strong commitment to the value of education together with a conviction that these attitudes are on the Left—are to be found in the Liberal parties of Britain and Scandinavia. The peculiarities of the French Radical Party arise from the role it has taken at the centre of French politics: an infinite capacity for both self-contradiction and survival.

Nothing illustrates this better than its history in the Fourth Republic. It started discredited along with the Third Republic which it had dominated. But within a few months the Radical politicians had staged their comeback. In March, 1946, the *Rassemblement des Gauches Républicaines* (RGR) was formed to unite the Radicals both with various cliques compromised by Vichy and also with the *Union Démocratique et Socialiste de la Résistance*. This latter was a federation of non-Communist Resistance organizations formed in June 1945, which, at the time, hoped to plant the seeds of a broad Labour or Social Democratic Party; had the SFIO been willing they might have indeed done so. In forming this cartel, the Radicals neutralized and pre-empted for the RGR the whole of the middle ground of French politics normally called Centre-Left, roughly defined as neither clerical nor Marxist. In fact the UDSR included a clerical element and had no *laique* tradition. Nevertheless, the UDSR fitted perfectly with the Radicals despite their opposite historical backgrounds; it consisted of a miscellany of local and national politicians without significant membership, ideology or common political purpose. Its deputies could therefore behave as they pleased, just like the Radicals.

After a brief period when they were in opposition to the Communist–SFIO–MRP governing alliance, the Radicals regained their governing role in January 1947. Thereafter no ministry was proposed to the Assembly without a complement of Radical or Centre-Left ministers. The first Radical Prime Minister came in July 1948, and thereafter Radical or Centre-Left politicians held the office for three quarters of the time. It gained also virtually permanent control over the Ministry of Education for the duration of the Fourth Republic. This remarkable return to power was not based on any increase in electoral support; the RGR vote remained steady until 1956.

The RGR groups (the Radicals and UDSR maintained distinct groups in the Assembly, although they united in the Senate) came to function as a forcing ground for young and able politicians. They offered both a remarkable tolerance of dissent and the quickest way to the top. A large number of later leading Gaullists found a temporary political home in the Radicals (e.g. Debré or Jacques Chaban-Delmas) or the UDSR (e.g. Réné Capitant or Jacques Soustelle). Tolerance was not indefinite; it did not extend to the Cot group on the Left who insisted on fellow-travelling with the Communists nor, eventually, to the Radicals who tried to retain their membership of the party and give their first loyalty to the

Gaullist *Rassemblement du Peuple français* (RPF). But it allowed two others groups—the so-called Neo-Radicals and the Mendèsists —successively to take control of the party (insofar as control meant anything in the Radical Party) although both had a very different idea of the role of the party from the mainstream of its members.

The Neo-Radicals were dominant in the party from about 1947 to 1955. The administrative President of the party during this period, Léon Martinaud-Deplat, the Secretary-General of the RGR, Jean-Paul David, and one of the period's Radical Prime Ministers, Réné Mayer, were Neo's; the other three Prime Ministers, André-Marie, Edgar Faure and Henri Queuille, were sufficiently close to leave the party with them in due course. Neo-Radicals shared the Radicals' political vocabulary and made due obeisance to their memories. They differed from them in representing certain interests (Parisian businessmen and North African *colons*) quite alien to the earlier Radical Party and in advocating right-wing economic and colonial policies (mainstream Radicals being disinterested rather than left-wing in economics). Ultimately the Neo's went too far in trying to line the party up on the Right and they were ousted by an alliance of Mendèsists with the most traditional Radicals of all—two surviving pre-war Prime Ministers, Edouard Daladier and Edouard Herriot, together with *La Depêche du Midi* and the South-western bastions of the party that it so influenced.

Mendèsism resembled Gaullism, with whom it shared some devotees, in its essential dependence on one man. It was conceived when Mendès-France made his first bid for the premiership with a remarkable speech on June 3, 1953, born with his premiership (June 1954 to February 1955), the most dazzling of the Fourth Republic, and baptised electorally in January 1956, under the name *Front Républicain*. It had much deeper roots, appealing to the Radical heart with its emphasis on the need for change and its dramatic challenge to powerful economic interests. However, its positive emphasis on economic growth policies and on withdrawal from colonial commitments were not particularly at home in the Radical Party. The object of creating a renovated and disciplined party of the Left was most ill at home in France's oldest and least disciplined party. This was an echo of what some had hoped for in 1945 in the UDSR, the larger part of which now rallied to the *Front Républicain* under Francois Mitterrand. The most characteristic inspiration was, however, the *Club des Jacobins*, which with its newspaper, *Le Jacobin*, provided a centre for Mendèsist activity and ideas. For a period Mendèsism swept all before it. The opinion poll popularity rating for Mendès-France's premiership was 55–60 per cent compared to some 30 per cent for his predecessor and 20–30 per cent for his successor. The administrative machinery of the party was taken over in May 1955, and by the end of that year party membership had increased by more than 50 per cent to over 100,000. In January 1956 Election, Mendèsist Radicalism made great strides in Paris and the industrial North-east. However, within a year the *Front Républicain* government had disappointed its most hopeful supporters, Mendèsism was losing ground within the Party and Mendès-France (who left the Government in May 1956) was finding it impossible to impose the discipline on the Assembly group which he regarded as essential. In June 1957, he resigned as first vice-president of the party and Mendèsism became another Radical memory.

Out of this shattering experience emerged four distinct parts of the Party:

1. The RGR which had remained in the hands of Mendès-France's opponents in 1955 and was converted by them from an electoral umbrella into a right-wing Radical party;
2. The *Centre Républicain* (CR) a group of dissidents centred round André Morice, who seceded following their defeat by Mendès-France at the Party Congress in 1956;
3. The *Centre d'Action Democratique* formed by Mendèsists in 1958;
4. What remained of the Radical Party proper, which had lost all its former Prime Ministers of the 1948–56 period.

The UDSR also split into two in 1958 over de Gaulle's constitution: a majority group round Mitterrand and a seceding minority round Réné Pleven. So thus, by the end of the Fourth Republic, the Centre-Left had given birth to six rival parties or groups. Of these the ex-UDSR Pleven group did not found a real party but stood for election under local labels. Mitterrand's UDSR continued as a convenient electoral label for him and a few friends. Mendès-France and his remaining associates decided to join the PSA as individuals in September 1959. The RGR dwindled as its members returned to the main Radical Party or preferred to join the CR. The CR flourished for a time; it returned 11 deputies in 1958 to the orthodox Radicals' 13 and became a centre for political sympathizers with the Algerian *colons*. None of them having enough deputies to form a group of their own, all the Centre-Left members elected in 1958 came together as the Entente Démocratique in the new Assembly; it was some time before its members were really able to work together. Meanwhile the Centre-Left had remained united in the Council of the Republic and in the new Senate the *Gauche Démocratique* was the second largest group (due to continued Radical strength at the local council grass-roots level).

Little was heard of the Radical Party during the interregnum period and once more the party was written off by many. However, it recuperated, reorganized its structure, built up a new team of officers and was better able to withstand the Gaullist tide than any of the other *Cartel des Non* parties in 1962. In July 1962, its new President, Maurice Faure, successfully negotiated the coming together of all the groups represented in the ED and GD as the *Rassemblement Démocratique*: the wheel was full circle.

The convulsions of the 1950s revolved around personalities and seem a peculiarly French way of behaviour for a peculiarly French party. However, from an international point of view they represented attempts to bring the French Radical Party into line with its nearest equivalents in other countries. Like parties as varied as the German FDP and the Danish *Radikale Venstre*, it is the lineal descendant of the late nineteenth century Left which has everywhere in Europe been replaced by Socialist parties. The Neo-Radicals offered it the course chosen by the German FDP or Italian Liberal Party: emphasis on economic liberalism and a place towards the Right of the political spectrum. The Mendèsists offered it the role claimed by the British and Scandinavian Liberal Parties: an emphasis on political liberalism combined with a radical empiricism in economics. Having rejected both these courses in turn, the party under Maurice Faure's leadership attempted both at once again in the RD.

The MRP

France differs from all other democratic Catholic countries in Europe, save Ireland, in not having a dominant Christian Democratic Party. Its substitute, which has never been quite sure whether it ought to be its equivalent, is the *Mouvement Républicain Populaire* (MRP). It was founded out of the Resistance and brought together two components, the one political and the other electoral, whose conflicting attractions were to dog its life and to contribute to its decision to commit suicide twenty years later.

The political component was a desire to reconcile Catholicism with the French Republic. At the same time it had a wider than purely political purpose and sought to infuse its ideas throughout French society. In this it resembled and competed with the Communist Party. To a significant extent it saw the MRP as the political parallel organization to the *Confédération Française des Travailleurs Chrétiens* in the trade union field and to Catholic Action organizations in the family and professional field. In 1959 all the 13 members of the National Bureau and 30 of the remaining 39 members[1] of the National Executive Committee held or had held positions in other Catholic-inspired organizations. The parties which had best embodied this component of the MRP were the pre-war *Parti Démocratique Populaire* and *Jeune République* (it drew its first President, Maurice Schumann, from the latter). These together polled less than 3 per cent in 1936; in 1945 the MRP polled 25 per cent and reached a peak in 1946 with 28 per cent.

The difference was supplied by the electoral component. Before the war the church-going, conservative voters of France had spread their votes among a fluctuating number of ill-organized right-wing formations, none of them proclaiming any particular clerical inspiration although none of them needed to since their loyalty to the Church could be taken for granted. Most of this vote opted for the MRP, untainted by Vichy, after the war. But it did not accept the political ideas of its party. This was shown in the referendum on the second draft constitution when the MRP switched sides, but most of its voters abstained or followed de Gaulle's advice to vote against. In the 1947 Municipal Elections the Gaullist tide cut the MRP to less than 10 per cent. The MRP started working in collaboration with the SFIO and Communists, which, its leaders hoped, would provide a broad-based stable government committed firmly

[1] As listed in W. Bosworth, *Catholicism and Crisis in Modern France*, Princeton University Press, 1962. Jean Lecanuet, who became MRP president in 1963, is one of the nine exceptions.

117

to socially progressive measures. The Cold War enforced a break with the Communists. The break with the SFIO was over the one policy of the MRP which tied it to the Right—*l'école libre*. Conscious of its electorate, its leaders could not risk not reacting against *laïcité* whenever the issue was thrown into the political arena—but their desire to make co-operation with Socialists work is shown by the fact that they refrained from introducing it. However, the Communists and Gaullists, for different reasons, periodically used the issue to prise the MRP and SFIO apart. In the 1951–55 Assembly it pushed the MRP into the hands of the Conservatives.

The MRP's vote declined steadily: 26 per cent in November 1946, 13 per cent in 1951, 11 per cent in 1956 despite the collapse of the Gaullist vote which largely explained the first fall. Some leaders, notably Georges Bidault, would have preferred a larger, more conservative party on the lines of the German CDU or Italian DC. But the membership were firmly committed to the role they had chosen for the party and, in particular, prevented Bidault's move towards the Gaullists. Between 1951 and 1954 the parliamentary leadership found itself balancing between militants who disliked the Conservative governments it was involved in and voters who approved them. Between 1944 and 1954 the MRP (in the person of Bidault or Robert Schuman) virtually monopolized the Foreign Ministry and dominated the formation of French foreign policy. This meant that, after an initial phase of anti-German feeling, it was they who led the way to the Franco–German reconciliation and the faith in European unity expressed in the ECSC, EDC and the EEC. Militant, voter and leader were united in what was probably the MRP's greatest contribution to France.[1] But Bidault's final 18-month tenure of office coincided with major colonial problems in Vietnam and North Africa. Mendès-France, scornful of this policy and of the MRP, came in, took the Foreign Office, made peace in Indo-China, reversed the direction of policy in North Africa, and presided over the death of the EDC. The MRP, firmly opposed

[1] Europe was one issue which could bring together the most reactionary of Catholic traditions and the hopes of the MRP militant. A united Europe was both a return to a pre-revolutionary pre-nationalist medieval situation and a brave move forward to the abolition of war between France and its neighbours. Accordingly, faith in European unity became almost the touch-stone of the MRP and was the issue which kept them apart from Gaullist governments from 1962.

to Mendès-France, linked itself with the Right under the banner of an illiberal colonial policy, and sealed its complete divorce from the Left. In the 1956 election, Radical-MRP hostility was greater than that between any other pair of parties.[1]

This was the climax to the MRP's failure to join a Catholic vote to Left policies. Many observers have agreed in describing them as really more progressive than the Radicals.[2] Yet at the one moment in the Fourth Republic when a Left-Right fissure opened up, the MRP were firmly on the Right and the official Radicals (then Mendèsist), on the Left. The other parties never understood or accepted the MRP. By the end of the Fourth Republic they had forced it into a position on the Right that they could understand but that it had never wanted. In 1958 Bidault split away with his *Démocratie Chrétienne* right-wing group and about that period a new generation of leaders came to the fore, trained in the attitudes of Catholic Action. The MRP spent the interregnum agonizingly unsure of its attitude to de Gaulle, but confident that it was building up a movement capable of playing the role it wanted to within the new institutions that it welcomed rather more whole-heartedly than any of the other Fourth Republic parties.

The CNIP

As the MRP went down election by election, up came the Conservatives or CNIP. Conservative is a term not used in France, but it is apt and convenient for those who would use for themselves *Modéré*, *Indépendant* or *Paysan*. The various groups within this political family were disunited in the Third Republic and started the Fourth in the same fashion. In 1948 three Senators founded the *Centre National des Indépendants* (*Paysans* added in 1951) with the modest aim of avoiding unnecessary electoral competition among those who were neither Marxist, nor Radical nor MRP. Departmental centres were set up, composed of local *élus* and of leading figures in farmers', employers' and commercial organizations. In its

[1] See A. Touraine's study in M. Duverger, etc., *Les Elections du 2 Janvier 1956*, Colin, Paris, 1957, pp. 299–300.
[2] Thus Dorothy Pickles in *The Fifth French Republic*, Methuen, London, revised ed. 1965, 'In matters of social and economic policy, the MRP is definitely farther to the Left than the majority of Radicals' (p. 78). Williams reverses the standard Left-Right order to place the MRP between the SFIO and the Radicals.

own words its function was a 'court of supreme arbitration which will accord at the national level "investitures" designed to indicate to the electors the candidates who are the most representative of their tendency'. Its investiture became a useful aid to both potential candidates and electors, although any Conservative winning against its investiture was generally welcomed as having proved that he was the choice of the Conservative electors.

Co-ordination at Parliamentary level proved more difficult; after 1951 it was found possible to simplify into two groups, but by the end of the Parliament there were four (due to a split among the *paysans* and the attraction of a part of the Gaullists). However, after 1956 all but a handful of *paysans* united in one group *Indépendants et Paysans d'Action Sociale* and full unity was achieved in 1958 with a special section within the group for agricultural interests. By the 1951–55 and 1958–62 parliaments Conservatives were able to achieve a strength and influence they had not known for 40 years. This success owes most to two men: Roger Duchet, the founder and first Secretary-General who organized it, and Antoine Pinay who found himself unexpectedly popular as one of the only two Conservative Prime Ministers.

It owed little or nothing to any upsurge of Conservative ideas. The CNIP refused at the outset to get involved in formulating policy and although it later diffused well-produced and well-researched political literature, this was designed to brief its candidates rather than to convey its views to the electorate. Some attempt was made earlier on to prevent the Extreme-Right jumping on the bandwagon but it did not last; ex-Vichyites and others on the Extreme-Right found a home with the CNIP. Possibly this flexibility avoided the growth of any significant party on the Extreme-Right. Dissension within the CNIP groups was rife but it centred round personalities and investitures. However, there was enough unity in the group for the majority of it to follow the realism of leaders like Pinay over issues such as European unity and North Africa. Originally they had specifically invited all whether of 'christian or *laique*' inspiration to join but later put much greater emphasis on the first. Certainly their increasing strength was at the expense of the MRP and brought them Catholic votes.

The vast majority of CNIP voters and *élus* would have been at home in Christian Democratic parties in any other EEC country.

Despite this the CNIP bore little resemblance to a Christian Democratic party. The nearest parallels are the British and Scandinavian Conservative parties but the differences here are also striking. It lacked the governing vocation and the cohesive character of the British Conservative Party and had no moderate wing to attract centre voters and provide forward thinking for the party; while it brought together the urban and rural interests which are split throughout Scandinavia. In fact most of its members are too concerned with defending their local interests and positions to care about such a matter.

The Gaullists

The CNIP is not, however, the party with least connection with any other in Europe; that distinction belongs to the Gaullists. There have been several parties proclaiming the unconditional devotion which was the hallmark of the Gaullist. From 1947 to 1953 there could only be one for the true Gaullist, the *Rassemblement du Peuple français* (RPF), created, inspired and led by de Gaulle himself. Earlier and afterwards until October 1958 there were small groups, some of them embodying very distinctive strands of Gaullism, together with odd individuals both within and without the other parties claiming the Gaullist inspiration but without any official position. In October the *Union pour la Nouvelle République* (UNR) brought together the majority of Gaullists; it never, however, claimed a monopoly of de Gaulle's followers.

In structure and functioning the RPF resembled a fascist movement rather than a democratic party operating within a parliamentary system. It was created and ruled from the top. Under its President, de Gaulle, were a secretariat and a 12-man Executive appointed by him; none of the latter might be parliamentarians. Originally it was hoped that it could appeal broadly both to members of the other parties and over their heads to the electorate without being another party in competition with them. An inter-group, linking Gaullist members of all parties, was constituted. But the parties' reaction to de Gaulle made this impossible; one-third of the inter-group constituted a separate parliamentary group at the end of 1948 and the rest remained with their parties. From then on until about a year after the 1951 Election, it came closest to the fascist parallel. The extra-parliamentary direction of the party (the

12-man body was enlarged to 20, with seven parliamentarians, appointed by de Gaulle in 1949) was imposed on deputy, candidate and militant alike. The rule of Paris was imposed on the departments in a way no other non-Communist movement would have dared; this was resented by and led to resignations among the many local Conservative leaders who had flocked to the Gaullist banner. A greater contrast with the CNIP could not be imagined. In the end the RPF broke on the attempt to control the deputies from outside. In July 1952 several broke ranks to vote with Pinay; some attempt was made to re-establish discipline on a more co-operative basis, but it failed as well and de Gaulle released his deputies from any allegiance in May 1953.

The fascist parallel is also strong in what the RPF stood for. Its attitudes were authoritarian without the conservative's reverence for traditional sources of authority. It combined demands for radical social change with intense nationalism. It was anti-parliamentary, anti-trade union and virulently anti-Communist. Its most distinctive positive policy, apart from the constitutional reforms demanded by its leader, was the 'association' of capital and labour in a way reminiscent of corporatism. Yet, with some Jewish leaders, it never succumbed to the anti-semitism that had earlier disfigured the Right in France, and the real parallels are perhaps Bonapartism and Boulangism. Finally, de Gaulle's determination to come to power legally probably prevented the RPF from developing further fascist characteristics.

The UNR during the period 1958–62 was quite different. It was formed to support de Gaulle in power, not to win power for him; it was formed by supporters of de Gaulle without his being involved, not by de Gaulle to attract supporters. It came into being as a union of six groups just before the 1958 Election, of which the three main ones were the *Centre national des Républicains sociaux*, the *Convention républicain* and the *Union pour le Renouveau français*. The first was the descendant of the leading deputies remaining from the RPF, mellowed by five years of participation in ministries. The *Convention* was a grass-roots creation in the summer of 1958, bringing together numbers of people and small groups (10,000 members were claimed) who had not been involved in politics with their leader. The *Union* was Jacques Soustelle together with the following and connections he had built up as an ardent *Algérie française* proponent as well as a Gaullist. There was some intention at the outset to involve all those (such as the groups round Bidault and Morice) who were of the same mind; the UNR was brought together by Soustelle with the intention of establishing an *Algérie française* electoral alliance. The UNR established its character as a democratic party straightaway by over-ruling Soustelle's hopes and deciding that it must have nothing to do with the old parties it was hoping to chastise.

De Gaulle made it plain that the UNR was not his official party and two other Gaullist parties fought the 1958 Election. The UNR, however, was sweepingly successful despite its youth and found itself the dominant party in the new Assembly. Although enough deputies from other parties supported the Gaullist governments on votes of censure to keep them in office so long as the Algerian war lasted, both Debré and his successor Georges Pompidou came to depend more and more on the consistent support of UNR deputies. De Gaulle's government had been composed of four ministers later UNR, twelve from other parties and seven technicians; Debré started with seven UNR, twelve others and eight technicians and finished with 10 : 8 : 9. Pompidou tried to involve the MRP but de Gaulle's attitude to Europe sabotaged the effort within a month and from May 1962 to April 1969 the government was not merely Gaullist but dominantly UNR-UDR.

Federal origin, electoral purpose and parliamentary role moulded the UNR into something far more like a typical political party than the RPF. Tension between loyal Gaullists and supporters of *Algérie française* dominated the first year and a half. This ended with the resignation or expulsion of the latter but, significantly, the battle took place and the decisions were made in the governing bodies of the party and its assembly group, and not laid down from above, although knowledge of de Gaulle's views was almost certainly decisive. After some hesitation the UNR developed into a loyal government party.

Outside the UNR, the most interesting group were the Gaullists who proclaimed themselves of the Left. In 1958 under the title *Centre de la Réforme républicaine* a group of Left-Gaullists competed with the UNR; they did very badly indeed (3,600,000 UNR to 150,000 CRR). However, undeterred, an earlier group, the *Union démocratique du Travail*, which had combined Mendèsism with

Gaullism, was revived and became from 1959 a sort of left-wing parallel to the UNR. It included a number of well-known Gaullists of progressive views but, as with its predecessor, never showed any evidence of a popular following. It was founded with de Gaulle's private blessing at a time when it was unsure whether or not his supporters would keep control of the UNR.

THE PARTY SYSTEM

No party could expect to achieve power on its own during the Fourth Republic. Thus each party had to decide on an attitude of co-operation with the others. For some this was a conscious decision expressed in votes for the investiture of Prime Ministers; for the Conservatives and Centre-Left the attitudes were often only the sum of individual conflicting attitudes. The following table shows how the groups lined up in the 40 votes to invest a Prime Minister during the Fourth Republic.

Prime Minister from	Votes in favour cast by					
	Communists	SFIO	Radicals	MRP	Conservatives	Gaullist[1]
Communists (1)	1	1	0	0	0	0
SFIO (9)	4	9	8	9	1	2
Radicals (16)	1	13	16	12	12	6
MRP (7)	0	5	5	7	5	1
Conservatives (5)	0	0	5	3	5	2
de Gaulle (2)	1	1½	1½	2	2	1

The willingness of the parties to combine in order to achieve power was practically confined to the four parties that were later to adopt the title *Cartel des Non*. Among them the CNIP members did not trust the SFIO and vice versa; otherwise support could be extended from any one of these four parties to any other. Of the 142 instances of a party supporting a Prime Minister, 114 (80 per

[1] No Gaullist votes could be cast until the formation of the group; hence the lack of a Gaullist vote for de Gaulle in 1945 when he was invested by the one unanimous vote of all the parties. Radicals, refers to Radical and Centre-left combined.

cent) occur within the area of the broken line in the table although only 40 per cent of the possible combinations occur here. It is striking that this *Cartel des Non* alignment was far stronger than the pull of Left and Right. Taking the Radicals as Left and the MRP as Right, the following line-up emerges:

Party or group voting for own Prime Minister	39
Left voting for other Left	27
Right voting for other Right	15
Right voting for Left	42
Left voting for Right	19

Quite clearly in combinations for power in the National Assembly, the Left-Right alignment, apart from mutual distrust between SFIO and CNIP, counted for very little indeed.

The other point at which the parties had to align together to achieve power was in front of the elector. Under the 1951–6 mixed electoral system there was much to gain from parties forming *apparentements*. In 1951 there were alignments of all the centre parties against Communists and Gaullists—indeed this had been the intention behind the law. The 1956 election, on the other hand, was sprung on the parties by a dissolution following a government defeat on the issue of the electoral system. *Apparentements* were hurriedly prepared and a very different line-up emerged (parties in brackets present in some cases only):

Left:	SFIO–Radical–(UDSR)–(Gaullist)	47
Right:	CNIP–MRP–(Gaullist)	37 } 49
	CNIP–MRP–RGR–(Gaullist)	12

The Left-Right fissure of 1956 divided the MRP from the Radicals, although they had played similar roles in Assembly alignments.[1] This implied that the basic demarcation line between Left and Right was over an issue which most politicians can agree to regard as broadly irrelevant: *laicité*. The Assembly alignments reflected the immediate policy preoccupations; the 1956 electoral alignment the passionate roots of French parties.

---

[1] The MRP and Radicals voted together on 30 of the 40 investiture votes, more than any other pair of parties.

STRUCTURAL CHARACTERISTICS

The very different origins of French parties means that few general statements can be made about their structure. With several, such as the RGR or CNIP there is some doubt whether the term 'party' is not being unduly stretched to cover them. On the Centre-Right the CNIP, RPF, MRP and RGR each base themselves on quite different conceptions of the role of a party. On the Left, the SFIO clearly borrowed from the Radicals, and the PSU from the SFIO, but they each gave their predecessor's pattern a twist before adopting it.

A mass membership is a luxury. The Communists do, however, have something closer to a mass membership than any other party. At the 1967 Congress it was reported that 425,000 membership cards had been issued but the true figure was probably little more than half this total. The SFIO has had a consistent membership of around a hundred thousand. Both the MRP and Radicals briefly touched this figure in 1945 and 1955 respectively but are normally far from it. The CNIP does not pretend to be interested in membership (nor really are most of the Centre-Left groups). The UNR has not sought the mass enthusiasm which momentarily gave the RPF over a million members. Despite claims made, the best estimate is that the UNR slowly climbed to 50,000 by 1961.[1]

The parties, particularly those with few members, prefer to proclaim their implantation among the people by their strength in local government. The tables in the Appendix (see p. 186) show how strength in municipal and cantonal elections differs from that in national elections. Conservatives and Radicals or Centre-Left are far stronger at local than at parliamentary level, less because of any political attraction to their views at this level than because their structure suits local councillors better. The MRP, Gaullists and Communists have found it very difficult to shift the loyalty of voters to outgoing councillors; hence this pattern persists. The SFIO is, however, now strongly implanted locally in most of its zones of parliamentary strength. This means that the Conservatives and Radicals have a grass-roots strength whose existence is scarcely noticeable in their national organization; this was almost certainly a major factor in the striking recovery of both from their initial

[1] J. Charlot, *L'Union pour la Nouvelle République*, Colin, Paris, 1967, Table, p. 116, makes illuminating comparisons between claimed and actual membership.

defeat after the war. Moreover, it makes the Senate, elected through local councillors, completely unrepresentative of France. The two parties which together took a clear majority of the votes in the 1962, 1967 and 1968 Assembly elections, Communist and Gaullist, have only a sixth of the Senate seats. The Senate groupings tend to fossilize older divisions; the line-up in 1968 is almost precisely what it ceased to be in the Assembly in 1955. The Senate does not count for a great deal in the constitution of the Fifth Republic, but this preservation of former divisions in one chamber of Parliament is a factor in the strength of these divisions in the political system.

If the Conservatives, Radicals and to a lesser extent the SFIO are prominent for their implantation in the local life of French communities, the Communists, the MRP and to a lesser extent the SFIO stand out for their implantation in French occupational and social organizations. The trade union movement in France has for some years been split into three factions, each running broadly parallel to a party; the pro-Communist CGT[1] is by far the strongest although many members do not accept Communist leadership, the Catholic CFDT ranks next—during the Fourth Republic it became a militant workers' body whose Christianity was less relevant—while the smaller FO was a split away from the CGT and corresponded fairly closely to SFIO voters. Trade union political loyalties are the more important because France has a system of elected social security councils in which trade unions play the role of parties. The farmers organization FNSEA aims to be non-party political, but different groups jockey for power inside it: immediately after the war the SFIO had built up some influence, but before long they had lost it to the Conservatives while the Catholic Action organization JAC steadily built their position to take over the secretaryship of the FNSEA in 1961. The lower middle-class businessmen's bodies, PME, together with the Poujadist UDCA were also game for political forces (the Communists were much involved in the beginnings of Poujadism), but they preferred to engage in politics on their own behalf. Family

---

[1] CGT signifies *Confédération generale du Travail;* CFDT, *Confédération français et démocratique des Travailleurs*, formerly the CFTC, *Confédération française des Travailleurs chrétiennes*; FO, *Force Ouvriere*; FNSEA, *Fédération nationale des Syndicats d'Exploitants agricoles*; PME, *Petits et moyens Entreprises*; UFF, *Union des Femmes françaises*; MFR, *Mouvement Familiale*; ANFANOMA, *Association National des Français d'Afrique du Nord et d'Outre-mer et Amis.*

organizations such as the UFF or the MFR are almost all in Communist or Catholic hands. The *Fédération des Locataires* (tenants) is largely but not wholly Communist controlled. The Communists and MRP alone ran successful large youth organizations—although the PSU is having some success in the university world where the SFIO had failed. The Gaullists alone lacked any sort of implantation either locally, occupationally or socially (unless one counts for a brief period the *rapatrié* body, ANFANOMA); this was in accord with their philosophy of despising all intermediary bodies which hindered direct contact from de Gaulle to the people. Initially the RPF did attempt to create its own structure of family, ex-servicemen and working-class bodies but they did not last. The UNR did not try seriously; after a rather embryonic youth group got infested with *Algérie française* ideas, it did not even have a youth organization.

There is no typical party structure in France but perhaps the most matured is that of the SFIO.[1] Its membership is organized into sections corresponding to communes or divisions of towns and departmental federations, the groupings of sections into constituencies being of minor importance. Federations send delegates to the Congress, armed with votes proportional to the number of members and with a right for a minority to have proportional representation within the federation delegation. As the Congress has the constitutional right to direct the party and elects the *Comité Directeur* to do this in effect, voting power at the Congress matters and the three federations from populous departments where the SFIO had a working-class following, Bouches-du-Rhone (the bastion of Gaston Deferre) together with Nord and Pas-de-Calais (that of Mollet), have a dominant role. The *Comité Directeur* consists of 45 members all elected by the Congress by majority voting; some representation is guaranteed to a minority of at least 20 per cent at the Congress which has seen its political views rejected by the majority. Between the *Comité Directeur* and the Congress lies a National Council, based on departmental representation as with the Congress. Extra-constitutionally the *Comité Directeur* has added a bureau to top the structure. The Socialist group in parliament are subject to the control of the party; the national council can decide on entry to the government, while the *Comité Directeur* decides

---

[1] This description is based on the party statutes last amended in 1946.

about parliamentary indiscipline. Similar controls exist from the federations over cantonal councillors and from sections over municipal councillors. But parliamentary influence is strictly limited: a maximum of 20 of the *Comité Directeur* may be deputies or senators. The Congress also elects a commission of conflicts (whose nine members must have spent at least ten years in the party, cannot belong to any other central body of the party and must include at least six non-parliamentarians).

This formal structure is more or less reproduced by the PSU except that sections may be based on place of work as well as residence, regional commissions correspond to the national planning regions and proportional representation by closed lists is the rule. The form is similar for the Radical Party except that the basic unit there is the parliamentary constituency, the Congress elects directly a President for a two-year period of office and there is no commission of conflicts. However, the position of *élus* is entirely different. Not only are there no provisions for outside control of parliamentary groups but all parliamentarians are *ex-officio* members of the Executive Committee (equivalent of the SFIO National Council) and all departmental councillors of the Congress. The Radical Party is much more an organization to link *élus* to members rather than one to control *élus* on behalf of members.

The MRP and UNR–UDT[1] go even further. The MRP was in concept a movement controlled by its members, but with considerable participation at the top from its parliamentary leaders. The UNR–UDT (which adopted the constituency as the basis of organization) had a hierarchy so filled with *ex-officio* members (including on the important Central Committee all former and current ministers of the party) and co-options that the element from the membership is diluted into very much a junior partner. Finally, the CNIP operated essentially as an extension of parliamentary groups (with the Senate having particular influence). At the opposite extreme, the RPF and Communist Party express the notion of the parliamentary group as the servant of the membership. In theory the first was organized from the top while the second is controlled by election from the bottom. The Communist Congress elects

---

[1] The UNR–UDT prior to its conversion into the UDVeR; for the modifications then introduced see below p. 144.

directly all the organs of the party: Central Committee, Political Bureau and Secretariat. In fact this direct control works downwards because all parts of the party are in turn responsible to the central organs. The basic unit in the party is the cell, ideally based on work-place, but more often (particularly in rural areas) based on residence, with departmental federations.

The relative formal role of parliamentarians in each party can be expressed in the form of a scale from one extreme to the other:

Party supreme		Balanced			Parliamentarians supreme
Communist	SFIO	Radical	MRP	UNR–UDT	CNIP
RPF	PSU				

In practice, this pattern does not entirely hold. The PSU has yet to put its statutory relationship into effect with a parliamentary group; de Gaulle failed to keep the RPF deputies faithful to their role while Mendès-France failed to impose the logic of the constitutional relationship on his.

French parties tend to be suspicious of leaders. Few of them have any single leading position. Variously the positions of Presidents (Radicals or MRP), Secretary-General (SFIO or Communist) or President of the Assembly Group (CNIP) confer the nearest recognition that there is. Traditional parties have been very suspicious of personalities. However, the Communist personality cult towards Maurice Thorez rivalled that of Stalin; de Gaulle dominated Gaullism, and, frequently, the small parties are formed round a popular personality (thus Giscardiens for the FNRI). A balanced attitude of conferring democratically on one man a position which is then clearly recognized as leadership, but still subject to re-election is rare. Prime Ministerial candidates tended to coincide only accidentally with positions of elected leadership. None of the Radical premiers was the party's President (though Gaillard became one soon afterwards). Mollet was so well established as SFIO leader that his choice was obvious in 1956, but he had occupied the same position when four other Socialists had come to the Assembly for investiture. De Gaulle let it be known that he did not want a President for the UNR and, in the absence of any involvement in the party from him, its leadership was in effect exercised by his appointed Prime Ministers: Debré and Pompidou. But after his dismissal as prime minister, Pompidou remained an unofficial leader of the UDR although holding no formal position in the party. The failure of the parties to produce clearly recognized leaders was one of the charges against them. Few Frenchmen knew much of the ever-changing Prime Ministers of the Fourth Republic and the only two who built up much popularity in the country (Mendès-France and Pinay) were allowed less than a year in office and no return to it.

Only the Communists, SFIO and Gaullists possess headquarters of any substance. All the Paris offices of the parties are scattered around the city and with these exceptions (and those of the MRP) they are small and hidden. Very few therefore employ any sizeable number of officials. Naturally headquarters activities are limited. However, most significant parties manage to publish a weekly or fortnightly newspaper for internal circulation, and some have attempted a daily for periods. Sometimes the precise allegiance of these papers can be important. The SFIO devotes a chapter of its statutes to the control of its newspapers. When the Conservatives split over Gaullism in 1962, the pro-Gaullists were able to capture the old *paysan* journal, *La France Rurale et Indépendante*, which they turned into *La France Moderne, Libérale, Centriste et Européenne* in April 1963, while the *Journal des Indépendants* remained in official CNIP hands.

Within these formal structures, parties create a social life of their own for their members. This has been particularly important on the Left. In the Communists, SFIO, Radicals and PSU, membership implies a certain acceptance of a system of internal values and vocabulary that each party has developed. The rules of each require a sort of probationary period before the member is considered fit to take any leading part in the party. For the Radicals, Congress delegates must have been members for two years; in the SFIO no member may become a parliamentary candidate or a member of any central organ of the party until after five years. For all its newness the PSU decided on similar rules. Such rules spring from an attitude that has been characterized by its opponents as the 'party-army', the party as a dedicated, self-selected *élite* working for certain ideological aims, rather than an open organization appealing to all those whose electoral support it is seeking. The MRP and RPF tried to constitute themselves in a deliberately more open fashion. However, it is not only on the Right that the closed character of the SFIO has been criticized; it was to become one of the main stumbling-blocks to the regrouping of the Left.

DEVELOPMENTS, 1962–1968

The Confrontation of Autumn 1962

The formal issue at the referendum of October 28, 1962, was whether the President of the Republic should be elected by universal suffrage or through an electoral college dominated by local councillors. However, many cross-currents were involved. For the opposition parties the referendum was a clear violation of the constitutional method of amendment and a deliberate snub to the Assembly. For the Gaullists, it was entirely appropriate that the people should be called on to exercise their sovereignty by amending their constitution and the opposition arguments showed a narrow legalism and a desire to put their parties' position above that of the nation. For de Gaulle's supporters, popular election was essentially in accord with the role which he had given to the Presidency; for his opponents, it was an entirely inappropriate way of choosing a figure-head or arbiter and gave a dangerous base to an office which they feared could be used to restrict the powers of the true reflection of the popular will—the Assembly. De Gaulle specifically put the issue in terms of himself or the parties of the bad old times. It was thus a straight confrontation; confidence in the traditional republican concept of parliamentary democracy, operated by the Fourth Republic parties, or confidence in the concepts and system of government of the Fifth Republic. France, by a 62 : 38 majority, opted for the latter despite the fact that the parties campaigning for the former had totalled over 80 per cent of the vote in 1958.

This was the first round of a three-round battle and the opposition parties were not particularly discouraged. It was widely assumed that their voters had voted for de Gaulle personally, but would return a good majority for the Traditional parties in the new Assembly. In the Senatorial elections in September, the UNR had lost seats and there were forecasts that it would be down to less than a hundred in the Assembly. Although the parties did receive some two-thirds of the votes cast at the first round of the November elections, they were disturbed by the high number of abstentions

(31·3 per cent),[1] and shocked by the good showing of the UNR. The second round was a Gaullist tidal wave and the candidates invested by the *Association pour la Cinquième République* (AVER) won an absolute majority; three-quarters of the CNIP and one-third of the MRP outgoing deputies lost their seats. The parties had been beaten on their own ground.

The reasons are not difficult to find. That there was widespread disillusion with political parties is apparent from opinion surveys, such as the following three taken by the *Institut français d'Opinion publique* in October, 1962:

Do you consider that political parties are necessary to the good functioning of a democratic system?

	per cent
Yes	53
No	26
No opinion expressed	21

Do you have the feeling that the interests of people like you are best defended by the action of unions or professional bodies, by the action of political parties or by the action of *élus?*

	per cent
Unions	54
Élus	10
Parties	8
No opinion expressed	28

In your view, if the majority of the political parties are opposed to the proposal submitted by General de Gaulle to the referendum, is this rather . . .

	per cent
. . . in order to defend their own interests	54
. . . out of concern for the good functioning of institutions	25
No opinion expressed	21

There is plenty of evidence that this attitude had been widespread well before autumn 1962; there had, after all, been the clear rejection

---

[1] Normally around one-fifth of registered electors do not vote; at the referendum the previous month this had risen to 23·2 per cent.

of outgoing deputies in the 1958 Election. But it was brought home in a dramatic way to the parties by the events of October–November 1962.

This battle was symbolic in another major respect. When the referendum was announced, it immediately aroused the Fourth Republic alliance of the four non-Gaullist, non-Communist formations. A vote of censure on the Pompidou government (for complicity in the violation of the constitution) was put down by them jointly and won with their votes working together for the first time since the Fourth Republic. The referendum campaign was conducted jointly. Even the CNIP and SFIO put out almost identical posters.[1] It was suggested, at an early stage, that this *Cartel des Non* should arrange, at the second round, one agreed, democratic *Non* candidate in each constituency. During the campaign before the first round cracks began to show; Mollet suggested that in a few cases (a dozen was mentioned) it might be necessary to support a Communist candidate in order to defeat the UNR. The other *Cartel des Non* leaders reacted in horror (including Maurice Faure, the Radical leader).

In the week between the two rounds the political alignment changed completely. The national leaders of the cartel still met and some attempt was made to carry out mutual desistments. In over half the departments popular front alliances were formed between the SFIO and Communists with the PSU and Radicals involved sporadically. The Ministry of the Interior estimated that Communist votes had elected some 52 anti-Gaullist candidates,[2] and more than a quarter of the Communist deputies elected clearly owed their seats to SFIO, PSU or Radical votes. Conversely, the majority of Conservative and MRP voters fled to Gaullist candidates in straight fights between them and Communist-backed SFIO or Radicals. A broad Left-Right alignment had reappeared. The *Cartel des Non* alignment was revealed as a grouping which was unable to stand up to an electoral system in which the electorate had to approve alliances. Similar anti-Communist, anti-Gaullist alliances had been made in 1951, but under the then electoral system they had not

[1] The CNIP added 'No to arbitration by the Communists' to the list of reasons for voting No given by the SFIO poster.
[2] These were 35 SFIO (out of 65), 10 Radicals (out of 42), both the two PSU deputies and five right-wing deputies.

needed the support of the electorate for them to operate. As in 1956, the division which was basically that of *laicité* appeared; a small part of the Centre-Left, both candidates and voters, came out on the Right of that division but in most of France it was Communist, Socialist and Radical on the one hand and MRP, Conservative and Gaullist on the other. Of the 227 straight fights at the second round, 197 were Left and Right in this sense. Only 95 were the cartel against a Gaullist.

Rethinking and regrouping 1963–65

The three-year period following the autumn 1962 confrontation was one of agonizing reappraisal for all the non-Gaullist parties. The main lesson of the confrontation—that the parties had to change —was well noted and all politicians engaged in intense debate about their parties. The pending Presidential Election, and the line-up on which it was to be fought, governed the debate. The secondary lesson of the confrontation—that the traditional Left-Right divide was the most natural election line-up—was largely ignored although in the event of the December 1965 Presidential Election it reasserted itself.

The debate about the parties consisted of two elements, not always clearly distinguished. On the one hand it was widely agreed that six, seven or eight parties were too many and that some simplification or regroupment was urgently necessary. On the other hand, some were arguing that this could only be properly achieved through a complete reform of French parties—their modes, purposes and structures—and that merely regrouping existing parties would not be enough. The evidence of opinion polls leaves no doubt that there was general agreement on the first point; one showed in December 1962:[1]

Some speak of the necessity of regrouping the existing parties into two or three. Are you

	per cent
Favourable to this idea	66
Unfavourable to this idea	10
No answer	24

[1] See *Revue Française de Science Politique*, 1963, p. 431.

But the second point was one of the most profound dividing lines in the whole debate over this period.

Earlier on the MRP took up an unequivocal position in favour of creating completely new parties. The MRP Congress in May 1963 agreed unanimously:

'Its conviction that a large union is possible between those determined to promote social, economic and political democracy and the United States of Europe. This large union cannot be realized by a simple regroupment of parties. It requires the creation of an entirely new formation . . .'

The Congress went on to express the willingness of the MRP to commit suicide in pursuit of this conviction and to elect as President and Secretary-General two comparatively new politicians firmly committed to this line (Jean Lecanuet and Jean Fontanet) in place of two Fourth Republic stalwarts.

No other party took up such a clear position, although the remnant CNIP half agreed. A similar demand was made on the Left, mainly outside the existing parties. Members of the Clubs which were springing up were looking for some such completely new party. The plan *Un parti pour la Gauche* proposed by the *Club Jean Moulin* called for the creation of an outward looking 'party of action' in place of the inward looking 'hard and pure party' it saw as characteristic of the traditional Left. The ex-Mendèsist group around the *Club des Jacobins* was similarly looking for some focus for the creation of a new party of the Left and found the existing parties unsuitable.

The SFIO Congress, which followed immediately on the May 1963 MRP Congress, was divided on the issue. Deferre was a partisan of political change—towards a truly presidental system of government and a new party system appropriate to it. Others were bitterly opposed to such a betrayal of the SFIO's traditions, and strongly attacked the *fureur novatrice*. The adopted resolution faced both ways, calling for a 'regrouping of those on the Left with a Socialist inspiration which will not result from the addition of a certain number of existing organizations', but asserting that the regrouping must be the product of efforts by the SFIO itself. Critics felt that this was no more than an invitation to PSU members, some Radicals and others on the Socialist Left to join a little-changed SFIO.

Elsewhere, the PSU were so involved with internal dissension as to be irrelevant to the main debate while the Radicals gave similar lip service to regrouping combined with proposals to achieve it by widening their own party. In fact, at the 1963 and 1964 Radical Congress steps were taken to fuse the small CR and UDSR with the Radicals. The 1963 Congress resolution envisaged a 'team' of 'democratic formations' to fight the Presidential Elections; by 1964 the Radicals had come much closer to the position of the MRP, which was 'unanimously conscious of the necessity of a profound change in political structures and methods', but was studiously vague about how it was to be achieved.

In practice the parties displayed all the instincts of self-preservation to be expected from established organizations. Although much of the impetus in opposition politics over these three years came from outside the framework of established parties (most noticeably the Deferre candidature), at the end of it the parties survived intact and proceeded to dominate the actual regroupment that took place. Even the MRP, for all its Congress resolutions, was to prove very anxious to avoid sacrificing its distinctiveness during the vital negotiations of May–June 1965. The organic strength of the old parties was to triumph over the widespread demand for completely new formations.

The impetus for change was increasingly channelled into new bodies—the Clubs. Most of these sprang up independently from about 1957 onwards, bringing together people interested in politics who were dissatisfied with the way politics was being operated in France. Some had particular geographical, occupational, religious or political attachments. The most notable were the old *Club des Jacobins*, which was long committed to the idea of a renewed Left and the *Club Jean Moulin*, smaller but containing many influential civil servants, which took a more detached view but became the channel for a series of non-doctrinaire but progressive publications about political problems. About 1962 contacts between some of these clubs began and groups of them, at first informal but later formalized, began to play a part on the political stage. Many who hoped for renewal by replacement rather than by regroupment saw in these emerging groupings the germ of a future Left or Left-Centre formation.

Meanwhile debate increasingly centred around what were in effect five projected regroupings of existing parties:

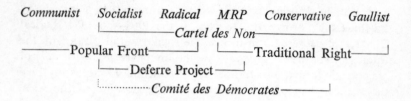

Communist   Socialist   Radical   MRP   Conservative   Gaullist
└──────────────*Cartel des Non*──────────────┘
──────Popular Front──────┘ └──────Traditional Right──────┘
└────Deferre Project────┘
············*Comité des Démocrates*────┘

Of these, the first three were quiescent; the running was made by the partisans of the Deferre project and to a lesser extent by the *Comité des Démocrates*. Nevertheless the first three traditional alignments were evidently in the minds of many and attachment to them was the basis of opposition to the rival proposals. Following the collapse of the *Cartel des Non* in 1962, no similar links remained other than through the *Comité des Démocrates*. But links on the traditional Right were carefully maintained. Two leading MRP Gaullists, Maurice Schumann and Charles de Chambrun, were able to wear both hats and avoid any clear breach between the MRP and Gaullism. The two rival Conservative groups, the anti-Gaullist rump CNIP and the pro-Gaullist Assembly group RI were careful not to rupture the existing links between them. In many departments, a local centre bridged the gap as did the two Senate groups. Meanwhile, close links grew up between the RI group and the rest of the Gaullist majority. Each group was keeping open its options.

As for the Popular Front grouping, the SFIO–Radical links were of long standing but even after the pact at the Second Ballot in November 1962 the Communist Party remained quite isolated. But changes within the Communist Party proceeded. In May 1963 the Central Committee declared that the theory of only one party in a socialist state was an error. At the Eighteenth Party Congress in May 1964, a notable rejuvenation of the leadership took place while the secret ballot was introduced for some internal elections. In his final oration to the party he had dominated in isolation for 17 years, Maurice Thorez played on memories of the Popular Front and emphasized the need for the unity of the Left in the face of Gaullism. About this period the Communist students were engaged in vigorous public debate about the changing role of the party, embarrassing hard-line loyalists but establishing by the fact of open debate that the party was changing. When Khrushchev fell in October 1964, the French Communist Party, once the most slavishly loyal to every shift in the Moscow line, demanded to know why and sent a delegation to Moscow to find out. By 1965 the party was looking distinctly less undemocratic and less unpatriotic. The collapse of the Deferre initiative opened the way for it to take advantage of the melting of hostility towards it.

The first project of regrouping was launched quietly in April 1963 as the *Comité d'étude et de liaison des Démocrates français* (usually shortened to the *Comité des Démocrates*), which included leading Conservatives, Radicals and MRP members with a sprinkling of less important Socialists. A year later all the SFIO members withdrew. The *Comité* served as a focus for discussion and preparation of a common attitude to the problems of regroupment. By May 1965 a manifesto was launched, proposing a *Centre Démocrate* which would synthesize 'the three fundamental streams which have inspired democratic beliefs of the nation: the liberal stream, the Socialist stream and the christian stream.'

However, the *Comité* had really succeeded in bringing together representatives of only the christian and liberal stream, whilst the presence of the CNIP leaders suggested that it was more likely to be anti-socialist. Moreover, although the Radicals' leader was heavily involved, he was out of step with his party (and his importance was declining since his term expired, without eligibility for re-election, in the autumn of 1965). The *Comité des Démocrates* was a limited success in that it prepared the way for the *Centre Démocrate* launched by Lecanuet, but a failure in that its political base was too narrow for it to hope to gain real influence.

The Deferre project was launched in a very different way and was inextricably involved with the candidature and personality of Deferre himself. After a build-up created by the Press and Clubs, Deferre declared himself a candidate for the Presidency in December 1963. A reluctant SFIO endorsed him but sought to limit his freedom of action. For some the Deferre candidature was to be the catalyst of a completely new social democrat or progressive democrat formation, formed out of his supports in the Presidential campaign and by-passing the existing parties. A group 'Horizon 80' was formed outside the parties to prepare a long-term political programme and it drew heavily on the resources of the Clubs. For a time it seemed that the existing parties might be brushed aside as a new movement took on substance. Some members of the MRP supported him but the May 1964 Congress failed to do so. Deferre retaliated by asking the Socialist members of the *Comité des Démocrates* to leave, but later in the same month declared 'that on all the essential questions there is agreement between the leaders of the MRP and me'. For twelve more months his candidature continued but failed to achieve the momentum that might have brought the parties to him.

In March 1965 the Municipal Elections provided an interesting commentary on the problems of realignment. Parties had to form alliances locally to stand any chance of winning the majority of votes which under the new electoral law took all the seats in each large town.[1] In the large towns 42 per cent of the votes were cast for lists including SFIO candidates, 39 per cent for ones with MRP candidates and 37 per cent for ones with Radical or Centre-Left candidates. These votes were distributed between the different types of alliance as follows:

Type of Alliance	MRP per cent	Radicals per cent	SFIO per cent
Traditional Right (UNR, Conservatives, MRP)	10·6	—	—
Popular Front (including Communists)	—	9·8	22·3
Anti-clerical non-Communists (SFIO, Radicals)	—	2·9	2·9
Cartel des Non (SFIO, MRP, Conservatives with or without Radicals)	13·4	11·2	13·4
Party alone	0·1	—	0·7
Anti-Socialist (Radicals plus Right)	12·2	13·9	—
Anti-Communist (UNR, Conservatives, MRP, SFIO)	2·7	—	2·7
Deferre Project (MRP, SFIO, with or without Radicals)	—	—	—
Total	39·0	37·8	42·0

[1] Defined in law as having more than 30,000 inhabitants.

These alliances reflected the necessities and inclinations of local politicians in French towns. They show very dramatically how little grass-roots sense was made by the three-party link-up that Deferre was about to propose. Roughly speaking the MRP split three ways: between being part of a traditional clerical right-wing front; being part of an anti-Socialist front; and being part of an anti-Gaullist traditional party alignment. The latter alignment still had its attractions for many local SFIO leaders but a clear majority had preferred the popular front link. The Radicals split evenly between allying to the Right, to the Left, and with both.

Despite this evidence, Deferre decided in May 1965 to stake all on the creation of a federation linking the MRP, SFIO and Radicals. This was to be put to the SFIO Congress in June; meanwhile it was discussed at the MRP Congress in late May. The MRP 'noted with interest' the proposed scheme, stated that the principle behind it was in accord with its own position and declared itself 'ready to study the putting into effect of the scheme'. The SFIO Congress was no more enthusiastic and laid down that the proposed federation must accept *laicité* in education and nationalization of commercial banks and building land; points which were clearly unacceptable to the MRP. In a series of meetings in mid-June, delegations from the three parties and from some Clubs tried to reach agreement on a charter to define the political aims of the federation. Eventually, after a nine-hour session on June 17–18 the negotiations reached deadlock on four points:

1. Relations with the Communist Party.
2. The schools question.
3. The inclusion of 'socialist' in the title (this was symbolic of what the MRP regarded as collectivism which the SFIO had obliged Deferre to accept).
4. The timing of the creation of the federation (the MRP wanted to postpone this until the Legislative Elections, due in March 1967).

It was the MRP who refused to accept what the others wanted on each of these points. But it was the SFIO, at any rate on the second and third points, which had taken a position likely to produce such an impasse.

That Deferre ever proposed his federation was itself a confession of failure of the idea that the parties could be by-passed by an entirely new creation. That his federation failed demonstrated, above all, that the traditional Left–Right cleavage in France could not be overcome. The first two points of disagreement are litmus tests of what Left has meant in France and demonstrate the inability of the MRP to fit into this tradition.

Both the *Comité des Démocrates* and the Deferre project were based on the creation of some sort of centre formation which would attract a natural majority. They differed only in where they placed the centre of gravity along the political spectrum (thus leaving the pivotal Radicals in the happy position of being able to support both proposals at once). Both refused to face the problems inherent in the creation of a truly two-party or two-bloc system. Both would have left blocs on both the Communist Left and the Gaullist Right. It would have been in the logic of such a three-party system that the Centre Party would have won every Presidential Election with the support of whichever extreme bloc came third against the other and that in the Assembly no government could be formed without it. The problems that such a system would create for democracy were little discussed. But so long as the Communist party was to be excluded from regrouping, such a three-party system was inevitable.

While the parties had been manœuvring for the Presidential Elections, a new grouping had appeared on the political scene. Various links between the Clubs had been established in 1963 and these led to two general meetings in 1964. At Vichy in April 1963 nearly a thousand delegates, representing 18 bodies, attended the *Assises de la Démocratie* on the initiative of the *Club Jean Moulin*. Five of the eleven clubs there had been associated with the launching of the Deferre candidature and, to some extent, the meeting gathered those who looked to his candidature. However, many of the bodies there did not wish to take up political positions and no party politicians were present. In June in Paris a *Convention préparatoire des Institution républicaines* was held on the initiative of the *Club des Jacobins* and attracted representatives from 54 clubs. This grouping brought together those with more specific political commitments and the meeting became the first of the CIR. Several Fourth Republic politicians were in evidence, notably Mitterrand. The CIR endorsed Deferre but it was never so closely associated with him as it was to be with Mitterrand later. By the April 1965 session of the CIR a new organization had been forged and was able to negotiate with the parties on behalf of the Clubs. When Deferre withdrew his candidature the CIR became an important forum for discussion on how to fill the gap.

On the Right the gap was filled by Lecanuet, whose candidature was launched by and a campaign was run from the *Comité des Démocrates*. Maurice Faure was loyal to him but the Radicals as a whole refused to follow him. Thus he became in effect the joint candidate of the non-Gaullist Conservatives and MRP. However, Lecanuet was determined to follow through the idea of a new party, resigned from his Presidency of the MRP and ran his campaign in part on the need to create a new party, the *Centre Démocrate*. On the Left, Mitterrand emerged as the best candidate behind whom the Communists, CIR, SFIO and most Radicals could unite. The day after he announced his candidature, the latter three agreed to constitute the *Fédération de la Gauche démocrate et socialiste* for which negotiations had proceeded quietly since the failure of the larger federation in June. The FGDS and the candidature were not at first directly associated but became so when the FGDS reorganized itself and elected Mitterrand its first President during the campaign.

In the heat of another election the much desired and talked about regroupment had taken place along the Left–Right cleavage, which had opened at previous elections in 1956 and 1962; not, however, across it as most of the discussion over the previous three years had presumed.

The Lines Harden, 1966–68
The alignment of December 1965 changed little. The political scene between January 1966 and March 1967 was dominated by the elections for the new Assembly which came in the latter month. More significant was the fact that the same line-up remained following the 1967 Election, and in all three camps the following year was spent thinking out the long-term future of their formations. The crisis of May 1968 and the snap election of June 1968 burst upon this process quite unexpectedly; none of the parties, hardly even the PSU, which overtly supported the students, was able to play any part in May. Indeed, one feature of that upsurge of ideas was a reaffirmation in much stronger terms of the feeling prevalent in

1962–63 that all parties were irrelevant. The June elections had certain immediate effects: the emergence of the *Centre Progrès et Démocratie moderne* and the growth of the gap between the *Fédération nationale des Républicains indépendants* and the *Union des Démocrates pour la République*. But the dramatic alteration of the relevant strengths of Gaullism and of the Left in the Assembly is bound to have much longer-term repercussions, and could facilitate a re-emergence of links between the non-Communist Left and the Centre.

In mid-1969 the future of all the political formations other than the Communist party looks more uncertain than ever before. The Chaban-Delmas government has looked beyond the Gaullist UDR and FNRI to the Centre for support; the Centre leaders split between Pompidou and Poher and the former FGDS vote split between Poher, Deferre and Duclos. It remains to be seen whether new groupings will follow these alignments, whether the lines which were clearly, if temporarily, drawn in 1966–68 will re-appear or whether, particularly on the non-Communist Left, there will now be established one or more quite new parties eschewing existing and discredited formations.

THE FORMATIONS 1966–68

The Gaullist Movement

The main body of the Gaullist movement to-day was constituted as the *Union des Démocrates pour la Vième République*, on November 26, 1967, in succession to the UNR–UDT. But although one purpose of this changeover was to enlarge the UNR–UDT, the UDVeR has no monopoly of Gaullism, which it shares with the *Fédération Nationale des Républicains Indépendants* (FNRI) and with a number of smaller groups generally referred to as the *Gaullistes de Gauche* (most of these are loosely grouped in the *Union de la Gauche pour la Vième République*). There is nothing in this particular nomenclature or arrangement of the various elements of the Gaullist movement to suggest that it will prove any more permanent than its predecessors have. For the June 1968 Elections another label, *Union*

144

pour la Défense de la République (UDR), was created to cover all UDVeR and most FNRI candidates. Indeed the shufflings that preceded the creation of the UDVeR show the problems involved in creating a permanent political party out of the supporters of the Gaullist regime. Following the election, there was pressure to keep the successful UDR etiquette so the UDVeR became the *Union des Démocrates pour la République*.

Despite its victory in 1962 and increasing importance during the period up to then, the UNR–UDT failed to capitalize on its position in 1963. With the incorporation of the UDT it had become, temporarily, the sole national vehicle for Gaullism (the *Républicains Indépendants* group in the Assembly refrained from setting up any national organization). Yet little or no effort was made to turn it into the one party for government supporters.

This was symbolized by the fact that Pompidou saw no reason to become a member of the UNR–UDT, although his predecessor Debré had been. After the third national sessions at Nice in November 1963 no further meetings were summoned despite Article 22 of the Statutes which required a meeting at least once a year. The Nice sessions were quite unlike a normal deliberative party congress; it was rather a panorama for the government—film shows about the achievements of the Fifth Republic in various fields, speeches by various public figures outside the party and a 'day of the majority' at which the *Républicains Indépendants* ministers were invited to speak.

Throughout the speculation during 1963–65 about whether or not de Gaulle would stand again for the Presidency, the UNR–UDT was totally irrelevant—it would have been quite unprepared to choose any successor had he retired. There was no issue dividing Gaullists to be fought over inside the organs of the UNR–UDT: in 1959–61 it had been important to keep the party with the President on his Algerian policy. Partly in consequence, the internal elections of the party after 1962 ceased to produce the competition and changeover they had previously.[1]

The March 1965 Municipal Elections underlined the relative failure of the party to achieve the local sort of implantation it needed to attract ambitious local politicians and to ensure its sur-

[1] Charlot, *op. cit.*

145

vival. When the 1965 Presidential Elections came, care was taken to ensure that the UNR–UDT was not too closely involved with de Gaulle's campaign.

From May 1966, the relegation of the UNR–UDT was confirmed as Pompidou formed successive *ad hoc* committees. In May 1966 the 21-member *Comité d'Action pour la Vième République* was formed under his chairmanship; the UNR–UDT had ten places, the *Républicains Indépendants* five, while the other six were mainly personalities such as André Malraux and Edgar Faure. This served as a clearing house for the 1967 Legislative Elections to ensure that there was only one official Gaullist per constituency. The investitures were given freely to non-UDR–UDT candidates: the *Républicains Indépendants* demanded and were given an increased share of places; all retiring *Centre Démocratique* and unaffiliated deputies who had supported de Gaulle at the Presidential Election were given the ticket and the little groups of *Gaullistes de Gauche* received a disproportionate 30 constituencies. This marked the government's desire to broaden and maximize its support, without being too dependent on a single instrument.

Following the elections, the UNR–UDT was simply taken over by the government. In May 1967 the post of Secretary-General was abolished. An Executive Committee was set up, to be chaired alternately by Pompidou and Roger Frey (the minister charged with co-ordinating the reorganization of the party) consisting of these two as Presidents, five joint-Secretary Generals and a few others. Pompidou, who had now clearly taken direction of the party, was not a member, and one of those moved in was a recent convert to Gaullism, de Chambrun, who in March 1967 had been re-elected as MRP with the CAVER ticket. This led to the creation in June 1967 of a new executive bureau to take charge of the UDR–UDT consisting of the five Secretary-Generals, five members elected by the bureau of the Assembly Group of *Démocrates pour la Vième République* (which had been set up in March to include all candidates who had received the CAVER ticket except the *Républicains Indépendants*), one from the Senate UNR group, the two presidents of the parliamentary groups, five elected by the political commission of the UNR–UDT and up to four co-options. All this rearrangement almost completely by-passed the statutory organs of the UNR–UDT through which the membership was supposed to be in control of the party (and even the political commission of the UNR–UDT included more ministers and ex-ministers sitting as of right than members elected from below).

It was this bureau that summoned and arranged the fourth and last national session of the UNR–UDT at Lille on November 25, 1967, after a gap of four years. This was purely a session to bury the old party and so clear the way for the new—the UDVeR—on the following day. The changeover did not take place entirely without hitches; there were some protests from old UNR militants and the name originally proposed, *Union des Démocrates Sociaux pour la Vième République*, was altered. More important, the militants insisted on a single national Secretary-General elected by the central committee and not a collective secretariat—thus ensuring that there could be a leader of the party organization distinct from the ministerial leadership.

The structure of the new party is much the same as the old. Changes include calling the national sessions once every two years, giving the planning regions a greater role, and cutting down the size of the national organs (the national council and central committee). These reductions greatly reduce *ex-officio* representation of ministers (previously all ministers and former ministers had sat as of right on the central committee and on its political commission). The statutes provided for the central committee to be composed of:

30 parliamentarians elected by the Assembly (25) and Senate (5) groups;

21 non-parliamentarians elected by the regional unions together with additional representation (currently 15) for larger regions;

20 elected directly by the national sessions, including ten of them parliamentarians;

The Prime Minister, one Minister appointed by him, the President of the Assembly and the Presidents of the Assembly and Senate groups together with any ex-Prime Ministers;

Two from overseas departments and territories;

Co-options up to 15 per cent of the above.

Not only does this composition reduce ministerial representation to three (though a few other ministers were elected or co-opted and ministers not members may attend meetings in a consultative capacity) but non-parliamentarians slightly outbalance parliamentarians. On paper the UDR is rather more subject to control from its rank and file members than the UNR was. It is too early to say whether this will matter in practice. One further change from the UNR–UDT was the introduction of double-membership if approved by the central committee. The purpose is to facilitate contact with other Gaullist groups: to allow them the opportunity to be involved in the UDR without surrendering their own independence.

There is, however, no evidence that the main rival Gaullist body, the FNRI, has any intention of being absorbed, even partially. The parliamentary group that appeared suddenly in 1962 as the *Républicains Indépendants* has meanwhile become a political party in its own right centred round Valery Giscard d'Estaing. For three years after its formation the parliamentary group played a very minor role. An early effort to form a parallel group in the Senate was repulsed and no national organization was formed beyond a *Centre d'Etudes et de Liaison des Républicains Indépendants*. A club supporting Giscard d'Estaing was set up in Paris in May 1965 under the title *Perspectives et Réalités*, but he maintained his declared refusal to set up a distinct political party.

The change came with the abrupt dismissal of Giscard d'Estaing from the government in January 1966. The former Finance Minister threw himself into building up his support in the country. A chain of provincial Clubs was set up, linked with *Perspectives et Réalités* and on June 1, 1966, the FNRI was launched as a party. The first nine months of its existence were spent bargaining with the UNR–UDT for more seats at the March 1967 Elections, with threats to fight the UNR–UDT at the first ballot. In the event the UNR–UDT lost about 40 seats whilst the strength of *Républicains Indépendants* group rose from 34 to 42. Giscard d'Estaing launched his part of the election campaign with the succinct slogan *Oui, mais* and this has increasingly characterized the role of his group. In August 1967 he publicly attacked de Gaulle over three issues: the Middle East War, the espousal of Quebec nationalism, and the taking of special powers to revise the social security laws; exactly the three issues on which the FGDS was currently attacking.

The FNRI took its distinct stance one step further in the June 1968 Election when some 50 of its candidates challenged the UDVeR at the first ballot. The Gaullist voters in those constituencies divided 63 : 37 in favour of the UDVeR candidates (who alone carried the official UDR label), a share for the FNRI which was much more favourable than its share of deputies or of the government posts. Indeed, if it could attract this proportion of the Gaullist vote over the whole of France, it would emerge with nearly as much popular support as the Communists or FGDS. This clearly demonstrated that, unlike Gaullism of the Left, which depends for any parliamentary or ministerial representation on the favours of the main Gaullist leadership, Gaullist Conservatism is an electoral force in its own right.

Its force was demonstrated in the April 1969 referendum when Giscard d'Estaing's *mais* became more important than his *oui*. The leaders of the parliamentary group, and a majority of RI deputies remained faithful to de Gaulle but the FNRI official position was *liberté de vote* while Giscard d'Estaing and his close associates were fairly hostile to the referendum proposals. This showed the schizophrenia of a body composed of a party created by one self-appointed leader (Giscard d'Estaing) and a parliamentary group of Conservatives formed to support de Gaulle.

The *Républicains Indépendants* have served the Gaullist regime as a bridge between it and traditional Conservative elements. They represent Conservatives who are prepared to support de Gaulle but who do not wish to accept Gaullism. From time to time the parliamentary group has voted against government measures—once six deputies voted for a motion of censure on the government's agricultural policy.

Great care has been taken to avoid rupturing the links with the non-Gaullist Conservatives. The two Senate groups both still unite the Giscardiens with strong opponents of the regime, although nearly a third of the Conservatives in the Senate are grouped in the *Amicale de l'Union Parlementaire Républicaine et Rurale* of Giscardien tendency. The FNRI is structured on the 21 planning regions, which neatly allows a good deal of vagueness about its relations with the old departmental *Centres des Indépendants*. In at least one case (*Alpes Maritimes* in September 1967) a departmental *Républicains Indépendants* organization has signed an agreement with its CD opposite number to put an end to the artificial division. It is evident that for many *Républicains Indépendants* their organization represents a way of keeping links with both Gaullists and Conservatives and that, with a realignment of forces on the Right in the post-Gaullist era, it may well become redundant.

On the other hand there is some evidence that the FNRI is building itself up to a position where it may be the most effective body on the Right if the UDR breaks up without its father figure. The FNRI has attracted a certain amount of business support on this basis. The regional organization created under Giscard d'Estaing after the March 1967 Elections does not seem built to fade away. If he can capitalize on his position as a supporter of the Fifth Republic without being too closely identified with the last years of de Gaulle, Giscard d'Estaing could emerge as leader of the most effective Conservative organization France has seen.

The left-wing of Gaullism has notably failed to establish itself in any parallel way. The UDT was submerged in the UNR–UDT and then in the UDVeR with little trace. At the first national sessions of the joint party in November 1963, the former UDT leaders won so few seats on the central committee that they threatened to re-form their party unless co-options were used to restore the balance (which they were). Two ex-UDT leaders, René Capitant and Louis Vallon, refused to go to the November 1967 national sessions arguing that the new UDVeR was to be an essentially conservative body. The growth of numerous other groups claiming the mantle of left-wing Gaullism during the last three years is further evidence that the merger has been a failure from the UDT point of view.

None of these groups is significant on its own. A number of them are grouped into the *Union de la Gauche Vième République*, which serves to channel official recognition from the government. But for the favours shown them by the main body of Gaullism in terms of seats and of public support, they would be of no importance. However, they contain a quite disproportionate number of personalities; former leading left-wingers who have given support to de Gaulle include ex-ministers from the Radicals, SFIO and PSU and even a former Secretary-General of the CGT. The enlargement of the Pompidou government in June 1968 brought several leading Gaullists of the Left into the government. One other group to the left of the UDR is the youth movement, *Union des Jeunes pour le Progrès*. The efforts to create an official UNR youth movement failed and this group was formed quite independently of the party. Its political line is generally fairly close to the old UDT, sharing its concern about the creation of the UDVeR.

Uniting all these bodies is loyalty to the person of de Gaulle and to the institutions of the Fifth Republic and belief in a shared experience. Around this loyalty there has grown a set of attitudes, perhaps a set of myths might be a more accurate description, which unites most or all Gaullists. It is impossible to classify these attitudes in terms of conventional political ideologies and they are difficult to define except in specifically French terms.

Charlot[1] identifies three categories of Gaullists: Gaullists of faith, empiricists and doctrinaires. For Gaullists of faith, the personal devotion to de Gaulle is the mainspring of their political views; the purest of the Gaullists, their presence throughout the movement gives it its most distinctive characteristics. The empiricist Gaullists are totally different; for them the justification of their loyalty to de Gaulle has been the practical successes of his rule in contrast to the failures of the Fourth Republic. Among the support that Gaullism has attracted since 1958, this element seems strongest; it has tended to predominate among the organizational leaders of the UNR–UDT— Charlot identifies most of those who have been its Secretary-General as empiricist Gaullists.

Doctrinaire Gaullists, according to Charlot, are of three sorts: a group whose ideas centre on the State, a group whose central idea is the 'common good', and the left-wing social Gaullists, each of them drawing on de Gaulle himself for their distinctive inspiration. For the first group, the creation of a strong and effective State together with hostility to all divisive elements in the nation is the core of its political doctrine. For the second group, the essence of Gaullism is the bringing together of all men and women in common purpose—an attitude that came to Gaullism from the MRP and Christian democracy. This attitude has something in common with those who see in Gaullism a continuation of the aims of the Left. For them, the institutional changes made by Gaullism have been aimed at restoring popular democracy, in place of a system in which a political class had effectively cut itself off from the people. For them the aim of social and economic policy should be (and they acknowledge that the Pompidou government has failed to attempt this) to reform French society so as to give the working class a much more worthwhile role.

To this classification, two elements ought to be added. Running

---

[1] Charlot, *op. cit.*, p. 276.

through all three versions of Gaullist doctrine is a common belief in the need for the renovation of France. At a time when France is undergoing profound social and economic changes, Gaullism is seen as the means of equivalent political change. One of the most common themes of Gaullist propaganda is the contrast of forward-looking Gaullism with the backward-looking old parties. For many Gaullists, the old concept of Left and Right in politics has been replaced by this distinction between the renovating and preservationist elements in France.

Nevertheless, perhaps the clearest characteristic of Gaullism in practice is that it has become the vehicle for the traditional Right of France. This is most clearly seen in electoral terms, as the following table shows:

PROPORTION OF SEATS WON ACCORDING TO DEPARTMENTAL VOTING TRADITION[1]

	per cent			
	1958 (UNR)	1962 (UNR–UDT)	1967 (CAVeR)	1968 (UDR)
Paris Region	56	77	60	73
Right-wing Departments	33	56	67	65
Intermediate Departments	42	49	39	66
Left-wing Departments	30	22	16	49
Whole country	40	49	48	63

Except for Paris, where Gaullism has always appealed, the electoral strength of Gaullism shifted dramatically between 1958, when many strongly left-wing seats fell to the UNR, and 1967 when the CAVeR relied amost entirely on the traditional bastions of the Right. At the 1968 election, the pattern was much closer to 1958, with an overall increase in strength of the Gaullists (see table above). It accords also with the government's policy in the social and economic fields. Although Gaullism has never particularly espoused the clerical vote, the Debré government's legislation on church schools

---

[1] Based on map of voting in M. Duverger *et al. Les Elections du 2 Janvier 1956,* p. 498. This table underestimates the extent of the Gaullists' reliance on areas of right-wing voting since it is based on departments; Gaullist-held constituencies in departments classed as left-wing are often in a part of the department which has always been more to the Right and vice versa.

placed it firmly on that side of the traditional divide. The atmosphere in which the UDVeR was launched marked a further acceptance of the role of the traditional Right; the dominant theme—the danger of Communism in France—was guaranteed to arouse traditional loyalties of both Right and Left, in support and opposition respectively.

Can Gaullism survive de Gaulle as a political force? Undoubtedly a memory will continue and will exercise a strong political fascination for many years to come. There is the possibility that the UDR will carry on as an essentially conservative party, attracting non-Gaullist Conservatives as its Gaullist characteristics decline. But no serious effort was made to develop the UNR–UDT into such a party, capable of surviving in its own right. It never acquired two of the essential roles of a political party—a source of political ideas and policies, and a channel for the recruitment and training of political leaders, either of which could have provided it with a *raison d'être* which could survive de Gaulle and with a common body of experience of functioning as a political party. The early struggle over Algerian policy and an attempt to thrash out a statement of doctrine at the second national sessions in 1961 were succeeded by six years during which the UNR–UDT seemed totally devoid of political ideas of its own. The political ideas in Gaullism came from members of the government outside the party like Malraux or Pompidou or from fringe groups such as those around Capitant and *Notre République*.[1] As for recruitment, Charlot's study shows how the leadership of the UNR–UDT has remained in the hands of an ageing group of Fourth Republic Gaullists. Of 29 ministers in governments from 1958 to 1965 who were members of the UNR–UDT all but three had been with de Gaulle in the Resistance and usually also in the RPF. In 1966–67 Pompidou widened his recruitment of ministers—but mainly among former Fourth Republic politicians rather than from the UNR–UDT. When in the 1968 crisis Pompidou brought in several more ministers they tended to be Gaullists of the Left who had not taken any leading part in the UNR–UDT.

The creation of the UDVeR was widely hailed, by both his supporters and his opponents in the Gaullist movement, as an attempt

---

[1] *Notre République* was the UDT weekly which continued to be published separately after the merger with the UNR, thus providing a focus for left-wing dissent within the larger party.

by Pompidou to create a broad-based conservative party capable of surviving de Gaulle. There was no reason why the same enterprise should not have been undertaken with the UNR–UDT in 1963, with much more time available. There is practically nothing in the constitution of the UDR to make it a more suitable vehicle for this purpose. So if this be the purpose, the change must be seen as essentially symbolic, designed to mark out the UDR for a different role in the future.

The Left

The Left in France consisted of two large, similar-sized bodies, together with one rather small party.[1] The Communist Party has changed least of all during the Fifth Republic and remains in strength, appeal to the working-class and internal workings very much as it was during the Fourth Republic. The FGDS was not a party but moved a long way towards becoming one following its constitution in September 1965. Meanwhile, the small PSU has pursued its own course, unable to achieve any significant growth, although in its persistence it is an uncomfortable reminder to the two larger bodies that they do not monopolize the Left.

One of the main criteria which had determined the boundaries of the FGDS in 1965 had been the question of relations with the Communists. The initial question in both cases was how to achieve an optimum result at the 1967 Legislative Elections; but closely following it has come that of how to make the FGDS, or the FGDS and Communists combined, a credible alternative government which could challenge the Gaullist regime. The questions of the ideological basis for unity (either FGDS alone or FGDS and Communist combined) and of the character of the new party to be formed out of the FGDS have taken second place to these more practical considerations.

In March 1966 Mitterrand took the initiative and proposed that the FGDS decide on three steps: the creation of a shadow cabinet,

---

[1] The May 1968 upsurge has thrown up a large number of left-wing groups which although they achieved remarkable effect during that month, have yet to show that they are anything but ephemeral. A Maoist *Parti communiste marxiste leniniste de France* was founded in January 1968 but was banned, along with most extreme-Left groups involved in the May upheavals, in June 1968. In April 1969 a Trotskyite *Ligue communiste* was formed, taking over many members from the banned *Jeunesse communiste révolutionnaire*, which took a leading part in May 1968.

the formation of a single group in the Assembly for all its supporters, and agreement on a sole candidate in each constituency for the legislative elections by July 1st. Mitterrand was recognized as 'Leader' for the coming elections by both the SFIO and Radicals in April. The shadow cabinet was agreed and announced in May. The other two proposals took longer to achieve but came in time. Mitterrand himself acted as a leader of the opposition, a role hitherto unknown in French politics. He systematically replied to de Gaulle's press conferences (with Mollet deputizing if necessary) and led the attack on crucial debates in the Assembly several times. Thus he kept himself in the forefront of press coverage of political news as an alternative president, to a greater degree than defeated presidential candidates in the United States normally achieve.

The autumn of 1966 was the crucial period in the relationship with the Communists. The newly-born FGDS and the Communists had not worked together in the 1965 Presidential Elections; they had merely worked individually for the same objective. During the first nine months of 1966 the two kept their distance in public. The Communist demand, as before the Presidential Elections, was the elaboration of a common programme (though they had been ready enough to drop that demand when it became expedient to support Mitterrand). However, the FGDS preferred to work out their own common programme for the coming Legislative Elections; this was done, and published symbolically on July 14, 1966. In October and November the matter was thoroughly discussed by the FGDS and the three constituent bodies, SFIO and CIR Congresses calling for an opening to the Left and the Radicals for an opening both to the Left and to the Centre. In December the Executive Committee of the FGDS decided to open negotiations with the Communists, nominating a delegation of three from each of its constituent groups. After three meetings over only eight days, this delegation reached a common agreement with the Communist Party on December 20, 1966, to bring about its re-entry into the mainstream of French politics after eighteen and a half years of bitter exile.

The agreement of December 20, 1966, stated as the main common objective the elimination of the Gaullist regime. The two parties agreed on the broad lines of their policy in the constitutional, social and economic fields and noted their disagreements in foreign policy.

155

The Communists agreed to drop their demand for a common pro-gramme and both parties agreed to fight the first round of the Legislative Elections with their own programmes and candidates. At the second, in all constituencies where the Left was in a position to win, 'the two formations will call on their electors to ensure the success of the candidate of the Left best placed by universal suffrage' (i.e. the votes at the first round). A few special exceptions might be made to this last provision.

The agreement worked better than most observers had expected. The two parties were able to agree with very little difficulty, on who should stand down, and both were able to impose the agreement on almost all their candidates.[1] This was a pronounced change from previous behaviour in France when local parties or candidates, particularly among the Radicals, had shown a marked propensity to adapt any national agreements to their own circumstances. Even more important, the voters of both camps followed the wishes of their leaders to a greater degree than had been expected.[2] This was most apparent in the change in the Left's strength in the Assembly: the Left vote had increased fractionally from 42·8 per cent to 43·6 per cent but their seats had shot up from 133 to 193. Subsequent analysis was to show that the solidarity of the FGDS was much less than it appeared[3] but the first impression—that the Left electorate had ratified the agreement—became the important political fact. As one speaker said to the Radical Congress in December 1967, the FGDS–Communist agreement had 'taken the character of a veritable contract with the country; it is an integral part of its (FGDS') public personality.'

After March 1967 there were several meetings between Com-munist and FGDS leaders and a degree of co-operation in the

[1] In only eight constituencies were there competing candidates on the second ballot and in none did the competition cost the Left a seat; in the 1936 popular front, in contrast, there had been 59 failures to follow the agreed tactics which cost the Left some six seats.

[2] In the three cases where it was evident from the figures of the first ballot that the maintenance of a second, rebel, Left candidate risked defeat for the Left, many voters for such candidates simply transferred themselves (the total vote for the three rebels fell from 21,957 to 10,342 in the week).

[3] See article in *Le Monde*, September 2, 1967, estimating, *inter alia*, that in straight fights between FGDS and Gaullist, the Communist vote split 80 : 10 (10 per cent abstaining). Between Communist and Gaullist, the FGDS vote split 59 : 38 (3 per cent abstaining).

Assembly. But the main effort was focused on a working-party composed of six Communists, three SFIO, three Radicals and three CIR which after eight months' work produced a Common Declaration of the Communist Party and FGDS of February 1968. This received much attention at the time, partly because of UDVER attacks on it, but in fact it did no more than spell out the rushed agreement of December 20, 1966. Agreement was reached on a large number of institutional, social and economic issues, with certain disagreements noted, particularly international issues.

However, there has been no suggestion that any formal links should be created between the FGDS and the Communist Party. There is no sign of the common programme demanded by both the Communists and the PSU; a suggestion that in the June 1968 elections the two might consider joint candidates at the first ballot was brushed aside by the Communist Party. Prior to December 1966 there was a long tradition of mutual hostility and whilst the popular fronting of 1966–68 was happily accepted by both sides in view of the success it brought initially, it broke up in May 1969, when rival presidential candidates were chosen.

Within the FGDS, there was much effort to ensure that the integration of the three parties would prove permanent. Immediately after the Legislative Elections, the three formed one group in the Assembly—although this meant the Radicals breaking their links with the members of the RD who had not come into the FGDS. In April 1967 two committees were set up to study the future structure and ideology of the FGDS; their reports were accepted by the congresses of all three partners in December 1967–February 1968. The CIR needed no urging; it has been the spur behind speeding up the progress towards fusion of the three partners. In July 1967 the CIR praesidium placed on the agenda of its November Congress a proposal for its own dissolution and called on the Radicals and SFIO to proceed likewise so that dissolution of the three bodies and fusion of them into a new party could proceed simultaneously. Neither the SFIO nor the Radicals have been prepared to move so fast or to give up their own identity. At the SFIO Congress in July 1967 there was much talk of the traditions of the 'old house' and of the danger of losing them. The Radicals in December 1967 accepted proposals for increased unity within the FGDS but emphasized their desire to retain a distinct identity within it. The FGDS needed some time to grow together and to create within it the sense of loyalty to one party that it had to have if it was to stick together in periods of adversity as well as whilst it was gaining ground. During the year of adversity following May 1968 the FGDS found that its cement was not yet strong enough. The memory of both unity and success in 1967–68, though, may prove a powerful factor in the debate about the future of the non-communist Left.

During its initial development, the FGDS has faced a series of problems. In the first place there have been persistent tugs in the directions of two other types of alignment—one round the PSU and the other towards the centre. It has had to sort out problems of internal balance between its partners, to consider the structure of the party to be created and to agree on a doctrine.

The PSU has continued to echo the former Communist demand for a common programme. It came into the Communist–FGDS agreement for the 1967 Elections after some hesitation but has refused to join the FGDS. At its June 1967 Congress three proposals were put: (1) for joining the FGDS; (2) against joining; and (3) to postpone any decision for a year. Voting on the three (second ballot system) was:

	First round	Second round
Proposal (1)	167	174
Proposal (2)	279	393
Proposal (3)	124	—

Part of the defeated minority broke away and has since formed the *Union des Groupes et Clubs Socialistes*, more notable for including several former PSA and PSU leaders (including one of their four deputies) than for its size. This group duly negotiated its entry into the FGDS and a few of its members fought the 1968 Election on the FGDS ticket.

At the same time the PSU has developed a new generation of leaders, who largely took over at this Congress from those who had come to it via the PSA from SFIO. The majority position represents the view of the most characteristic members of the PSU, younger intellectuals—whose attitude towards the regrouping of the Left is expressed in the words of one of its student leaders 'neither pro-American Social Democracy integrated into the system, nor the bureaucratic Communist Party increasingly reformist, but the development of a revolutionary current fighting here and now for Socialism'.[1] The PSU has failed to make any electoral impact (the four seats won in 1967 were all owed to personal votes or local strength taken from a local section of the SFIO which left the Party in 1958 and were all lost in 1968) but it has real strength in the universities. Because of this the PSU has the power, if nothing else, to deprive the FGDS of the sort of critical intellectual support which it could otherwise expect.

The success of the FGDS and of the FGDS–Communist alliance implied the failure of the PSU concept of the future of the Left, although with the upsurge of ideas and groups in universities in May 1968, it is very likely that further efforts will be made to create a new movement, by-passing the FGDS and Communists.

At its beginning, the FGDS established the principle of equality of representation between the three families: the SFIO, the Radicals with the UDSR, and the Clubs, both in and out of the CIR. In November 1965 the Executive Committee was fixed at 17 SFIO, 17 Clubs, 14 Radicals and 3 UDSR, with a smaller bureau similarly balanced. Voting was to be by a two thirds majority. After the 1967 Legislative Elections, the persistent SFIO demand that its superior strength to its two partners be reflected was agreed. From May 1967 the FGDS Bureau was composed of 11 SFIO, 5 Radicals and 5 Club representatives. In March 1968 the balance was altered to 33 : 18 : 18 in the Executive Committee and 13 : 7 : 7 in the Political Bureau.[2] There have been SFIO demands for the Radicals and the CIR to publish their membership as the SFIO does; the Radicals have demanded that weight be given to the number of *élus* possessed by each party. The adopted formula gave the SFIO the largest influence, equated the Radicals and the Clubs, but allowed the two latter to just outvote the SFIO. One factor however gave the Clubs more than their numerical share of power and meant that the Radicals have tended to be the third partner. When

---

[1] *Tribune Etudiante.*

[2] Four of the SFIO members in the Executive Committee and two of them in the Political Bureau were to be from SFIO Clubs: two and one respectively of the club representatives were to be from the *Union des Clubs pour le Renouveau de la Gauche*, with the remainder from the CIR. Until autumn 1967 the *Club Jean Moulin* had also been separately represented but it then withdrew from the FDGS. The UDSR ceased to have separate representation in 1966. As from March 1968 all voting was by individuals and by simple majority.

Mitterrand was elected the first President of the FGDS in 1965 it was agreed that the office should rotate every six months. This has not happened and, with Mitterrand the only President and Hernu occupying a powerful position in the Secretariat, the Club element in the FGDS remained prominent. In the reconstituted FGDS in March 1968 Mitterrand was elected President for two years.

When the common Assembly group was formed in April 1967, the SFIO found itself in a controlling position.[1] The composition of the group, and of its organs as elected in April 1967, was as follows:

	Group	President	Officers	Bureau
SFIO	76	1	5	10
Radicals	24	—	3	7
CIR	16	—	2	5
PSU	4*	—	—	1
Other	1*	—	—	—

* Affiliated to the group.

Thus a rough balance between the principles of equal and proportional representation was met, analogous with voting inside the EEC.

After June 1968 the group was reduced to 42 SFIO, and 13 Radicals together with Mitterrand himself and one other, both formerly in the RD. All the CIR deputies who had gained seats in March 1967 lost them fifteen months later, as did most of the younger SFIO and Radical deputies. So the FGDS group lost its leavening of deputies who had initially won their way into the Assembly under the FGDS label and became a grouping of long-established SFIO and Radical members, dominated by the former. Nevertheless it has maintained its unity despite the break-up of extra-parliamentary organization of the FGDS.

All these have been *ad hoc* compromises pending agreement on the type of party to be created. The two main schools of thought favoured either a 'multi-form' party or a completely fused single party. The multi-form concept, favoured by the Radicals, envisages that the constituent bodies would retain their individual membership and identity within a common discipline based on common policy-

[1] A demand at the SFIO Congress that SFIO deputies should continue to meet separately was met by Deferre with the statement that such meetings were unnecessary because of the SFIO's predominance inside the combined group.

making organs. The British Labour Party, a little misleadingly, has been cited as an example of this type of party.[1] Complete fusion is envisaged by several means. One has been the creation of a fourth family of direct members of the FGDS who might ultimately out-number those joining indirectly through the other three families. Another has been to achieve fusion by departments, at speeds varying according to local conditions, with national organs being built up in due course, simply replacing the previous confederal structure. The SFIO has hesitated between the alternatives; it shares the Radical attachment to its own traditions but in view of its size, not so much their fear of submergence. One variant has been espoused by Deferre: immediate fusion between the SFIO and the CIR as 'Socialist' bodies with the Radical Party remaining in a federal relationship to them. In December 1967 and February 1968 all three partners agreed that fusion should take place in 1969.

But the failure of the FGDS-Communist pact in the June 1968 elections had as disastrous an effect on both the pact and the FGDS itself as the success in March 1967 had had in the opposite direction. The Soviet invasion of Czechoslovakia, coming soon afterwards, deepened the rift between the Communist and non-Communist Left and helped further to discredit the Mitterrand leadership, closely associated as it was with the idea of unity of the Left. Mitterrand resigned his presidency of the FGDS in November 1968 and with his non-replacement, the FGDS itself ceased to function as an organiza-tion. It was not wound up but simply discarded as the SFIO, the CIR and two smaller groups (the UGCS and UCRG) agreed on creating a *Nouveau Parti Socialiste* in 1969 from which the Radical party opted out. Significantly when the Senate in October 1968 elected a new president the united Left tactic was tried but failed on the first ballots and the SFIO and Centre-Left members ended voting in a typical Fourth Republic alignment for the MRP candidate, Alain Poher, with Communist and Gaullist members in defeated minorities.

However considerable doubt came to shroud both the project for a new party for the non-Communist Left and its relations with the Communist party by the autumn of 1968. The Radical half

---

[1] Though the example of the ILP's independent status inside the Labour party is a possible parallel to Radical demands.

pulled out of the project at their congress in November, leaving the SFIO, the CIR and the two smaller groups to plan a new Socialist party—which by this stage looked much like the SFIO enlarged. But the plans to launch the new party in first April and then May 1969 were completely overtaken by first the referendum and then the presidential election.

Some local sections of the proposed new party were created out of the departmental FGDS groups in the early months of the year. A congress was held in early May, at which the bulk of the delegates were in fact SFIO but which also included the UCRG and some only of the newly-created local sections. The SFIO and UCRG recognized this as the foundation of the new party; the CIR and UCGS denounced it. The Radicals, apart from two leading members who joined the new party, were busy re-forming their links to the Right through the Poher condidacy. In this confusion the non-Communist Left floundered in mid-1969.

THE CENTRE

The Centre and derived terms such as *Centrist* and *Centrisme* have become increasingly used as general terms for all those who are neither of the Left nor Gaullist. This gives a wholly misleading impression both of the unity of this third group and of the position of much of it in the political spectrum. It comprises the remnants of three Fourth Republic parties, the CNIP, the CR and the MRP; each of them for different reasons probably dying. Most of it is now covered by two complementary but distinct bodies, the *Centre Démocrate* launched in February 1966 and the Assembly group, *Progrès et Démocratie Moderne* formed in April 1967. Otherwise various extreme right-wing groups may be included if only by themselves; at the 1967 Legislative Elections there were two candidates sponsored both by the CD and Tixier–Vignancour's *Alliance Républicaine*. Finally a curious group, *Objectif 72*, leads off to the Left.

Objectif 72 was launched in 1966 by Robert Buron, a former MRP Minister. Condemning the FGDS as a *cartel des gauches* and the CD as the *bloc national* of 1919, Buron appealed to those outside the parties who looked for a new political lead and were unhappy with the traditional parties' domination of the regrouping process. He broke his determination to turn his back on the traditional parties by circulating all the MRP departmental federations with a protest against the betrayal of the MRP's aims by the rightward-looking CD and calling for support for his *Objectif 72*. His body was set up with officers and a bureau at a convention in December 1967, attended by some 250 people (a fifth of whom were estimated by *Le Monde* to have come from the MRP).

It is, probably deliberately, not clear how far *Objectif 72* intends to act as a distinct political party and how far it intends to be a cross-party and non-party group, preparing the way for a different alignment. Its standpoint seems closest to that of the Deferrists in 1963–65 (Buron claims that they failed because Deferre worked through traditional parties) and it includes some of his supporters now in the FGDS. But it has refused for the moment suggestions that it should join the FGDS. It clearly acts for the left-wing conscience of the old MRP and represents the last hope of the intention of attaching devout Catholics to a progressive political party.

Lecanuet had promised to launch a completely new party out of his Presidential campaign. Its novelty was somewhat compromised when he launched it in February 1966. With himself as President, he had ranked himself with two of the four leaders of the erstwhile *Cartel des Non*, the Radical Maurice Faure and the CNI leader Bertrand Motte as Vice-Presidents. The carefully balanced 20-man managing committee consisted of five MRP, five CNI, five RD and five others (two of them in the existing Assembly group *Centre Démocratique*). Although the CD avoided any formal links with any existing party and all members of the managing committee took office in a personal capacity, at the start the CD seemed rather to be fulfilling the cartel function of the FGDS only in a different form.

The Radicals' involvement was short-lived—and showed the relevance of existing parties to the question of what was to constitute the CD. Eight days after the latter had been launched, the bureau of the Radical Party decided that membership of itself was incompatible with membership of the CD; Maurice Faure and other Radicals thereupon withdrew from the CD, though some non-Radical RD members remained. It was agreed to keep in being the *Comité des Démocrates* in order to maintain links between the CD and the Radicals. At its second convention in Nice in November 1967, the officers elected were balanced thus: President and

Secretary-General, ex-MRP; the three Vice-Presidents, Motte (for whose election as first Vice-President Lecanuet had to make a special appeal to delegates), one ex-MRP and one Catholic Trades Unionist. The complete change of balance since the launching is indicative. Observers have tended to see the CD more and more as the MRP reincarnate but shifted to the Right. In May 1967 a commission was set up to prepare the second convention consisting of six parliamentarians nominated by Lecanuet and 12 non-parliamentarians elected by the CD political council. Of these, 15 were formerly or currently MRP, two CNIP and one GD.[1]

Meanwhile the MRP has confirmed its intention of giving way to the CD. The dissolution of the MRP can be pronounced only by a national congress (which has not been summoned since 1965) and the formal dissolution has been left indefinitely. But the effective withdrawal of the MRP as a body came in September 1967 when its Executive Committee announced that it would be transformed into a sort of *club de pensée* with study groups. It will remain the French correspondent of Christian Democracy, which a centrist party with its wide appeal will not be able to do. The withdrawal was symbolized by the journals of the MRP and CD. The MRP weekly *Forces Nouvelles* and the fortnightly *Courrier des Démocrates*, originally the organ of the *Comité des Démocrates*, ceased publication simultaneously; a new CD weekly *Démocrate Moderne* replaced both in September 1967.

However, the MRP is not dead. A fortnight after this withdrawal, a former MRP leader Pierre-Henri Teitgen warned that it was only sleeping and that it would be revived if hopes for an enlarged CD were disappointed. Fontanet, the caretaker leader since no successor as President was elected to follow Lecanuet, was ostentatiously absent from the second CD convention. The MRP is still alive enough to be used by those of its members who are unhappy with what Lecanuet makes of the CD.

The most serious failure of the CD was its performance at the 1967 Legislative Elections and its inability to establish its own parliamentary group. Only 27 CD candidates were elected (30 being the minimum required for a parliamentary group) and most of these

[1] See *Le Monde*, May 4, 1967. One of the CNIP members refused to serve in protest against the imbalance.

were retiring deputies with personal followings in their constituencies (the CD had been generous in extending its sponsorship to almost anyone who wanted it). The necessities of representation on the Assembly organs brought together the whole of the Centre in a 41-member group, *Progrès et Démocratie Moderne* (PDM). The diverse character of this group can be seen in the former party affiliation of the 31 members who had previously sat in the Assembly.[1]

MRP		13
CNIP		10
Centre Left:		7
UDSR[2]	3	
CR	3	
RGR	1	
UNR		1

PDM elected as its President, Jacques Duhamel, who had been a prominent member of the CD without belonging to any of its constituent parties, had supported Lecanuet in 1965 and joined in the launching of the CD but had stood without any party affiliation at the election. Lecanuet, a member of the Senate, had not stood for election to the Assembly; he stood in 1968 but was not elected.

His absence from the Assembly may prove to have been one of the biggest errors of his career and has proved one of the biggest obstacles to his attempt to build up the CD. The PDM has developed into a rival pole of centrism, despite the fact that two thirds of its members were CD candidates. Within a few months there was talk of *Centrisme Lecanuetist* and *Centrisme Duhamellien*. In July 1967 Duhamel announced the formation of a Club to back up PDM (*Centre d'études progrès et démocratie moderne*). In October only one quarter of the PDM group voted for a censure motion which Lecanuet had urged the whole group to do. In November Duhamel was ostentatiously absent from the CD convention. In view of the pivotal position of the PDM in the Assembly the government has negotiated with Duhamel about his group's support and he has been considered as the spokesman of the Centre in parliament, whatever Lecanuet may feel. By 1968 Duhamel was being regarded in the press as the successor to Lecanuet as leader of the Centre.

[1] Another was the former Gaullist minister, Sudreau.
[2] The Pleven Group of the UDSR which had moved from the Centre-Left ED to the Centre Démocratique already in 1962.

To avert the effects of this potentially dangerous divergence, the *Comite d'entente centriste, organisme de liaison entre le Centre Démocrate, le CNIP et le group PDM* was formed in October 1967. The role of this link is not yet clear but if the CD and PDM are to keep in touch it will inevitably increase in importance. The separate role in this body of the CNIP is interesting: it marks the feeling of many Conservatives that the CD is now only the MRP and that the CNIP will have to remain a separate body on a par with the CD to safeguard Conservative interests. The formation of such a body perhaps also marks the failure of Lecanuet's belief that he could create a totally new unitary party, by-passing previous formations. Already the June 1967 political council meeting of the CD talked of a compromise between a unitary and a federal party which would permit the CNIP to retain its identity within the CD. A distinct unitary party remains, however, the CD's aim and its second convention confirmed that membership of the CD and other parties would become incompatible as from July 1, 1969.

In the May 1968 crisis and June 1968 Elections, the lead was taken entirely by Duhamel and the PDM group. Duhamel personally launched the compromise label CPDM for the elections to include both parliamentary PDM and the extra-parliamentary CD. It seems that despite Lecanuet's initiative and the widespread belief that parties could be formed round the Presidential Election, a party is being formed in the most classic manner of all—out of a group of parliamentarians who found the need to work together in the Assembly. The Centre in its PDM manifestation is less anti-Gaullist, less dominantly ex-MRP and generally broader in its extent than the Centre in its CD manifestation. But they are still running in parallel, with the CD the only body in the Centre which is really trying to be a political party.

PROBLEMS OF REALIGNMENT

The idea that the party system is related to the electoral system runs deep in France. The advantages of various types of electoral system have been much debated in terms of how they might produce desired effects on the parties. A French political scientist, Maurice Duverger, has become one of the most prominent advocates of a presumed relationship between proportional representation and a multi-party system on the one hand and a single-member seat plurality voting and a two-party system on the other. Party list proportional representation was introduced at the start of the Fourth Republic partly because its supporters believed it would facilitate the creation of stable, disciplined and responsible parties. Throughout the Fourth Republic the Radicals championed a return to a constituency system because they believed it would help deputies to build up bastions of personal support which would protect them from overmighty governments or party leaderships. The two ballot system was reintroduced for the Fifth Republic within single-member constituencies, much to the regret of many Gaullists who feared it would drive the Socialists and the Communists together. The idea of direct election of the President was supported by many who hoped it would aid a simplification of the party system. With all these hopes as part of the background to the regrouping process, it is worth enquiring how far the electoral system may have affected it.

The electoral system for the Assembly incorporates three main features:[1] it is a majority system in that it denies all representation to the minority in each constituency; it is a single member constituency system; and it operates by means of two ballots with voluntary withdrawal between the two.[2] Regarding the first feature, there is no evidence that the denial of fair representation to minority parties without the necessary geographical concentration of votes has been a factor in bringing the parties together. The second feature has certainly had some effect on the sort of representation secured by parties; the smaller parties have depended very much on locally entrenched deputies for representation in the Assembly. This very much affects the character of the PDM group and differences between it and the CD. So long as France keeps a single-member seat system and so long as French voters are prepared to vote for personalities as well as parties to the extent that they do, there will always be a number of deputies who are essentially free of any party restraints and who find it convenient to operate from the centre of the spectrum. Thus a fairly loosely united Centre group is likely to be a permanent feature of the scene and the problem of how to fit it into the party system will remain. Up to 1967 the Radicals, although

[1] There are certain differences in some overseas territories.
[2] Except that candidates with less than 5 per cent at the first ballot (1958 and 1962) or less than 10 per cent (1967 and 1968) must withdraw.

declining, constituted that group. It was a marked change of role for the Radicals to enter into the discipline of the FGDS.

The third feature, the two-ballot system, has undoubtedly had a significant effect on the regrouping. Inside the Assembly, or under an electoral system with *apparentement*, parties can make alliances on the basis of common policies or antagonisms with little problem of ensuring that their electorate will follow. Under the two-ballot system it is absolutely essential that a party's electorate approve of any alliance for without that approval the alliance is null and void. This was the lesson of the failure of the *Cartel des Non* in 1962. It is hardly an exaggeration to say that the two-ballot system ensures that the division between Left and Right will be over the question of co-operation with the Communists. In the Assembly it is possible for the non-Communist Left to ignore the Communist Party (especially if it has been reduced by gerrymandering the system as in 1951) and make alliance to the Right. But at the polls, where the Communist vote can decide defeat or victory, it is a different matter. So long as Communist and Socialist candidates competed at the second round, it was mathematically almost certain that the Left could never win a majority in the Assembly, whatever its majority in the country, unless the Right indulged in a similar division. And once there was a *rapprochement* between the Communist and non-Communist Left, it was natural that this should extend to the Radicals but not to the MRP. The Radicals have always regarded themselves as being on the Left, along with the Communists; the catholicism of the MRP's voters imposed on it a profound hostility towards Communism. It is easier to induce the voters for a fairly conservative Radical càndidate to switch to the Communists than it would be for those of a progressive MRP candidate. Once the die was cast with the Radicals agreeing to work with the Communists, the division between them and those much closer to them on their Right was sealed. This is closely related to the issue of *laicité* and it ensured that this traditional Third Republic Left-Right division reappeared in 1967. Not for nothing did the UDVeR anti-Communist propaganda later that year emphasize that the Communist party was committed to 'a direct struggle against religion'.

The presidential electoral system incorporates the two-ballot system and therefore will be likely to encourage the same division. Furthermore, it ensures that the question of the Communist vote is faced directly: there can be no question of making different alliances in different parts of the country. The presidential electoral system also has the effect of encouraging the formation of two blocs at the second round. At this round, the candidate running second is almost bound to seek to maximize his support by gathering together all those who voted against the leading candidate at the first round;[1] provided the supporters of the leading candidate are one recognizable political bloc, the others are likely to become one as well. Situations where one candidate has a massive non-partisan personal vote or where three equally strong candidates compete could hinder this process, but once two blocs have become established at one election the forces of inertia are likely to preserve them. The two blocs need not necessarily become parties. The distinction between the creation of 'two large tendencies' as opposed to a genuine two-party system was foreseen as the consequence of the direct election of the President some while before the idea became a matter of practical politics.

The presidential electoral system thus allows the growth of two national blocs, grouping smaller political parties in a way which blurs the question of what is a political party. This of itself is nothing new in France but it does now seem that the two blocs are likely to be rather more permanent and national than the cartels and electoral blocs which have been created so frequently in the past.

This is one really new element in the type of parties that has evolved. Despite all the hopes of the reformers of 1963–65 that new, open, mass parties could be created in place of what they felt to be the introverted, narrowly-based parties of the past, remarkably little else has changed. This is most strikingly seen in the personnel of the party-leaderships. The UNR–UDT and UDVeR have been run by a small clique of long-time Gaullists. During the Debré ministry a number of technicians were brought into ministerial posts and so into political parties. During the Pompidou ministry, recruitment into the government was almost exclusively from the ranks of people moulded by Fourth Republic politics—either former ministers from other parties such as Edgar Faure or Maurice

---

[1] Thus between the two ballots in December 1965 Mitterrand changed his title from 'sole candidate of the Left' to 'Candidate of the Republicans' with a view to attracting support from Lecanuet.

Schumann, or Gaullists who had established their faith by working in the RPF. When Pompidou reorganized his government in 1967, nine years after the inauguration of the Fifth Republic, the ministers he introduced included three who had entered the Assembly in 1945 (two MRP, one SFIO), a Conservative who had been a minister in the Pinay government fourteen years previously, two who had worked for the RPF and two others. The two others were Debré's brother-in-law and a member of Pompidou's personal cabinet.

The failure was even more striking in the shadow government of Mitterrand. In its leading personnel it was almost a repeat performance of the *Front Républican* government of 1956–57, with Mendès-France now, as then, a disturbing influence just outside. Indeed, one of the most striking features of political leadership in the Fifth Republic has been the steady return of Fourth Republic politicians: at the 1958 Legislative Election only nine members who had held ministerial office in the final Parliament of the Fourth Republic were re-elected. In 1962 another four made their way back; in 1967, three others re-appeared. The only parties which can claim seriously to have evolved a Fifth Republic generation of leaders are the FNRI and the PSU, whose respective leaders Giscard d'Estaing and Michel Rocard come from strangely similar backgrounds as *inspecteurs des finances*. Both the CD and CIR claimed a large influx of new members immediately following the 1965 Presidential Election (there is no doubt that this event did mark a reawakening to politics among many Frenchmen) but they have been strangely silent about such claims since. The CIR, a completely new party based on political clubs, contributed 16 deputies to the 1967 Parliament, but offered no sign of a broadening base of recruitment. Fifteen of the sixteen lost their seats in June 1968. The number of joining parties has continued to stagnate; the UNR–UDT has not the mass membership of the former RPF although it has polled more votes. The Communist Party has claimed, on the basis of an internal survey completed in 1966, to have undergone a certain rejuvenation of membership since 1959 particularly in Lorraine.[1] But once again

---

[1] See report on the 18th Congress, *Le Monde*, January 7, 1967. It was also claimed that the proportion of women among members had increased from 22·9 per cent to 25·5 per cent and that 40,000 members had joined since 1962. The electoral performance of the Communist Party in Lorraine in March 1967 did show local gains.

perhaps the best claim to have attracted completely new types of members could be made by the PSU and the FNRI, though for both in a very small way.

The PSU and FNRI are also the only two parties to have adjusted their structures properly to the significance of the planning regions in France, in which political decisions are begining to be taken and pressure groups are operating.[1] The traditional parties have been reluctant to make themselves into political entities at this level. The UDR is the only large party which has really recognized the single-member constituency electoral system in its structure. But perhaps the most striking failure of the parties to adjust their structures to new conditions is the total failure of all of them to make any allowance for the need to nominate candidates for the Presidency.

The 1965 Presidential Election was fought despite, rather than by political parties. All the candidates either nominated or seriously suggested were promoted outside party channels;[2] the choices and the methods of campaigning emphasized the unimportance of, indeed the desirability of dissociating oneself from, political parties.[3] In the 1969 election the main nominations (except the Communist Duclos) were made by consultation between political factions and personalities rather than by or through political parties. Pompidou announced his candidature before getting the support of the UDR, the FNRI and some PDM leaders; Poher's was promoted by a motley collection of individual politicians.

The first, formative popular election of the President may prove very important in determining the character of parties in France. If the parties are to regroup round the presidential electoral system into something recognizable as a two-party system, the unifying point will be the selection of their candidates. If the 1965 experience of fumbling around for candidates without any proper machinery for getting agreement inside or among the parties is to form the pattern for the future, it will mean that the parties as such are liable to be excluded from presidential politics. In so far as presidential elections are likely to be regarded by many Frenchmen as their best

---

[1] The SFIO youth movement announced that it was doing so in January 1968.

[2] Pierre Marcilhacy was nominated by a convention but this was summoned by and consisted largely of friends of other minor politicians.

[3] For discussion on the relations between candidates and parties during the campaign see Schwartzenberg, *La Campagne présidentielle de 1965*, pp. 133–5.

opportunity of participating in the democratic process, this can only worsen the estrangement of parties from the electorate. Many have recognized this: the CD (though rather less the CNIP element), Deferre and some in the CIR have urged the parties to accept the presidential electoral system (all of them outside the Gaullist movement opposed it in 1962). Deferre and several CD leaders go further and have called for, along with the FNRI, a true presidential system on the United States model. The FNRI has gone furthest with calls for a primary system. There is less recognition that it is in the parties' hands to adjust themselves to the popular election of a President: there were some calls for nominating conventions in the 1963–65 period (though little understanding of the problems involved) but the question has hardly been raised since.

Insofar as the parties have accepted the dualism inherent in the presidential electoral system it has been on what academic observers in France have termed a bi-polar rather than a bi-party basis. If this is indeed the pattern of the future, it is neither a two-party nor a multi-party system. The system will allow as great a multiplicity of parties as at any point of the Fourth Republic; but it will require them at intervals to coagulate round two points. The intervals are frequent enough and the distinction between the two points almost certainly fixed enough for the periodic coagulations each to possess a permanent character. However, they will not formalize into a pair of parties unless the nature of the parliamentary system produces it.

One of the changes of character that was urged on the parties by the reformers of 1963–65 was that they should be of *vocation majoritaire*. It is the only change which seems to have been accepted by them. The UNR–UDT is the first party in French history to provide the parliamentary base of support for a government. The left has acted in imitation with the calls for a common programme from the Communists and PSU and the shadow cabinet of the FGDS. In the Assembly the Gaullists have shown greater cohesion than any past Conservative group, whilst the FGDS are relatively united despite being only a coalition. The result is that a Left-Right cleavage is not purely an electoral phenomenon.

However, if one is to sum up how far parties have been changed following the period of intense rethinking, the answer must be: very little. There has been no realignment, only a regrouping. In one respect they are perhaps worse than their critics had felt they were

SOURCE OF VOTES FOR PARTIES

Per cent

Characteristic category		Year	Comm.	SFIO	Radicals	MRP	Cons.	Gaullist	All
Catholicism	Devout	1952	00	9	14	73	56	50	31
	Non-practising	1952	87	67	60	4	15	24	35
Sex	Men	1952	61	59	64	47	47	47	48
		1962	65	58	60	50	51	49	51
Age	Under 35	1952	42	30	11	31	30	38	34
		1962	35	26	21	32	26	28	31
	Over 50	1952	23	37	65	34	45	37	37
		1962	34	42	52	32	44	48	41
Rural	Communities under 5,000 population	1952	48	50	60	53	55	45	48
Occupational	Farmers	1952	5	9	31	20	35	18	16
		1962	5	17	22	16	21	13	13
	Business and managerial	1952	5	8	12	10	18	15	10
		1962	6	6	21	14	17	12	11
	Salariat	1952	10	13	6	14	9	9	12
		1962	13	18	10	13	13	16	15
	Workers	1952	54	34	15	18	14	22	26
		1962	51	27	21	26	16	21	28
Income	Under 8000 NF p.a.	1962	60	56	65	57	49	49	54
Education	Not beyond primary stage	1962	79	70	71	70	54	60	66

173

in the Fourth Republic. One constant piece of advice for the parties to make contact with the *forces vives*, the various occupational interest groups which emerged as more significant with the relative eclipse of parties in the early years of the Fifth Republic. The reverse has happened: the *Confédération Générale du Travail* and *Force Ouvrière* are less involved with their equivalent parties whilst the CD has nothing of the close ties with the *Confédération Française Démocratique des Travailleurs* that the MRP had with the *Confédération Française des Travailleurs Chrétiens*. The PSU's strength among the staff and student university bodies has tended to cut the rest of the Left off. The Clubs of the CIR are composed of individuals, often from a cross-section of professions.

Each of the parties, nevertheless, is based in part on the attachment of particular social or other groups to it. From survey evidence one can see how far this applies to the character of each party's support. The table on p. 173 shows this for selected categories in 1952 (the mid-point of the Fourth Republic in both time and political development) and in 1962 (the last election fought on the basis of the traditional party line-up).[1]

Voting by class is marked for the Communists but hardly for the other parties. Class polarization on a Left-Right basis is very low compared to other countries unless one takes the Communists alone:

	Alford Index of Class Voting[2] (1962 Election)
Communist	36
Socialist (Communist plus SFIO)	10
All Left (Communist plus SFIO plus Radicals)	2

A party not only often tends to draw on particular groups for its electoral support; it may also act as the channel for particular groups to achieve direct representation in the parliamentary system. The following table examines the occupational breakdown by party

[1] The 1952 figures are taken from Williams, *op cit.*, except for those on Catholicism. The 1962 figures are from F. Goguel *et al.*, *Le Referendum d'Octobre et les Elections de Novembre 1962*, Colin, Paris, 1963, pp. 228–40.

[2] See R. Alford, *Party and Society*, Murray, London, 1964, p. 102.

of all deputies elected in the 1956, 1958 and 1962 elections:[1]

					Per cent			Pouja-dist[3]
Occupation[2]	All	Comm.	SFIO	Rads.	MRP	Cons.	Gaullist	
Workers	7	43	4	0	4	0	0	0
Employés	4	12	3	1	7	1	3	0
Fonctionnaires	10	3	16	13	8	7	13	0
Professional:								
Teaching	12	17	31	14	13	2	6	2
Medical and								
Chemist	10	0	13	12	3	10	13	7
Legal	13	1	11	20	14	21	13	2
Army	1	0	0	0	0	0	4	2
Other	9	4	9	11	12	12	10	0
Farmers	10	11	3	7	17	20	6	0
Cadres	7	2	7	7	8	4	11	2
Commercants	6	0	3	3	4	7	5	81
Industrialists								
and Directors	9	0	0	12	11	14	13	0
	100	100	100	100	100	100	100	100

The table shows that the parties are much more differentiated in the sort of person they have as deputies than according to voting support. The function of the Communist party as the only party through which the French working-class can achieve direct representation in the Assembly is prominent. The domination of the SFIO by state employees and particularly by teachers, the fact that

[1] This table combines the individual tables in the studies of the 1956 (M. Duverger *et al., op. cit.*), 1958 (F. Goguel *et al., op. cit.*) 1962 (F. Goguel *et al., op. cit.*) elections drawn up by M. Dogan. The 1967 Assembly is not included because of the difficulty of fitting its party line-up to that of previous ones; interesting features are that only 23 per cent of Communist deputies were workers, and that among Gaullists farmers were much more noticeable in the *Republicain Independant* ranks (23 per cent) than in the UDR (7 per cent). Further details were published in *Le Monde*, February 7, 1968.

[2] French categories without exact English equivalents are left untranslated: *Fonctionnaires* covers all state employees from higher civil servants to postmen; *Employés* is roughly equivalent of white-collar workers; *Cadres* refers to those in managerial positions; *Commerçants* refers essentially to small businessmen.

[3] 1956 only.

the peasant vote for Radical candidates does not go to fellow peasants but to small town professional candidates such as doctors and lawyers, and the attempt of the MRP to represent all groups in society are also prominent.

The two tables above show how far the parties have had different functions representing groups in society. The non-Communist Left and Right as such are scarcely differentiated: it is quite evident that this division in France is not based on socio-occupational allegiance. On the Right the only significant difference lies among the peasantry, for whom the CNIP has been the most preferred means of representation while the Gaullists made a greater impact in the towns (although in 1968 the movement to Gaullism was greater in rural areas). On the Left, the division between Communists and non-Communists is shown to be to a large extent based on the role of the working-class. The SFIO has failed to achieve the position of Anglo–Scandinavian Social Democratic parties as the party of the politically-conscious working-class. The strength of the Communists rests on its role as such a party. In this function it is the French Communists who are more like the British Labour Party than the French Socialist Party. But this position is based on class-consciousness rather than economic deprivation. Judging the lower section of French society in terms of income or education shows little difference between any of the parties on the Left or indeed between them and the MRP. But the Conservatives and Gaullists have distinctly more support among the better-off and better educated.

Another sphere in which the parties represent different interests is that of the different political fields they espouse. This is very clearly seen in the distribution of ministries in the Fourth Republic. Some ministries were almost monopolized by one or two parties, whatever the coalition in office. The MRP dominated the Foreign Office for most of the time but were never allowed to get their hands on Education (which was indeed never allowed out of the hands of the *laique* Radicals or SFIO). The Conservative interests were closely shown up in that the only two ministries in which they clearly led the way were Agriculture and Ex-Servicemen. The four ministries most popular with each party, in descending order, were:

SFIO   Interior, Labour and Social Affairs, Industry, Works and Transport

176

Radical and Centre-Left	Education, Interior, Justice, Defence
MRP	Foreign Affairs, Health, Colonies, Agriculture
Conservative	Agriculture, Ex-Servicemen, Finance, Reconstruction

The Radicals' preoccupation was with the functions of the nineteenth-century state; the SFIO and MRP showed most interest in fields of social welfare added to the state's function in the twentieth century. To a considerable extent the parties were differentiated according to the subjects in which they took an interest: a sort of functional rather than ideological or economic interest differentiation.

It is clear from the foregoing discussion that the division between Left and Right in France, as it has been re-established by the recent regroupment, does not revolve around socio-economic differences in electoral support or in representational function. How far does it lie in ideological differences? The problem here is that ideas cannot be defined and measured in the way that socio-economic characteristics can be. The question is whether there are consensus recognitions about the ideological identifications of parties which can be taken as having some validity. There are in France, as elsewhere, many critics of the relevance of labels such as Left and Right. Thus one can very easily point out that the most purely 'Left' government of post-war France, that of Mollet in 1956–57, pursued a particularly reactionary North African and foreign policy while the Gaullist regime, resting on an essentially 'Right' electoral base, has pursued Left-inclined foreign policies in several fields. But in France, rather more than elsewhere, parties have an urge to identify themselves in such terms (thus the current use of Left and Centre as party labels).

The first question is that of identifying how many ideological groups, or political families, there are in France. During 1963–67 the argument ranged round whether there are two, three or four natural groupings. Some grouped Communist and Socialist together as the collectivist Left; others made a clear distinction. If a distinction was made, some then grouped socialism as part of a broad area of progressive and democratic ideas to be distinguished from the totalitarian Left and the democratic but conservative and nationalist Right. Others regarded socialism as a naturally distinct grouping of its own. In the Centre and Right various distinctions were made:

between democratic and authoritarian (i.e. Gaullist to the anti-Gaullist); between reformist and conservative nationalist (an MRP point of view);[1] or between a governmental Centre (Gaullism) and the classic Right.[2] Others identified all to the Right of what they regarded as Socialist or Left as being one political family. Thus Duverger identified 'three fundamental ideologies' early in the realignment debate as 'a conservative Right (CNI, MRP, UNR and Radical) . . . a socialist Left . . . and communist Extreme-Left'.[3] It is noticeable that two historic currents of French political ideas, the Radical and the Social Catholic (or Progressive Christian), were largely ignored in this debate—both were assumed to have lost their force or to have been submerged in a broader current.

In practical terms, the question resolved itself into one of whether there was a 'progressive centre', a body of political ideas linking democratic socialism with progressive humanism and progressive Christianity: in other words, the SFIO–Radical–MRP link-up championed by Deferre. If not, then there must be a significant ideological division between a fairly evenly balanced Left and Right, whether the Radicals were to one side or the other of it, or split by it, with or without the MRP similarly divided and whether either the Left or Right or both ought to be sub-divided. The critical period from June 1965 (the collapse of the Deferre project) to January 1966 (when the Radicals stopped Maurice Faure from keeping open their options) decided both that there was such a division, and also that it lay between the Radicals and MRP. Once the SFIO and the Radicals had made a decision which implied accepting sufficient unity of purpose with the Communists to allow co-operation with them, it was automatic that this should be so.

What, then, is the ideological basis of that division? In most industrialized countries the difference between Left and Right relates, at least in part, to a conflict between socialism and capitalism, or between nationalization and free enterprise (or the same conflict in any other terminology). During the preparation for his campaign,

[1] Thus in 1963 Jean Colville urged a regrouping between 'Reformism both individualist and communalist' (Radicals and the MRP) on the one hand and the UNR and CNIP, distinguished as being both conservative and nationalist, on the other.

[2] The view of Terrenoire, quoted in Charlot, *op. cit.*, p. 290.

[3] *Le Monde*, May 2, 1963.

Deferre put his emphasis on a socialism which did not seek systematically to extend the public sector of the economy but which sought, in the common interest, to ensure economic growth and equitable distribution of its fruits.[1] Several MRP leaders in May and June 1965 accepted that this was close to their own ideas. But there were those in both the MRP and SFIO who were determined to emphasize the differences: Lecanuet at the MRP Congress demanded that the SFIO choose between modern socialism and traditional socialism. The SFIO replied by reasserting its traditional definition of socialism. When the Deferre project broke up in June 1965, agreement had been reached on certain fields of economic policy, including national planning and municipalization of building land though not over the nationalization of commercial banks. But the essentially symbolic character of the division was demonstrated by the fact that a major point of disagreement was whether the term Socialist should be included in the title of the proposed Federation.

Since then, this ideological division has been emphasized by Lecanuet who has frequently termed the FGDS as collectivist[2] while the SFIO reasserted its 'traditional socialism' with the following resolution at its July 1967 congress:

'Congress confirms that such a fusion (of the FGDS) requires an accord on the fundamental principles and objectives of socialism, recalls that the distinctive character of socialism is the replacement of the system of capitalist property by a system where natural wealth such as the main means of production and exchange will become collective property.'

The link of the MRP with CNI elements in the CD had meant that the latter has clearly shifted to the Right on this issue: left-wing members of the MRP have accused the CD of having become entirely subservient to the employers' interests. So between the CD and the SFIO element of the FGDS an ideological divide on this issue is quite clear. Insofar as the Deferre reinterpretation of socialism repre-

1 *Un nouvel Horizon* (a book published as part of his campaign for the Presidency), Paris, 1964, p. 126.
2 F. Goguel (*Revue Française de Science Politique*, 1967, p. 450) makes the point that Lecanuet reintroduced the term collectivism into the active French political vocabulary in June 1965.

sented a similar change to the revisionism of the Bad Godesberg programme or of Gaitskellism, the SFIO has refused to touch it.

This leaves the Radicals in an odd position. They have no symbolic objection to the term Socialist, which after all is in the full title of their own party. Historically, they have been willing to envisage nationalization of major monopolies (more from the point of view of opposition to concentrations of power rather than from opposition to capitalism).

But there is no doubt that in the sense of the word that the SFIO insists on retaining, French Radicalism is not socialist.[1] Some would go further and regard Radicalism as being a variant of economic liberalism—thus Remond's study of the Right in France concludes 'at least in the social sphere, the radical family has rejoined liberal conservatism of which it forms a third variant'.[2] Yet the Radical Party has found it possible to agree within the SFIO on both an election programme (which included demands for 'Extension of the Public Sector to companies whose market is monopolized by the State' and 'Nationalization of Commerical Banks') and a statement of doctrine. Nevertheless there was an element of truth in Tixier–Vignancour's remark in May 1965: 'It would have been wiser to re-unite two federations, the one comprising the MRP and socialists under the etiquette of *dirigisme*, the other Radicals and *Indépendants* both being liberals.'

There remains one sphere in which the Radical–SFIO link in opposition to the MRP is entirely explicable: that of the *laique* versus the social catholic philosophy. Deferre and the then Radical leader Maurice Faure attempted in 1965 to avoid the schools question. But the SFIO Congress insisted on making it one of the basic principles of the proposed federation; this proved an absolutely unacceptable condition to the MRP and naturally the Radicals found themselves on the *laique* side of the fence. Since then the FGDS has espoused the legalization of contraceptives and made one of its main slogans 'Priority above other priorities for State Education'. The CD has abandoned the specifically Christian commitment of the

---

[1] Felix Gaillard has argued that the FGDS offers a synthesis between Socialism and Progressive Liberalism; this suggestion (in February 1968) was not welcomed by Communist or SFIO spokesmen.

[2] R. Remond, *The Rightwing in France from 1815 to de Gaulle*, University of Pennsylvania Press, Philadelphia, 1966, p. 340.

MRP but with Gaullists always ready to remind its electorate of the ungodly character of Communism and of the threat to the Debré government's legislation in favour of private schools, it cannot afford to lose its clerical associations if it wanted to. The table on page 173 showed that Catholicism is a far greater determinant of party allegiance between Left and Right than any other measurable characteristic. It is therefore evident that the events of 1965–66 have made the clearest ideological divide between Left and Right that of *laicité* versus clericalism.

It is quite clear that this corresponds to the popular identification of Left and Right. An IFOP survey in December 1962 showed:

'Among the following parties, which do you consider as parties of the Right, of the Centre or of the Left?'

	Left	Centre	Right	No answer	Left polarization[1]
Communist	85	1	0	14	100
PSU	57	10	4	29	93
SFIO	60	14	3	23	81
Radical	24	34	12	30	67
MRP	3	30	44	23	6
CNIP	3	32	39	26	7
UNR	4	22	55	19	7

Source: *Revue Française de Science Politique*, 1963, p. 432.

Furthermore, it is quite clear to French politicians that the electorate will follow this identification in its voting behaviour. This comes out in the analysis of the relationship between party identification and voting in 1962. For MRP and Radical identifiers, both of whom did not have a candidate in many constituencies in 1962, the problem was solved very differently despite the very similar policies of the two parties in most fields:

1962 GENERAL ELECTION VOTE[2]

	Radical identifiers	MRP identifiers
Communist, PSU or SFIO	31	4
Radical	53	3
MRP	2	58
Conservative or Gaullist	13	35
	100	100

[1] Left polarization is calculated as the proportion of those who identify the party as either Left or Right (i.e. excluding those who saw it as Centre or gave no reply) who saw it as Left.

[2] Recalculated from Table 24, p. 219, in *Goguel et al., op. cit.*, on 1962 elections.

The ideological identification of Left and Right which crystallized out in France in 1965–66 and which has defined the political boundaries of the FGDS and CD is thus based on a very deep-rooted and strong identification among the electorate which is in turn mainly based on attitudes to the Church.

The struggle against the Church is historically very strongly associated with the struggle for the Republic. An ideological division on the clerical issue also involves, therefore, a division in terms of attitudes to traditional Republican values in France. Because the Left has been defined as the *laique* Left rather than the Socialist Left, it is also a Republican Left united by certain conceptions of democracy. Conversely, because the Right is now largely Gaullist, and Gaullism involves many sharp breaks with Republican traditions, the Right that is in opposition to this Left is also largely in opposition to these conceptions. The odd group out in this respect are those conservatives in the CNIP who share an attachment to Republican traditions; the MRP, on the other hand, has been most willing to accept some parts of Gaullist ideas on democracy.

There are several ways in which this division has been related to political issues. In seeking to reform the Senate and local government, where the FGDS is strongly entrenched, the Gaullists have attacked the vested interests of the latter whilst projecting themselves as building for the future. The basic institutions of the Fifth Republic have themselves become electoral issues. Towards the end of the March 1967 campaign, the likely consequences of a majority for the Left became the major issue. The Left accused the government of seeking to subvert democracy, whilst the Gaullists charged the Left with not accepting the spirit of the constitution although it had received a popular mandate. In 1969 President de Gaulle returned to the attack. His projects for the reform of Senate and local government were pretexts for, rather than objects of, the referendum. His defeat and the election of Pompidou as his successor suggested a balanced view on the part of the electorate. However, it also justified the UDR propaganda associating itself with the Fifth Republic and its institutions rather than with the person of de Gaulle. By mid-1969 the inherent contradictions between the presidential and parliamentary aspects of the Fifth Republic remained to be resolved. At the same time, the Left still faced the basic issue of its future orientation, unable to decide finally if its vocation should be to work for the reform of the new institutions or their capture. Because of the way the parties have approached the institutional problem, it may well be that this will become one of the major issues dividing Left from Right in the future.[1] It is noteworthy that the FGDS–Communist declaration of February 1966 devoted nearly as much space to institutions as to economic and social problems.

If one could sum up the ideological regrouping in terms which are relevant to other European countries, one could describe it in the following terms. A political tradition which, while distinctively French, has much in common with the anti-clerical liberalism of Germany or Italy and with the political liberalism of Britain or Scandinavia, and the French Socialist tradition, have for some years sought hesitantly to merge with no definite result as yet. The attempt to create a political force which was both Catholic and socially progressive has failed; and the creation of a more broadly based and rightward-looking movement inspired by Christian Democracy, analogous to the German CDU or Italian DC, is being attempted too late to succeed (and in fact is much less inspired by Christian Democracy). In its place a broad movement inspired by very peculiarly French ideas occupies most of the Right of the political spectrum but, like Christian Democratic parties, has a wing to the Left. It may break up as the father-figure of those ideas departs; but if it survives him it may find itself in a very strategic position in any evolution of European political parties. For, all its peculiarly French elements apart, it is in effect something of a cross between an Anglo–Scandinavian Conservative Party and a continental Christian Democratic Party and might therefore form a useful bridge between them.

International Links

These can be summarized in three groups: clear and long-established for the Communists and Socialists; virtually non-existent for the Gaullists; and uncertain and changing for the other groups.

Both the Communist Party and the SFIO have origins in an international movement and have always subsequently played a

[1] An opinion poll in September 1966 showed that a clear majority on the Right thought it would be a good thing for one party to have an absolute majority in the Assembly whilst a clear majority on the Left thought it would be a bad thing. See *Revue Française de Science Politique*, 1967, p. 76.

part in it. The French Communist party, as befits its popular following, has enjoyed a weight in European Communist circles along with the Italian party. Conversely, international Communist developments have had an enormous effect on its standing in France. The development of the cold war in the late 1940s, the Soviet attack on Hungary in 1956 and invasion of Czechoslovakia in 1968 have each in turn opened a chasm between the Communists and the rest of the Left in France. The French Communist party did adopt an attitude of initial disapproval over Czechoslovakia, but was badly divided over it and has had great difficulty in interpreting the event to its followers.

The SFIO has always played an active role in the international socialist movement since its foundation. It is one of the larger parties in the Socialist International, though this is only through the size of France and in spite of having a lower proportion of its national vote than most of its main equivalents in other countries. The PSU has established some contacts with similar parties in other mediterranean countries (such as EDA in Greece and PSIUP in Italy) but has not linked up with the somewhat similar Socialist Peoples' parties in Northern Europe.

The peculiarly French origins and distaste for European integration of the Gaullist parties makes it hardly surprising that they should not have been concerned to create any links with foreign parties. After an early period in the Liberal group in the European parliament, the mainstream Gaullist UNR deputies withdrew in 1962 but the representatives at Strasbourg of the *Républicain indépendant* group remained with the Liberals. However, all three of the current RI members there had entered the French parliament as *Indépendants* before the formation of the Giscardien group and so are probably representative of its Conservative rather than its Gaullist wing. The Gaullist youth body, the *Union des Jeunes pour le Progrès*, has tried to make international contacts with groups as varied as the British Young Liberals and the German Young Christian Democrats—but its limited success with the latter probably owes more to the state funds available under the Franco-German treaty for youth exchanges than to any ideological sympathies.

Fifteen years ago the MRP and the Radicals had as clear international links as the Communists and Socialists. The MRP was one of the leading Christian Democratic parties of the 1940s, although it was always a little more left-inclined than some of its equivalents. By 1962 its youth group preferred to be an observer rather than a member of the international group of Christian Democrats and Conservative students because it found the other members too right-wing. The Radical party had played a leading part in interwar European Liberal-Radical circles; for the first ten years after the war the RGR was an active member of the Liberal International. But with the break-up of the RGR, Radical interest in such links dwindled and for some years it has participated little in Liberal International meetings. The Conservatives in France have happily fitted into the Liberal group at Strasbourg but have no organized international links with other parties.

Since 1962 the links of the MRP and Centre-Left have grown confused. In 1962 Pleven, president of the Liberal group at Strasbourg, moved into the MRP dominated *Centre Démocratique* in the French Assembly but, to the annoyance of *laique* 'Liberals' in France remained a 'Liberal' at Strasbourg. Both the present PDM representatives at Strasbourg (both with Centre-Left rather than MRP origins) are in the Liberal group but the two members from the equivalent Senate *Centriste* group (which is the MRP senate group simply renamed) are in the Strasbourg Christian Democrat group. The MRP itself has decided that it will continue for international Christian Democrat but not for domestic purposes; since the new *Centre Démocrate* seems determined to de-emphasize its clerical affiliations and will therefore probably prefer to be 'Liberal' in European terms, it is difficult to see how such a decision could work. Meanwhile Morice of the CR has attempted without much success to bring together the 'various expressions of French Liberalism' (i.e. Conservatives, Peasants, Giscardiens, Centrists and Radicals) in a French group of the Liberal International, also working inside the *Mouvement européen pour l'Europe unie*. However, the Radicals by joining the FGDS have half moved out of the 'Liberal' camp. When Maurice Faure was renominated for membership of the European parliament by the FGDS after the 1967 elections,[1] he had to give a pledge to switch his membership from the Liberal to the Socialist group while the two senators from the Radical GD group still sit with the Strasbourg Liberals.

[1]After much wangling, the Gaullists succeeded in vetoing his election and obliged the FGDS to sponsor another candidate.

APPENDIX I

Party Strengths

General Elections (Metropolitan France) (votes in thousands)

	Communist	Socialist	Radicals, etc.	MRP	Conserva-tives	Gaullist	Others	Total
October 1945	5,005	4,561	2,131	4,780	2,546	—	165	19,190
June 1946	5,154	4,188	2,295	5,589	2,540	—	115	19,881
November 1946	5,431	3,434	2,136	4,989	3,073	—	155	19,218
June 1951	4,934	2,784	1,980	2,454	2,295	4,266	239	18,952
January 1956	5,517	3,229	3,246	2,362	3,180	837	2,815	21,478
November 1958	3,908	3,455	1,999	2,273	4,007	4,165	534	20,485
November 1962	4,004	2,726	1,430	1,666	2,493	5,856	159	18,334
March 1967	5,030	FGDS: 4,714		CD: 2,864		8,453	1,331	22,392
June 1968	4,435	FGDS: 4,528		CPDM: 2,290		9,664	1,221	22,139

Assembly Groups (including overseas deputies)

	Communist	Socialist	Radicals, etc.	MRP	Conserva-tives	Gaullist	Others	Total
October 1945	161	150	28+29	150	64	—	4	586
June 1946	153	129	32+21	169	67	—	15	586
November 1946	183	105	43+27	167	71	—	22	618
June 1951	101	107	76+19	96	98	120	10	627
January 1956	150	99	75+19	84	97	22	50	596
November 1958	(10)	47	40	64	129	206	81	578

November 1962	41	67	39	CD: 55	RI: 37	233	10	479
March 1967	73	FGDS: 121		PDM: 41	RI: 44	201	7	487
June 1968	34	FGDS: 57		PDM: 31	RI: 64	296	5	487

Senate Groups (Fifth Republic only)

April 1959	14	51	64	34	94	44	6	307
September 1962	14	52	49	34	84	31	10	274
September 1965	14	52	50	38	81	30	9	274
September 1968	17	54	50	40	80	29	13	283

Local Elections (Fifth Republic only)

Cantonal								
1961	52	298	409	142	415	166	21	1,504
1964	99	326	401	148	369	123	15	1,562
					(+81)	(+81)		
1967	95	652		148	379	200	7	1,573
					(+92)	(+92)		
Cities								
1959	993	1,062	608	688	1,252	663	36	5,524
1965	996	1,172	678	614	1,191	684	17	5,524
					(+172)	(+172)		

187

NOTES

Sources

Williams for 1945–58 voting figures (except that UFD has been transferred from the Radicals to the Socialists and the Centre Republicain from the Conservatives to the Radicals); Ministry of the Interior figures for 1962 and 1967. All election figures published in France are unsatisfactory because of the complex and changing labels used by lists and candidates. The simplification to the six tendencies involves many arbitrary judgements.

All local election figures are based on Ministry of the Interior figures, which are regularly contested by the parties. However the serious disputes usually revolve around the divisions drawn between classifications which have been grouped together here.

Assembly and Senate figures are those of the official groups.

Communists

Includes Progressives.

Socialists

Includes extreme-left votes and seats (only significant for general elections from 1958 and for local elections: UFD in 1958–59 and thereafter PSU).

Radicals, etc.

Includes all the centre-left groups. During the Fifth Republic these normally amount to about half of the votes or seats, except in the cities where two thirds of the total are centre-left. The Assembly groups in the Fourth Republic show first the Radicals (or RGR) and then the UDSR. In the Fifth Republic the groups are *Gauche Démocratique* (Senate) *Entente Démocratique* (1958 Assembly) and *Rassemblement Démocratique* (1962 Assembly).

MRP

Includes *Démocratie Chrétienne* in 1958 votes (one fifth of total).

Conservatives

All the various Conservative, Moderate, Peasant or Independent groups but not the Poujadists, extreme-right groups or right-wing groups of Radical origin. In local elections also those classified by the Minister of the Interior as Local or Municipal Interest Alliances. The Senate groups are *Républicains Indépendants* (1962 and 1965: 64; 1968: 62) and the *Républicains d'Action Rurale et Sociale* (Peasants) (1962: 20; 1965: 17; 1968: 62).

Gaullists

RPF in 1951, *Républicains Sociaux* in 1956, UNR and all other Gaullist groups in 1958 (the latter forming one eighth of the total), UNR–UDT in 1962 and CAVER in 1967 for general election figures; equivalents for other figures. The *Républicains Indépendants* classified separately for local elections are shown in brackets after both the Conservatives and Gaullists.

At the 1962 Elections nearly 700,000 votes were cast for non-UNR–UDT candidates who had the backing of the *Association pour la Cinquième République* as well as their own party (24 Ind., 11 MRP-ED).

Others
Mainly Extreme-Right. Poujadists in 1956 and Algerian deputies in 1958 Assembly.

1967 General Election
FGDS includes Extreme-Left (mainly PSU), just over one tenth of the total, but not the votes cast for Centre-Left candidates without FGDS support; most of them were with the *Centre Démocrate*. The *others* heading includes about a million votes cast for dissident Independents (mostly), Gaullist or Centre-Left who did not have the backing of the three main organizations. About one million of the CAVER votes were cast for candidates who were not UNR–UDT in 1962.

1968 General Election
FGDS includes PSU (nearly one fifth of total). The Gaullist total refers to those with the official UDR label; RI candidates without this label are included in the *others*, their votes constituting one third of the *others'* total.

Local Elections
All take place at six year intervals; in the cantonal elections (for the department general councils) half the seats come up every three years. The 1967 figures include only half those elected in the Paris area (where there were complete elections following redrawing of boundaries). The Cantonal figures are for all general councillors elected in each year; the Cities figures are for those elected to municipal councils in towns of more than 30,000 inhabitants. In 1967 Extreme-Left (24), FGDS (455) and Centre-Left (173) are grouped together.

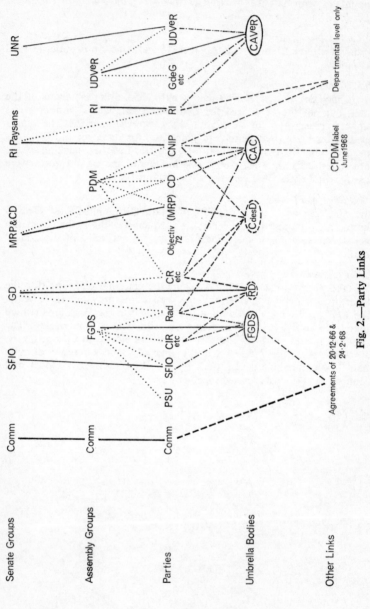

Fig. 2.—Party Links

This diagram shows the links between French parties as they were in 1968 as follows:

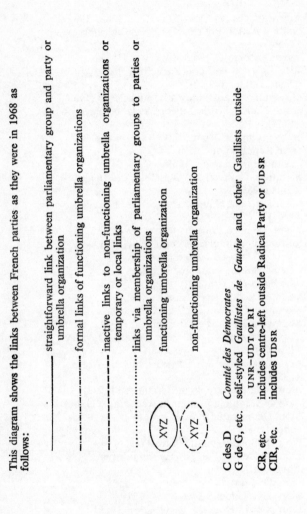

———————— straightforward link between parliamentary group and party or umbrella organization

—·—·—·—·—· formal links of functioning umbrella organizations

— — — — — inactive links to non-functioning umbrella organizations or temporary or local links

·············· links via membership of parliamentary groups to parties or umbrella organizations

(XYZ) functioning umbrella organization

(XYZ) non-functioning umbrella organization

C des D *Comité des Démocrates*
G de G, etc. self-styled *Gaullistes de Gauche* and other Gaullists outside UNR–UDT or RI
CR, etc. includes centre-left outside Radical Party or UDSR
CIR, etc. includes UDSR

LIST OF PARTIES REFERRED TO BY THEIR INITIALS

Initials	Party/Group
AVeR	Association pour la Cinquième République (1962)
CAVeR	Comité d'Action pour la Cinquième République (1966)
CD	Centre Démocrate (1966) (N.B.—Not to be confused with the Centre Démocratique (1962))
CIR	Convention des Institutions Républicaines (1964)
CNIP	Centre National des Indépendents et Paysans (1948)
CPDM	Centre Progrès et Démocratie Moderne (1968)
CR	Centre Républicain (1957)
ED	Entente Démocratique (1958)
FNRI	Fédération National des Républicains Indépendants (1966)
FGDS	Fédération de la Gauche Démocrate et Socialiste (1965)
GD	Gauche Démocratique (1946)
MRP	Mouvement Républicain Populaire (1945)
PDM	Progrès et Démocratie Moderne (1967)
PSA	Partie Socialiste Autonome (1958)
PSU	Partie Socialiste Unifié (1960)
RD	Rassemblement Démocratique (1962)
RGR	Rassemblement des Gauches Républicaines (1946)
RPF	Rassemblement du Peuple Français (1947)
SFIO	Section Français de l'Internationale Ouvrière (1905)
UDCA	Union de Défense des Commerçants er Artisans (1953)
UDR	Union de la Défense de la République (1968)
UD R	Union de Démocrates pour la République (1968)
UDSR	Union Démocratique et Socialiste de la Résistance (1945)
UDT	Union Démocratique du Travail (1959)
UDVeR	Union des Démocrates pour la Cinquième République (1967)
UFD	Union des Forces Démocratiques (1958)
UGS	Union de la Gauche Socialiste (1957)
UNR	Union pour la Nouvelle République (1958)
UNR–UDT	Union pour la Nouvelle République–Union Démocratique du Travail (1962)

CHAPTER 5

ITALY

BACKGROUND

Italian politics has been permanently affected by the manner in which the unification of the country was achieved. First, the fact that unification was the work of an 'heroic' minority has meant the domination of the Italian Parliament by a tiny *élite*, originally social but now governmental. Indeed, the politics of the pre-fascist period was a parliamentary battle between a very restricted class of factions. In 1861, the national electorate was less than 2 per cent of the population and although successively enlarged it was still less than 25 per cent as a result of Giolitti's introduction of so-called universal male suffrage in 1913. Turnout in this period averaged only 50 per cent. Women, moreover, only received the vote in 1945. In this, it must be remembered, Italy differed little from other European countries. But there was one significant difference: the loss of his temporal power led the Pope to decree the abstention of Catholics from participation in the public life of the new nation, thus depriving the country of an important section of the population eligible in other respects. As elsewhere in Europe the parties or factions were recruited from the land-owning gentry in general. The Historical Right, which brought to the government of the new nation a high concept of the functions of the State based on Hegelian philosophy, represented the large, landed, commercial, industrial and professional classes with a regional bias towards the North, while the more democratic Historical Left was based on the smaller gentry and urban artisans with a regional bias towards the South. Party differences were in methods and not in ideas. Chabod has written that 'in pre-1914 Italy, the parties had virtually no policy—policy lay with Parliament and Members of Parliament',[1] so that once

[1] F. Chabod, *L'Italie contemporaine*, Conférences faites à l'Institut d'études politiques de l'Université de Paris, 1950, multigr, p. 16 (English translation, *A History of Italian Fascism*, London, Weidenfeld and Nicholson, 1963, p. 192; incidentally, the title is a complete misnomer).

Depretis had ensured his position in power and inaugurated the system of *trasformismo*,[1] even the differences between Right and Left were blurred away. There was, in fact, no organized opposition to factions, cliques and camarilles, which skirmished in Parliament until the rise of the Socialists at the end of the century. Moreover, organized parties were of no consequence in Italian politics until after the First World War. Of this period, it has been said, 'neither ideas nor practical programmes were used as weapons in the fight for national power; they became the instruments of transactions, jobs and influence, elections and places'.[2]

Secondly, unification secured the supremacy of the Northern ruling classes in the new nation, while national subordination secured for the Southern gentry continued predominance in their own local bailiwicks. This colonial relationship based on the so-called alliance of Northern capital and Southern land, which was nothing less than the submission of the Southern ruling classes to their would-be conquerors, if not responsible for creating that economic and social disparity between North and South known as the 'Southern Question',[3] was at least instrumental in its progressive aggravation. Indeed, it can be said that the annexation of the Kingdom of the Two Sicilies by the House of Savoy enabled the Northern industrial bourgeoisie, within the structure of a highly centralized state, to reduce the South to the position of a colonial market. Northern industrialization was encouraged by a protective tariff which provoked the closing of the French market and severely damaged Southern agriculture. The North, thus, systematically pumped the South of the little capital resources that it had. The South was forced to accept the imposition of this damaging system because its ruling classes benefited from the arrangement; they were

[1] This was the name given to the practice of many deputies supporting and opposing different governments without any reference to their policy or programmes. For a description of it, see C. Seton-Watson, *Italy from Liberalism to Fascism, 1870–1925*, London, Methuen, 1967, pp. 246–64.

[2] W. A. Salomone, *Italy in the Giolittian Era: Italian Democracy in the Making, 1900–1914*, Philadelphia, University of Pennsylvania University Press, 1945, 2nd ed., 1960, p. 14.

[3] For an economic analysis of the 'Southern Question', see V. Lutz., *Italy, A Study in Economic Development*, London, Oxford UP, Royal Institute of International Affairs, 1962, pp. 91–152; for a political analysis, see A. Gramsci, *The Southern Question* in *The Modern Prince and other Writings*, London, Lawrence and Wishart, 1957, pp. 28–43.

ensured of state support for the protection of their local privileges as a *quid pro quo* for economic freedom of manœuvre.

It is unnecessary to describe here the economic and social differences which have developed between North and South. It is sufficient to state that the North is now a largely developed industrial society organized along the typical West European pattern while the South is still a backward rural society where the norms and structures of the classical Mediterranean civilization are found. Nevertheless, it must be remembered that neither region is homogeneous since there are regions of the North which are predominantly rural, such as the Venetias, known as the 'Italian *Vendée*', and zones of the South in the process of industrial development, such as Naples, Taranto and Syracuse. More important for our purpose is the contrast in the political system which has developed from this relationship between North and South, because of its effects on party organization and activity. In the North political organization is based on economic and social class groupings. In the South, on the other hand, such political organization as exists is built on the vertical system of a personal clientele. Thus, in the North the political arena is the scene of battles between well-organized group interests and in the South it is the site of the small trading of favours down the hierarchical chains of personal acquaintances. In this way Northern economic interests have succeeded in dominating Italian national politics while the role of the Southern politicians has been to provide the required parliamentary majority because their target has remained local government for its petty patronage.

The last decade of the nineteenth century saw, as has been mentioned, the rise of the first real political party in Italy, the Socialist Party. It played only a small part in the Italian Parliament before the First World War because the restricted suffrage limited its representation. Moreover, its policy of keeping faith with Marxist revolutionary principles excluded active participation in a bourgeois government. This policy was maintained, in contrast to other European Socialist Parties, during the war. In January 1919 a second real political party appeared with the aim of being a party and not just a collection of Members of Parliament. This was the Popular Party or Catholic Party. Its advent represented the official return of Catholics into Italian public life and they returned not as individuals but as a compact organized mass with a programme of their own.

In the election of 1919, the two organized mass parties won more than half the seats in the Chamber of Deputies, and the old parliamentary groups found themselves in a position where they could not govern without previous agreement with either of these two parties. Thus, the political struggle became, for the first time, a genuinely inter-party affair. Giolitti and the old style parliamentary leaders could not understand that matters of State had henceforth to be discussed with party leaders who might not be Members of Parliament. This misunderstanding of the new direction of politics ushered in by the war, the failure of the Socialist Party to accept the rules of the parliamentary system and the burden which the Popular Party imposed as allies proved too much for the leaders of the old parliamentary groups. Italian politics had taken a new turning and the old remedies no longer sufficed.

It was into this turmoil that the Fascist Party, organized on military lines from 1919–20, was able by a combination of terrorism and ruse to conquer power in 1922. The March on Rome was, in Chabod's words, 'not a revolution, but a parade'[1] because the parliamentary leaders were prepared to negotiate with the Fascists where they had failed with the Socialists and Catholics. In the early years, Mussolini was prepared to rule through Parliament, but after the Acerbo Majority Electoral Law of 1923, the Matteotti murder and the Aventine secession of 1924, the pretence of parliamentary government was abandoned. 1926 was the crucial year in the creation of the dictatorship and the first move was the prohibition of all political parties except the Fascist Party. It was followed by the setting up of the Corporate State. In 1928 the single national list was introduced for the Chamber of Deputies and the following year Mussolini made peace with the Church in the Lateran Pacts. Thus, the 1930s saw the high summer of the Fascist Corporate State, when even the Chamber of Deputies was replaced by a Chamber of Corporations whose members, called National Councillors, were appointed by the government.

The Fascist interregnum was responsible, nonetheless, for two major developments with important consequences for the post-war parliamentary scene. One was the reintegration of the Catholic Church into Italian national life. The Lateran Pacts were very

[1] F. Chabod, *op. cit.*, p. 41.

favourable to the Church, which was given control of education and culture. Mussolini's desire to legitimate his regime encouraged him to give the Church a position of leadership, particularly in local life. The autonomy which the pacts accorded to its organizations enabled it to train a whole generation of leaders on the margin, if not outside the regime. Thus, they placed the Catholics in a privileged position to take control when Fascism fell. The other was that the integration of the Fascist Party into the State forced local leaders to legitimate their rule through Party membership and control of the *podestà*. However, it is also true that Fascist policy was to appoint local leaders to these posts, except in the big cities, which enhanced rather than destroyed clientele structures. Both these developments were of greater consequence in the South than in the North because of the general lack of autonomous organized associative groups.

THE POLITICAL SYSTEM

Since the fall of Fascism, Italy has returned to a parliamentary system of government. The government is formed from Members of Parliament commanding a majority in both Houses of Parliament, the Senate (upper House) and Chamber of Deputies (lower House). A vote of no confidence in the government leads automatically to its resignation. A new government is formed by a Member of Parliament on appointment by the President of the Republic after consultation with the principal political leaders. Election to both Houses of Parliament is by proportional representation of party lists on a modified version of the d'Hondt system for the Chamber of Deputies and a mixed system for the Senate.[1] The electoral system recognized the primary role of parties in the formation of the parliamentary representation. This recognition is written into the Republican Constitution of 1948, which states in Article 49: 'All citizens have the right to associate freely in political parties in order to contribute through democratic procedure to the determination of national policy.' Thus, it can be said that the role envisaged for political parties in Italy is the generally accepted liberal democratic one of representing group and private interests, forming public opinion and translating it into public policy.

[1] For details, see W. J. M. McKenzie, *Free Elections*, London, George Allen & Unwin, pp. 90–2.

In assessing the role of Italian parties in the political system, it is necessary to remember that they not only existed prior to it but that it is their brain-child. By this, is meant not only that the most important parties were founded under an earlier regime and reconstituted clandestinely, but also that they were the formal and actual holders of power under the aegis of the Allies in the constitutional vacuum which existed between the fall of fascism and the election of the Constituent Assembly. All attempts, in fact, to exclude them failed and moreover, the most important political crisis[1] for the orientation of postwar Italian politics—the fall of Parri and the accession of De Gasperi as Prime Minister in December 1945—took place in this period. Parties have thus formed the basis of Italian politics and the functioning of the country's Republican institutions, at both the national and local level.

It should, however, also be recalled that at the end of the war, Italy was a devastated country under Allied military occupation.[2] Reconstruction and the reacquisition of national sovereignty were pursued by a succession of national governments. In place of the national unity initially imposed by the urgency and homogeneity of those needs, a divergence grew increasingly between the social and economic 'haves' and 'have-nots' which coincided with the beginning of the cold war. Italy was in the Western and capitalist camp under the wing of the United States. Einaudi's restoration of the lira coincided with the expulsion of the Communists and Socialists from the government. Acceptance of the Marshall Plan was a condition of the political alliance between De Gasperi and Costa, President of *Confindustria* (the Italian Confederation of Industry), based on a comprehensive agreement covering the whole range of problems from economic policy to the financing of government parties. These included the control of wages as the counterpart to a national economic policy aimed at keeping consumption as low as possible. It was believed that this was the only way to achieve reconstruction. In addition it required the reorganization of production on the

[1] For testimony on the importance of, and reasons for, this crisis, see the discussion among the surviving participants in *L'Espresso* in December 1965.

[2] What follows owes a great deal to the suggestive paper by A. Pizzorno, 'Le parti communiste dans le système politique italien', presented to the colloque on *Le communisme en France et en Italie*, Paris, 1968, mimeographed, pp. 2–3; see also M. V. Posner and S. J. Woolf, *Italian Public Enterprise*, London, Duckworth, 1967, pp. 1–18.

basis of the uncontested power of management in the factory.[1] In consequence, factory committees set up during the Resistance were rendered powerless where they were not actually dismantled.

Wage restraint was at its height during the years of the Italian 'economic miracle'. In the early 1960s, workers' wage demands and trade union activity revived with a violence which had been unknown for more than a decade. In 1962, the annual rise in wages reached 14 per cent and it coincided, not accidentally, with the 'opening to the left'. The leading economic groups reacted with hostility to this political movement and the economic system responded with a depression, the flight of capital abroad, the fall in investments and of share prices on the stock markets. Certain political and military leaders conceived or prepared authoritarian *coups*: for example the Tambroni Government of 1960 and the De Lorenzo affair of 1964.[2] These developments suggested, as Pizzorno has commented, that the functioning of the type of system characteristic of the 1950s—delegation of political responsibility to economic interests at a period of increasing state intervention in the economy—was breaking down. The major political question had ceased to be the need of reconstruction and economic development at any price. Instead, controversy centred on the question of reorganizing specific sectors of the social and political system. At the same time, pressures for general reforms of all types—the tax system, educational system, hospital system, etc.—was growing.

To appreciate the basic problems confronting the Italian political system, it is necessary first to consider how the party system has, in fact, worked. Italy is widely considered, particularly since the passing of the French Fourth Republic, to provide the classic case of a multiparty system. There are eight parties operating nationally as well as a number of local parties, such as the Sardinian Action Party, the *Union Valdôtaine* and the *Südtiroler Volkspartei*, which

[1] One only has to recall the moral pressures and police violence which the employers used to try and break the trade unions. The greatest success was at Fiat motor-car works in Turin with the formation of an autonomous pro-employer union, SIDA. See the classical study of A. Carocci, *Inchiesta alla Fiat*, Florence, Parente 1960.

[1] The De Lorenzo affair concerned the supposed attempt of General De Lorenzo, head of Italian Counter-Espionage, to organize a military *coup* if the Socialist Party refused to agree to the DC terms for solving the cabinet crises of July 1964, under the aegis of President Segni, see R. Martinelli, *SIFAR, Gli atti del processo De Lorenzo-L'Espresso*, Milan, Mursia, 1968.

are able to elect one or two Members of Parliament as spokesmen for their localities. Moreover, none of the national parties has succeeded in winning a majority of the popular vote in any postwar election. Government has been by a coalition of centre parties, now right, now left, and marked by cabinet instability (average life of 9 months). However, the classical view of the Italian party system engenders more confusion than understanding of postwar Italian party politics. First, the system has been dominated by a permanent government party, the Christian Democrats (DC), which has consistently polled two-fifths of the vote in all postwar parliamentary elections and has been the kernel of all government coalitions since 1946. Indeed, one of the key factors of postwar Italian politics is that no government can be formed which is not acceptable to the DC. Secondly, the principal opposition party, the Italian Communist Party (PCI), which has consistently had the support of between one-fifth and a quarter of the electorate, is by origin and definition an anti-system party. Although the party has never explicitly denied its Marxist goals, it has followed a reformist line, proposing structural reforms for the construction of socialism. This acceptance of parliamentary government has not generally been believed. Its opponents have preferred to believe that the PCI would destroy the parliamentary system, should it ever come to power, and the electorate so far has followed them. For this reason, it has systematically been excluded from national power. Thirdly, the minor right-wing and left-wing parties (including the Socialist Parties) have rarely, if ever, totalled more than a third of the electorate and so have not been able to provide a credible alternative government to the Christian Democrats. Their highest aspiration, in fact, could only be the conditioning of the Christian Democrats towards either conservative or reformist policies.

Cabinet instability has been a major characteristic of the system, but so too have electoral stability and its corollary political immobility. Cabinets may fall and Ministers may change office but the same persons remain Ministers.

In one sense, therefore, the Italian system has worked in Parliament in a manner remarkably similar to that which Namier[1] con-

---

[1] For the most complete statement of the Namier party system, see his Romanes Lecture at Oxford in 1952, *Monarchy and the Party System*, Oxford, Clarendon Press, 1952, p. 23.

structed for England in the eighteenth century. There has been a
permanent government or 'in' party (DC), a permanent opposition or
'out' party (PCI), a group of government supporting parties (the
minor coalition partners) and, finally, a group of alternative government supporting parties, temporarily in opposition (the minor
would-be coalition parties, opposing this coalition). The similarity
between the Namier model and the present working of the Italian
party system is useful in so far as it draws attention to the relevance
in analysis of the Italian system of one of its characteristics, namely,
the independence or distance of parliamentary representation from
its electoral base. However, it should not blind one to the great
differences, of which the nature of the links between party and
electorate in the two systems is not the least important. This independence or distance between electorate and representatives, which
gives considerable room for parliamentary manœuvre, is provided
in Italy by voting stability. Four reasons can be given for voting
stability:

(i) The ideological tradition of the two leading parties. Both the
DC and PCI are heirs of particular Italian subcultures, the
Catholic and Marxist, which date from the second half of the
nineteenth century;

(ii) The parties, particularly those in government, have acted as
channels of patronage and defence of small group and
sectional interests;

(iii) The cold war with its tendency to divide the world into two
blocks has acted as an element of polarization between the
supporters of the United States and those of the Soviet
Union. Inside Italy the line of demarcation between these
two groups passed through the Socialist Party, which explains
much of its postwar history;

(iv) Finally, the proportional representation system, by relating
accurately parliamentary seats to votes won and lost, accentuates the stability of representation of major parties while
encouraging that of minor parties because voting landslides
rarely occur. On the other hand, the simple majority single-
ballot system accentuates electoral landslides because it turns
small changes in votes into large turnover of seats while, at the
same time, discouraging the representation of minor parties.

In these circumstances, it can be argued that the Italian party system has operated as one of defence or consolidation of the regime rather than of democratic development. It has been dominated by parliamentary intrigue and factionalism with interminable debates over minor issues and cabinet crises provoked by questions of patronage. The DC, because it cannot forseeably be replaced as major governing party by election, has had virtually no interest in promoting policies which might lead to an attenuation of the distance separating Parliament from the country. It has acted as the dominant bourgeois party and its leaders' constant preoccupation—outside the advancement of its members to key posts in all sectors of Italian society and satisfying individual Catholic organizations—has been the disqualification of its greatest rivals by limiting 'the democratic area', and the preservation of its own internal unity, since a schism is the one sure way in which it could lose power. This attitude has fostered political immobility because, in the words of Lord Samuel, 'there is only one way to sit still, but there are many ways of going forward'. Similarly, the PCI, although ideologically opposed to parliamentary government, has, from its imposed place of permanent opposition, become, paradoxically enough, its staunchest defender. One of the PCI's greatest successes was to force the government to set up the constitutional court, one of the fundamental institutions of the Republican constitution, nearly ten years after the constitution came into force. Finally, the minor parties, because of their aspiration for power, in spite of the fact that they cannot hope in present circumstances to control the government by replacing the DC, are continually forced to renounce the various policies which they claim to be their *raison d'être* for fear of worse. If by chance they push their support of principle to the point of resignation, they can be replaced by one of the alternative government-supporting coalition parties or even by a military *coup*.

THE MAJOR PARTIES[1]

I *The Italian Communist Party*
History and strategy. The PCI was founded in January 1921 from a schism in the iItalan Socialist Party (PSI) at the LeghornCongress

---

[1] Information on the PCI and DC organizations comes from the recent research project carried out by the Istituto Carlo Cattaneo of Bologna (see bibliography). Some results have already been published by G. Galli, *Il bipartismo imperfetto*, Bologna, 1966, Il Mulino. Most of the data in this chapter comes from this

over the acceptance of the twenty-one conditions of the Third International (Comintern). The Comintern had been set up in March 1919 to promote Soviet style revolutions in other countries and the PSI had been the first foreign party to adhere. The conditions included the expulsion of 'reformists' which meant that the PSI had to reject its parliamentary leaders. Defeated in the vote on the final motion, the Communists declared their secession and the foundation of a new party. The PCI, was, therefore, born under the aegis of the Comintern and has preserved throughout its history the double nature of its birth: the historical traditions of the Italian working class and subordination to Soviet Communism.

The two leading groups which formed the new party were Bordiga's abstentionist faction centred on Naples and the paper *Il Soviet*; and the Turin Communists round Gramsci and the paper *Ordine Nuovo*, who included Terracini, Tasca and Togliatti. Bordiga preached the necessity of abstention from all parliamentary activity in order to concentrate the party's forces on organizing the workers in 'soviets' and in revolutionary military formations. The Turin group visualized a new party built on the workers' councils, set up in large factories for the purpose of gaining control over the management of the factories, and which would be the organized *avant-garde* of a new state and civilization.

Conflict between the two factions and semi-legality imposed by fascism meant that, in the early years, the party was limited to a hard-core of militants. Moreover, arrests of party leaders facilitated Comintern control of the party and it seized this opportunity for ensuring the success of the Turin group and the total liquidation of the Bordighist faction. Prohibition of parties forced it underground where it managed to maintain a more or less continuous organization throughout the fascist period, but only at the expense of increased dependence on the Comintern. Its policy followed the fluctuations of the Comintern line between a united anti-fascist front policy, attacks on the Social Democrats as 'social fascists' and offers of collaboration[1].

source and I am much obliged to the Istituto Cattaneo for permission to consult and incorporate their data in this chapter. Information on the PSI comes from A. Landinolfi, *Il partito socialista, oggi e domani*, Milano, Azione Comune, 1963; and F. Cazzola, *Carisma e democrazia nel socialismo italiano*, Roma, Istituto L. Sturzo, 1967, which also contains a bibliography on post-war Italian socialism.

[1] For these violent policy fluctuations from the Pact of Unity of Action with the PSI of 1934, to their attacks on the PSI in the 'thirties and its offers of collaboration with the Fascists in 1936 and 1939 (Molotov–Ribbentrop Pact) etc., see G. Galli, *Storia del partito communista italiana*, Schwartz, Milano, 1958, pp.117–212.

The party's role in the resistance, for which its activity in the Spanish civil war had been a perfect preparation, not only enabled it to gain virtual control of the working masses but also to penetrate circles where it was previously unknown. At the same time, Togliatti's dramatic return to Italy with the offer of collaboration in the Allied supported, but popularly discredited, royal government marked a decisive turning point in the anti-fascist struggle. It placed him overnight in the front rank of Italian national leaders in addition to bringing the party participation in government. He stressed the importance of the new orientation by declaring: 'we are no longer a sect of agitators but have assumed the responsibilities of a great party'.[1]

The policy, which has determined the party's whole postwar action, was one of collaboration with other parties in Parliament and local government, and the promotion of broad-based 'People's Democratic Blocks' and, hence, the support of programmes of very moderate political reform.[2] Its declared objective has been the creation of a democratic socialist state. Its strategy was based on the idea of the progressive insertion of the working class as subjects within the Italian political system, and on the Gramscian concept of hegemony through which an emancipated working class, by its presence in civil society and the modernity of its culture, would transform society and hence the state.[3] This strategy differed both from the classical Social Democrat one of organizing the working class outside the state in organizations which would anticipate the structure of the future socialist society and the reformist one which proposed transforming society on the basis of a parliamentary majority. It was not a Leninist strategy either.

[1] Quoted in *Rinascita*, No. 3, 1944, p. 1.
[2] For example that adopted at the Fifth Party Congress which met in January 1946: '. . . to declare the Monarchy obsolete . . . and to ensure that the Italian state shall be a democratic republic of manual and intellectual workers supported by a representative parliamentary régime in which the fundamental liberties of the citizen shall be guaranteed and defended'. In *La politica dei comunisti dal quinto al sesto congresso—risoluzioni e documenti raccolti a cura dell'ufficio di segretaria del PCI*, Roma, 1948, La Stampa Moderna, pp. 6–14.
[3] See A. Pizzorno, *op. cit.*, pp. 4–8, who argues that the strategy owes more to an analysis of Italian history than to the theoretical writings of Gramsci or the events of the Comintern after 1935, which are given as the usual origins. It was based on an interpretation of the Giolittian policy of the first decade of the century as made manifest in Croce's *Storia d'Italia*, see Togliatti's *Discorso su Giolitti*, Roma, 1950, Ediz. di Cultura Società; now in *Momenti della storia d'Italia*, Rome, 1963, Editori Riuniti, pp. 79–117.

In practical terms, the strategy meant: (i) the construction and consolidation of a large mass party and its auxiliary organizations—achieved in the period 1945–50—to occupy as large a place in civil society as possible; (ii) the support and pursuance of those policies and alliances which coincided with the widest and most plausible conception of the national interest; and (iii) finally avoiding a test of strength with the Allied-supported government parties. The party saw itself as one of government and its expulsion in May 1947 came as a shock. Its leaders were well aware that Italy was within the Western sphere of influence and that a rash move would lead to the outlawing of the party and a situation such as had arisen in Greece. Hence, at the height of the cold war in winter 1947–48, despite pressure from the Cominform to step up party militancy, the party leadership did not press street demonstrations with real determination but devoted more attention to attempting to win a parliamentary majority.[1] The failure of the party-promoted Popular Front to win more than a third of the vote in 1948 and the open unwillingness of the leadership to organize a bid for power by force demonstrated the impotence of the party's revolutionary strategy to the Northern workers. It lost influence and prestige because it was clear that the revolution was no longer an immediate prospect.

The day-to-day tactics of the party were consistent with its strategy, although there was a certain ambiguity arising from the cold war and its relations with the Soviet Union, and were carried on at two levels: in Parliament and in the country. In Parliament, it proposed and supported the most progressive measures it thought acceptable, often embarrassing the government with its votes, and in the country it organized large popular demonstrations attacking American 'imperialism' (the party never criticized the USSR's foreign policy in these years)[2] or in defence of sectional groups

[1] For the circumstances of the setting up of the Cominform and the pressure put on the Italian and French parties recounted by one of the PCI's principal representatives, see E. Reale, *Nascita del Cominform*, Milano, Mondadori, 1957, p. 176.

[2] See, for example, Togliatti's speech, quoted in *L'Unità* of September 29, 1957, which contained the following passage: '... the tie with the Soviet Union has been our life, it has been the essential part of the life and conscience of the working class and its vanguard; therefore this tie is put above and beyond the debate which we all want to conduct and which has always been conducted, on the way to resolve determinate problems, on the criticisms which must or must not be made'.

(workers, peasants, shopkeepers, small businessmen, intellectuals, etc.). This constitutional practice was helped by the crisis of 1956. Khrushchev's denunciation of Stalinist errors and his suggestion that Communist parties, in some countries, might eventually come to power by parliamentary means permitted Togliatti to formulate explicitly the doctrines of 'polycentrism' and the 'Italian way to Socialism'.[1] Despite a falling off in recruitment, the party was progressively 'de-Stalinized'. In 1961, the method of democratic centralism had returned to something like its original Leninist conception. Disagreements were known to exist in the Central Committee. After Togliatti's death in 1964 two openly factional positions were being canvassed: one associated with the name of Amendola (new unity, a single party of the working class and democratic forces from PCI to PSDI, which would be capable of winning a parliamentary majority); and the other with that of Ingrao (dialogue with the Catholics and a new majority based on a complete and organic programme, an overall strategy and a general theory of the new class situation).[2] At its XIth Congress in 1966, the party, while not rejecting the second alternative favoured the first, by placing on the agenda 'the problem of the formation of a unified working class party', in spite of the fact that it was opposed to the unification of the PSI and PSDI which was in the process of realization. In August 1968, it denounced the Soviet invasion of Czechoslovakia in forthright terms. Moreover, its denunciation was maintained at its XIIth Congress (January 1969) in which it re-

[1] The concept of polycentrism was first formulated in an interview which Togliatti gave to the review *Nuovi Argomenti* of June 1956; he said: 'The Soviet model should no longer be obligatory . . . the complex of the system is becoming polycentric, and in the communist movement itself one can no longer speak of a single guide . . .'. For an interpretation of what it has meant to the PCI, see G. Galli, 'Italy' in W. Laqueur and L. Labedz, *Polycentrism, The New Factor in International Communism*, New York, Frederick A. Praeger, pp. 127–40.

[2] Amendola's position was first expounded in 'Ipotesi sulla riunificazione', *Rinascita*, Vol. 21, No. 47 of November 28, 1964, pp. 8–9, and at more length in '6 Domande su Riforme e Riformismo' in *Critica Marxista*, Vol. 3, Nos. 5–6, September–December 1965, pp. 15–38; Ingrao's position in 'Democrazia socialista interna di partito' in *Rinascita*, Vol. 21, No. 17, April 25, 1964, pp. 3–5, and 'Ancora sul rapporto democrazia-socialismo', *ibid.*, Vol. 21, No. 21, of May 23, 1964, pp. 3–4. See also the discussion in the *International Socialist Journal*, Vol. 1, No. 4, August 1964, entitled 'A debate in the Italian CP' pp. 486–91, and J. Halliday, 'Structural Reform in Italy; Theory and Practice' in *New Left Review*, No. 50, July–August 1968, pp. 73–92.

affirmed the validity of its Parliamentary strategy, 'The Italian way of Socialism'.

Structure. The PCI is an ideological party with a highly articulated branch-type structure. Its basic units, each with self-elected executive bodies, are cells, which are located in work-places; sections, which are located geographically, and federations. Above the federations is the supreme party body, the National Congress, which elects the Central Committee. All executive bodies are responsible to their superiors as well as to their rank and file members. This hierarchical arrangement permits maximum penetration and agitational activity with ease of political control from above since the central or provincial leadership can intervene to appoint or remove local officials if need be. The party leadership also keeps a tight reign on all party activities by careful advance preparation of congresses and street demonstrations, as well as appeals for discipline. Thus, for example, cell members are encouraged to discuss the party line because this informs the leaders of its reception and of any heresy that might be being perpetrated. Unorthodox opinions and criticisms are discouraged, although since 1956 the party has become much less draconian than in the early postwar years. Membership of the Central Committee and other important bodies has been controlled in the same way: Togliatti and his associates have used their skill in manœuvre and personal prestige to settle its composition.

In addition to the formal structure, the party sponsors and supports a panopoly of permanent auxiliary organizations, including a Youth Movement, a Women's Movement, Sports Societies, and Cultural and Recreational Associations. Other branch-type features of the PCI include a daily press comprising a national daily, *L'Unità*; two supporting papers, *Paese Sera* of Rome and *L'Ora* of Palermo; a women's magazine, *Noi Donne*; and a national weekly, *Vie Nuove*; not to mention the theoretical review *Rinascità* (founded by Togliatti in 1944) and the publishing house, *Editori Riuniti*. More important than the auxiliary movements as a source of strength in providing the party with a social base in the country has been its close links with the Trade Unions (CGIL) and the League of Co-operatives. The PCI very skilfully managed to postpone the first postwar congresses until its activists had gained control of these organizations (i.e. after the PSI schism in January 1947). Both organizations act as very efficient channels of social communication. It is in the local chambers

207

of labour and co-operative centres, as often as in the cells, that workers learn the meaning of a strike and a vote for the PCI.

The work-place cell, with an average membership of 20–30 persons, is an ideal instrument for agitation and street demonstration. From the early postwar years to the height of the party's expansion in the mid-1950s, they ensured the party's capillary penetration into the roots of Italian society. As one would expect, they were more numerous in the industrial centres of the North and Centre than in the South. Following the 1956 crisis, however, party members' preference for the section based on residence as a meeting place resulted in the territorial section supplanting the cell as the pivotal structural unit. The task of the section was seen as one of democratic political education along the lines of the English non-conformist parishes;[1] they generally meet six or seven times a year for political discussion—less frequently than in the immediate postwar years. These changes indicate a gradual shift in the nature of the party from mass action to one of opinion.

Membership. The PCI is a mass party; its membership passed the million mark soon after the war and reached over two million in the mid-1950s. Since then it has lost members but it still has a membership of over 1·5 million. Its distribution over the country is uneven in several respects. Over a third of its members are found in two regions of Central Italy, Emilia and Tuscany, which have earned the reputation of being a 'red belt' because of their old Socialist traditions and the PCI's control of local government. Membership levels in the North and South (as proportions of the population) are now the same. Whereas in the North membership has declined in the postwar period and turnover is low, in the South it has increased but the turnover level is double that of the North. Similarly, while Northern membership is concentrated in the large and medium sized cities, Southern members are dispersed in the countryside and agro-towns.

The PCI is also a proletarian party. About three-quarters of its members are recruited from the proletarian classes. Nonetheless, social composition follows the same uneven pattern of geographical distribution and recruitment. In the early postwar years, the backbone of the party was formed by the industrial working-class; this

---

[1] Galli, *op. cit.*, pp. 177 ff.

has latterly become one of working-class families. Many industrial workers have left but the family members of those who have remained have joined. Regional differences are also strong:[1] while the industrial working-class family is strong in the North and the Centre, it is the peasantry which is the bulwark of the party in the South: a reflection of the weakness of Southern trade unionism and relative lack of industry. Similarly, the proportion of intellectuals is much higher in the South than in the North; this is a significant point, given the role of intellectuals in the South and in Italian national life. Moreover, one of the party's weaknesses has been its inability to attract the new northern urban classes. Finally, the high proportion of share-croppers in Emilia and Tuscany is due to the long socialist tradition and the activity of Red co-operatives in these regions.

Party officials. Four grades can usually be defined in the party hierarchy. At the lowest level, there are the party activists, a veritable army of over 100,000 members (5–10 per cent of members) who are prepared to be mobilized for proselytism at any time; at the next level are found the local party officials (50,000) who man, generally unpaid, the local sections; the third level is that of provincial officials (about 5,000, threequarters of whom are paid career officials) who are the prospective recruits of the Italian political class; finally, at the top are the national party leaders and parliamentarians (not more than 400 persons) who control the party.

The geographical distribution and social composition of the first group mirrors, as one would expect, that of the membership. Thus, the activists faithfully represent the party, but on the other hand only half the local officials are workers and peasants. Nonetheless, such wide access to positions of public responsibility to persons of humble origin makes the party already a vehicle of social promotion. It is at the level of provincial officials that the situation changes, since only two fifths of this group have a proletarian background. As full-time bureaucrats these cease to be workers. Hence, although the avenue of social promotion is much narrower, it is still sufficiently large to provide a model for aspiring party workers and local officials.

[1] On regional differences in the party, see S. G. Tarrow, *Peasant Communism in Southern Italy*, New Haven, Yale University Press, 1967, p. 389, Chs. 7, 8 and 9, pp. 162–246.

Finally, the quality and initiative of the PCI's regional leadership has been noted in several studies. It has been attributed to the long period of underground activity under Fascism, which led to the acquiring of an expertise and autonomy that not only helped it to assume leadership of the Resistance but also helped it in the building of the party's territorial organization in the postwar period. Certainly, it outclasses all its rivals today in this respect.

National leadership and parliamentarians. There is no clear distinction between these two groups because party leaders, and many officials, are given seats in Parliament. Almost all the important party leaders have sat there and so do nearly all the Central Committee. Membership of Parliament brings prestige and the candidature of important leaders can help to swell the party vote in parliamentary and local elections. The number of seats which the party wins is of more practical consequence than mere propaganda value, since the party draws the parliamentarians' salaries and pays them only part as a wage. In addition, the party likes to switch candidatures to give as many members as possible the experience and satisfaction of sitting in Parliament, and to emphasize that a parliamentary seat is subordinate to position in the party hierarchy. Parliamentary representation, nonetheless, takes one stage further the opportunity of social advancement for persons of humble origin. The proportion of proletarian members in this group is more restricted than among party officials, and there are signs that it is declining further. It goes without saying that they are few among the southern leaders, for these are drawn mainly from the middle and upper class with urban backgrounds. Indeed, the southern leader is much more likely to have had a professional career or to be recruited while at university than his northern counterpart who is more likely to have come from the labour movement. A further point must be made which accounts for some of the parliamentarians of upper class social origin: that is the tendency of the PCI to give places on their lists to intellectual celebrities, such as Carlo Levi and Alberto Carocci, to increase their poll.

Two things remain to be stated about the leadership. Very few of the important leaders have a working-class background; Bordiga, Terracini, Tasca, Togliatti, Pajetta, Spano, Serini, Amendola, Reale, Ingrao and Napolitano were all university students with middle-class backgrounds. Gramsci and Di Vittorio were of proletarian, but rural, families. Only d'Onofrio, Longo and Secchia have anything like working-class experience. Second, the province of Emilia, despite supplying one quarter of the members, has no national leader. This is vital for the stability of the party since with the support of Tuscany he could challenge the Secretary General. It was no coincidence that when Amendola launched his revision of the party-line, he should have had himself elected as delegate of the Bologna federation.[1]

Electoral support. The electoral support which the PCI wins in parliamentary elections follows very closely that of its membership in both geographical distribution and social composition. Indeed, there is a very high correlation between party membership and electoral support.[2] The party's strength lies in the 'red belt' of Central Italy, where it now polls two-fifths of the electorate. It is weak in the North-east, the so-called 'white provinces', where its vote is down to under 15 per cent. In the remaining areas (industrial triangle, the South and Islands) it polls the national average of 25 per cent. However, even here its electoral record has tended to follow its recruitment trends: it has tended to lose votes in the industrial triangle since the war and gain them elsewhere. This movement, which was clear before the 1963 elections, has become confused as a result of the migration of southern labourers to northern cities. In the 'red belt' its control of local government has been responsible for its progressive increase in support.[3]

The social composition of the Communist electorate is predominantly lower class and male: workers in the North and peasants in the South. To these basic groups must be added the share-croppers and middle-class in the 'red belt', and a part of the lower middle-class

---

[1] Galli, *op. cit.*, pp. 341–50. For a study of the Bologna federation, see R. H. Evans, *Coexistence: Communism and its practice in Bologna, 1945–65*, Notre Dame, Notre Dame University Press, 1967, p. 225, and G. L. Degli Esposti, *Bologna PCI*, Bologna 1966, Il Mulino, p. 263. The party viewpoint can be found in P. Togliatti, *Discorsi sull' Emilia*, Bologna, Arte Stampa, 1964, and as expressed by one of the new Bolognese leaders (present Mayor of Bologna) G. Fanti, 'Il PCI in Emilia' in *Critica Marxista*, Vol. 1, Nos. 5–6, September–December 1963, pp. 246–63.

[2] *Ibid.*, p. 132: it was $0 \cdot 82$ with party organization; $0 \cdot 72$ with CGIL membership; and $0 \cdot 64$ with the distribution of *L'Unità*. The next highest correlation was $0 \cdot 43$ with the 1946 vote for the Republic.

[3] See P. A. Allum, 'The Italian Election of 1963' in *Political Studies*, Vol. XIII, No. 3, October 1965, p. 337; and for the effects of migration, see R. C. Fried, 'Urbanization and Italian Politics' in *Journal of Politics*, Vol. 29, No. 3, August 1967, p. 522.

and urban poor in the big southern cities. In addition, the proportion of women voters has progressively increased. Many explanations have been put forward to explain the continued electoral success of the party. Its support has been called a 'protest' vote, but this is to underestimate the very solid traditions, both anti-clerical and co-operative, on which it is based. Moreover, it can be argued that the PCI represents the only realistic opposition party to the clerical and conservative Christian Democrat Party. In any case, it enables large masses of the people to identify themselves with the proletariat and to feel that they are participating in the class struggle.

Financial support.[1] Italian parties keep secret their sources of revenue. Thus, any discussion of party income must be largely hypothetical. Nevertheless, a number of sources can be indicated. The first and most obvious is party dues and periodically requested special contributions. A second source is parliamentarians' salaries. Third is the annual fund-drive for the party press. These sources of direct contribution raise approximately 20 per cent of party revenue. A fourth source arises from control of local government and is twofold. Members can be put on the pay-roll of local organizations, etc., within local government patronage. More important are commissions on contracts where public money is being spent. Here the party achieves a double aim: that of favouring party members by awarding them contracts wherever possible and that of collecting large contributions to be credited against the cost of its local organization. In addition, the party can hope to receive smaller contributions from entrepreneurs in those communes where it is in opposition but has hopes of coming to power.

A fifth source of revenue has been commercial activities. It is

---

[1] The information on all parties' finance comes almost entirely from Passigli's contribution to the Special Number of the *Journal of Politics* devoted to *Comparative Political Finance*, edited by A. J. Heidenheimer and R. Rose, S. Passigli, 'Italy', Vol. 25, No. 3, August 1963, pp. 718–36; it is perhaps necessary to point out that in Italy, unlike England, money for political parties was not always available from the large funds accumulated by trade unions and by business. Since standard subscriptions from ordinary party members were not sufficient to finance parties, other sources, such as profitable contracts and public appointments, were developed. These can be considered as the transfer of public funds from one type of political expenditure to another. The whole problem of party finance is under discussion at the moment, particularly with regard to introducing financing directly from public funds, but no decision has so far been reached.

known that the party operates a number of industrial and commercial enterprises, including a large garment concern which maintains retail stores in most Italian towns. It has also attempted the creation of a chain of department stores, without much initial success. However, it is fairly certain that the major flow of income to the party has come from the transactions with the Soviet Union by communist-controlled enterprises which contributed most of the profits to the party. It is claimed that the recent financial problems which have beset the party, particularly those of the party press,[1] have been caused by the liberalization of trade with the East which has reduced this major source of revenue. Galli[2] considers that it has been greatly reduced over a period and now estimates that it does not exceed a third of the party's needs.

Power analysis. The pre-eminence of the leadership within the party is not in doubt, as a result of its Leninist structure and the emphasis placed on discipline. The leadership is elected but, in fact, has been able to control election and dismissal. A system of co-option has in reality been in operation in the postwar period. The crux of this control is the method of 'democratic centralism' which, in practical terms, means bureaucratic centralism. It is based on the career pattern of party officials. The PCI is the only Italian party which acts as a vehicle of social promotion for the proletarian classes. A political career for persons of modest origin meant becoming a full-time party official. Entry into the national leadership was possible only for those who had reached office-holding positions at provincial level and over three-quarters of provincial party officials, regardless of social origin, are full-time paid career men. Since the party apparatus is in the hands of people whose livelihood depends on their party career, it is easy to see how the party leadership controls the party apparatus.

The PCI is an apparatus, rather than a parliamentary party. Whilst its top leaders have simultaneously been Members of Parliament, their power base is always their position in the party hierarchy. Moreover, strict discipline ensures that the party retains full control

1 One reason for the party's difficulty in financing its press is that *L'Unità*, despite a circulation of about 500,000 copies, has an almost total lack of paid advertising; Passigli (p. 722) states that it can count on 6 per cent as against over 40 per cent for the big independent dailies *Il Corriere della Sera* and *La Stampa*.
2 *Op. cit.*, p. 219.

over who is elected as a Member of Parliament. The electoral system does give the voter limited rights to change the order of a party list, but, although some Communists take advantage of this, the practice has nowhere reached a level at which a parliamentarian could consider himself elected despite, rather than because of, the party machine. It follows that parliamentarians have little freedom of action in opposition to the Central Committee.

All this points to the monolithic party structure western writers often associate with Communist parties, but it would not be a completely accurate description of the PCI in the 1960s. The Italian leaders,[1] unlike their French counterparts, have permitted revisionist discussion and criticism at the risk of a breakdown of the party's unity and discipline. Galli[2] has indicated the party's three strong points: the inheritance of the power positions and traditions of the key organizations of the labour movement, the trade unions and the co-operatives; the control of local government and a whole network of subsidiary organizations in the 'red belt'; and the amount of time which the parliamentarians, without governmental responsibilities and obligations, can devote to following and defending the sectional interests of various groups in the population. The limits of the party leadership in imposing a particular line on the party emerge when the contradictions between the reality of the line and the reality of the interests of these three groups become too painfully apparent. Already there has been discontent about 'the mode, the quality and the character of the debate'[3] within the party. The party cannot demand for too long what the members of the CGIL or the 'red belt' do not want. If it does it will suffer a similar crisis to the one the French party suffered in the late 1950s and early 1960s; a greatly reduced membership and a much narrower sphere of influence.

II The Italian Socialist Parties

History and Strategy. The First International Working Class movement founded by Bakunin was active during the period of his

---

[1] In this connection, it is necessary to bear in mind the rôle of Togliatti, who on his return to Italy in 1944 can be said to have had a charismatic personality, based on the part he had played in the party's foundation and the heroic period of its history which was its clandestinity as well as his membership of the Comintern.

[2] Op. cit., p. 248.

[3] Ingrao, P., in Rinascità, Vol. 21, No. 26, July 4, 1964.

residence in Italy (1864–76). After a decade of conspiracy it petered out on the morrow of the failures of the Bologna commune and S. Lupo insurrection in 1876–77, and was followed by years of small group activities with individual MPs of socialist leanings. An organized socialist party which accepted Marxism as its doctrine was only founded in 1892 at a Congress in Genoa. It adhered to the Second International and shared in the passionate theoretical debate of that organization. Two factions, a revolutionary one and a reformist one, quickly appeared.

The pre-First World War period was dominated by the figure of Turati but characterized by uncompromising clashes between the various factions and a number of spectacular schisms: 1908 saw the departure of the revolutionary syndicalists and 1912 the expulsion of the moderate wing of Bernstein revisionists. The Turatian heritage, in fact, was to become an important element in Italian socialism. He and his followers, despite their confidence in the progressive tendencies of the industrial bourgeoisie, were never prepared to renounce their belief in the revolution nor in the concrete autonomy of the working class, as a method of thought and action in the class struggle.[1] In contrast to the other European socialist parties, the PSI opposed the war and maintained a policy of strict neutrality.

In the postwar period, the conflict between maximalists and reformists was resumed despite the party's parliamentary success in 1919, and culminated in the communists' secession at Leghorn in 1921. In addition, the PSI's refusal to participate in a parliamentary coalition facilitated the success of fascism. It participated in the Aventine secession after the fascist murder of Matteotti, one of its leading MPs in 1924. Its leaders were either arrested or forced into exile and, after the prohibition of opposition parties, it ceased to exist in Italy. During the rest of the fascist period, it maintained a foreign centre in Paris, where Nenni developed his critique of post-First World War Italian socialism in the form of the dilemma: either revolution or participation in bourgeois government, but not both at once. In this he was to remain consistent for the rest of his life. Initially, he chose the possibility of revolution and led the PSI into the anti-fascist popular front.

[1] See V. Foa, *Italian Social Democracy, Yesterday and Today*, Reading, 1968, Occasional Paper of the Centre for the Advanced Study of Italian Society, No. 2, p. 3.

Reorganization of the party was initiated on the fall of fascism, but factional in-fighting soon reappeared. This time maximalists and reformists split over collaboration with the communists. The maximalists led by Nenni defended such collaboration (which was based on the Pact of Unity of action between the two parties) on the grounds of the need to preserve working-class unity, since in his analysis it was precisely this division which had permitted the rise of fascism.[1] The reformists, led by Saragat, complained of the totalitarian methods of the Italian Socialist Party of Proletarian Unity (PSIUP), as it was then called, which they alleged resulted from collaboration with the PCI. The conflict was made the more bitter because of the development of the cold war. At the Rome Congress of January 1947 Saragat and a quarter of the party deputies chose secession and founded a Social Democrat Party aided by American labour[2] and COMISCO (The Socialist International). In December 1947 the Saragat party accepted membership of the DC-led centre coalition, a membership which has continued, on and off, throughout the whole postwar period.

The postwar history of the Socialist Party (now PSI) under the leadership of Nenni can, with simplification, be divided into two phases,[3] with the year of 1956 as the dividing line. In the first period, working-class unity and collaboration with the PCI were the underlying policies. This was the period when Morandi built up the party organization and succeeded in eliminating party factionalism, but he was unable to elaborate a strategy or an ideological position sufficiently distinct from the PCI to give the party more than a semblance of autonomy. Even his organizational structure was modelled on that of the PCI. Nenni was well aware of this failure and chose the alternative reformist strategy. Hence, in some ways he anticipated the policy *volte face* which the events of 1956 precipitated, i.e., the road to social democracy, participation in bourgeois government and socialist reunification, which was the object of the

---

[1] Nenni's analysis is contained in his *Storia di Quattro Anni*, 2nd ed., Rome, 1946, Einaudi.

[2] See the text of the letter of the PSLI Party Secretary G. Faravelli to Saragat of March 17, 1947, published in *L'Unità*, October 13, 1947, the authenticity of which was confirmed by Saragat the next day.

[3] An account of the Socialist politics of this period can be found in R. Zariski, 'The Italian Socialist Party, A Case Study in Factional Conflict' in *American Political Science Review*, Vol. LVI, No. 2, June 1962, pp. 373–81.

second phase. The path was difficult—it prompted the reappearance of factionalism—and full of detours; and it proved possible only because the PSI had such a prestigious leader as Nenni. The price was high. The secession of the left-wing faction which founded the new PSIUP in January 1964 in protest at the PSI entry into the government coalition meant the loss of valuable leaders and also undermined Nenni's strategy.[1] He was committed to going through with it without any alternative, since the only way the party could have brought pressure on the DC and PSDI was the threat of a renewal of the alliance with the PCI. The credibility of this threat was removed by the schism. Thus, when reunification with the PSDI was achieved in November 1966, the Unified Socialist Party (PSU) was not a new party, but the re-alignment of the PSI on the PSDI positions. In consequence, its participation in government followed the pattern of the PSDI 15 years earlier and it had to watch its programme being sacrificed on the altar of governmental solidarity.

The PSU still has a programme of reforms, then, but they do not differ essentially from what a modern, progressive and far-seeing non-socialist party may put forward. Indeed, the PSU faced the parliamentary elections of 1968 more with the hope of preserving as much of its electorate—and so political influence—as it could, through government patronage, than with any clear idea of what it wanted to achieve or of a strategy for achieving it. The new PSIUP, on the other hand, took its stand on a platform critical of both PCI and PSU, although more favourable to the former; it considers that a Marxist socialist force is an indispensable element of both the unity and strategy of the Italian working class. Hence, it proposes a continuous dialogue with the PCI as a basis for collaboration.

All this does not conceal that the real weakness of the Socialist parties in the postwar period has been lack of autonomy: the old PSI and the new PSIUP towards the PCI and the old PSDI and new PSU towards the DC. Lack of an original strategy has been one cause, weak organizational structure has been another.

Proof of the truth of this assessment was provided in spectacular fashion at the last Congresses of both Socialist Parties in late 1968, in which both exhibited kaleidoscopic factional tendencies. The PSU

---

[1] For a fairly recent statement of Nenni's position see his 'Where the Italian Socialists Stand' in *Foreign Affairs*, Vol. 40, No. 2, January 1962, pp. 213–23.

Congress was unable to decide on a majority motion and its factions agreed to disagree, while at the PSIUP Congress a similar situation was avoided by the leaders using their control of the party apparatus to impose their line.

Structure. The organisation of both the PSU and new PSIUP are based on that of the PCI. They too have branch-type structures, but their collateral organisations and activities are much less well developed than those of the Communist Party. The PSU's auxiliary organizations (Women, Youth and Sports) are weak and it has virtually no control of left-wing cultural associations (ARCI). Its party newspaper, *Avanti!*, one of the most famous in the country, is in irresistible decline and it has lost control of its publishing house to the new PSIUP; its theoretical magazine, *Mondo Operaio*, has become a monthly (while the new PSIUP has *Mondo Libero*) and it has neither a weekly nor a women's magazine. Worse still, its trade union members are now split between the CGIL (under PCI—PSIUP control) and the weak UIL (controlled by the PSDI but shared with the PRI); the same situation exists in the co-operative field.

The basic territorial unit of both parties is the section, but they can be organized in work-places in nuclei of 5–15 members (NAS). Sections and nuclei depend on federations which depend, in turn, on the Central Directorate and Central Committee, which are the highest party bodies in periods between National Congresses. The parties have, therefore, a pyramidal structure, but there does not appear to be the same direct responsibility of lower units to their superiors noted in the PCI. Nuclei have never been strong—at the height of the PSI's organisation under Morandi they operated in less than 10 per cent of Italian enterprises—and can be assumed to be less important since schism and reunification respectively. In addition, socialist sections were absent in three-eighths of the communes in the country in 1961 and, assuming an improvement since then, it still leaves an appreciable area uncovered.

The geographical distribution of sections indicates that the areas where the former PSI was best organized were in Lombardy, Liguria, Emilia, Tuscany and Sicily, and that it was worst organized in Piedmont, the Venetias and the mainland South. Finally, it must be borne in mind that participation at the section and NAS level is slight and has permitted the building up of local power positions. Delegates to Federal and National Congresses are often appointed without a vote being taken. Similarly, delegation to the Central Committee and Party Directorate is made by a small group of leaders charged with forming the list of members on the basis of the requests of local and national groups. Control is, therefore, concentrated at the top.

Membership. The PSU is still a mass party. It now claims over 600,000 members, compared with 700,000 in the PSIUP before the Saragat schism in 1947 and 440,000 of the PSI and 192,000 of the PSDI before reunification. The figures for the new PSIUP are given as 164,000 members. Geographical distribution of members of the PSU is even more uneven than of the PCI. The latter has a general regional distribution, while the former has strong federations side by side with weak ones. In the North and Centre, socialist strength in Lombardy and the 'red belt' would appear to be tied to socialist traditions, but in the South in Campania and Sicily to the personal position of national and local leaders. It is interesting to note that in the Venetias it is stronger than the PCI; a result of the maximalist tradition in that region. Most of the areas where it has made recent advances are where it was previously weakest (the South), while it has declined where it was previously strong ('red belt' and North), although no precise pattern can be ascertained. Data for the new PSIUP indicates that its membership is evenly distributed over the country.

The Socialist parties are not basically working class in composition. Before unification only a third of the members were workers and another third peasants. Of the latter, over two-thirds were peasant farmers. It is certain that, since reunification, this proportion has diminished in the PSU while that of the middle classes in it has increased, although it is impossible to be precise. There is some evidence to suggest that the new PSIUP has been more successful in retaining the allegiance of the socialist members of the working class. In the North, the PSU recruits a fair number of members from the new urban middle classes and technicians as it does from among the traditional intelligentsia in the South. The principal reason for membership still appears to be family tradition, son following father, and the chief motive for going along to the party section is recreation; members go to play cards or watch television and seldom discuss politics.[1]

[1] P. Pavolini, 'I sette socialismi' in *Il Mondo*, August 26, 1958, p. 3.

Party officials. An important difference is apparent at the lowest level in comparison with the PCI; the Socialist parties recruit as activists only one member in fifty. This gives them barely 15,000 persons for the important work of proselytism, a seventh of the Communist number. No information is available on geographical distribution or social composition of activists of either party. By analogy, there is no reason to suppose that the activists differ greatly from members. At the next level, that of the local party official, it has been noted that in the mid-1950s there was a growing tendency towards a social distinction between members and local officials; increasingly, the latter were being selected from lawyers, chemists, shopkeepers and accountants rather than peasants and workers.[1]

At the provincial level, two groups of the former PSI have been analyzed:

(i) The directive committees (4,000 persons) of whom two-thirds were professional men and civil servants and only one-sixth workers;

(ii) The executive committees (real centres of federations—1,500 persons), which were found to be composed before the 1964 schism of 70 per cent full-time career officials and 30 per cent professional men. Of these less than 20 per cent came from proletarian backgrounds; they were twice as numerous in the North as in the South in contrast to the distribution for professional men.

The importance of southern intellectuals in the party repeats a point already noted in the PCI.

National leadership and parliamentarians. The proportion of parliamentarians in the Central Directorate of the former PSI was so great (over 85 per cent in the last decade) that Landinolfi commented:

'The almost total parliamentarization of the national leadership of the party carries with it the danger of an identification of the party with its parliamentary representatives and of serious moral and political consequences (moral in making party posts a launching pad for parliamentary and ministerial careers; political in placing all the decisional power within the sphere of clientelistic interests and

---

[1] P. Pavolini, 'I sette socialismi' in *Il Mondo*, August 26, 1958, p. 3.

parliamentary alliances) likely to reduce the party organization to a simple propaganda machine for collecting votes.[1]

In fact, this group in the Socialist Party has never been conspicuously compact either socially or politically. Nevertheless, it is possible to group members in two nuclei, which correspond to two different generations and two different types of politician. On the one hand, there are the younger, more modern and intellectually alert members of varied experience, the former bright young party officials, the former Communists and the former Action Party leaders. On the other hand, there are run of the mill MPs, lawyers and local bosses, who constitute the 'notables', a phenomenon known to all Italian parties, except the PCI. Their interest is strictly personal and generally local and since membership of Parliament is the key to the system, it is the summit of their ambition.

Social composition of the PSU national leadership and of the parliamentarians displays a situation similar to, but more accentuated than, that seen in the PCI, i.e., a more restricted basis of recruitment than among members and lesser officials. Over four-fifths of them come from the upper and middle classes. Thus, in this respect too the PSU fails to be a valid competitor to the PCI as a working class party. Data for the new PSIUP leadership are not available, but it must be similar to the PSU since most of the leading members held office in the former PSI. It is worth noting that the larger proportion of them came from the North and so, presumably, more came from the newer generation distinguished above.

Electoral Support. The Socialist electorate since the war has remained stable at around 20 per cent. Indeed, the combined proportion of the vote won by the new PSIUP and PSU in 1968 was within 1·7 per cent of that polled by the old PSIUP in 1946. Such stability, however, masks a certain movement, since it is clear that the Socialist parties lost a part of their electorate to the PCI as a result of the 1948 Popular Front experience, but have since regained it from the Centre Right-wing parties. Regional distribution of the Socialist vote has changed considerably since the war. In 1946, it was three times as great in the North as in the South (30 per cent against 10 per cent),

---

[1] A. Landinolfi, *Il Partito socialista oggi e domani*, Milano, Azione Comune, 1963, p. 98.

but in 1968, the difference was less than one third (21 per cent against 16 per cent). Hence, although still stronger in the North than in the South, the Socialist parties are no longer as closely linked to industrial Italy as they once were. Indeed, the PCI has capitalized on socialist traditions much more than the Socialist parties have since 1946. However, the PSU has penetrated, like the PCI, but less so, regions where socialism was virtually unknown before fascism. It has become more of a national and less of a sectional party.[1] The vote of the new PSIUP totals 4·5 per cent and is fairly evenly spread over the whole country with strongholds of over 5 per cent in the White Provinces and the Islands (Sicily and Sardinia) and a weak spot (3·4 per cent) in the continental South.

The social composition of the socialist electorate confirms these trends. It is less specifically working class than it was in the immediate postwar years. A greater proportion is now both peasant and middle class, which is consonant with the movement of its centre of gravity towards the South. In addition, the bias towards a male electorate appears also to be on the increase, in contrast to its decline in the PCI, owing almost certainly to the Socialist parties' inherent anticlericalism. At present, only just over two-fifths of their vote comes from industrial workers as against a third from the different agricultural groups, farmers, labourers etc. Finally, the remaining fifth comes from the urban middle classes. There is also recent evidence to suggest that socialism has had some success among technicians and better skilled workers. The strength of socialist traditions and a policy of democratic reforms have been suggested as the explanation of socialist support among the composite elements of its electorate. The strength of socialist traditions is evident if it is recalled that it polls two-thirds of the PCI vote, with one-third of its members, one-seventh of its activists and a considerably weaker party organisation.

Financial support. Many of the Socialist parties' sources of revenue are common to all Italian parties and particularly the PCI, at least until recently. About 20 per cent of the Socialist Party's needs also came from direct contributions, such as party dues, special contributions and fund-drives for the party press (*Festa dell'Avanti!*). In addition, substantial sums come from local and, since 1966,

---

[1] Allum, *op. cit.*, p. 337.

céntral government patronage. The former, it has been said, 'vary according to the nature of the coalition, or rather to the amount of power they (the parties) enjoy. Thus, the PSI secures certain departments when allied to the Communists but controls others when engaged in coalitions with the DC'.[1] Similar factors apply to the national government coalition which the PSI joined in 1963. It is difficult to assess how the PSU has fared—the indications are that it has been disappointed—but the importance of the patronage at stake is obvious from the struggles which have been going on among the members of the 'Centre-Left' coalition to secure the appointment of their protégés and which have often paralysed the coalition, if not yet suffocated it. Participation in national government, and the possibility of being able to share public funds, either from public corporations and state-owned industries, has been responsible for a major change in Socialist Party revenue, even if it has not prevented it from remaining the Cinderella of the mass parties. Unlike the PCI, neither the PSI nor PSDI could count on industrial activities and highly lucrative commercial enterprise, with the exception of trade with Yugoslavia, which is believed to have favoured the PSI. In addition, its weakness in the co-operative movement meant that it could not count on much help from that source. Indeed, during the period of the party's closer collaboration with the PCI, it was said to be largely dependent on the resources of the Communist Party. The PSDI was believed to be largely endowed with money from 'Confindustria' (The Confederation of Italian Industry) and, in its early years, it received financial assistance from American trade unions. A final source of funds is the Socialist International. Nothing is known of the importance of this but it was sufficient to play a role in socialist reunification.

No information on the finances of the new PSIUP is available. It has clearly been able to retain those sources which were available to the pre-schism left-wing faction (*carristi*) of the PSI. It may well have received financial help from the PCI in its early stages.

Power Analysis. Control of the parties by the leadership has been much less secure than in the PCI. In general, Nenni and Saragat maintained fairly effective control of their respective parties by a

---

[1] Passigli, *op. cit.*, p. 730; he refers to a study of his on the distribution of departments in different types of local government alliance in the *Annuario Politico Italiano* of 1963, pp. 478–98.

combination of caution in policy realignment and charismatic appeal. Indeed, it has been argued that in certain moments in the factional struggle over socialist autonomy and reunification, Nenni's charismatic personality enabled him to prevail over a hostile party 'apparatus'. At present, the new PSIUP has no charismatic leader. Nevertheless, neither Nenni's nor Saragat's dominance over fellow party leaders was great enough to prevent schisms. However, schisms and factions were largely leadership affairs and never concerned more than a very small proportion of local officials and members. One observer has written:

'The rank and file . . . participates very little in political discussions in the true sense; contenting itself with affirmations about socialism and depreciating factional struggles considered unpropitious for unity and harmony among Socialists. The leaders, whether party officials or elected office-holders, are the only ones to concern themselves with politics in the true sense, which thereby becomes an encounter and clash at the summit, leaving the rank and file more or less indifferent . . . at a higher level, on the key issues of general policy, only a few groups take part: Members of Parliament (not all), a few communal and provincial councillors, officials of the principal federations, and a small nucleus of young intellectuals, who have become members of the party relatively recently. . . .'[1]

Thus, it would seem that even the relatively weak party 'apparatus', which the PSU now has, is generally able to keep control of the party. It has, however, to take account of the power positions built up by local 'notables' (doctors, lawyers, shopkeepers and trade union officials) on the basis of personal clientele. In 1960, confronted with the opposition of Nenni, heading such a coalition of local and provincial notables allied with the ex-Action Party intellectuals, the party 'apparatus' proved incapable of maintaining its own cohesion, let alone blocking Nenni.[2] The role of the leadership group in the PSU is likely to increase because the alternative to going along with local 'notables'—their exclusion—means loss of votes. The former PSI's acceptance of autonomy and socialist reunification was built

---

[1] Pavolini, *op. cit.*, p. 3.
[2] For details, see Zariski, *op. cit.*, p. 389.

on a parliamentary power strategy. Hence, this very much limits the undoubted right of the PSU apparatus to control candidatures to public office. This shift would indicate a change in the nature of the party from an apparatus party to a parliamentary party. Nevertheless, since members of parliament dominate the central directorate, the apparatus is in their hands and, therefore, such a distinction is not so crucial as it is in, for example, the new PSIUP which is more like the old German SPD.

III. *The Italian Christian Democrat Party*
History and strategy. The Italian Catholic movement arose as an 'intransigent' protest against the Liberal regime which unification under the House of Savoy had introduced, and was aimed at restoring the temporal power of the Church in Italy. The first militant Catholic movement, the Catholic Congresses which were founded in 1874, was an auxiliary of the Holy See for the integral restoration of its rights. From the beginning, however, it showed a concern for the lower classes; as Webster has said, 'Slighted and bespoiled by the bourgeoisie, the Church turned to the masses'.[1] And it was this concern which led the Liberal Government to lump the 'clericals' together with Republicans and Socialists as 'subversives'. However, it was above all by its organizational activity that the Catholic Congresses laid the foundation for a mass Catholic party in Italy. They founded rural banks and co-operatives to assist peasants and landowners and which have remained the backbone of Italian Catholicism to this day. Politically, they implemented Leo XIII's *non-expedit* counsel which hardened into a formal prohibition against participation in public life.

At the same time, a 'conciliatorist' tendency developed in the Catholic movement, particularly among Bishops and landowners. They saw the Liberal State, despite its past wrongs to the Church, as not only an established fact, but, more important, as a bulwark of the social order. The conciliatorists never formed a mass movement but rather an *elite* group which took advantage of the limited increase in the suffrage of 1882 discreetly to re-enter public life. The Church itself turned to a conciliatory policy only two decades later;

---

[1] R. A. Webster, *Christian Democracy in Italy, 1860–1960*, London, Hollis and Carter, 1961, p. 5.

and even then policy fluctuated between encouraging the compactness of the mass movement by shows of intransigence and permitting the gradual integration of the Catholics into public life by a policy of wittingly turning a blind eye to Catholic candidatures. The first open Catholic deputies were elected in the first decade of the century. On the one hand, the Church supported those who wanted Catholics to enter parliamentary politics only when they had a mass party of their own, and on the other, it did not oppose those who thought it necessary to accept the Italian State and defend it. The matter was not very important while the suffrage remained restricted because this kept a limit on Catholic representation. But in 1913, Giolitti's introduction of virtual male suffrage brought the contradictions of these two positions into the open and they were resolved only *in extremis* by the Gentiloni Pact in which Catholics undertook to support Giolitti's Liberal candidates in return for certain *private* promises of respect for Catholic views. In addition, the pact relieved the Church of the danger of the formation of a Catholic political party which would have been independent of the ecclesiastical hierarchy and could easily have imperilled the unity of Church command.

The Catholics took a further step towards their complete involvement in Italian politics with their patriotic activity in the war and Catholic parliamentarians' acceptance of office in the War governments. The final move, however, came at the end of the war, when Don Luigi Sturzo founded the Popular Party in 1919 with Vatican approval. The Holy See removed the last barriers to Catholic participation in national public life while at the same time declaring that the party did not represent the Church. To emphasize this Sturzo himself resigned from Catholic Action, which now gave up its political role and became a specifically religious organization for promoting the lay activities of its members. The Popular Party's programme was one of democratic reform, appealing to voters of all social classes. It was to be the party of 'Catholics', but not a Catholic Party. Unfortunately for Sturzo, the party became prey to the contradictions inside the Catholic movement because while the traditional Clerical leading strings remained, there were groups on the left even advocating outright collectivism. From the start, the party was torn between factions and never became a reliable political instrument. It also suffered from the oligarchic tendencies

226

of pre-Fascist politics. In such conditions, it was unable to make a coherent contribution to a particularly troubled period of Italian history. After the Fascists came to power, the Catholic hierarchy gradually abandoned the party, first letting it be known that it was an embarrassment, and later, intervening directly to denounce autonomous Catholic political action. The Pope reserved for himself the political direction of Italian Catholicism. Thus, De Gasperi, who had succeeded Don Sturzo on the latter's resignation in 1923, was also forced to resign in December 1925. When all political parties were prohibited in January 1926, the Popular Party ceased to exist.

The Church's abandonment of the Popular Party was inspired by its desire to negotiate a new Concordat with the Fascist regime and effect a reconciliation between Church and State. These negotiations took three years and resulted in the Lateran Pacts of 1929. They were very favourable to the Church and gave it wide powers in matters of direct concern to the State. 'In short,' it has been said, 'Italy became a confessional state, unique among the great powers of contemporary Europe.'[1] One clause of particular importance for its effects on postwar politics was Article 43, which recognized the immunity from State (Fascist) pressure of Catholic Action and its dependent organizations. This placed the Catholics in a privileged position during the Fascist period because their organizations not only preserved an enviable continuity but most important of all, they were able to recruit and train a whole generation of future leaders relatively untouched by Fascism. The Catholics did not fail to take advantage of this privilege since it was in these organizations that the seeds of the Christian Democratic Party were sown.

The party was founded in 1943 as a result of contacts between Catholic leaders towards the end of Fascism. The ground had been prepared by the various but often divergent Catholic groups. From the Salerno Government (April 1944), the DC began its participation in government, which has continued throughout the postwar period. The Catholic groups in occupied territory took part in the Resistance, making an important contribution. The party's organization was able to take advantage of ecclesiastical organization, particularly the parish, to build itself up quickly and efficiently.

The decisive moment of its history came in December 1945 when it allied with the Italian Liberal Party(PLI)in ensuring the resignation of the partisan Prime Minister Parri and the appointment of De Gasperi in his stead. Since then a member of the DC has always been Prime Minister of Italy. Although the party led a tripartite coalition until 1947, it was the dominant bourgeois party and hence became ever more decisively the pillar of Italian anti-Communism. It was under the menace of the cold war and in the face of US pressure that De Gasperi expelled the PCI and PSI from the government and formed a Centre coalition with right-wing support which won a great electoral victory in 1948, led the country into the Western Alliance and enabled it to reconstruct a capitalist economy with Marshall aid. The De Gasperi period also saw the introduction of limited agrarian reform and the setting up of the Southern Development Fund, and Italy's support for European unity. Within his own party De Gasperi had to defend his conception of a democratic coalition against those who wanted the introduction of an integral Catholic state.[1]

De Gasperi's death in 1954 coincided with a new phase in the history of the DC, one in which the DC no longer controlled power but had to share it, at least partially. While successive Prime Ministers fought to keep the various Centre and Centre-Right coalitions together, Fanfani, who won control of the party in the same year at the Congress of Naples, endeavoured to reorganize the party on branch-type lines in order to give it a certain autonomy from Catholic Action organizations. This policy provoked opposition from the hierarchy and other quarters and gave rise to intense factional in-fighting within the party.[2] Party organization became more efficient and membership rose, but Fanfani was unable to impose sufficient discipline to control the party and his resignation was confirmed at the Florence Congress in 1959.

Moro, Fanfani's successor, tried a more subtle policy of attempting to conciliate factions and orient the party towards a new coalition with the Socialists. The 'opening to the left' was accepted in 1962

[1] The most notorious example of Church intervention in DC affairs occurred in April 1952, in the so-called 'Sturzo Affair'. For accounts, see M. R. Catti-De Gasperi, *De Gasperi Uomo solo*, Rome, Mondadori, 1964 and G. Andreotti in *Concretezza*, August 1965.

[2] For an account of this, see R. Zariski, 'Intra-Party Conflict in a Dominant Party: The Experience of Italian Christian Democracy' in *Journal of Politics*, Vol. 27, No. 1, February 1965, pp. 6–19.

and the PSI entered the government the following year. Unfortunately, Moro's conciliation did not reduce factional in-fighting; so much of his energy as Prime Minister was used in keeping the coalition together that he was unable to prevent it from settling into a comfortable immobility.

Thus, the DC has seen itself throughout the postwar period as a government party. It does not have a political ideology in the sense that the ideology dictates specific social objectives, but rather in the sense that catholicism supplies the limiting framework. Within it the party pursues vague policies of modernization deformed and accentuated by its chief task, that of interest brokerage. Its proclaimed strategy is, therefore, one of 'social synthesis' which, in practical terms, means administering political power in the interests of its strongest *clientele*. It is the dominant bourgeois party, with political power as its chief aim. Power is required not to implement a specific policy—the party rarely has the coherence to formulate a specific policy—but rather to prevent others from doing anything to which it, the Church and the great economic groups, would be opposed.

Structure. Formally, the DC now has a branch-type structure. It is based on the territorial section and articulated in provincial federations, subordinate to the National Council, Directorate and Secretariat, all of which are elected at the biennial National Congress. It also sponsors the full range of auxiliary organizations and a party press responsible for the publication of a national daily, *Il Popolo*, five regional newspapers and 34 provincial weeklies. Like the PCI, it has its own publishing house, *Cinque Lune*, and party review *La Discussione*; and organizations which provide it with a social base in the country: the CISL, the Catholic trade union, the *coltivatori diretti*, the Catholic-controlled peasant union and the Catholic-controlled Confederation of Italian Co-operatives, in addition to the whole panoply of Catholic Action organizations.

In its formal structure and organizational relationships, the DC resembles the PCI, the 'apparatus' party, *par excellence*. Indeed, it could be argued that the only difference is its lack of that specifically Leninist institution, the cell. In fact, the party has no need of it since it can find its equivalent in the church parish. However, the relationship between the DC's formal and actual structure is complex. In the early postwar years it owed its success more to its control of government and the support of the ecclesiastical hierarchy than to its own structure. Thus, when Fanfani attempted to give it its own autonomous organization after 1954, he ran up against the established positions of powerful groups which eventually defeated him.

This relationship makes it difficult to assess the party's structure. Party information indicates that the number of sections increased during Fanfani's secretaryship, when he concentrated on building up the party. But Congress discussions suggested that many of them existed only on paper,[1] particularly in the South. In the North and Centre where the party's structure is more solid, the number of sections is both greater and more rationally located. In any case sections rarely meet more than two or three times a year. Thus, there can be little doubt that the party is still very dependent on the parish, particularly in rural areas, for the continual penetration which ensures the massive DC vote in successive parliamentary elections.

Membership. The DC is a mass party; its membership exceeded one million in 1948 and again in the mid-1950s, whence it rose to the 1·5 million mark round which it appears to have settled. Recruitment figures for this period show two interesting facts: first, unlike the other mass parties, DC membership increased right up to the 1960s and any decline has been both recent and limited; and secondly, the increase has not been linear; it has been more rapid in Congress and electoral years and slower or negative in the other years. This reflects the DC's position as a dominant party in a government-orientated political system; and also suggests that membership is manipulated for Congress purposes.[2]

Territorial distribution does not follow any expected pattern. Southern membership levels (as proportions of the population) now exceed those of the 'White provinces' as well as those in the North and Centre. This penetration of the South reverses the immediate post-war situation. But southern annual membership turnover is often

[1] See discussion quoted in J. P. Chassériaud, *Le parti démocrate chrétien en Italie*, Paris, Colin, 1965, p. 48.

[2] For example, at the National Council meeting of March 14, 1959, former Prime Minister A. Zoli said: 'I know very well that this year our friend Branzi will tell you that the number of members has increased, we are in a congressional year . . .' quoted in *Il Popolo*, March 15, 1959; at the National Congress in October of the same year, Donat-Catin stated: 'As regards organization, inflationist tendencies in membership must be deplored, particularly in those regions where there are masses of unemployment or underemployment . . . all groups are responsible . . . from the situation in Latium and in particular in Ciociara . . . right down to certain Southern regions . . .' quoted in *Il Popolo*, October 27, 1959.

close to half the members in some provinces, which provides further striking confirmation of the artificial nature of many of the southern federations' 'congressional' membership figures.

The DC is, as it claims, an all-class party, i.e., it recruits members from all classes of Italian society. The proletarian percentage is only half that of the PCI, but still represent almost a third of its members. The bourgeois groups also number a third of party members and are composed of the urban and rural middle classes in a proportion of 2 to 1. The percentage of this group has increased in the postwar period and shows that the DC now recruits the professional people who formed the cadres of the Liberal parties before Fascism.[1] This is a consequence of the DC's dominant position. But it must not be forgotten that the majority of this group is made up of professional people from the Catholic organizations (e.g. teachers). Over a third of the members are women; the largest percentage in any Italian party.

Party officials. DC activists are second only in number to those of the PCI and represent a similar proportion of party members (5–10 per cent). Their social composition reflects the all-class membership of the party. However, divergence already appears with the local officials. Working-class elements are reduced to a mere 15 per cent and the agricultural labourers are absent altogether. The professional middle classes constitute the majority (60 per cent), while the other groups, peasant farmers, artisans, shopkeepers, and employers, each contribute 8 per cent of these officials. Once again, however, as with the PCI, the qualitative jump in the formation of the DC leadership comes at the level of the Federation. Over four-fifths of this group came from the upper and middle classes and not one was either a worker or a peasant. Indeed, the two professions which predominate are teachers (in the North) and lawyers (in the South), and both groups are extensively recruited from Catholic organizations (Catholic Action, Catholic graduates etc.). Over two-thirds of DC party officials begin their political careers in this way.

National leadership and parliamentarians. This group is approximately twice as large as that of the PCI, emphasizing the wider responsibilities of a dominant party. Moreover, there is less real division between the national leadership and parliamentarians than in the PCI, because those who are not MPs aspire to sit in Parliament.

[1] See Galli, *op. cit.*, pp. 176–7.

In most cases, in fact, membership of Parliament is necessary to be recognized as a potential party leader. All heads of factions, without exception, sit in Parliament.

The social composition of this group is even more restricted than at the provincial level, since over 94 per cent comes from the upper and middle classes. Only four wage-earning members of the DC have broken into this circle. Recruitment from Catholic Action is considerable, more than 85 per cent of DC parliamentarians have belonged to Catholic organizations. Such a situation suggests three conclusions: (i) although the DC is an all-class party in its membership and activists, this is not true of its officials, and particularly, of its provincial and national leadership; (ii) as an instrument of social promotion, the party serves only the middle classes. For the working class, it is not a serious competitor of the PCI. It has increasingly become, as has already been indicated, the party of those individuals and groups whose ambition is *fare politica*, and (iii) that the main path to office in the DC passes by membership of (and preferably office in) Catholic organizations.

Finally, no region has had a monopoly of party leadership. DC Prime Ministers have been very widely spread: De Gasperi from Trento, Pella from Piedmonte, Scelba from Sicily, Segni from Sardinia, Zoli and Fanfani from Tuscany, Tambroni from the Marche, Leone from Campania and Moro from Apulia. Such rotation of leadership is a recognition of the nature of the party which has resulted from its dominant governing status. The decision to give cabinet posts to prominent leaders of all regions has meant that continuous cabinet service has enabled them to build up a wide network of interests. Thus, they have become, in effect, entrenched local bosses, often controlling whole regions. And in serving their own interests, they have served the interests of the party because by becoming immovable they have helped preserve party unity.

Electoral support. The party's vote in the postwar period has fluctuated round two-fifths of the electorate. It follows membership in geographical distribution and social composition in some respects, but differs in others. The differences reflect the double nature of its electoral support. Hence, although there is a correlation between membership and vote in the nation as a whole,[1] it is not as rigorous

[1] *Ibid.*, p. 132; it was 0·50 with party organization; and 0·31 with CISL membership.

as for the PCI. The DC is strongest in the 'white provinces' where it regularly polls half the vote and it is weakest in the 'red belt' where its vote is only around 30 per cent. In the North and the South its support was similar to the national average in 1948. In 1968, it held its own in the North, whereas in the South it improved its vote by more than 5 per cent. Thus it would appear that its vote has increased in keeping with increased membership in the South. It must be noted, however, that membership in this region has increased much more rapidly than votes. The DC would seem, therefore, to tap two sources of electoral support: (i) Catholics, particularly in the 'white provinces' where Catholic traditions and organizations are strong; (ii) conservatives, particularly in the South where the DC's position as a permanent government party has enabled it to control local government.

Social composition of the DC electorate seems to confirm its double nature. First, it wins support from all classes. One-fifth of its electorate is provided by the urban proletariat; almost half comes from the rural classes, in majority peasant farmers; and the remaining third is made up of the urban middle classes. Secondly, two-thirds of DC voters are women. Thirdly, it is nearly twice as strong in communes of less than 1,000 inhabitants than in the six cities with populations of over half a million. The final two points emphasize the importance of the Church as the principal agent ensuring the massive DC vote in successive elections. The greater religious feeling of women makes them likely to heed the numerous appeals which the Church makes to Catholics 'to vote together' and to remember their duty to 'place their fidelity to fundamental Christian principles and the needs of the common good before their personal opinions and individual interests',[1] as well as to take advice of their local priests. Similarly, the rural vote is evidence not only of the social homogeneity and more intense religious feeling of these areas, but also of the strength of the *coltivatori diretti*, which controls all aspects of farmers' lives through its dominance of the *Federconsorzi* (local self-managed agricultural organizations which manage all state aid to agriculture). But, as has already been noted, the DC is not only a rural party; it also has an important urban following. Nearly a third of all its voters live in cities of over 30,000 people.

[1] Appeal of the Conference of the Italian Episcopacy of March 13, 1963, quoted in Allum, *op. cit.*, p. 331.

These urban voters have a social composition in stark contrast to that of their rural counterparts; they tend to be male, middle class and politically more active and informed. Moreover, many are even crypto-anticlericals and opposed to the intervention of the clergy in politics. They represent the other face of the DC electoral coin, the conservative middle classes.

Financial support. For the DC, as for the PCI and PSI, direct contributions, even allowing for special contributions and fund-drives, are far from providing the necessary amount of money to meet party expenditure. Moreover, the party does not touch parliamentary salaries. Commissions on public contracts, however, are of considerable importance. In local government, the share-out of departments depends on the type of coalition and the power relations of the constituent parties. The position of the DC is usually dominant and so it does not surrender key financial departments such as those of Public Works or Welfare. In addition, since the DC does not seem to be engaged in commercial or co-operative activities, it must count on other powerful sources of income as, for example, that which comes from its long control of the central government. Passigli discounts the idea of commissions on government contracts because these are performed by the administration, but, on the other hand, accepts the notion that funds flow into party hands from the various public corporations and state-owned enterprises; most notably from ENI (Italian National Petroleum Corporation). He writes:

'In spite of being accountable to Parliament for their operations, public corporations enjoy in fact a considerable degree of autonomy. Moreover, most state-owned industries are formally private corporations where the state, through having a controlling interest, acts as a private shareholder. Their real budgets are then largely disguised and offer, under various miscellaneous headings, possibilities for direct financial contributions. The fact that the actual recipients of these contributions tend to be various organizations and individuals does not substantially change the role of public money, though it has far-reaching consequences since it allows a careful discrimination among the various groups in the Catholic party; the final recipient of support tends to be the individual faction rather than the party.'[1]

[1] Passigli, *op. cit.*, pp. 730–1.

Another source of direct contribution to the DC is reputed to be *Confindustria.* However, the relations between the DC and Italian industry are complex. They were much closer in the De Gasperi era. Today it is necessary to bear in mind two factors: fluctuations in the reactions of industrial leaders to changes in the party's internal leadership; and differing assessments of the various industrialists about a particular party policy. Thus it is known that some groups, such as FIAT and Montecatini, supported the 'opening to the left' and so can be taken as having been likely to contribute to party funds, while others, like Edison and Assolombarda, (Association of Lombardy Industrialists) vigorously opposed it. The main channel of such funds is in the form of direct contributions from individual companies, often given to the auxiliary organizations rather than to the party. This procedure, like that adopted by the public corporations, has important consequences since it enhances greatly the power of the auxiliary organizations and groups in the party, accounting for the discrepancy between the influence of certain faction leaders and their support among party members.

The government party also benefits from considerable indirect financial support. Four newspapers[1] are more or less directly state-owned, three by the Bank of Naples and one by ENI. They support the DC, but speak with widely different voices, as backing different groups within the party. Italian radio and television have been another important source of support for the DC. At the end of the 1950s, they came under severe criticism for alleged abuse because of the use they made of their monopoly of these forms of communication. A rule was established of equal time allocation to all parties during electoral campaigns. However, the rule does not affect coverage and editorial management of news broadcasts during electoral campaigns or, indeed, at any other time. Finally, the most important source of indirect financial help goes under the name of *sottogoverno* which can be interpreted as 'patronage' in the widest sense. It is impossible to measure its importance but it would seem difficult to underestimate it. It is necessary to

---

[1] They are: *Il Mattino* and *Il Corriere di Napoli* of Naples, and *La Gazetta del Mezzogiorno* of Bari controlled by the Bank of Naples; and *Il Giorno* of Milan controlled by ENI. Moreover, FIAT controls *La Stampa* of Turin; Crespi and Sons owns *Il Corriere della Sera* of Milan; and Perrone and Sons *Il Messagero* and *Secolo XIX* of Rome, the principal so-called independent newspapers.

mention only two facts which illustrate this point of view: (i) the DC has been careful, since it came to power in 1945, to keep within its hands, except for very brief periods, the key ministries which control this field, i.e., the Ministries of the Interior, Defence, Finance, Agriculture and Education, as well as the new key Ministry founded in 1958, the Ministry of State Industrial Holdings;[1] (ii) despite numerous political scandals, party solidarity of the DC has been such as to prevent leaders implicated in scandals from being tried. In other cases, where investigations have begun, the government has succeeded in ensuring that evidence was not made available to the investigating magistrate, so that they have had to be dropped. In fact, the only persons to have been condemned have been members of the minor coalition parties.[2]

Power Analysis. The complex nature of the DC as a party is apparent from what has been said. This is no less true at the top than at the base. It is, in essence, an ideological party whose vocation is government; but continued dominance can be won only at the cost of attracting the support of groups critical of, if not opposed to, its ideology. The need to reconcile contradictions is ever present in its power structure. This is impossible to characterize with any certainty, since it has varied over time; all that one can do is to outline some of the factors involved.

In the De Gasperi period, the party appears to have been a parliamentary party. Certainly De Gasperi so considered it, as is evident from his last speech to the Party Congress, since known as his political testament.[3] In his postwar political activity, he always took more account of the reactions of the electorate than of the

---

[1] See Galli, *op. cit.*, p. 199.

[2] The most notorious example of DC solidarity preventing a parliamentary enquiry was the Trabucchi case.

[3] 'La Lotta per la democrazia' in *I congressi nazionali della DC*, Roma, 1959, SPES, pp. 478 ff., in which he emphasized the importance of Article 67 of the Constitution: 'Every member of Parliament represents the Nation and exercises his function without any mandate-ties', and which contains the following passage, 'Its (the party's) specific function is to give a political direction to its representatives and legislators . . . and this function they exercise democratically, i.e. from decisions of its militants in their assemblies and its directive organs. But the party is, at the same time, part of a larger reality which should interest the electorate and through it the people. And here besides the numbers, experience, personal capacity and social position is important. It is here that the so-called "notables" have a role, either in their quality of people of intelligence or as representative of important social and local nuclei.' p. 484.

party and more of certain economic groups than either since he believed that the support of the electorate depended on successful reconstruction. Moreover, his position in the party was reinforced not only by his prestige as the pre-Fascist leader of the party but also by his position as Prime Minister in the politically dramatic period of the cold war. Thus, although De Gasperi's position as party leader was never in doubt, this did not free him from difficult battles with different party groups at various times.

De Gasperi's death and Fanfani's attempt to strengthen the party organization complicated rather than simplified the internal party situation, because it increased the number of contesting elements at the very moment the political lynch-pin disappeared. This was because the DC does not control, much less lead, its own electorate. Its electorate is controlled and provided for the party by the Catholic movement as a whole, which is, in turn, subject to the ecclesiastical hierarchy. Galli[1] has noted the tasks which Catholic organizations have been given as three in number: (a) to look after the sectional interests of the group for which the organization caters; (b) to be prepared to respond to the call of the ecclesiastical hierarchy; (c) to reinforce the hegemony of the DC over the catholic and conservative electorate. In consequence, not only do politicians with the most divergent viewpoints cohabit in the DC but its unity is preserved only by the Church and the realization that the result of a schism would be the party's loss of its dominant position and power. Moreover, a disobedient leader would at the next election lose the support of the Church and hence his local power base.

In these circumstances, it is not surprising that the party is a heterogeneous alliance of interest groups organized in a kaleidoscope of factions, of which the party apparatus is one contender. This state of affairs is encouraged by the 'polycentric' flow of funds and the party's dominant status. Top leadership sits in Parliament, as it does in other parties. However, this does not make the DC a parliamentary party in the English sense, since decisions can be taken independently of a DC Prime Minister. Parliamentary membership plays a more important role in party decisions than in the PCI, and perhaps even than in the PSU, because of the prestige which it confers on would-be leaders, although this would be difficult to

1 Galli, *op. cit.*, p. 202.

substantiate. However, an important new development must be mentioned. This is the slow emergence of new technocratic leaders, such as Bassetti in Milan, whose career is oriented towards the new local planning centres and not the traditional parliamentary seat. The influence of Bassetti,[1] and others like him, is difficult to assess but it is more important than that of many parliamentarians and is likely to increase. What is certain at present is that a relatively small group of leaders, either of the party or of collateral organizations, most of whom sit in Parliament, control the party. The greater part of the membership, through sheer lack of interest, is happy that this should be the case.

MINOR PARTIES

The Italian minor parties are a mixture of permanent minority and personality parties. All try to give themselves an organization in the country, although some depend on a personality for any importance they might have.

The Italian Republican Party, which has polled between 1 and 2 per cent of the vote in postwar elections, is heir to the Mazzini tradition. Its support is strongly centred on areas of central Italy and the Romagna. Although it has been on the verge of losing national representation—the institutions of the Republic in 1946 meant the loss of its principal *raison d'être* and the defection of many of its troops to the PCI, a more vociferous defender of their interests—it has played a more important role in postwar Italian politics than its numbers would warrant, principally owing to the activity of its leader, Ugo La Malfa. It has recently oriented itself into a more modern radical party and in the 1968 elections improved its parliamentary position, in both votes and seats, for the first time since the war.

The Italian Liberal Party was founded by Croce in his home on the morrow of the Liberation in the tradition of pre-Fascist liberalism from Cavour to Giolitti. Its credo is liberty and initially it provided a political home for pre-Fascist 'notables' and southern landowners, who found the newly organized mass parties distasteful. Despite its success in the monarchist South in 1946, it suffered

---

[1] For Bassetti's opinion, see his replies to the questionnaire at the *Seminario sui Partiti* in September 1967, mimeographed, p. 26.

successive defections during the cold war years because its organization was inadequate for the political realities of that harsh period. It reached its lowest ebb in 1953, after which it was taken over by a newer generation representing northern business interests, under Giovanni Malagodi. The party was reorganized and given a branch-like structure. It now depends on revenue from local companies and national business associations since, as can be understood from its history, contributions from large land-owners have greatly diminished. In 1963, its opposition to the 'opening to the left' mobilized the discontent of the well-to-do urban middle classes with the steady rise in the cost of living, which was one of the consequences of the Italian 'economic miracle', and doubled its poll to 7 per cent. The centre of this vote was located in the fashionable residential districts of the big cities, Milan, Turin, Rome and Naples. The creation of the centre-left coalition and the mildness of its reforms blunted the party's appeal; this was evident in the 1968 electoral results in which it had the greatest difficulty in limiting its losses.

The Italian Monarchist Party was founded on the morrow of the referendum ostensibly to group all those who had voted for the Monarchy in a single party to fight for a restoration. In fact, it has been no more than the political expression of the vested interests of a number of conservative politicians, of whom the most important was the Neapolitan ship-owner, Achille Lauro. Hence, its postwar history has been marked by schisms, reunifications and defections. In the mid-1950s it mobilized regional antagonism in the South against the Central Government and the North. In this period, it won between 5–10 per cent of the poll, localized in the big southern cities, particularly Naples. Its voters comprised, in the main, nostalgic elderly aristocrats and the big city poor. Its inability to do anything for these groups and the DC's administrative attack on its control of local government were sufficient to precipitate an irremediable decline. It was virtually devoid of any grass-roots organization and its activities and costly political clienteles were openly financed by Lauro from his personal fortune, one of the largest in the country.

The Italian Neo-fascist Party was founded clandestinely by the Fascist small fry on the basis of the 18 points of Mussolini's Verona Charter of 1943. It took advantage of the cold war situation to come out into the open and contest parliamentary seats in the 1948 election. Fortunately for Italian democracy, it has remained remarkably sterile and unsuccessful in attracting support. At the height of its expansion in the early 1950s, it failed to win 10 per cent of the poll, and has been saved from complete collapse recently only by the Monarchist débâcle. Despite possessing a formal structure and satellite organizations (the trade union (CISNAL)), it depended greatly on the local reputation of a number of 'notables' for its electoral strength. It is alleged to have been financed by extreme right-wing Italian business groups but this is far from certain. More probably, it has been helped with funds from the personal fortunes of a few nostalgic beneficiaries of the former regime.

RELATIONS WITH PARTIES IN OTHER COUNTRIES

Four of the eight Italian parties have relations with parties in other countries. They are the PCI, PSU, DC and PLI. Two have none, PRI and Monarchists, partly because they are anomalies in modern Europe. The Monarchists have an international link, but that is with the ex-King, in exile in Portugal. Two further parties, the PSIUP and MSI, would probably like to have international links but have so far found no party (or parties) with which to have links. As regards the latter, it is perhaps as well to remember that the Italian National Fascist Party had links with other European Fascist Parties in the 1930s in the belated and ill-fated Fascist International.

Italian Communist Party

The PCI has had close international links since its birth in 1921. Founded with the help of the Third International, it had links with the Comintern until its dissolution in June 1943. Indeed, its international links were particularly important during the Fascist period as they enabled it to preserve an organizational continuity which otherwise it would not have had.[1] Moreover, its leader Togliatti rose to high office within the organization, becoming Secretary of the Executive Committee under Dimitrov in the late 1930s and responsible for the organization's relations with Spain during the Spanish Civil War. Similarly the PCI was a member of the Cominform when

[1] For the role of the Comintern in the life of the PCI, see *Per la Libertà e L'independenza d'Italia*, relazione della direzione del PCI al V Congresso, Roma, 1945, Soc. Edit L'Unità.

that organization was founded in Autumn 1947. The Cominform like its predecessor was an international organization of foreign Communist Parties subordinate to the Communist Party of the Soviet Union (CPSU). The PCI followed its directives but refused to press them to the point where its own future might be endangered.[1] The Cominform's lack of success led to its rapid dissolution Since then there has been no formal international Communist organization.

Until Khrushchev's denunciation of Stalin's crimes in 1956, the PCI accepted Soviet leadership of the world communist movement. This deference to Soviet primacy was based on the prestige of the Soviet Union as the first socialist state and financial support which the USSR gave the PCI. In subsequent years, the PCI has demonstrated increasing autonomy towards the USSR and its world revolutionary strategy. Togliatti developed the notion of the 'polycentrism' of the world communist movement and the 'Italian way to Socialism' as the party's own strategy. Polycentrism can be interpreted as meaning the autonomy of each party within the world movement. Practical effect was given to this policy in the PCI's role in the Sino-Soviet split, now enshrined in Togliatti's political testament, the Yalta Memorial.[2] This pleaded for 'unity in diversity'. The party opposed the CPSU's demand for a meeting of the 81 Communist parties to condemn Mao Tse-tung's deviationism. Togliatti stated that the PCI would attend a preparatory Congress but only to resist the convening of a World Conference. This is what the party did when the consultative meeting of 19 parties finally met in Moscow on March 1, 1965. The PCI position was supported by the majority of parties represented and the CPSU did not press its proposition. This was, therefore, a clear and public challenge to the authority of the CPSU in the international movement. It showed that the PCI has

[1] See footnote on p. 205 referring to Reale's book, *Nascità del Cominform*. The Party published a collection of documents covering cominform activity at its VII Congress in 1951, see *Risoluzioni e documenti dell' Ufficio d'informazione dei partiti communisti e operai*, 1947–51, Roma, La Stampa Moderna, 1951.

[2] This was published in *Rinascità*, a 21, n. 35, of September 5, 1964; for the general position of the PCI, see also *Interventi della delegazione del PCI alla Conferenza agli 81 partiti communisti ed operai*, Roma, 1962, GATE. For a study of the PCI's relations with the International Communist Movement in the last decade, see D. L. M. Blackmer, *Unity in Diversity, Italian Communism and the International Communist Movement*, Cambridge, Mass., Press, 1968.

reversed its priorities from supporting the CPSU and developing its political power in Italy, to the point where the latter came first. Moreover, it maintains its solidarity with the USSR not only through habitual loyalty but because the link gives the PCI political prestige and aid as well as protecting it from the threat of an 'alternative to the left' in Italy.

Thus the PCI supports an international movement open to the free and pragmatic interplay of ideas and trends. It also maintains close relations with Communist parties in other countries. In 1965 it sent delegations to Prague, Moscow, Peking, Hanoi and Djarkarta for interparty talks. However, its closest links are with East European parties and the French Party, in which it attempts to encourage them to change towards an acceptance of the revisionist path recommended by Togliatti in his Yalta Memorial. Cultural delegations have been sent to Czechoslovakia and Hungary and there are frequent interviews in its weekly theoretical review, *Rinascita*, with East European and French economists and writers. In this connection, it must be remembered that, unlike France at least until recently, Italy has an indigeneous Marxist theoretical tradition associated with the names of Labriola and Gramsci which permits the party considerable autonomy in the cultural field.

Unified Socialist Party. The PSI was a member of the Second International from the last years of the last century; it was also the first foreign party to adhere to the Third International, but it was expelled in 1921. The Second World War swept away the remnants of the international labour movement. Nonetheless, the British Labour Party founded a new organization COMISCO to which the PSIUP adhered in 1944 but it expelled the PSI under Nenni after the socialist schism of 1947 for its pro-communist orientation, and recognized the Saragat Social Democrat Party. Moreover, COMISCO's successor, the new Socialist and Labour International, also recognized the PSDI and probably helped it financially through its early lean years. In keeping with its social democrat orientation it also played an important but obscure role in Socialist reunification, since, after Nenni's break with the PCI in 1956, it encouraged his struggle for autonomy by letting it be known that it would welcome him back into the social democrat fold. At the same time, the PSDI also wished to avoid being disavowed on the return of the prodigal son.

The PSU, therefore, has links with all democratic socialist parties which are members of the Socialist International. At triennial congresses, regular Leaders' Conferences, etc., the Italian party is fully represented.[1] The party also maintains close informal contacts with social democrat parties in neighbouring countries, sending delegations to their conferences and meetings. It is, of course, a member of the Socialist group in the European assemblies, and supports and promotes all the common activities of the Socialist Group, such as its bureau and press service, etc.

Christian Democrats. Despite the party's supranational ideological commitment, international links have in practice been restricted by the slow development of a 'Christian Democrat International'.[2] The World Union has made its headquarters in Rome and this gives a role of some importance to the Italian party. Although the European equivalent—Nouvelles Equipes Internationales, later the European Union of Christian Democrats—established its headquarters in Paris, the Italian and German parties were naturally dominant. Until recently, Rumor—then Secretary of the Italian Christian Democrats—was President of the European Union. Outside these formal international channels, the Italian party has informal bilateral relations with equivalent parties in Europe, particularly in Germany and with the former MRP in France. However, it has taken the lead amongst continental Christian Democratic parties in objecting to any institutionalized link with the British Conservatives.

Liberal Party. The PLI is a member of the Liberal International and also the Liberal group in the European Parliament. The former has been a largely ineffectual body through its ideological differences and the Italian party has contributed to this by their extreme right-wing position on many issues, in particular contrast to the British Liberals. However, the party has always been a prime mover for further European integration.

[1] For an Italian appreciation of the role and activities of the Socialist International, see the PSDI publication, *Il Centenario dell'Internazionale Socialista* (a cura dell'Ufficio Internazionale della Direzione del PSDI), Roma, Tip. Moravia, 1964.

[2] For details of Catholic Parties' international organization and collaboration, see *Democrazia Cristiana, realta internazionale* (a cura di A. Bernassola), Roma, Ediz. Cinque Lune, 1968.

PARTICIPATION IN EUROPEAN ASSEMBLIES

The Italian Government played a leading role in the postwar movement for European unity. Indeed, De Gasperi has rightly been
considered, alongside Robert Schuman and Konrad Adenauer, as
one of the fathers of the Six. Two reasons can be advanced for
Italy's interest in European integration: the cosmopolitan[1] nature of
Italy's cultural traditions stemming from the Renaissance and the
need to overcome the ambiguous heritage of Fascism and the
Resistance—that despite the Resistance, Italy was still associated
with the Axis and military defeat. European unification provided a
means whereby Italy might become fully reintegrated in the community of nations.[2] Thus, the government, after having proposed a
customs union with France in 1948, vigorously supported the
Schuman Plan and subsequent European initiatives.

This European commitment of the Italian Government was, like
so many things in Italian politics, an *elite* commitment. Survey
information on knowledge and attitude to the Common Market
indicate that the Italian public is the least informed of all the members
of the Six: only 57 per cent of Italians had heard of the Common
Market as against over 87 per cent in the other five countries in
1963.[3] Of the 57 per cent, only 37 per cent thought that the Common
Market had been of advantage to their own country. In addition,
this support came principally from the upper and educated classes.
Nonetheless, it goes some way to explaining the attitudes of the
parties of Europe and the European assemblies.

The PCI opposed the government initiatives in the European field
from the start and although it has remained generally hostile, its
hostility has been much more flexible than that of the French
Communist Party. Indeed, in the early 1960s, the CGIL leaders
were prepared to accept that the workers could gain some benefits
from the Common Market. Communist opposition was based on
its analysis that the movement was a stage in the development of
neo-capitalism, that of the international concentration of monopoly
capital. Its activity was, of course, restricted to anti-European

[1] See Count Sforza's book, *Europe and the Europeans*, published in exile in
New York in the inter-war years, (London, Harrap, 1936).
[2] For the European content of Italian Foreign policy, see N. Kogan. *The
Politics of Italian Foreign Policy*, London, Pall Mall, 1963.
[3] See *Reader's Digest European Surveys, 1963*.

propaganda in the country so long as the party was not represented in the European assemblies.

The Socialist parties have taken different approaches to Europe: The left-wing party (PSI then PSIUP) has followed the position of the PCI closely and been largely hostile while the right-wing party (PSDI then PSU) has been in favour of European co-operation. The Socialist parties which formed part of the various government coalitions supported all their European initiatives, but their activity in the European Parliament has been limited because the Italian delegation was not renewed after the first election of representatives in 1957 until 1969. In 1957, the Centre-party government coalition (DC, PSDI, PRI & PLI) used their majority to limit the delegation to their members. Thus, Socialist experience of the European Assembly was limited to the activity of two PSDI members. The PSU's attitude towards them has been, therefore, largely negative because representatives[1] are not elected by direct universal suffrage in all member countries. Italian representation has often not been complete. From 1957 until 1968 the delegation was not renewed and until the latter year PCI and old PSI members were excluded. Interest has also been limited by the lack of real powers of decision vested in the European Parliament, particularly in the financial sphere, and also the long distance to Strasbourg.

The DC, as the leading member of all postwar government coalitions, has been the prime mover of Italy's European policy, but its participation has been more active in the Community governmental institutions than in the European Parliament. In fact, the DC representatives have been disappointed with its work in Strasbourg, although much of the blame rests with themselves. The DC group elected in 1957 was the largest single group but participation by most members has been irregular. They claim this situation is a result of the work-burden and the responsibilities which most of them have assumed in Italy. Moreover, the Assembly's lack of real power dampens any enthusiasm which might have persuaded them to make the journey from Rome to Strasbourg more often. As it is, many of them consider the debates purely academic[1]. Recently,

---

[1] It was the leader of the PSDI, Saragat, when Foreign Minister in 1964, who announced Italy's intention to pursue this objective as a cardinal part of its European policy.

however, it is claimed that there has been a rebirth of interest in European problems within the party in reaction to Gaullist policies which, it is believed, have been gaining ground through lack of participation by Italian representatives. In consequence, the party has sponsored a bill for the election of Italian representatives to the European Parliament by universal suffrage, but so far agreement has not been reached with the PSU and PRI for its enactment and implementation.

The PRI and PLI have also made notable contributions to Italian Europeanism despite their size. This has been the work mainly of Sforza (as Foreign Minister) and La Malfa for the PRI, and Martino (as Foreign Minister) for the PLI.

CONCLUSIONS

The similarity between Italian parties is striking. All claim, more or less, to represent an exclusive ideological point of view.[2] In addition, they have all attempted to follow the PCI and give themselves a highly articulated branch-type structure and to sponsor permanent satellite organizations and a party press. Two parties, PCI and DC, have been more successful than the rest. Nonetheless, despite local differences, control of all parties lies with the party leaders through the paid career officials who control, in turn, local section meetings and the provincial congresses which elect the delegates to party congresses. Factionalism exists in all parties; it is more severe in the DC and Socialist Parties than in the minor parties and PCI. In the latter its existence is formally denied; in other parties the practice has been to have each faction represented on the national organs. Party policy, therefore, is debated and decided at the top.

In spite of the evident control of parties by a restricted *elite*, direct membership is considerably higher than in any comparable Western European country. However, as has already been suggested, membership is for the most part purely passive; it has tended to be that of a

[1] This view was not limited to the European Parliament. In 1963, Piero Malvestiti, former DC Minister, resigned from the Presidency of the ECSC High Authority in 1963 to seek re-election to the Italian Parliament for Milan.
[2] I.e., Communism, Socialism, Republicanism, Catholicism, Monarchism and Fascism.

vague act of faith rather than a rational political decision. Many studies have documented the low level of political education of the majority of the electorate. The parties have catered for this situation by trying to impose their subculture on as large a part of the population as possible by providing supporters with a closed social system where most of their needs and aspirations can be fulfilled and where the degree of identification with the party is not limited to politics. The origin of this system is to be sought in the backward economic development of the country in the late nineteenth century. The Fascist Party developed the 'membership card' mentality by making it obligatory for appointment to certain posts. It has remained and been exploited by all parties in the Republican period, but its efficacy has depended on what each individual party has been able to provide. For the reasons explained above, the PCI and DC have been most successful since in certain areas their party-sponsored centres are often the only gathering places.

This situation has a number of implications which explain the *elitism* characteristic of Italian politics and the working of the party system.[1] In the first place, the large number of ideological party choices which so many all-inclusive systems present to the electorate call for a considerable degree of sophistication on its part. This it does not have through lack of education, both formal and political. Hence, it is unable to understand the consequences of the basic party choices, much less appreciate those offered by the subtleties of party factions. Most members of the electorate tend to react either by joining the strongest party in the neighbourhood for protection or by ignoring politics altogether.

In the second place, political participation, and, in fact, educational attainment rather than social class is the most important single direct factor determining entry into party political leadership. Of course, social class is the key to educational opportunity. Today 45 per cent of the PCI national leaders have a university degree and only 2 per cent are either self-taught or do not have a primary school-leaving certificate. All the mass parties have tended, in fact, to split themselves into two levels: (i) at the grass-roots, where a co-operative and associative life is organized which is oriented,

[1] This and other points are outlined in A. Pizzorno, *Schema teorico sui partiti in Italia*, paper presented to the Congress on parties held at Sinisgalia in September 1967, mimeographed MSS., pp. 43–61.

within a particular system of values, towards recreational activities rather than towards political discussions; (ii) at the federal and national levels, where political discussion is the centre of activity. The local sections comprise homogeneous social and cultural groups in which formally educated people seem out of place. Thus, those interested in a political career must accede to the federal level: a university education normally permits a person direct entry.

In the third place, implicit in the isolation, in terms of communication and comprehension, of party leaders from their rank and file supporters, is the pressure to complicate political issues instead of simplifying them. In this way small groups justify their assumption of greater power than would be warranted if more people could understand the issues involved and so demand a voice in what was said. Hence the multiplication of factional positions at the top of Italian parties. Moreover, since no party can pretend to a clear majority, the subtle work of ideological distinction presented by the party *elite* to the rank and file in defence of its activity is usually passed over in the vulgar compromises of place distribution which are the basis of each successive coalition cabinet. These ideological subtleties are often, therefore, no more than fictions to justify the present *status quo* which must be judged advantageous to the *elites* of all parties, since they continue to promote them in all earnestness.

The principal characteristics of the working of the Italian party system have already been described as cabinet instability based on electoral stability and resulting in political immobility. The nature of cabinet instability is the 'musical chairs' of continuous coalition between the same partners: frequent change of office but rare changes of personnel. The number of persons holding ministerial office has been restricted. During the period 1946–63, 102 persons became Ministers (of whom 63 were in the DC) in 17 cabinets. Moreover, although it was easier to reach office in one of the minor parties, the chances of holding office for any length of time were correspondingly less. DC ministers have often retained office for long periods; in the cases of some, like Andreotti, Taviani and Colombo, almost continuously for twenty years. Finally, the systematic exclusion of the PCI from government responsibilities since 1947 has meant not only a wilful limitation on the source of potential ministerial personnel, but, more importantly, has restricted the social area of recruitment of ministers. It has been seen that, whereas the PCI is the only party which recruits national leaders and parliamentarians in any numbers from the working class and the peasantry, the DC almost exclusively recruits its national leadership from the middle classes.

This situation is very important in the appreciation of government performance. It has been argued that the system has promoted political immobility because it gives no incentive to the government parties to pursue dynamic forward-looking programmes. On the contrary, it has placed a premium on passivity because it is feared that a breach of the *status quo* would destroy the fragile equilibrium which has been so laboriously established. Despite the big build-up of pressing reforms, the introduction of new forces in the 1960s, in the shape of the 'opening to the left', almost brought about the collapse of the party system. Yet it can also be argued that the political system does function. Any assessment of the working of the political system as opposed to the party system means widening the scope of the discussion to include the relations between the government and other institutions, such as the administration and the powerful economic groups. In terms of power, the question can be formulated thus: what degree of autonomy do the political leaders have in relation to economic and bureaucratic leaders? This is an extremely complex problem and it is not easy to come to any concrete conclusions. Lack of information is one difficulty; the fact that the politician and the financier, industrialist or civil servant often have similar goals is another. Moreover, the probability of common goals is likely to be increased in a society, such as in Italy, where the economic, bureaucratic and political leaders come from similar social backgrounds. In fact, over 80 per cent of Italian Ministers come from the upper middle class and over 90 per cent have a degree (two thirds in law!).

One of the principal elements dictating the relationship between politicians and industrialists has been the conditions governing postwar politics, namely, the fact that Italy found itself in the Western camp and chose the reconstruction of a capitalist system. Development in the complexity of the capitalist system has led to a *rapprochement* between the public and private sectors of the economy. Despite the extension of the public sector the government has not chosen to orient the economy in new directions. Control has even benefited the private sector. For example, there have been financial sacrifices by the State to encourage certain activities, the profits of which have accrued to private individuals. Meynaud considers that this situation demonstrates the subordination of the government to business interests. 'It tends to confer on public servants the status of devoted administrators of capitalist interests. On this basis, the degree of autonomy of political leaders to private business is obviously limited'. He adds, however, that it is impossible to state categorically that political leaders have no autonomy of economic leaders: rather they have preferred not to act autonomously.

The position of bureaucratic leaders is somewhat different from that of economic leaders. Firstly, it is necessary to bear in mind the *meridionalizzazione* of the administration. Two-thirds of the top civil servants are recruited from the southern intelligentsia, who have had a humanist and legal training and so are less well armed to compete with the technical competence of northern industrial personnel. Secondly, the Italian civil service is notoriously inefficient, resulting from a spread-the-work policy, antiquated and time-consuming methods, and general lack of an overall plan. Finally, there has been the growing politicization of the administration which has coincided with growing intervention by the state in social and economic activity. In concrete terms, this means that a greater proportion of posts now fall within executive appointment. The justification for this is the need to co-ordinate policy, but since the government has increasingly been unable to come to an agreement among its members on what that policy should be, the ability to appoint to these posts has become a symbol of a party's political strength, which it cannot afford to renounce.[2] Appointment becomes a mechanism for ensuring the support of certain groups. Although political leaders in Italy would seem more independent of the administration than in some European countries, such as France, the machine is much less capable of carrying out a coherent policy. Its greatest achievement is the carrying on of routine administration.

For the reasons outlined, it can be said that the political system has been oriented in the interests of the great industrial groups (FIAT, Montecatini, Edison etc.) and many of the important decisions, particularly in the economic sphere, have been taken

[1] J. Meynaud, *Rapport sur la classe dirigeante italienne*, Lausanne, 1964, Etudes de Sciences Politiques, No. 9, p. 318.

[2] A typical example is the letter of C. Santoro of the PSDI National Secretariat to A. Corsi, President of INPS, of March 11, 1963, published in the supplement to *L'Espresso* of March 13, 1966.

outside the formal institutions of government. It was to introduce some order into an area that was becoming increasingly chaotic that new machinery for economic planning (*la programmazione*) was set up in the 1960s.

The stability of the party system, it was stated at the outset, was due to the combination of four factors: two of which can be considered structual and the other two environmental. The structural factors are the avoidance of problems touching the fundamental interests of powerful groups and the proportional representation electoral system. It need only be said of the former that all governments and particularly the 'centre-left' coalition have had to rue the day they tried to overlook the importance of this factor. However, the back-log of uninitiated and incomplete reforms is becoming such that a point may be reached in which immobility can become as dangerous for the party system as feverish reforming activity. The two environmental factors are the consequences of the cold war and the ideological tradition of the leading parties. Their impact has been diminishing. The effect of recent economic developments is to destroy the subcultures on which the present party structures were chiefly built. There has already been a crisis of membership and participation in advanced urban industrial zones to which the parties have responded, as it were, by 'electoralizing' themselves. But since elections cannot alter the political situation, in the immediate future, their nature has imperceptibly changed. They are no longer an intra-party battle with a clear political choice but have become a party rite, as in single party states, for the celebration of the renewal of their legitimacy, i.e., the parties use electoral campaigns not to win adhesion to a particular political platform but rather to extract from an unwilling electorate recognition of the right to occupy ministerial office (for the government party) and to sit in Parliament (for the opposition).[1]

---

[1] The personal advantage to be gained from a parliamentary career can be seen from the following privileges which members enjoy: free first-class travel on all Italian trains; free first- and second-class tickets for members of their family and dependants; free carriage by rail of heavy luggage; 48 free journeys annually by sleeper; free hair-cut in Monecitorio and Palazzo Madama and free permanent wave and *mise en plis* for women members; free bath and shower service; free transport on Rome municipal bus service; free entry to all cinemas, members of AGIS; reduction on price of theatre tickets; free tickets for sporting events; and exemption from all taxes and contributions. Quoted in M. C. Sforza, *L'Uomo Politico*, Florence, Vallecchi, 1963, p. 241.

All parties have tended to imitate the PCI's strategy and see their role as the occupation of many of the key posts in civil society, with the difference that whereas the PCI hoped by occupation to transform society, the government parties' operation has been one of patronage; the occupation of key posts *per se*. This operation has reduced them almost to the role of defenders of sectional interests. They can achieve more than interest groups, not because they embody general interests, but because control of state apparatus at national and local level gives them the right to patronage. It was because the government parties had so reduced the sphere of their action that the 'opening to the left' and Socialist reunification were promoted. In this way, it was hoped to introduce a certain mobility into the system as well as effect a number of urgent reforms. It failed, as was forseeable, because the Socialist parties were too weak to provide a credible alternative to the DC and were quickly assimilated to vassal status. To provide a credible alternative, the PSU needed to be autonomous of both DC and PCI. Autonomy from the DC meant it being in the position to form an alternative parliamentary majority with the PCI, while autonomy from the PCI meant it being a serious electoral rival of it. But, as has been stated, it lacked both these conditions: there is no chance at present that a left-wing coalition would win a parliamentary majority; and in such an alliance the PSU would inevitably fall under the hegemony of the PCI because it is weak where its rival is strong (i.e. among the workers, in the CGIL, in the League of Co-operatives, as a 'vehicle' of social promotion for the proletarian classes, etc.).

The Italian party system is static and yet the economic and social framework in which it operates is changing. The elements on which its stability were founded are dissolving, albeit slowly, and yet all attempts to introduce political mobility have so far foundered, or so it seems. Moreover, the number of urgent reforms are piling up. In this light, it is easy to view the system with despair. But it must be remembered that the Republican regime has already outlived Fascism and there are no inherent reasons why, in the absence of external crises, it should not be able to tackle the problems facing it individually and resolve them within the existing system. To do this it would need to associate new forces in government, as it has already done in 1947 (association of the Social Democrats) and 1963 (association of Socialists) to prevent the antithesis between the government and the country becoming irreparably great. In this perspective, movement towards an Austrian-type situation (permanent coalition between the two principal parties, DC-PCI) rather than a French-type situation (new bi-polar left and right-wing alliances) is likely to be the rule. Such a development, however, could be thrown into the melting-pot by unforseen changes in the international situation, or in the direction of the Church. Already, an external event, the First World War interrupted Italy's first experiment in parliamentary democracy and some recent activities show that such solutions are still dreamed of in some quarters. Total disinterest in Italian politics by the Catholic Church could lead to a split in the DC between its conservative and progressive wings and the formation of two Catholic parties with incalculable consequences. This could bring about a political mobility which the party system has not yet known. In spite of the Second Vatican Council, however, it must be remembered that the Church still considers Italy its temporal dominion and is still a long way from permitting the development of a situation which it would be prepared to support or even encourage elsewhere.[1]

At the present time, the gravest danger to the system would still appear to come from within: a danger resulting from its inefficiency. So far, it has done sufficient to prevent the antithesis between the viability of the institutions and the credibility of the country from becoming unbearably great, although, on occasions, it has come, at least to the outside observer, perilously close to the brink.[2]

[1] In this connection, it is significant that Paul VI has reinstituted the Civic Committees in something like their Pre-John XXIII position of influence. On the politics of the Church, in general, see the recent study by *The Times* correspondent, P. Nicols, *The Politics of the Vatican*, London, Pall Mall, 1968, particularly, pp. 216–28.

[2] Areas where the belief in the viability of the parties and, particularly, their parliamentary role has broken down are the trade unions, the ACLI, and more recently, the student movement.

APPENDIX A

Election Results of National Parties 1946–1968 (votes, percentage and seats)

	1946			1948			1953			1958			1963			1968 (May 19, 1968)		
	Votes (mn)	%	Seats	Votes (mn)	%	Seats	Votes (mn)	%	Seats	Votes (mn)	%	Seats	Votes (mn)	%	Seats	Votes (mn)	%	Seats
PCI (FDP)	4·4	18·9	104	8·1	31·0	183 →	6·1	22·6	143	6·7	22·7	140	7·8	25·3	166	8·6	26·9	177
PSIUP/PSI/PSIUP	4·8	20·7	115				3·4	12·7	75	4·2	14·2	84	4·3	13·8	87	1·4	4·5	23
US/PSDI/PSU				1·9	7·1	33	1·2	4·5	19	1·3	4·5	23	1·9	6·1	33	4·6	14·5	91
PRI	1·0	4·4	23	0·7	2·5	9	0·4	1·6	5	0·4	1·4	6	0·4	1·1	6	0·6	2·0	9
DC	8·1	35·1	207	12·7	48·4	304	10·8	40·1	263	12·5	42·3	273	11·8	38·3	260	12·4	39·1	266
UDN/PLI	1·6	6·8	41	1·0	3·8	19	0·8	3·0	13	1·0	3·5	14	2·1	7·0	39	1·9	5·8	31
BNL/Mon	0·6	2·8	16	0·7	2·8	14	1·9	6·9	40	1·4	4·8	25	0·5	1·7	8	0·4	1·3	6
UQ/MSI	1·2	5·3	30	0·5	2·0	6	1·6	5·8	29	1·4	4·8	25	1·6	5·1	27	1·4	4·5	23
Others	1·4	5·6	20	0·6	2·4	6	0·7	1·8	3	0·7	1·8	6	0·4	1·6	4	0·7	1·4	3
Total	22·9		556	26·2		574	27·0		590	29·5		596	30·7		630	31·9		630

Notes

PCI   includes FDP in 1948.

PSI   includes PSIUP in 1946 and 1968.

PSDI includes US in 1948 and PSU in 1968.

PLI   includes UDN in 1946 and BN in 1948.

Mon includes BNL in 1946, PNM in 1948 and 1953, PNM plus PMP in 1958 and PDIUM thereafter.

MSI   includes UQ in 1946.

Sources: For the elections of 1946, 1948, 1953 and 1958, G. Schepis 'Analisi statistica dei risultati' in A. Spreafico and J. La Palombara, *Elezioni e comportamento politico in Italia*, Milano, Comunita, 1963, pp. 329–406; for the 1963 election, P. A. Allum, 'The Italian Elections of 1963' in *Political Studies*, vol. XIII, No. 3, October 1965, pp. 326–45, at p. 333; for the 1968 elections, the Italian Press for May 21, 1968.

APPENDIX B
Parties' Share of National Vote*

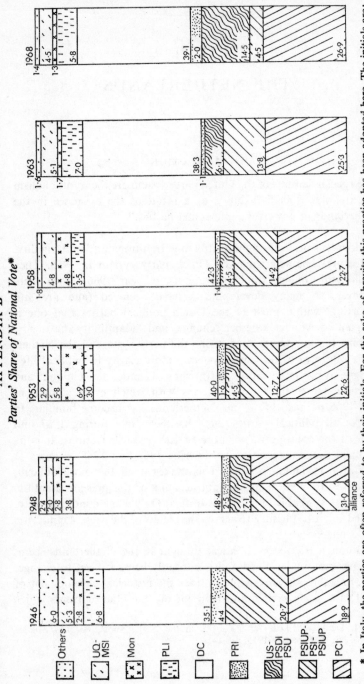

* In Italy, the parties are often referred to by their initials. For the sake of brevity this practice has been adopted here. The initials are: Italian Communist Party (PCI), Italian Socialist Party of Proletarian Unity (PSIUP), Unified Socialist Party (PSU), Italian Socialist Party (PSI), Italian Social Democrat Party (PSDI), Italian Republican Party (PRI), Christian Democrats (DC), Italian Liberal Party (PLI), Monarchists (PDIUM) and Neofascists (MSI).

CHAPTER 6

THE NETHERLANDS

INTRODUCTION

'The special features of the Dutch party system are the traditionalism and rigidity which it exhibits as a result of the existence in the Netherlands of powerful confessional parties.'[1]

Daalder was perfectly right in stressing 'traditionalism' and 'rigidity' as features characterizing the Dutch party system in 1955. They would still roughly apply till about the year 1966. Since then, however, so many developments have occurred (and are still occurring) within most of the Dutch political parties that one is tempted to wonder whether 'change' and 'adaptibility' have now become the key words to describe the party system of the Netherlands. 'Reform of the party system', 'more clarity in political life', 'progressive concentration', 'Christian Democratic Union', and 'election agreements' are the terms with which every student of post-1966 political life in the Netherlands has become familiar. In almost all political parties there has been talk during 1967 and 1968 of the splitting off of more or less 'radical' factions. It is by no means an exaggeration to describe 1967 and 1968 as years of confusion in Dutch politics. This makes it all the more difficult, therefore, to write a meaningful account of the present situation. The party system is in a process of flux. Only when conditions have settled will it be possible to survey the results of the present confusion and change.

Although traditional political thought in the Netherlands seems to have been undermined and is currently being subject to change, it is, nonetheless, worthwhile to trace the historical development of the Dutch party system and to point out the main currents which

[1] H. Daalder, 'Parties and Politics in the Netherlands', *Political Studies* Vol. 3, No. 1, February 1955, pp. 1–16.

have hitherto divided political thought in the Netherlands. A knowledge of the history of Dutch political parties is a necessary pre-requisite to understand the present desire for change.

Traditionally, three pillars (*zuilen*) carry the roof of Dutch society: the Roman Catholic, Protestant and 'general' or neutral pillar. These three *zuilen* are found in all fields of social and economic life. Trade Unions, employers' organizations, students' clubs, radio and television corporations, farmers' unions etc. are set up mainly along religious lines. A Dutchman cannot enter a club or organization without choosing beforehand between the three *zuilen* (although for many people this choice is made the moment they are born). *Verzuiling*, in its extreme form, is a typically Dutch phenomenon and not surprisingly this three-fold division exists in political life as well.

There have always been two major cleavages dividing the country into parties of the 'right' and parties of the 'left'.[1] One dividing line is formed by the difference between religious, or 'confessional' parties and the other parties. The three major religious parties are the Catholic People's Party (KVP), and two Protestant parties, namely, the Anti-Revolutionary Party (ARP) and the Christian Historical Union (CHU). The other dividing line between 'right' and 'left' is based on socio-economic factors, as in several other countries; representing the well-known dichotomy between 'conservatives' and 'progressives.' On the one hand, there are parties that stress the rights of free enterprise in a capitalistic society where government regulations and taxes should be held at a minimum and where the rights of the private individual should be strongly guaranteed. The Liberals who have operated throughout the years under various names and now call themselves the People's Party for Freedom and Democracy (VVD) fit in this category. The Farmers Party (BP), formed in 1958, is closer to the Liberals in this respect. On the other hand, there are those parties that stress the importance of underprivileged groups in society, who claim a special concern of the state and for whom the state should take the necessary social measures, which might go as far as the introduction of a greater or lesser degree of socialism, implying the nationalization of the

---

[1] Daalder, *op. cit.*, p. 6; and Arend Lijphart: *The Politics of Accommodation: Pluralism and Democracy in the Netherlands*, Berkeley and Los Angeles, University of California Press, 1968, pp. 16–58.

major means of production. The Labour Party (PVDA), the Pacifist Socialists (PSP) and the Communists (CPN) fall into this category. The three main religious parties have always claimed that they can combine both the 'progressive' and 'conservative' strains of thought thus eliminating the need for a political division along these lines. The Socialists and Liberals maintain on the contrary that there is no need for religious parties.

One result of all these differences of opinion is that there exists a great number of parties in the Netherlands. In March 1968 12 political parties were represented in Parliament, and 23 had participated in the elections of February 1967.

HISTORICAL ROOTS

The primacy of parliament in the Netherlands dates from the second half of the nineteenth century. In 1848 full ministerial responsibility was written into the constitution. It is commonly agreed that the parliamentary system of government was established in the cabinet crises of 1867–68, when it became the accepted practice for the cabinet to have the support of a parliamentary majority. No longer could the King form cabinets against the will of the majority of Parliament.[1] It was in this period that the first political parties were founded. In the beginning they consisted mainly of 'conservative', 'liberal', Protestant and Catholic Members of Parliament, who were loosely held together by their common political views. 'Political parties' in the modern sense developed when the grant of subsidies to religious schools and the extension of the suffrage became political issues. The Liberal cabinet of 1878 felt that all people had a right to free, 'neutral' state education, but that those parents who wanted to send their children to religious schools should pay for this privilege out of their own pockets. Many Protestants and Roman Catholics, however, considered it anti-religious discrimination to pay taxes for the neutral schools as well as paying for the religious education of their own children. A petition movement against the Education Act of the government was organized, attracting 300,000 signatures out of the total population of a little over 4 million.

[1] E. van Raalte, *Het Nederlandse Parlement,* 's-Gravenhage, Staatsdrukkerij en Uitqeverijbedrijf, 1960, pp. 3–4.

The Protestant Parties

Out of the petition movement of 1878 the oldest Dutch political party was born, the Anti-Revolutionary Party, which rejected the principle of popular sovereignty of the French revolution (therefore 'anti-revolutionary') and stressed instead the sovereignty of God. It consisted mainly of strongly Calvinist elements. The Anti-Revolutionary Party became the party of the *kleine luyden* ('small people'); including Calvinist farmers and shopkeepers, most of whom belonged to a separate Calvinist church, the *Gereformeerde Kerk*. This party now draws its intellectual strength from the Free (Calvinist) University in Amsterdam, founded in 1880, where many of its most famous politicians and statesmen received their education.

In 1894 a group of less orthodox Protestant parliamentarians, who were opposed to the extension of the suffrage, left the Anti-Revolutionary Party. In 1908 they founded the Christian Historical Union, which to this day is the second important Protestant political party. It differs from the ARP in that most of its voters belong to the *Nederlands Hervormde Kerk*, the largest Protestant church in the country. Its party organization is less tight than that of the ARP. Indeed, members of the CHU often stress the fact that theirs is a 'union', not a party, suggesting that a wide range of individual opinion is allowed within its ranks. It usually supports the cabinet, whether or not it is represented there. Even for many Dutchmen it is hard to understand the essential difference between ARP and CHU;[1] for many Protestants it is mainly a matter of having been born in one or the other. It has often been suggested that the two parties should merge. Although at the local level they often work closely together, the CHU—being the weaker of the two—has always been opposed to a national merger. Such a joint Protestant party would probably be dominated by the leaders of the ARP, whose party is the more militant and better organized. It is also

[1] Daalder's remark written in 1955 is still entirely valid: 'It is extremely difficult to explain to foreigners what a world of difference lies between the adherents of these two parties. The Christian-Historicals insist more strongly on the positive Calvinist character of the state, but are opposed less strongly to "pagan" elements and are thus potentially less isolationist; they will give the government of the day either active co-operation or the benefit of the doubt. The Anti-Revolutionaries, on the other hand, are more militant, more of a *parti de masse*, and more sternly against non-Calvinists, although they tend to insist less that the state should be positively Calvinist and to assert rather more the doctrine of "spheres of sovereignty".' Daalder, *op. cit.*, p. 3, note 3.

generally conceded that such a joint party might receive fewer votes at the polls than the combined total of the two. The two ultra-orthodox Calvinist parties, State Reformed Party (SGP) and Reformed Political Association (GPV), who regularly receive around 2 per cent and 0·7 per cent of the national vote respectively, are not seriously considered in any plans for merging the Protestant parties.

The Roman Catholic Party

Roman Catholics have traditionally formed a minority group in the Netherlands. Heavily concentrated in the two southern provinces of Noord-Brabant and Limburg they were for a long time treated as second-class citizens. For 150 years after the Peace of Westphalia of 1648, the southern provinces were virtually governed as colonies of the north and retained the status of occupied territories (*generali-teitslanden*). One of the reasons for this discriminatory treatment may have been that the Protestants in the north did not trust the Catholic south; fearing that it might try to join the other Roman Catholic provinces in what is today Belgium, which remained under Spanish and later Austrian rule. This discrimination was formally ended under the French rule (1795–1813). During the nineteenth century the Roman Catholics fought for, and gradually achieved, full equal rights and treatment with the rest of the population.

It took a long time before the Roman Catholics organized themselves politically. Roman Catholic Members of Parliament worked, at first, closely with the Liberals; this resulted in the restoration of the episcopal hierarchy (1853).[1] Later they switched their support to the Anti-Revolutionary Party, with whom they shared an interest in obtaining state financial aid to religious education. This led to the 'monster alliance' of Roman Catholics and orthodox Protestants, which formed the first coalition government of 1888. There were many more to follow in later years.

In 1896 the Roman Catholic representatives in Parliament agreed

---

[1] Bone notes, citing Van Eekeren, that the alliance was a very one-sided affair, with the Catholics running behind the Liberal chariot and eagerly trying to be the best of clients in hope of further favours. He calls the Liberal–Catholic alliance 'a classic illustration of a political *marriage de convenance*'. See Robert C. Bone, 'The Dynamics of Dutch Politics', *The Journal of Politics*, Vol. XXIV, 1962, p. 33, note 31, quoting Wilhelmus A. M. van Eekeren, *The Catholic People's Party in the Netherlands*, unpublished Ph.D. dissertation, Georgetown University, Washington D.C., 1956, pp. 19–27.

on a common programme, and in 1904 a Roman Catholic union of electoral associations was founded. However, it was only in 1926, after general suffrage and proportional representation had been adopted, that the Roman Catholic State Party was formed. After the Second World War the party was reborn as the Catholic People's Party, which on a more progressive programme again drew the majority of the Roman Catholic voters.[1] It is not an ecclesiastical party, but considers itself to be founded on Christian principles and on the moral norms embodied in the natural order and divine revelation as explained by the authoritative teachings of the Church. Everyone who adheres to these same principles is invited to join the party. This means, in practice, that probably only Catholics are members of the party, while few non-Catholics vote for it. Its representatives in the two chambers of Parliament are all Roman Catholics. With the exception of the elections of 1952 and of 1956, the Catholic People's Party has always emerged as the strongest political party in the postwar period (see Table I). Being the largest party and a party of the centre, no coalition could be formed without it. The KVP has been represented in all postwar cabinets. The cabinets of 1946–48, 1959–66 and the present cabinet were led by a Catholic Prime Minister. Roman Catholics now form the largest religious group in the Netherlands, although the country is often wrongly referred to abroad as a Protestant nation. The era of discrimination against Roman Catholics is over.[2]

The Liberals

The Liberals were most influential during and after the reforms of 1848, which were introduced by their great leader Thorbecke,

[1] Bone comments however: 'In December 1945, the then Roman Catholic State Party changed its name to Catholic People's Party and went through the motions of turning itself into a Christian Democratic Party. But neither in terms of policies nor electoral support has there been any notable difference between pre- and post-war period, and the party has continued as the political spokesman for the Catholic "camp" in the Netherlands.' (Bone, *op. cit.*, p. 37, note 39.)

[2] However, compare Bone's quotation from Van Eekeren's unpublished dissertation on the Catholic People's Party, where he cites a secret report of 1954 of the Catholic Institute for Social-Ecclesiastical Research. The report noted that, although as of 1954 Catholics constituted 38 per cent of the population of the Netherlands, Catholic civil servants in the leading ministries averaged only about 10 per cent of total personnel. Van Eekeren, *The Catholic People's Party in the Netherlands*, as quoted by Bone, *op. cit.*, p. 27, note 14.

TABLE I

Dutch Election Results for the Second Chamber of Parliament, 1946-67

	1946		1948		1952		1956	
		% Seats		% Seats		% Seats		% Seats
Number of registered voters	5,275,888		5,433,663		5,792,679		6,125,210	
Number of votes cast	4,912,015		5,089,582		5,501,726		5,849,652	
Number of valid votes cast	4,760,711		4,932,959		5,335,745		5,727,742	
Catholic People's Party (KVP)	1,466,510	30·8 / 32	1,531,326	31 / 32	1,529,464	28·7 / 30	1,815,363	31·7 / 49
Labour Party (PvdA)	1,347,664	28·3 / 29	1,263,366	25·6 / 27	1,545,414	29 / 30	1,872,131	32·7 / 50
People's Party for Freedom and Democracy (VVD)	305,202	6·4 / 6*	391,982	7·9 / 8	471,005	8·8 / 9	502,377	8·8 / 13
Anti-Revolutionary Party (ARP)	614,177	12·9 / 13	651,717	13·2 / 13	603,269	11·3 / 12	567,556	9·9 / 15
Christian Historical Union (CHU)	373,191	7·9 / 8	453,211	9·2 / 9	476,175	8·9 / 9	482,886	8·4 / 13
Communist Party (CPN)	502,935	10·6 / 10	381,953	7·7 / 8	328,571	6·2 / 6	272,210	4·8 / 7
Other parties	151,032	3·1 / 2	259,404	5·4 / 3	381,847	7·1 / 4	215,219	3·7 / 3

	1959		1963		1967	
		% Seats		% Seats		% Seats
Number of registered voters	6,427,864		6,748,611		7,452,776	
Number of votes cast	6,143,409		6,419,964		7,076,328	
Number of valid votes cast	5,999,531		6,258,521		6,878,030	
Catholic People's Party (KVP)	1,895,914	31·6 / 49	1,996,865	31·9 / 50	1,822,904	26·5 / 42
Labour Party (PvdA)	1,821,285	30·3 / 48	1,750,808	28 / 43	1,620,112	23·5 / 37
People's Party for Freedom and Democracy (VVD)	732,658	12·2 / 19	643,236	10·3 / 16	738,202	10·7 / 17
Anti-Revolutionary Party (ARP)	563,091	9·4 / 14	545,438	8·7 / 13	681,060	9·9 / 15
Christian Historical Union (CHU)	486,429	8·1 / 12	536,521	8·6 / 13	560,032	8·1 / 12
Communist Party (CPN)	144,542	2·4 / 3	173,457	2·8 / 4	248,422	3·6 / 5
Other parties	355,612	6 / 5	612,196	9·7 / 11	1,206,298	17·7 / 22

* The figure for 1946 is the figure of the Party for Freedom, which was the predecessor of the People's Party for Freedom and Democracy.
Sources: Most of the figures in this table were obtained from: G. H. Scholten and G. Ringnalda, An International Guide to Electoral Statistics: Chapter on the Netherlands, Amsterdam, mimeographed paper, 1962.

founder of the present constitutional set-up of the country. In 1885 the Liberal Party was formally established, but it soon split into a radical and a more conservative wing. Though both were overwhelmingly anti-clerical, they sharply disagreed on such matters as labour laws and the extension of the franchise. The introduction of general suffrage and the system of proportional representation in 1917 weakened the more conservative Liberal Party, which declined from 15 per cent of the national vote in 1918 to 7 per cent in 1937. The more radical Liberal-Democratic Party remained at a steady level of 5 per cent of the national vote.

After the Second World War the Liberals reunited. The Party for Freedom founded in 1946 merged in 1948 with groups from other parties and this led to the establishment of the People's Party for Freedom and Democracy (VVD), which is now the third strongest party in Parliament (see Table I). It draws its support at the polls mainly from the higher and middle income groups: businessmen, doctors, lawyers, secondary school teachers, high and medium-level employers, managers, civil servants, shopkeepers and farmers. The party stresses the virtues of free enterprise, individual initiative and freedom of choice, both in the intellectual and in the economic fields.

The Socialists
The first Socialist Member of Parliament was F. N. Domela Nieuwenhuis who entered the Second Chamber in 1888. His Social Democratic Union became more and more anarchistic and anti-parliamentarian. This was one of the reasons why P. J. Troelstra and others founded the Social Democratic Workers Party (SDAP) in 1894, which explicitly wanted to use parliamentarian methods to improve the working conditions in industry and to shorten working hours. Its aim was to establish the common ownership of the means of production. General suffrage was to become a weapon in the class struggle. Later, when general suffrage did not bring the party the clear and overwhelming majority it had hoped for, it stressed socialization, national disarmament, state pensions and (since 1935) a planned national economy. When the fascist movements gained strength in Germany and Italy, the Dutch socialists abandoned their programme of national disarmament. In the period between the two world wars, the SDAP never received more than 20–24 per

cent of the popular vote. It remained an uneasy opposition group in Parliament until 1939, when two socialist Ministers entered the cabinet. After the Second World War the Socialists merged with radical Liberals, progressive Roman Catholics and members of the CHU into the Labour Party (PvdA) which in vain tried to 'break through' the old divisions along religious lines. The PvdA broke away completely from the anti-clerical past of its predecessor and tried to enclose Catholics and Protestants within its ranks. Although it became larger than the prewar SDAP, the 'break-through' failed to materialise to any large extent. Until 1959 the Labour Party participated in all postwar coalitions. In 1965 and 1966 it became again a coalition partner. During the rest of the time it formed the largest opposition party. It draws its support mainly from skilled industrial workers, white collar workers and also from civil servants.

In 1957 a group of left-wing socialists and pacifists founded the Pacifist Socialist Party (PSP), which has fought for unilateral disarmament and withdrawal of the Netherlands from the NATO alliance. It receives between 2–4 per cent of the vote and draws its support from workers and left-wing intellectuals.

In 1909 a group of Marxist intellectuals seceded from the Socialist Party and founded the Social Democratic Party, which was later renamed Communist Party of Holland (CPH) and which is now known as the Communist Party of the Netherlands (CPN). It draws its strength mainly from industrial and dock-workers in Amsterdam and neighbouring districts and the agrarian north. The party obtained its largest number of votes in 1946, when, due to the excellent work of many Communists in the resistance movement and the war-time alliance of the Netherlands with the Soviet Union, it polled 10 per cent of the vote. Since then, it has steadily declined in strength. It received 3 per cent of the vote in 1967 (see Table I). In recent years it has shifted its focus from Moscow to a more independent course.

RECENT DEVELOPMENTS

The present condition of political change and uncertainty in the Netherlands originated with the success of the Farmers Party, which was founded in 1958. It received 2·1 per cent of the vote at the parliamentary elections in 1963. At the provincial elections of

March 1966 it increased its overall percentage to 6·7 per cent and, later, at the municipal elections of June 1966, it received its highest percentage when it polled around 9 per cent of the overall vote.[1] In the parliamentary elections in 1967 it got 4·8 per cent of the votes, which resulted in seven parliamentary seats. The Farmers Party had been established in reaction to what was thought to be too much of governmental interference in areas regarded as preserves of a private citizen. Many farmers were especially annoyed with the activities of the *Landbouwschap*, a semi-governmental agency having regulatory and taxing powers in the field of agriculture. They protested against the levies of this agency. which many refused to pay. In a few cases this led to the forced sale of farms by writ of execution, which increased the bitterness. Apart from this, a more general feeling of uneasiness and dissatisfaction (*onbehagen*) about the way the government was running affairs as well as the inability of ordinary people to change conditions was beginning to prevail in the mid-1960s. This uneasiness was symbolized and voiced by the Farmers Party, whose voters were by no means restricted to farmers; in 1966 it received 9·4 per cent of the vote in Amsterdam, 7·2 per cent in Rotterdam and 10·9 per cent in The Hague. The success of the Farmers Party can be attributed to a large extent to the demagogic but popular presentation of its leader, Hendrik Koekoek, who continually campaigned against the growing bureaucratization of the nation's government. In contrast to most other politicians he spoke in a language which the common man could understand. As his party offered only few positive alternatives,[2] he was often ridiculed in Parliament by his fellow-parliamentarians, although, when seen on television, this helped to increase his popularity among some of the voters.

In addition to the success of the Farmers Party, Daudt has pointed to several other signs of growing dissatisfaction among the

[1] As the same parties did not participate in all municipal elections, it is hard to give an entirely valid overall result. In 131 of the 928 municipalities with 6·7 million inhabitants (54 per cent of the national population) the Farmers' Party received 8·8 per cent of the vote (see *Keesing's Historisch Archief*, June 10, 1966, p. 358).

[2] 'Its ideology is a curious mixture of authoritarianism, individual self-reliance, direct interest appeal and considerable demagogy.' See H. Daalder, 'The Netherlands: Opposition in a Segmented Society', in Robert A. Dahl (ed.), *Political Oppositions in Western Democracies*, New Haven, etc., Yale University Press, 1966, p. 234.

voters.[1] He mentions the decline in the aggregate strength of the five major parties from 91·5 per cent (in 1956) to 78·8 per cent (in 1967); the findings of a 1966 sample survey in which 53 per cent of the respondents said that the voters ought to have more influence and that political parties ought to reflect better the voters' preferences, and where 68 per cent said that there was hardly any difference in the activities of the five major parties;[2] and the findings of a 1967 sample survey in which 46 per cent of the respondents agreed with the statement: 'the main parties are all alike', and 50 per cent of the respondents agreed that the voters should elect not only the Members of Parliament but the Prime Minister as well.[3]

Towards the end of 1966 a new party appeared on the Dutch political scene, 'Democrats '66' (D'66), which was founded by a group of journalists, civil servants and university members. They had several objections to the existing system of government, one of which was that the political composition of the cabinet should not be changed without consultation of the voters, as had happened in 1965 when VVD and CHU left the coalition and PvdA came in. They proposed several constitutional reforms which would give the voters a greater say in the formation of the cabinet. This, they suggested, could be achieved by having the Prime Minister directly elected by the voters. The candidates for office would present themselves to the voters with a proposed programme of government and a suggested list of ministers. In addition, in order to bridge the gap between the electors and the elected, they advocated that proportional representation should be abolished and a majority system of voting based on electoral districts introduced. Agreeing with those voters who feel that the five major parties offer insufficient alternatives D'66 expects to achieve an 'explosion' of the party system; doing away with most of the existing political parties (including D'66 itself) and replacing them by two or three major political blocs which could offer the voters clearer alternatives at

[1] H. Daudt, 'Party System and Voters' Influence in the Netherlands', mimeographed paper for the Third International Conference on Comparative Political Sociology, Berlin, January 16–20, 1968, p. 6.

[2] 'Politiek in Nederland,' *Revu*, December 17, 24 and 31, 1966, and January 7, 14 and 21, 1967; the material collected by Attwood Statistics is available at the 'Steinmetzstichting' in Amsterdam.

[3] Material collected by the Institute of Social Sciences of the Free University in Amsterdam.

the elections. This 'anti-party party'[1] surprised all Dutch politicians —and most Dutch political scientists—by winning 4·5 per cent of the vote at the 1967 election.

The success of D'66 has served as a catalyst to spur the other political parties into action. The new coalition cabinet, consisting of members of the Catholic People's Party, the Liberal and Anti-Revolutionary Party and the Christian Historical Union, announced the establishment of a Royal Commission to study the need for constitutional and electoral reforms. If possible, the government intended to introduce certain electoral reforms before the next parliamentary elections scheduled for 1971.

In the three main religious parties 'christian radical' groups have emerged, which attempt to make their parties steer a more progressive course. These christian radical groups, which operate within the Catholic People's Party, the Anti-Revolutionary Party and the Christian Historical Union, objected especially to the coalition that these parties formed with the Liberal Party in 1967. The three groups also held several joint meetings. In February 1968 a group of radical Catholics, including four Members of Parliament, left the Catholic People's Party and formed a new Radical Party. Partly in answer to the aspirations of the radicals, the leaders of the three largest religious parties have made proposals which would lead to an eventual merger of the three parties into a Christian Democratic Union. It remains to be seen what will be the final result of the developments within the religious parties. It should be added that in the Labour Party also, and even in the staid Liberal Party, 'radical' groups have emerged. The 'New Left' in the Labour Party, particularly, has argued strongly for a more radical socialist approach to economic policy, a sharp increase in economic aid to developing nations and a foreign policy that would be more independent of the United States. One of the leaders of the New Left group was elected to the parliamentary group of the Labour Party and several of its representatives were elected to the Party Executive. They have exerted an important influence on the composition of the party programme of the Labour Party.

Daalder, when writing in 1954, still considered a break-up of the

[1] See Sidney Verba, 'Some Dilemmas in Comparative Research', *World Politics*, Vol. XX, No. 1, October 1967, p. 124.

traditional alignments not very likely.[1] He could still mention the great aggregate strength of the five major political parties, pointing out that 'all other groups *combined* have at no time contained more than 16 per cent (in 1933) of the valid national vote.' In this respect, the results of the February 1967 elections were beyond all expectations, when the combined percentage of the 'other' parties rose to 21·2 per cent. It would be rash, indeed, to make any concrete predictions at this moment about the future course of Dutch political life. It is, however, worthwhile mentioning in this connection that dissatisfaction with the party system does not necessarily mean that there is an overall, fundamental dissatisfaction with life in general. Daalder writes for instance:

'Does all this point to fundamental dissatisfaction? Other data reveal a very high degree of satisfaction with present living standards and future economic prospects. Younger people sometimes seem to take a more positive attitude toward politics than older ones and rising educational levels tend to make for greater knowledge of political affairs. Perhaps the best conclusion one can draw is that most people are neither much worried nor much interested at the present time, and many realize that Dutch politics is not actually so important in view of the overwhelming role of international factors'.[2]

Other findings seem to offer support to this conclusion. Thus Daudt and Stapel found in 1965 that a majority of the voters (65 per cent) were satisfied with the working of the parliamentary system as a whole. Only 19 per cent felt that it did not work well, and 16 per cent gave no answer.[3]

CHARACTERISTICS OF THE PARTY SYSTEM

It should be clear by now that any description of the characteristics of Dutch political parties necessitates extreme caution. When such an attempt is made, it can only apply to data of the recent past,

[1] H. Daalder, 'The Netherlands: Opposition in a Segmented Society', Robert A. Dahl (ed.), *Political Oppositions in Western Democracies*, New Haven, etc., Yale University Press, 1966, p. 230.

[2] Daalder, *ibid.*, p. 232.

[3] H. Daudt and J. Stapel, 'Parlement, politiek en kiezer: verslag van een opinieonderzoek', *Acta Politica*, Vol. 1, Nos. 1–4 (1965–66), p. 55.

laying no particular claim for any applicability to the future.

Relations between Party and Parliamentary Group

The constitutional system of the Netherlands provides for a sharp distinction between the party organization and individual Members of Parliament. Article 96 of the constitution states: 'The members (of parliament) vote without mandate from or consultation with those who have elected them'.[1] Parliamentary groups often stress the fact that they have a special responsibility towards their *voters*, apart from what their *party* may think or want. However, the party organization retains a great deal of influence, since, in the system of proportional representation based on lists, it decides which members shall be candidates at the next parliamentary elections. In most parties the local branches may suggest names for the list of candidates, which are put in alphabetical order. The national party executive has the greatest influence, as it may add names to the lists suggested by the local branches and as it has a great say in the final composition of the list of candidates that is put before the voters.[2]

The executive of the Catholic People's Party has even greater powers. The regulations provide for a system of 'reserved seats' for people 'who are experts in important fields of political and public life'. These are safe seats, which are allocated apart from the regular procedure. The party executive may reserve one third of all available candidacies for this purpose. The electoral council, which consists in majority of members of the party executive, then decides on the precise places these experts may occupy on the lists of candidates. The individual members of the party cannot make changes in the places allocated to these experts. In view of this it is not surprising that Lipschits concluded that the nominating procedure in the Catholic People's Party has strongly oligarchical overtones.[3] Even

[1] This rule was inserted in the constitution to rule out traditional practices in the old Republic, where the members of the confederate assembly were required to consult with and obey the instructions of their respective provincial governments.

[2] I. Lipschits, 'De politieke partij en de selectie van candidaten', *Sociologische Gids*, Vol. X, No. 5, September–October 1963, p. 273–81; and 'Partijbestuur en fractie', *Acta Politica*, Vol. I, Nos. 1–4, 1965–66, p. 156–7.

[3] I. Lipschits, 'De politieke partij en de selectie van candidaten', *Sociologische Gids*, Vol. X, No. 5, September–Octobber 1963, p. 276.

the voters cannot change the order of candidates. Theoretically, a member of parliament may be elected by vote of preference outside the normal order of candidates. This happens very rarely. In the Catholic People's Party candidates are required to sign a statement prior to the elections that they will not accept their seats, if elected by preference vote, unless this is explicitly permitted by the party executive. In view of this regulation, it is no wonder that many people were shocked when in February 1968 four KVP members of parliament left the party, three of whom retained their parliamentary seats. This was obviously contrary to what the KVP Party Executive desired!

In the other political parties the influence of the executive is equally strong or almost as strong as in the Catholic People's Party. In one case it is even stronger: the regulations of the Communist Party entrust the executive with the composition of the lists of candidates in consultation with the district executives. In the other parties, the composition of the lists of candidates offers a slightly greater say to individual members. However, as there are no primary elections in the Netherlands and no law dealing with this matter, it is entirely left to the parties as to how much influence they give to individual members. Lipschits argues quite rightly that, if a law were made dealing with the organization of parties, as has occasionally been suggested, this important matter should not be left out of consideration.[1]

In view of the foregoing it should not be surprising to find that in all political parties there exists a strong relationship and much co-operation between the party executive and the parliamentary group. Basing himself on figures for 1965 Lipschits found that the executives of all major Dutch parties contained members of parliament. In the Catholic People's Party 14 per cent of the members of the central executive were members of parliament; in the Labour Party 36 per cent; in the Liberal Party 3 per cent; in the Anti-Revolutionary Party 7 per cent; in the Christian Historical Union 25 per cent; and in the Communist Party 9 per cent. In the daily executives of four parties this percentage was even higher: 44 per cent in the Catholic People's Party; 55 per cent in the Labour

[1] Lipschits, *ibid.*, p. 281; see also *Eindrapport van de Staatscommissie van advies inzake het hiesstelsel enfwettelijhe regeling der politieke partijen*, The Hague, 1958.

Party; 25 per cent in the Anti-Revolutionary Party; and 33 per cent in the Communist Party.[1] Lipschits concluded that there are strong personal ties between the parliamentary groups and the party executives. He also suggested that the party executives normally do have a great say in the composition of and the policies followed by its parliamentary groups.

Party Membership

Recently all parties have lost members, except for the Liberal People's Party for Freedom and Democracy, which conducted a successful membership drive in 1967 and gained 5,800 additional members. Although it is hard to come by reliable data, the following facts seem reasonably trustworthy:

the Catholic People's Party has lost members in recent years and has now 220,000 members, who pay an annual fee of three guilders;[1] the Labour Party lost 4,000 members in 1967 and has now 131,000, who pay between 5 and 30 guilders annually, depending on their income;[2] the People's Party for Freedom and Democracy has 38,000 members paying 25 guilders; the Anti-Revolutionary Party has 93,000 members who pay an annual fee of 12 guilders; the Christian Historical Union has 45,000 members, paying amounts of between 12 and 25 guilders; the Pacifist Socialist Party has 5,000 members paying an average of 30 guilders; Democrats '66 have 4,000 members who pay a minimum of 25 guilders, depending on their yearly income.[3]

A Dutch political party has on the average a membership that is about 10 per cent of its electoral strength. Only the Catholic

---

[1] I. Lipschits, 'Partijbestuur en fractie', *Acta Politica*, Vol. 1, Nos. 1–4, 1965–66, p. 168.

[2] £1 = 8·7 guilders.

[3] Figures from *Het Parool*, February 14, 1968. J. van den Berg, writing in 1967, listed the following membership figures: Catholic People's Party: more than 300,000; Labour Party: 140,000; Liberal Party: 35,000; Antirevolutionary Party; about 100,000; Christian Historical Union: 50,000. (J. van den Berg, *De Anatomie van Nederland* I (Amsterdam, De Bezige Bij, 1967), p. 69–85).

People's Party and the Anti-Revolutionary Party have a membership that is larger. Based on the election results of 1967, the Catholic People's Party has a membership of 12 per cent of its electorate; the Labour Party has 9 per cent; the People's Party for Freedom and Democracy 5 per cent; the Anti-Revolutionary Party 14 per cent; the Christian Historical Union 8 per cent; the Pacifist Socialist Party 2 per cent; and D'66 1 per cent.

No overall study has been made so far of the way in which the Dutch political parties are financed. Van den Berg quotes the official budget of the Anti-Revolutionary Party amounting to 576,700 guilders for 1967, 84 per cent of which is paid out of membership contributions.[1] It is often said that the Labour Party gets financial support from the socialist trade union, NVV, while the VVD is said to receive financial support from big industry and business interests. In 1965 Cramer published an account of receipts and expenditures based on figures furnished by the parties themselves. The annual expenditures of the five major parties were as follows: Catholic People's Party (1965), 1,084,500 guilders; Labour Party (1962–63), 1,571,450 guilders; Liberal Party (1963), 463,650 guilders; Anti-Revolutionary Party (1964), 473,100 guilders; Christian Historical Union (1963), 83,793 guilders. All except the Liberal Party stated that they were financed largely by contributions from their membership. The Catholic People's Party paid 96 per cent of its expenditures from membership contributions; the Labour Party, 91 per cent; the Anti-Revolutionary Party, 93 per cent; the Christian Historical Union, 98 per cent. The Liberal Party paid 28 per cent of its expenditures from membership contributions, while it financed 70 per cent of its budget from 'gifts and donations.'[2] Most of the parties seem to be greatly in need of funds. The Catholic People's Party and Democrats '66, among others, have repeatedly appealed to their voters to make financial contributions to the party. The government provides free radio and television time to all parties represented in Parliament. It has recently been suggested that it might subsidize other activities of the parties such as research work and study centres.[3]

[1] Van den Berg, *op. cit.*, p. 74–77.
[2] N. Cramer, 'Kasboek van onze partijen', *Het Parool*, March 6, 1965.
[3] Geld en Politiek, *De Volkskrant*, January 25, 1968.

Organizational Structure

The organizational structure of the various political parties shows much similarity. The complaint is often heard that members do not participate sufficiently in the activities of the parties and that there is too much of a gap between leaders and members. The organizational structure of the parties does not facilitate the bridging of that gap.[1] Most have several tiers of regional organs, culminating in the national organs of which there are usually four that are most important: the Congress, the Council, the Executive and the Daily Executives. The names differ for each individual party,[2] but the organs at similar levels of the hierarchy are more or less the same. Nevertheless, there are some differences. For instance, the regulations of the Catholic People's Party provide a much more limited role for the congress than those of the other political parties. Whereas the congresses of the Labour Party and the Christian Historical Union can give 'policy directions' to the party, elect the whole or part of the chief executive body and determine or change the party statutes, the congress of the Catholic People's Party can only 'discuss' the policy of the chief executive body. Only the congress of the People's Party for Freedom and Democracy can influence the lists of candidates for the parliamentary elections. Lipschits notes that the influence of the party congress is not as great as might be expected of this 'highest organ' of the party. They certainly cannot take any short-run decisions, if only because they meet only annually or once every two years.[3]

Most of the parties have a 'council' which takes over the functions of the congress, when the latter is not in session. The councils of all five major parties have some influence in determining the content of programmes and regulations. The councils are generally more important than the congresses in deciding party matters; they meet more often and are smaller in membership, thus presumably more efficient.

The size of the executive body varies between ten and fifty members. It conducts the general leadership of the party and has much influence upon the composition of the lists of candidates for the

[1] I. Lipschits, 'De organisatorische structuur der Nederlandse Politieke Partijen', *Acta Politica*, Vol. II, No. 4, 1966–67, p. 272–3.

[2] See for the variety in designations, Lipschits, *ibid.*, p. 270–1.

[3] Lipschits, *ibid.*, p. 283.

parliamentary elections. It calls meetings of the party congress and party council, of the chief executive itself and of the daily executive. Party members can only indirectly elect members to the chief executive, by electing representatives to the party congress. The daily executive has the day-to-day leadership of the party; it prepares and executes the decisions of the chief executive body. In some parties the daily executive is elected from the ranks of the chief executive body. In other parties the chairman, vice-chairman, secretary and treasurer are elected directly by the council or the congress.

Party Support

According to a nation-wide sample survey held in 1966 the Catholic People's Party draws the bulk of its support from the countryside, and the Labour Party from the cities and towns. Supporters of the Anti-Revolutionary Party, the Christian Historical Union and the Liberal Party seem to be about equally distributed over cities and the countryside. None of the major parties, however, is based solely on cities or the countryside.[1] (Sample survey information on the social characteristics of the 'voters' of the various political parties is used here as no similar data is available with regard to party 'membership'. A study of the members of the parties might, however, produce different results).

As far as age is concerned, the figures for the 1967 Election Study by the Free University show a great preponderance of young people (21–30 years) among the voters of D'66; 42 per cent, which is twice the overall percentage of this age group (see Table II). Also a relatively high percentage of voters of the Pacifist Socialist Party is found in the lowest age group. Both parties have relatively high percentages among the 'middle age' group, but fall off sharply in the oldest group. The Christian Historical Union has a relatively high percentage of voters (47 per cent) in the highest age group. The distribution of age among the voters of the Catholic People's Party, the Labour Party, the Liberal Party and the Anti-Revolutionary Party does not differ much from the overall age distribution.

[1] God in Nederland, Amsterdam, Van Ditmar, 1967, pp. 226–27; see also H. Daalder, Nederland: Het Politieke Stelsel, in *Repertorium van de Sociale Wetenschappen: Politiek*, L. van der Land (ed.), Amsterdam and Brussels, Elsevier, 1958, p. 236, and Lijphart, *op cit.*, p. 18.

TABLE II
Distribution of votes at 1967 election (by age group)

Party	Age-group (per cent)		
	21–30	31–50	51 and older
Catholic People's Party	20	40	40
Labour Party	18	41	41
Liberal Party	19	42	39
Anti-Revolutionary Party	21	38	41
Christian Historical Union	18	35	47
Farmers' Party	24	41	35
Pacifist Socialist Party	30	47	23
Democrats '66	42	44	14
Other parties	18	41	41
Total	21	40	39

Source: Social-Wetenschappelijk Instituut Vrije Universiteit Amsterdam, *De Nederlandse Kiezers in 1967*, Amsterdam, Agon Elsevier, 1967, p 50.

Figures available for the elections of 1967 showed a slight preference among women for voting for religious parties, and among men for non-religious parties. The percentage of women was especially high among the CHU voters; of men among the voters of the Farmers Party, the Pacifist Socialist Party and Democrats '66 (see Table III).

TABLE III
Distribution of votes at 1967 election (by sex)

Party	Men	Women	
	(per cent)		
Catholic People's Party	47	53	(100 = 1,045)
Labour Party	53	47	(100 = 1,001)
Liberal Party	50	50	(100 = 487)
Anti-Revolutionary Party	49	51	(100 = 397)
Christian Historical Union	39	61	(100 = 334)
Farmers' Party	60	40	(100 = 131)
Pacifist Socialist Party	64	36	(100 = 78)
Communist Party	54	46	(100 = 84)
Democrats '66	59	41	(100 = 257)

Source: Communication to the author supplied by courtesy of the staff of the Institute of Social Sciences of the Free University in Amsterdam.

Daalder's 1958 assessment of the distribution of incomes among the voters of the various parties is still substantially correct. He noted that the voters of the various parties can be put in the following order (from lowest income to highest): Communist Party, Labour Party, Catholic People's Party, Anti-Revolutionary Party, Christian Historical Union, Liberal Party.[1] Figures from the 1967 Election Study of the Free University show that no substantial changes have occurred (Table IV). Many supporters of the Farmers Party are

TABLE IV

Distribution of votes at 1967 election (by personal income) £1 = 8·7 guilders

Party	6,000–9,000	9,000–18,000	more than 18,000	No answer
		per cent		
Catholic People's Party	45	35	7	13
Labour Party	55	35	4	6
Liberal Party	23	35	28	14
Anti-Revolutionary Party	41	39	10	10
Christian Historical Union	49	31	8	12
Farmers' Party	57	26	5	12
Pacifist Socialist Party	50	39	8	3
Democrats '66	34	43	12	11
Total	45	35	9	11

Source: Sociaal-Wetenschappelijk Instituut Vrije Universiteit Amsterdam, *De Nederlandse Kiezers in 1967*, Amsterdam, Agon Elsevier, 1967, p. 50.

found in the lowest income group. This is probably true of the Communist party for which no information is available. The Pacifist Socialist Party follows closely after the Labour Party, while the Anti-Revolutionary Party and the Christian Historical Union seem to have changed positions. The new party, Democrats '66 fits in between the Anti-Revolutionary Party and the Liberal Party. Daalder noted that there were many industrial workers and pensioners amongst voters of the Communist and Labour Parties while the religious parties had many supporters amongst farmers and agricultural workers. The Liberal Party, in particular, counts

[1] Daalder, *ibid.*, p. 236.

many professional people among its voters. On the other hand, all parties have representatives of all skills and professions among their voters. Daalder noted in 1958 that about 86 per cent of the Roman Catholic voters voted for the Catholic People's Party. This figure is supported by the findings of the sample survey conducted by the Free University in 1967.[1] (see Table V).

TABLE V

Distribution of votes at 1967 election (by religion)

	Roman Catholic	Dutch Reformed	Reformed Church ('Gereformeerd')	Other No answer	No church
			per cent		
Catholic People's Party	98	—	—	—	2 (1045)
Labour Party	9	44	1	8	38 (1001)
Liberal Party	17	40	2	12	29 (487)
Anti-Revolutionary Party	5	23	61	8	3 (397)
Christian Historical Union	1	91	2	4	2 (334)
Farmers' Party	31	37	1	10	21 (131)
Pacifist Socialist Party	13	19	3	14	50 (78)
Communist Party	10	8	—	18	64 (84)
Democrats '66	32	22	3	9	34 (257)
Total	35	29	7	9	20

Source: Communication to the author supplied by courtesy of the staff of the Institute of Social Sciences of the Free University in Amsterdam.

INTERNATIONAL CONTACTS

Many contacts of political parties are established through membership of international assemblies. In 1960 Daalder published an

[1] Using a different method Kusters reached a similar conclusion, see W. J. J. Kusters, 'Stembusgedrag en maatschappijstructuur', *Sociologische Gids.*, Vol. X, No. 5, September–October 1963, p. 233.

account of the relationship between the Netherlands Parliament and international parliamentary assemblies.[1] With slight modifications this account is still valid. Five international assemblies have Dutch parliamentarians among their members: the European Parliament; the Consultative Assembly of the Council of Europe; the Parliament of the Western European Union; the Interparliamentarian Benelux Council; and the Assembly of the North Atlantic Treaty Organization. Delegations attending the Assembly of the Council of Europe and the WEU are identical. But apart from this, there is relatively little overlap among the membership of the various international bodies. In 1967 none of the Dutch parliamentarians belonged simultaneously to both the European Parliament and the Assembly of the Council of Europe. Four members of the Interparliamentarian Benelux Council belonged also to the Assembly of the Council of Europe, and one parliamentarian was both a member of the Benelux Council and of the European Parliament. Of those five, three belonged also to the NATO Assembly in 1967. Another three members belonged to the Council of Europe and the NATO Assembly and one was a member of the European Parliament and the NATO Assembly. All in all, there were in 1967 nine members of parliament who belonged to more than one interparliamentarian assembly in the field of foreign affairs (see Table VI).

Dutch members of these assemblies are designated by a joint decision of the presidents of the two chambers of Parliament after

TABLE VI

Members of Parliament who belonged in 1967 to more than one inter-parliamentary body

	Catholic People's Party	Labour Party	Liberal Party	Anti-Revolutionary Party	Christian Historical Union
I	–	1	1	1	–
II	2	1	1	1	1

I = Members of the First Chamber of Parliament.
II = Members of the Second Chamber of Parliament.

[1] H. Daalder, 'The Netherlands', in Kenneth Lindsay (ed.), *European Assemblies*, London, Stevens and New York, Praeger, 1960, pp. 115–32.

having received the necessary authorization from the chambers. This authorization is not needed, however, in the case of the NATO Assembly. The division of representatives among the parties is roughly proportional to the relative strength of the parties. This has meant thus far that only members of the five major parties have been appointed to the European Parliament, the Assembly of the Council of Europe and the NATO Assembly. This was also the case for the Interparliamentary Benelux Council until 1967 when one member each of the Farmers Party and Democrats '66 was appointed to that body.[1] The method by which the presidents of the chambers arrive at the distribution of seats among the parties leads in effect to the exclusion of the smaller parties, whose opportunities for international contacts are thus effectively limited.[2] This procedure has recently come under criticism from the leader of the Labour Party in the Second Chamber, Den Uyl, who received support from the then newly elected leader of Democrats '66, Van Mierlo. They were willing to grant the customary authorization to appoint members to the European Parliament and the Assembly of the Council of Europe for one more year, at the suggestion of the President of the Chamber. In the meantime, Den Uyl contended, a more objective mathematical system of distribution should be developed by which smaller political groupings would get a chance of being represented in the European Assemblies. The President of the Chamber had no objections to this procedure, but pointed out that it might be very difficult to devise a completely objective and fair method of distribution in view of the limited number of seats available for the Netherlands: seven for the Council of Europe; 14 for the European Parliament; and 21 for the Consultative Inter-parliamentary Benelux Council.[3]

Table VII illustrates the distribution of the permanent and alternate seats among the various parties in 1967. It shows a preponderance of members of the Second Chamber of Parliament in the international assemblies as compared to members of the First Chamber. Daalder, in commenting on a similar division between

[1] *Handelingen Tweede Kamer der Staten Generaal*, Buitengewone Zitting, 1967, 8th meeting, May 10, 1967, p. 177; and 11th meeting, May 24, 1967, p. 293.

[2] Daalder, *op. cit.*, p. 117.

[3] *Handelingen Tweede Kamer der Staten Generaal*, Buitengewone Zitting, 1967, 4th meeting, April 19, 1967, p. 39.

TABLE VII

Distribution of permanent and alternate seats in four international assemblies among the Dutch political parties in 1967

		Catholic People's Party	Labour Party	Liberal Party	Anti-Revolutionary Party	Christian Historical Union	Farmers' Party	Democrats '66
Council of Europe	I	1	1	1	1	1	—	—
	II	3	3	1	1	1	—	—
European Parliament	I	1	1	1	—	1	—	—
	II	4	3	1	2	—	—	—
Benelux Council	I	4	4	2	2	2	1	—
	II	10	8	2	2	2	1	2
NATO Assembly	I	1	1	1	1	1	—	—
	II	3	3	1	1	1	—	—

I = Members of the First Chamber of Parliament.
II = Members of the Second Chamber of Parliament.

Note: In the case of the Council of Europe and the Interparliamentary Benelux Council both permanent and alternate members are included.

the two chambers in 1959, noted that the members of the First Chamber have more commitments outside their political work than the members of the Second Chamber and that the latter tend to be more active in the work of the international assemblies.[1]

To a certain extent expertise in foreign affairs and a successful political career seem to go together. No less than eight ministers and state secretaries were previously members of the Assembly of the Council of Europe or the European Parliament.[2] On the other hand, frequent absences from the domestic scene have drawbacks. Members may not be able to attend crucial party meetings or give important speeches, etc. This may have been the reason why several foreign policy experts disappeared from the lists of candidates for the 1967 Elections. The chairman of the foreign affairs committee of the Second Chamber, a member of the Labour Party, who had occupied several important positions in the international assemblies, was not put up for re-election in 1967. It should be added, however, that there were other reasons as well; his political views on domestic and foreign affairs did not coincide entirely with the main currents of thought within his party where he is considered to be too much of a 'conservative'. Two leading foreign policy experts in the Catholic People's Party lost their seats as well.[3]

Apart from these assemblies, some parties have other international contacts. The Labour Party belongs to the Socialist International while the People's Party for Freedom and Democracy is a member of the Liberal International. No study has been made of the practical results of these contacts. It would seem that in neither case does this affiliation have great influence on policy. The leaders of these parties meet their colleagues from abroad at cordial meetings, and sometimes act as hosts. The international contacts of the Communist Party are sufficiently known, but it should be repeated that the CPN has followed a line in recent years that is relatively independent from Moscow. Among other things, it did not attend the International Conference of Communist Parties of March 1968 in Budapest.

[1] Daalder, *op. cit.*, p. 119.
[2] 'Samenstelling van de Europese Assemblees,' *Nieuw Europa*, Vol. XX, No. 3, March 1967, p. 89.
[3] 'Nederlanders in Straatsburg,' *Nieuw Europa*, Vol. XIX, No. 12, December 1966, p. 205.

CHAPTER 7

AUSTRIA

THE EMERGENCE OF THE POLITICAL *LAGER*

'Continental European parties', one of their veterans has written, 'are the remnants of the intellectual social movements of the nineteenth century. They have remained glued to the spots where the ebbing energy of such movements deposited them some decades ago'.[1]

Of few European countries is this observation more apt than of Austria. The present structure of Austrian parties is rooted in the conflicts—linguistic, religious, and economic—of the Habsburg Empire in its constitutional era (1861–1918), at any rate of the Western, Austrian half of that Empire. Until the middle 1880s, under a franchise that extended to 6 per cent of the total population, parties were informal groupings of parliamentary notables with little or no constituency organization. The Liberals represented the German-speaking urban middle class, particularly business and the civil service, and a section of the aristocracy. They favoured a centralized administration, based on Vienna, economic individualism and a breach between Church and state. The Conservatives represented most of the nobility, the non-German nationalities and the interests of agriculture. Under the impact of industrialization and franchise reform these loose associations disintegrated, but the successor parties took over much of their ideological ballast.

The Habsburg Period

The Austrian party system emerged in its present shape in the 1880s. Its three main groupings correspond closely with the 'sub-cultures' of continental European politics identified by Gabriel Almond:

(*a*) preindustrial, primarily Catholic, rooted in the *ancien régime*;

[1] O. Kirchheimer, 'The Waning of Oppositions in Parliamentary Régimes', *Social Research*, Vol. XXIV, No. 2, 1957, p. 147.

(*b*) the older middle classes . . . still primarily concerned with the secularization of the political system itself;

(*c*) industrial components.[1]

Within all three sub-cultures the new generation of leaders sought to emancipate the underprivileged, at the lower end of the middle class and in the proletariat, at the expense of the older Liberal-Conservative *elite*. Among Catholics, social reformers, including many of the lower clergy, formed the Catholic Social Union in 1887 and began fighting elections. With anti-liberal and anti-Semitic slogans they gained the support first of the lower middle class in Vienna and later of the peasantry. By the mid-1890s they had emerged as a fully-fledged political party. Among Liberals, dissident groups around Georg von Schönerer rebelled against the upper middle-class leadership of the party, demanding a more militant defence of German-speaking interests and economic and franchise reforms. Schönerer's Pan-German League, founded in 1882, offended many by its extreme anti-clericalism and racialism, but parties with more moderate versions of his programme—the German People's Party (1896), the German Radicals (1903), and the German Agrarian Party (1905)—gained the support of the provincial middle-class, as well as some anti-clerical farmers, particularly in the areas of German-Czech rivalry in Bohemia and Moravia. Similar Christian-social and radical-nationalist parties were soon formed among the other nationalities of the Empire. Finally, in 1889 the Social Democratic Party was founded, uniting under a Marxist programme the hitherto disparate revolutionary sects and appealing to all industrial workers, irrespective of nationality.

These new parties shared characteristics which distinguished them from their predecessors. Their aim was to recruit the masses into political participation. Their organizational strength lay outside parliament; inside parliament they could begin to supplant the older parties only after the franchise extensions of 1882 and 1896. The introduction of universal suffrage in 1906 completed their conquest of the political arena. In the parliamentary elections of 1907 and 1911 the parties of 'the masses' virtually monopolized the representation of the German-speaking areas. At the same time

---

[1] G. A. Almond, 'Comparative Political Systems', *Journal of Politics*, Vol. XVIII, No. 3, 1956, p. 406.

there also took place a further rationalization of party alignments along the lines which have persisted to the present day (see Diagram, p. 319). The Christian Social Party absorbed the remainder of the old Conservative party and from then on had complete control of the preindustrial, Catholic sub-culture.[1] The Social Democratic Party, which had prided itself on being a 'little International', putting class before language, split in 1910 on the question of autonomous trade unions for Czech workers; the withdrawal of the bulk of the Czech-speaking organizations left the 'official' party as an overwhelmingly German-speaking one.[2] In the same year the various liberal-national parties, which had always been the weakest organizationally, combined into the *Deutscher Nationalverband*, leaving out only a small liberal segment, based mainly on the Jewish middle-class in Vienna,[3] and an extreme racialist body which was to become, after 1918, the National Socialist Party.[4] In the last Parliament of the old Empire the Christian Social Party held 74 of the 233 constituencies with predominantly German-speaking voters, the *Deutscher Nationalverband* 98 and the Social Democrats 47.

Though all three party groupings set out, with some success, to emancipate a population accustomed to passive and deferential political habits, they did so very much on their own terms. The masses were to be brought into the political market-place, but under the tutelage of their educators. The party was to cater for the citizen's every need from the cradle to the grave and meet, with its subsidiary organizations, every economic or leisure interest. The mass political parties therefore tended to emphasize, even institutionalize, the manifold cleavages among the Empire's inhabitants. There was not a single party in the *Reichsrat* of 1914 that represented more than one nationality, class or ideological attitude. The siege mentality, which made each sub-culture aim at internal self-sufficiency and view its rivals with unqualified hostility, has led historians to

[1] N. Miko, *Die Vereinigung der Konservativen in der Christlichsozialen Partei*, unpublished dissertation, Vienna, 1949, pp. 71–75.

[2] J. Joll, *The Second International, 1889–1914* London, 1955, pp. 118–21.

[3] P. G. J. Pulzer, 'The Austrian Liberals and the Jewish Question, 1867–1914,' *Journal of Central European Affairs*, Vol. XXIII, No. 2, 1963, p. 139.

[4] See A. G. Whiteside, *Austrian National Socialism before 1918*, The Hague, 1962.

describe as *Lager*[1]—armed camps—what André Siegfried has, in the French context, christened *familles politiques*.

The resilience of the *Lager* to the cataclysms which Central Europe has undergone in the twentieth century is inversely correlated with the weakness of the state within which they have operated. It is the parties which provide the historical continuity of modern Austria; it is they who stepped into political vacuums in both 1918 and 1945 to create new forms of the state.

The First Republic

In October 1918, even before the Emperor's abdication, the *Reichsrat* deputies for the German-speaking constituencies formed themselves into a 'provisional national assembly'; they created an executive council, drew up a provisional constitution and appointed the Social Democrat Karl Renner as Chancellor. On the Emperor's abdication they proclaimed a Republic and arranged for the election of a Constituent Assembly which ratified the terms of the provisional constitution. Even more extraordinary was the performance of the parties in April 1945, after a lapse of 11 years in free political activity. Karl Renner, by now 75 years old, was called on by the Russian military commander to form a provisional government. He consulted with leaders of the main parties—still formally subject to their enforced dissolution by the Dollfuss regime in 1934 and at a time when large parts of the country were under German military control—and within a week succeeded in his task. On April 27 the members of this government acting as 'executives of the political parties of Austria' proclaimed the 'restoration of the democratic republic of Austria'.[2] A leading constitutional theorist has commented on the way in which:

'at a time of almost completely disrupted communications the same political parties everywhere constitute themselves at a local level, their leaders gradually establish contact with each other, freely

---

[1] The two best analyses along these lines are: A. Wandruszka, in *Geschichte der Republik Österreich* (ed. H. Benedikt), Vienna, 1954, pp. 289-485; and A. Diamant, 'The Group Basis of Austrian Politics', *Journal of Central European Affairs*, Vol. XVIII, No. 2, 1958.

[2] *Staatsgesetzblatt* 1, §1. Quoted by A. Schärf, *Österreichs Wiederaufrichtung im Jahre 1945*, Vienna, 1960, p. 74.

subordinate themselves to other leaders, until finally the whole of party life is built up around two great political parties, under men who are able to command authority at a moment when it is scarcely possible to speak of a sovereign state.'[1]

On May 13 the provisional government reinvigorated the constitution of 1920 (as amended in 1929) and on November 25 the first parliamentary elections took place. It is therefore true to say that the force of the present constitution in Austria, though it affirms the sovereignty of the people, rests neither on the decision of an elected constituent assembly, nor on confirmation by plebiscite, but on a treaty between political parties whose legal existence derives only from their own constitutional *fiat*.

If the character of Austrian political alignments is to be explained by the sectionalism of political life in the last years of the Empire, the demagogy and intransigence of the parties was encouraged by a shadow parliament which provided a public platform but no share in the responsibilities of government. When, therefore, a parliamentary republic with ministerial responsibility arose out of the defeat of 1918 it was no match for these well-established states within the state. The notion of a prior loyalty to a state, which comes naturally to parties that have evolved inside the legislature, did not and could not come easily to parties which, by their exclusion from all decision-making processes, had been encouraged to concentrate either on the mere exertion of group pressure or on the achievement of all-embracing eschatological objectives. No longer inhibited by an Imperial army, bureaucracy, censorship or government by decree, the *Lager* prepared to penetrate every branch of public life. Indeed, as the major parties now formed their own paramilitary organizations—the *Republikanischer Schutzbund* on the Left and the *Heimwehr* on the Right—the term *Lager* ceased to be a metaphor.[2]

Even the revolution of 1918 produced no more than a slight shift in the relative strengths of the *Lager*. The Social Democrats and Christian Socials, both possessing secure mass bases, increased their

---

[1] G. E. Kafka, 'Die verfassungsrechtliche Stellung der politischen Parteien im modernen Staat', *Veröffentlichungen der Vereinigung der deutschen Staatsrechtslehrer*, Vol. XVII, 1959, p. 58.

[2] The best description of these organizations is: C. A. Macartney, 'Armed Formations in Austria', *International Affairs*, Vol. VIII, No. 6, 1929.

support compared with before the war. The liberal-national groups, weakened by the loss of their main source of votes, Bohemia and Moravia, to Czechoslovakia, organized themselves into the urban *Grossdeutsche Volkspartei* (pan-German People's Party, 1920) and the rural *Landbund* (Agrarian League, 1922). However, the intensification of class antagonisms meant that the Christian Socials, as the chief anti-Marxist party, were able to attract middle-class support that was not specifically clerical, while the Social Democrats gained the support of professional and intellectual *strata*, mainly Jewish, who were repelled by the illiberalism and anti-Semitism of the other two *Lager*.

The excellent organization and ideological intransigence of the parties ensured an almost complete politicization of Austrian society. Elections become formalities which confirmed the established frontiers between the *Lager*. Left and Right were returned in the almost unalterable proportions of 42:58. The two main parties never gained below 75 per cent of the total votes. Communism made no headway at all; totalitarian extremism on the Right made no headway until 1930, when it polled 9 per cent, and considerably more in subsequent local elections. Although the Social Democratic and Christian Social parties dominated the political scene, it would be wrong to talk of a two-party system. In the first place, the system of proportional representation adopted in 1919 ensured that neither of the parties secured an absolute parliamentary majority. In the second place, neither of the parties expected the Republic to be ruled by regular alternations in power and loyal opposition in the life-time of the First Republic. From 1918 to 1920 they governed in coalition. When the election of that year made the Christian Socials the strongest party, the Social Democrats preferred the role of militant opposition *pour mieux sauter*, concentrating in the meantime on their administration of Vienna, which had been raised to the status of a province. Though they were committed, both formally and in practice, to parliamentary methods, most of them envisaged the achievement of majority support as equivalent to the overthrow of class rule, liable to be reversed only by violent bourgeois counter-revolution.[1] The Christian Social Party, on the other hand,

---

[1] Detailed accounts of these debates in: C. A. Gulick, *Austria from Habsburg to Hitler*, Berkeley, 1948, Vol. II, pp. 1363–1400; K. L. Shell, *The Transformation of Austrian Socialism*, New York, 1962, pp. 126–37, 157–64.

was only too anxious to exclude the Social Democrats from government, and for the remainder of the Republic's life formed *Bürgerblock* cabinets with the liberal-national groups.

Until 1927 the *Lager* succeeded in co-existing. After the violent Socialist demonstration of that year—in protest against the acquittal of right-wingers who had killed two participants in a Socialist procession—they were in a state of cold civil war, which became three-cornered after the rise of Nazism in the 1930s. In 1933 Dollfuss' government suspended parliament; in 1934, after the abortive workers' rising in Vienna, he proclaimed an authoritarian, corporative constitution. All existing parties were dissolved; a new, single party, uniting all anti-Marxist and anti-Nazi forces, the Fatherland Front, ruled the country until its annexation by the Third Reich in 1938. The Front retained the support of most of the old Christian Social camp, somewhat attenuated by defections to Nazism. The Social Democrats, however, underwent a severe crisis in the four remaining years of the First Republic. After the civil war of 1934 the majority of the leaders fled the country and set up a headquarters in Brno, Czechoslovakia, willing to admit that their tactics, but not their theory, had been wrong. Some of the younger cadres who remained behind, however, concluded that there was no future for a 'menshevik'-type workers' party in Austria: they formed a separate group of Revolutionary Socialists, dedicated to the violent overthrow of capitalism, in co-operation, if necessary, with the Communists.[1]

THE SECOND REPUBLIC

Nothing illustrated more clearly the strength and stability of the sub-cultures than the speed with which political parties revived in 1945 and the way in which the first elections revealed a virtually unchanged balance of forces. On paper each of the major parties was a new creation; in substance it was the lineal successor of a First Republic party. Changes in programme and structure have been more substantial since 1945 than they were between 1934 and 1945. The Austrian Socialist Party (SPÖ) and the Austrian People's

[1] e.g., O. Bauer, *Zwischen zwei Weltkriegen?* Bratislava, 1936, esp. pp. 233–350. On the Revolutionary Socialists, J. Buttinger, *In the Twilight of Socialism*, New York, 1953.

Party (ÖVP) were both constituted in April 1945. At the same time the Communist Party (KPÖ) emerged out of illegality. It was these three parties that were invited to form—in approximately equal proportions—the coalition government and these three parties alone that the Allied military authorities were prepared to license.

The Socialist Party

The new Socialist Party resulted from a merger of the old Social Democrats and the Revolutionary Socialists (RS). Indeed, for a time the two constituent partners were specifically recognized in the official subtitle—*Sozialistische Partei Österreichs (Sozialdemokraten und Revolutionäre Sozialisten)*. Within a few months the unwieldy parenthesis was quietly dropped.[1] Although the party offices were initially shared equally between Social Democrats and Revolutionaries, the RS contingent contributed little to the character of the new party. The new SPÖ, like its predecessor, was to be a mass-membership party; this, however, was inconsistent with the RS view of leadership through revolutionary cadres. Moreover, the SPÖ was specifically committed to the principles of parliamentary government, and therefore the legitimacy of multipartism, thus rendering irrelevant the slogans which the RS had inherited from the days of illegal activity. Only one ex-RS functionary seriously challenged the evolution towards orthodox Social Democracy. He was Erwin Scharf, who was expelled in 1948 and shortly after became editor of the main Communist daily, *Die Volksstimme*.

TABLE I

Membership of Austrian Socialist Party, 1929–66

1929	718,083
1932	648,479
1945	375,818
1948	616,232
1960	727,265
1966	699,423

Source: *Jahrbuch der Österreichischen Arbeiterbewegung*, 1929, 1932; *SPÖ, Bericht an den Parteitag*, 1965, 1967.

Not only did the RS element fail to move the party to the Left; it did not even prevent it from moving to the Right of the interwar

---

[1] K. L. Shell, *op. cit.*, p. 36.

Social Democratic Party. The old Austro-Marxist leadership was dominated by intellectuals, many of them Jewish. It was to a considerable extent discredited by the failure of its policy in 1934. Some of the old leaders died in exile or in concentration camps; others, such as Julius Braunthal or Friedrich Adler, preferred not to return to Austria; those that did, such as Julius Deutsch, were fobbed off with minor posts. The leading positions in the reconstituted party therefore went to those men associated with the Renner wing of the party who were on the spot: Dr Adolf Schärf (party chairman and Vice-Chancellor from 1945 until his election to the Presidency in 1957), Oskar Helmer (vice-chairman and Minister of the Interior from 1945 to 1959), Karl Waldbrunner (a central secretary of the party from 1946 to 1956 and a member of the cabinet from 1949 to 1962). Even when they are professional men with university backgrounds, they have no taste for theorizing or oratory and concentrate on tactics and administration. There has also been a much higher recruitment of party leaders from the trade unions, including Johann Böhm (President of the Austrian Trade Union Congress, 1945–59 and a member of the Renner cabinet), and Karl Meisel (Minister for Social Security, 1945–56, Vice-President of the Trade Union Congress, 1948–59).

The greatest contrast with the interwar period lies in the reduced influence of Vienna. Before 1934 the preponderance of intellectuals among the leadership and the geographically concentrated, militantly class-conscious proletariat in the capital contributed to the party's radicalism. The rise of provincial influence since 1945 has helped to accelerate the trend towards pragmatism. In part Vienna has lost the lead through the disappearance of the Jewish intellectual stratum; in part the drift of membership and voting power has merely followed the shift of economic expansion towards the Western, Alpine provinces (see Table II).

In other respects the party has maintained its original traditions: the emphasis on individual membership, the proliferation of ancillary associations and a centralized organization. Between the wars about half the regular Socialist voters and about 20 per cent of the total electorate were organized in the party. Within three years of the end of World War II the party had almost succeeded in equalling the prewar figure; after that membership rose more slowly, reaching an all-time peak in 1960.

TABLE II

Contribution of Vienna to total population, qualified electors, members and voters of Socialist Party, 1930–62

	Population			Electors		
	1934	1951	1961	1930	1953	1962
Total	6,760,233	6,933,905	7,073,807	3,687,082	4,586,870	4,805,351
Vienna	1,874,610	1,616,125	1,627,566	1,193,072	1,233,321	1,264,397
Vienna per cent of total	27·7	23·7	23·0	33·3	26·3	25·9

	Party members			Socialist voters		
	1932	1951	1961	1930	1953	1962
Total	648,497	607,283	708,871	1,516,913	1,818,517	1,960,685
Vienna	400,484	262,498	290,268	703,718	590,532	595,265
Vienna per cent of total	62·3	43·2	40·9	46·5	32·6	30·4

Source: *Österreichische Statistische Jahrbücher; SPÖ, Bericht an den Parteitag,* 1965, pp. 54–5.

The social structure of the membership has changed over the years in step with the general evolution of the occupational structure (see Table III).

TABLE III

Occupational structure of Socialist Party membership
(Per cent)

	1929	1947	1961
Workers: industrial	51·2	38·8	39·2
agricultural	—	3·1	2·0
Employees: in private employment	11·8	7·9	10·1
in public service	8·6	11·9	14·0
Professions	1·5	1·9	1·3
Self-employed: industry and trade	4·3	4·4	2·3
agriculture	—	2·5	0·8
Pensioners	2·2	7·4	14·4
Housewives	16·1	20·1	14·6

Source: Shell, *Transformation of Austrian Socialism,* p. 50; *SPÖ, Bericht an den Parteitag,* 1965, p. 57.

Equally important in the work of political mobilization are the 28 affiliated 'socialist organizations', which cover every activity from mountaineering to stamp collecting. Some, like the parents' organization *Kinderfreunde* or the sports league ASKö have several hundred thousand members;[1] at the other extreme is the *Austria Sozialista Liga Esperantista* with a membership of 102.[2] Membership of these organizations does not imply membership of the party; only office-holders and delegates to the party conference need to be full members.[3] The party has lost direct control of the most important of its former dependencies, the trade unions. Before 1934 these were divided according to party-political allegiance, the Social Democrats dominating the largest of these, the *Freie Gewerkschaften*. Since the war, there has been a unitary, non-party (or rather, since this is Austria, all-party) organization, the öGB. Although the great majority of its officials are Socialists, trade union funds and publications can give the SPö only limited help.

The party is kept together by a strictly hierarchical and highly centralized organization. Before 1934 this centralization merely reflected the preponderance of Viennese influence. The postwar rise of provincial influence has not led to any 'federalization' of the party, but it has enabled provincial delegates to have a progressively greater say. In 1945 the provincial organizations were allocated half the seats on the *Parteivorstand* (party executive) and all but two on the *Parteikontrolle* (party control), the two bodies which were elected by the annual party conference and which between them constituted the *Parteivertretung* (party presidium).[4] Under the new statutes, adopted in 1967, the various provincial organizations are allotted 40 seats out of the 54 in the new unitary party executive in proportion to their membership, calculated according to the d'Hondt system; any province which thereby receives only one seat is entitled to one of the remaining 14 seats.[5] The party executive, together with co-opted members, among whom the provinces again feature strongly, constitute the *Parteirat*, one of whose main

---

[1] *SPÖ Bericht an den Parteitag*, Vienna, 1967, pp. 121, 149.

[2] *SPÖ Wien. Jahresbericht, 1966*, p. 92.

[3] *Programm und Statut der Sozialistischen Partei Österreichs*, 1967, §20, pp. 56–7.

[4] K. L. Shell, *op. cit.*, p. 78.

[5] *Programm und Statut*, §§33–6, pp. 66–7.

tasks is the selection of parliamentary candidates for the entire country.[1] The lower levels of provincial, district and local branches are served by an army of voluntary officials known collectively as *Vertrauenspersonen* ('persons in positions of confidence'). In 1966 they totalled 66,579,[2] almost one tenth of the party membership. One of their most important tasks is the collection of dues, which they do with a success that rarely falls below 95 per cent.

The biennial party conference is, in accordance with the theory of intra-party democracy, the sovereign legislative and elective body. It only fulfils this role in a nominal way. Thus, in electing members to the pre-1967 presidium, delegates were free to cross out names on the approved list drawn up by the election committee, and write in substitute names; in fact, since the war the 'platform' ticket has always triumphed in its entirety. No platform resolution has ever been defeated.[3] Only two postwar conferences have been marked by real controversy. The more recent was the extraordinary congress which followed the party's election defeat in 1966. This was considered a revolt against the leadership of Dr Bruno Pittermann, who had succeeded Dr Schärf in 1957. In his place the conference elected Dr Bruno Kreisky. Although personalities as well as policies were involved in the dispute, Kreisky was the candidate of the more pragmatic, coalition-minded provincial organizations and a strong opponent of any co-operation with the Communists. The other heated congress was also an extraordinary one; that of 1958 when the new 'revisionist' programme was adopted. The party had not given itself a new programme in 1945; in so far as any text was valid it was still that of 1926 which bore the Austro-Marxist stamp of Otto Bauer. The intellectual lassitude which has characterized the party since the war left theoretical debate to a small group of addicts. Only by the late 1950s was it considered necessary to draft a document which would recognize the party's final disillusionment with Communism, its continuing participation in coalition government and its *de facto* acceptance of the mixed economy. The new draft evoked 1,070 amendments, mainly in favour of theoretical traditionalism.[4] The final text, though paying

1 *Ibid.*, §§46–7, pp. 74–5.
2 *SPÖ. Bericht*, 1967, p. 32.
3 K. L. Shell, *op. cit.*, pp. 107, 10.
4 *Ibid.*, p. 102.

tribute to Marx and some of his formulations, committed the party 'unconditionally' to democracy and, by implication, to multi-partism; to 'a juster system of property'; to private ownership of agricultural land and to nationalization only where justified by the common good.[1]

The People's Party

The Austrian People's Party which filled the political vacuum in the Conservative *Lager* bore rather fewer resemblances to its inter-war predecessor than the Socialist Party. On the one hand, the involvement of most Christian-Social leaders in the unpopular Fatherland Front regime of 1934–38 had discredited them. A fresh start was, therefore, desirable and most of the founders of the new party—Leopold Figl, a peasant leader from Lower Austria (Federal Chancellor, 1945–53; Foreign Minister, 1953–59), Dr Felix Hurdes (general secretary of the party, 1945–51), Alois Weinberger (deputy Lord Mayor of Vienna, 1945–59)—had redeemed themselves by their detention in Nazi concentration camps. On the other hand, the ÖVP was anxious to achieve the uniting of all anti-Socialist forces that had always eluded the Christian-Social Party. It was helped in this by the decision of the Allied Control Council not to license any parties that might speak for the liberal-national *Lager* on the grounds that any such party would be Nazi-dominated. This had the effect of introducing into the party a stronger 'liberal' (i.e. non-Catholic) element, exemplified by the Tyrolean Dr Karl Gruber (Foreign Minister, 1945–53). In addition, the leader of the prewar national-liberal *Landbund*, Vinzenz Schumy, had in any case decided not to revive his party and joined forces with the ÖVP. This step was important in depriving any future national-liberal party of an agrarian base.

In accordance with the ideology of Austrian conservatism the party structure is corporative and federal. Members are recruited into three constituent leagues according to their occupation: the Farmers' League (*Österreichischer Bauernbund*, ÖBB), the Business League (*Österreichischer Wirtschaftsbund*, ÖWB) and the Employees' League (*Österreichischer Arbeiter- und Angestelltenbund*, ÖAAB). Direct individual membership of the party is possible, but excep-

[1] K. Berchtold, *Österreichische Parteiprogramme, 1868–1966*, Munich, 1967, pp. 291, 295, 298.

tional. It numbered 1,518 at the last count.[1] Within the leagues there is a high degree of provincial autonomy, so that the ÖVP may be said to comprise 27 confederate units. For instance, the rate of membership subscription is fixed by each provincial league, subject only to federal headquarters receiving 10 per cent of the contribution.[2] The selection of *Nationalrat* candidates, in contrast to the SPÖ, takes place at constituency level.[3] In view of this fragmentation of control it is difficult to assess membership levels realistically. Figures supplied by party headquarters give the following totals of league members:

TABLE IV

Membership of ÖVP by constituent leagues, May 1967

		Per cent
Farmers' League	408,959	50·0
Business League	146,089	32·1
Employees' League	263,054	17·9
Totals	818,102	100·0

Source: Dr Peter Diem, ÖVP.

However, membership of the farmers' and business leagues is open not only to the entrepreneurs themselves (*Stammmitglieder*) but to dependents working with them (*Familienmitglieder*). Detailed breakdowns by category are not available for all provinces; a projection of those that are available suggests the following federal total of full members:

Farmers' League	200,000
Business League	65,000
Employees' League	250,000
Total	515,000

Even this is a very high figure by the standards of other European Christian-Democratic parties. Taken together with SPÖ member-

---

[1] A. Pelinka, 'Die politischen Parteien in Österreich,' *Politische Studien*, No. 168, July–August, 1966, p. 393.

[2] *ÖVP. Bundesorganisationsstatut und Geschäftsordnung*, Vienna, 1965, §3, pp. 28–9.

[3] *Ibid.*, §41, p. 32.

ship it shows that at least one registered elector in four in Austria is a card-carrying member of a political party.

The figures also show that the traditional predominance of agrarian interests in the Catholic-Conservative *Lager* continues, and is being only slowly eroded by the changing social structure. Farmers have an absolute majority of league members in Lower Austria, Upper Austria and Styria; employees in Vienna; in the remaining five provinces the balance between leagues is fairly even. Equally traditional is the predominance of Lower Austria over the organization of the other provinces. Lower Austria provides 31 per cent of the country's farmers, but 47 per cent of the members of the Farmers' League; 17 per cent of the country's entrepreneurs, but 37 per cent of the members of the Business League. Lower Austrians held most of the leading positions in the ÖVP at its foundation;[1] they have provided two of Austria's four postwar Chancellors (Figl, 1945–53; Raab 1953–61) and two of the four postwar Ministers of Agriculture (Kraus, 1945–52; Hartmann, 1959–64). Nevertheless, by the mid-1960s the balance had changed somewhat away from the old Christian-Social occupational and geographical pattern. The most dynamic of the ÖVP's three leagues has been the ÖAAB, with a rise in membership from 221,000 to 250,000 in five years. True, fewer than a third of these are industrial workers,[2] but success in recruiting has helped to raise the ÖAAB from its former status as the party's step-child. In the ÖVP single-party cabinet formed in 1966 the ÖAAB received four ministries, the ÖWB four, and the ÖBB only two.[3] In the Cabinet re-shuffle of January, 1968, these proportions were changed to 4:3:2.

Like the Socialists, the ÖVP relies on supplementary organizations to mobilize support: the women's and youth organizations, which have a status co-ordinate with that of the leagues, and five professional and vocational associations ('*Zweckverbände*')[4] which do not confer full membership of the party but are entitled to send conference delegates. Compared with the Christian-Social Party,

---

[1] A. Vodopivec, *Die Balkanisierung Österreichs. Die grosse Koalition und ihr Ende*, Vienna, 1966, pp. 30–4.

[2] D. Marwick (ed.), *Wahlen und Parteien in Österreich. Österreichisches Wahlhandbuch*, Vienna, 1966, Vol. II, p. 43.

[3] A. Vodopivec, *op. cit.*, p. 401.

[4] *ÖVP Bundesorganisationsstatut*, §8, p 6.

however, the ÖVP has lost one important source of direct support: the Church. Following the Church's disastrous courtship with Caesar, first during the corporative regime of 1934–38 and then at the time of the *Anschluss* in 1938, the Archbishop of Vienna, Cardinal Innitzer, in 1945 prohibited any political activity on the part of the clergy. Given Austria's ideological traditions, this could not mean a significant shift in the party loyalties of Catholic laymen. It was, and is, rare for a practising Catholic to be a Socialist voter, even rarer to be a Socialist functionary, although the SPÖ has deliberately avoided any revival of a *Kulturkampf*. What it did mean was that the ÖVP could not count on the collective support of the highly effective network of Catholic lay organizations, with their member-ship of over half a million.[1] The political neutralization of the Church was accelerated after Innitzer's death in 1956, by his successor, Cardinal Franz Koenig, one of the leading advocates of ecumenism and improved relations with the Communists. From 1959 onwards the Austrian hierarchy has not, in its pastoral letters at election time, given any partisan guidance.[2] Though the ÖVP proclaims support for 'Christian-occidental culture' and 'Christian social teaching', it disclaims specific bonds with any denomination.[3] The party is also committed to multipartism, to the principle of private property and to 'a market based on the competition of economic forces'[4]—doctrines which are derived at least as much from liberalism as from the Party's Christian-Social antecedents.

Minor Parties

The ÖVP's hopes of constituting a federative *Bürgerblock* were dashed when the Allied Control Commission, largely at the urging of SPÖ, licensed a fourth party for the elections of 1949. This, the 'League of Independents' (VdU), led by two Salzburg-based journa-lists, Herbert Kraus and Viktor Reimann, neither of whom had a Nazi past, appealed most obviously to what remained of the liberal-national *Lager*, in particular the 480,000 former members of the

1 E. Bodzenta, *Die Katholiken in Österreich. Ein religions—soziologischer Überblick*, Vienna, 1962, p. 30.
2 U. W. Kitzinger, 'The Austrian Election of 1959', *Political Studies*, Vol. IX, No. 2, 1961, p. 136.
3 *ÖVP Bundesorganizationsstatut*, §1, p. 3; Berchtold, *op. cit.*, pp. 397, 400.
4 Berchtold, *op. cit.*, pp. 398, 399.

Nazi party disfranchized in 1945 but now once more entitled to vote. Weakened in the rural areas by the amalgamation of the *Landbund* with the People's Party, the new party revealed itself as primarily the party of the medium and small-town bourgeoisie. It gained 11·7 per cent of the total votes, but 23·6 per cent in the provincial capitals.[1]

This initial success compared quite favourably with the interwar results achieved by the equivalent parties. Thereafter support declined consistently. In part this was because the vdu had set out to speak for all 'victims' of the postwar political system, but prosperity, the passage of time and patronage by the coalition parties has integrated more and more of the politically maladjusted. The other major reason is the unresolved tension in the party between liberals and ex-Nazis. This came to a head just before the 1956 elections with the departure of Kraus and Reimann, to be replaced by undisguisedly Nazi elements. The party renamed itself *Freiheitlich* (FPÖ), a tribute to the ideological traditionalism of Austria, for the description was that which the pan-German/anti-clerical/constitutionalist opposition had adopted in the pre-1848 era. The new leader of the party was Anton Reinthaller, a member of the 48-hour Seyss-Inquart cabinet which in March 1938 effected the *Anschluss*. The FPÖ sank to 6·5 per cent in 1956, but was able to achieve some improvement and stabilization in its support in the following years. Its leadership was rejuvenated in 1959, when Reinthaller was succeeded by Freidrich Peter, also an ex-Nazi but not of the old guard.

Not all FPÖ voters and functionaries are Nazis, and former Nazis are to be found in plenty in the ÖVP and SPÖ; nevertheless, surveys reveal a harder core of unreconstructed views in the ranks of the FPO than elsewhere. Supporters of different parties agreed with certain statements on the extermination of the Jews in widely different proportions.[2]

---

[1] i.e. Salzburg, Linz (Upper Austria), Graz (Styria), Klagenfurt (Carinthia), Innsbruck (Tyrol), Bregenz (Vorarlberg). Vienna has the status of a province. Lower Austria has no capital, its administration being accommodated in Vienna. Eisenstadt (Burgenland) is too small to be statistically significant.

[2] H. Kienzl, 'Der Österreicher und seine Schande', *Neues Forum*, No. 154, October 1966, pp. 655-7.

	FPÖ	KPÖ	ÖVP	SPÖ	All
			Per cent		
(a) 'The extermination of the Jews was the greatest disgrace of the century'	9	66	38	50	39
(b) 'The Jews caused their misfortunes through their own behaviour'	48	6	10	6	10

Asked, 'At what period do you think Austrians had the best time?' 45 per cent of FPÖ supporters chose the period 1938–45, compared with 5 per cent of the total sample; asked in what country they would like to live, 56 per cent of FPÖ supporters chose Germany, compared with 13·5 per cent of the total sample.[1]

Since 1962 the FPÖ decline has resumed. Its real difficulty is that its ideological position is seen as increasingly archaic; the debate about whether there is a separate Austrian nationality, distinct from German,[2] is of little interest to the bulk of the electorate, and anti-clericalism is a dying cause. Its economic policy does not differ markedly from that of the ÖVP. Exclusion from the coalition deprived it of influence and patronage: the party's vote has, significantly, held best in Salzburg, where it participates in the provincial coalition. Organizationally, the FPÖ suffers from the traditional weaknesses of the national-liberal *Lager*; the individualism of its followers and the lack of an identifiable economic interest of which it can claim to be the exclusive defender. Its membership is small: 22,000 in 1959, when figures were last published.[3] It is endemically short of funds and was partly kept going in the early 1960s by a secret subsidy from Socialist funds, channelled by the then General Secretary of the ÖGB, Franz Olah.

Extremism on the Left has had an even poorer run than on the Right. During the First Republic the Social Democrats managed, thanks to their oppositional stance and continued adherence to Marxism, to keep their Communist rivals completely at bay. Following the Social Democrats' failure to defend the Republic in 1934, and the generally good performances of Communist parties throughout Europe at the end of the war, one might have expected a Communist advance in Austria too. But *Lager* discipline proved

[1] *Die Meinung*, Vol. V, No. 1, 1965, p. 9.
[2] Berchtold, *op. cit.*, pp. 493, 496.
[3] A. Pelinka, *op. cit.*, p. 396.

too strong, and distaste for the Russian occupation did the rest. The Communist (KPÖ) never exceeded 5·3 per cent of the total vote. Following the ending of the occupation in 1955 their few strongholds, which had mainly been in the Russian occupational zone, disintegrated, a process which was accelerated by the crushing of the Hungarian revolution. By 1965 their membership, once more than 150,000, had sunk to 36,400. Half the members were office holders; only one-fifth were aged under 40. A radical rejuvenation was undertaken: their veteran leader Johann Koplenig retired in favour of 35-year-old Franz Muhri; 33 of the 87 members of the central committee were replaced.[1] The party decided to withdraw from electoral contests which it regarded as hopeless; in the 1966 general election it fought only one of the 25 multimember constituencies, recommending its followers to vote for the SPÖ elsewhere.

Party Loyalty and Party Finance

Much that characterizes Austrian parties, particularly the ÖVP and the SPÖ, can be explained only in terms of habit and an often deliberate traditionalism. In the days when the party was an ideologically based movement aiming at the conquest of the state on behalf of its vision of society, the mass membership, the impassioned theoretical debates and the proliferation of subsidiary organizations made sense. The party had to be an autarchic state within the state. But have these devices not degenerated into a pointless game, in an age when parties argue with electors' votes rather than the size of their demonstrations, when they strive for compromises on behalf of the interests they represent rather than summoning their rifle squads? The answer is a qualified 'yes'; and the chief qualification is that membership is a source of funds. The frequency of election campaigns—presidential, parliamentary, provincial and municipal—causes heavy financial drain. The best estimate[2] is that a parliamentary election costs 120,000,000 *schillings*;[3] one for a provincial diet 35,000,000 *schillings*. Only the SPÖ is able to live 'of its own', with an annual income of some 80,000,000 *schillings*;

[1] *Ibid.*, p. 397; *The Economist*, London, June 12, 1965, p. 1265.
[2] A. Vodopivec, 'Zur Finanzierung von Parteien aus Steuergeld', *Berichte und Informationen* 1084, May 19, 1967, p. 1.
[3] £1 = 62 schillings.

TABLE V
Austrian election results, 1945-66

	1945			1949			1953			1955		
		%	Seats		%	Seats		%	Seats		%	Seats
Electors	3,449,605			4,391,815			4,586,870			4,614,464		
Turn-out	3,253,329	94·3		4,250,616	97·0		4,395,519	96·0		4,427,711	96·0	
Valid Votes	3,217,354			4,193,733			4,318,688			4,351,908		
ÖVP	1,602,227	49·8	85	1,846,581	44·0	77	1,781,777	41·3	74	1,999,986	46·0	82
SPÖ	1,434,898	44·6	76	1,623,524	38·7	67	1,818,517	42·1	73	1,837,295	43·0	74
FPÖ	—			489,273	11·7	16	472,866	10·9	14	283,749	6·5	6
KPÖ	174,257	5·4	4	213,076	5·1	5	228,159	5·3	4	192,438	4·4	3
Others	5,974	0·2		21,289	0·5		17,369	0·4		2,440	0·1	

	1959			1962			1966		
		%	Seats		%	Seats		%	Seats
Electors	4,695,860			4,805,351			4,886,534		
Turn-out	4,424,658	94·2		4,506,007	94·0		4,583,948	93·8	
Valid Votes	4,362,856			4,456,131			4,531,864		
ÖVP	1,928,043	44·2	79	2,024,501	45·4	81	2,191,128	48·4	85
SPÖ	1,953,935	44·8	78	1,960,685	44·0	76	1,928,922	42·6	74
FPÖ	336,110	7·7	8	313,895	7·1	8	242,599	5·3	6
KPÖ	142,578	3·3		135,520	3·0		18,638	0·4	
Others	2,190	0·1		21,530	0·5		150,577	3·3	

Source: Österreichisches Statistisches Zentralamt: Die Nationalratswahlen von.

301

some 10 per cent of it from subscriptions.[1] The ÖVP's income from subscriptions is estimated at no more than 7,500,000 *schillings* per year, but this money goes, in the first place, into the coffers of the Leagues and, in the second place, into the coffers of the provincial organizations. Both the federal party headquarters and the Viennese organization are in permanent financial embarrassment. A further source of income for both parties consists of directly owned commercial enterprises, particularly printing and advertising, and here again the SPÖ, whose investments go back over 70 years, have the advantage. Less easy to document are subsidies from organizations over which the parties have only indirect control, such as co-operatives and insurance societies. The ÖVP's financial shortfall has traditionally been made good by donations from private industry. In the late 1950s these were estimated at about 2,500,000 *schillings* per year.[2] All parties except the SPÖ suffer from an endemic shortage of money, hence the growing demand for subsidies out of public funds,[3] in extension of a principle already adopted by some provincial governments. (Vorarlberg, for instance, pays each party represented in the assembly 2·50 *schillings* (10d.) per five-year legislative period for every vote gained in the preceding election.) The SPÖ, which has least to gain from such an innovation at a federal level, has turned down proposals along these lines from the ÖVP Government.

A major consequence of the surviving *Lager* mentality has been the extraordinary stability of partisan loyalty shown at postwar elections up to (but not including) that of 1966. The proportion of electors who in 1962 declared themselves to be firm supporters of one of the established parties is 74 per cent[4]—not very different from levels reported in other Western countries. However, it turned out that of those who claimed to be non-partisan, the great majority had already made up their minds how to vote before the election campaign began; in other words, their party identification is almost as intense as that of overt partisans.

[1] *SPÖ Bericht*, 1967, pp. 44–5, Table 6.
[2] A. Vodopivec, *Wer regiert in Österreich?* Vienna, 1960, pp. 62–5.
[3] e.g., R. Marcic, 'Sentenzen zur Parteifinanzierung', *Österreichische Monatshefte*, Vol. XXIII, No. 1, January, 1967, pp. 22–9; W. Mantl, 'Plaidoyer für Parteifinanzierung', *Neues Forum*, 164–5, August–September, 1967.
[4] K. Blecha, R. Gmoser, and H. Kienzl *Der durchleuchtete Wähler. Beiträge zur politischen Soziologie in Österreich*, Vienna, 1964, p. 42.

TABLE VI

Percentage of Party supporters making voting decision before start of election campaign, 1962

	Per cent
KPÖ supporters	98
SPÖ supporters	96
ÖVP supporters	88
FPÖ supporters	83
Non-partisan	76

Source: Blecha, Gmoser & Kienzl, *Der durchleuchtete Wähler*, p. 37

It is fair to say that between 1949 and about 1964 there was virtually no direct transfer of support between the ÖVP on the one hand and the SPÖ/KPÖ on the other. The slow but steady rise in the SPÖ's share of the vote during the 1950s may be accounted for by four factors:

1 ÖVP over-representation among the old;
2 SPÖ majorities among voters coming of age;
3 conversions from the KPÖ;
4 conversions from the FPÖ, especially in Upper Austria, Carinthia and Styria.

The reasons for the stagnation of the SPÖ thereafter appear to be a stabilization of KPÖ and FPÖ support; it also seems likely that what remained of FPÖ voting strength was predominantly middle-class and heavily anti-Socialist, so that further erosion of the FPÖ strength would benefit the People's Party. By 1966 an entirely new factor, an unmistakable loosening of ideological loyalties, had emerged.[1] The stability of the first twenty years of the Second Republic was enhanced by the system of proportional representation inherited from the First Republic.[2] One curiosity of this is the allocation of seats by population rather than registered electors. This favours rural areas with high birth rates (64 per cent of the population is electorally qualified in Vorarlberg and Carinthia) at the expense of industrial areas (79 per cent of the population is qualified in Vienna),[3] and, is, therefore, slightly biased against the Left; in

---

[1] See below, p. 313.
[2] U. W. Kitzinger, 'The Austrian Electoral System', *Parliamentary Affairs*, Vol. XII, Nos. 3–4, 1959, pp. 397–8.
[3] O. Lackinger, *Die regionale Verteilung der Wähler*, Vienna, 1966, p. 6.

both 1953 and 1959 the SPÖ emerged as the largest single party, but still trailed the ÖVP in seats.

The fragmentation of social life and of economic interest groups along ideological lines is not an exclusively Austrian phenomenon, though only in Austria has it contributed so directly to the breakdown of fragile consensus as to result in a civil war. When, therefore, the *Lager* reassembled their ideological and organizational lumber in 1945 there was every reason to fear that nominally new dogs would stick to old tricks. That partisan animosity has steadily diminished may be traced to three causes. The first is the common concentration-camp experience which united some of the founders of the ÖVP and the SPÖ. The second is the general decline in ideological fervour in Western countries since the war, generally attributed to growing affluence and exemplified in Austria by the SPÖ's jettisoning of Marxism and the Church's growing political neutrality. The third and most important is the coalition which governed Austria from 1945 to 1966, instilling, by example, a lesson in co-existence which no precept could ever have taught so convincingly.

THE 'PERMANENT' COALITION

The Origins of the Coalition

The provisional government which Karl Renner had formed at the request of the Soviet military command consisted of the three 'antifascist' parties: ÖVP, SPÖ and KPÖ. The Russians had consented to this arrangement because they were confident of Communist success in free elections, the anti-Communist politicians because they were confident of the opposite. In consequence of their defeat in November 1945, the Communists were reduced to one seat in the cabinet; in November 1947, they left the coalition altogether. From then on, until April 1966, the two main parties remained in continuous coalition. The immediate incentive for this collaboration was unity in the face of Allied military occupation. But the coalition continued after the achievement of the State Treaty in 1955, which freed Austria from external control, and this revealed further and more deeply felt inducements to coalition politics. The desire, strengthened by the emergence of moderate leaderships in both parties, to avoid the mistakes of the First Republic was supplemented by continuing distrust of the other party's bona fides. Among the major interest groups there predominated a preference for non-competitive distribution of the national wealth.

The coalition was not the outcome of an *ad hoc* bargain between the participants, but subject to a formal treaty which well illustrated the primacy of party over the institutions of the state in Austria. The earliest of these coalition pacts, that of February 1947, embraced only the öVP and sPö, although the Communists were at that time still in the government: it pledged the two parties to joint responsibility for any currency reform and confirmed the 'watchdog' function of state secretaries, who were appointed from the opposite party of the responsible minister.[1] The first fully fledged coalition pact was that following the 1949 election; it and the pact of 1953 were secret. The 1949 pact was, however, leaked to the press, and all subsequent pacts have been published.[2] The common feature of all the pacts lies in the commitment to collective responsibility and to collaboration to the exclusion of other parties, until the next election. Policy-making is shared with a 'coalition executive' (*Koalitionsausschuss*) in which both parties are equally represented though not, except for the party leaders, by cabinet ministers. This insistence on unanimity distinguished the institutionalized Austrian coalition from the 'collegiate' systems of Switzerland and the Austrian provinces, where majority voting prevails. Decisions thus agreed are binding on the two parliamentary parties; the chief function of the weekly meetings of the parliamentary *Klubs* (party groups) was to receive instructions from the whips. This represented a devaluation of the powers of parliament even more drastic than in most modern constitutional states, especially since all coalition pacts up to 1962 were 'rigid', i.e. leaving virtually no topic to extra-coalition bargaining. Since party discipline, in tune with Austria's monolithic political habits, was complete, the *de facto* possibility that parliament might reject or even amend a proposal submitted by the government was considerably less than even in Britain. Moreover, since parliamentary oratory enjoys no prestige, debates lacked even the educative function sometimes attributed to proceedings at Westminster. Only the 1962 coalition pact conceded

[1] A. Schärf, *Österreichs Erneuerung, 1945–1955* (revised ed.), Vienna, 1960, p. 281.
[2] *Wiener Zeitung*, June 27, 1956; July 29, 1959.

some topics to be *koalitionsfrei*; the chief effect of this was to increase distrust between the partners.

Granted the permanence of Austrian political loyalties the outcome of all elections could be predicted to within two or three seats; granted the main parties' mutual commitment to continued coalition, the outlines of the new government were already known before the election. The one attempt by the ÖVP to strengthen anti-Socialist representation by introducing VDU ministers, made in 1953, was vetoed by President Körner on the grounds that the VDU was not reliably democratic.[1] Even had he not done so, the Allied Control Commission would almost certainly have interposed its veto. Elections were decisive none the less. In the first place they determined the distribution of office within the cabinet. Of the departments of state, five have been regarded as ÖVP preserves, viz. Education, Finance, Commerce, Agriculture and Armed Forces; four have been regarded as SPÖ preserves, viz., Justice, Interior, Social Welfare and Transport; two are marginal, viz., Foreign Affairs and Nationalized Industries other than transport. In the negotiations after the 1966 elections, which resulted in an absolute ÖVP majority and the end of the coalition, Justice was also treated as marginal. In addition there are state secretaryships, also awarded on the basis of electoral strength, which facilitate 'opposition' control in a rival preserve. Most important of all, however, is the *Proporz*, the right of appointment, recognized by the coalition pact, within the allocated preserve. This patronage is, in the light of the very large public sector of the economy, considerable. It does not invariably mean promotion for party hacks irrespective of merit, as hostile critics of the system tended to imply; it does, however, mean politicization of most of administrative and much of professional life and, at any rate, the risk of intimidation. (In SPÖ administered Carinthia the Socialist Teachers' Association has 1,628 members, in ÖVP administered Tyrol, with a similar population, 22 members.)[2]

Electoral competition, therefore, was not between opposition and government, for the opposition parties, diminutive, fragmented and tarnished with the odium of totalitarianism, have no opportunity of office. Instead it resolved the rivalry between 'two parties per-

[1] A. Schärf, *op. cit.*, p. 335.
[2] *SPÖ Bericht*, 1965, p. 130.

manently in coalition with each other [which] nevertheless continue to compete uninterruptedly between themselves. Each of them is simultaneously government and opposition party'.[1] This formulation, by a leading socialist commentator, refers to the concept of *Bereichsopposition* (departmental opposition)—the right of each coalition partner to criticize, not merely in private (through the state secretaries and within the Cabinet) but also in public, the administration of the other partner's government.

Interest Groups and the Coalition

A feature of Austrian government which further devalued the role of the legislature was the political negotiating power given to the representatives of the major economic groups. Again the observer of advanced Western systems sees nothing strange in these corporative devices; what characterizes the Austrian version is its thorough-going institutionalization. Moreover, though the prevalence of collective bargaining shuts out those organs which ought, according to the constitution, to be the policy-makers, it does not shut out the parties. While the parties cannot, of course, afford to ignore the wishes of the pressure groups which provide them with votes, they can, through the universal politicization of public life, channel many of the demands and policies of the pressure groups in the direction of partisan expediency.

The chief instrument of interest representation are the chambers. There are eleven of these, for different occupations and professions, of which the three most important are those of Labour, Business and Agriculture. The chambers are statutory bodies. Membership is compulsory. Their main functions are:

1 to report to, and advise, legislative and executive bodies;
2 to act in the common interest of their members by reporting unanimously;
3 to participate in the work of regulatory boards, e.g. the wage and price commission;
4 to undertake research.[2]

1 F. Scheu, 'Die Kritik in der Demokratie', *Die Zukunft*, February 1956, p. 36.
2 H. P. Secher, 'Representative Democracy or "Chamber State". The ambiguous Role of Interest Groups in Austrian Politics', *Western Political Quarterly*, Vol. XIII, No. 4, 1960, pp. 892–5.

Elections within the chambers are carried out on partisan lines; as a result the SPÖ permanently dominates the Chamber of Labour, the ÖVP those of Business and Agriculture. It is by no means easy to determine whether it is the interest groups that speak through the parties or the parties that speak through the interest groups. When, in 1947, the system of wage-price commissions was set up, negotiations were entrusted to the three main chambers. This, however, resulted in a political imbalance in favour of the ÖVP. To redress this, the non-statutory, non-partisan (but SPÖ dominated) trade unions were brought in as a fourth partner. Both the interest groups and the chambers are recognized routes for the recruitment and promotion of political leaders. Julius Raab was federal President of both the Business Chamber and the ÖVP's Business League on becoming Chancellor in 1953; Karl Maisel became President of the Chamber of Labour on ceasing to be Minister of Social Welfare in 1956; Franz Olah combined the Presidency of the ÖGB with the Vice-Presidency of the National Assembly in 1959 and became Minister of the Interior in 1963.

The coalition, whatever its defects in terms of decisive policy-making, had its merits as a force for political education in a country haunted by civil war. It made a virtue of political equilibrium. Throughout the duration of the Second Republic the ÖVP has held the chancellorship (thanks, in part, to the accidents of electoral arithmetic); the SPÖ the elective presidency. The coalition remained, albeit decreasingly, popular. According to surveys 90 per cent of the electorate approved of it before the 1959 elections, 75 per cent before the 1962 election.[1] But even on the assumption that all KPÖ voters supported Socialist presidential candidates—which they probably did—the SPÖ could gain, and hold, the presidency only by winning normally 'bourgeois' votes. These come principally from national-liberal electors who feel that they can, in a presidential election, give priority to ideological, anti-clerical sentiments over economic interests. Whether there are, in any presidential or parliamentary election, electors who vote as they do specifically to preserve a balance is difficult to establish. The parties believe that such electors do exist and appeal to them in their propaganda. In 1959,

[1] F. C. Engelmann, 'Haggling for the Equilibrium. The Renegotiation of the Austrian Coalition, 1959', *American Political Science Review*, Vol. LVI, No. 3, 1962, p. 653, n. 13; *Die Meinung*, Vol. III, No. 1 (1963), p. 1.

when the ÖVP was one seat short of an absolute majority in the outgoing parliament, SPÖ posters showed a listing ship, one part labelled '82', the other '74', and bore the legend '82 + 1 = monopoly power'.[1] Voters were warned against 'single-party dominance' (*Alleinherrschaft*) in terms which exploited the electorate's fear of the abuse of power. Many commentators have regarded coalition *à l'autrichienne* as a unique and admirable device. According to Adolf Schärf 'the Roman system of two consuls seems to be repeating itself at a higher level of social evolution';[2] Gustav Kafka, an eminent constitutional theorist, predicted in 1958 that 'a return to free political competition would amount to a revolution'.[3]

Strengths and Weaknesses

Many individuals and groups felt that their interests were better protected in the larger market-place of the coalition than the smaller one of single-party government. This was true of organized labour in general, which saw the coalition as a device for getting the justice of its demands formally ratified; it was true of the greater part of agriculture and small business, which preferred the *dirigisme* of corporative bargaining to the cold blast of competition. In retrospect, the evidence seems to confirm the ÖVP's suspicions that the SPÖ benefited most from the coalition system. They gained equality of influence in a country in which there was, throughout, a 'bourgeois' majority, and in which they had been traditionally type-cast as opposition. They gained, through the *Proporz*, an entry into the bureaucracy which would otherwise probably have been denied them. They were able, through the convention of 'departmental opposition' to exercise a watching brief over the elaboration of general government policy which the ÖVP, through their tenure of the chancellorship and the Ministry of Finance, regarded as their prerogative.

From 1963 onwards the signs of strain within the coalition became more evident. Within the ÖVP the leadership was tending away from agriculture and small business, associated with the first

[1] U. Kitzinger, 'The Austrian Election of 1959', *Political Studies*, June 1961, p. 125.
[2] A. Schärf, *op. cit.*, p. 412.
[3] G. E. Kafka, *op. cit.*, p. 90.

two Chancellors, Figl (1945–53) and Raab (1953–61), towards industry, the least coalition-happy of the major interests. Raab was succeeded by Alfons Gorbach, identified with the 'reformist' wing of the party who aimed at a looser coalition structure. Gorbach was succeeded in 1964 by Josef Klaus, another 'reformer' and the first Chancellor previously to have been Minister of Finance, the office with the closest links to the views of private industry. Within SPÖ there was a short-lived anti-coalition upsurge associated chiefly with Franz Olah. In 1963 passions were stirred by the application of Dr Otto Habsburg, the pretender to the throne, for an Austrian passport. The ÖVP was in favour, the SPÖ and FPÖ against; for the first time since the formation of the coalition one of the partners voted with the opposition against the other. It was a badly chosen issue, of more interest to traditionalist party activists than the man in the street, but it demonstrated that the FPÖ was available for an opening to the Left instead of only—as had hitherto been assumed—the Right.

When at the beginning of 1966 the coalition decided on premature elections because of disagreements on the budget, the future of a rigid, equilibrial coalition—though not of the coalition itself—was raised. The ÖVP entered the campaign with a demand for a 'clear majority' and did so at a time most unfavourable to the SPÖ. Olah's financial dealings with the FPÖ gave those within the party who objected to his overbearing and intransigent temperament a chance to end his career. In 1964 he was expelled from the party and deprived of his trade union functions, whereupon he founded his own Democratic Progressive Party (DFP). Its programme was vague, but it was clearly intended to appeal to proletarian distrust of a distant, intellectual, revisionist party leadership. The DFP polled 3·3 per cent, of which an estimated 65 per cent came from discontented Socialists and 10 per cent each from former Communists or FPÖ supporters.[1] Olah's rhetoric soon took on ultra-nationalist and anti-Semitic overtones, and a splinter which could have inflicted lasting damage on a scelerotic Socialist party has degenerated into a superfluous, poujadist rival of the FPÖ. In the local elections of autumn, 1967, and spring, 1968, it polled negligibly.

[1] K. Blecha and H. Kienzl, *Die Zukunft*, May 1966.

THE END OF THE COALITION

The general election of March 6 gave the People's Party 85 seats, the Socialists 74 and the Freedom Party 6. For the first time since 1945, and the second time in the history of the Republic, the voters had given one party an absolute parliamentary majority. This verdict has in retrospect been regarded as a mandate for ending the coalition. There is no evidence that this is how the electorate saw it at the time. Pre-election surveys showed that the majority of the voters of all parties did not expect single-party government even in the event of an outright victory by one party.[1] During the campaign the SPÖ emphasized its desire to continue the coalition and the ÖVP asked only for 'the guarantee of renewed collaboration through a clear majority',[2] Other reasons for the upset must therefore be sought. On paper it had looked as though the Socialists were more likely to emerge as the strongest party. The SPÖ had trailed the ÖVP by only 60,000 votes in 1962; and the Communist withdrawal made about 120,000 votes 'available'. The threat of a Popular Front victory was emphasized in ÖVP propaganda and appears to have swayed some voters. As it turned out, by no means all the disenfranchised Communists followed their party's advice to vote Socialist; and Olah's DFP deprived the SPÖ of at least as many votes as the Communists had delivered.

Nor did it immediately occur to the two coalition parties that the election result spelt the end of their partnership. Their initial reaction was to set about the familiar routine of bargaining. Nevertheless, something fundamental had changed in the Austrian political system. The equilibrium of social forces had been an essential characteristic of the coalition era. The equilibrium justified the coalition and the coalition seemed to perpetuate the equilibrium. For the moment, at least, the equilibrium was no more, and any new coalition would have to reflect the changed ratios. It was not merely a question of those government departments—principally Justice and the nationalized industries—which the SPÖ would have to yield to the ÖVP, but more fundamentally of the nature of the coalition pact. An absolute parliamentary majority gave the ÖVP

[1] Information kindly supplied by *Sozialwissenschaftliche Studiengesellschaft.*
[2] *Wiener Zeitung*, March 6, 1967.

a sanction which neither coalition partner had possessed since 1949; it was therefore bound to hold out for a less rigid pact, one which could conceivably devolve some policy decisions on votes in parliament. On the other hand, its new minority status obliged the SPÖ to press for as many built-in guarantees as possible, in particular with regard to the minimum duration of the coalition; anything else would look too much like responsibility without power. The maximum that the ÖVP felt justified in conceding was less than the minimum that SPÖ felt bound to demand. On April 18 the Socialist Party Executive turned down the ÖVP's final offer; in less than an hour Chancellor Klaus was able to present the names of his one-party cabinet to the President.

The incompatibilities between the negotiating partners, though not insuperable, were reinforced by those elements in both parties—the industrial interests in the ÖVP and the Viennese organization in the SPÖ—which were more strongly tempted to go it alone, in office or in opposition. The decision to end the coalition was also made easier by the growing disrepute which the immobilism and the patronage of the latter years had, rightly or wrongly, inflicted on it. It was easy to see that the system by which Austria had been governed for two decades was dead; more difficult to discern the shape of the future. It is certainly premature to conclude, as does one prominent Austrian commentator that

'the new era represents nothing other than the transition to those political conditions which characterize a parliamentary democracy of the Western type'.[1]

This assertion must be subjected to three reservations: the first, that the idea of coalition government itself is by no means finally discredited in Austria; the second, that it is not yet obvious that single-party government is better qualified to solve those problems that the coalition failed to tackle; the third, that the possibilities of a genuine alternation of power on the Anglo-Saxon model have not yet been tested.

If Austria today seems to be on the threshold of parliamentary government of the mature Western type, the credit for this must

[1] Vodopivec, *Die Balkanisierung Österreichs*, p. 367.

go to the parties and the manner of their past co-operation. When the representatives of the historic *Lager* pooled their efforts to recreate an Austrian state in 1945 they took over liabilities which dated back to the limited constitutionalism of Imperial days—the inability, indeed unwillingness, to conduct a meaningful dialogue with political opponents; the temptation to put ideological purity above the survival of the common weal; and the tendency to penetrate every cranny of public and private life with party-oriented activity. In 1934 the *Lagermentalität* had found its apogee in a short but ruinous civil war. The politicians of the Second Republic made a genuine attempt at basing their country's political style on con-ciliation and compromise. Whether the ten years that elapsed between the end of the war and the state treaty would have sufficed to habituate citizens and the party rank and file to the new style is doubtful; after 21 years success was a good deal more likely. The image of the coalition is, therefore, not exclusively one of indecision and log-rolling; it is also one of co-operation, supra-partisanship and stability.

In addition, the öVP administration will have to prove itself as a more incisive decision-making organ than the coalition. It is rather badly placed to do this. Its federal, corporative structure makes it a coalition in miniature, as much plagued by overmighty subjects as its predecessor. The strength of its centrifugal forces was well illustrated by Cabinet disunity over the Budget in the autumn of 1967, involving much publicized summit meetings (*Bündegipfel*) of the leaders of the Leagues; an operation as far removed from the letter of the constitution as any in the coalition days.

Lastly, there is the question how far, in terms of electoral trends, the conditions exist for an alternation of power. Can the Austrian pendulum swing? The SPö defeat in 1966 cannot be explained solely in terms of Communist abstentions and DFP defections. Even if the Communists had withdrawn in all constituencies and all their votes, as well as the DFP's, had gone to the Socialists, the öVP would still, under the Austrian electoral system, have gained an absolute majority.[1] What had happened was the first major loosening of party-political loyalties, the first major direct transfer of support from one *Lager* to another since the foundation of the Republic.

[1] G. Golltz, 'Fast hatte es zum 86 Mandat der ÖVP gereicht', *Berichte und Informationen*, 1025, March 25, 1966.

An elaborate opinion survey found that, in contrast with previous elections:

1. three months before polling day over a million electors, out of 4,800,000, were undecided;
2. a few days before polling day 350,000 electors were still undecided;
3. the number of voters who changed allegiance reached 450,000 or about 10 per cent of the total;
4. the öVP had a majority among those voting for the first time.[1]

In this, if in no other respect, Austrian political behaviour does now resemble the Western norm. There is no inherent reason why this new electoral volatility should not, in due course, benefit the SPÖ. But to secure a reversal of the 1966 situation, i.e. a working majority of five, would require a 'swing' of 6–7 per cent, a turnover for which there is no precedent.[2] A working majority of its own is therefore not, in the short term, a realistic alternative for the SPÖ. Sitting it out in opposition is unattractive for other reasons. The habits of public patronage which blossomed in the coalition atmosphere have not, understandably, disappeared overnight. The coalition may be dead, the *Proporzmentalität* is not. In the first two years the öVP have made relatively few changes in their favour in the nationalized industries and broadcasting, but have moved in rather energetically in army and police administration. It is obvious that the Socialists cannot afford to let their opponents enjoy a monopoly of federal spoils over, say, two legislative periods while they revamp their image with the electorate. The SPÖ, therefore, has as much to gain from a revival of the coalition as from a competition for absolute majorities. As the Socialist leader, Dr Kreisky, readily admits, it would have to be a more flexible coalition than that of the 1950s and 1960s, with a greater number of topics reserved for free parliamentary votes;[3] the decline and possible disappearance of the FPÖ would then make the provision of some

[1] K. Blecha and H. Kienzl, *op. cit.*, pp. 26–7.

[2] Provincial elections in the autumn of 1967 and the spring of 1968 produced an average swing of 5·5 per cent from the öVP to the SPÖ; municipal elections in a number of major cities produced swings of between 4 and 12 per cent. But this may demonstrate no more than the continuing volatility of the Austrian electorate, and the tendency of single-party governments to suffer from mid-term unpopularity.

[3] Interview with *Die Furche*, September 30, 1967, p. 3.

sort of 'opposition within the government' more important than ever. Austrian party politics can never again be quite what they were before March 1966, but the change is unlikely to be of those 'revolutionary' dimensions which observers like Professor Kafka foresaw.

EUROPEAN INTEGRATION AND THE PARTIES

Placed in the centre of Europe and conscious of their country's supranational past, most Austrians are internationally minded. The ideological traditions of the Socialist and the Catholic *Lager* do not encourage the idealization of the sovereign nation-state. The idea of 'united Europe' is as attractive to many Austrians as it is to many West Germans—it provides a deutero-patriotism, untarnished by the symbols of the past. The only limitation placed on Austria's treaty-making powers is the obligation to 'permanent neutrality' imposed by the State Treaty. This provision was no obstacle to Austria's joining either the United Nations or the Council of Europe, which it did as soon as possible on regaining sovereignty; nor to Austria's becoming a founder member of EFTA. It has, however, bedevilled the question of Austria's relations with EEC, whether of full membership, association or 'special agreement'.

It is accepted that the neutrality clause rules out membership of EEC under Article 237. Austria's policy-makers initially assumed that it did not rule out association under Article 238. In concert with the other two neutral members of EFTA, Sweden and Switzerland, they applied for association at the end of 1961. The USSR, as a signatory of the State Treaty, has, however, made it clear that it regards EEC as an instrument of the cold war, and Austrian association with it as a disguised *Anschluss*. Whatever one may think of the merits of these objections, there is every likelihood of a Soviet veto, should the occasion arise. A further difficulty arose out of Austria's own desire to preserve not only the spirit but the substance of her neutrality. This was embodied in the three major reservations with which Austria qualified her application, and which did not endear her case to the EEC council:

1. continued treaty-making power *vis-à-vis* third powers;
2. the right to suspend articles of association in the event of a war involving EEC members;

3. the unrestricted right to import and stock food and drugs in the event of a war.[1]

The first of these reservations referred to Austria's 'most favoured nations' trade relations with the USSR, in the light of Articles 111(2), 113 and 114 of the EEC treaty; the second to the right to unilaterally restrict strategic exports. Negotiations with Brussels were resumed in 1965, the objective being a more vaguely defined 'special arrangement' instead of formal association. These, too, have come to nothing. One reason for this is purely contingent: Italy, anxious to force Austria to take stronger measures against irredentist terrorism in South Tyrol, has barred all discussion. A weightier reason is the opposition of France, which does not want further institutional complications inside EEC and sympathizes with the Soviet Union's interpretation of the neutrality clause.

The initial application for associate membership was made by the coalition government in which the Socialists held the Foreign Ministry. It was therefore a bipartisan move. Nevertheless, partisan divisions on Austria's European policy have never disappeared and have, since the failure of the Brussels initiative, come into the open. The SPÖ has always regretted more strongly than the ÖVP the failure, in the 1950s, to create a greater European Free Trade Area, which would have been the ideal solution to Austria's problems. The ÖVP has looked more favourably on the Common Market, attracted by its Christian-Democratic inspiration and the prevalence of free enterprise; the SPÖ has a preference for EFTA, with its stronger parliamentary institutions and Social Democratic bias. The chief advocate within the ÖVP of links with EEC is Dr Fritz Bock, Minister of Commerce before, Vice-Chancellor since the end of the coalition, and a spokesman for industrial interests; the chief sceptics within the SPÖ are those, like Dr Pittermann, who wish to promote Austria's bridge building with the East, or, like Karl Czernetz, one of the party's delegates to Strasbourg, who distrust the link between EEC and NATO.

As long as the coalition lasted these cleavages were more apparent among electors than party leaders. An opinion survey in 1965 elicited the following responses:[2]

---

[1] *Österreichische Zeitschrift fur Aussenpolitik*, Vol. II, No. 5, 1962, p. 293.
[2] *Die Meinung*, Vol. V, No. 1, 1965, pp. 1–2.

1. 'How do you value Austria's membership of EFTA?'

Per cent

	FPÖ	KPÖ	ÖVP	SPÖ	None
Favourably	37	46	47	59	41
Neutral	26	13	12	8	11
Unfavourably	17	22	9	9	10
Don't know	20	19	34	24	38

2. 'How would you value Austria's membership of EEC?'

Per cent

	FPÖ	KPÖ	ÖVP	SPÖ	None
Favourably	76	14	52	58	46
Neutral	nil	8	5	6	10
Unfavourably	6	67	13	19	15
Don't know	18	11	30	17	39

3 'Should Austria stay in EFTA or change over to EEC?'

Per cent

	FPÖ	KPÖ	ÖVP	SPÖ	None
Stay in EFTA	9	42	15	19	14
Change to EEC	37	4	16	9	9
Other answers	54	54	69	72	77

It is evident that Communists and Freedom Party supporters both view the issue in terms of relations with Germany, arriving at opposite conclusions, and that Socialists have a slightly greater preference for EFTA than the People's Party. There were some differences of emphasis in the parties' election manifestoes in 1966, the ÖVP pressing for 'continuation of attempts to integrate the present EFTA countries into a European market', while the SPÖ hoped for 'the realization of a great unified market of the countries of EEC and EFTA, serving 300 million people'.[1] The extent of the split between the parties was revealed on July 8, 1967, when the SPÖ voted against Dr Bock's report on his Brussels negotiations, ostensibly on the grounds of his failure to safeguard Austria's treaty-making autonomy vis-à-vis third parties. To the SPÖ's

[1] Österreichische Zeitschrift fur Aussenpolitik, Vol. VI, No. 1, 1966, pp. 24, 27.

opponents this apparent *volte-face* betrayed that they had never been sincere in their support for association; in fact it merely revealed the Opposition's superior perception of the imminent failure of Austria's European strategy, confirmed two months later when M. Pompidou, on a visit to Vienna, turned down all requests to mediate.

It is evident that political considerations are weightier than those of economic self-interest in determining the rival attitudes, since the evolution of Austria's foreign trade provides ammunition for both sides. Those who favour closer links with EEC argue that the greater part of Austria's trade must always be with her immediate neighbours, Germany and Italy; those who oppose such links argue that exclusion has enforced much needed diversification on her trading patterns. The premium on public unanimity has dampened debates within the major parties and interest groups. The independent press is pro-EEC. Those considerable branches of agriculture and industry which have most to suffer from exposure to EEC competition have not raised their voices inside the ÖVP Leagues, and the topic of economic integration was not even mentioned at the quadrennial Trade Union Congress in 1967.

In the absence of wider opportunities, Austria's European efforts are directed at the Consultative Assembly of the Council of Europe. Austria is entitled to six of the 138 seats; three each for the SPÖ and ÖVP. The SPÖ members belong to the Socialist group, those of the ÖVP to the Christian Democratic group. One of the alternative delegates has always been drawn from the FPÖ, at the expense of one or other of the big parties. The delegations have tended to be prestigious: that of the ÖVP was led by Dr Lujo Toncic-Sorinj until his appointment as Foreign Minister in 1966; that of the SPÖ has always included Dr Pittermann, the party leader and Vice-Chancellor until 1966. Karl Czernetz, another SPÖ delegate, was elected Chairman of the Socialist group in 1964. Dr Pittermann also became President of the Socialist International in 1964. The People's Party, lacking the seniority and intellectual prestige which the Socialists enjoy within their International, are apt to be overshadowed by the major Christian Democratic parties of the EEC states both at Strasbourg and within international Christian Democracy generally. The Austrian Communists have never been represented at the Consultative Assembly and count for very little in international Communist circles.

It cannot be said that participation in the Strasbourg assembly has affected the structure or policies of any of the parties, but the contributions of Austrian delegates are widely reported in the press.

APPENDIX B

Parties' share of national vote by election

I. AUSTRIAN PARLIAMENTARY ELECTIONS, 1911–1966

Percentage of total votes cast for main ideological blocs

	1911	1919	1920	1923	1927	1930	1945	1949	1953	1956	1959	1962	1966
Marxist Parties	29	41	36	40	43	42	50	44	47	47	48	47	43
Liberal-National Parties	18	✳ 18	17	13	7	16		12	11	7	8	7	✳ 5
Christian-Conservative Parties	53	36	42	45	48	42	50	44	41	46	44	45	48

Source: Österreichische Statistische Jahrbücher.

CHAPTER 8

SCANDINAVIA

This chapter on political parties in Scandinavia deals with the five countries represented on the Nordic Council, often referred to as the Nordic countries, viz., Denmark, Finland, Iceland, Norway and Sweden.

It consists of six parts. Part I provides the background—with a brief reference to the origin of the five countries as sovereign states—and the emergence of representative, responsible and democratic government which is accepted as the necessary prerequisite for the development of modern political parties. Part II deals with the general structure of the party systems and their bases and the variables conditioning their development and actual character. Part III outlines the roles of the parties in the political systems, Part IV deals with the significance for the parties of proportional representation, while Part V is concerned with the party organization, power structure and party finance. Part VI is devoted to a discussion of international and European aspects.

PART I BACKGROUND

The Countries

The five Scandinavian countries have travelled different roads to their present position as small, independent and democratic states. The three monarchies, Denmark, Norway and Sweden, existed as sovereign states more than a thousand years ago. Norway lost its independence as a result of Danish efforts towards the end of the Middle Ages to create a large all-Scandinavian state; Norway virtually became a Danish province. When Finland first emerged as an organized society it formed part of the Swedish Kingdom. In 1809, however, Sweden had to give up this eastern part of its territory to Russia. Until the Russian Revolution in 1917 Finland held the position of a Principality under the Russian Czar, retaining, however, the political institutions established during the Swedish era. Iceland came under the Norwegian Crown in the thirteenth century, and when about two centuries later Norway became a Danish dominion Iceland too fell under Danish rule. Norway severed its link with Denmark in 1814, only to be forced into a union with Sweden in the following year, with, however, its own constitution and political institutions and with complete home rule on all domestic matters. In 1905 Norway and Sweden managed to agree on a peaceful dissolution of the union. Norway elected its own King and became a sovereign state.

The two Scandinavian republics, Finland and Iceland, became independent only during the present century. Finland declared itself independent of Russia in 1917. In Iceland a kind of home rule gradually evolved from the 1870s. In 1918 it was recognized as an independent state, remaining in 'union' with Denmark under the same King until 1944, when the Republic of Iceland was proclaimed.

The Systems of Government

Here we are concerned with the development of representative, responsible, and democratic government. As in other countries, the growth of political parties in the Scandinavian countries is closely related to the emergence of representative government. For Denmark the crucial year in this respect was 1849, when the absolute monarchy, which in the seventeenth century had superseded aristocratic rule, vanished and a modern constitution with remarkably democratic features was adopted. In Norway the brief spell of revolutionary independence, 1814–15, was used to adopt a constitution. It provided for a modern parliament and served as a framework for national constitutional and political development during the enforced union with Sweden. In Sweden a parliament of four estates (nobility, clergy, burghers and peasants) emerged during the fourteenth and fifteenth centuries. For some fifty years during the eighteenth century the estates even provided a parliamentary basis for an interesting experiment in representative and responsible government. During this remarkable phase of Sweden's constitutional history parliamentary parties of great vitality, the 'Hats' and the 'Caps', played a prominent part. This so-called Era of Liberty turned out to be only an historical episode. Not until 1866 were permanent conditions for representative government created when the estates were abolished and replaced by a bicameral parliament. In Finland the parliament of four estates, inherited from Sweden, led a precarious existence during the century of Russian government. However, it was abolished in 1906, eleven years before independence, and a unicameral parliament was established. Iceland may claim to have the oldest parliament in the world. Its *Althing* can trace its history as far back as the ninth century. For several hundred years of foreign rule its political powers and functions were almost completely suspended. Only as the country moved towards independence were they gradually resumed.

The establishment of viable representative institutions, however, did not immediately create the necessary conditions for the emergence of modern party systems. Certainly political parties of some sort appeared everywhere during the nineteenth century. Insofar as these parties could wield direct political influence they were in most places, with one or two notable exceptions in Denmark, organizations existing inside the parliaments only, and not nationwide parties. Other conditions had to be fulfilled before the present pattern and role of parties were established. The governments had to be made responsible to the parliaments. They had to be based on the confidence of the parliamentary representatives, or, at least, on the tolerance of the majority in that body, rather than on personal support of the head of state. The franchise had to be widened to include most significant groups in the countries.

Norway led the way to a modern type of responsible government. After a protracted struggle with the King (of Sweden and Norway) the Norwegian Parliament won the right in 1884 to decide who should be tolerated as a government. Denmark followed suit in 1901 and in Iceland responsible government was recognized two years later, during the brief period of 'home rule' before independence. Sweden witnessed a gradual development with a first breakthrough towards parliamentary government in 1905, prompted by the desire to solve the crisis over the dissolution of the union with Norway in an atmosphere of national unity. After a brief interruption during the First World War responsible government was definitely vindicated in 1917. In Finland the Russian bond placed obvious difficulties in the path of attempts to base home rule on parliamentary, responsible government; the principle was recognized and written into the 1919 constitution. In the other Scandinavian countries it was still based on practice only, not on law. This situation remained unchanged until 1953 when Denmark codified the principle of parliamentary responsibility of the government in its Constitution. In Sweden a similar provision forms part of the current constitutional reform.

The Danish Constitution of 1849 provided for a wide and equal suffrage for men. A conservative reaction followed the disastrous war with Prussia and Austria in 1864, which deprived the country of the duchies of Schleswig and Holstein. It led *inter alia* to dual voting for privileged groups and other anti-democratic safeguards, entrenching conservative interests in the still-powerful Upper House. When the franchise restrictions were again removed, under the 1915 Constitution, it was also widened to admit women to the vote. Iceland, at that time still under Danish rule, but enjoying a considerable amount of home rule, was also covered by these regulations.

Finland was, in fact, the first country in Europe to adopt political rights for both sexes in 1906. In Norway, fully democratic suffrage, for men and women, was established in 1913. Sweden witnessed a piecemeal process in this respect, beginning with men in 1909 and proceeding to full and equal suffrage for men and women in 1918 for local elections and in 1921 for parliamentary elections.

PART II   THE BASES OF THE PRESENT PARTY STRUCTURE

Some important factors in the configuration of the party structure are virtually common to all the Scandinavian countries. These are, on the whole, variables of a socio-economic character. Other factors differ from country to country; such as historical traditions, religious issues, nationality and language problems.

The origins of modern party structures can, in general, be traced to the last decades of the nineteenth century. In Iceland and Finland important structural changes have also occurred since that formative period. The various liberation movements, religious and social, economic and political, brought about the establishment of liberal groupings. Against the organized efforts of these groupings counter-groups rallied in defence of the traditional society. On the whole, these liberal and conservative parties were parliamentary groups rather than national mass parties. In the constituencies party members based their support on civic respect and personal allegiance; not on permanent political organizations of nation-wide significance. Only gradually, as the electorates grew in number, was the need for a firm organizational basis for the parliamentary parties recognized by the late-nineteenth-century liberals and conservatives. The political labour movements, on the other hand, emerged as extra-parliamentary parties, based on mass recruiting of members. In the pre-democratic era, the franchise qualifications normally excluded the majority of workers from the ballot box.

With the growing urbanization and the ensuing increase of the urban middle class the conservative and liberal parties slackened their hold on the rural population. Special farmers' parties were formed in all countries except Denmark where the agricultural industry long retained its position as the leading branch of the country's economy and, hence, could count on sufficient support from the traditional parties. A differentiation has, however, gradually taken place in Denmark also, assigning a specific role as a farmers' party to the moderate Left Party (*Venstre*).

Since the Russian Revolution, Communist parties have emerged in all the five countries. In Denmark, Norway and Sweden they have always led a precarious existence, torn between external and internal loyalties. In recent years the Communist parties, in both Denmark and Norway, have been completely annihilated as parliamentary forces; other less Moscow-oriented parties have assumed their place on the political Right–Left continuum. The Swedish Communist Party has escaped the fate of its Danish and Norwegian counterparts only by a complete transformation, through which it has tried to adjust itself both to the new traditional patterns of welfare democracy and to the expectations of the new left. After set-backs in the 1968 election, however, the future of the Swedish Communist Party also appears highly uncertain.

Another new development in Denmark, Norway and Sweden has been the efforts towards closer co-operation or even amalgamation among the bourgeois parties in order to balance the long overwhelming domination of the Social Democratic parties. These efforts, which seem to be prompted both by socio-economic factors and by concepts of the necessity for a regular change of power in a successful parliamentary system, have brought about political changes in Norway (1965) and Denmark (1968). In both countries non-socialist coalition governments have taken office. But the efforts towards bourgeois co-operation have not yet affected the formal party structure of any of the three countries.

Religious issues have played a limited role in the development of the Scandinavian party structure. Political parties with the word 'Christian' or its equivalent exist only in Norway and Sweden. Of the two parties the Norwegian is alone of any practical significance in national politics. The Swedish Christian Democratic Party is not even represented in the *Riksdag*. In general, religious issues play a minor role in comparison with economic, welfare and security problems. However, most parties adopt some kind of attitude towards religious questions. In general it tends to be rather neutral, but it is obvious that Conservative parties normally take a more positive stand than Liberals in relation to matters concerning the traditional religious establishment. Liberal groups and parties, however, have since their formative years in the nineteenth century drawn considerable support from deeply religious movements formed in opposition to traditional orthodoxy in the State churches. This opposition has been expressed partly in the formation of dissenting 'free churches', and partly in low church revivals inside the establishment. There are very few Roman Catholics in the Scandinavian countries and as a group they have no political significance.

Ethnic issues are on the whole of little importance in Scandinavian politics. Only in Denmark and Finland have language or nationality minorities formed separate parties. Until 1960 the Slesvig party, representing the German minority in the southern border area of Denmark, could rally a sufficient number of voters to return one member to the Danish Parliament. Subsequently, it has been unable to achieve this. Among other minorities those of Faroe islands and of Greenland are guaranteed two members each by the Constitution itself. In Finland the Swedish People's Party—representing the dwindling Swedish-speaking minority—retains a certain influence. The Åland islands, with a purely Swedish population, are by law assured one seat in the Finnish Parliament. In Sweden, ethnic minorities, Lapps and Finns, have always been too small and too scattered even to dream of having an independent voice in national politics.

In the post-war period a new form of ethnic problem has emerged which may possibly in the future assume political significance in relation to parties. This development may be characterized as a reflection of the Europeanization and general internationalization of the post-war world. In Sweden the long booming economy has attracted a large amount of foreign labour. As a result some 6 or 7 per cent of the total population are either naturalized Swedes or aliens. So far the new minority groups have not made any visible impact on party politics. Most groups are too small and the only large minorities, from the other Scandinavian countries, especially Finland, still retain regular connections with their home countries and may, hence, be regarded as cross-border commuters.

Some reference should also be made to the curious 'language' issue in Norway, which had its greatest political significance during the latter part of the nineteenth century and the early part of the twentieth. This issue took the form of a struggle to substitute a new Norwegian language, built on rural dialects, for the traditional, official and Danish-influenced city language. Formal equality between old and new Norwegian was recognized in the 1880s. The language issue reflected, however, a cultural and a social struggle, not a conflict with ethnic roots. Recent efforts to overcome the split created by the century-old language battles may be regarded as a recognition, long overdue, of the fact that the issues underlying the conflict are all obsolete, solved or dead.

In view of the foregoing, one can conclude that Scandinavian party systems generally operate amongst peoples of great homogeneity. The patterns which emerge, despite some notable exceptions, tend to be remarkably similar.

TABLE I

Parties represented in the parliaments of the Scandinavian countries, 1969

CONSERVATIVE PARTIES

Denmark: *Det konservative folkeparti* (Conservative People's Party)
Finland: *Kansallinen kokoomuspuole* (National Unity Party)
Iceland: See Conservative and Liberal
Norway: *Høyre* (The Right Party)
Sweden: *Högerpartiet* (The Right Party)[1]

CONSERVATIVE AND LIBERAL PARTIES

Finland: *Svenska folkpartiet* (Swedish People's Party)
Iceland: *Sjalfstaedisflokkurinn* (Independence Party)

[1] In 1969 the Swedish Conservative Party decided to change its name to *Moderata samlingspartiet* (Moderate Unity Party).

CHRISTIAN PARTY

Norway: *Kristelig folkeparti* (Christian People's Party)

LIBERAL PARTIES

Denmark: *Det radikale venstre* (The Radical Left)
Finland: *Liberaalinen kansanpuolue* (Liberal People's Party)
Iceland: See Conservative and Liberal, also Farmers—Centre parties
Norway: *Venstre* (Left Party)
Sweden: *Folkpartiet* (People's Party)

FARMERS—CENTRE PARTIES

Denmark: *Venstre* (the Left Party)
Finland: *Keskustapuolue* (Centre Party)
           Suomen maasutupuolue (Small Farmer's Party)
Iceland: *Framsóknarflokkurinn* (Progressive Party)
Norway: *Senterpartiet* (Centre Party)
Sweden: *Centerpartiet* (Centre Party)

SOCIAL DEMOCRATIC PARTIES

Denmark: *Socialdemokratiet* (Social Democracy)
Finland: *Sosialidemokraattinen puolue* (Social Democratic Party)
           Työväen ja pienviljelijäin sosialidemokraattinen liitto (Workers'
           and Small Farmers' Social Democratic League)
Iceland: *Alpthyduflokkurinn* (Social Democratic Party)
Norway: *Det norske arbeiderparti* (the Norwegian Labour Party)
Sweden: *Sveriges soialdemokratiska arbetareparti* (Swedish Social
           Democratic Labour Party)

LEFT SOCIALIST AND COMMUNIST PARTIES

Denmark: *Socialistisk folkeparti* (Socialist People's Party)
           Venstresocialisterne (Left Socialists)
Finland: *Suomen kansan demokrattinnen liitto/Demokratiska førbundet
           för Finlands folk* (Democratic League for the people of Finland,
           or The People's Democrats)
Iceland: *Alpthydubandalgi* (People's Alliance)
Norway: *Sosialistisk folkeparti* (Socialist People's Party)
Sweden: *Vänsterpartiet kommunisterna* (Communist Left Party)

The parties (see Table I) are primarily arranged according to the traditional ideological Right–Left continuum. Two exceptions have been made to this rule. The Farmers' parties have been put in a special group. Generally these parties come, in ideological terms, close to the Liberal parties. This is especially true of the Danish Left Party and the Icelandic Progressive Party. Both are sometimes labelled as Liberal rather than as Farmers' parties. It is becoming increasingly true also of the Centre parties of Norway and Sweden.

The Norwegian Christian People's Party is basically a religious party but has, by choosing its general position first in opposition to the Labour Government until 1965 and, subsequently, as a coalition partner in the bourgeois Government, justified a place close to the category: 'Conservative and Liberal parties'.

PART III THE ROLES OF THE PARTIES IN THE POLITICAL SYSTEMS

The study of the role of parties in the political system of a country or group of countries can be approached in several ways of which two will be followed here. One is to look at the parties in terms of systems analysis; the other is to state the part that the various parties have played in politics over a selected period of time.

In analytical terms the role of a political system is to distribute values in an authoritative manner accepted as binding by the members of the system. A political system has certain input and output functions. The input functions, in Almondian terms, are those of socialization and recruitment, of the articulation and aggregation of interests, and of communication. The output functions are defined as rule-making, rule application and rule adjudication.[1] The roles of political parties are primarily related to the input functions in a political system.

Input Functions

Socialization, defined as the process by which young (and other new) members of societies are educated into the political values of the civilization in which they live, is a wide and comprehensive function. Several factors contribute to this process: families, schools, various voluntary associations, local and national public institutions; indeed, the whole influence or pressure exercised by the total national environment.

By and large the political parties in the Scandinavian countries play a significant part in this process. The national parties constitute mass organizations with widespread educational activities, in both indirect and direct forms, as one of their major tasks. The signifi-

[1] Gabriel Al Almond, A Functional Approach to Comparative Politics, in Almond and Coleman, *The Politics of the Developing Areas*, Princeton, N.J., Princeton University Press, 1960.

cance of political youth organizations, which exist among most parties, should be obvious. Special women's party organizations are also notable participants in this process. Many of these bodies, based on currently criticized ideas of special 'sex roles' were formed when women had to be 'socialized' and 'recruited' to participate in the political system during the struggle for female suffrage.

Another instance of social education is provided by associations for voluntary education, many of which are sponsored by political parties, although often in conjunction with other organizations. Of equal or possibly greater significance is the fact that there is constantly—and traditionally—a lively party debate through various mass media, books, newspapers and periodicals, radio and television, which exercises a permanent educational influence. General loyalty to the same basic principles, marking practically all political parties in Scandinavia—perhaps with a question mark in the margin for some minor groups which have at times propagated ideas foreign to the ideals accepted by the system as a whole—is probably the strongest single element in the socialization contribution by the political parties. The same idea may be expressed in the simple statement that the Scandinavian societies are non-revolutionary, homogeneous, stable and contented.

Socialization may, however, be looked upon not only in terms of induction into the political culture but also of preservation. Loyalties and acceptance of the rules have not only to be fostered in the younger generation but also maintained among those who have been 'recruited' into specific roles in the system. Here the political parties serve a useful and necessary purpose in all the Scandinavian countries, although not in exactly the same manner or to the same extent. It is a purpose that is easy to assert but difficult to measure. On the whole, the parties have a strong organizational structure, with relatively large memberships (measured in percentage of total national votes at general elections) and with a fairly large number of members performing tasks of varying importance in the work of their party.

In general systems terms, the input role assigned to political parties is primarily that of aggregating interests articulated by various interest groups and similar bodies. The ideal model is that of well-socialized citizens who articulate their interests through numerous, well-organized voluntary associations and find their interests aggregated in well-balanced proportions in political parties.

Now, the role of political parties is not as simple as that. Some parties may be aggregates of different interests while others tend to articulate the interests of one major, distinct interest in the society. We have noted that all the Scandinavian countries have multiparty systems. Such a structure may obviously provide better possibilities for representation of limited group interests than basic two-party systems; e.g., the British or the American type.

Some parties in the Scandinavian countries show this tendency to reflect distinct and limited interests. The general development, however, is clearly in the direction of diminishing this tendency. In an increasingly diversified society it is necessary for all parties to seek support outside the original groups or interests for which the party may originally have catered. This is clearly the case with the labour parties which started as political organizations with the very definite purpose of representing the interests of manual labour and with goals and ideals in accordance with the recognized needs of the 'proletariat'. Later, they have everywhere found it necessary to widen their appeal to other groups and interests, in order to gain the necessary strength in votes to preserve or win, as the case may be, a clear majority support among the electorate.

The Farmers' parties, especially in Finland, Iceland, Norway and Sweden, have found themselves in a similar situation. For a long time they regarded the pure articulation of farmers' and rural interests as their chief or even sole function. In postwar years, however, the farmers have decreased in numbers and hence also in political significance. As a consequence, the Farmers' parties have everywhere tried to broaden their support to include other groups as well, with some important interests similar to those of the farmers, such as other rural groups, artisans and small entrepreneurs. Beginning in Sweden in 1957 and later followed in Norway and Finland, previously exclusive farmers' parties have transformed themselves into 'Centre' parties.

Stretching the definition, ideology may also be regarded as an 'interest' that has to be 'articulated'. If ideology is taken in the traditional nineteenth century sense, most modern parties may be regarded as bearers of 'synthetic' ideologies drawn from conservatism, liberalism and socialism. Parties, hence, represent aggregates both of interests and of ideologies, although differing in the proportions of the elements in the mixture. This is true of all the parties representing by name or tradition the classical ideologies—conservative parties, liberal parties, and social democrats. On the whole it applies also to Farmers' parties some of whom have, nevertheless, at times, explicitly disclaimed any ideological heritage of this kind.

In one or two cases ideology may be seen as an overriding interest which the parties concerned regard as the chief interest that they have to represent. This was for a long time definitely the case with the Communist parties, representing a specific kind of ideology, dominating their whole political behaviour. This ideology provided an unusually unambiguous profile, but it also limited the electoral appeal. In recent years the Communists have been more or less completely superseded by, or transformed into, left-socialist parties; in some cases even abandoning the former label completely. Their ideological attitude has changed and their international allegiance has been abandoned.

This development leaves only one category of party which may be said to have reserved, as a basic function, the articulation of very special and limited ideological interests, viz. the Christian parties (in Norway and Sweden). In a general way they could be considered as bourgeois parties, but they represent different interests and strata in the societies concerned. In actual fact, their social composition seems to be of subordinate importance. Their wish to promote what they regard as true Christian interests provides the overriding common concern and cohesive element.

The role of the political parties as representatives of various socio-economic groups in the Scandinavian countries has been the subject of several studies. Some of the results are indicated in the following tables. It should be noted that the data have not been compiled according to the same pattern and at the same time in all the countries. The tables should, nevertheless, help to illustrate the aggregational aspect of the parties' functions in the political systems of the countries concerned. The tables cover the four major countries. For Iceland no relevant data are available.

The Danish figures refer to 1963. It is to be regretted that in the Danish Gallup poll, on which Table II is based, the categories housewives and pensioners have not been split up among the other groups.

331

TABLE II

Danish parties and social groups
(Percentage composition of parties by social groups)

Parties	Socialist PP	Social Democrats	Radical Left	Left Party	Conserva- tive PP
Workers	59	34	18	8	10
White collar	11	14	11	6	27
Farmers	0	1	16	31	3
Entrepreneurs	1	3	5	9	18
Housewives	22	28	36	33	28
Pensioners	7	18	12	10	9
Not gainfully employed	—	2	2	3	5

Source: Danish Gallup and Berlingske Tidende

The Finnish material is ten years old but may still be considered to be fairly representative. In his work on *Structural Cleavages in Finnish Politics* Erik Allardt divided the electorate into three groups, farmers, workers and intellectuals. His results are shown in Table III.

TABLE III

Finnish parties and social groups
(Percentage break-down of social groups according to party preference)

Parties	Farmers (308)	Workers (431)	Intellectuals (133)
Social Democrats	3	34	14
People's Democrats	9	34	5
Farmers (now Centre)	54	5	5
Other bourgeois	17	11	61
No answer	17	16	15

The Norwegian data are on the whole organized according to the same pattern as the Finnish. They emanate from an investigation of voters' attitudes before the 1957 Election and are taken from Henry Valen's and Daniel Katz's *Political Parties in Norway.*

TABLE IV

Norwegian parties and social groups
(Percentage break-down of social groups according to party preference)

Parties	Fishers and farmers (283)	Manual workers (479)	White collar (336)	No occupa-tion (31)
Communists	1	3	1	—
Labour Party	41	61	26	32
Liberals	4	3	4	6
Christian Party	7	4	9	10
Farmers (now Centre)	17	1	1	—
Conservatives	7	7	34	10
Uncertain	8	10	15	16
Non-Voters	15	11	10	26

In Sweden the Central Bureau of Statistics gave the following data from a sample investigation of party affiliation among different social groups at the General Election in 1964.

TABLE V

Swedish parties and social groups
(Percentage break-down of social groups according to party preference)

Groups	Major employers in higher posts, etc.	Farmers	Smaller employers	Other salaried employees	Agricultural workers	Other workers
Conservatives	46	13	15	14	4	3
Centre	3	64	17	6	21	8
Liberals	30	12	34	25	14	7
Socialists	8	7	25	46	51	74
Communists	—	—	1	2	4	4
Others	9	2	3	4	1	2
Not known	4	2	5	3	5	2

The fourth input function in the Almondian pattern is represented by communication. Here the role of the parties is obvious. Communications have, from the point of view of the parties, several different aspects, and concern both the informal flow of information from the parties themselves to the core of the political system, viz. the institutions charged with formal decision-making, primarily parliament and government. Information and propaganda fulfil an integrating, cohesive function within the parties and also carry the party message through various channels to the electorate.

The techniques employed for securing information from supporting interests differ from party to party. As a broad generalization, it may be said that Labour parties usually maintain a strong organizational link with their chief supporters, i.e. the trade unions and the workers. This link may be formalized in collective or bloc affiliation; as in Norway and Sweden. Trade unions may also be represented on various party bodies without formal party affiliation. This kind of relationship has been adopted in Denmark, where trade-union interests are guaranteed *ex officio* representation on the governing bodies of the national party organization of the Social Democratic Party (see Chart I, p. 353). In Finland and Iceland the workers are split between two or three parties. In Iceland the Communist-dominated People's Alliance has, for a long time, been the chief beneficiary of the relationship between trade unions and labour politics. In Finland trade unionism is split in its political allegiance.

For other parties this kind of contact with supporting interests is not possible. Not even the farmers, in spite of the heavy concentration of their vote for various parties specifically representing them, have dared to suggest anything approaching bloc affiliation. Combination of leading posts, e.g. in farmers' organizations with a leading position in the relevant party, can often serve as an effective, albeit, informal link between interest and party. Frequently, parties try to create inside their own organization machinery for contact with important interests. This may take the form of various party sub-committees or *ad hoc* working parties with the task of providing sympathetic or, otherwise, important interests with an opportunity to voice their opinions inside the formal party structure.

Communications also mean an opportunity for the parties to convey their messages to the electorate. This brings the role of mass media into focus. As a broad generalization, it may be said that the social democratic press is weaker, in both absolute and relative terms than the bourgeois press. The difference is primarily caused by the notorious weakness of the metropolitan Labour press. In Sweden there is no Labour morning paper in the capital. In the other countries the labour papers in the national capitals lead a very precarious existence, usually saved by lavish support from the trade unions. The provincial Labour press is on the whole more vital.

Radio and television provide, on the whole, equal opportunities for all parties. These mass media are put at the disposal of the parties on equal terms and free of charge as a public service. Political broadcasts and television programmes are a regular feature. During election campaigns they form a major part of the radio and television productions. On the whole television is regarded as the most important medium of political communication; more as an instrument for information—and, perhaps, serious entertainment—than for direct influence on voting behaviour.

Output Functions
The input functions of the political parties are, on the whole, identical for the party systems in all the Scandinavian countries. On the output side, parties in office play a major role in all the countries through responsible, parliamentary governments. Opposition parties, too, perform useful and important output functions. The functions in which the parties represented in the parliaments have a share fall, according to the model followed here, into the categories of rule-making and of rule application. All parties represented in a legislature participate in the former function. The latter function, that of rule application, is on the whole reserved for the party in office, in its role of providing political leadership for the administrative machinery.

Under the parliamentary system of government, parties in office have a predominant influence, whenever they are supported by a working majority. The role of the opposition, which works mainly by criticizing the activities of the government and the policies of the party or parties responsible for keeping the government in office, is primarily that of indirect influence and modification. When minority governments are in office, the role of the opposition parties in formulating compromises between various interests and party attitudes is, of course, much more significant.

So far this section has been descriptive of the situation prevailing in parliamentary countries in general. With some qualifications it is also applicable to the Scandinavian countries. If a widespread spirit of compromise exists, opposition parties can exert a direct influence

TABLE VI
Political parties in Denmark, 1945–1968
(Strength of parties in Folketing elections and seats in the Folketing)

Parties		1945	1947	1950	1953 : 1	1953 : 2	1957	1960	1964	1966	1968
Social Democratic	%	32·8	40·0	39·6	40·4	41·3	39·4	42·1	42·0	38·2	34·2
	M	48	57	59	61	74	70	76	76	69	62
Radical Left	%	8·1	6·9	8·2	8·6	7·8	7·8	5·8	5·3	7·3	15·0
	M	11	10	12	13	14	14	11	10	13	27
Conservative People's Party	%	18·2	12·4	17·8	17·3	16·8	16·6	17·9	20·0	18·7	20·4
	M	26	17	27	26	30	30	32	36	34	37
Left Party	%	23·4	27·6	21·3	22·1	23·1	25·1	21·1	21·0	19·3	18·6
	M	38	49	32	33	42	45	38	38	35	34
League of Justice	%	1·9	4·5	8·2	5·6	3·5	5·3	2·2	1·4	0·7	0·6
	M	3	6	12	9	6	9	0	0	0	0
Communists	%	12·5	6·8	4·6	4·8	4·3	3·1	1·1	1·3	0·8	1·0
	M	18	9	7	7	8	6	0	0	0	0
Socialist People's Party	%	—	—	—	—	—	—	6·1	6·0	10·9	6·1
	M	—	—	—	—	—	—	11	10	20	11
Socialist Left Party	%	—	—	—	—	—	—	—	—	—	2·0
	M	—	—	—	—	—	—	—	—	—	4
Liberal Centre	%	—	—	—	—	—	—	—	—	2·5	1·3
	M	—	—	—	—	—	—	—	—	4	0
Independent Party	%	—	—	—	—	2·7	2·3	3·3	2·5	1·6	0·5
	M	—	—	—	—	0	0	6	5	0	0
Danish Unity	%	3·1	1·0	—	0·6	—	—	—	—	—	—
	M	4	0	—	0	—	—	—	—	—	—
Slesvig Party	%	—	0·3	0·3	0·3	0·4	0·3	0·7	0·3	—	0·2
	M	—	0	0	0	1	1	1	0	—	0
Total participation	%	86·3	85·8	81·9	80·8	80·6	83·7	85·8	85·6	88·6	89·3

of considerable significance, even if they are in a clear minority. This does not only apply to a country—like Denmark—where the necessity of compromise has been fostered by frequent coalitions and minority governments. It may be equally true of a country of seemingly monolithic party stability and strength, like Sweden. Many issues, dealing not only with vital problems of national security (defence, foreign policy) but also with domestic questions, have often been solved by broad interparty agreements.

Government and Oppositional Roles

The roles of various parties in Scandinavian countries can best be considered by a summary review of the parts they have played during the postwar years in relation to the major roles of government and opposition. Again, sweeping generalizations are as difficult as they are dangerous. The situations in the five Scandinavian countries are in many respects influenced by special conditions. For this reason, the present aspect of the role of the parties will first be considered on a country-by-country basis.

It should be noted that Table VI does not include the special seats assigned to the Faroe Islands and to Greenland (since 1953 two seats for each area). The table invites many comments. The steady but usually still-born attempts to form new parties is a typical feature of Danish politics. What emerges clearly is the leading, although not completely dominating, role of the Social Democrats. Only three times since 1945 have they been in opposition—during the Left-Party minority government of 1945–47; during the Left-Conservative minority coalition of 1950–53; and since January 1968 throughout the Liberal–Farmer–Conservative (Radical Left, Left Party, Conservative People's Party) majority coalition. These data, however, may give a false idea of the strength of the Social Democrats and also an exaggerated impression of political stability.

The most crucial factor has not been the strength of the Social Democrats, who have never commanded an independent majority, either in the electorate or in the *Folketing*, but rather weakness and disunity in the opposition parties. On the whole, the party constellations during the postwar years have led to weak governments. Only during the years 1957–64 and since January 1968 were the governments supported by a clear, albeit heterogeneous majority. Political instability is an adjunct to parliamentary weakness. In

TABLE VII

Political parties in Finland, 1945–1966

Parties		1945	1948	1951	1954	1958	1962	1966	Number of Governments on which party represented
National Unity (Conservative)	%	15·0	17·1	14·6	12·8	15·3	15·0	13·8	4
	M	28	33	28	24	29	32	26	
Swedish People's Party	%	8·2	7·7	7·5	7·0	6·8	6·4	6·0	13
	M	15	14	15	13	14	14	12	
Finnish Liberals	%	5·9	3·9	5·6	7·9	5·9	6·5	6·5	11
	M	9	5	10	13	8	14	8	
Centre Party (Agrarians)	%	21·3	24·3	23·2	24·1	23·1	23·0	21·3	19
	M	49	56	51	53	48	53	50	
Small Farmers' Party	%	—	—	—	—	—	—	1·0	
	M	—	—	—	—	—	—	1	
Social Democratic Party	%	25·1	26·3	26·3	26·2	23·1	19·5	27·2	11
	M	50	54	53	54	48	38	55	
Social Democratic League	%	—	—	—	—	1·7	4·4	2·6	1
	M	—	—	—	—	3	2	6	
People's Democrats	%	23·5	20·5	21·5	21·6	23·2	22·0	21·2	3
	M	49	38	43	43	50	47	42	
Total participation	%	74·9	78·2	74·6	79·9	75·0	85·1	83·0	Total number of party governments 20

Danish politics this fact is demonstrated by the frequency of general elections.

It may, nevertheless, be argued that Danish politics have for long periods been marked by some kind of stability. This may be illustrated by the fact that all the governments between 1953 and 1968 *all?* were led by Social Democrats, with or without coalition or independent support by other parties. In part, this permanence of one party in a leading position may be explained by the role performed by the Radical Left. Normally this is a very small party (see Table VI) but it has, with few exceptions held a decisive position between socialist and bourgeois parties. For long periods—in or out of government—the Radical Left has supported the Social Democrats. Only in recent years does this situation seem to have changed. From 1966 the Social Democrats openly relied on unofficial support not from the Radical Left but from a party on their own left, the Socialist People's Party. In the 1960 Election the latter party had routed the Communist Party—from which its own leader had been expelled—as a parliamentary force and assumed the role of left-wing critics of the Social Democrats. This unofficial coalition obviously meant a Social Democratic swing to the left but also a move to the right for supporters of the Socialist People's Party.

This situation produced two important political effects. In 1967 the Socialist People's Party split. As a consequence the Social Democratic government lost its parliamentary majority. The Radical Left, on the other hand, reinforced its new orientation towards the other bourgeois parties. All this led in January 1968 to a situation in which the Danish electorate was faced with an unusual, rather unambiguous choice between the Social Democrats and the bourgeois parties. Such a situation, in close conformity with the ideas underlying British two-party notions, are in clear conflict with Danish political traditions—and hence, perhaps, unlikely to persist over a long period. The immediate effect, however, was to substitute a bourgeois coalition for the Social Democratic minority government.

Finnish politics resemble, in some respect, French politics during the Third and Fourth Republics. Since April 1945 there have been 23 governments. Among these three were 'non-party' governments, while the remainder represented different combinations of parties. This instability, characteristic of Finnish parliamentarianism, arises in part from deep-rooted historical antagonisms. The French parallel should, however, not be carried too far. The Finnish political system has clearly proved more viable than that of the Fourth Republic in France. To point to any single explanation would be an oversimplification. In part, it may be explained by the restrictive influences exercised by Finland's rather precarious position in the international system.

One party stands out as the dominating actor on the Finnish scene, viz. the Centre Party (formerly called the Agrarian Party and still basically representing the Finnish small farmers). The Centre Party participated in 20 of 21 party governments since 1945, supplying 12 with the Prime Minister—in five cases Mr Kekkonen until he, in 1956, became President of the Republic. One party government was a Social Democratic minority cabinet.

In view of their parliamentary strength and normal position as the largest party among the electorate, and of their participation in 12 governments, the Social Democrats come second in importance as a government party. The fact that they have been out of office for long periods marks them also as the leading opposition party in the postwar years. In the last ten years the Social Democrats have been weakened by the formation of a break-away party, the Social Democratic League.

The People's Democrats (or the Democratic League for the People of Finland), led by the Communists, hold a special position. In size they are about equal to the Centre and the Social Democrats. Historically they represent both the socialist critics of the second Finnish–Russian War (1941–44) and the old Communist Party which was outlawed in 1930 and remained out of open politics for 14 years. After the war they held leading positions in the governments until 1948. In that year a Communist *coup* on the Czech model was averted and the People's Democrats were then kept out of responsible politics until 1966 when they were readmitted to ministerial office.

On the right wing the National Unity Party has also, as a rule, been avoided as a government partner, as being too identified with pro-German war-time movements. These restraints, both to the left and to the right, did in fact for long periods limit the possible basis of governments to the Agrarian Centre, the Social Democrats, the Swedish People's Party and the Finnish Liberals. The limited basis—due to these self-restraints—of Finnish parliamentary politics ex-

TABLE VIII

Political parties in Iceland, 1946–1967

Parties	%	1946	1949	1953	1956	1959 : 1	1959 : 2	1963	1967
Independence Party	%	39·5	39·5	37·1	42·4	42·6	39·7	41·4	37·5
	M	20	19	21	19	20	24	24	23
Progressive (Country) Party	%	23·2	24·5	21·9	15·6	27·3	25·7	28·2	28·1
	M	13	17	16	17	19	17	19	18
Republican Party	%	—	—	3·3	—	—	—	—	—
	M	—	—	0	—	—	—	—	—
Social Democrats	%	17·8	16·5	15·6	18·3	12·4	15·2	14·2	15·7
	M	9	7	6	8	6	9	8	9
Nationalist Party	%	—	—	6·0	4·5	2·5	3·4	—	—
	M	—	—	2	0	0	0	—	—
Communists	%	19·5	19·5	16·1	19·2	15·2	16·0	16·0	17·6
	M	10	9	7	8	7	10	9	10
Total participation	%						90·1	91·1	90·4

plain the concentration towards the middle of politics by most coalitions.

As in Finland, politics in Iceland are marked by coalitions, recurring in various patterns. But unlike Finland, Iceland represents a picture of considerable governmental stability. Seven—or, technically speaking, nine governments in 24 years imply an average life far longer than that of the governments in Denmark but much less than in Norway or Sweden. Icelandic governments have been dominated by the Independence Party, in shifting coalitions. Only from 1956 to 1959 was this large bourgeois party of both liberal and conservative traditions in opposition, first to a coalition of all the others and then to a Social Democratic minority government. The coalitions in which the Independence Party has participated were either grand coalitions of all parties (1944–47) or all except the Communists (1947–49), or with the non-socialist Progressive Party (1950–56), or—since 1959—with the Social Democrats.

TABLE IX
Political parties in Norway, 1945–1965

The Norwegian party table is arranged in order to indicate the effects of special party coalition lists. On Table IX the number of members elected for each party is given under the vote percentage for the 'pure' party lists. However, some of these members were obviously elected on the party coalition lists which are specified below the parties.

Parties		1945	1949	1953	1957	1961	1965
1. Conservative Party	%	17·0	15·9	18·4	16·8	19·3	19·6
	M	25	23	27	29	29	31
2. Farmers' Centre Party	%	8·0	4·7	8·8	8·6	6·8	9·6
	M	10	12	14	15	16	18
3. Christian Party	%	7·9	8·4	10·5	10·2	9·3	7·8
	M	8	9	14	12	15	13
4. Liberal Party	%	13·8	12·5	10·0	9·6	7·2	10·1
	M	20	21	15	15	14	18
5. Labour Party	%	41·0	45·7	46·7	48·3	46·8	43·2
	M	76	85	77	78	74	68
6. Communist Party	%	11·9	5·8	5·1	3·4	2·9	1·4
	M	11	0	3	1	0	0
7. Socialist People's Party	%	—	—	—	—	2·4	6·0
	M	—	—	—	—	2	2

Party Coalitions

1 + 2	%	—	2·0	0·6	2·5	—	—
1 + 3	%	—	—	—	—	1·0	1·8
1 + 4	%	—	—	—	0·3	—	—
2 + 4	%	—	1·3	—	—	4·1	0·6
1 + 2 + 4	%	—	2·6	—	—	—	—
Total	%	76·4	82·0	79·3	78·3	79·1	85·4

After the end of the war and of German occupation, Norway resumed normal political activities with an attempt to preserve national unity under a broad coalition government. This experiment failed and from 1945 Norwegian political affairs were led by the Labour Party—often supported by a rather narrow majority in the *Storting*. After the 1961 Elections the Labour Party had two fewer seats than the other parties combined and was maintained in office only by the support normally provided by the two members of the Socialist People's Party. At one time, in 1963, the two turned their influence against the government, causing its resignation and an

TABLE X

Political parties in Sweden, 1944–1968

Parties		1944	1948	1952	1956	1958	1960	1964	1968[1]
Conservative	%	15·9	12·3	14·4	17·1	19·5	16·5	13·7	13·9
Party	M	39	23	31	42	45	39	32	32
Farmers' Centre	%	13·6	12·4	10·7	9·4	12·7	13·6	13·4	16·1
Party	M	35	30	26	19	32	34	35	39
Liberal	%	12·9	22·8	24·4	23·8	18·2	17·5	17·1	15·0
Party	M	26	57	58	58	38	40	42	34
Christian Democratic	%	—	—	—	—	—	—	1·8	1·5
Party	M	—	—	—	—	—	—	—	—
Bourgeois Unity	%	—	—	—	—	—	—	1·5	—
Movement	M	—	—	—	—	—	—	3	—
Social Democratic	%	46·7	46·1	46·1	44·6	46·2	47·8	47·3	50·1
Party	M	115	112	110	106	111	114	113	125
Communist	%	10·5	6·3	4·3	5·0	3·4	4·5	5·2	3·0
Party	M	15	8	5	6	5	5	8	3
Total participation	%	71·9	82·7	79·1	79·9	77·4	85·9	83·9	88·7

[1] Bourgeois party coalition votes distributed among the parties.

experiment lasting less than a month with a bourgeois coalition government. This cabinet proved to be a rehearsal for the government that followed the defeat of the Labour Party in the 1965 Election. By proving able to co-operate in an effective coalition government, the bourgeois parties in Norway may be said to have set an example—before the Danes who followed in 1968—of how to overcome the traditional effects of a multiparty opposition, facing a monolithic government party.

The figures in Table X refer to elections to the Lower House of the Swedish *Riksdag*. Sweden has, even more than Norway, in practice divided up the functions of the parties between the Social Democrats and the non-socialist parties in seemingly permanent roles of government and opposition. As in Denmark and Norway the greatest source of strength for the Social Democrats may be claimed to have been the notorious disunity of the opposition.

The only element of mobility in the Swedish postwar system has been provided by Social Democratic tactics in looking for outside support in critical situations: in 1951–57 from the Farmers (now Centre) by means of a formal coalition government; and in recent years, until 1969, without any formal arrangements, by leaning more to the left in order to catch the wind of left-socialist revival from which the Communists (now reformed as the Communist Left Party) emerged as the first political beneficiary.

Efforts by the bourgeois parties to mobilize the strength necessary to make them into a viable alternative government have, on the whole, been limited to increasing co-operation—with the possibility open for future formal unification—between the Liberal Party and the Centre Party. The Conservatives have been left outside joint efforts by these two parties to increase their own credibility as a progressive alternative to the Social Democrats. A countermovement in favour of co-operation between the two 'middle' parties and the Conservatives aiming at a united bourgeois opposition, and later government, has had a disturbing effect on the unity movements by being neither a success nor a complete failure.

The Art of Compromise

In systems theory the role primarily assigned to political parties is that of aggregating interests. The ideal party in such a pattern is one which embraces a sufficiently wide range of interests to produce something that may be called truly national policies. The model is formulated by Americans and fits the American party system, the two dominating actors in which, by and large, represent the whole social and economic range in interests.

In the Scandinavian countries, characterized by multiparty systems, individual parties may be regarded as insufficient or imperfect instruments for representing all the interests necessary to formulate national policies. This theoretical weakness, which is not necessarily a practical defect, has been met in different ways. Under the Scandinavian multiparty systems, most parties, indeed all parties not representing extreme policies, have a tendency to look to the moderate, average man, thereby reducing the impact of whatever special and limited interest the party may represent. Apart from this, the problem of aggregating special interests into national policies has prompted different solutions, connected with the characteristic features of the national party systems and with various national traditions. In Denmark, minority governments have been the rule. This has contributed to enhancing the significance of the *Folketing* itself as a major factor— a scene rather than an actor—in the process of interest-aggregation and policy-making. In Finland and in Iceland, governments are normally based on coalitions, often including both ends of the ideological continuum: bourgeois and socialist parties. Here the final aggregation of interests can, to a large extent, be effected by the government itself. The lack of stability in Finnish politics indicates, however, that this process of interest aggregation and policy-making often meets with great difficulties. Hence compromises reached between parties outside the government, in the *Eduskunta* (Parliament) or by informal party contacts, can also play a significant part in the process.

Sweden and Norway have been dominated by Social Democratic Labour governments during most of the postwar era. Proposals introduced by the government in the respective parliaments, the Norwegian *Storting* and the Swedish *Riksdag*, have, with a few exceptions, been 'finished products' from the point of view of interest aggregation. They represent the compromises between interests that the government, in view of their own basic policies and underlying party tactics, are ready to accept. This means that the final aggregation of interest, to a large extent, has been effected before its introduction in parliament. The function of aggregating interests into national policies has, on the whole, taken the form of what may be called 'antecedent consultations'. Procedures of this kind are obviously part of the systems of working out viable compromises. They may, however, be assumed to be of special significance in countries dominated by a single party with a rather limited interest base.

The most elaborate method for this purpose is probably represented by the Swedish system of investigations by 'expert commissions' often including representatives of the major parties and interest organizations. The commission reports, normally available to the general public immediately on their delivery to the government, are followed by a process which invites comments and recommendations on the reports from all interests concerned, whether private or public. The whole process bears clear similarities to British Royal Commissions—with the difference, however, that in Sweden the method is used far more frequently (the annual average is about two hundred per year) and, like the whole Swedish administration, is more open to public inspection and, hence, also more effective in provoking an informed debate in mass media. Another method, less dramatic but probably at least as effective, of providing for the aggregation of interests necessary for viable policies consists in continuous consultations, both formal and informal, between the ministries and representatives of important interests. These consultations are often carried out by top-level administrators (civil servants) rather than politicians. This rather unspectacular form of 'antecedent consultation' is used in all the Scandinavian countries.

PART IV   THE ROLE OF PROPORTIONAL REPRESENTATION

So far we have mainly been dealing with the role of the political parties according to the concepts of political systems theory. Obviously, the functioning of parties is related not only to their place in the political process but also to the conditions imposed on their activity by public legislation. In the five countries under consideration the state intervenes very little in the activities of the parties. Its chief function is to provide guarantees for the freedom of the parties to fulfil their vital functions in a democracy. It has also to provide a set of basic rules in the form of laws governing elections to representative bodies.

The electoral law is of great significance for the parties. Firstly, the distribution of seats between constituencies and the method of assigning seats according to votes to the various parties determine whether the parliamentary parties—and similar groups in various elected municipal bodies—may be regarded as truly representative. Secondly, the very structure which is laid down for the constituency organization in electoral law is of fundamental importance for the structure of party organization. The first aspect will be dealt with here, while the second will be discussed in Part V.

All the Scandinavian countries have adopted proportional representation. In Denmark, Norway and Sweden it is based on the Sainte-Lague system; in Finland and Iceland on the d'Hondt system. The basic philosophy behind proportional representation is simple and seems, on democratic grounds, to be irrefutable. In the words of a Norwegian *Storting* Committee report of 1963–64, 'franchise regulations should provide a reasonable relationship between the number of votes polled by a party at an election and the number of representatives returned to the *Storting*'. However, there is also an acute awareness of the practical difficulties in the application of such a principle of pure democracy. The Norwegian Report added: 'it is an important demand of a democratic franchise that the parties, supported by a majority among the electorate are also in a position enabling them to form a Government'.

In other words, the electoral system should be able to produce a workable government as well as an opposition able to assume the reins of power. 'In this connection the Committee majority (representing the Labour Party) will underline that the franchise regulations should not be formed in such a way that it encourages the formation of small parties, making it difficult to get a workable majority in the national assembly.' For small parties would then be able to act as controllers of the political balance and 'acquire an influence on the country which is not justified by their numbers'. Here is, then, the dilemma: to provide for proportional justice and, at the same time, to encourage the establishment of strong governments, supported by majorities both in the country and in the parliaments. What are the methods followed in order to provide for all parties a fair share in proportion to their strength, and what are the safeguards used in order to avoid some of the disadvantages usually connected with proportional representation? After a discussion of these two problems the net result of the different methods employed will be analysed in the light of the results of the most recent elections in the five countries.

A reasonable basis for any system is that the number of enfranchised citizens or, alternatively, the number of inhabitants electing a member should be approximately the same. This is usually very difficult to attain, both for such technical reasons as mobility of people and intervals between the redistribution of seats (as indicated by British experience) and because of the different demands of densely populated urban areas and of vast regions with a sparse population. In Norway the number of persons entitled to vote in the metropolitan area is around 27,000 for each *Storting* member; for the rest of the country the maximum is less than 19,000, and in the far North it is just above 11,000. In Sweden the national average number of inhabitants for each seat in the Lower House was around 33,000 in the 1964 Election. The maximum exceeded 35,000 while the minimum, as in Norway represented by a constituency in a special geographical position, was less than 18,000.

The basic principle of proportional representation is that each vote should carry the same weight. No vote should be lost by not participating in the election of a member. To ensure a fair representation to all parties—or at least to most parties—the constituencies should be fairly large. Looking again at Norway and Sweden we find that the average number of members per constituency is 7·5 and 8·3 respectively. In Finland it is 12·5, while in Denmark and Iceland, representing the low extreme, it is about 6. In these two countries, however, another device has been adopted similar to that in the German Federal Republic for ensuring a fair distribution of seats in relation to the votes polled by the parties. In Denmark 40 seats and in Iceland 11 seats, out of totals of 175 and 60 respectively are not distributed in the constituencies but assigned to the parties in relation to the number of votes which have not participated in returning members in the constituencies. A similar device has recently been accepted in Sweden for the new unicameral parliament, effective from 1971, in which 40 out of a total of 350 seats will be used to ensure a fair over-all distribution of mandates between the parties.

The conflict between the aim of arithmetic justice and the wish to avoid proliferation of small parties and political instability is also evident. The simplest method to fulfil the second of these objectives is through small constituencies. Special devices are normally built into the arithmetic methods of distributing the mandates between the parties, e.g. the Sainte-Lague series of divisors is applied in Denmark, Norway and Sweden (the number of votes of a party is to be divided by 1·4, 3, 5, etc. in order to establish the comparative figures for a party before the first, second, third, etc., seat is assigned to it). The d'Hondt method used in Iceland and Finland may also have similar effects (here the divisors are 1, 2, 3, etc.). Another possibility which is applied in Denmark and Iceland, and adopted as part of the 1971 reform in Sweden, is to prescribe that a certain minimum percentage of votes, nationally or regionally, is necessary for a party to be entitled to participate in the sharing of the parliamentary seats.

What is the net effect of the different principles and rules governing the application of proportional representation in the five Scandinavian countries? The answer can in fact be gathered from a close analysis of the figures on Tables VI–X. The relevant data to illustrate the working of the electoral system, in this respect, at the most recent parliamentary election in each of the countries are given in Table XI. This table follows the subdivisions of Table I but takes no account of parties without parliamentary representation. In each country column two figures, the one representing the percentage of the popular vote, the other the percentage of parliamentary seats, are provided for each party.

Distortion is obviously too strong a word for the deviations from an ideal proportional pattern. There was an obvious bonus for large parties, clearly indicated by the Social Democrats in Denmark, Norway and Sweden, as well as by the Finnish agrarian Centre Party and the Conservative and Liberal Independence Party in Iceland. Farmers' parties normally draw support from concentrated agricultural areas and are hence also favoured. The disadvantage of being small is particularly great in Norway and Sweden as indicated by the position of the Communist parties. It must, however, also be remembered that only parties actually returned to the parliaments concerned are included in the table. A number of small parties, especially but not only in Denmark, failed to qualify for a single seat. With all these minor reservations the final conclusion is nevertheless obvious: parliaments in the five Scandinavian countries are on the whole representative. The electoral laws provide sufficient

TABLE XI

Election results and parliamentary representation

(V = % share of popular vote;   S = % share of parliamentary seats)

Party \ Country	Denmark V	Denmark S	Finland V	Finland S	Iceland V	Iceland S	Norway V[1]	Norway S	Sweden V	Sweden S
Conservatives	20·4	21·1	13·8	13·0	—		20·0	20·7	13·9	13·3
Conservatives and Liberals	—				37·5	38·3	—		—	
Liberals	15·0	15·4	6·0	6·0			9·9	12·0	15·0	15·0
Farmers	18·6	19·4	6·5	4·0	28·1	30·0	9·0	12·0	16·1	16·7
			21·3	25·0						
			1·0	0·5						
Social Democrats	34·2	35·4	27·2	27·5	15·7	15·0	43·0	45·3	50·1	53·6
			2·6	3·0						
Left Socialists and Communists	6·1	6·3	21·2	21·0	17·6	16·7	6·0	1·3	3·0	1·2
	2·0	2·3								
Christian party	—		—		—		7·8	8·7	1·5	—

[1] Norwegian party coalition votes are distributed among the parties.

350

safeguards to ensure each organized group of a reasonable size a fair representation according to strength.

PART V PARTY ORGANIZATION, POWER STRUCTURE AND PARTY FINANCE

Party Organization

The preceding survey has shown that Scandinavian parties vary greatly in strength. Nevertheless, all are mass parties in the technical sense. They are built on the basis of open recruitment; they try to attract the largest possible number of members; and they depend—more or less—on members' dues and on the voluntary activities of the members as loyal workers in periods of 'mobilization', i.e. primarily during election campaigns.

A primary function of the national party organization is to mobilize support at national, regional and local elections. This purpose is reflected in the whole structure of party organization. By and large the party machines are tailored to the needs ensuing from the rules of electoral law. The internal party organization is also designed as a system of party democracy and leadership; of communication, information and consultation, authority, influence and control.

The standard pattern of party organization includes local associations or clubs, sometimes based on formal municipal subdivisions but often providing a more elaborate organizational network. They are the main instrument for membership recruitment, internal information and consultation, and for general party work at the grass-roots level, as well as for tasks connected with municipal politics.

On the whole the constituencies for parliamentary elections, 23 in Denmark, 16 in Finland, 20 in Norway and 28 in Sweden, are based on the county (or 'provincial') administrative subdivisions of the countries. Hence the constituency organizations of the parties are also based on these administrative subdivisions. In many countries, especially with directly and separately elected regional councils, there is also a need for some form of party organization based on the constituency subdivisions for these elections, i.e. units between the parliamentary constituency organizations and the basic, municipal party bodies.

At the top of the organizational pyramid are the central organs of the national party, always including a Congress and an Executive Board and Committee. The Congress is the highest authority in the party—although not necessarily the most powerful. It appoints the leaders of the party as well as the chairman and the elected members of the Executive Board. It decides, in form or in fact, the programme and matters concerning party organization. In some socialist parties the members at large, in a party referendum, constitute an authority above the party Congress, however rarely it may be called upon to function. Some parties have established Representative Councils between the Executive and the Congress, to deal with more important problems between the sessions of Congress. The significance of such intermediate bodies is especially great in parties which have prescribed long intervals between Congress sessions (up to four years).

It is sometimes said that the practice of long intervals between party congresses helps to protect unity and to minimize dissensions. The labour parties may in this way have avoided some of the difficulties encountered by the British Labour Party. Sweden may be cited as the opposite extreme to Britain in this respect. The Congress of the Swedish Social Democratic Labour Party, unless summoned for an extra session, which has happened only twice during the whole history of the party, meets only in years of ordinary elections to the Lower House of the *Riksdag*. This gives a normal interval of four years between the sessions. Since Congress meets before the election, the party considers its problems and reviews the position of the leadership in a situation dominated by all the restraints that follow from the need for cohesion, unity and discipline in the coming election.

A condition for a system of this type is, of course, that the dates for elections are definitely set and known beforehand. This is obviously the case in Norway where the government has no right at all to dissolve the *Storting*. In Finland and Sweden election dates are also fixed in law, although there is a right, prescribed in constitutional law, to dissolve in between election dates. Denmark and Iceland follow both the theory and the practice of the British system, with the difference, however, that, the maximum length of a *Folketing* and of an *Althing* is four years. As indicated by a comparison between Tables VI and VIII the Icelandic pattern of dissolutions reflects nevertheless greater stability than the Danish.

CHART 1

The Swedish Social Democratic Labour Party Organization

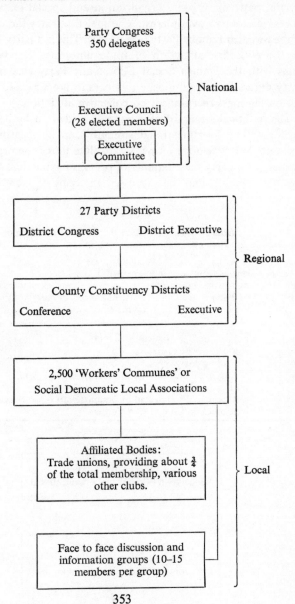

Party Congress
350 delegates

Executive Council
(28 elected members)

Executive
Committee

} National

27 Party Districts

District Congress   District Executive

County Constituency Districts

Conference   Executive

} Regional

2,500 'Workers' Communes' or
Social Democratic Local Associations

Affiliated Bodies:
Trade unions, providing about ¾
of the total membership, various
other clubs.

Face to face discussion and
information groups (10–15
members per group)

} Local

M

353

The structure of party organization may be further illustrated by two charts. The charts are selected in order to demonstrate both general patterns of party organization and special features of considerable comparative interest. The first illustrates the organization of the Swedish Labour Party (see p. 353). This is a party based partly on the collective affiliation of trade unionists. The second chart deals with the Danish Social Democratic Party (see below). This party differs from its opposite numbers in Norway and Sweden in not basing mass recruitment on collective affiliation.

The 'political strength' of a party is evidenced by its support in elections. The 'organizational strength' can be measured both in absolute and in relative terms. In absolute terms the organizational strength of a party is the number of persons paying dues to the party. Relative strength may be expressed in terms of membership as a

CHART 2

Danish Social Democratic Party Organization

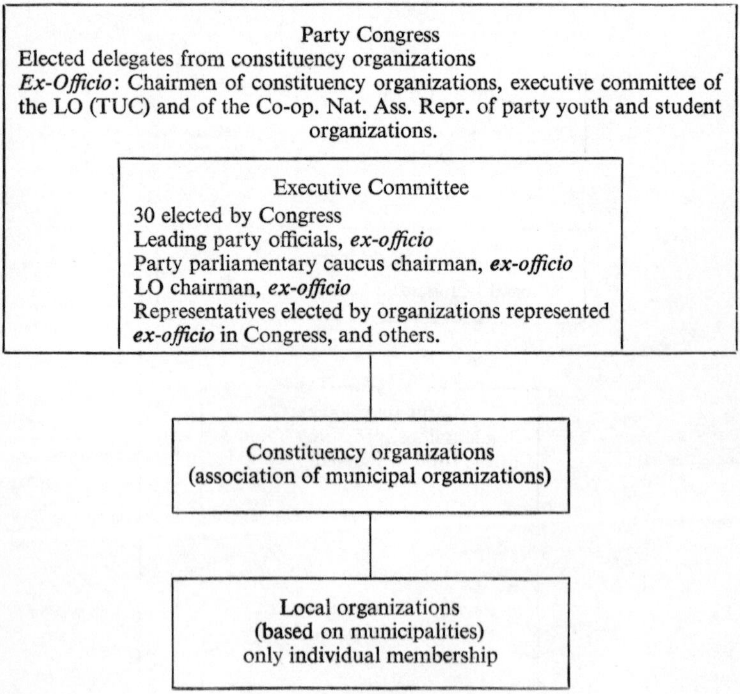

Party Congress
Elected delegates from constituency organizations
Ex-Officio: Chairmen of constituency organizations, executive committee of the LO (TUC) and of the Co-op. Nat. Ass. Repr. of party youth and student organizations.

Executive Committee
30 elected by Congress
Leading party officials, *ex-officio*
Party parliamentary caucus chairman, *ex-officio*
LO chairman, *ex-officio*
Representatives elected by organizations represented *ex-officio* in Congress, and others.

Constituency organizations
(association of municipal organizations)

Local organizations
(based on municipalities)
only individual membership

354

percentage of the total party vote. Here organizational strength refers to relative strength: for the four major Scandinavian countries the averages for all parties together have, in recent years, been between *c.* 20 and *c.* 30 per cent: Sweden and Finland *c.* 30 per cent, Norway *c.* 25 per cent, and Denmark *c.* 20 per cent. From Tables II–V it is evident that the Labour parties of Norway and Sweden have been outstanding in political strength. In both parties the membership is to a considerable extent inflated by collective affiliation, primarily of trade unions. This affiliation takes place at the bottom of the party structure; local trade clubs join local Labour organizations. There is no affiliation at the top as there is in Britain. One obvious advantage of the 'Scandinavian' system seems to be that the trade unions do not maintain a separate identity inside the Labour parties. Whatever tension exists between trade unionists and other Labour party members is not stimulated and enhanced by artificial devices of party organization.

It is difficult, perhaps even impossible, to make valid generalizations concerning the significance of organizational strength as defined above. The pattern is very irregular. If we pick out the dominating parties in each of the four major Scandinavian countries, it is obvious that great political strength and great organizational strength go together in the cases of the Finnish Centre (Agrarian) Party and the Swedish Social Democrats. For the former party about half the number of voters are also party members; for the latter more than 40 per cent.

It is, however, clear that political strength is not necessarily accompanied by organizational strength nor is such strength necessarily a property of large parties. The Norwegian Labour Party has, in spite of block affiliation by trade unions, a membership of less than 20 per cent of its normal voting strength. In Denmark the Social Democrats had a high percentage in the late 1940s and in the 1950s (approaching the Swedish figure). In recent years it has, however, declined and now hardly reaches 20 per cent. The Finnish Social Democrats, through the years the major competitor of the Agrarian Centre for the leading position, also had (in 1962) an organizational strength of less than 20 per cent.

The Liberal Party in Sweden, which has been the leading opposition party since 1948, has always had a low ratio of party members among its supporters at elections, shifting between some 10 and

355

15 per cent. This seems, on the whole, to be typical of the Scandinavian Liberal parties (Finland 9 per cent; Denmark, the Radical Left normally has c. 15 per cent, though after the electoral success in 1968 this probably fell to much less than 10 per cent; Norway 15 per cent).

Farmers' parties and Conservative parties usually have high organizational strength. The Finnish Agrarian Centre, with 50 per cent, represents not only the strongest Farmers' party but also a record in organizational strength, unlikely to be surpassed in many other countries; generally, the organizational strength of Scandinavian Farmers' parties ranges around 30–35 per cent. Conservative parties are usually somewhat, but not much, weaker. Conservative organizational strength was in Denmark and Finland c. 25 per cent, in Norway c. 30 per cent and in Sweden 35 per cent.

Power Structure

There are several aspects to the problem of the power structure in political parties. In part it is a question of the relations between the national party organizations and the regional-local subdivisions of the parties. It concerns the position of elected leaders and their strength and authority within their respective parties. There are the relations between the parliamentary party and the national party.

In most parties the regional constituency organizations, responsible for the elections to the national parliament, are traditionally anxious to assert as much independence as possible from the national organizations. Where regional sentiments are strong, this tendency seems to be reinforced. Norway provides a clear example. Obviously the independence of a branch of a national party organization must always be limited. At constituency level it is emphasized primarily by independence from national party headquarters in the nomination of candidates for parliamentary elections. With minor exceptions the national party has neither the right nor the prospect of controlling or interfering with such nominations.

In Finland it has been observed that, although the left-wing parties are centralized they are at the same time especially concerned with the problem of providing viable democratic methods for the operation of their organization. Parties on the right, on the other hand, are said to be decentralized and also less concerned with the problem of democratic participation. How far this observation is generally applicable has not been investigated. It is very likely that it is true also for other Scandinavian countries, and indeed that it has even wider applicability. Labour parties have been formed in opposition against established interests. In order to be successful the labour movements, both political and industrial, have had to act with unity, co-ordinated under centralized leadership. There is, however, reason to believe that these differences have been reduced. The 'parties of the left' have become representatives of recognized and established—indeed predominating—interests in the welfare state. On the other hand, the 'parties of the right' have had to accept and follow the standards of party organization set by their opponents in order to hold their own in a democratic era.

Irrespective of the significance of these developments it is clear that the tendency towards centralization has received new impetus in all parties. This is partly related to the role of the mass media. As party-affiliated newspapers are gradually reduced in number, outlets for propaganda and information are available less often than before in the local press. Fewer newspapers serving larger areas are less likely to propagate party policies editorially.

Parties have to rely more than hitherto on the central media of propaganda and information, especially television and radio. This development tends to increase the importance of the central party organization at the expense of the lower levels in the party structure. In Sweden, where data concerning party finance have been published, this development is confirmed by the relatively greater increase in the costs of central party organization as against those of regional and local party bodies.

By and large party leadership is strong in Sweden and Norway. Iceland also seems to fit into this category. However, a comparison between Sweden and Norway suggests some differences. In Sweden all parties have united the leadership of the national party organiza-tion with that of the parliamentary party or—if the party also holds office—with the post of Prime Minister. In Norway the Labour Party follows the same principle, while split leadership has been the rule in the bourgeois parties (now in office).

The same lack of uniformity in the structure of party leadership is also characteristic of Denmark. A division of authority between a national chairman and a parliamentary chairman exists in all the major parties except for the Social Democrats. Several parties have gone one step further by dividing the parliamentary leadership between a chairman and a 'political spokesman'.

In Finland the leadership situation is even more complex. Split leadership is the rule but owing to special factors the actual leadership of a party may be exercised by persons holding no formal chairmanship. This often leads to situations in which a party may include several members who may be regarded as possible candidates for the post of Prime Minister, should the political situation make it suitable to select the holder of this office from the party in question.

Another aspect of party leadership concerns continuity and stability. It is obvious that in most countries and parties the situation has been marked by considerable stability. In Sweden the Social Democrats have had three leaders during the 80 years' history of the party. The present leader was elected in 1946. He is likely to retire, but for age reasons only, in 1969. Norway presents a similar situation. The first change of leader since 1945 in the Labour Party came in 1965, partly because of his age and partly as a result of electoral defeat. Denmark has witnessed a succession of five Social Democratic leaders since 1945, but in all cases death or failing health have provided clearly non-political explanations. This stability in the Social Democratic parties seems to be natural; success and power easily go together with stability. The Icelandic Independence Party, dominating the political scene through the whole postwar period, may be cited as a further instance in support of this generalization. So may the Agrarian Centre Party in Finland, for many years under the domination of the present President of the Republic, Mr Kekkonen. In actual fact the opposition parties, many of whom have been in the political wilderness for several decades, also present, on the whole, a picture of remarkable stability. In many cases split leadership, especially the troika-system existing in Denmark and the leadership structure in Finland, makes direct comparisons difficult.

Obviously, continuity need not be equated with concentration of power in the hands of the incumbent, whose position may rest more on skilful brokerage than on powerful leadership. It does, however, normally indicate absence of major party crises. Internal tensions, leading to changes in leadership, have on the whole been rare. Notable exceptions are provided by the Danish Conservative and Left Parties in the 1940s and by the Swedish Conservatives in the 1960s.

Party Finance

Party finance is generally a very difficult subject for scholarly treatment. For various reasons political parties, especially on the bourgeois side of the right-left continuum, are reluctant to reveal their sources of income. Nowhere in Scandinavia has legislation been passed in order to force the parties to disclose their financial contributors and benefactors or to limit their expenditure. Some scattered items of information are, however, available in most countries, and a general outline, vague in contours and details, may be attempted. The best data are available in Sweden. They may be used as a concrete illustration of the general position, as the Swedish situation, to judge from data from the other countries, seems to be typical. In one respect, however, it is not typical. Since 1966 the chief source of income for the Swedish political parties is state support; appropriated by (the parties in) the *Riksdag* for the benefit of the national party organizations, among whom the grant is distributed according to principles which rule out arbitrary application. A similar system of party subsidies has been adopted in Finland. In Norway proposals have been made for this while in Denmark the idea of a system of party subsidies provided by the state has so far been clearly rejected.

Apart from direct subsidies, income comes mainly from two different sources, membership fees and voluntary contributions of various kinds: for labour parties usually trade union support and for bourgeois parties support from various organizations representing private enterprise. Norwegian data from 1950 indicate that party dues varied greatly in significance for the different party budgets. The maximum—80 per cent of total party income—was represented by the Communists, followed by the Liberals and the Farmers (now Centre) with 70 and 65 per cent respectively. The Conservative Party and the Christian Party covered 50 per cent with membership dues but the Labour Party only 37 per cent. In Finland it was estimated that in 1951 only $8 \cdot 4$ per cent of the total income of all the political parties came from membership dues. For Denmark very little definite information is available. On the whole the Danish situation seems to come closer to the Norwegian than to the Finnish.

Swedish data on party finance are available for 1948, 1949 and 1966. The 1949 figures may be compared with the Norwegian figures for 1950 and the Finnish for 1951. In Sweden the membership dues accounted for the following rough proportions of the party budgets:

for the Conservatives *c.* 20 per cent, for the Farmers (now Centre) 70 per cent, for the Liberals 12 per cent and for the Social Democrats 75 per cent. Complete figures for the Communists are missing. Like 1950 in Norway, 1949 was a non-election year in Sweden. In 1948, which was the year of a general election, contributions provided for a much larger proportion of the income of the parties.

If averages, based on a series of years, were available, better material would also exist for a general evaluation of the significance of different sources of party income. The trend during the past two decades is, however, reflected in the Swedish figures concerning the sources of income of the national party organizations, excluding the district (constituency) and local organizations, which were included in the previous Swedish percentage figures. Two election years form the basis for the comparison: 1948 (Lower House election) and 1966 (local elections—equal in intensity and propaganda techniques to the Lower House elections).

TABLE XII
Party Finance in Sweden ('000 kronor)

Party	1948		1966		
	Dues	Total income	Dues	State support	Total income
Conservatives	—	3,243	600	3,540	9,240
Centre	165	447	342	3,423	4,250
Liberals	35	2,658	202	4,245	6,926
Social Democrats	684	1,615	2,111	11,520	19,600
Communists	157	818	150	645	1,435

PART VI INTERNATIONAL RELATIONS

The subject of the international relations of political parties raises several questions. In what do such international relations consist? To what extent are the international attitudes of the parties coloured by the special situation of the country in which they are operating? To what extent have European organizations with parliamentary bodies affected the attitude and approach of the political parties to European problems, regionally and universally? To what extent is it possible to distinguish specific effects of this or that European movement or branch of the European movement? As far as the Scandinavian countries are concerned, given the present state of research and general knowledge it is not possible to give answers which go beyond the level of generalizations based on scattered information and impressions.

In general, it is clear that international relations—i.e. contacts with related parties in other countries—play a subordinate part in the work of political parties. Their chief interests are focused on internal, national problems, not on international issues. This does not exclude regular, indeed increasing contacts of various sorts with political parties in other countries. These contacts are obviously related to the various international sub-systems in which the Scandinavian countries operate. All the countries participate in the Nordic Council which is a symbol of, and, stimulus to, Nordic co-operation. Denmark, Norway and Sweden are members of EFTA, which they are officially hoping to merge with the EEC. Finland is associated with EFTA. Denmark, Iceland, Norway and Sweden are members of the Council of Europe. The former three are members of NATO and all the Scandinavian states belong to the United Nations.

International links are primarily with other Scandinavian parties, but broader contacts have also developed. For the Communist parties, which until the recent polycentric development in the Communist world formed part of a seemingly monolithic international movement under the dominating leadership of Moscow, such contacts were for a long time a natural and necessary part of their activities. The Social Democrats also have a strong international tradition. However, they differ from the Communists—at least those of yesterday—in having little direct community of interest in primary goals for joint action in a larger context than the national system in which they are operating. Like the relations between Conservative, Liberal and Farmers' Parties, international Social Democratic links involve little more than exchange of information, on recent developments and on new techniques and devices. The most positive interpretation that can be put upon the development of international party relations is that they indicate a growing general awareness of larger contexts than the limited national systems for which they have been established.

It seems to be typical of small countries that international affairs and especially in relation to security—always the primary responsibility of the party or parties in power—are usually conducted in a spirit of national unity. This is clearly true of a country like Sweden, with its self-imposed non-alignment in relation to the present great power blocs and with neutrality in any future conflict as its basic goal. It is also characteristic of Finland which since the mid-1950s has moved towards a position similar to that of other neutral countries. Its attitude is, however, conditioned by one overriding consideration. In view of its history during the 50 years of national independence and of the 1948 treaty of friendship and assistance with the USSR, Finland finds it absolutely necessary to maintain total and unquestionable credibility among other countries for its will and ability to maintain good relations with its eastern neighbour. That is both the condition and the limitation of her neutrality. In both Finland and Sweden credibility is thought of as demanding an almost complete unity of purpose and attitude, shared by all parties. For both countries this demand is of some significance for their possibilities of participation in various forms of co-operation with other western democratic countries.

The three west-Scandinavian countries are all members of NATO. This membership alone, with all the political and technical commitment involved, has so far proved sufficient to create credibility for their international position. Total national unity, between or inside the parties on all major issues, is not so necessary in Denmark, Iceland and Norway as it is in Finland or Sweden with their enforced or self-imposed positions. (In fact, Denmark joined NATO only because no other road was open to solve her security problems after Norway and Sweden had failed to reach agreement on the conditions for a Scandinavian Defence Alliance, 1948–49). The same is true of Iceland which (in spite of the fact that the principle of neutrality is inscribed in the constitution), unlike Denmark and Norway has foreign troops stationed on her territory in peace-time. In all three NATO-aligned countries criticism has at times been voiced against this commitment. On the other hand, it is also clear that no party in office, however critical in principle, has made any serious attempt to change the situation. NATO seems to be respected, at least as an *ad hoc* necessity.

The alignment of Denmark, Iceland and Norway with NATO has influenced their attitudes to European problems in general. One current instance of this is of special interest and importance. For the three NATO-aligned countries future membership of the EEC does not necessitate a clash of basic principles. In Sweden it seems to be widely accepted in influential circles that its non-aligned position would lose in credibility, should it subscribe to all the conditions, tenets and possible future ambitions of the EEC. The interesting consequence of this situation is that a more open, at times violent, debate has taken place in the NATO-countries than in Sweden. In Sweden the parties are more or less completely forced to moderation by the accepted need for maintaining maximum credibility for non-alignment. The critical observer should not be deceived by the fact that moderation in substance is sometimes couched in a very polemic phraseology. For Finland any consideration of a closer connection with the EEC is at present an absolute impossibility. This fact is also recognized by the parties.

Within the limitations just indicated the political parties in the Scandinavian countries have, by and large, assumed a positive attitude towards European co-operation. In general, it may be said that the less direct commitment involved in such international collaboration, the more enthusiastic the support for it. Participation in various forms of European organization during the two last decades has increased the awareness of Europe among the five countries. The Common Market has contributed more than any other issue to this increased European consciousness. Even a limited and cursory survey of parliamentary debates in the countries concerned bears out the validity of this assertion. In view of the dominating impact on public opinion of the 'market' issues it is very difficult—or rather impossible—to isolate the importance of the Council of Europe and the effects in all the Scandinavian countries, excluding Finland, of their participation in its activities. A general educational value for those who have participated in the European experiment at Strasbourg is obvious and self-evident. However, only the emergence of the 'market' issue has made Europe an issue of prime importance.

The attitudes of the political parties to the EEC, or rather to the question of whether the country in question should join it, follow certain patterns, conditioned by varying economic and political interests. In Sweden there has always been stronger sympathy towards full membership of the EEC among Liberals and Conservatives than among the Social Democrats and the Centre Party. But the

Communists alone are, as a party, outright in their hostility towards the idea. In Norway the EEC issue created a veritable political storm in the early 1960s. The idea of Norwegian membership was criticized, especially among left-wing Socialists and Liberals. Trade union Labour and Conservatives have alone stood out as staunch supporters of Norwegian membership of the EEC. The Norwegian Farmers, Christian Party and Liberals have demonstrated a more hesitant attitude as to the best method of connecting Norway with the Common Market.

Denmark has found herself in a somewhat different situation. For her agricultural industry, membership of the EEC would become absolutely crucial were Britain to join. Even without Britain, membership of the Common Market has considerable attractions. The urgent need for easier access for Danish food to the markets of industrialized Western Europe is clearly recognized. Even so, it is clear that the issue has not generated much enthusiasm and engagement. This may partly explain the relative success of the anti-NATO, anti-defence, anti-EEC Socialist People's Party in recent elections. Among the major parties, however, there are very substantial majorities supporting Denmark's policy of seeking entry into the EEC with full member status. Gallup polls have also clearly indicated that the degree of support is increasing from left to right on the party spectrum.

Membership of the EEC has not yet appeared for the Scandinavian countries concerned as an immediate possibility. So far General de Gaulle's successful attempts to bar Britain—and her 'economic friends'—from membership of the EEC have probably had a negative effect on the growing European awareness in the Scandinavian countries.

The immediate response to the frustration suffered in relation to the EEC has been a serious effort aimed at greater co-operation and integration between the Nordic states themselves. A Nordic customs union within the EFTA free trade area seems to be a primary goal. The fall of de Gaulle may, however, possibly raise new expectations for a broad European solution of the trade interests of the Scandinavian countries and reduce the enthusiasm for a narrow, Nordic approach.

CHAPTER 9

SWITZERLAND

INTRODUCTION

Political science in Switzerland has only recently established its autonomy as a branch of enquiry. In French Switzerland it has flourished longer than in German-speaking areas, but the market for books within the former is small. Consequently, until recently, there were few published studies of Swiss parties, and interest was concentrated upon the juridical status and constitutionality of the activities of parties and interest groups—a barren field where a few arguments have been repeated by a succession of scholars. Even today, there are satisfactory studies only of the Socialists and the Landesring.

A partial explanation of this is a tradition of secretiveness that is only just starting to break down. Switzerland is constitutionally a very advanced democracy, but socially it is controlled by a loose confederacy of *elites*, who do not see any advantage to their own position accruing from investigations into their public-spirited activity. Financial support is not freely offered for such enquiries and replies are not freely given to impertinent questions. The perfect working of democratic arrangements is also important for Switzerland's international prestige—the referendum (and the International Committee of the Red Cross) can be set against non-membership of UNO and a very modest place in the list of State assistance to underdeveloped countries. The secrecy goes very far: membership figures of all parties, except the socialist, are a closely guarded secret As regards the historic party of Switzerland, the Radicals, figures have been winkled out and published for three cantons—they are widely different.

Furthermore, what really matters for the bourgeois political parties is the cantonal organization. The question to be asked for comparative purposes is: 'What is the relationship between the National Councillor and his cantonal party bureaucracy, and his cantonal electorate?' This would involve a very considerable

365

inquiry: there are 25 cantons, and it might be necessary to examine as many as a dozen of them to establish a pattern.

THE POLITICAL FRAMEWORK

Much though Switzerland has in common with its continental European neighbours, its governmental system has three characteristics that give a peculiar cast to political parties in the central government—localism, the collegiate executive, and the referendum.

Localism

Swiss political life is strongly localized. There has been no major sudden social upheaval during this century and the local units of quasi-sovereign self-government, the cantons, have individual characteristics that make generalization insecure. Federalism is deeply rooted historically, but it has a further basis in linguistic differences—German, French and Italian. The language frontiers can be drawn with a single uninterrupted line (which cuts across many cantonal frontiers), but the boundary between religious areas, those dominated by Roman Catholicism, by cantonal Reformed churches, or which are traditionally of mixed religious confession, is not continuous. It pays no attention to the French–German frontier, but does largely follow the old cantonal frontiers. For the study of political parties one can almost overlook the linguistic differences, but the religious difference is of fundamental importance.

The formal structure of cantonal constitutions is not markedly different from that of the Central Government, though the general position of the Parliament, against the Executive, is stronger. On both levels the logic of proportional representation is accepted, there is a collegiate executive, and there is the referendum; indeed, on the cantonal level the referendum is more developed. The major difference is that the Central Government alone is bicameral, and the cantonal executive councillors are elected by the people at large. The national parties are by no means equally distributed. Some cantons are dominated by one party, and the mixture of parties in the multiparty cantons varies. The right-wing parties vary considerably in their local policies, while the left-wing is less willingly regional.[1] The degree of political involvement also varies. In the

[1] The best first introduction to the cantonal political and social scene is now F. R. Allemann, *25 mal die Schweiz*, Piper Verlag, Munich, 1965.

more traditional cantons, and in some where the balance is a fine one, life is still deeply politicized—though there are a few, such as Geneva, where party allegiance is a fairly superficial attribute of personality. Where life is fully politicized, party does much more than merely articulate the relations of Parliament and Executive, it extends into the judiciary and the administration and into commercial and family life, and becomes an indelible part of a man's status. Because of the more deeply politicized style of cantonal public life, the parties are more significant at that level.

The Collegiate Executive

The Federal Executive (*Bundesrat, Conseil Fédéral*, Federal Council) is a sort of collegiate body of seven members, chosen for the whole four-year term of the legislature (by the two chambers in joint session).[1] Its members have a certain claim to re-election, at least so long as they do not totally lose the allegiance of their own parliamentary party. (A recent book, *The Parliament of Switzerland* by C. J. Hughes examines the relation of this body to parliament and its structure, at considerable length). The three main parties (in 1968) have each two members in the Federal Council, and the next party has one member. This 2 : 2 : 2 : 1 structure fairly represents the proportional entitlement according to voting strength in the country.

---

[1] There is a proposal for a Total Revision of the Swiss Constitution. The project is a fertile topic for seminars in Law Schools in Swiss universities. It is not easy to account objectively for 'the Helvetic malaise', and there are suggestions that it is an imaginary malady. From abroad, one thinks of Switzerland as enjoying a relaxed good health, but within the country there is a feeling that Switzerland has lost her position of leadership in democraticness among democracies. There is a search for a mission, or at least, for excitement. The patient takes his temperature, feels his pulse, both are normal for healthy middle age. The bank balance is sound. There is no bad conscience. And yet. . . .

Even if this revolution of the professors is successful the result is likely to be a redactional improvement, removing some of the defects and most of the national character from the Federal Constitution. The main institutions of government are likely to remain unaltered. The most likely changes are an increase in the size of the Federal Council to nine (under the impression this will lighten work) and a strengthening of the position of the Federal Chancellor, an officer of state whose political significance has been minimal for a century. The problem of increasing the power of elected representatives is likely to elude the framers of the new Constitution, if it comes to be. In the meanwhile, the inability of Switzerland to subscribe to the European Convention for the Protection of Human Rights has been embarrassing.

The government acts as a corporate body and its actions seldom now give effect to an identifiable party-political philosophy. As a result one can rarely consider party A as responsible for action Z. The role, therefore, of political parties is profoundly different from that elsewhere in Western Europe; the last link in the chain of responsibility to the electorate, political action, hangs loose.

Furthermore, party strength in the popular chamber (chosen since 1919 by PR) varies very little from election to election. The three large parties (Radical, Catholic, Socialist) command a quarter of the votes each, and the Peasants' Party one half of the remaining quarter. Power is not within the reach of any party on the federal level, but if proportionality had not been decided on by a sort of consensus among the ruling group for its own sake, power in the sense of a monopoly of the Federal Council by two parties would certainly be within the reach of a Radical-Catholic coalition, and it would be equally within the reach of an anti-Radical or of an anti-Catholic coalition comprising more parties. The arithmetic of the matter is complicated by the necessity of considering also the 44-member Council of States—where the Socialists can count on being under-represented and the Catholics upon being over-represented.

The Referendum

The two politically important forms of semi-direct democracy are the Initiative (of constitutional amendment, but this can include a guaranteed price for carrots), and the Challenge (of a federal law). The effect of this institution on political parties is very complex. Probably no single Swiss federal party organization can quite afford from party funds the expense of launching an Initiative or a Challenge, but the parties have so close a connection with interest groups (such as the Radicals with the *Vorort*, the Confederation of Swiss Industries, and the Socialists with the Trades Unions) that this hardly matters. The referendum can be used by a party to advertise itself and gain adherents, but there is ample evidence that voters do not necessarily follow instructions on how to vote, if the issue is one which they happen to understand. The question of how people vote in referendums is difficult. Public opinion is partially determined by people committed to a political party, but the leadership cannot deliver its popular vote on request.

In this connection, the newspapers are relevant. The Swiss male (who alone has the vote in strictly federal matters) may be expected to read a local daily paper, which is written in his native tongue, which adheres to his own religious confession, and espouses his own political doctrine. If he reads a second paper, it will probably be Liberal or Radical, for these parties monopolize the Swiss journals of international standing.[1] The Swiss press is wonderfully Olympian and well informed on non-Swiss matters, and intensely incapsulated in place and ideology on domestic issues. The great variety of Swiss periodicals ensures that no one need ever query his own prejudices, but behind each impoverished editorial office stands a helpful news service,[2] said to be in right-wing radical hands.

The chief rivals of the parties are the lobbies (*Verbände*)[3]. These interest-groups are consulted while legislation is being drafted. The parties are consulted, during the parliamentary process, though there is said to be a tendency to assimilate them to interests and to involve them too at the drafting process. However, the distinction between interests and parties is not absolute. Major interests have parliamentary spokesmen and frequently make contributions to party funds. A large number of parliamentarians have an acknowledged connection with a particular interest.

In spite of the power of the *Verbände* (an indirect consequence of the referendum), the political parties remain important for the selection of persons for posts. The parties help to integrate society with the State, and to educate the public, even if they are not really

[1] *Neue Zuercher Zeitung*, Zurich, Radical; *Gazette de Lausanne*, Liberal; *Basler Nachrichten*, Liberal. Close on the heels of these, *National Zeitung*, Radical, Basle; on its way up. Finally, *Journal de Genève*, Liberal. Several highly respectable journals, however, make a claim to be above parties.

[2] In Switzerland it is seldom in point to speak of 'monopoly'. There is rather a system intermediate between liberty and suffocation, which may be called 'cartellization' in the commercial sphere. The editorial boards may be rather thoroughly integrated into local financial and economic society, and the source of news is likely to be the Schweizerische Depeschenagentur. The source of advertisements is likely to be an agency also, probably rather close to the news agency. The supplementary news agencies are also likely to be poltically controlled. Once within this system, nonconformity is possible, but not particularly easy, and the system does not exactly encourage it. Yet it is only recently that there have been signs of the sort of press empire to which Britain has become accustomed—the Ringier group—which might make nonconformity still more hard.

[3] There is a good recent case-study of the medical pressure groups. See Gerhard Kocher, *Verbandseinfluss auf die Gesetzgebung*, Franike, Berne, 1967.

a part of the decision-making process in the narrower sense.[1] Thoughtful observers sometimes regret that parties are so relatively far from the centre of power at federal level. At cantonal level it is different, the *Verbände* being more centralized than the parties.

Even though the constitutional and social structure of Switzerland have peculiarities, there is nothing very surprising about the ideological currents, though their character is somewhat distorted by Swiss history.

In general, Federal parties did not begin to emerge until the 1890s. In the cantons the Liberals were the first political group to emerge during the years after 1815, causing Catholics to be self-conscious politically, and giving rise to opposition from the Conservative side also in the Protestant cantons. Next to emerge to the left of the Liberals were the Radicals, representing a socially lower and a more numerous class. Later, in various cantons, a left-wing rebellion against radical hegemony occurred at very varied dates, usually calling itself 'Democrat'. Meanwhile, a new political class formed a Social Democratic movement, polarizing into socialist and communist at various dates, but perhaps finally under the influence of the threat of Hitlerism. The introduction of proportional representation in the popular chamber in 1919 coincided with the emergence of the Peasants as a new party, chiefly at the expense of the Radicals in certain cantons, notably Berne. Finally there is the small Landesring party, a significant phenomenon peculiar to Switzerland.

The party history of the Federal Council is set out in the following table:

	Radicals	Catholics	Peasants	Socialists
1848–91	7[2]			
1891–1919	6	1		
1919–29	5	2		
1929–43	4	2	1	
1943–53	3	2	1	1
1954–59	3	3	1	0
1959–	2	2	1	2

[1] At the Conference of the Swiss Political Science Association of 1968 this assertion was made by Professor Sidjanski of Geneva, and not disputed.

[2] A whole political spectrum is concealed behind this apparently solid figure 7. The style of politics within the Radical family was more passionate, bitter, uncompromising—at times—than it now is within the 2 : 2 : 2 : 1 coalition.

	Radicals		Catholics		Socialists		Peasants		Landesring		Liberals		Democrats and Evangelicals		Communists		Unclassified		Total	
	NC	CS	NC	CS	NC	CS	NC	CS	NC	CS	NC	CS	NC	CS	NC	CS	NC	CS	NC	CS
1947	52	11	44	18	48	5	21	4	9	–	7	2	5	2	7	–	1	2	194	44
1951	51	12	48	18	49	4	23	3	10	–	5	3	5	2	5	–	–	2	196	44
1955	50	12	47	17	53	5	22	3	10	–	5	3	5	2	4	–	–	2	196	44
1959	51	13	47	17	51	4	23	3	10	–	5	3	6	1	3	–	–	3	196	44
1963	51	13	48	18	53	3	22	4	10	–	6	3	6	3	4	–	–	1	200	44
1967	49	(14)	45	18	51	(2)	21	3	16	1	6	3	6	3	5	–	1	1	200	44

NC = National Council, CS = Council of States
Source: (Modified from) *Annuaire statistique de la Suisse.* The figures for the election of October 1967 are from the Swiss press

371

The relative size of the parties is given in the table on page 371, showing representation in the two Councils. For consideration of parliamentary business the delegations of the party within the two Councils sit together, and the Federal Councillors who belong to that party attend. For electing Federal Councillors, and certain other officers, the two Councils come together in Joint Session. For other business, and in particular for legislation and approval of the budget, accounts, and the conduct of the administration (*gestion*), they have formally equal powers and sit apart. There are some joint committees. The National Council is chosen by proportional representation, and therefore the size of the parties on that Council fairly closely corresponds with the number of electors voting for it. The constituencies are the cantons, the biggest of which are about 30 times as populous as the smallest, which are too small for proportional representation to work.

The figures for the National Council are not necessarily reliable in detail. They are based on the 'parliamentary group' (*fraction*) in the Council, which may alter in the course of the year. Moreover, a member may have run under one label and adhere to another *fraction*. During most of the period in question the minimum number recognized as a *fraction* was five. Small groups band together to have a chance of representation on committees, etc. The Communist parties, however, found no allies; this was foreseeable when the figure was fixed at five.

The figures for the Council of States should be used with still more caution in detail. The period of election is determined by each canton, though the election at large for four years is now usual. Retirements during the period are not infrequent, and there must then be a new election (whereas no by-elections for the National Council occur). Thus the Landesring was represented in the States for two years (1949–51), but this does not appear in the above table. The excessive representation of the Catholics (and, for a different reason, of the Liberals) is constant, and so is under-representation of the Socialists. But particular figures are misleading here also (e.g. in 1967 a second scrutiny was pending).

THE MAIN PARTIES

The Radical Party (*Freisinnige Partei der Schweiz*)
This is the typical party of the non-Catholic middle class in towns,

but its appeal is much wider than this, and probably its support is, as an average of the whole country, evenly distributed among all social classes. This may also be the case within some towns (notably Geneva), but regional variations are enormous. In some cantons, notably Vaud, the Radicals are the farmers' party, but in Berne much of its rural support has seceded to the Peasants. A broad-minded Catholic may belong to the party, and in some parts (Solothurn, for example) this would give rise to no comment. In much of the former Sonderbund— the cantons who fought and lost a war of secession in 1848—such an allegiance would, until ten years or so ago, have been almost provocative. In the past, in fact, the Radical party has been anti-clerical, free-enterprise, nationalist, but its traditions differ in almost every canton.[1]

Though the party makes up only a quarter of the National Council, its prestige is enormous. Down to 1919 it ruled Switzerland, and today it is the only party represented in every cantonal government (except Appenzell Inner Rhodes, which has scarcely reached the stage of development in its internal politics that acknowledges the existence of parties). The institutions of Switzerland are either the creations of this party or survivals of the old regime. Most of the

[1] The Grisons (Graubünden), the largest in area of the cantons but the sixteenth in population, has a political life and tradition of its own in stronger measure than any other canton. Protestant and Catholic villages and valleys are mingled in this labyrinthine area, and so are German and the residual Romantsch dialects, while three Italian-speaking valleys protrude south of the Alps. The patrician families, one can almost say the nobility, long retained a greater prestige than elsewhere, while (by a paradox that can be paralleled in other parts of Switzerland, and indeed of Europe) there is a tradition of an extreme democracy and decentralization. The Christian Conservatives had here, unlike other parts of Switzerland, a claim to be genuinely bi-confessional, and it was the homeland of an attractive, rather English-seeming, type of Christian Socialism. The Radicals, in the period between the wars, suffered the same sort of eclipse that they underwent in other parts of Switzerland a half-century earlier at the hand of a 'Democratic Party' revolt, and the Democrats in the Grisons comprise a quarter or more of the canton's representation in the National Council.
The Democrats of Grisons were long under the leadership of a controversial personality, Dr Gadient, and followed the political pilgrimages of their leader. Their rise coincided with a shift in social and economic power in the canton— away from the great Radical hotel-owning families and, after an interval, towards the management of certain large, semi-private, economic enterprises which are gradually giving a new character to the canton. There is certainly some connection between the social and political evolution. The Democrats can, back home, be classified as radical-Radicals, but the political style of the Grisons is traditional, so they may not make this type of impact on the Federal level.

Swiss whose names one has heard of, as artists, writers, lawyers, statesmen, philanthropists, financiers (or even seen on the wrappings of chocolates), are Radicals—or old-Liberals. The Radical party, for many purposes, *is* Switzerland and together with the tiny group of old-Liberals it dominates Swiss intellectual and commercial life.

The ethos of the party is that of the liberals and radicals throughout continental Europe and of many conservatives in Britain. It includes, for example, a moderate free enterprise according to the rules of the game, and these rules include the sanctity of private property, of the dignity and the dynamism of the individual, and the feeling for law, nation, and formal legal equality. The surprises come chiefly from other movements, such as the Peasants or the Landesring, that have rivalled or surpassed the party in some cantons.

The pressure groups supporting the party are as one might expect. The greatest of these is the *Vorort*, whose reputation is almost legendary in Switzerland, but in general all the employers' organizations are at one with the Radicals. Of course no great pressure group wishes to identify itself totally with a 25 per cent party, hence support for other bourgeois parties, notably the Catholics and the Peasants. However, the managerial class will quite naturally find that the Radicals share its views.

The size of the cantonal parties (the number of fee-paying members) is a closely guarded secret. It was always thought that this secrecy arose from a feeling of inferiority to the Socialists, but there are now some suggestions that the opposite is the case: in a democracy one tries, if one is rich, to appear to be of mediocre wealth.

The Catholic Party

The Catholic Party (Christian–Socialist Conservative People's Party) claims to represent all shades of opinion and all social classes of Christians, but has not followed the postwar European trend of *effectively* seeking support among non-Roman Catholic Christians, though its latest manifesto does so in words, and there has been a tradition of bi-confessional moderate conservatism in the Grisons. On the one hand, there is a temptation to seek Protestant support as Protestants are the majority. On the other hand, the lot of a minority is easily tolerable and this status has long been the only possibility for any party on the federal level. The easiest way 'to become a CDU' would be to take into partnership either the small old-Liberal party, or one of the small religious (Evangelical) parties to be found on the cantonal level.

The claim to represent all social classes, in rural and semi-rural Catholic districts, can be readily upheld, and it is the only party really to do this. In such districts it may well happen that the tension between the Christian–Social left wing and the clerical–Conservative right wing is intense, and in other parts, where there is insufficient fuel for doctrinal differences, personal or traditional rivalries can achieve a rare intensity. The influence of church, of co-operative, and of neighbours generally (in a country where far-reaching powers are exercised in the commune) can never reach the stage of actual tyranny, since every part of Switzerland is now open to outside influences; the spiritual atmosphere is not that of Ireland or rural Bavaria. Moreover, the Church itself is more democratically structured than usual, and under the influence of the Second Vatican Council is loosening its involvement with lay political organizations and newspapers. What is the future of a confessional party when the Church moderates her claims?

The party is strongly localized and, since most of the really tiny cantons are Catholic, it is passionately attached to localism. (As is well known, the federal formula on which Switzerland is constructed is that language-minorities, *plus* religious minorities *equal* a majority of cantons, and therefore usually a majority in the Council of States. The power to block a constitutional amendment is a by-product of this situation.) The tiny cantons are safe seats for the Catholics, and this is a part of the federal bargain. On the federal level, the party will readily co-operate with the Farmers' Party and the Socialists in favour of protection for agriculture and rural industry and for social, notably 'family', benefits. On the other hand, it will also readily co-operate with other bourgeois parties, including the radicals, to protect the values enshrined in private property against socialism. This fits it for the role of the Centre Party, although psychologically this is difficult, because of the party's origins as an organization of defence against the Radicals, who feel themselves to be the natural governing party of Switzerland. On the federal level the party has a reputation for attention to personnel politics. It is reputedly less interested in the few commanding posts of the bureaucracy proper (for which it might find difficulty in obtaining candidates, since the politically-Catholic parts are rather underdeveloped) than

375

in the lower, numerous, electorally significant posts, e.g. in the railways. However, this is difficult to substantiate.

Not all Catholics, and very few others, adhere to the party. At federal level, religion does not really enter into politics, since the important questions are within the legal competences of the cantons. The big interest groups, which form a sort of phantom social-parliament, court the party, and more particularly its individual members, but none dominates it. Although intensely local, paradoxically it is also a very natural point of contact with Switzerland's neighbours, most of whom are dominated by Christian Democratic parties, and since the late 1920s it has been a member of the 'Catholic International'.[1] In some ways it is the most European of Swiss parties, but because of its policy of maintaining the prosperity of the small land-owning peasantry: in other ways it is one of the most narrowly national.

The Social Democratic Party

The Social Democratic Party is less peculiarly Swiss than the parties to its right. At federal level it was founded in 1888, but the much older Gruetliverein (founded 1838), associated with it in 1901 and later absorbed by it, has a claim to be considered the Swiss ancestor of social democracy. Unlike the other parties, the federal (i.e. central) organization is much more important than the local. Statistics and information are made available, and there is a serious and valuable academic study of it.[2]

In 1950, 25 per cent of its voters paid subscriptions to the Social Democratic Party. For long it has been assumed that the readiness to publish membership figures implied that they made up a higher percentage of voters than other parties enjoyed: in private conversation, however, I have heard this doubted. In the context of Swiss society and its tradition of discreetness—a tradition enforced by popular political rights—it may be better to conceal strength. The Radicals may be much stronger than they imply, and the Catholics may have difficulty in disentangling corporate from private membership.

[1] UEDC and NEI (Nouvelles équipes internationales). The Swiss Catholic Party was not one of the founding parties in 1925, but gave the impetus to the refounding after 1944. See Charles Dechert, 'The Christian Democrat International', *Orbis*, vol. xi, No. 1, Spring 1967.

[2] Francois Masnata, *Le parti socialiste et la tradition démocratique en Suisse*, Neuchâtel, 1963.

The shifts of doctrine in the party are to some extent revealed in successive programmes; bearing in mind that a class party is almost certain to assert that it is *not* a class party. The programme of 1888 was preoccupied with the issue of centralization, which the party espoused against cantonalism. In 1904 a larger dose of socialist doctrine was introduced. The programme of 1920 represents the high-water mark of doctrinaire-Marxist, class-war, dictatorship-of-proletariat, liturgy. It was composed under the influence of the Russian Revolution, and of the unsuccessful two-day general strike of 1918 which brought Switzerland to the brink of at least the attitudes of civil war.[1] In 1935, the danger of fascism was more apparent, and the programme became such that socialists could be considered allies and candidates for a share of power by the liberal parties. The programme of 1959 is diffuse and undoctrinal.

These shifts often represent a quite small change in the number of congress votes. They follow widespread changes in the climate of opinion, but they also reveal tactical necessities. At one time the left wing, or communism, is the danger, and words must be introduced to propitiate Marxist comrades, at another time strength can be gained by decoying the average educated citizen. As in other countries, a moral impulse, which is very widely shared, has got caught up both with a centralized political machine and with a rigid system of ideas which it does not follow or reject. There is an inner unhappiness, which is very close to an inner strength. In social terms the two streams of doctrine, natural law and Marxism, can be seen as a conflict between a large number of loyal workers, interested in the moral issues and in certain quite practical problems arising from their working life and companionships, and a small number of graduates to whom doctrinal tokens are the real currency.

Electoral statistics show that the rigidity of organization answers a need of the adherents. At all levels, more socialists vote the straight ticket than do others. This attitude is reciprocated in that a pro-socialist vote by adherents of other parties is rarer than other cross currents. The air of being besieged by enemies is congenial to the party: it has a grievance-wish stronger than that of other minorities.

---

[1] Two books were published in 1968 which will certainly supersede the previous literature on the General Strike of 1918. These are: Willi Gautschi, *Der Landesstreik, 1918*, and Paul Schmid–Ammann, *Die Wahrheit über den Generalstreik von 1918*.

In some ways Switzerland is a difficult environment for social democracy, because on paper the proletariat have enjoyed a dictatorship time out of mind, and public ownership is a part of the old regime.

Gripped in a perpetual coalition, Swiss socialists have at times been allies of the Radicals, as being anti-clerical and interested in political rights, but more recently they have explored common ground with the Peasants and Catholics, as being interested in protection, *étatisme*, paternalism, and generally in the priority of social-moral principles over economic expediency: the 'red-green-black' alliance.

As with other Social Democratic parties, the internal structure may be regarded from an ascending or descending point of view. From the ascending viewpoint there are: individual members, forming a local section, and electing from there a cantonal and a federal representation to respective congresses. These three levels nominate candidates for the parliamentary bodies of commune, canton, and confederation, and the national party Congress is led by a large Central Committee and a smaller Directing Committee, each with a chairman. Members of Parliament (National Councillors) participate in a personal capacity at all levels. The descending and more realistic interpretation, on the other hand, sees the parliamentary party and its chairman taking decisions, and submitting its policy for the applause of inferior, and larger, groups. The same interpretation can be applied to elections, when a list of candidates is prepared by committees, and then accepted by that grade in the hierarchy which the statutes of the party declare to be competent.

There are many more workers in the working-class trade union movement than there are socialist voters, and there is no organic connection between the two formal organizations: nevertheless, the Swiss Syndical Union and the Social Democratic Party regard each other as natural partners, sharing many leaders, and many ideals, each with its own source of strength. We may note that the Catholic Unions are similarly linked to the Catholic Party and the Peasants' Union to the Peasants' Party. Nevertheless, the relationships are not the same. The aims of the Peasants' Union at Brugg (e.g. protection) can often only be obtained through legislation, while the Trades Unions can obtain their ends through their own action. Co-operatives are not very important in this context.

The Peasants' Party

The Peasants' Party (Party of Farmers, Citizens and Tradesmen as it prefers to be called) is an offshoot of the Radicals, rather to its right, representing the interest its popular name denotes. In Berne, it has edged the Radical party out of first place.[1] This canton is so large as to have an undeniable claim to one seat on the Federal Council, which goes to the Peasants. This perpetuates its position, since an ambitious man in Berne must see that the most dazzling prospect of all, the federal presidency, is reserved in his canton for this particular party. Proportional representation for the National Council was introduced in 1919 and this led to the formation of the party as a result of an already existing split in the Bernese Radicals.

In Vaud, however, the Radicals have kept the upper hand with the peasantry, particularly on the federal level and since there is usually a Vaudois seat in the executive, this situation also perpetuates itself. In other cantons the situation is rather complex, and it may well happen that an elector or even a politician is Radical on the federal level, but locally is within the Peasants' Party. The Catholic Party is, of course, often a peasants' party and its ethos has points of contact. The appeal of the Peasants' Party, as its official name indicates, is not merely to small rural landowners, but to Protestant, protectionist, and conservative middle classes in towns, particularly, it is said, to officials.

The Landesring (Forum) of Independents

The least numerically important of the substantial parties is, in some ways, the most interesting phenomenon. Just as the Peasants' Party is a submerged element in most western European countries, which in Switzerland has become explicit and selfconscious, so the Landesring is a part of the political subconscious that has seen the light of day. There may, for example, be points of contact with Poujadism. Moreover, it is the only Swiss party apart from the Social Democrats that has received full-length treatment in a learned study—by Jean Meynaud.[2]

Within Switzerland, the Landesring receives attention because,

[1] For an account see: Beat Junker, *Die Bauern auf den Wege zur Politik. Die Entstehung der Bernischen* BGB *Partei*, Berne, 1968.

[2] Jean Meynaud and Adelbert Korff, *La Migros et la Politique*, Lausanne, 1965.

not being represented in the Federal Council, it is the only sizeable legal opposition party on the federal level. It groups round itself the bourgeois elements of opposition. In a mischievous way it also sometimes upsets the bargains made above the heads of the people by party leaders—'You have the judgeship and the seat in the National Council, and leave us the seat in the Council of States'— which are the normal way of life of the smallest cantons. It thus serves a rather useful function.

The party was started by Gottfried Duttweiler. Duttweiler was a free-lance grocer of genius, undercutting established oligopolies in the 1930s. The established firms used their federal influence and control of the cantonal legislatures against him, as well as their powers of economic boycott, so he was forced into ever-widening ambitions that ultimately led him to create a political party, with the same function in the political world as his chain store, Migros, in the economic. The party has survived him. Claiming to be above faction, it has not avoided the reproach of opportunism. But there must be many democracies (including Britain) that could envy Switzerland this one open window in a stuffy room.

Other Parties

The Old-Liberals are a small but very distinguished party, representing the Protestant high bourgeoisie in Basle and Geneva, vineyard owners in Vaud, bankers and the great dynasties of professors. It can today be regarded as a right wing of the Radicals.

The Communists muster a still smaller number of members, concentrated in Vaud, Geneva, and, potentially, in Neuchatel and perhaps Basle. Their affairs are characterized by the usual tergiversations and crises, passions and justifications. In July 1967, the orthodox party was considered to be the 'Party of Work—Peoples' Labour Party' under Jean Vincent, a gifted Geneva lawyer with a pleasant personality. But the 'League of Communists' and the 'Communist Party of Switzerland' assert of the former and of each other that the others betray the true doctrine, and are tools of the Evil One. The League of Communists, 'The Organization of the Swiss Marxists–Leninists', is said to sympathize with Chairman Mao. Some of these strands have been unravelled by Walter Hollstein in a series of articles in the (Basle) *Nationalzeitung* during June and July 1967.

There are other small parties, often important in a particular canton, that sometimes surface into federal politics. Moreover, to be an independent candidate in a National Council election one must give oneself a party name: such names often promise much, but do not enjoy longevity or success.

The expelled leader of the socialists in the Valais formed such a one-man party at the 1967 elections, and was elected. In accordance with a general rule of political symmetry, the radical right wing may be expected over the years to recruit the same number of supporters as the radical left wing. The modern rallying point for the survivors and successors of the right wing or Nazi 'Fronts'[1] of the 1930s is the resentment felt against the large disenfranchised body of foreigners who perform much of the manual labour of Switzerland. These right-wing groups seldom surface on the federal level, but they obtained one seat in the most recent federal election. The other point of interest in the most recent election (October 1967) was the increase in the votes of the 'opposition' parties, the Landesring and to a less degree the Communists. This is the only way open to the electors to give expression to the 'feeling of malaise' which, it is often said, has come over Switzerland in recent years. It is a vote against the system of coalition government, as well as against the parties in the coalition.

EUROPE

Relations with Europe are seen, in public discussions, as economic necessities. Behind the scenes, because it is embarrassing even to discuss neutrality in public, the military question (NATO) may also be considered. Beyond the economic problem lies the social one, especially the preservation of a viable peasantry, for the peasantry are near the heart of Swiss social values. In some aspects, the Swiss are intensely incapsulated, but in activities that look beyond the national frontiers, there is no people so free of prejudice and so well informed, though sympathies cease abruptly and totally at the iron curtain, and 'the smaller country is always right'.

Because Switzerland privately prefers the old international regime in Europe with four powers in independent competition at her

---

[1] A study, which appeared too recently to comment, of the Swiss right wing radicals, is W. Wolf, *Faschismus in der Schweiz. Die Geschichte der Frontenbewegungen in der deutschen Schweiz, 1930–1945*, Zurich, 1969.

borders, she is only reluctantly 'European'. The Swiss tradition, however, is to be the last to take a thing up, but to note and avoid the mistakes of others, and, when the device is eventually adopted, to surpass all others in perfection.

It is said that the Swiss group in the Strasbourg Consultative Assembly act closely together, rather than with their party-colleagues from other states. Within the Assembly, the group often follows the weaker line, for example, trying to avoid any condemnation of the Greek military regime in case the Greek government feel hurt. The word 'neutrality' can sometimes be used as an alibi, and when one expresses surprise that there can be a connection between the action proposed and neutrality, one is told that there is a very special sort of Swiss neutrality. Under Petitpierre, as Minister for Foreign Affairs, this sometimes bordered on the grotesque—as in the refusal of Switzerland to contribute to UNRRA in 1944.

There is a 'Swiss Movement for Unification of Europe' which spans all the respectable parties, and which has a weekly *Europa*, which is now (1968) in its thirty-fifth year. This Society acts as a forum of discussion, and as a sort of loose pressure group. It recently had 'a Gallup poll' among the 1,264 candidates for the 200 National Council seats. Of these, 40 per cent responded, including about the same proportion of those who in the event were elected. The following is an extract from the result of this poll.[1]

	Joining EEC		Association with EEC		Joining UNO		Mercenary service with UNO	
	Yes	No	Yes	No	Yes	No	Yes	No
Radicals	46	41	79	9	42	50	33	46
Catholics	47	27	60	6	40	33	34	32
Socialists	81	13	61	10	89	3	61	19
Peasants	6	31	38	5	13	32	12	33
Liberals	8	5	9	1	4	13	7	6
Landesring	42	9	35	5	35	12	35	18
Communists	1	6	0	6	1	5	1	5

[1] Thanks are due to M. Henri Stranner for some of this information, and permission to reprint these figures.

The position of the Peasants' Party is conspicuous, and so is that of the Landesring. It is clear from the answers, and from other suggestions, that the arguments of one group do not meet the arguments of the others. The capitalist parties look to the trade advantages above all, and the left-wing parties to nationalism as a good in itself. Other figures support (what is expected to be the case) that there is rather more international feeling in the non-German speaking parts of Switzerland, and the figures should be taken as expressing a willingness to join the EEC in the situation where Britain and other EFTA countries are members, 'the wider community', and not the EEC as it is at the moment.

Switzerland is a member of the more harmless international communities, but not of UNO. It cultivates these with a sort of redoubled ardour as an insurance against joining the more disturbing or effective organizations.

The question of the influence of membership of certain European communities upon Swiss political parties is a rather artificial one: it would not occur to the observer of parties to ask this question. The delegation to the Consultative Assembly of the Council of Europe is constituted as a simple committee of the two chambers—a sort of ante-chamber and annex to the committee on foreign relations. But all parties are rather well informed of what their opposite numbers in neighbouring countries are doing and thinking: it is difficult to see that this close observation of the people next door has been altered by formal participation in European activities.

NATIONAL COUNCIL ELECTION 1963 AND 1967
Relative size of Parliamentary groups

	Radicals % Vote 1963	Radicals % Vote 1967	Radicals Seats 1963	Radicals Seats 1967	Catholics % Vote 1963	Catholics % Vote 1967	Catholics Seats 1963	Catholics Seats 1967	Socialists % Vote 1963	Socialists % Vote 1967	Socialists Seats 1963	Socialists Seats 1967	Peasants % Vote 1963	Peasants % Vote 1967	Peasants Seats 1963	Peasants Seats 1967
Zurich	16·2	14·8	6	5	12·5	10·7	5	4	27·3	22·2	10	8	13·8	13·0	5	5
Berne	17·6	17·5	6	6	6·6	6·3	2	2	36·1	34·4	12	12	32·3	30·9	11	10
Lucerne	36·2	33·8	3	3	49·6	48·6	5	5	9·1	9·1	1	1				
Uri	93·0	95·2	1	1												
Schwyz	21·7				49·5	97·8	2	1	28·9		1					
Obwald	34·5				64·5	69·6	1	1								
Nidwald		29·0		1	95·0		1							9·0		1
Glarus																
Zug	22·9	49·0	1	1	54·1	51·0	1	1	12·9	17·8	1	1				
Fribourg	41·8	25·5	2	2	24·6	47·7	3	3	33·6	30·2	1	1				
Solothurn	25·0	44·4	3	3	13·1	25·3	1	1	32·1	29·5	3	3	10·1		1	
Basle Town	23·7	16·8	1	1	14·6	13·8	1	1	34·5	33·1	2	2				
Basle Land	43·1	22·8	1	1					45·2	42·0	2	2	15·4	14·5	1	1
Schaffhausen		40·3		1												
Appenzell-Rh. E.					85·3	96·2	1	1								
Appenzell-Rh. I					47·4	47·8	1	1								
St Gallen	27·5	28·1	4	4	41·6	40·4	6	6	18·2	16·8	2	2	14·4	14·7	2	2
Grisons	15·4	15·0	1		22·9	20·2	2	2	13·0	11·3						
Argau	19·6	15·4	3	2	26·8	26·7	3	3	31·0	28·3	4	4	24·9	23·3	2	2
Thurgau	40·8	21·6	3	1	36·8	37·0	1	1	28·3	27·4	2	1	3·4	2·7		
Ticino	31·9	41·0	3	3	5·4	4·7	3	3	19·0	15·7	1	1				
Vaud	20·7	31·9	6	6	64·1	57·9	1	1	27·9	26·1	4	4	8·0	8·7		
Valais	26·0	18·3	1	1			5	5	15·2	19·1	1	1				
Neuchâtel	20·1	23·4	2	2	15·7	13·9	1	1	39·1	34·5	2	2				
Geneva		18·5		2			2	2	24·9	16·0	2	1				
Total	24·0	23·2	51	49	23·4	22·1	48	45	26·6	23·5	53	50	11·4	11·0	22	21
Switzerland (total number of votes) 1963	230,200				225,160				256,063				109,202			
1967	230,095				219,184				233,873				109,621			

Cantons	Landesring % Vote 1963	Landesring % Vote 1967	Landesring Seats 1963	Landesring Seats 1967	Old Liberals % Vote 1963	Old Liberals % Vote 1967	Old Liberals Seats 1963	Old Liberals Seats 1967	Minor Parties (Democrats and Evangelicals) % Vote 1963	Minor Parties % Vote 1967	Minor Parties Seats 1963	Minor Parties Seats 1967	Communists % Vote 1963	Communists % Vote 1967	Communists Seats 1963	Communists Seats 1967
Zurich	13·2	23·0	5	9					10·7	7·8	4	3	2·1	2·6		
Berne	4·0	7·4	2	2					1·9	2·8		1				
Lucerne	5·1	8·5														
Uri																
Schwyz																
Obwald																
Nidwald																
Glarus																
Zug																
Fribourg																
Solothurn																
Basle Town	11·2	15·8	1	1	11·8	16·7	1	1					6·8	6·8		
Basle Land	11·7	10·8														
Schaffhausen		17·7														
Appenzell-Rh. E																
Appenzell-Rh. I.																
St Gallen	6·9	7·3	1	1												
Grisons	5·5	11·7	1	2					29·4	33·3	2	2				
Argau									2·8	2·6						
Thurgau																
Ticino					14·4	12·7	2	2					12·3	3·6	2	2
Vaud		1·4												41·3		1
Valais					22·3	22·8	1	1					12·6	19·3		
Neuchâtel		12·1		1	16·9	13·8	2	2								
Geneva					2·2	2·3							18·9	20·9	2	2
Total	5·0	9·1	10	16			6	6	3·4	3·0	6	6	2·2	2·9	4	5
Switzerland (total number of votes) 1963	48,224				21,501				32,668				21,088			
Switzerland (total number of votes) 1967		89,950				23,208				29,989				28,723		

Notes:

In some small Cantons there was no election, as the number of seats was not less than the number of candidates. In Uri, seats in the Council of States were traded against the seat in the National Council. The Canton is in fact overwhelmingly Catholic. Similar bargains are common in the smallest Cantons. A number of small parties, in many cases representing only the personal following of a single candidate, upset the accuracy of some of these percentages. The figures may thus vary between one person's mode of reckoning and another's. Furthermore, the grouping in the Assembly diverges slightly from the listing of parties in the cantons for electoral purposes.

Reproduced and adapted from *Année Politique Suisse Schweizerische Politik 1967* (pp. 26–27), published by *Forschungszentrum für Geschichte und Soziologie der schweizerischen Politik an der Universität Bern*, 1968.

CHAPTER 10

THE UNITED KINGDOM

INTRODUCTION

Parties do not exist in a vacuum. They have to be viewed in the context of the political society within which they operate. Britain is the European country with, perhaps, the most polarized two-party system: two large parties alternate in being in complete control of the government. Most factors conditioning this are themselves so inter-related that cause and effect become obscured. However, two phenomena—homogeneity and stability—and two pieces of political machinery—cabinet government and the electoral system—are crucial. Together these factors make any trend towards a two-party system overwhelming.

Homogeneity

The United Kingdom consists of England, Scotland and Wales (constituting Great Britain) and Northern Ireland. The country is small and compact and its population is ethnically similar in all areas. England tends to dominate the island, and English is the first language of the vast majority. Ninety per cent of the population is Protestant. The only identifiable minorities are coloured immigrants. Whilst these occasion particular political problems, their presence has as yet made no fundamental difference to political society.[1] There is a close and thorough system of transportation which tends to radiate from London. The capital, in fact, dominates commercial and cultural life. Almost unique to European countries, Britain's daily newspapers are national, although of necessity there is some deconcentration in the places of printing.[2] Generally, the

---

[1] Two studies have so far been made of this problem: Institute of Race Relations, *Colour and the British Electorate*, Allen and Unwin, London, 1965; and P. Foot, *Immigration and Race in British Politics*, Penguin Books, London, 1965.

[2] In England there are printings of some national newspapers at Manchester and other provincial centres, but these tend to differ little from the basic London edition. Most Scottish newspapers are directly linked to an English counterpart.

provincial press is confined to evening newspapers with their traditional emphasis on local news. The mass media are also run on national lines. The British Broadcasting Corporation (BBC) has monopoly of sound radio and controls two thirds of the television channels. Even the independent television companies have done little to foster regionalism.

In Britain centralization is both accepted and expected. A useful comparison can be made with France. The latter has a good deal more formal centralization in the governmental machine, but there is also a great deal more deconcentration in the siting of administrative offices. Britain has less formal centralization and less deconcentration. Final evidence of homogeneity comes from the economic sphere. The industrial revolution started in the north of England but its ultimate impact has been felt almost universally throughout Britain. Living standards do vary in different parts of the country, but the differentials are much smaller than in many other European countries.

The most striking exceptions to this homogeneity are Scotland and Wales. It is possible to look back to independent national traditions, with their cultural connotations including ancient languages. Regionalism in England may have an artificial flavour, but nationalism in Wales and Scotland is becoming once again a force to be reckoned with. So far it has not been strong enough to have a basic impact on British political society, but it could pose a long-term threat to the stability of British institutions and the two-party system.

Stability

It is almost 300 years since Britain had a major upheaval in her political structure, and it is possible to present history since 1688 as a pattern of orderly progress from a still-strong monarchy to constitutional democracy and, eventually, to the welfare state and the mixed economy. One reason for this has been external. It is 900 years since Britain was last invaded. Internally, the political system has always been sufficiently flexible to canalize major discontents. Those who have, at different times, been unreconciled to the prevailing system have tended to be too few and too weak to mount a meaningful challenge. Two factors have been crucial—the political skill of the aristocracy and the willingness of the working class to operate substantially within the system. The British aristocracy proved itself the most far-sighted in Europe by its handling of the major political crisis of 1832. In giving a share in political influence to the commercial and industrial classes, it was able to cling successfully to its own more dominant role. After three reform acts, Lord Salisbury's 1886 cabinet could still contain ten peers out of 14, and it was not until the Liberal landslide of 1906 that the aristocracy found its power limited to the Upper House of Parliament.

It took nearly a century for the representatives of the commercial and industrial middle classes to lever themselves into positions of political leadership to which their economic weight entitled them. Skilful resistance to change by the aristocracy helped to stabilize the structure of the political system. Nineteenth-century politics revolved around the clash between the Whig-Peelite-Liberal factions and the Tories and each side was eager for reinforcement. Consequently, Gladstone and Disraeli vied with each other to extend the franchise to the urban working classes in the hope of earning their gratitude, and electoral dividends. The repeat of this operation in 1884 meant virtual manhood suffrage. Painlessly the working class was brought within the existing system. This fact, coupled with the gradual development of trade unionism in the later part of the nineteenth century, made possible a fresh evolution: the emergence of the Labour Party and its replacement of the Liberals, after a brief alliance with them, as one of the two major political forces.

Cabinet Government

In the bicameral legislature, the House of Commons has won full supremacy; the party which dominates that chamber automatically forms the government. General elections take place at intervals of up to five years, and the Prime Minister can always, if he so wishes, bring about a dissolution of Parliament. Elections tend to be contests on a nationwide scale between the rival political parties. As soon as the results are known, the leader of the largest party is automatically invited by the Monarch to form a government. The government is formally subject to parliamentary control; this is attenuated by the fact that it always wields some kind of parliamentary majority, usually absolute. The leader of the biggest opposition party receives the office of, and payment for, Leader of Her (His) Majesty's Opposition. This increases the gladiatorial nature of, what has become in some ways, a contest between rivals for Prime Ministerial office. Legislative power is in theory vested almost completely in the House of Commons. The House of Lords has a delaying power of only one year. In practice, the government controls both executive and legislature through its majority in the House of Commons.

Electoral System

The electoral system employed in Britain is a necessary but not sufficient cause of the two-party system. Taken, however, in the total political context, it gives overwhelming reinforcement to the tendency towards the two-party system. The country is divided into 630 constituencies with an average of 57,000 electors[1] in each. All constituencies return a single member by a straight plurality. There is no transferable vote and no attempt at any kind of proportionality. Third parties operating on a national scale are likely to find themselves considerably under-represented in Parliament and this is the dilemma of the modern Liberal Party. On the other hand, the system is also likely to give the party with the largest number of votes a disproportionately large number of seats.[2] Thus, although at no general election since the war has any party won an overall majority of the popular vote, one party has always gained an absolute parliamentary majority.

Within this context the British parties fulfil the traditional functions ascribed to political parties. They aggregate, and help to arti-

[1] This was at the 1966 General Election. In 1945, 640 constituencies had an average electorate of 51,000. In 1966, the smallest constituency had only 23,000 voters, as against 102,000 in the largest.

[2] At most postwar elections, the electoral system has contained a small inherent bias towards the Conservative Party. This implies that if the two parties won the same share of the national vote, the Conservatives would win more seats. This bias was reflected by the 1951 result when Labour received a greater popular vote than the Conservatives, but still won fewer seats. The major reason for this was the large number of Labour votes 'wasted' in piling up huge majorities in safe seats. At the 1964 Election, the bias disappeared. Although, the difference in the popular vote of the two parties was the same as that in 1951, Labour was able to win a majority of seats. A major factor in the change was that many seats with relatively small electorates were won by Labour. Ironically, if the government accepts the Report of the Independent Commission on Constituency Boundaries which, amongst other things, attempts to equalize the numbers of voters in different constituencies, then the bias towards the Conservatives will be recreated.

culate, interests. Given the dominant role played in alternation by each major political party, both become an obvious object for infiltration by pressure groups. As might be expected, only the largest pressure groups can gain a position of real influence over *majoritaire* parties of the British kind. The parties also supply personnel of the government (but not the civil service) and Parliament, and the system ensures the permanent existence of a complete alternative government. Operating within the British political system, the parties also fulfil a unique role in providing a buckle to bind legislature and executive. It is the existence of relatively tightly organized parties which characterizes and creates the conditions for the form of cabinet, perhaps even Prime Ministerial government, which has replaced the more classical parliamentary system of the nineteenth century.

Stress has been laid on the ability of the British political system to accommodate the strongest class differences. However, the basic cleavage between the two dominant parties today is class.[1] A distinction is sometimes made between party-forming and party-formed issues. French politics would appear to have at least three party-forming issues. In Britain there is only one: Labour against Capital. Intellectuals deride this as an out-of-date issue, and some of the force of the clash has certainly been removed by mutual acceptance of the mixed economy. Nonetheless, class is a fundamental factor in the British party system. The Conservatives are a party of moneyed and managerial classes seeking the support of sufficient of the working class to gain political power. Labour is a party founded on an alliance between trade unionists and socialist intellectuals. In practice, a large section of the working class (particularly amongst the non-unionized) habitually vote Conservative but various surveys show the nature of the party. One at Greenwich in 1950[2] showed the working class as 79 per cent of all voters. The same class supplied the Labour Party with 92·5 per cent of its supporters and the Conservatives with 60 per cent. On the other hand, only 9 per cent of officers in the local Conservative Party came from this class compared with 44 per cent in the Labour Party. Mark Abrams, looking at the 1964 General Election[3] suggested that 42 per cent of

---

[1] See Robert Alford, *Party and Society*, Murray, London, 1964. This is a valuable account, but he may over-emphasize the importance of class factors.

[2] Benny, Grey and Pear, *How People Vote*, cited in Pulzer, *Political Representation and Elections in Britain*.

[3] Article in the Spring, 1965, issue of *Twentieth Century*.

the skilled manual and 44 per cent of the non-skilled manual voted Labour. Equivalent percentages for the Conservative Party were 26 per cent and 23 per cent. Despite the spread in Conservative support, their parliamentary party is narrowly based. After the 1966 General Election, 42·7 per cent of its MPs gave as previous profession 'Company Director', 'Farmer' or 'Landowner'. Labour's equivalent was 2·5 per cent. As many as 25·1 per cent of Labour MPs had been manual workers as against 0·4 per cent of Conservatives.[1] The Labour elite—party leaders, Members of Parliament, etc.—contains an increasing proportion of the middle class, but a basic orientation remains. Labour policies favour the working class and less well-off sections of the community. The trade unionist finds economic and social pressures militating in favour of support of 'his' party. Much of the Labour leadership retains close links with the trade union movement, and the party's finance comes overwhelmingly from the unions. Conservatives, on the other hand, favour rewards for initiative and private enterprise. The non-intellectual bourgeois finds it natural to vote for this party. In the higher echelons, there is virtually nobody of working-class origin and the major source of the party finance is business.

The voting strength of the two parties is spread fairly evenly throughout the country, save for Labour's domination in Wales and that of the Conservatives in Northern Ireland. However, the nature of the electoral system results in a dependence by the Conservatives on Southern England for at least two fifths of their parliamentary seats. Ever since 1950, the Conservatives have held a big lead in this part of the country: even in 1966 they took two thirds of the parliamentary seats. Over this period Labour has increased its dominance in terms of seats in Northern England and Scotland, whilst it completely dominates Wales. Were it not for Labour strength in what was the County of London, a north-south polarization would have appeared.

There are no really significant divisions along religious lines. Catholics are more Labour than non-Catholics, but Alford ascribes this to more heavy class voting and the disproportionate number of working-class Catholics.[2]

[1] See *Times Guide to the House of Commons, 1966*.
[2] Alford, op. cit. A 1962 survey by the British Institute of Public Opinion showed that Labour were favoured by 57 per cent of manual workers and 22 per cent of other groups. Amongst Catholics the respective figures were 78 per cent and 19 per cent.

TABLE I
(percentage of popular vote by area)

Share of votes by each in seats contested

1966	Labour	Conservative	
	49·9	40·7	London
	38·8	47·4	South
	51·5	43·2	Midlands
	54·3	38·8	North
	60·7	27·9	Wales
	49·9	37·6	Scotland
	39·3	61·8	Northern Ireland

1959	Labour	Conservative	
	43·9	49·1	London
	35·4	54·5	South
	47·2	49·2	Midlands
	48·9	47·3	North
	56·4	33·8	Wales
	47·6	46·7	Scotland
	31·6	77·2	Northern Ireland

Source: Butler and Freeman, *British Political Facts, 1900–67.*

This monopoly by the existing major parties of the two classes big enough to form a political base poses a serious problem to would-be third parties. The working of the electoral system distorts in an unfavourable direction the number of seats they gain for their votes. Thus in 1966 it took 36,000 votes to elect a Labour MP, 45,000 to elect a Conservative and 193,000 to elect a Liberal. This in turn may produce a further distortion. The unwillingness to 'waste' a vote may cause supporters of third parties to switch to the lesser evil of the two big parties. Clearly, at all elections in the 1950s this second factor militated heavily against the Liberals.[1] Table II shows the votes and seats at seven general elections since the war:

[1] Financial stringency after their disastrous showing in the 1950 Election forced the Liberals to reduce the number of constituencies contested from 475 to 109. Throughout the 1950s many potential supporters were deprived of the opportunity of actually voting Liberal.

TABLE II

General Election Results, 1945–1966

	1945	1950	1951	1955	1959	1964	1966
Labour:							
Votes	11,632,891	13,266,592	13,948,605	12,404,970	12,215,538	12,205,814	13,064,951
Seats	393	315	295	277	258	317	363
Conservative:							
Votes	9,557,667	12,502,567	13,717,538	13,311,936	13,749,830	11,979,708	11,418,433
Seats	213	298	321	345	365	303	253
Liberal:							
Votes	2,197,191	2,621,548	730,551	722,405	1,638,571	3,092,878	2,327,533
Seats	12	9	6	6	6	9	12
Others:							
Votes	674,853	381,964	198,969	321,182	275,304	370,502	452,689
Seats	21	2	3	2	1	0	1
	+ Speaker	+ Speaker		+ Speaker		+ Speaker	+ Speaker
Turn-out (per cent)	73·3	84	82·5	76·8	78·7	77·1	75·9

Notes:

Electoral statistics vary considerably due to inaccuracies and genuine difficulties of classification. I have here generally followed the figures in the Appendix to Butler and King, *The British General Election of 1966*. These include in the figures for 'others' any Speaker who, seeking re-election to the House of Commons, stands as Mr Speaker. Normally, he would be unopposed by any official party candidate. In fact, where there is a contest, Mr Speaker's votes are likely to come almost exclusively from previous supporters when he was a party candidate.

N*

393

The best prospects for third parties (whose object is continued existence as a third party rather than the hope of replacing a major party) must lie in finding a regional basis. The Liberals have never quite decided what their basic objective ought to be. Table II shows a considerable revival at the two most recent general elections; far more seats were contested than at the three previous elections. A strand of Liberal thought adheres to the idea of replacing one, or even both, of the existing major parties. Geographical analysis, though, of relative Liberal success makes it quite clear that the party has been based for 30 years now on the Celtic fringes: Wales, Scotland and in England, the West Country. If we contrast Liberal performance at elections in 1950, 1951, 1964 and 1966, an interesting pattern emerges (see Table III). The realistic alternative to attempting to become a major party appears to be reliance on regional bases, confinement to the Celtic fringe, but a more secure future as a permanent third minor party.

During the same period, other parties have done much worse.[1] Since 1950 none has won any English seat in the House of Commons, although it can be argued that two Communists who lost their seats in that year were more the victims of the cold war than the political system. Outside England the position is different. Mention might here be made of Northern Ireland which is united politically to Britain and dominated by the Ulster Unionists who are allied with the Conservatives. At different times other political forces have won some of the twelve Northern Ireland seats.[2] Wales and Scotland both have nationalist parties and since the 1966 Election each has won one seat at a by-election, but it is too soon to discover whether

[1] Frequently this is attributed to the electoral system, but this is an over-simplification. Unlike the case of the Liberals, the share of votes going to 'other' candidates has not normally significantly exceeded their share of seats.

[2] The basic policy of the Ulster Unionists is the continuation of the United Kingdom, and they can also be styled the 'Protestant Party'. Since 1945 they have always held a minimum of 9 out of Northern Ireland's 12 seats. The remainder have at various times been held by Nationalist, Sinn Fein, Independent Labour and Civil Rights candidates. The Northern Ireland Labour Party has never won a seat for its own candidates. Major Northern Ireland political issues have concerned partition, relations with the United Kingdom, civil rights and discrimination against Catholics. During 1968/9 there was a split within the Unionist party on the last two issues. At the Northern Ireland election in 1969, there were rival Unionist candidates in many constituencies. Even so, the Unionists emerged as much the largest force and attempts were made to heal the rift.

TABLE III

Liberal performance in selected areas at certain general elections

	1950	1951	1964	1966
Liberal seats in Parliament,	9	6	9	12
of which in England outside the West Country	2	2	1	3
% share of vote in seats contested				
England	(413) 11·4	(91) 12·4	(323) 18·3	(273) 15·6
London	(98) 8·6	(7) 8·5	(71) 15·8	(64) 11·5
Lancashire	(47) 9·7	(23) 7·9	(25) 18·9	(22) 14·7
West Country	(14) 20·2	(9) 17·5	(14) 29·7	(13) 27·2
Scotland	(41) 11·5	(9) 24·8	(26) 22·7	(24) 22·2
Forth	(9) 9·3	—	(4) 13·5	(4) 10·9
Clyde	(14) 6·6	(2) 9·1	(6) 18·3	(3) 17·2
Highlands	(6) 25·7	(3) 28·1	(6) 38·3	(6) 37·2
Wales	(21) 21·2	(9) 32·6	(12) 21·9	(11) 19·5
Rural Areas	(9) 30·0	(8) 37·6	(8) 28·1	(9) 22·0
Industrial Areas	(12) 11·8	(1) 8·4	(4) 12·8	(2) 10·6

Note: Figures in brackets show number of seats contested.

Sources: Nicholas, *The British General Election of 1950*; Butler, *The British General Election of 1951*; Butler and King, *The British General Election of 1964*; and Butler and King, *The British General Election of 1966*.

or not this is a new trend. What it does demonstrate once again is the necessity for small parties to acquire a local or regional base if they are to attain parliamentary representation.

Before proceeding to a structural-functional analysis of the major parties, two theories about the contemporary political structure are worth discussion. The first challenges the concept of two-party domination by the ingenious argument that, at many earlier periods, there have been three or more parties in Parliament, often without there being an absolute majority. In particular, it is argued that from 1885 to 1945, there were always three sizeable parties in Parliament and sometimes four with several coalition governments. In fact, for much of this time one of the parties was the Irish Nationalist Party. With the achievement of independence for Eire they more or less disappeared as a parliamentary force. On the other hand, during the period 1905 to 1931 the Labour Party was struggling to replace the Liberals as one of the big two. After 1931, Britain had clearly reverted to the two-party system and the so-called National Government was heavily dominated by the Conservatives. On balance, it would appear that the argument cannot be sustained. The Irish Nationalists were a regional phenomenon and this is a continuing possibility in the context of the British two-party system. The system, moreover, retains the flexibility to permit the replacement of one major party by another as one of the big two. What seems fundamentally improbable is that a genuine three-party system can emerge with the three parties alternating in government through various coalitions.

The second theory concerns the so-called 'swing of the pendulum'. This was fashionable in the early 1950s and suggested that not only did the two parties share political power but that their periods of office would alternate one with the other. This postulates a norm of a party winning no more than two elections consecutively and, frequently, only one with an inevitable electional swing against the party in power. Today this theory is discredited. There remains only a broad assumption that each party must have the possibility of occasionally wielding power if the system is to be maintained. Since the war, two general elections have produced changes of government, one has weakened the existing government and three have strengthened it.

Having placed the two-party system in its proper framework, we will now pass on to a detailed analysis of the structure and function of the parties. In view of their dominant role in British political life, most space will be given to the Labour and Conservative parties.

THE LABOUR PARTY

Introduction

The Labour Party is the formal embodiment of an alliance between left-wing intellectuals and the organized trade union movement. It began as a federation of Socialist Societies (of which the Independent Labour Party was the most important) and trade unions. Individuals could not join the Labour Party directly and could only be 'members' through affiliated bodies. The present constitutional structure of the party dates back to 1918 and is a hybrid between the original federal organization and a more normal mass membership party.

Today there are two types of member: individual (belonging to a constituency branch); and indirect (belonging to an affiliated trade union or Socialist Society). Individual members are required to pass an eligibility test of not being a member of any other party or ancillary organization. No such test is required of affiliated members, and some of these, as will be shown, cannot even be classed as party sympathizers. Officers, at local and national level, must be individual members of the party.

Different categories make it difficult to form a reliable estimate of the number of members. On the individual membership side, all constituency parties are credited with having a minimum of 1,000 members. In practice a good many have fewer. In 1967 there were officially 735,000 individual members.[1] This was the lowest figure since 1949. The highest annual figure was over one million in 1952. At present 58 per cent of individual members are men, a proportion which seems fairly constant. On the trade union side, apparent membership is affected by Acts of Parliament regulating their right to indulge in political activities. A trade union wishing to use funds for political activities cannot simply take this from the general membership subscription. A secret ballot must first be held

[1] Official figures are issued each year in the Annual Report of the National Executive Committee to the Party Conference. Subsequently they are reprinted in the *Annual Conference Report*.

to ascertain if the majority of members favour the establishment of a political fund. If this turns out to be the case, a separate political levy can then be added to the general subscription. Members not wishing to pay the levy may contract out. At one time, those wishing to pay had to contract in, thus switching the onus. The majority of trade unions now use part of the proceeds of their political fund to affiliate members to the Labour Party, although they need not affiliate all who pay the levy. The affiliation fee is only one shilling per year per member, so most Trade Unions retain a balance in their political fund for making special contributions to the party. Clearly, not everybody 'affiliated' may really wish to be a member of the Labour Party and the figures are inflated by inertia. It is significant that in 1946—the last year of contracting in—affiliated trade union membership was 2,635,000, whilst for the following year under the new system the figure jumped to 4,386,000. In 1967 the figure was 5,540,000. The final category of members of the Labour Party is those affiliated through Socialist Societies; in 1967 about 21,000. The total number of members is thus approximately 6,300,000, but the only real significance of this figure is to give an indication of party income.

Structure

The function of the Labour Party's mass membership is essentially to represent the party at a local level and to act as the machinery for contesting elections. The commitment of the individual who joins will vary from simply paying a subscription to working for the party by canvassing or addressing election literature. Some will aspire to party, local government or parliamentary office. The basic party unit is the ward or polling district committee and this only involves individual members, all of whom are entitled to share in running the ward party, particularly in electing officers and choosing a candidate for local elections. The form of organization[1] varies somewhat according to whether a parliamentary constituency is equal to, greater or less than the related unit of local government, but the basic structure is the same. The next tier upwards from the ward committee is usually the constituency party which exists through its management committee only as a delegate body. The management committee may

[1] A series of model rules is issued by the NEC and these normally form the basis for the constitution of a constituency Labour Party.

meet as often as required, but the norm is quarterly, and it runs the affairs of the constituency. It contains delegates of the ward parties and also of those trade union branches and Socialist Society branches which are locally affiliated. Not all branches of nationally affiliated unions bother about local affiliation; this may pose a financial problem for the constituency. Constituency parties, in fact, differ greatly in membership and resources. The biggest individual membership in 1967 was over 5,000, whilst the real membership of some constituencies was probably no more than 300 or 400. The management committee elect an executive committee to run party affairs between meetings. In theory the smaller body can only recommend; in practice it usually has a great deal of influence. Formal powers of decision-making reside in the management committee and of these the most important is the selection of a parliamentary candidate. Any affiliated organization or ward may nominate. The executive then draws up a short list to which the management committee may add names, and the management committee resolves itself into a selection committee to make a final choice; the central organization will have a representative present during the final stages of selection, and the National Executive Committee must approve all candidatures. In practice, though, the National Executive and party leadership have little control over constituency choice. Theoretically, at by-elections the National Executive discusses potential candidates with the management committee but, contrary to popular belief, there is rarely direct interference. Where a constituency has a sitting Labour Member of Parliament, procedures for candidate adoption differ in such a way as virtually to ensure his readoption.

In most constituencies, the working-class element is strongly entrenched in party organization, but increasingly candidates for parliament are being selected from the professional and middle classes. Of successful candidates at the 1966 General Election, 230 can be described as coming from the middle, managerial and professional classes; 42 can be classified as clerical and technical workers or engineers; and 6 were party officials. This leaves 97 as manual workers, of whom 40 were trade union officials at the time of first election. A contribution the trade unions make to the party is to sponsor candidates. The union pays the bulk of election expenses and also part of the salary of a full-time agent, if one is employed. About 150 MPs are sponsored candidates, although a good number of these have never worked at the occupations theoretically represented by their union. Over half the Labour MPs had a university education and over 60 per cent attended public or grammar schools, but 20 per cent had no secondary education at all.[1]

Constituency parties send delegates to the Annual Conference of the Labour Party as do nationally affiliated trade unions. In theory Conference is the governing body of the party, but this has never been the case in practice. Today it is a very large, if not unwieldy, body which is one of the centres of power, but by no means the most important, in the movement. Party leaders can resist temporary bouts of Conference criticism. Resolutions must pass Conference by a two thirds majority in order to be added to the party programme. Whilst the leadership is occasionally defeated, it is never by this kind of margin. Frequently, the leaders are able to persuade the wider party to change its collective mind. Thus in October 1960, Conference passed by a simple majority a resolution calling for unilateral renunciation by Britain of nuclear weapons. This would have implied Britain's leaving NATO and was unacceptable to Hugh Gaitskell, then the party leader. In the subsequent 12 months his supporters campaigned successfully for a reversal of the vote. This places conference powers in perspective. Clearly, a situation in which leaders and Conference remain out of step is intolerable. Conference has to be taken note of, but the greater powers of persuasion belong to the leaders.

Decisions at Conference are made by a system of block voting. Constituency parties and trade unions cast a vote on behalf of their entire membership with no division of vote. This means that the Transport and General Workers' Union casts more votes than all the constituency parties together. Six large unions have an absolute majority. It should be noted, however, that there have been few occasions when the majority of constituency parties voted differently from the majority of unions.[2] The real criticism is that in many

[1] *The Times Guide to the House of Commons, 1966.* Not having secondary education should not be taken as an indication that all formal education ended before the age of 14. Many later participated in courses arranged by the National Council of Labour Colleges and other forms of adult education, c.f. E. Janosik, *Constituency Labour Parties in Britain*, Pall Mall, London, 1968.

[2] For a more detailed study of this point see M. Harrison, *Trade Unions and the Labour Party since 1945*, Allen and Unwin, London, 1960.

affiliated bodies the membership never express themselves on Conference issues and thousands of votes are thus determined by a small group and, perhaps, by one man. Traditionally, the largest unions supported the party leaders, but the defection of the Transport and General Workers' Union with the succession to its General Secretaryship of Frank Cousins altered the balance. Decisions are now very dependent on the volatile Amalgamated Engineering Union, which has moved to the left in its selection of Hugh Scanlon to succeed Lord Carron as President.

Annual Conference elects the National Executive Committee (NEC) to run the affairs of the party during the year. It is elected in several sections. Trade union delegates elect 12 members, and these places are traditionally 'carved up' by agreement in advance. Generally speaking big unions send their best men to the Trade Union Congress General Council and the second string to the National Executive. Affiliated Socialist Societies elect one member. Constituency Labour Parties elect seven members. The entire conference elects five women. This is clearly a relic from the past, and this section is eschewed by some of the more able women in the party, who prefer to seek election in the constituency section. The entire conference also elects a Treasurer who is an *ex-officio* member of the National Executive. Also *ex-officio* are the Leader and Deputy Leader of the Party. It follows that 18 out of 28 members owe their position to trade union support. It is also normal for slightly more than half of the total to be MPs. The post of chairman of the NEC is filled annually by virtue of seniority of service. It carries with it the right of presiding at the year's Annual Conference.

Infrequent meetings and structure ensure that Conference is not the real centre of decision-making in the Labour party. This role is shared between the NEC and the leader. The latter will in his person bridge any gap between the formal party machine and its parliamentary wing. The traditional assumption is that the NEC will work in close liaison with the leader, and thus be subsumed into the leadership. In government, the Prime Minister's position should also be aided by the fact that some leading Ministers will be members of the NEC and, theoretically, bound by collective responsibility to voice no criticism of government policy. In the past the NEC has certainly sought to give no public embarrassment to a Labour government. During 1968 and 1969 a new situation was created by the growing rift between the Prime Minister and the NEC. First there was a vigorous assertion that the party machine was not simply an adjunct of the Prime Minister's office when the nominee of the Prime Minister for the party secretaryship was turned down. Some Cabinet Ministers voted 'against' Harold Wilson on this occasion. Later on there was a growing rift over government proposals to introduce trade union legislation. The NEC came out formally against this, and whilst this cannot in itself change government policy, it must create difficulties. It would for example mean that at a subsequent party conference the spokesman for the executive with the right to make a long speech from the platform would be against the government, whose representative would, in theory, only have five minutes from the floor. The NEC does not have the decisive influence in determining party policy when in government, but it is still an important locus of power, and it undoubtedly controls the party organization.

The NEC's control of party organization is co-ordinated through sub-committees and also a regional organization. Sub-committees also help in the preparation of the party's programme. Particularly when the party is in opposition, there is a flow of policy documents for approval by Conference. If passed by a two thirds majority, they become part of the party programme but not necessarily of the manifesto for the next General Election. The manifesto is worked out jointly by the NEC and the Parliamentary Labour Party, with the cabinet playing a major role when the party is in government. The General Secretary, effectively selected by the NEC (although subject to formal approval by Conference), is responsible to that body for the entire organization. He is a full-time official and is not allowed to be a Member of Parliament. Since this rule was inaugurated the holder of the post has tended not to be a major political figure.

The party's regional organization is centralized, although by definition deconcentrated. Power and authority flows downwards. The country is divided into eleven regions and in each a regional organizer is responsible to Transport House. Regional offices give assistance to constituency parties and also help, without normally trying to influence, the process of adoption of parliamentary candidates. Constituency parties are grouped into a kind of federal structure through regional councils, but the council secretary is always the regional organizer. These bodies are not allowed to discuss topics of national or international importance.

Finally, mention must be made of the Party's Youth Section. For a Party so dedicated as Labour is to progress and the future, there has been a surprising inability to build up a powerful vanguard of young people actively working for and supporting the party. In practice, the traditional kinds of political work such as canvassing have had limited appeal to the young who have shown great keenness to debate major issues of the day, pass resolutions and demonstrate their opinions. Moreover, organizations to the left of the party have shown considerable ability at infiltration. The result is that the Young Socialists are continually being reorganized by the party, and today the section is very much a dependant of the party, permitted to affiliate only at local level.

The Parliamentary Party (PLP)

The organization of the Parliamentary Labour Party is separate and independent. Originally it had been intended that the PLP would be an ancillary of the whole party and subject to its control. In practice the PLP has, since 1918, been virtually independent. After the 1931 disaster attempts were made to reverse the process, but their failure was marked in 1945 by Attlee's terse rejoinder to a suggestion by Harold Laski (then Chairman of the NEC) that the whole party be consulted on the question of whether to accept a royal request to form a government after the election.

Just as the PLP has asserted its position at the expense of the wider party, so it has found that the leader it elects tends to become its ruler. One of the PLP's most important tasks is the selection of the Party Leader. In opposition he is nominally subject to re-election every year by multi-ballot-absolute majority system. In fact, the PLP shows a great loyalty to its leaders of whom there have been five since 1922. Until then, the nominal leader was really little more than a chairman, but in that year MacDonald became the first real leader. He was unopposed until he left the party in 1931. Had he attempted then to appear before the PLP to seek support for the national government he was forming, he might well have been successful. He was succeeded by George Lansbury who alone of Labour leaders was virtually ejected from office by a decisive defeat at Party Conference on the issue of armaments. Attlee had been Deputy Leader in 1931 because almost all the chief figures lost their seats at the general election. He succeeded Lansbury and after the 1935 General Election retained his position in a three-cornered contest. He was never again challenged. Gaitskell who succeeded him in 1955 was challenged twice in a seven-year spell, but in each case won quite easily. Wilson, elected in 1963, has since been unchallenged. The PLP also elects a deputy leader and when in opposition a chief whip and a committee of twelve who form the basis of the shadow cabinet. Although the leader can make additional appointments, this limits his freedom of action which, however, is unrestricted should he become Prime Minister. In government, the machinery is different, and the PLP is run by a liaison committee. This consists of a back-bench chairman and two (since 1967 three) vice-chairmen elected by the PLP, a representative of the Labour group in the House of Lords, the Chief Whip and the Leader of the House of Commons.

The position of the PLP as the power base for the party leadership gives it a certain authority but this is much greater in opposition than in government. In opposition, meetings of the PLP are a crucial factor determining the party's stand on many issues. The study groups, of which there are a large number on all kinds of areas of interest, group front and back benchers and have some influence in making policy. In government this is diffused into the general melée through which back-benchers seek to influence the government. Details of policy come from the civil service machine, probably along the lines of the party programme. Ministers rarely pay special attention to the PLP at the pre-policy-making stage. Meetings of the full parliamentary party provide an arena in which critics can offer a challenge, but members of the government (almost one third of the PLP) are mandated in the way they vote. In government the PLP is simply another part of the movement to be taken into account by the leadership in making policy decisions. Clearly, because of the significance of parliamentarians in the opinion-forming process the PLP's position is important, but it is probably not crucial. This should be contrasted with the firm and decisive support given by the PLP to Gaitskell during 1961 and 1962. Without such support, he would have lost the battle over unilateralism and his own position as Leader.

Labour candidates at general elections must agree in advance to accept the rules of the PLP if elected, and these rules require that voting in the House of Commons shall be in accordance with the majority decision. In office, the PLP take very few decisions and the rule is interpreted to mean support of government policies. Abstention for reasons of conscience is allowed and in practice 'conscience' is liberally interpreted. Discipline is less rigorous now than it was immediately after the war, but there are still strong pressures against voting against an official decision.[1]

Finance

The bulk of regular income comes from subscriptions. At a national level, each trade union, constituency party, and other affiliated organization pays one shilling per member per year. Annual income totals about £400,000 of which 70 per cent is from trade union affiliations. Small surpluses were made in 1965 (£32,000) and 1966 (£45,000), but in 1967 there was a loss of £25,000. The party's financial resources are insufficient to meet the obligations of a major party. In 1967 the total wages bill at Transport House, the party headquarters, was £140,000 and a further £110,000 was spent in the regions.[2] The party's research and publications departments are inadequate, and very little help goes from the centre to the constituencies save at election time. One way out of the dilemma would be to double affiliation fees to two shillings per year per member. This would increase income by £320,000 of which £280,000 would come from the trade unions.

The reserves of the Labour movement are healthier. At successive general elections, special appeals tend to raise much more than is spent. The Labour Party made a 'profit' on the 1966 Election of almost £200,000 and this has brought reserves up to £800,000. Typically, almost the whole is invested in gilt-edged securities whilst gross investment income is only 4·5 per cent. The trade unions are less conservative in investment policy and have built up considerable reserves in their political funds which, in 1965, totalled £1,700,000, although this is by no means automatically available to the party.

At constituency level, there is a good deal of enterprise in money-

---

[1] After the Labour victory in 1966 PLP standing orders were suspended. Following various 'rebellions' by back-bench MPs and dissension inside the PLP a 'code of conduct' was accepted as the basis for new standing orders.

[2] Annual accounts in NEC Report, 1968, *op cit.*

raising schemes. Even so, only one third of the parties employ a full-time agent. A recent estimate[1] suggests that average constituency party income is about £800 per year. The regular source of income is again from subscriptions. In theory, all individual members pay 12 shillings of which 11 shillings is kept by the constituency party. Moreover, trade union branches affiliating locally pay sixpence per member per year. Constituency parties, too, are likely to have special appeals for the general election, although about one third of the cost is likely to be born by Transport House.

One cause of the great variation in financial strength between different constituency parties is the system of sponsored candidates. Trade Unions have lists of candidates whose election they are prepared to sponsor and this implies meeting the bulk of election expenses plus a large proportion of the costs of keeping a paid organiser in the constituency. In 1964 and again in 1966, 138 candidates were sponsored of which 120 and 132 respectively were successful.[2]

Lack of professionalism and financial stinginess causes great problems for the party. It is not easy to attract the right kind of people at the low salary rates which are offered. Changes, though, seem improbable. In 1966 the NEC set up a sub-committee to report on finance and organization. There is little sign as yet of likely action on some of its more challenging proposals.[3]

Dogma and Ideology

As an ideological movement, British Socialism, epitomized in the Labour Party, is almost unique. Amongst European Social Democratic parties it can be singled out as the one in which Marx's idea have had least influence. The writings of such thinkers as Morris, Shaw, Cole and Tawney have helped furnish a native Socialist tradition more influential than imported continental ideas. On the other hand such writers reflect the mood and spirit of British Socialism; they rarely mould it. The party's policies and aspirations seem to be determined far more by prevalent political circumstances than by pre-conceived philosophies. In the early 1960s the academic revisionist controversy between Crosland and Crossman offered an

---

[1] Richard Rose, *Influencing Voters*, Faber, London, 1967.

[2] Butler and Freeman, *British Political Facts*, 1900–67.

[3] First report by the so-called Simpson Committee contained in the *Annual Conference Report, 1967*.

intellectually fascinating blow by blow account of a major political struggle, but it did not of itself determine the outcome of that struggle.

The crucial factor in the evolution of British Socialism has been the alliance with the trade unions. In the words of Tawney—'The trade union base . . . has ensured that Socialism in this country rests on broad popular foundations; has averted the deadly disease of dogmatic petrification which afflicted the pre-1914 German Social Democrats; and has saved British Socialism from the sterility which condemns to impotence a party, like the French, severed from working-class roots'.[1] Obviously, though, the basic motivations of Socialists and trade union leaders may be very different, for the latter will certainly place economic and social improvement above the creation of a wholesale new system. What has perhaps helped to ensure the success of the marriage has been the fact that the fundamental impulse of socialists in Britain has tended to be ethical rather than economic. Crossman states that 'the Labour Party was founded as a movement of moral protest'.[2]

In a recent book on British Politics Professor S. H. Beer stresses the Labour Party's adoption of socialism in 1918.[3] This gives a misleading impression. The Labour Party adopted its constitution in 1918 since when it has been virtually unchanged. The broad and general programme, which was then laid down, has become a kind of Bible. Some of this approximated to the more rigorous kind of Continental socialist thinking. Later on, Beer argues more convincingly that this adoption of socialism should be seen as a function of Labour's final assertion of independence of the Liberals—it gave a faith for the party. Indeed, in the conduct of the party in its two periods of office in the 1920s, there is little to suggest any deep socialist commitment in a Marxist sense, and if 'the common ownership of the means of production, distribution and exchange' did become a hot gospel for stalwarts, party policy was never subsequently moulded in such a way that wholesale nationalization seemed a real possibility. The Labour Party's brand of socialism has been tempered by the

---

[1] Article in *Socialist Commentary*, June 1952; reprinted in R. H. Tawney, *The Radical Tradition*, Allen and Unwin, London, 1964.

[2] Article in *Encounter*, April 1960; reprinted in *Planning for Freedom*, Hamish Hamilton, London, 1965.

[3] S. H. Beer, *Modern British Politics*, Faber, London, 1965.

exercise of power. The chief aim has become the establishment of a Labour government rather than the bringing about of socialism. On the other hand, this view has never been unchallenged—its critics reverting to a more continental ideological tradition. This helps to explain most cleavages in the party.

In practice the aims have been those of social democracy: the welfare state; economic planning; income redistribution and equality of educational opportunity. Hugh Gaitskell summed up the aims under three heads: social equality, economic security and industrial democracy.[1] C. A. R. Crosland, leading spokesman for the revisionists, has made two attempts to list or define Labour Party objectives. In May 1960 he produced ten broad aims; by October there were 11, not wholly identical.[2] Summarizing the two formulations, we have greater provision for social welfare; more equal distribution of wealth; fundamental reform of the education system; a greater allocation of resources to the non-profit-showing public sector; urban and transport planning; consumer protection; faster economic growth; libertarian reforms on subjects like homosexuality, capital punishment and immigration; entry into Europe; continuation of the Western Alliance; and a greater amount of overseas aid. This has been the type of programme that Labour in office has tried to fulfil with the major exception of immigration policy. Since 1966 Harold Wilson has emerged as a kind of managerial socialist.

Labour's nearest approach to the more dogmatic brand of socialism has come through its nationalization policies. Clause 4 of party constitution lays down as one of the party objectives: 'To secure for the workers by hand or by brain the full fruits of their industry and the most equitable distribution thereof that may be possible, upon the basis of the common ownership of the means of production, distribution and exchange, and the best obtainable system of popular administration and control of each industry and service'. Over the years, nationalization came to have a central place in Labour beliefs. G. D. H. Cole argued in 1938 that socialists sought 'a classless society in which economic activities are directly conducted under public auspices, on a basis of public ownership of the means of production, and democratic control of the uses to

[1] Hugh Gaitskell, *Socialism and Nationalization* (Fabian Tract No. 300).
[2] Fabian pamphlet and *Encounter* article reprinted in C. A. R. Crosland, *The Conservative Enemy*, Jonathan Cape, London, 1962.

which capital and labour are to be applied. The essence of Socialism is not public interference but public ownership.[1] What may be more surprising than this statement by a guild socialist is that Evan Durbin, perhaps the founding philosopher of modern revisionism, places maximum emphasis on the strategic importance of nationalization.[2] Having cogently argued that a democratic socialist programme should consist of four types of measures—amelioration; socialization; prosperity and egalitarianism—he is definite that socialization should take priority. He wants a self-denying ordinance: socialists should be willing to place further ameliorative measures in their order of priority after, and not before, the socialization of industry. In 1956 Hugh Gaitskell, whose later views on nationalization were to be a mainspring of the 1960–61 controversy, wrote that nationalization had often been treated as an end in itself rather than a means to the end: 'The fact that it is nevertheless often treated as an end, as indeed, more or less identical with Socialism, is because it has been regarded not as a means to achieve the ideals of Socialism but as the only possible means which could not fail to produce the desired ends.'[3] Gaitskell went on to list the four main bases of the case for nationalization. The first was Marxist, based on an application of the labour theory of value. The second related to the belief that a capitalist system must produce poverty in the midst of plenty. The third suggested that power must belong to those who owned capital. The fourth was an ethical argument against the whole capitalist system. Although public ownership was never more than one part of Labour's election programme, it should be remembered that as recently as 1959 when trying to present a modern up-to-date image in *The Future Labour Offers You*, the party was able to state that industries failing the nation would be taken over. At the same time, there was reference to the 600 firms which dominated Britain's economy. 'Labour believes the time has come when public control must be extended, so as to ensure that the decisions of these Boards, which vitally affect our economy, are in line with the nation's interests.' It is against this background, and the inevitable importance which many of the Labour rank and file had come to attach to nationalization that the events of 1959–61 should be considered.

[1] G. D. H. Cole, *Socialism in Evolution*, Penguin Books, London, 1938.
[2] Evan Durbin, *The Politics of Democratic Socialism*, Routledge, London, 1940.
[3] Gaitskell, *op. cit.*

The Revisionist Controversy

Labour's election defeat in 1959 was in every way a shattering blow to the party. Before that election, the theory of the 'swing of the pendulum' in its crude form was upheld by most political observers. 1955 was seen as an exception. Before the 1959 Election Labour had healed the divisions in its ranks. By general consent, too, Labour seemed to have won the campaign, yet the result was a worse defeat even than in 1955. Surveys made then and later suggested that Labour lost ground because of its over-close association with a working-class image and with nationalization.[1] Nationalization was held to be dogmatic and irrelevant by an increasing section of the electorate. Above all, Labour could only hope to win by making a clear appeal to the growing middle class. It is to Hugh Gaitskell's credit that he saw most of this fairly clearly. It says much for his honesty, but little for his political skill, that he resolved to attack the problem frontally by urging the dropping of the section of Clause 4 of the party constitution dealing with public ownership. His argument was that since the party was not in practice going to act on this clause, it was futile to flaunt it as an article of faith and thus frighten away voters. There followed the clash over revisionism.

The revisionists argued that in the existing state of society there was so much to be done that the fundamental necessity was for the Labour Party to gain power, even if to do so it had to drop cherished beliefs. Crosland was the leading intellectual figure to press this line of argument. He felt that the party image was out of date and likely to lose votes, in particular by the 'vaguely threatening' but uncertain attitude towards nationalization. Crosland went on to argue that even without its traditional class orientation and socialist dogmas there were still plenty of progressive radical measures for the party to adopt which, for years to come, would emphasize its dissimilarity from the Conservatives. Were the party to adopt such a programme, Crosland saw a clear future: 'If British socialism succeeds in adapting itself and its doctrines to the mid-twentieth century, it will still find plenty of genuine battles left to fight. Besides it might even get back into power, and have a chance to win them'.[2]

To this, the intellectual reply came from Richard Crossman argu-

[1] Abrams and Rose, *Must Labour Lose?*, Penguin Books, London, 1960.
[2] Article in *Encounter*, March, 1960, reprinted in *The Conservative Enemy*, *op. cit.*

ing a more fundamentalist case. He denied the Crosland premise that capitalism had adapted and could now produce regular affluence. Indeed, 'we can predict with mathematical certainty that, as long as the public sector of industry remains the minority sector throughout the Western world, we are bound to be defeated in every kind of peaceful competition which we undertake with the Russians and the Eastern bloc.[1] Crossman felt that there was still an impending crisis in capitalism and that if Labour did not change its views because of temporary defeats it would be well-placed to benefit from this situation in the future. He felt that radical governments were only likely to come into power once in 30 or 40 years. Above all, 'In a period of complacent prosperity, a vigorous Socialist opposition will have far more power for good than a weak Labour government with a small majority'. It is doubtful whether Crossman continued to subscribe to these beliefs in 1965, when the Labour government had a majority of only three!

The Gaitskellite attack on fundamentalism failed in one sense, for the party would not adjust Clause 4 or even accept a new form of words with vague reference to taking over the commanding heights of the economy. In the row over nuclear weapons which dominated 1960 and 1961 some of Gaitskell's opponents clearly took revenge for what they thought had been an attempted betrayal over Clause 4. The aftermath was strange, for when the dust settled Gaitskell had defeated his unilateralist critics and cemented his position 12 months later with his anti-Common Market speech at Brighton. Gaitskell died at a time when he was completely in control of a machine which had threatened to engulf him. His successor, Wilson, was on the centre left of the party. However, the 1964 election manifesto made little reference to nationalization other than the suggestion of nationalizing steel and water (which was mostly already under public ownership). In office, Wilson has acted in a Croslandite manner save for being somewhat less radical. The party has shown little desire to attempt a fundamental reorganization of the structure of the society or the economy. Beyond nationalizing the steel industry there has been no serious move towards extending further the public sector of the economy. Reforms during the first five years of Labour

[1] R. H. S. Crossman, *Labour in an Affluent Society* (Fabian Tract No. 325); reprinted in *Planning for Freedom*.

rule have been concentrated on economic reconstruction and on the social services. In addition measures such as the abolition of capital punishment and the liberalization of the laws on abortion and homosexual practices have been passed by free votes of the house of Commons with a certain amount of government procedural help. One might conclude that the revisionists have in practice won the battle. It would be more accurate to suggest that the Labour government from 1964 has acted rather as its predecessors in the 1920s and 1940s.

The Left Wing

It should not be suggested from the foregoing that the evolution of the Labour Party's own brand of Socialism has been unchallenged. Precisely because the Labour Party has gained a virtual monopoly over British Socialism, it contains within its ranks those who in other countries might join parties based further to the left. 'Left wing' in the Labour Party covers a whole variety of political beliefs, but there are certain common features. The acceptance of the mixed economy as anything other than a temporary device is challenged. The 'left wing' advocate a rapid and radical extension of the public sector with the introduction also of certain measures of workers' control. Solutions to economic problems such as the balance of payments are not to be found in deflationary remedies, but rather in neo-autarchic efforts to cut the British economy away from the international liberalization of the capitalist world.

During the 1950s the 'left wing' could on occasion muster as many as 80 MPs to join in 'rebellions' against official policy. They could also rely on considerable constituency support particularly amongst the militants and party workers. On occasion the clash was characterized as one between the entrenched right wing Trade Union leadership and the militant rank and file. In the parliamentary party of the 1960s, the significance of the latter kind of clash has declined with the entry of a younger generation, many from the teaching profession. This group may be even more pragmatic than their predecessors in approach to social and economic problems. On the other hand, they may link up with the traditional left in pressing for more institutional reforms—an area in which successive Labour governments have been highly conservative. The decline of the regular 'left-wing' group to about 35 MPs now known as the 'Tribune

Group' together with the relative drop in the number of trade union MPs must create some uncertainty about the future policy orientation of the parliamentary party, but it seems unlikely that any change will be in the direction consistently advocated by the traditional 'left-wing'.

Associated Groups

A brief mention must be made of the Co-operative Party. This is a nominally separate body which is financed by the co-operative movement. It is associated with the Labour Party and policies are harmonized through joint committees. The Co-operative Party does not affiliate at a national level, but local societies frequently affiliate to constituency parties. As a result joint candidates are sponsored. If successful they are required to join the PLP and act in every way like other members. The bulk of expenses will be met by the Co-operative Party. Fear of the attraction to constituency parties of the financial resources of the Co-operative movement coupled with the increase in 'Co-op' candidates from 21 in 1935 to 33 in 1945 and 38 in 1955, led to an agreement to limit candidates to 30. In fact at the general elections of 1964 and 1966, there were only 27 and 24 respectively. Of these 19 and 18 respectively were elected.[1]

Finally, special mention should also be made of the Fabian Society. This is the oldest of the socialist societies with a continuous membership of the Labour Party. It comprises a large proportion of the intellectuals of the movement, although most of its members are individual members of the party as well. The society exists primarily for research and discussion and adopts no political attitudes. There are some 80 local societies throughout the country, although the existence of some of them is rather ephemeral. On the research side, most work is done at the national level and there is a continuous flow of tracts and pamphlets. These deal with many of the major problems, at home and abroad, which face the Labour Party and the socialist movement. In both quantity and quality this research work is much superior to that undertaken by the official Transport House department, even though most contributors and authors are unpaid.

Conclusions

Power analysis of the Labour Party is complicated. In the past

[1] Butler and Freeman, *op. cit.*

observers have erred in taking too literally the theoretically democratic bases of the movement and a constitutional tradition which made the PLP and the leader the servants of the whole movement. The best modern critic, Robert McKenzie, may go too far in the other direction when he suggests that 'annual conference has no control whatever over the actions of a Labour government'.[1] It is not the function of a British political party to govern, but rather to form the power base for a government. It follows, and here practice and theory coincide, that party leaders—in or out of government—must pay a considerable amount of attention to the views expressed within the party through various representative organs. The normal political processes of adjustment and persuasion take place, and although the leader has many built-in advantages, he cannot ignore in the last analysis the aspirations of party members.

In this connection, some members necessarily have greater power and influence than others. A Labour leader must always pay the greatest attention to big trade unions and not simply because they control most votes at conference. These same unions supply the bulk of Labour's funds and their members most of its votes (although any threat by a union leader to withhold these votes would have a rather hollow ring). Perhaps, it is more appropriate to consider the Labour Party as a very elaborate machine. The leader is given full access to the controls but he needs to be an excellent mechanic to retain his position. Conference, the NEC, the trade unions and the PLP are all minor centres of power. In trying to keep his grip on the party the leader can rely on traditional loyalty to the man in command. When a situation arises in which a divergence appears between the leadership and the party expressing itself on occasion through Conference, harmony must be restored. Frequently the leader persuades the mass party to support him, but on other occasions he may change his views. Labour leaders have an entrenched power of persuasion, but in their own interests they have learnt the art of adjustment.

Historically, the major difference between the Labour party and most other democratic socialist parties has been the institutionalized links with the trade union movement. This assures the party a firm political and financial base, but it also tends to associate

[1] McKenzie, *British Political Parties*, Heinemann, London, 2nd ed., 1964.

Labour with the image of the trade unions which is not always popular today. Both the Labour party and the trade union movement have now become a part of the establishment. This has caused the Labour party to moderate both its socialism and its undiluted advocacy of trade union interests. The Labour party is thus neither a socialist party nor a trade union pressure group. For their part the trade unions find themselves recognized as being a major economic force, and this means they must be prepared to work in some harmony with all governments. It remains to be seen if the interests of a political party and the official trade union movement will remain sufficiently in harmony for the institutional links to be retained for all time.

THE CONSERVATIVE PARTY[1]

Introduction

Conservatives can be characterized by their belief in the organic evolution of society, and the Conservative Party itself symbolizes the application of the theory. The party, as a whole, has no written constitution and is divided into three virtually autonomous parts: the parliamentary party, the National Union and Central Office. The unifying factor is at the apex—the Leader.

The Conservative Party originated as a parliamentary group, supported by *elite* caucuses in the country. From the caucuses developed constituency associations and these, ultimately, grouped themselves into the National Union of Conservative (and Unionist) Associations. During the latter part of the nineteenth century the National Union decisively failed to take control of the party as a whole.[2] Today it is the mass wing of the party, entirely autonomous in running its 'own' affairs, but able only to advise the leader in the making of policy. As a result, constituency associations and the National Union alike resemble supporters' clubs. Their sanction is not the use of votes to alter the movement's policy, but the displaying of greater or lesser enthusiasm. Policy making is the responsibility of the leader operating through the complex structure of the party machinery.

[1] The editors are grateful to David Howell, MP, for reading this section and making valuable comments.

[2] For the constitution of the mass-membership wing of the party see *Rules o, the National Union of Conservative and Unionist Associations.*

The National Union and Mass Membership Structure[1]

Constituency associations are largely autonomous bodies, wielding no direct powers over party policy. Membership is direct and signifies possibly a rather smaller degree of commitment than individual membership of the Labour Party. The total membership of the party is the sum of all the constituency associations and is presently about 2,225,000.[2]

The Annual General Meeting of a constituency party is open to all the members, although in practice participation is usually a great deal less than the average 3,500 who are thus eligible. The elected Executive Council, which is theoretically in charge of constituency affairs, meets at least once a quarter. In turn it elects various committees, of which one—the Finance and General Purposes Committee—includes all the officers and is the most influential body in the constituency party.

The chief function of a constituency association is to select a parliamentary candidate. The Council establishes a selection committee to draw up a short list of people for interview. The selection procedure is more rigorous than in the Labour Party. Exhaustive enquiries tend to be made into the personal life of the prospective candidate. His social status and acceptability may be factors. Even his wife is liable to be interviewed by the Council. The Conservative Central Office gives advice and help in the selection process but rarely tries to influence the outcome. Names on the short list must be approved by the standing advisory committee on candidates of the National Union. It is extremely rare for such approval to be withheld. As in the Labour Party readoption of a sitting Member of Parliament is virtually automatic. The case of Nigel Nicholson who was in effect deposed as MP for Bournemouth by action of his local

---

[1] Randolph Churchill sought to make the National Union his base in the struggle for power in the Conservative Party in the 1880s. His resignation from the Salisbury cabinet marked his failure, since which time there has never been any serious suggestion of control over the whole party by its mass membership wing.

[2] Official figures are not published on any regular basis and none have been given since 1953 when more than 2,800,000 were claimed (as against less than 1,000,000 in 1946). The present estimate is supported by McKenzie, *op. cit.* whilst Rose, *op. cit.* puts the figure rather lower. Any estimate is bound to be speculative since it is unclear just what act constitutes 'joining' the Conservative Party. There is no requirement on local associations to report precise membership.

party is an exception.[1] Significantly, although Nicholson's activities had not particularly endeared him to the Conservative leadership, Central Office influence was clearly—and vainly—exercised on his behalf. The average MP has little difficulty in retaining support from his constituency association.

Ward or polling district branches are set up, if possible, by the constituency association to which they are subordinate. As in the Labour Party, membership at this lowest level is direct, but members meet normally only once a year at an Annual General Meeting. Branch affairs are run in the interim by a small committee. In many parts of the country scions of traditional families retain positions of considerable influence, often as major benefactors of the party. Despite major efforts to broaden the base of membership of the party in recent years, local associations tend to be bourgeois dominated. A study of the parties in Newcastle-under-Lyme[2] showed 18 per cent of the Conservative membership as being from the working classes (objectively rather than subjectively defined), as against 37 per cent of Liberal and 77 per cent of Labour members. Not surprisingly and despite the attention paid by the National Union as a whole towards the small trade unionist membership of the party, candidates selected for general elections show an orientation towards the middle classes. One study[2] suggests that only 3 per cent of all Conservative candidates are from the manual, wage earning classes who make up 64 per cent of the population. The same study later makes it clear that these candidates are not very likely to be selected for winnable seats. After the 1966 General Election, the Conservatives in Parliament had only one former manual worker, compared to 55 from the legal profession, 26 from journalism or publishing, 38 farmers and landowners and 70 company directors. Another significant point of contrast with the Labour Party is that only three came from the teaching profession. However, two thirds of Conservative MPs had been to university, and, perhaps most significantly of all, four-fifths had attended public schools.

[1] Ultimately there was a ballot of all members of the local association to decide Nicholson's future. Narrowly defeated, he has not at the time of writing been adopted elsewhere. This tentative move towards US style primary elections has been echoed latterly by other Conservative associations.

[2] Bealey, Blondel, McCann, *Constituency Politics—A Study of Newcastle-under-Lyme*, Faber, London, 1965.

[3] Ranny, *Pathways to Parliament*, Macmillan, London, 1965.

Only three had received no form of secondary education.[1] This should not, incidentally, be taken to imply any correlation between a high level of education and support for the Conservatives. A clear correlation exists in Britain between family income level and education. There is a strong correlation between income level and support for the Conservative Party. At a given income level there is, however, unlikely to be a correlation between the amount of education and likely support for the party.[2]

It would not be appropriate to dismiss the Conservatives as simply a class party. The nature of British society and a two party system force the Conservatives to seek working class support, and in this they have achieved a considerable amount of success. However, the above evidence of the nature of local associations and also the composition of MPs and party leadership make it clear that the party can be categorized as a bourgeois group appealing to the support of as much of the working class as possible. It seems to be the case that this support is more likely to come from non-trade unionists who are exposed to contradictory social pressures. The party also has a general appeal to anybody with a small amount of personal property which they may feel needs protection against collectivizing zeal and also to those who are in process of moving upwards from one class to another.

Generally speaking local headquarters of the Conservative Party tend to be better organized than in the Labour Party. Whilst Labour frequently have to make use of Trade Union accommodation, the Conservatives usually own their own building, and in towns it is normally in the more prosperous area. It is rare indeed for the Conservatives to employ no office staff and the norm is a full-time agent and at least one other employee.

There are two bodies to which constituency parties send representatives: the Annual Conference and the Central Council. Both of these are organs of the National Union. Neither formulates policy and the Annual Conference resembles a rally of the faithful in that it does not even determine the policy of the National Union. This is

---

[1] *The Times Guide to the House of Commons, 1966.*

[2] See article by Mark Abrams, *op cit.* He produces figures to show that only 11 per cent of those who were Middle Class by occupation (objective) and self-assertion (subjective) actually voted Labour. He goes on—'broadly this minority consisted of electors who had received more full-time education than the average middle-class person'.

the task of the Central Council. On the other hand, the Annual Conference receives a great deal more publicity and its deliberations are accepted as a good gauge of party opinion and morale. The National Union of Conservative and Unionist Associations actually groups together only branches in England and Wales, although it works in close harmony with the Scottish Conservative and Unionist Associations, and the Ulster Unionists. The organization of these bodies is fairly similar, so that it is necessary to consider only the National Union structure in detail.

The Central Council is itself an unwieldy body and its membership is as large as that of the Labour Party Annual Conference. It meets twice a year, determines the policy of the National Union and elects its officers who are a President, a Chairman and three Vice-Chairmen. Since the post of President is largely honorary, it is the Chairman who is the most important figure. He represents a vital liaison between the party leaders and the mass membership organization. Representation on the Central Council includes five from each constituency and a large category of *ex-officio* membership, including all members of the Conservative groups in both Houses of Parliament. These bring the total to well over 3,000, although in practice nothing like this number attends. Formally, the Central Council determines the policy of the National Union. In practice, votes are rarely taken and party chiefs have little difficulty in exercising effective control over meetings.

The next body upwards is the Executive Committee which considers broad aspects of policy. It also approves the admission of associations to the National Union and arbitrates disputes within or between associations. Composition is laid down in the rules and is not subject to the Central Council. The Committee recommends to the Council officers for the National Union and also appoints sub-committees, known as national advisory committees. The Executive Committee is much too large a body to carry out the detailed work of policy programming, consisting as it does of some 160 members. This is therefore delegated to the General Purposes Sub-Committee, most of whose composition is again laid down in the rules. The Executive Committee only makes 12 direct appointments out of a total membership of 55, many of whom are *ex-officio* by virtue of positions held in the central and regional machinery. This sub-committee can fulfil many of the duties of the Executive

Committee. It prepares the agenda for the Central Council and an annual report. National advisory committees cover the following subjects: Women, Young Conservatives, the Conservative Political Centre, Trade Unionists, Local Government, Education and the Federation of Conservative Students. In addition, there is the standing Advisory Committee on Candidates.

Co-existing with all this machinery is the Annual Conference. This is an annual rally in support of the Conservative Party by its own active workers; with none of the pretensions of its Labour equivalent. (During the war, the Conservative Party lost little by cancelling annual conferences. Labour conferences were taking place, but so too were meetings of the Central Council.) Conference membership is larger than that of the Central Council, all of whose members attend automatically. In addition, each constituency association has two more representatives, all agents and organizers can attend and various others are included, making a total of about 5,500. Since attendance is usually not far short of 3,500, the Conference is not only larger than that of the Labour Party but possibly the largest in the world. Although motions may be submitted by any constituency association and by certain other bodies, the General Purposes Committee determines the agenda. Debate frequently takes place round a motion, but there is very rarely a vote. The officers note the sense of the meeting which they promise to convey to the leaders. Virtually the only recorded votes in recent years were in 1950 on the question of the size of Conference, and in 1967 on comprehensive education. Outbursts of enthusiasm from the floor occasionally sway events. Thus the Conservatives adopted the target of 300,000 houses as part of their 1951 election manifesto as a result of Conference enthusiasm, but this was hardly a case of leaders changing course. In 1963 the announcement of Macmillan's resignation came just as Conference was meeting. Conference showed overwhelming enthusiasm for the claims of Lord Hailsham (now again Mr. Quintin Hogg). In retrospect this did not significantly advance his claim, and Lord Home hardly owed his ultimate triumph to this particular quarter.

The entire National Union is thus essentially advisory. Certainly, Conservative leaders need, as does any politician, to keep the support and enthusiasm of party workers, but this should not be interpreted as control by the National Union of party policy. The leader has many more built-in advantages in dealing with Conference than the Labour leader. Amongst the rank and file activists, at least, there is a great deal of deference, although this does not necessarily extend to those echelons just below the rank of leader; for the Conservative Party has a tradition of powerful figures based on the regions. Rank and file deference does ensure that the work of the king-makers is likely to be approved. The lack of a formally democratic constitution coupled with the conservative tradition give the rank and file no great expectation of being able to exert any particular influence, so there is little disappointment at the minor role accorded to their representative organs.

One of the most successful branches of the Conservative Party has been its youth organization, the Young Conservatives. Interestingly, the Conservatives have had less difficulty than any other British Party with their youth movement from a political point of view. The basic reason lies in the nature of the Young Conservatives. Generally speaking they are a social rather than a political body, and in many branches dances are a more regular activity than meetings. Although many Young Conservatives never later become active in the wider party, the organization is of immense benefit. It is a useful medium for propaganda directed towards young people and at election times a source of workers. The Young Conservatives are fully integrated into the structure of the National Union at all levels, and through constituency associations they receive considerable representations at the Conference and Council. The Central Office attaches great importance to the movement and at no time has needed, or wanted to consider it an embarrassment.

The Conservative Party in Parliament
In recent years, the parliamentary wing of the party has acquired a considerable increase in formal powers by the establishment of a settled system for the selection of party leader. Previously there had been no fixed means for selecting the leader. If a vacancy occurred whilst the party was in government, then the Monarch in choosing a Prime Minister would give the party a new leader. On the other hand, since the beginning of this century, the Monarch would hardly act without taking some advice of senior statesmen in or linked to the party. Hence the tradition of taking soundings. Whilst, though, there was controversy over Baldwin's replacement

of Bonar Law in 1923, the succession of Neville Chamberlain in 1937 was anticipated and obvious, as was that of Eden in 1955. Churchill was Prime Minister in 1940 for some months before he formally acquired the party leadership. His accession to the former post was the result of negotiations involving other political parties as well. Most discussion and argument has, in fact, arisen over Macmillan's succession to Eden in 1957 and his own replacement by Home in 1963. In each case, senior statesmen in the party made enquiries as to who were the first and subsequent choices of different groups in the whole party. It also appears that a further enquiry was made as to which candidates were least desired by any section. Possibly this amounted to a kind of blackballing procedure. The result in each case was that the apparent front runner, Butler, was passed over. In the second case, the controversy became more acute since a few weeks earlier Home had apparently had no following. Moreover, under his leadership the Party lost the General Election of 1964.[1]

Subsequently, a new formal procedure has been established for three ballots. On the first ballot a winning candidate would need an absolute majority and a 15 per cent plurality over his nearest competitor. For subsequent ballots, existing candidates may withdraw or new candidates be nominated. On the second ballot an absolute majority is still required. On the third ballot, a transferable vote system is used to ensure a result, if there are still more than two candidates. The 15 per cent requirement is a relic of the idea that a leader should emerge from consensus rather than by majority, but it may turn out to be unimportant. In 1965 there were three candidates. Heath had an overall majority which was less than 15 per cent, but his chief rival, Maudling, promptly withdrew. Interestingly, this was the first selection of a leader whilst the party was in opposition since 1911.[2] There had then been some expectation of an election, but consensus was preserved by two candidates withdrawing

[1] For a detailed discussion of the succession to the leadership of Macmillan and Home, see McKenzie, *op. cit.*

[2] In 1922 a meeting of MPs and candidates at the Carlton Club determined upon withdrawal from the Lloyd-George coalition. This necessitated the resignation from the leadership of Austen Chamberlain. The willingness of Bonar Law, who had resigned the leadership the previous year on health grounds, to make a come-back obviated the need to find suitable machinery to choose another leader.

in favour of the third.[1] From 1965 onwards the establishment of regular electoral machinery is a sharp move towards formal democracy and away from traditional consensus in the internal organization of the party.

The parliamentary party has thus become the major power base for future leaders, instead of being only one peculiarly important group amongst others. On the other hand, there is no annual re-election of the leader and no provision for an elected deputy. Nowhere in the machinery is there formal provision for 'firing' a leader, although in the past the position has in practice been less secure than that of the Labour leader. Since 1923 the Conservatives have had seven leaders of whom four have departed under some pressure. Although Neville Chamberlain was still nominally leader when he died, he had in practice already been pushed out when he was forced to resign as Prime Minister. During Eden's brief reign as leader, he was subject to certain pressure. The combination of the Suez affair and his own ill health finally brought about his resignation. Pressure for Macmillan's resignation was mounting when he was taken ill in October 1963 and a combination of these events produced his departure. Home was quite clearly forced out of the leadership. It may seem curious that the party with less insistence on democracy has less respect for its leaders. In fact, all these leaders retained to the end much support from the rank and file. Where they tended to lose support was in the upper echelons of the party machine, amongst powerful regional figures and in the parliamentary party.

The organization of the parliamentary party differs in several ways from that of the PLP. In accordance with general Conservative practice it is fully autonomous in running its own affairs, but it does not determine policy either for the whole party, or even for it to pursue in Parliament. There is no meeting of the whole parliamentary party as such. The 1922 Committee is for back-benchers, and its structure is similar in government and opposition. A chairman, five other officers and a committee of twelve are elected from amongst the back-benchers. In government, ministers are not present and party whips only attend in an advisory capacity. In opposition, only

---

1 Walter Long and Austen Chamberlain withdrew in favour of Bonar Law. In retrospect the best potential leader, he initially was the least well-known of the three with the least support as first choice.

the leader is barred from attending (unless specially invited), but members of the shadow cabinet and whips have no voting rights. In fact, as in other Conservative institutions, formal voting is relatively rare. Discipline is traditionally less rigid than in the Labour Party. Candidates are not required to make such an all-embracing pledge of loyalty in case of election.

The detailed work of the parliamentary group is carried out in various subject and area committees. Officers on the subject committees carry some importance when the party is in opposition. The official party spokesmen selected by the leader become chairmen of the appropriate committees but the elected vice-chairmen and secretaries can expect to be called on for occasional appearances on the front bench when their subject is being discussed in Parliament. The Conservatives have, however, no direct equivalent of the PLP's election of a shadow cabinet.

Central Office

The third section of the Conservative structure is the Central Office. This is the party machine and, in contrast to Labour's, it is under the personal control of the party leader. It is in no way subject to decision-making by the National Union at any level. The leader of the party appoints a Chairman for the Party Organization and together they appoint two Vice-Chairmen as well as directors for the various departments which, at present are: organization; publicity; speakers; industrial; local government; Young Conservatives; and teachers and universities. Significantly, these parallel various advisory committees of the National Union and in addition one Vice-Chairman has a very special responsibility for all matters concerned with parliamentary candidature. Whilst the central departments listen carefully to the opinions of the mass membership branch, their own role is essentially one of direction. Since, though the National Union is theoretically as autonomous as the Central Office, it is essential for the chairman of the party to have a strong measure of support up and down the country.

The central organization of the party also includes two other semi-autonomous bodies: the Conservative Political Centre (CPC) and the Research Department. In each case their responsibility is to the Chairman of the Party Organization rather than to the Central Office itself.

The CPC is essentially concerned with general political education, whilst the Research Department concentrates on preparing briefs for MPs and party spokesmen. A relatively new innovation is the Public Sector Research Unit which is concerned with long term plans for government. Since the Conservatives also benefit from the research work of the Bow Group, a section of younger, more left-wing party members, they have many advantages over Labour in this sphere. In fact, the Conservatives employ a considerably larger number of people at national level and at higher salaries than Labour. Consequently, a much greater range of assistance is available to constituencies. In both quantity and quality, Conservative literature and printed propaganda is superior to that of the Labour Party.

The Central Office possesses a regional organization paralleling the federal organization of the National Union. The key official in each of the 11 regions is the Central Office Agent and he serves as secretary to the Area Council of the National Union. This means that a similar link exists to the one in the Labour Party. The essential difference is that in the Conservative Party both the organization downwards from Central Office and that going upwards from constituencies are autonomous. In practice, this means that Conservative area councils have greater independence than their Labour counterparts.

Finance

The Conservative Party never published any official accounts until 1968, the change being possibly occasioned by the new law requiring companies to divulge details of contributions to political parties. Traditionally, the Conservatives have disposed of considerably more in the way of financial resources than have their Labour rivals. This is readily demonstrated in the quantities of literature published, various national advertising and propaganda scales, and the number of officials employed. At all levels, the Conservative Party employs more officials and pays higher salaries. This makes a particular impact at constituency level. Whilst a Labour agent receives from £800 to £1,200 per annum, his Conservative counterpart receives a minimum of £2,000. The relationship between financial resources and political professionalism is also demonstrated in the more rapid conversion of the Conservative Party to public relations techniques and the exploitation of the mass media. Harold Macmillan may have been the first political figure to have been sold in Britain like a brand of soap powder. What is even more significant is that he was sold successfully.

Prior to the publication of the first official accounts, much detailed research was undertaken by Professor Rose.[1] His basic estimate was that Central Office spent about £1,250,000 per year in the period before 1965. This figure allows for an annual average of £250,000 general election expenditure. 1967–68 was not a general election year, and the official accounts do not allow for any expenditure under this heading. Given that the official total expenditure is less than £1,100,000 on this basis, 1967–68 would appear a fairly typical year. Almost half the total expenditure was incurred in servicing areas and constituencies. The bulk of this went on area organization, which is thus incomparably better financed than in the Labour Party. Just over half of total expenditure was for central services. The biggest shares (20% each respectively) went on general administrative expenditure at party headquarters and the research department (including market research). The presentation of Labour's accounts makes it difficult to compare research expenditure, but it seems certain that the Conservatives spend at least five times as much.

The income picture presented in the first accounts may be rather less typical. Rose detected no noticeable deficit in the early 1960s, although Lord Carrington was to claim in 1967[2] that this was running at an annual rate of £400,000. The deficit for the year 1967–68 was in fact £200,000. One slight mystery is that an admitted £900,000 reserves only yielded a gross investment income of about £30,000. Rose had suggested that the party earned £100,000 a year from investment and trading. In the official accounts 60% of income arises from donations—individuals, one man companies and big business. Much of this is channelled through the Central Board of Finance which raises money for political purposes from big business. The autonomous British United Industrialists also raise money for unspecified purposes in connection with the preservation of free enterprise. There is a strong suspicion that part of its funds may go to the Conservative Party. The remainder of the party's income

[1] Rose, *op. cit.*
[2] Speech at Conservative Annual Conference, 1967 when he launched an appeal for £2 million.

arises from quotas placed on constituency associations according to their means.

Support amongst rich individuals and business gives the party the ability to raise quickly considerable sums of money. The 1947 appeal for £1 million was rapidly successful and it would appear that the 1967 appeal for twice that amount has met with similar success. Again there is some confusion by virtue of the fact that a note with the official accounts claims that the income figures for 1967–8 include donations and contributions which accrue to the £2 million campaign. Ultimately, publication by companies of political contributions will make available a fresh source for calculating the income of the Conservative Party and industrial groups, like those against nationalization, which are generally in support. These groups spent about £1·5 million before the 1964 election.[1] So far study of company balance sheets suggest that annual expenditure by industry for political purposes must be running at well over £900,000 per year.

At constituency level, subscriptions are much more important as a source of revenue. This is the basis for the oft-asserted claim that millions of ordinary people pay for the party's activities. Even if all the membership paid only the minimum 2s. 6d. subscription, £500,000 would be raised. In fact, many pay more than this. Total constituency party income was calculated by Rose at about £1.8 mn per year. The average constituency association thus has an annual income almost four times that of its Labour equivalent. Outside of subscriptions, this may be raised in a variety of ways, bazaars being more, and football pools less, typical than in the Labour party.

The Philosophy of Conservatism
Conservatives can be categorized as the party of resistance to change. The binding link is a refusal to accept any broad theory for reforming society; measures are considered strictly on their merits. Although the Conservatives have never claimed to have any all-embracing ideology, their traditions can be dated back quite clearly to the writings of one man: Edmund Burke[2].

The cataclysmic French Revolution afforded Burke the historical

[1] Rose, *op. cit.*
[2] Particularly in his *Reflection on the French Revolution.* (Various editions, latterly Penguin Books, London, 1969).

opportunity for stating the advantages of stability. His fundamental principle is that the order of society as it exists, at any moment, is the product of the cumulative wisdom of past generations. Any one generation should not, therefore, have the imprudence to take it on itself completely to upset this order. It is worth contrasting this with a definition of progress by Quintin Hogg, an apostle of modern conservatism: 'Something miraculous by which man, over countless millenia, clambers from the proverbial slime to something a little lower than the angels.'[1]

Fundamentally, the Conservative Party views itself as a natural governing group which has fought against a liberal heresy and now opposes socialism. Most Conservatives consider it vital that the party should be in government, and to achieve this objective compromises in belief can easily be made. The Conservative will justify this by the assertion that beliefs and policies applicable at one stage may not be relevant later. There is an element of opportunism about this, but also a degree of intense practicality. Between their catastrophic election defeat in 1945 and their return to power in 1951, the Conservative Party underwent a historic reversal in belief without any major internal upheaval comparable to that which wracked the Labour Party ten years later. There was no hint in the 1951 election manifesto that the Conservative Party had ever held serious reservations about the social services. Although only 15 lines were devoted to the social services, housing was specifically accorded a 'priority second only to national defence'. The Conservatives offered the nation better social services for the same outlay and promised special help for pensioners.[2] By 1964, after 13 years in government, the party had moved yet further in trying to outbid Labour. The biggest single section in the manifesto dealt with housing whilst the 31 lines devoted to the rest of the social services boasted generally about past achievements and offered a fresh general review of the whole sector.[3]

Indeed the record from 1951 to 1964, if not one of outright

[1] Quintin Hogg (Lord Hailsham), *The Conservative Case*, Penguin Books, London, 1959.

[2] Election manifesto of the Conservative and Unionist Party, 1951, reprinted in the *Times Guide to the House of Commons, 1951*.

[3] Election manifesto of the Conservative and Unionist Party, 1964, reprinted in the *Times Guide to the House of Commons, 1964*.

expansion in this sector, must be considered one of consolidation. In general, the Conservatives have not tried to reverse the work of previous Liberal or Labour governments. Liberal reform of the House of Lords was allowed to become permanent despite vigorous opposition at the time. The National Health Service was retained after 1951, and of various industries nationalized, only two—road services and steel—were handed back to private enterprise. Now that steel has been renationalized it seems improbable that a future Conservative government would revert back fully to free enterprise in this sector, although financial re-organization is quite likely.

The two most fundamental principles of the Conservative Party today arise from its historic links with the bourgeoisie; the desire to limit the role of the state and the importance of private property. In the nineteenth century the Conservatives were sometimes willing to use the state to support the weaker members of society. Today the Conservative Party has inherited beliefs traditionally associated with the Liberal Party. In the nineteenth century the latter stood for *laissez faire* and free trade. Although the Conservatives are more moderate in approach, the party would still accord a relatively modest role to the state which should take on only those tasks which cannot be adequately fulfilled by individuals or voluntary groups. R. J. White, the chronicler of Conservative thought, has listed the limited functions which are to be granted to the state: the minimum use of force in the interests of public order and justice; the administration of justice according to a known body of law; the removal of obstacles in the path of individual self-agency.[1]

This approach is justified by a strong insistence on liberty, although in a different context from the socialist insistence on the same thing. Socialists will argue that full liberty necessitates a considerable degree of economic equality. The conservatives are more concerned for the liberty to do whatever one wishes to and can do for oneself. Thus Lord Hugh Cecil argued that it is better if the weak can manage without the help of the state.[2] The fundamental bastion, though, of individual liberty is held to be the institution of private property. Hogg argues that private property is a right of the individual; the natural right and safeguard of the family which is

---

1 See R. J. White (ed.), *The Conservative Tradition*, A. and C. Black, London, 1950.
2 Lord Hugh Cecil, *Conservatism*, 1912.

the natural unit of society; provides an incentive for work; and ensures liberty by preventing the state from acquiring a monopoly of economic power.[1] It is interesting to note how insistence on natural rights and natural laws, once a radical gospel, has become the preserve of those resisting change.

There is something unsatisfactory about trying to define conservative philosophy and ideology in the same way as can be done for the Labour Party. Whilst the latter has never been based on dogma in the same way as continental socialist parties, it has nonetheless a close relation with a coherent set of ideological beliefs. The same simply is not true of conservatism. The British Conservative Party is almost unique in its longevity and adaptability. One can only indicate an approach, for it is not really possible to rationalize for this party a systematic philosophy. The Conservative Party today is fundamentally pragmatic, but oriented chiefly to western style capitalism, and sometimes balanced uneasily between the conflicting claims of traditional small business and modern technocratic firms. Finally, as the legatee of the imperial tradition since the time of Disraeli, Conservatives tend to be rather the more nationalist of the two parties, particularly anxious that Britain should play a vigorous and independent role in world affairs.

Conclusion

Reverence for authority is considerably greater in the Conservative than in the Labour Party and there remains far less insistence on formally democratic institutions. In a sense the party is not a mass membership one. The party is something separate from its members who are formally cast in the role of supporters. In practice this may not make much difference to the kind of pressures which normally affect the leader of any political party. There may be no block votes to worry a leader, but then as already shown the major power of trade union leaders in the Labour Party comes from the purse strings.

On the other hand, the Conservative Party must in policy terms pay some heed to the aspirations of its powerful business and financial supporters.

Once he is placed in office, the Conservative leader is given full

[1] R. J. White, *op. cit.*, p. 91.

control of the party machine—unlike his opposite number. He does not have to battle for control initially, but his position is nonetheless not always entirely secure. Lately opposition within the party has tended to push for a greater amount of formal democracy. This is partly the result of a feeling that any appearance of authoritarianism may not be good for the Conservative image. On the other hand, it is felt that there is something undignified in Labour's constant squabbles; Conservatives should argue out their differences in private.

Above all the Conservative Party is one of government and administration. The modern Conservative Party can trace back an unbroken link to Peel's Tamworth Manifesto in 1835. Since then the Conservative Party has been in office, exclusively or in coalition, for 75 years. Since 1900, the party has been out of office for only 25 years. This has tended to place a premium on the need for unity and on the tradition of government. This being the case, the Conservative Party is only likely to fight pressures for reform until they appear irresistible. Ever since the Duke of Wellington's acceptance of Catholic Emancipation in 1827, the motto that the 'King's government must be carried on' has remained with the party. What the party seeks to do is to supply good government for the country, and to this end it is pragmatic in approach to particular problems. Moreover, once in office, the party does not necessarily reverse reforms which were carried out against its original opposition. Perhaps they too have become a part of the legacy of the past which is to be respected. This means that in the mid-1960s, the Conservative Party have undergone an evolution parallel to that of Labour. They too accept, without seriously trying to change, the mixed economy and the welfare state.

OTHER PARTIES

The Liberals

Although Liberal history goes almost as far back as that of the Conservatives, it may not be altogether fruitful to consider the party in the same kind of way as the other two parties or as it might have been itself 50 years ago. The Liberal Party retains a national structure and is a genuinely national party in the sense that it operates to some extent in all parts of the country. Nonetheless, the party for all its present pretensions and hopes has to be considered as minor. Since the war the Liberals' best overall performance at a

General Election was in 1964, but they only won about 11 per cent of the popular votes. No more than 13 seats have been held at any one time since the war. Nor is the party at all well-entrenched at local government level, where it controls no major authority and only contests a small minority of seats on local councils.

The basic problems confronting the party spring from those facets of political society which have already been considered. Without a base in a large class, the Liberal Party have found it extremely difficult to raise sufficient finance for nation-wide activities.

The attempt to gear a small party with limited resources to political action on a national scale poses obvious difficulties given the nature of the British electoral system. Moreover, in so doing the party could jeopardize its entire future. Liberal strength in recent years has been disproportionately based on Wales, Scotland (especially the Highlands) and the West of England (see Table III, p. 395). At each of the 1951, 1955 and 1959 elections these areas gave the party four of its six parliamentary seats. In 1966 when the Liberals pushed their partliamentary representation up to 12, nine seats came from these areas. A major cause of this advance has been the appeal to discontents against a political system dominated by the large parties which can be characterized as London based and English oriented. It is noticeable that a purely anti-system appeal, divorced from regionalism, has had little success and won, perhaps, only one parliamentary seat (Orpington). Attempts by the Liberals to play a more significant role in the national political system could result in some loss of touch with the party's regional bases. This problem is likely to be exacerbated if Nationalist parties emerge as strong forces in Wales and especially Scotland at the next general election. On the other hand, no amount of discontent with the major parties seems to give the Liberals a real chance of a national break-through[1] and this must now recede further with the

---

[1] The nearest the Liberals came in recent years towards bridging this 'credibility gap' was early in 1962. In March they gained a seat from the Conservatives at the Orpington by-election. The following month a Gallup Poll showed that over 20 per cent would vote Liberal at an immediate General Election—the highest figure since the war. At the borough council elections in May, Liberal candidates achieved their best postwar results taking one-eighth of the seats. The peak was passed by August and subsequent polls never showed the Liberals with more than 15 per cent support. From 1964 to 1966, the figure was under 10 per cent and the Liberals in 1965 lost two-thirds of the local authority seats gained in 1962. Butler and Freeman, *op. cit.*

resignation from the leadership of the popular, and genuinely charismatic, Jo Grimond.

Structurally, there is nothing particularly significant about Liberal organization. The parliamentary party elects the leader and enjoys a considerable degree of autonomy. Modern attempts to make the parliamentary group more subservient to the mass party have not been altogether successful. As in the Labour Party, an annual assembly is the theoretically supreme body in the party. Each constituency party—at present there are about 400—may send up to 20 delegates, although the attendance, in practice, is nothing like as large as this might suggest. Another rather smaller body, the Council, meets quarterly and shares in the making of broad party policy. However, the most important bodies are the Executive Committee and, at least up to 1966, the Organizing Committee. This group worked closely with the leader in planning overall party direction and arose out of the 1959 election campaign. It ceased to function after the 1966 election and no replacement has so far emerged.

Membership of the party is direct through constituency associations and totals approximately 200,000.[1] The annual subscription, normally five shillings, is retained by the constituency party. The latter, however, must affiliate by a subscription of 25 guineas to the central party. In addition, special quotas are imposed on the constituencies and in theory each one should be giving a total of £100. Since there are 400 constituency parties and in 1967 the income from quotas net of the affiliation came to only £24,500, it is clear that this target was often not realized. Constituency parties have full autonomy and even greater freedom than in the major parties to choose their own candidate. There are numerous examples in recent years of candidates with views out of line with the party on major matters and of candidates selected where the central organization felt the seat should not be contested. Constituency parties are grouped into area federations, but underneath the federations there is an extra tier of area groups. The party has very few full-time officials. About 40 are employed by the central organization, but only a small handful of constituencies can boast an

---

[1] Official figures are not published, but this estimate has been privately agreed with senior party spokesmen.

agent. The party's youth movement has become the most lively of those attached to political causes, although this is not necessarily advantageous in the smooth running of the party. The Young Liberals have constantly tried to push the leadership towards more left-wing policies.

The limited improvement in party finances during the early 1960s has not been sustained and resources remain clearly inadequate for the projected scope of activities. In general election years (1964 and 1966) the party is able to cover its normal expenditure as well as the costs of the campaign. In other years, there is a loss. Expenditure has grown steadily to about £130,000 in 1967, when there was a loss of nearly £40,000, bringing the accumulated deficit up to £70,000.[1]

A major crisis was only averted early in 1968 by an anonymous donation of £20,000. Meanwhile a special committee had been established with the task of raising £1,000,000 in four years, in the hope of placing the party on a sounder financial footing. The party admits to disappointment with the progress made in this respect, although no detailed figures have been issued. Few constituency parties have much in the way of resources and during a general election there is no question of financial assistance from the central organization. Rose estimates that for the 1964 General Election the central organization spent £250,000 and constituency parties collectively about £225,000. In view of the fact that only 365 seats were contested, the amount spent by constituency parties during the election period does not work out all that much less than the average per constituency spent by the large parties.[2] Partly as a result of the financial strain imposed, though, only 311 seats were contested at the 1966 General Elections. The fact that this accounts for the major share of the drop in the total Liberal vote at that election illustrates once more the difficulties facing the party.

The present policy of the Liberal Party differs strikingly from its

[1] See *Annual Report of the Liberal Party, 1968* and article by John Bourne, *Financial Times*, 13 September, 1967.

[2] Official returns of election expenditure show that the average Liberal candidate spent £579 in 1964 and £501 in 1966. Comparable figures for Labour candidates were £751 and £726 and for Conservative £790 and £766—Butler and Freeman, *op. cit.*

characteristic nineteenth century ideology. Then the party's twin articles of faith were *laissez faire* and free trade. Today most of the real enthusiasts for *laissez faire* are to be found in the Conservative Party whilst Liberal enthusiasm for the European Economic Community has rather tended to drown attachment to free trade. Broadly the Liberals argue that the class orientation of politics is wrong and irrelevant to the real national interest. They feel that Conservatives exaggerate the role of the individual and Labour that of the State. Liberals would accord the state a positive role in bringing about a situation in which individuals can satisfactorily run their own affairs. Thus the Liberal alternative to state nationalization or private enterprise is a mixture of profit-sharing, co-ownership and workers' participation in management. Passionate support for individual liberty runs throughout the party whose leading members tend to be strong advocates of humanitarian reforms. The power of trade unions and big business are alike distrusted. In foreign affairs, the party is influenced by its broadly anti-imperial traditions.[1] For many years the most distinctive item of its programme was advocacy of entry into Europe, although here as in other things the Liberals have seen their clothes stolen by their larger rivals.

Finally, a great deal of stress at home is placed on regional devolution, which has been partly caused by, and partly accounts for, success in Wales and Scotland. In recent years the party has undoubtedly moved leftwards, and this policy seemed likely to yield returns during the early 1960s when the Conservatives were in power and Labour was tearing itself to pieces. Today the Liberals face a fresh dilemma that any swing away from the Labour Government is more likely to benefit the Conservative Party.

Liberals have frequently argued that their party is more democratic and individualistic than its larger rivals, and there is a good deal of truth in this. The Liberals impose much less discipline in Parliament than either Labour or Conservative, and dissent is expressed fairly openly. However, at times when the Liberals have seemed on the verge of breaking through to become once again a major party, their behaviour has begun to resemble the two large rivals. If the

[1] The anti-imperial tradition associated with Gladstone and Asquith has been dominant over the imperialism of Rosebery and the neo-imperialism of Lloyd-George.

Liberals ever did replace one of the major parties it is doubtful if they would be strikingly different in organization from them. Perhaps the biggest difference arises from the fact that the Liberals cannot appeal to the mass loyalty and financial support of the bourgeoisie, as can the Conservatives, or the trade unions, as can Labour. The resulting lack of a powerful political base constitutes perhaps the biggest handicap towards the aspiration of achieving major party status.

Minor Parties

Brief consideration ought to be given to three more parties in Britain: the Communists, Welsh Nationalists and Scottish Nationalists.

The Communists have operated for over 40 years, but have never held more than two seats in Parliament. At the last two general elections no Communist candidate has polled more than one eighth of the votes. Total votes received in 57 constituencies where there was a candidate at the 1966 General Election amounted to 62,000. Membership is rather over 30,000 with about 6,000 in the Communist League of Youth. The party has always operated in the shadow of Labour and a major part of Communist activities has been concerned with attempted infiltration. This has been more successful in certain trade unions and in Labour youth movements than it has been in the party as a whole. Unique amongst British parties, the Communists have an official daily newspaper: the *Morning Star*. Its circulation is less than 60,000.

The Welsh Nationalists won their first parliamentary seat at a by-election in 1966. The Scottish Nationalists followed this achievement with a victory of their own in 1967 and major gains in the 1968 local elections[1] when they took one third of the total vote in the large cities. It is too early to ascertain yet whether these successes are a temporary phenomenon or a harbinger of things to come. The parties are seeking at least Home Rule and preferably virtual independence for their two countries. Advances by them at general elections would present Labour with a major problem since they usually win a majority of seats in the two countries. The two

[1] Earlier a Scottish Nationalist sat for three months in the House of Commons before the 1945 General Election.

436

parties are gradually spreading branches all over their countries and claim respectively 40,000 members (Wales) and 115,000 (Scotland). No exact information is available on the financial resources of the two parties, but in each case the annual subscription is five shillings and there are considerable fund-raising efforts. The Scottish Nationalists are generally considered to possess superior financial resources[1] possibly running to several hundred thousand pounds. They intend to contest every Scottish seat at the next election.

Increasing support for these parties once again demonstrates the necessity of a regional base for would-be third parties in the context of British politics. The appeal of the Nationalist parties is to people living within clearly defined frontiers in which there is a national tradition and an historic culture and language. In both cases it is possible to comment on the remoteness of London, and skilfully to exploit all existing discontents. In the past a root cause of third party failure has been the ability of existing large parties to canalize the discontents on which the smaller groups rely. The near future is certain to witness the reaction by the major parties who are threatened by the latest political phenomena in Wales and Scotland.

INTERNATIONAL RELATIONS OF BRITISH PARTIES

Institutional Links

Labour has the closest ties with equivalent parties in other countries through the Socialist International. Labour usually sends a high-level team to the triennial Congress, the Council Conference and the Executive Bureau. The latter meets monthly, frequently in London where the secretariat is sited. Successive Labour leaders have attended and very frequently acted the host to the leaders' conference. The International Union of Socialist Youth contains much less British participation, owing to recent difficulties with the Young Socialists. Labour sends observers to the Annual Congress of the Socialist parties of the Six, but otherwise has no special link with them. Representatives to the Consultative Assembly of the Council of Europe and the Assembly of Western Europe have traditionally been selected by the Whips. Latterly, selection has been much more sought after and with Labour in power and committed to entry into

---

[1] On Scottish Nationalism see article by J. P. Mackintosh, in *Political Quarterly*, October-December, 1967.

the Common Market, there has been some intervention in the selection process by the Foreign Office and possibly the Prime Minister. Membership of these assemblies has played some part in the European education of those attending, but the delegations never report back on their work to formal party meetings. Two Labour members, Edwards and de Freitas, became Presidents of the Assembly.

The Conservative Party has not been able to develop the same kind of institutional links with foreign parties, largely owing to its own uniqueness. In the past there has been considerable reservation about open links with predominantly Catholic Christian Democrat parties. Latterly, the Continental Christian Democrats, particularly the Italians, have begun to doubt the wisdom, in their turn, of close identification with an avowedly capitalist and anti-dirigiste party. For these reasons the only regular meetings with other parties by the Conservatives are with their equivalents in Scandinavia, but so far no formal link has resulted from these friendly relations.

The Conservatives select their delegates to European assemblies in a similar way to Labour, but participation seems to have been more highly prized over the years, and Conservative delegates have certainly played a larger role in the work of these bodies[1]. Finally, the *Nouvelles Equipes Internationales* (now the European Union of Christian Democrats), built up certain British contacts over the years with some participation in their congresses. Those taking part have frequently been active Conservatives, but their participation has been on an individual basis.

The Liberal Party participates in the Liberal International where they are well to the left of most other constituent parties and find little in common with the German Free Democrats and nothing at all with the Italian Liberals. The Young Liberals have played a bigger role in the World Federation of Liberal and Radical Youth.

Attitude towards European Integration

Cleavages on the issues of European unity have tended to be within rather than between parties. Until 1959 there were strong advocates of British participation in European unification in both major parties, but they were a small minority. Party differences have tended to be caused not so much by basic attitudes towards Europe

[1] One, Mr Peter Smithers, later became the Council's Secretary General.

as by whether or not the party was in power and what the national foreign policy, in which there has been a great deal of bipartisanship, happened to be. Only the Liberals early adopted a characteristic pro-European policy which they have tended to maintain throughout.

Until 1959 succeeding governments tended to doubt the practicality of uniting Europe and the wisdom of tying Britain to a 'declining' continent. After the war, the Labour Government was instrumental in shaping the limited institutions and powers of the Council of Europe. Alleged preference for functionalism as against federation was really founded on opposition to any form of supranationalism. The Conservatives, out of government, affected to be the European party and Churchill, an Honorary President of the European Movement, enjoyed tremendous prestige on the Continent. However, after 1951 the Conservative Government in no way reversed Labour policies.

Britain still showed no interest in membership of the Coal and Steel Community and was unwilling to join the projected European Defence Community, despite Churchill's one-time sponsorship of the idea. After the collapse of the EDC, Britain took the lead for the last time in contemporary European affairs, in creating WEU, and making it a framework for German rearmament. After this, the Six began to look to themselves and the Conservative Government showed little interest in moves which led to Euratom and the EEC. The Labour opposition remained as aloof as it had been in government. It was only after the failure of the British sponsored plan for an OEEC-wide Free Trade Area, containing the EEC as a unit, that either party began to question in any serious manner the fundamental direction of British policy.

The initial reaction to the failure of the Free Trade Area was for Britain to sponsor a small EFTA—the Seven—in the hope of building a bridge. The refusal by the Six to enter into multi-lateral talks effectively baulked this hope and set the stage for the historic reversal in Britain. Today, both major parties have formally adopted 'Europeanism', although the Conservative conversion was earlier and more sweeping. A number of reasons for this can be adduced. There is certainly an element of opportunism in that the Conservatives happened to be in office in the early 1960s when the evident success of the European Communities and their refusal to form a wider

economic association first made British membership a real proposition. It is also true, though, that over the years, at the highest
levels, individual Conservatives had taken a greater interest in
Europe than their Labour opposite numbers. Labour's dedication
to creating a new social order at home has tended to give a domestic
orientation to party policies. Moreover, despite the links with
Continental social democratic parties, Labour tended until very
recently to look down on them, both for their alleged lack of
socialism and because none had ever won absolute power in their
own country. Labour infinitely preferred the Scandinavian Socialist
parties with their tradition of being in office, and this made EFTA a
special favourite. Finally, it was Labour, ironically, who felt the
greatest affection for the multi-racial Commonwealth, which they
claimed to have created out of the Tory Empire. These emotional
reservations about Europe were rationalized in 1962 by the Labour
Party into five formal conditions for British membership. These
postulated that any agreement between Britain and the EEC must
safeguard the interest of the Commonwealth and EFTA countries as
well as British agriculture, and also ensure that Britain retained the
right to plan her own economy and pursue her own independent
foreign policy. For a short time it seemed that the Common Market
might become an electoral issue between the two major parties.
De Gaulle's first veto prevented this and Labour in office have faced
the same problems as did the Conservatives. Moreover, the irre-
levance of the five conditions has become apparent, as the basic
economic difficulties facing the country have deprived Labour of
the opportunity either to plan the domestic economy as they would
ideally wish or to pursue an independent role in world affairs. In
addition, the centripetal attractions of the European Communities
have become more apparent with other EFTA countries pressing
Britain to heal the split in Western Europe and some Commonwealth countries, like Nigeria, even making their own arrangements
with Brussels. Hence, when the Labour Party came round to applying
for admission, it did it without any prior conditions, and it was
made fairly clear that all that needed to be 'arranged' was the way
in which the British agricultural system should be adjusted to that
of the Community.

Meanwhile, the permanence of the Conservative conversion to
Europe had been evinced by the fact that in opposition they have

generally pressed the government to be more positive in attitude. As a result, all three political parties now formally seek Britain's rapid entry into the European Communities. At the parliamentary level, policy seems to be endorsed by all the Liberals, 85 per cent of Conservatives and 70 per cent of Labour MPs. Outside parliament, support for British entry is fairly evenly divided between proponents of the two major parties.

Labour's post-1964 conversion has been for fundamentally economic and technological reasons, and these are generally the most common causes of pro-European attitudes. The Liberal Party is most enthusiastic for some kind of political union, but support for this is also spread fairly evenly amongst the other two parties. On the other hand, there are only a small number of formally committed federalists. Finally, there are in the Conservative Party a small number of British 'Gaullists' who would like Europe to form a strong third force between the USA and the Communist World. For them the choice of Europe implies the rejection of the Atlantic link.

With all three parties advocating British entry into Europe, opponents of EEC membership have had to concentrate on independent organizations or on minority groups within the parties. The latter are becoming increasingly well-organized in the Labour Party, predominantly on the left but with some support in all sections. Here the fears of dilution of socialism and intensifying the cold war are strongest. In the Conservative Party, it is the traditional imperialist wing which supplies most of the opponents. Finally, the few Liberal opponents seem to be a relic of the old 'free-fooders'.

CONCLUSIONS

Most of this chapter has been devoted to the two largest political parties. The justification for this is their virtual stranglehold on British political life at all levels. Since 1950, they have always between them held at least 85 per cent of the popular vote at general elections; and dominated local government in towns and counties. There are protests at this domination, particularly at by-elections when a section of the population opts for other parties. However, it is two parties which virtually monopolize political discussion. The mass-media tend to present political controversy as being essentially between government and opposition. On occasions of national crisis: Suez, Rhodesia, devaluation, etc., it is extremely difficult for any third force to establish a position in the argument. Whilst the government always has a special position as against the opposition, the chief party in the latter always has an entrenched constitutional and traditional position as against others.

Any society requires that interests be aggregated if any kind of order is to be possible. In democratic countries, both parties and governments carry out this function. Where government is normally through a coalition, parties themselves fulfil only a part of the interest aggregation function and thus each can be relatively homogeneous. In Britain the parties aggregate many interests and are thus heterogeneous. The dividing line between the major parties is necessarily artificial. Not only are the moderates in each party closer together than either is to the respective extremists, but the right wing of the Labour Party is likely to be much less progressive on all kinds of issues than the left wing of the Conservative party. Since both parties are *majoritaire* each tries to win the support of the centre. It was once believed that floating voters were those who weighed up most carefully the rival claims of different parties. Now, psephology suggests that the floating voters include a disproportionately large number of those who think least about politics and are most impressed by images. Hence the stress in party propaganda has switched from issues to images, and elections have come to resemble a lottery with the parties moving closer together in mutual attempts to capture the centre. In the 1950s supposed similarity in economic policies of Gaitskell and Butler led to the coining of the phrase 'Butskellism'. There is little doubt that in selecting Heath to succeed Home, the Conservatives were consciously looking for a leader in the Wilson image. Just as Labour has shed much of its socialist ideology, so Conservatives have ceased to attempt to reverse major policy reforms inaugurated by Labour governments. In some ways Britain seems to be moving increasingly into an era of opinion poll politics in which rival groups of would-be administrative leaders battle for power, essentially through the mass media. At general elections, the national campaign directed through the press, radio and above all, television is increasingly gaining in importance at the expense of traditional methods in constituency elections.[1] As a result, the functions of the political party must undergo changes.

Already there has been reference to a possible conflict in party organization between amateurism and the professional method. Constituency parties manned by untrained people cannot be efficient. The Labour Party has eschewed a national agency system, so that in two-thirds of the constituencies there is not a single paid official. Mass membership parties have traditional specific functions of involving more people in the political process and acting as election-winning machines. Today these considerations must be balanced against the importance of mass media and associated methods. People who attend party conferences and those who send them there are clearly involved in politics, but it is not clear that they are having very much more influence than those whose opinions are faithfully recorded by the opinion polls. When it comes to elections the similarity in results, in different parts of the country where Labour and Conservatives may have local parties of very different degrees of strength and efficiency, suggest that party machines may make very little difference to the outcome. Although there have been variations in swing at successive general elections, notably on a regional basis in 1959, nonetheless the country seems to move sufficiently in the same direction for it to be possible to make scientific use of an overall swing concept. Thus in 1955, against a national swing to the Conservatives of $2 \cdot 15$ per cent Labour only gained one seat. In 1966, against a crude swing to Labour of $2 \cdot 6$ per cent, Conservatives did not gain a single seat.

The phrase 'party machine' can be given a rather different connotation. Some suggest that the 'machine' as such has gained a dominant position in political life, and that only the existence of two alternatives preserves any kind of democracy. It is certainly true that the road to any kind of formal political influence lies through membership of one or other of the two big political parties, although the system of government eschews all kind of placemenship in the civil service. On the other hand, membership of party cannot exactly be described as a supreme moral commitment. British politics may not have reached the stage where the would-be political leader

---

[1] Rose, *op. cit.* also Trenaman and McQuail, *Television and the Political Image*, Methuen, London, 1961; and Blumler, *Television in Politics*, Faber, London, 1968.

simply looks for the party most likely to help him in his aspiration, but somebody wishing to enter politics might very well find the choice as between parties by no means clear cut.

This chapter has given a detailed account of how the two big machines are constituted and also attempted to indicate where and how theory and practice differ. In neither the Labour nor the Conservative parties can there be any pretence that the mass membership is in control. The centre of gravity may not be at the apex, but in practice it is not far below it. When the leader of a big party is also Prime Minister, he has at his disposal an almost frightening concentration of power, and the party machine is likely to become quite subservient to him. Policy ideas will be coming from Ministers rather than from formally constituted party sub-committees.

Despite all this, the parties retain valuable functions. They are still almost the sole means of recruitment for governmental and parliamentary office and they do offer very many people, who would not otherwise be involved, the chance of playing some minor role in the political process. Above all, the parties keep open the possibilities of political controversy. Britain today, like other democratic countries, faces the problem of bureaucratization. It has been suggested that in Britain the civil service machine runs the country through alternate sets of nominal political masters. In such a situation the problem of preserving some popular, parliamentary control over government and civil service becomes paramount. It is a crucial advantage of the two-party system that it maximizes the possibility for doing this: there is always an opposition and there is always an alternative government. The first will not be true in a one-party system and the second is frequently not the case in a multiparty system. The two parties in Britain today help to keep open the political processes by which the government operate. The twin guarantees of stability and democracy retain considerable value. It means that despite the criticisms of governmental and political machinery for failure to adjust to the demands of a techno-cratic age, British political parties still have useful roles to fulfil.

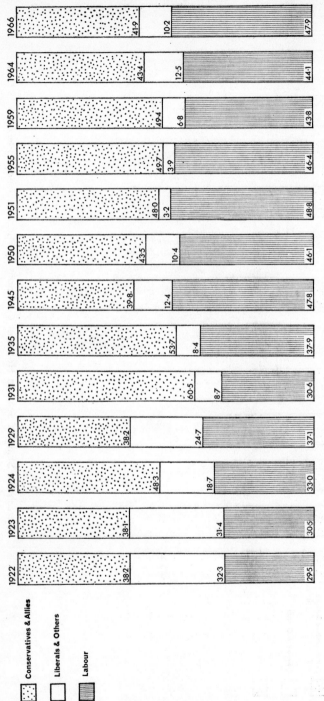

Percentage Share of Votes gained by Party at General Elections 1922–66

Conservatives & Allies	
Liberals & Others	
Labour	

1922 — Conservatives & Allies 38·2 — Liberals & Others 32·3 — Labour 29·5

1923 — Conservatives & Allies 38·1 — Liberals & Others 31·4 — Labour 30·5

1924 — Conservatives & Allies 48·3 — Liberals & Others 18·7 — Labour 33·0

1929 — Conservatives & Allies 38·2 — Liberals & Others 24·7 — Labour 37·1

1931 — Conservatives & Allies 60·5 — Liberals & Others 8·7 — Labour 30·6

1935 — Conservatives & Allies 53·7 — Liberals & Others 8·4 — Labour 37·9

1945 — Conservatives & Allies 39·8 — Liberals & Others 12·4 — Labour 47·8

1950 — Conservatives & Allies 43·5 — Liberals & Others 10·4 — Labour 46·1

1951 — Conservatives & Allies 48·0 — Liberals & Others 3·2 — Labour 48·8

1955 — Conservatives & Allies 49·7 — Liberals & Others 3·9 — Labour 46·4

1959 — Conservatives & Allies 49·4 — Liberals & Others 6·8 — Labour 43·8

1964 — Conservatives & Allies 43·4 — Liberals & Others 12·5 — Labour 44·1

1966 — Conservatives & Allies 41·9 — Liberals & Others 10·2 — Labour 47·9

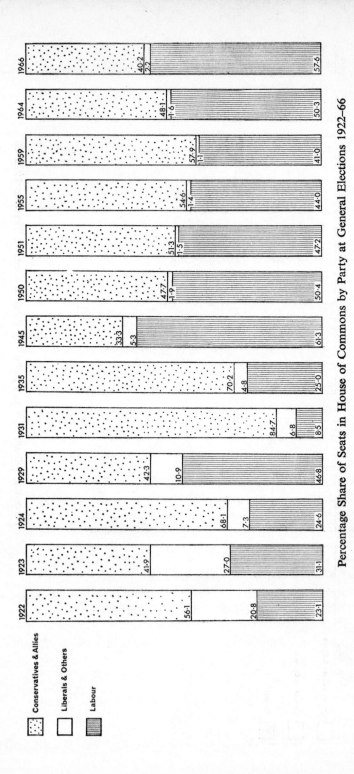

Percentage Share of Seats in House of Commons by Party at General Elections 1922–66

CHAPTER 11

THE REPUBLIC OF IRELAND

I

In general form and in its working the Irish political system resembles the British pattern on which, of course, it was modelled. The successful transplantation of British forms and practices was due largely to the fact that Irish people had for so long and to such a considerable extent absorbed willy-nilly the culture and shared in the educational and social development of the United Kingdom. Hence, at independence, Ireland was a comparatively advanced country whose people had educational standards comparable to those of Britain; with a GNP per head lower certainly, but not all that much lower, than Britain's; with a political culture markedly influenced by British ideas; with some experience of democracy and developed administration; with a population who accepted liberal–democratic values; and with leaders who, while they had little direct experience of participation in British-type politics, certainly knew no other political system. As it happened also, the circumstances of independence precipitated a major political division and, reflecting it, a markedly bi-polar party system and strictly competitive (as opposed to coalition) politics.

The result of this combination of circumstances was that Ireland developed a cabinet system of government and cabinet-parliament relationships similar to those that obtain in Great Britain, one-party governments for all but six years (see Table I), a 'Government' and an 'Opposition', the alternation of party leaders in power in an 'ins and outs' pattern and, consequently, elections that involve essentially a choice of government and leaders from among known alternatives. To win an election was, and is, to win the right to a virtual monopoly of legislative and policy initiative and the power to manage and control the *Oireachtas* (Parliament). Consequently, it is to be expected that the role of political parties and of the component institutions of the parties are also in many respects similar.

TABLE I

Nature of Irish Governments, 1922–65

Single party governments with majority of own supporters	1922, 1923, 1933, 1938, 1944, 1957, 1965
Single party governments without majority and dependent on others	June 1927, Sept. 1927, 1932, 1937, 1943, 1951, 1961
Coalitions	1948, 1954

On the other hand, the British mass parties which developed from the 1860s onwards, being the product of British social structure and divisions, were never relevant to Ireland and Irish conditions and acquired no real basis of mass support in the country except in the case of the Ulster Unionists. While Great Britain rapidly became an industrialized, urbanized and class-polarized society, Ireland remained largely rural and agricultural and, with land reform from the end of the century, became increasingly a society of small holders, owning and working tiny family farms. In the countryside and particularly in the west, the remnants of a peasant, pre-industrial culture lingered on to an extent that depended on distance from Dublin and from town influences generally.

As a consequence, the parties that developed in the Irish Free State had little element of continuity with British parties, or, because of the debacle of the Irish Parliamentary Party, with Irish party life before independence. Only the Labour Party, founded in 1912, continued to exist, and even it had been much changed by the events of 1916 and after. Moreover, since Great Britain so effectively screened Ireland from continental Europe and because Ireland was,

448

and is, a Catholic country whose Catholicism is of a very conservative kind, Marxist or other continental influences were few and made no impact. We need, therefore, look no further back than independence and, indeed, the main bases of the Irish party system are to be found in the circumstances of independence itself.

II

The two major Irish parties derive from the split in the independence movement over the terms of the Treaty with Great Britain. This disagreement, partly over constitutional issues and partly personal, led to civil war which in turn caused a deep cleavage in Irish society, a cleavage which polarized the relatively peaceful and constitutional politics that followed. Reflecting it, Irish politics tended to be composed of two groups though, as a result of the operation of the election system (proportional representation by the single transferable vote) and of the continued existence of the Labour Party, there have never been less than three parties with seats in the *Dàil* (House of Commons) and sometimes as many as six (see Diagram, p. 464).

The product of disagreement over the Treaty, the two main parties tended by their very existence to perpetuate the division on a nation-wide basis. The supporters of the Treaty became Cumann na nGaedheal, later Fine Gael; the opponents of the Treaty, except those diehards who would not concede a jot of principle to engage in constitutional politics, became Fianna Fáil. They attracted enough support to allow, first the one and then the other to form governments composed exclusively of their own leaders. Until 1948, other parties and politicians tended to identify themselves with one or other and to be known as dependable allies, and there existed a chasm between the parties which no politician would cross. Hence, governments without a majority of their own supporters were in fact rarely defeated and quite secure in office. And though, by the 1950s, the issues which had divided the parties were settled or no longer of consequence, they continued, with hardened traditions and distinctive images, with those of their original leaders who survived still in charge and accustomed to strictly competitive politics, and with aspirants waiting to pick up the reins whenever the old men at last shuffled off. Since then, as we shall see, the two

P   449

major parties have no doubt changed in their aims and to some extent in character, but the continuity from the 1920s is still preserved unbroken, and the images they evoke are still different. Both have been able to continue attracting mass support. Between them, they have always polled more than 60 per cent of first preference votes and at the last election, in 1965, Fianna Fáil's share of the poll was 48 per cent and Fine Gael's, 34 per cent. The great stability of Irish politics, some would say stagnation is due to this and particularly to the fact that, since the early 1930s, Fianna Fáil has always been able to hope for, and sometimes to attain, an overall majority of seats (see Diagram). In these circumstances it will naturally not seek the ties of coalition.

Apart from the extreme republicans who, not accepting the regime, have been on or beyond the fringe of constitutional politics, it is only the existence of the Labour Party that has consistently marred the stark simplicity of this pattern. Its presence constitutes, without doubt, an important modification of bi-polarity, but it should not be exaggerated for two reasons. In the first place, the party has never attracted more than 16 per cent of the electorate and, at one point, support fell to as little as 6 per cent. Secondly, both parliamentary logistics and the competitive mentality of party leaders have usually prevented it from playing a critical role in the formation and preservation of governments.

The Labour Party was founded by trade union leaders and was intended to be the same sort of alliance of socialism and trade unionism as had been established in the United Kingdom. What element of extreme socialism there was in the party evaporated after the departure of Larkin to the United States and the execution of Connolly in 1916. Arguing that the issue on which Sinn Féin split was not the most important one for the Irish people, its leaders accepted the Treaty and co-operated in constitutional and parliamentary politics. It was, indeed, the major opposition party until 1927 and the advent of de Valera to constitutionalism.

Cogent and responsible as this attitude was it did not strike a chord with Irish public opinion which was polarized on the Treaty issue. The Labour Party found itself in the valley between the twin peaks of Irish political opinion—Treaty and anti-Treaty—and it became and remained a minor, third party. Cut off from its greatest single source of strength, the industrial north-east, it was now operating in a predominantly rural country of small holders in which a trade union-based proletarian party was largely irrelevant. Moreover, this was a country in which the priests taught that socialism of whatever variety was next to 'atheistic communism' and must surely lead to it. Consequently, a socialist alternative to bourgeois parties had little chance. Because of the dominance of national issues, it never even established itself in strength in Dublin where, one would have thought, its natural strength should lie. Instead, it was strongest in rural Leinster and the south, areas in which numbers of agricultural labourers and landless countrymen were high and where it had early on established itself through the support of rural workers' organizations.

Opposed to Cumann na nGaedheal on socio-economic grounds in the 1920s and 1930s, Labour became an independent ally of the then more radical Fianna Fáil, a role not likely to bring it governmental office whatever the parliamentary situation because coalition and compromise of any description were personal anathema to the messianic and charismatic de Valera. In the 16 years from the accession of de Valera to power in 1932, the Labour Party moved progressively away from the increasingly conservative and bourgeois Fianna Fáil. When in 1948 the opportunity presented itself, it tried coalition in an 'Inter-party' government dominated by an even more conservative and bourgeois Fine Gael. Two periods of coalition, 1948–51 and 1954–57, were enough to bring disenchantment. Labour once again turned to its independent and comparatively uninfluential role and Fine Gael to its pretensions to a majority position which, despite its inability to win the votes of more than one third of the electorate, it had never abandoned. Thus, constrained by the competitive attitudes and strategies of the two big parties and handicapped by its failure to appeal to more than about one-sixth of the electors, Labour has never played the part in Irish political life which conceivably it might.

The deep and nation-wide division over the Treaty and the consequent existence of two highly competitive national parties explains, to a great extent, the failure of other parties (apart from the already existing Labour Party) to establish themselves on a permanent basis, despite the use of an election system which, in its operation, at least does not weigh the scales against new or small groups. Only two minor parties of the dozen or so that have come and gone contested elections for more than a decade. Today, none at all of any consequence exist. Most have been the product of differences over the dominant national and constitutional issues, dissidents or extreme groups of one sort or another splitting away from, and then being reabsorbed into, the bigger parties. Because of the dominance of the constitutional issues, the development of parties based on other community interests or cleavages has been inhibited. Not even a farmers' party has established itself permanently, though two such have come and gone.

The electoral system has also allowed individuals, including party rebels, who could appeal to some local feeling, loyalty or gratitude to win popular support and even seats. Indeed, there is little difference between such Independents and small electoral or parliamentary alliances calling themselves parties. In the case of most Independents, as of the minor parties, there has usually been little doubt where they stood in relation to the constitutional issue and the major parties, and some have been more or less campfollowers. At every election up to 1965, 20–30 such Independents competed, and always some—as many as 16 in the 1920s, as few as 5 in 1954—were elected. Only in the 1965 Election did they virtually disappear.

III

While it is not possible to explain the division over the Treaty and support for Cumann na nGaedheal or Fianna Fáil wholly in socioeconomic or cultural terms, some broad generalizations may be made. De Valera and Fianna Fáil represented, and at first drew much instinctive support from, many of the small farmers, especially of the west; to some extent from landless labourers and the land hungry; from the erstwhile poor countryman turned urban worker; and from some of the middle class who had risen from the small farmer background or who had radical republican leanings. Mr de Valera's vision of a frugal, gaelic, republican Ireland of small holders was theirs also. In contrast, Cumann na nGaedheal was the party of the Treaty and Commonwealth status, of peace and stability. It attracted the business community; the medium and large farmer, especially those who wanted independence but whose economic ambitions had been satisfied by land redistribution;

452

former unionists as they accepted the inevitable and became integrated in the new Ireland; and those who feared or hated de Valera. It was middle class and conservative in character.

Both parties have changed. The moderation in opposition of Fianna Fáil after 1927 and its growing conservatism in office, once constitutional matters were settled to de Valera's satisfaction, brought it support from other sections of the public and particularly an increasing number of the commercial and industrial middle class, perhaps largely made up of small family business people who prospered modestly under Fianna Fáil's policy of protection. Fine Gael, suffering though it did from the growing respectability of Fianna Fáil and the success of that party in implementing its programme, continued in the thirties and forties to harbour the thought that it might once again win power. From 1948 when it entered a coalition and, by sponsoring the Republic of Ireland Act, threw off its Commonwealth image, it, too, could hope to appeal more widely.

As the old issues were resolved or softened by the passage of time, new and mainly socio-economic issues took their place and Ireland faced up to the possibility of a closely linked European community. As politicians slowly recognized that their business had now to do with such matters as growth rates and planning, attracting foreign investment, and agricultural support policies, both parties have tended to become non-ideological, broad-based, pragmatic, welfare-oriented parties engaged in the producer and consumer politics typical of the prosperous and satisfied western communities—'catch-all' parties as they have been called. To some extent Labour, too, fell into this mould and never presented a radical or socialist alternative until suddenly, in early 1969, it lurched to the left.

Since the two major parties are national parties, appealing to all in a country that is not deeply class divided, one might expect to find their supporters in all sections of the population, with the third party, Labour, drawing mostly from the poorer sections. It might be supposed, too, that the original appeal of Fianna Fáil to the smaller farmer and of Fine Gael to the more prosperous in the farming and business communities are still reflected to some extent in the social composition of their support today. However, such differences may well be diminishing under the impact of 'catch-all' policies and consumer politics. Unfortunately, there have been no surveys to analyse party support and impressions are all that are possible at this stage.

Something can, however, be said about the socio-economic status of those who are active in party politics. Politics in Ireland, as in so many countries, is a middle class activity. Farmers (or, rather, the better off farmers) on the one hand, and shopkeepers, publicans and small businessmen on the other predominate, with professional people more prominent at national level and dominant when it comes to ministerial office (almost 60 per cent of all Irish ministers from 1922 have been professional men). Few of the non-agricultural working class and the poorer farmers and farm workers play an active part. And, while Fianna Fáil and Fine Gael do not differ much in the social composition of their 'actives', the working-class character of the Labour Party is confirmed by the presence in it of a large number of trade union officials, by the paucity of professional and business people and by the greater proportion of working-class people, mainly white-collar workers and artisans, than in the other parties.

Besides the parties 'in the system', as it were, there is at the extreme edge of constitutional politics, and beyond it, a very small and diminishing, but persistent, radical republican element. From this element have come the recruits for the Irish Republican Army. Besides its appeal to individuals of a certain temperament, extreme republicanism has always had its main social basis in the poorer small farmer element and, hence, has tended to occur in the west, and especially in County Kerry, and, for obvious reasons, in the border counties. In other areas, and particularly in Dublin, it has attracted a small amount of radical working-class support.

Apart from this tiny extremist wing, there is a considerable uniformity in the aims, character and even mass support of the Irish parties, with only the Labour Party at last providing something of an alternative in outlook and something of a contrast in its social composition. This situation reflects the successful resolution of the deep divisions of the past and the comparative social cohesion and uniformity of a community that does not see itself as socially highly stratified and may only now be on the brink of a rural-urban split. To the extent that social divisions *do* exist, they are not really reflected in the party system. Indeed, government in Ireland today is more a process of the steady and incremental appeasement of interest groups by direct negotiation than of implementing distinctive programmes of constitutional, social and economic policies placed before the electorate by parties, representing or intending to appeal to this or that class or section.

IV

In considering organization, it is with the three main parties that we are concerned. Minor parties, which have all been ephemeral, have occasionally attempted to reproduce the organizational pattern of the big three, but have always failed for lack of resources. More usually, small parties have been content to remain parliamentary alliances of TDS (members of the Dáil) who were virtually 'Independents'.

Irish parties, like those in Great Britain, have three main functions. Firstly, they mobilize the electorate, a task which involves communicating demands to the political centres and policies to the public. Secondly, they recruit political leaders at all levels and provide candidates for offices that are filled by election and representative posts generally. They do not, however, fill many other public offices since the 'spoils system' does not obtain to any great extent. The civil service and local government service are recruited by competition and are career services, their relationships with their political masters being very similar to that which exists in Great Britain. Similarly, the staffs of state enterprises and other non-departmental administrative and regulatory bodies tend to be recruited by competition. It is only the boards of these 'state-sponsored bodies', as they are called, which are filled by Government nomination, and even here blatant 'jobs for the boys' appointments are more the exception than the rule. Apart from these, the only appointments where party politics decide the issue are one or two comparatively minor appointments such as rate collectors. Thirdly, parties assume responsibility for 'government', meaning here both policy-making and administration of public services, central and local, and, more widely, parliamentary and representative processes for the discussion, scrutiny and criticism of government policy and its execution.

The organization and procedures which parties use in the performance of these tasks resemble in form those of the British parties, but naturally there is a vast difference in scale and in the resources which they are able to bring to bear. Because of this, and because of the local bias of Irish politics, parties look somewhat amateur and undeveloped as compared with those of Britain. The term 'party machine' is not one that has much currency or justification in Ireland. This weakness is exacerbated by the effects of the electoral system, since the method of the single transferable vote in multi-member constituencies offers the elector a chance to put the candidates of his own party in *his* order of preference and forces candidates to base their appeal on grounds of service to constituents both personally and as a local community. To get and keep a 'quota' of first preferences, politicians must operate a considerable 'contact man' service at local and central administration levels, thus building up a personal connection of clients. In such circumstances, party executives and central offices have little control over local branches and machine politics cannot develop in the face of more personal links.

The main institutions of the three parties, which resemble one another very closely, are—local clubs or branches on a parish or ward basis, linked to a rather sketchy constituency organization; an annual delegate convention; a national executive; a 'parliamentary party' with a leader who is also the party leader; and a central office. None of the parties have youth movements or other ancillary organizations of any consequence.

Both Fianna Fáil and Fine Gael have branches throughout the country. In 1967 Fianna Fáil had 2,015 of them registered, the number in each constituency varying from 20 to 70, while Fine Gael had almost 1,700. In both parties, however, some of these branches are moribund, perhaps as many as one half to two thirds in the case of Fine Gael. Labour, which does not cover the whole country, had about 500. Individual membership of a party is obtained through a branch but the Labour Party, as in Great Britain, has a large trade union affiliated membership. The functions of the branches are to recruit members, nominate candidates and fight elections both at national and local level. Although much depends upon the enthusiasm of the local TD or other local representative or party official, most branches engage in comparatively few activities between elections, springing to life only at election time. Activities which, one would think, are in the long run basic to winning elections, like political education, recruitment of members and constant fund raising, are in fact in most cases not engaged in on any regular basis. Nor do branches act to any great extent as channels of information and opinion between the periphery and the centre or between the members and the representatives. This function tends rather to be pre-empted by the councillors and TDs whose seats depend upon appearing personally both assiduous in attending to the needs of their constituents and influential in getting the right decisions at the centres of power.

In such circumstances it is no wonder that individual party membership is low. Accurate figures are unobtainable, for the parties really do not themselves know exactly. Fianna Fáil claims between 40,000 and 45,000 members; Fine Gael puts their membership even higher; Labour has about 5,000. Many observers would regard Fianna Fáil's claims as optimistic, let alone Fine Gael's. The effective membership of the latter party may, indeed, be not much more than 12–15,000. Rightly or wrongly, many branches are probably not much concerned with formal membership; it is votes on election day upon which party workers concentrate.

Branches have the right to send delegates to conventions to nominate candidates at constituency level. It is their major pre-occupation to get their own local nominees accepted, for everyone believes that it is important to have a person from the district in office, local or national, in order to obtain the full benefit of public services and public money. Though party leaders preside over the constituency conventions to choose general election candidates, and nominees must be approved by the party, the centre by no means controls the nomination process. As a result, parliamentary candidates are almost always local people and there is no room for carpet-baggers from outside. This has important effects upon the composition of the Dáil. Local candidates, locally selected, to a large extent fight their own campaigns, for the amount of support that they can expect from the centre is very limited. In such circumstances, strong central control and machine politics are clearly impossible.

The annual delegate meeting of each party—called *Árd Fheis* (grand congress)—is, in theory, the supreme policy making organ. In practice, it is far from being so; serving instead as an occasion for local 'actives' to hear and meet their leaders and to bolster party loyalty and enthusiasm. The resolutions that are passed are little more than suggestions which the real policy makers might take into account when appropriate. For policy-making and the formulation of party strategy are confined to the parliamentary party and the national executive and, indeed, largely to the leaders of the parliamentary party. Prominent, though sometimes not pre-eminent among them, will be the leader of the parliamentary party who is chosen by them and who is the party leader. In the case of the party in power, he will be the *Taoiseach* (prime minister), an office which almost inevitably puts its holder into a position above his colleagues.

The monopoly of the leaders of the parliamentary party in formulating policy is virtually complete. Neither the branches nor the annual convention have much influence here, while the rank and file Deputy tends to leave this function and, indeed, the weight of parliamentary comment and criticism on general matters, to his leaders, being content to follow them and to support them loyally with his vote. He is, in fact, often more concerned with the task of servicing his constituents. The parliamentary parties do hold regular meetings when the *Oireachtas* is in session, but there is no network of active party committees to debate or comment on party policy and, of course, no official parliamentary committee system. In this respect, the *Oireachtas* has lagged behind even the very limited British developments and must now be one of the worst organized, equipped and informed parliaments in the democratic world.

Because the parties, as centralized organizations, are compara-tively poor and weak, the central offices are tiny and their functions circumscribed. They each employ a secretary and a handful of staff, but are in no position to provide more than the most sketchy information and research services to their members. There is not even any attempt to provide party organizers on a systematic or universal basis. At election time, central offices produce and distri-bute handbooks, notes for speakers and publicity material and they handle what national publicity there is. However, the biggest of them, Fianna Fáil's Mount Street headquarters, had a published total annual expenditure of little over £10,000 in the mid-1960s.

Since the services the parties give to their branches and to their parliamentary representatives are very meagre and since, also, the

458

branches tend not to engage in regular fund-raising or expensive education and recruiting activities, party annual income and expenditure are very low. Of course, political party finances are notoriously difficult to probe and it is impossible to obtain a complete and satisfactory picture, but the broad pattern is clear enough. The main regular source of funds is in each case an annual collection made by the branches, part of which goes to the central party for expenses and the remainder of which is used by the branch, mainly as an election fund. Individual members pay small annual subscriptions which finance the activities of the branches, such as they are, and in the case of the Labour Party affiliated unions pay annual subscriptions according to the number of their members. Until 1967 these amounted to only about £1,600; with the affiliation of the Irish Transport and General Workers Union to the Party in that year, this figure was more than doubled.

What does this regular income amount to? It is surprisingly small. Fianna Fáil has a regular declared income of £20,000 per year, mostly from the national collection, and of this about half goes on the central office. The Labour Party has perhaps about £8,000 per year, while Fine Gael, which does not publish any accounts at all (for what publication is worth) is almost certainly in between.

Of course, parties and individual party candidates spend much more than this at elections, for which special collections and appeals, public and private, are made and special contributions given. It is widely believed, indeed, that there is much private soliciting and giving both to the parties and to individuals. If so, it is certainly not reflected in the candidates' returns of election expenses for, with a few exceptions, a candidate's declared expenditure is unlikely to be more than a few hundred pounds. Returns of expenses, however, may well not tell the whole story since, to say the least, in the words of the Fianna Fáil election handbook, 'rigid accuracy is not possible, nor is it expected'. Fianna Fáil, more thoroughgoing in its approach than the others, has evolved from its *ad hoc* election expenses committee, a more permanent organization, *Taca* (support), composed of 200 invited members, mostly business people, who each subscribe £100 per year to provide a fund of £20,000 per year to fight elections. The newly affiliated Transport and General Workers' Union is said to have available a political fund of £92,000 and, together, the unions have political funds of more than £120,000, but it would be a mistake to regard these funds as at the disposal of the Labour Party. Hitherto they have been used in a discriminating way, e.g. to help subsidize union candidates. These candidates are helped as individuals by grants in aid running up to as much as £500–600 per man. Incomplete as it is, this is in general, clearly a picture of modest, even meagre, finances.

v

The inability of the Irish nationalist movement to win a complete victory in 1921 and the consequent constitutional and border problems have had a profound and lasting effect upon the political perspectives of Irish politicians and people. Nowhere is this more clearly illustrated than in attitudes towards Europe. Ireland was in the nature of things bound to be greatly influenced, if not dominated, socially, economically, and culturally, by Great Britain, a country itself notoriously 'un-European'. To this was added an obsession with unfinished national business, also closely involving Great Britain. Together, these have been the major factors in Irish political life and until recently they were predominant. If, viewed from Europe, Ireland is, in the words of Jean Blanchard, 'une île derrière une île',[1] Europe has been blotted out for Ireland by Britain and, until recently, has been regarded as of little political consequence.

Because of the inhibitions and self-imposed restraints arising from the unending dispute about the border, Ireland became and remained myopic in its international perspective. As those few of her original leaders with a knowledge of Europe or with European horizons relinquished power, Ireland lost sight of Europe and Europe of Ireland. Only de Valera as President of both the Council and the Assembly of the League of Nations in the 1930s made any significant contact or impact, and with the war and self-imposed neutrality, even that link was severed. As a consequence, the country was increasingly cut off from the mainstream of European life until the late 1950s. Refusing to subscribe to the postwar Western European defence arrangements and, moreover, precluded from joining some other European and international associations, including the UN

---

[1] *Le Droit Ecclésiastique Contemporain d'Irlande*, Paris, 1958, p. 11.

to which she was not admitted until 1955, she played little part in European affairs. True, Sean MacBride, Minister for External Affairs from 1948–51, was personally active and interested in European affairs but, like de Valera in the 1930s, he was virtually alone; neither his party nor his government showing much interest in his activities. The great social, economic and political changes which took place in postwar Europe made practically no impact on a society that was stagnating and, indeed, they went largely unremarked.

Since the late 1950s, however, the position has been changing. Irish membership of the United Nations Organization brought obligations and opportunities for Irishmen to serve upon a world stage and in the glare of publicity. The achievements of the Irish serving in the UN forces and of her diplomats at the UN Headquarters in New York—it was an Irishman who broke his chairman's gavel calling Mr Khrushchev to order in the Assembly—evoked a patriotic pride and awakened some interest in international affairs. More important, the prospect of British entry to the Common Market suddenly brought the Irish Government, if not immediately the people, face to face with postwar Europe and European realities. From 1960, first the then *Taoiseach*, Mr Séan Lemass, and gradually his government and the political leaders of the other parties attempted to hammer home to Irish agriculture and business and to the community generally the social and economic realities of contemporary Europe against considerable and enduring indifference and inertia. Their interest and concern, it would be fair to say, arose out of the development of economic planning and the exigencies of promoting economic growth from 1958 onwards. Europe is not 'foreign affairs' so much as a factor in economic development like, for example, British cattle prices. Even yet, the *political* consequences of closer European union are hardly canvassed or, apparently, fully perceived even at political-leader level.

It will be obvious from the foregoing that there simply is no tradition of interest or feeling of involvement in Europe, and that it is only a growing awareness of harsh economic realities that has led in recent years to the Irish Government and other political leaders attempting with not much vigour to persuade the community to adapt to the new Europe. The narrowness of this European involvement needs stressing. It is largely confined to political leaders and senior public servants, and it is limited to recognizing the need for integration or uniformity in economic affairs and some public social services in order to ensure Irish prosperity. The ordinary parliamentary representative is still only peripherally concerned. In the Irish governmental system he plays a small role in policy formation in any case, and particularly is this so in external affairs. Neither Mr de Valera nor Mr Aiken, who between them have been in charge of the Department of External Affairs for 31 out of the last 37 years (to early 1969), have encouraged back-bench interest or participation in foreign policy issues. There is no foreign affairs committee of the Dáil.

Not that the average member minds; he has other and more pressing business looking after his constituents and, thus, his seat. At no election has any question involving Europe come to the fore or been an 'election issue'. Consequently, the public in its turn is mostly both ill-informed and unconcerned, though the national daily newspapers and the television service, to their credit, carry an increasing amount of foreign news in an attempt to educate their audiences and evoke their interest. The normal TD standing between his uninterested constituents on the one hand, and his leaders and the Administration, who do not need his contribution, on the other, does not find any demand or necessity to take up European affairs.

There are a few—mostly professional and cosmopolitan men with some acquaintance with Europe—who do not conform to this pattern. They and some party leaders, including some members of the Government, conduct what little public debate there is on European matters. It is people from this group who are likely to be found at interparliamentary conferences or the Consultative Assembly of the Council of Europe where the Irish have tended to present a united national front rather than to seek ties with representatives of other countries on an ideological basis. However, for the first time 'a sharp difference of opinion' among Irish delegates over the military implications of membership of the Community was expressed at the Council of Europe's Consultative Assembly in October 1967. Perhaps significantly, also, the Labour Party affiliated to the Socialist International late in 1967.

Of course, ministers are more and more tending to become involved in ministerial meetings and conferences of European and other international organizations. These ministers and, more importantly, civil servants are no doubt increasingly influenced by their contacts and their experiences in Paris, Strasbourg, Brussels and elsewhere, and the signs are evident that the Administration, to an ever growing degree, appreciates European realities and the needs and opportunities of the situation. On the other hand, there is very little feed-back to the rank and file of the political parties, to the agricultural and business communities, and least of all to the public as a whole. Ireland is still, very much 'une île derrière une île'.

TABLE II *Election Results, 1948–65*

	1948	%	Seats	1951	%	Seats
Electors	1,800,210			1,785,144		
Turnout	1,336,628	74·2		1,343,616	75·3	
Valid votes	1,323,443	99·0		1,331,573	99·1	
Fianna Fáil	553,914	41·9	68	616,212	46·3	69
Fine Gael	262,393	19·8	31	342,922	25·7	40
Labour	149,088	11·3	14	151,828	11·4	16
Others	359,048	27·0	34	220,611	16·6	22
	1954	%	Seats	1957	%	Seats
Electors	1,763,209			1,738,278		
Turnout	1,347,932	76·4		1,238,559	71·3	
Valid votes	1,335,202	99·1		1,227,019	99·1	
Fianna Fáil	578,960	43·4	65	592,994	48·3	78
Fine Gael	427,037	32·0	50	326,699	26·6	40
Labour	161,034	12·0	19	111,747	9·1	12
Others	168,171	12·6	13	195,579	16·0	17
	1961	%	Seats	1965	%	Seats
Electors	1,670,860			1,683,019		
Turnout	1,179,738	70·6		1,264,415	75·1	
Valid Votes	1,168,404	99·0		1,253,122	99·1	
Fianna Fáil	512,073	43·8	70	597,414	47·8	72
Fine Gael	374,099	32·0	47	427,081	33·9	47
Labour	136,111	11·6	16	192,740	15·4	22
Others	146,121	12·6	11	35,887	2·9	3

A general election was held in June 1969. Provisional figures give Fianna Fail 45·6% of votes and 75 seats; Fine Gael 34·1% and 50; Labour 16·9% and 18; Others 3·2% and 1. Turnout was 75·9%.

The Party Composition of Dáil Éireann, 1923–1965 (Percentage of Seats held)

Notes (1) In 1923 and 1927(I) Fianna Fáil deputies did not take their seats. (2) In 1927(I) and 1957 Sinn Féin deputies did not take their seats

CHAPTER 12

EUROPEAN ASSEMBLIES

The proliferation of international parliamentary assemblies in Western Europe since the war has been one of the more notable developments in the recent history of international institutions. The Consultative Assembly of the Council of Europe, the Assembly of Western European Union, and the European Parliament of the Common Market are probably the three best-known assemblies of this type. Alongside them are the Nordic Council and the Consultative Assembly of the Benelux Union. Recently (in 1966) the NATO Parliamentarians Conference, which has been meeting for many years, transformed itself into the 'Atlantic Assembly'. It seems as if no international organization can now be complete without what M Spaak has called *la coiffure parlementaire*.

It has been a further notable development that within at least some of these assemblies there have emerged transnational party groups with a certain amount of cohesion. It is the purpose of this chapter to examine the nature of these new party groups, and to assess their importance in the work of the organizations to which they belong.

THE TYPES OF EUROPEAN ASSEMBLY

The feature common to all the European assemblies is that they are composed of persons, chosen from the national parliaments of the member states, who are not necessarily members either of national governments or of government parties. This feature of their membership makes the assemblies quite different from, for example, the General Assembly of the United Nations. Beyond the common nature of their membership, the European assemblies differ considerably not only in terms of size, age, length of sessions and financial resources, but also in powers and functions.

The oldest is the Consultative Assembly of the Council of Europe, established in 1949, and composed today of 147 representatives from 18 member states. Most Western European countries are members, together with Turkey, Iceland, Cyprus, Greece and Malta. The Assembly meets in Strasbourg, and its annual sessions, divided into two or three parts, last about one month. The Nordic Council, established in 1953, consists of 69 representatives from the five Scandinavian countries. It is an itinerant body meeting in the various capitals of its member states and holding one annual session lasting from seven to ten days. The Assembly of Western European Union, set up in 1954, consists of 89 representatives from the United Kingdom and the six countries of the Common Market. It meets in Paris and holds two annual sessions each lasting about a week. The NATO Parliamentarians Conference (to call the 'Atlantic Assembly' by its original name) was set up in 1955 and consists of about 180 representatives from the 15 NATO countries. It holds one annual session in Brussels lasting five or six days. The Benelux Interparliamentary Consultative Council was set up in 1955; it consists of 49 representatives from the three Benelux countries and holds three sessions annually, each lasting two days. Like the Nordic Council it is an itinerant body, meeting one year in Brussels, another in the Hague, and a third in Luxembourg. Finally, the European Parliament, established in 1958 in succession to the former EC SC Common Assembly, consists of 142 representatives from the six countries of the Common Market. It meets in Strasbourg for an annual session divided into six to eight parts, lasting a total of about 35 days. In terms of financial resources the assemblies vary significantly. The European Parliament has an annual budget of well over £2 million, the Consultative Assembly one of about £2 million, and the NATO Parliamentarians Conference (NPC) one of under £100,000.[1]

In terms of powers and functions there are also major differences between the assemblies. All of them, except the Nordic Council, are parts of larger organizations, which have differing objectives. The EEC, the Benelux Union, and the Council of Europe, each aim, in their own way, at integration. NATO and Western European Union on the other hand, are defensive alliances, with certain formulae about co-operation added to them. The Nordic Council itself aims purely at co-operation. The most that is common to the assemblies is that they aim at promoting closer links between

[1] Estimates from J. A. Hovey, *The Superparliaments*, Praeger, New York, 1966, p. 158.

nations. None of them have the objective of preserving national sovereignty and independence which is one of the tasks of the United Nations and its Assembly.

The European assemblies have certain supervisory and quasi-legislative functions which again vary considerably. All of them can pass resolutions on the subjects coming within their sphere. All of them can pass recommendations which may, or may not, eventually be transformed into laws by the governments. Only the European Parliament has the right to be consulted over laws (Regulations) while they are being made. The supervisory powers of the NPC, of the Consultative Assembly of the Council of Europe, and of the Benelux Assembly are very limited. The WEU Assembly can reject the annual report of its Council, while the European Parliament has, in theory at any rate, the power to sack the Common Market Commission. The Nordic Council has no other institution to supervise, but is entitled to hear from the national governments what they have done about its recommendations.

One further function which the assemblies share is that of airing publicly issues of common interest to the countries which belong to them, and thus of 'educating' both their members and the wider public. The success of this educational process depends, of course, on the degree to which the work of the various assemblies is reported, and made known to the public.

It is clear that the various assemblies can be grouped together according to many different criteria. Perhaps the most significant distinction for the purposes of this analysis is that between those assemblies which have been set up to provide a forum of discussion, and a place of co-operation, between the various national parliaments, and those intended to be independent quasi-parliamentary bodies in their own right. If this criterion is followed, the Nordic Council and the NPC come into the first category, while the Consultative Assembly, the WEU Assembly, the European Parliament and its predecessor the Common Assembly all come into the second. Rather more difficult to place is the Consultative Interparliamentary Council of Benelux. As its title suggests and its Convention specifies, it is designed to bring about 'regular co-operation between the three Parliaments of Belgium, Luxembourg and the Netherlands'.[1] It was

---

[1] The Convention setting up a Benelux Interparliamentary Consultative Council, reprinted in A. H. Robertson, *European Institutions*, Stevens, London, 1966, p. 416.

however, established by decision of the governments rather than by the parliaments themselves, and the Convention shows certain similarities with the Statute of the Council of Europe. The Benelux Council thus stands midway between the two categories described above.

THE FORMATION OF PARTY GROUPS IN THE ASSEMBLIES

It is interesting that the formation of transnational party affiliations has been almost non-existent in the assemblies created to promote co-operation between the national parliaments, but significant in those that have been set up as independent bodies. The Nordic Council is instructive in this respect. It is expressly designed as 'an organ for consultation between the *Folketing* of Denmark, the *Riksdag* of Finland, the *Althing* of Iceland, the *Storting* of Norway and the *Riksdag* of Sweden, as well as the governments of these countries, in matters involving joint action by any or all of the countries'.[1] Representatives in the Council (five from Iceland and 16 each from the other four) reflect the strength of the various political parties in the national parliaments, and can include, in contrast to the delegations of most of the other assemblies, members of the Communist parties. The remarkable feature of the Council is that it is a single-tier, not a two-tier organization. There is no Committee or Council of Ministers which the Council supervises; rather members of governments attend and take part in the Council's debates (though they are not allowed to take part in its decisions) and provide information about the action they have taken on the Council's recommendations. This makes the Council, perhaps, the outstanding example of an international organization which is purely parliamentary in nature.

Despite this, no transnational party groups have been formed in the Council. The members sit in alphabetical order. In nominating the officers and committee members of the Council proportional national representation is the main consideration, though an effort is made to ensure that there is a fair representation of party political trends in each of the committees and amongst the chairmen of the committees. In the plenary sessions of the Council it is extremely

[1] From the translation of the Statute of the Nordic Council contained in Stanley V. Anderson, *The Nordic Council, A Study of Scandinavian Regionalism*, University of Washington Press, Seattle, 1967, p. 151.

rare for there to be divisions of a party political nature. The main exception was in 1954 when the Norwegian centre and right-wing parties—the Liberal, Agrarian, Conservative and Christian People's parties—voted together against a number of proposed recommendations, in particular one which asked the governments to make preparations for the establishment of a common Nordic market. The Finnish Communists—the People's Democratic League—have also occasionally voted as a separate group, in opposition not only to their fellow Finns but also to the other members of the Council. Only a very small number of the proposals put forward by members of the Council—11 out of 151 in the first eight years—have been introduced by authors sharing the same political affiliation, but of different nationalities: of these 11, five had only two authors.[1] The vast bulk of recommendations adopted by the Nordic Council are passed unanimously.

The NATO Parliamentarians Conference shows the same lack of transnational party affiliations. The aim of the Conference is again to link together national parliaments in relation to a particular problem. 'The Conference, by virtue of its membership, drawn from the various national parliaments, provides an informal link between the responsible NATO authorities and these parliaments. Through its discussions, it helps to promote a feeling of Atlantic solidarity in the various legislative assemblies and to further the aims of the Atlantic Alliance.'[2] The NPC came into being 'under exclusively parliamentary sponsorship, unencumbered by official responsibility or status'.[3] Its members sit with their national delegation, which votes as a unit. Votes both in plenary sessions and in the committees are weighted. For example, in plenary sessions the United Kingdom, France, Germany and Italy have 18 votes each, while the United States has 36, and Canada 12. Transnational party groups play no part either in the election of officers and committee members or in discussions, and energetic individuals such as the American Senators Javits and Jackson seem to provide the main motor for action. As in the Nordic Council 'virtually all measures have carried unanimously or with a few abstentions.'[4]

---

[1] Anderson, *op. cit.*, esp. p. 63 and pp. 92–100.
[2] NPC, Rules of Procedure, cited in Hovey, *op. cit.*, pp. 17–18.
[3] *Ibid.*, p. 15.
[4] *Ibid.*, p. 21. There has been a movement within the NPC to transform it into a consultative parliamentary body for both NATO and OECD, but little has happened yet beyond the change of name.

Before looking in more detail at why transnational party groups have not evolved in these assemblies, it is worth examining two of the assemblies in which such groups have emerged, namely the Consultative Assembly of the Council of Europe and the WEU Assembly. (The European Parliament will be examined in detail later on.)[1]

The Consultative Assembly was clearly not intended to be simply an organ of interparliamentary co-operation like the Nordic Council. In the official statement issued when the Statute of the Council of Europe was signed in 1949 it was stated: 'The Consultative Assembly will provide a means through which the aspirations of the European peoples may be formulated and expressed, the governments thus being kept continually in touch with European public opinion.' And the Statute itself stated that 'the Consultative Assembly is the deliberative organ of The Council of Europe'.[2]

Transnational party groups did not, however, form immediately. The seating arrangement adopted by the Council places the delegates in alphabetical order. There seems to have been some desire in the early years to get beyond not only national but also traditional party affiliations.[3] More important than this, in the early years of the Council the main issue which dominated the debates was that of the ultimate form of integration, and this issue divided the delegates along lines which were national rather than party political. Essentially the division lay between those—chiefly the British, the Norwegians and the Swedish—who wished to create a 'functional' Europe, and those—the bulk of the representatives from the six countries which now form the Common Market—who wanted a 'federal' Europe. There were exceptions—the socialists of France and Germany were also opposed to federal proposals at this time— but the main line of division was national. The successful formation

[1] As the Benelux Interparliamentary Council will not be treated further, it should be added that the principal role within it is played by party groups, of which there are three: Christian Democrat, Socialist and Liberal.

[2] A. H. Robertson, *op. cit.*, p. 40.

[3] See the contribution of M Levy in *Les Elections Européennes au Suffrage Universel Direct*, Editions de l'Institut de Sociologie, Solvay, Paris, 1960, pp. 131–33. M Levy still considers that the European 'left' and 'right' should be defined in terms of their adherence to the cause of European integration. Party groups formed along traditional lines 'are only parasitical elements which prevent the development, separation, and articulation of deep trends within the European assemblies' (pp. 132–33).

of the European Coal and Steel Community in 1952 not only lessened the sharpness of this dispute between federalists and functionalists, but also provided an example for the formation of transnational party groups (see p. 477). By 1953, according to Haas,[1] a Liberal, a Socialist and a Christian Democrat party group had begun to function in the Consultative Assembly. During the presidency of Guy Mollet (1954–56) they consolidated their organizations. At first their role was limited to proposing candidates for posts in the Assembly and its committees, but during the presidency of Fernand Dehousse (1956–59) they became associated with the planning of the debates. They also began to receive a financial subsidy from the Assembly budget, and in October 1956, for the first time, a 'group viewpoint' was presented in a plenary debate of the Assembly. A high point was reached in January 1959 when group viewpoints were expressed on behalf of all three political groups.

Although the British Socialists had been active members of the Socialist Group from an early date the British Conservatives did not join the Christian Democrat Group. In 1958, however, the British Conservatives, together with the conservative parties of Scandinavia and Ireland began to organize themselves into a group which is now known as the Independent Representatives. Finally in January 1964 the Assembly's Rules of Procedure were modified to take account of the political groups. In 1968 the strength of the groups was: Socialists 41, Christian Democrats 37, Liberals 21, and Independents 15. There were 19 delegates not attached to any group—including the whole Turkish delegation and the French Gaullists—and there were no delegates present from Greece or Cyprus.

There has thus been a gradual evolution of the political groups within the Consultative Assembly. However, their importance should not be exaggerated. The party groups meet regularly during sessions of the Assembly in rooms provided by the Council. They share secretariats with the corresponding groups in the WEU Assembly, and, in the case of the socialists, with the corresponding group in the European Parliament.[2] The groups do not meet between sessions.

[1] Ernst B. Haas, *Consensus Formation in the Council of Europe*, Stevens, London, 1960, p. 39.
[2] Peter H. Merkl, European assembly parties and national delegations, *The Journal of Conflict Resolution*, Vol. VIII, 1964, p. 54. I am indebted to this article for much of the detail regarding group behaviour in the Consultative and WEU Assemblies.

In the organization of the Assembly the groups play a role which is roughly equal to that of the national delegations. The President of the Assembly is chosen by general consensus, regard being paid to both national and party rotation. Membership of the Bureau, which drafts the daily agenda of the Assembly during session, is decided by negotiation between national delegations and party groups to ensure a fair representation of both. The group chairmen are advisory members of the Assembly's Standing Committee—consisting of the Bureau and the various committee chairmen—which acts for the Assembly between sessions. Membership of the Assembly's committees is determined by the national delegations who try to ensure that national parties are represented in a balanced manner. The groups are faithfully reflected in the bureau of each committee, but the chairmen are chosen on grounds of their aptitude alone, regardless of national or party affiliation.

The groups play a less decisive role in influencing the debates and voting in the Assembly. It is true that in the deliberations of the Assembly's committees the groups function as 'negotiating agents'.[1] Efforts are chiefly directed towards reaching a generally acceptable committee viewpoint, however, and sharp partisan debate is rare. In plenary sessions, statements by group spokesmen are very infrequent, and one is more struck, on reading the accounts of debates, by the lack of mention of party viewpoints than by their presence. Statements of personal opinion are the predominant feature. Furthermore, a large number of the decisions of the Assembly are taken unanimously, or with a few abstentions, and even when there is not unanimity, the majorities tend to be very large. When there is a division over highly charged political issues such as relations between EFTA and EEC, national and regional loyalties tend to be predominant. On other divisive issues loyalty to the transnational party groups is important. However, an overall assessment shows that party group cohesion is lower on average than that of the national delegations.[2] Only the Christian Democrat group shows a level of cohesion greater than that of the average national delegation. Surprisingly, the Socialists, although they are the most highly organized group, show a much lower level of homogeneity.

[1] Hass, *op cit.* p. 67.
[2] Merkl, *op. cit.*, p. 57.

The second assembly in which party groups have evolved is that of the Western European Union (WEU). This held its first meeting in 1955, having been set up almost by chance as part of an organization which is concerned essentially with defence and the control of armaments. Inspired by the examples of the Consultative Assembly of the Council of Europe and of the ECSC Assembly, the WEU Assembly quickly asserted its independence and parliamentary authority, and succeeded in gaining for itself certain rights which the older Consultative Assembly did not possess. Once again it saw itself not as an interparliamentary body on the model of the Nordic Council, but as a separate institution performing the 'parliamentary function arising from the application of the Brussels Treaty'.[1]

The WEU Assembly is composed normally of the same parliamentarians which its member countries—Britain and the Six—send to the Council of Europe. From the start, the Assembly made provision in its standing orders for the formation of party groups, and these organized themselves with considerable speed, the Liberal Group constituting itself in January 1956, and the Socialist and Christian Democrat Groups following in April of that year. Neither the British Conservatives nor the French UNR are affiliated to any party group in the Assembly. In the organization and procedure of the WEU Assembly the party groups play a more important part than they do in the Consultative Assembly. Debates in the WEU Assembly are also marked by a more partisan flavour. However, in terms of voting behaviour, the groups show slightly less cohesion than in the Consultative Assembly. This seems to be because defence matters, which are the primary occupation of the Assembly, stand far closer to the vital interests of the member states than many of the issues coming before the Consultative Assembly.[2] It should also be noted that in the debates on British membership of the EEC which have recently occupied a considerable amount of the Assembly's time the division is chiefly along national lines; Britain, the 'Five' and the non-Gaullist French being opposed to the French UNR.

[1] From the first article of the Charter and Rules of Procedure of the WEU Assembly, cited in A. H. Robertson, *op. cit.*, p. 125.

[2] Merkl, *op cit.*, p. 63. See also the article by Ernst B. Haas and Peter Merkl, Parliamentarians against Ministers: The case of Western European Union, *International Organization*, Vol. XIV, 1960.

SOME GENERAL FACTORS RELATING TO THE FORMATION OF PARTY GROUPS

At this point, having looked briefly at the role of party groups in four European assemblies, and before considering in detail their role in the European Parliament, a few general observations may be made. It has been shown that party groups have formed in those assemblies which have been constituted, and regard themselves, as independent quasi-parliamentary institutions in their own right, rather than in those formed to link together national parliaments. However, it would be naïve to suppose that this is the only factor which leads to the formation of party groups in some assemblies and not in others. The number of countries belonging to each organization is clearly a relevant factor. The larger and more variegated the number of member countries, the less likely it is that there will be strong transnational party ties. Thus, it can hardly be expected that the NPC, which is composed of representatives from 15 countries, including the United States and Canada, will find it as easy to form common party political links as a body like the WEU Assembly with only seven European members, or the European Parliament with only six. The Consultative Assembly of the Council of Europe, with 18 members, is also handicapped in this respect. On the other hand it must be stressed that the number of member states alone is not the decisive factor, for the Nordic Council with only five members, showing considerable ethnic and political homogeneity, has not developed transnational party groups.

The status and power of the respective assembly is another relevant factor in determining the emergence of strong party groups. A body like the NPC, of peripheral and informal status and no formal powers, will be far more anxious to speak unanimously, without any divisions of a national or party political nature, than one such as the European Parliament, with a relatively more assured position, which can afford the luxury of internal division.

The nature of the subject-matter coming before the assembly in question must also be considered. It can be argued, for example, that the Nordic Council's preoccupation with technical matters, its deliberate avoidance of major political issues, means that party political debates will not emerge. It may also be pointed out that when the highly technical activities of Euratom are discussed before the European Parliament it is very unusual for a party political debate to occur. On the other hand, it is precisely when highly charged political issues such as the relations between the Six and the Seven, or the future shape of European integration come before the Council of Europe that national blocks tend to replace transnational party lines. Similarly defence issues in the WEU Assembly seem to have a fragmenting effect on group voting. In other words, it seems as if transnational party lines become well-defined in an intermediary zone between the highly technical and the highly political.

The specificity of function of the organization to which the assembly belongs will affect the role of party groups. When an organization has very general tasks to fulfil—this is the case with the Council of Europe, the Nordic Council, and the NPC—it is more difficult to establish clear-cut partisan positions than when the organization has precise and specific tasks. WEU and the Common Market both have such specific functions, and the correspondingly greater degree of partisanship in the debates of their assemblies owes much to this.

The length of session of each assembly is a further relevant factor. In an assembly like the Nordic Council, which meets in plenary session for only seven to ten days, and where much of the work is done in specialized committees which meet between sessions, it is likely that when an issue comes up for discussion it will have been effectively 'depoliticised' by committee discussion beforehand. It is also unlikely that in assemblies such as this, with infrequent plenary sessions, there will be enough time for transnational links to consolidate.

Finally, one factor which has clearly affected the growth of political parties in certain European assemblies has been the force of example, or the 'demonstration effect'. In particular, the example of the party groups which formed in the ECSC Assembly and its successor, the European Parliament, has clearly influenced the growth of such groups in the Consultative Assembly and the WEU Assembly. To quote only one small case, in supporting a demand for increased subsidies to political groups in the Assembly of the Council of Europe in 1964, Mr Zimmer of Germany drew express attention to the 'exemplary work' of the European Parliament, stating that 'the successes of the European Parliament are largely due to the work of . . . political groups'.[1] Whether this example will be sufficient to lead to the growth of party groups in the new Atlantic Assembly or in the Nordic Council remains to be seen.

Having examined some factors encouraging or discouraging the growth of political groups in international assemblies, there remains one further general aspect to be discussed, namely the tasks which these groups perform. As the preceding account has indicated, there are two broad categories of tasks which party groups, in greater or less degree, assume. The first is that of organization, which includes not only nominating candidates for the various offices of the assembly in question, but also deciding upon, and influencing, its procedure. The second may be termed ideological, by which is meant the articulation and promotion of certain commonly held viewpoints in the discussions and voting of the assembly.

To understand the significance of these two tasks, it is worth making a brief comparative survey. There would seem to be three main ways in which an international assembly can organize its work and administration. The first is through the medium of the national delegations, which means either that there must be enough offices to satisfy each delegation, or where there are fewer offices than delegations, a system of rotation must be agreed. The second is through the medium of blocs of nations, each bloc agreeing on candidates for nomination, and competing with one another if necessary. The last method is through transnational party groups which may again compete if necessary. The first method is that of the Nordic Council; the second is that of the General Assembly of the UN; and the last, as will be shown, is that of the European Parliament. In some assemblies, of course, the methods are mixed.

It is less easy to be categorical about the second task, namely, the articulation and promotion of viewpoints in discussion. There would, however, seem to be four common variations in practice. National delegations can either group themselves together in permanent blocks or they can align together as the issue demands. Alternatively, individuals within different national delegations can band together to promote specific interests; one can talk here

[1] Council of Europe, Consultative Assembly, *Official Report of Debates*, Sixteenth Ordinary Session, 1964, p. 226.

loosely of an international pressure group. Or, finally, transnational party groups can be formed cutting across the national delegations. In the General Assembly of the UN, the first and second methods predominate. In the European Assemblies, as had been indicated, the fourth form sometimes shows itself. It is now appropriate to look at the assembly in which this form has made its most advanced appearance, namely the European Parliament.

THE EUROPEAN PARLIAMENT

The very appropriation, by the Assembly of the European Communities, of the title 'European Parliament', shows the kind of body which it considers itself to be. Of all the European assemblies, it is the one which has gone furthest in asserting that it is a new parliament in its own right, distinct from the national parliaments which nominate its members. It has some legal justification for the claims which it makes. The Treaties establishing it declare that its members are representatives not of the member states, but of the peoples of the member states, and they also make provision for its eventual election by direct universal suffrage. It possesses the right to censure a body—the joint executive of the three Communities—which itself has substantial powers, and it has the right to be consulted on measures which in many cases become directly binding law on the citizens of the states who belong to it.

A comparative glance at the records of the debates of the European Parliament and those of the Consultative Assembly of the Council of Europe reveal clearly the more intense parliamentary atmosphere of the former. Spokesmen for party groups appear very rarely in the Consultative Assembly, while in the European Parliament it is their speeches, together with those of the committee *rapporteurs*, which tend to dominate the debates. The very appearance of the two assemblies in session is different, the members of the Consultative Assembly sitting, as has been mentioned, in alphabetical order, while those of the European Parliament sit according to party affiliation, the Socialists being on the left of the hemicycle, the Christian Democrats in the centre, the Liberals and *apparentés* (associates) to the right of them and the European Democratic Union on the extreme right.

The history of these party groups in the European Parliament requires a brief review of the Common Assembly of the ECSC, which the present European Parliament replaced in 1958. The Common Assembly, established in 1952, had within its own sphere substantially the same powers as the present Parliament. Party groups appeared within it with remarkable speed. Thus in the constitutive meeting of the Common Assembly, the first important vote, over the election of the President, showed an alignment along party lines. The German Socialists voted together with all the other Socialists for the Belgian Socialist candidate, M Spaak, rather than for the German Christian Democrat candidate, von Brentano. Four months later, in January 1953, it was agreed that the membership of the Assembly's committees should reflect political tendencies as well as a balance of nationalities. By March 1953 political groups had come to be organized, and in June 1953 they were formally recognized in standing orders; at the same time, they were allotted a financial allowance from the Assembly's budget to cover their administrative expenses. This practice of subsidy has been continued; the groups each receive a uniform lump sum and an additional payment in proportion to their numbers. Thus a sum of £44,000 was earmarked for the groups in the Parliament's budgetary estimate for 1968.[1]

From their official recognition in June 1953 onwards, the political groups—only three in number at this time, the Christian Democrats, the Socialists and the Liberals—spread their influence rapidly through the organization of the Assembly and asserted their presence in the debates of the plenary sessions. It is interesting, however, that it was not until 1958, when the Common Assembly was replaced by the present Parliament, that an alphabetical order of seating was replaced by one in which members sat with their own party groups.

In the new Parliament, which was larger than the Common Assembly (142 members as opposed to 78), the three party groups consolidated and in certain fields expanded the position which they had won in previous years. The main change in their composition was in 1959 when the Liberals, who had been consistently the smallest group in the Common Assembly, ousted the Socialists from their customary position in second place. This was due to the appearance in the Liberal Group of a substantial UNR representation, and a simultan-

---

[1] Parlement Européen, *Rapport sur L'état prévisionnel des dépenses et des recettes du Parlement européen pour l'exercice 1968*, Rapporteur, M. E. Battaglia, Document 74, June 14, 1967, p. 27.

eous reduction in the French membership of the Socialist Group.

Late in 1962, after the French elections held in November had swollen their numbers to 15, the Gaullists broke away from the Liberal Group and formed a bloc of *non-inscrits*. At this time, they did not have the minimum number of 17 required to constitute themselves formally into a party group. However, as a result of some vigorous campaigning Parliament agreed in January 1965 to reduce the minimum to 14, and it was from this time that the European Democratic Union Group, consisting wholly of Gaullist members, came into being.

The following table gives a breakdown of the four groups as they existed in 1969.

TABLE I

Composition of the Party Groups in the European Parliament in March 1969

1 *Christian Democrat Group. President: Joseph Illerhaus (Germany)*

		Number
Belgium:	Parti social chrétien (PSC)	2
	Christelijke Volkspartij (CVP)	4
France:	Mouvement républicain populaire (MRP)	2
Germany:	Christlich—Demokratische Union (CDU)	14
	Christlich—Soziale Union (CSU)	4
Italy:	Democrazia cristiana (DC)	15
	Südtiroler Volkspartei (SVP)	1
Luxembourg:	Parti chrétien social (PCS)	3
Netherlands:	Katholieke Volkspartij (KVP)	5
	Anti-revolutionaire partij (AR)	2
	Christelijk Historische Unie (CHU)	1
	Total	53

2 *Socialist Group. President: Francis Vals (France)*

		Number
Belgium:	Parti socialiste belge (PSB)	3
	Belgische Socialistische Partij (BSP)	1
France:	Fédération de la Gauche démocrate et socialitse (FGDS)	4*
Germany:	Sozialdemokratiishe Partei Deutschlands (SPD)	15
Italy:	Partito socialista italiano (PRI)	6
	Partito repubblic italiano (PRI)	1
Luxembourg:	Parti ouvrier socialiste luxembourgeois (POSL)	2
Netherlands:	Partij van de Arbeid (PVdA)	4
	Total	36

* Includes two French Senators who continue to describe themselves as members of the French Socialist Party (SFIO).

3   *Group of Liberals and Associates. President: René Pleven (France)*

		Number
Belgium:	⎰Parti de la liberté et du progrès (PLP)	3
	⎱Partij voor vrijheid en vooruitgang (PVV)	1
France:	Centre Nationale des Indépendants et Paysans (CNIP)*	4
	Gauche démocratique (GD)	2
	Progrès et démocratie moderne (PDM)	2
	Républicains indépendants (RI) (Giscardiens)	3
Germany:	⎰Freie Demokratische Partei (FDP)	2
	⎱Demokratische Volkspartei (DVP)	1
Italy:	Movimento sociale italiano (MSI)	1
	Partito democratico italiano di unità monarchica (PDIUM)	1
	Partito liberale italiano (PLI)	2
Luxembourg:	Parti démocratique (PD)	1
Netherlands:	Volkspartij voor Vrijheid en Demokratie (VVD)	2
	Total	25

* Of which Centre républicain d'action rurale et sociale (CRARS) 1.
Républicains Indépendants (RI) (Senate Group) 3.

4   *European Democratic Union. President: Raymond Triboulet*

		Number
France:	Union des démocrates pour la République (UDR)	18

5   *Non-affiliated*

Partito communista italiano (PCI)	7
Partito socialista italiano di unità proletaria (PSIUP)	1
Indipendente di Sinistra (IS)	1
Non-affiliated (French)	1
Total	10

This, of course, is only a 'snapshot' of the groups at one particular moment. It is untypical chiefly because of the presence of the Italian Communists, the PSIUP, and the IS, who only obtained representation in the Parliament in January 1969. Before that date the Parliament's status as a representative body was severely weakened by the exclusion of both the French and Italian Communists, and of the smaller groups of the extreme left in these two countries. This practice of exclusion, inherited from the Consultative Assembly of the Council of Europe, was enforced by the French and Italian methods of designating members to the Parliament. Whereas in other delegations political parties were represented in proportion to their strength in the national parliaments, the French and Italian delegations were chosen by a majority vote system which was used to ensure the exclusion of the Communists as well as of the Nenni Socialists. This system began to be attacked in Italy with the 'opening to the left' (1962). However, because left and right were unable to agree on the issue, no new Italian delegations was chosen after the 1963 general election, and the old delegation—incomplete and non-representative—continued in office. Not until after the 1968 general election was an Italian delegation chosen on a proportional basis and Communist membership of the European Parliament for the first time secured. It is now possible that French Communists will also gain admittance, and that Communists will obtain representation in some of the other European assemblies which at present exclude them.

The relative strength of the three main party groups in the Parliament has not changed much during its lifetime. The Christian Democrats have been consistently the biggest, the Liberals consistently the smallest group—except for the years 1959 to 1962 when Gaullist membership of the Liberal group raised them into second place. The number of Gaullists has increased steadily from 8 in 1959 to 18 now.

The following sections will consider the internal organization of the European party groups and their links with the national parties. This will be followed by an examination of the groups' activities in relation to the two tasks described earlier, namely, the organization of the Parliament, and the articulation of ideas in its debates.

Each of the three main parties is headed by an executive, elected, usually unanimously, from their number, and consisting of a president and six to ten members. (The UDE has an executive of three.) Each party group also has a small secretariat in Luxembourg; these secretariats can play a highly important role in ensuring the effectiveness and continuity of the groups' work. During plenary sessions of the Parliament additional staff (about 15) are taken on to help service the groups.

Both the Socialists and the Christian Democrats, but not the

Q 481

Liberals, are closely linked with the national parties from which they are composed. The Socialists have the oldest and strongest tradition of co-operation. The links, in their case, take the form of a 'Liaison Bureau' and a Conference. The former has its seat in Luxembourg, sharing a secretary-general with the Socialist Group of the Parliament. The Bureau consists of a representative from each of the national parties, together with one representative each from the Socialist International, and the Socialist Group in the Consultative Assembly. It meets at least twice a year and generally holds its meetings together with the executive of the European party group. The Bureau makes pronouncements on questions relating to European integration, and occasionally on matters farther afield. For example, the meeting held in Brussels in June 1967 under the present President M Radoux of Belgium issued a statement to the press on the situation in the Middle East, 'affirming its solidarity with the state of Israel'.[1] The other organ of liaison, the Conference of the Socialist parties of the six Common Market countries, has met regularly since 1957; the seventh Conference was held in Berlin in November 1966. This consists of representatives of the national parties, the members of the 'Liaison Bureau', and members of the European party group. At each meeting the President of the latter makes a report on the group's activities. The Conference discusses European problems and usually ends with a number of joint resolutions. It should also be mentioned that the 'Liaison Bureau' keeps in regular contact with the *Gauche Européenne* movement, which has a wider membership than the Conference (Britain is, for example, a member, and Sir Geoffrey de Freitas the present President), and holds congresses from time to time. Information on these various liaison activities is readily available from the *Courrier Socialiste Européen*, the joint publication of the 'Liaison Bureau' and the Socialist group of the European Parliament, which comes out very frequently and presents a steady stream of socialist comment on all aspects of European problems.

For a long time the Christian Democrat Group in the Parliament was far less closely in touch with the national parties than the Socialists. Until 1965 the Group's links were maintained primarily through its representation on the Steering Committee of the

---

[1] *Courrier Socialiste Européen*, No. 7, 1967, p. 2.

Nouvelles Equipes Internationales, and its participation in the annual congress of the latter. The leader of the European Christian Democrat Group also attended meetings of the 'Conference of the Presidents and Secretaries-General of the Christian Democratic Parties' which held meetings regularly after 1958 outside the framework of the NEI.

In 1965 the old statutes of the NEI were replaced by the statutes of the European Union of Christian Democrats, UEDC, the European wing of the World Union of Christian Democrats, UMDC and in 1967 the Secretariat of the UEDC and that of the European Christian Democrat Group in Luxembourg were amalgamated. Under the aegis of UEDC there are also regular conferences of the presidents and secretary-generals of the Christian Democrat parties of the Six—these can be summoned if necessary at the request of the President of the European party group—and of the Eight (the Six, Austria and Switzerland). Details of some of these activities can be found in the *Cahiers Européens,* the organ of the European Group, which is published in Luxembourg. It is a more formal, less aggressive publication than the *Courrier Socialiste.* It comes out much less frequently than the latter and is confined largely to the texts of addresses by prominent European Christian Democrats.

The Liberal Group in the European Parliament has no such outside contacts and no publication. Its sole link would seem to be with the Liberal International, to which it is affiliated. The UDE also has no publication; its only outside contacts seem to have been unofficially with the German CDU–CSU, probably to try to improve German–French relations.

Turning to the role which the party groups play in the organization and procedure of the European Parliament it can be seen at once to be all-pervasive and decisive. Candidates for nearly every office from the presidency downwards are nominated by the party groups, and there is often a contest between them to secure the successful election of their nominees. It is true that for a long period after the election of M Spaak in 1952, the Presidents of both the Common Assembly and the Parliament were elected by a unanimous decision of all parties. Since 1960, however, this practice has ended and elections in which party considerations play the prominent role have come to the fore. The last two elections, those of the Belgian Christian Democrat M Duvieusart and of the French Christian

Democrat Alain Poher were straightforward partisan contests. Nominations to the nine-man Bureau of the Parliament are also in the hands of the party groups, though every effort is made here to ensure that there is a proportional representation of the member states.

More significant is the role of the party groups in the nomination of the 12 standing committees. These play a vital role in the working of Parliament for all debates are based on a report previously drafted by the appropriate committee. Moreover, committees also perform much of the Parliament's supervisory role, meeting frequently between sessions and often asking members of the Community executives to attend and explain their policies.

The Parliament's standing orders state that in nominating members of the committees, account should be taken both of the fair representation of member states and of political affinities. In fact, it is the latter which play the decisive role. Representation on the committees is proportional according to the numerical strength of party groups. No account is taken of the national delegations in the process of nomination. Although there is no strict allocation of either committee chairman or committee *rapporteurs* according to national or party political lines, party political considerations play a strong part in determining their election, along with other factors such as the specialized knowledge of the candidate in question.

In the procedure of the Parliament the impact of the political groups is also apparent. The presidents of the groups are members of the Committee of Presidents which helps draft the Parliament's agenda, and also join the Bureau to decide on the same. Official spokesmen of the party groups can, at request, take precedence over other speakers in the order of debates. They frequently do. Such spokesmen are also given longer to expound their views than those who speak independently.

Turning to the second task of the groups, namely the articulation and promotion of certain common standpoints, one may start conveniently from Neunreither's observation that 'no important matter is treated in plenary sessions without having been discussed previously by the political groups'. He adds that it is not unknown for 'the plenary session to be interrupted when new facts present themselves, in order to allow the political groups to discuss them'.[1]

[1] K. Neunreither, *Europa-Archiv*, No. 22, 1966.

Each group meets every day of a plenary session, before debate begins. Two of the groups—the Socialists and the Christian Democrats—also meet from time to time between sessions of the Parliament to discuss European problems, and sometimes set up specialized working groups to deal with specific issues. In the meetings immediately preceding the debates each group tries to agree on a common viewpoint, and appoints a spokesman to express it. The UDE and the Socialists are almost invariably able to do this; the Christian Democrats have more difficulty; and the Liberals find it hardest of all. Sometimes two spokesmen are appointed.

These preliminary meetings are private, and it is difficult to find information about them. However, Neunreither, a member of the Parliament's Secretariat, has provided this account of them:

'National points of view play a more important role in the formation of the opinion of the political groups than in that of the plenary assembly. One can say that before appearing in the plenary session, national elements have already been "filtered" or "arranged" through the exchange of views in the groups. (This naturally does not apply to the UDE, whose national character becomes even more accentuated by this process) . . . Not only are national positions more accentuated—compared with the plenary session—but within the group the members of the relevant committees have an influence which it would be wrong to underestimate. As a general rule, one of the members of the relevant committee, perhaps the *rapporteur*, makes an exposé on the subject which appears on the agenda for the day. When it is the *rapporteur* who gives an account of his report before his own political group he has a tendency to defend, over and above his own position, the result of the deliberations of his committee. Furthermore, where members of a group have been put in a minority when a draft resolution has been adopted in committee, they will tend to use their group spokesman to put forward an amendment. Thus, even if there is no absolute loyalty with regard to decisions taken in committee—and this loyalty is nowhere demanded from anyone—each person's position is nevertheless subjected to the influence of this first phase in the deliberations.'[1]

[1] *Ibid.*, p. 10.

This interplay of group and committee opinions need only be noted at this point. In the debate itself the spokesmen put forward their party views. However, it is not unusual for an individual member of a party to disagree in the debate with his party's spokesman. There are no 'whips' in the European Parliament or in any other European Assembly, and the pressure to keep together as a group is very delicate.[1] Nevertheless, as the following table shows, at least some of the groups have achieved a considerable record of cohesion in voting.

TABLE II

Voting Cohesion in the European Parliament*

Delegations	Per cent of seats in European Parliament	Cohesion Index average	
		1958–63	1963–66
Germany	25·35	35·9	26·5
Italy	25·35	4·4	3·2
France	25·35	11·8	24·6
Belgium	9·85	30·8	19·8
Netherlands	9·85	6·0	9·1
Luxemburg	4·25	28·0	9·6
Average of national delegation		19·5	15·5
Parliamentary parties			
Christian Democrats	43·7	15·2	14·9
Socialists	24·7	1·7	2·0
Liberals	18·3	13·7	17·6
UNR–UDT (UDE)	10·6	—	4·5
Average of the supranational groups		10·2	9·7

* The cohesion index is calculated from the percentage deviation of national or ideological groups from unanimity in roll call votes. The higher the percentage of deviation, the weaker the cohesion.

Source: Gerda Zellentin, Opposition in the European Communities, in *Government and Opposition*, Vol. 2, No. 3, April–July 1967.

[1] That the Socialist Group formally decides when to allow its members to vote freely is indicated by M Dehousse's intervention on May 11, 1967, cf. Parlement Européen, *Débats*, VI/67, No. 91, p. 119.

The Socialists have been the most cohesive of any political or national group. They have been drawn, generally from six or seven national parties, and have been dominated numerically since 1958 by members of the German SPD. What policy does the group represent? On energy its views have been fairly consistent. It has called for greater co-ordination and programming of the energy market by the High Authority, and for more vigorous intervention by the latter not only to meet the continuous recession in the European coal industry which began in 1959 but also to alleviate the social dislocation caused by pit closures. It would be wrong, however, simply to label the Group's policy as one of dirigisme, for in most debates it has recognized that, even if increased intervention is necessary, the coal industry must gradually change and adapt to new competitive conditions. Voices such as those of M Toubeau—significantly from the Walloon area—calling for nationalization of the European coal industry and a form of European state control of the petroleum industry are exceptions rather than the rule.

The Socialists' policy on farming has also been consistent. They have continuously championed the European consumer and called for low food prices. M Mansholt, himself a Socialist, has called attention to the Socialists' somewhat ambivalent policy of helping the coal industry and yet wishing to expose the farmers to the full blast of market forces.[1] In taking a stand on low food prices the Socialists have sometimes, but more often not, been successful in determining the Parliament's opinion (see below). The group has also, under the influence of the SPD, called for strong measures to counter industrial cartelization and monopolization at the Community level. It was largely the pressure of the Socialist Group in the debates on this issue which ensured that the Parliament's opinion did not represent a weakening of the Commission's proposals. Regarding economic policy as a whole, the group has favoured medium-term programming for the Community, as well as an incomes policy covering not only wages but other forms of income as well, and full implementation of the Treaty's social provisions.

The Socialist Group has always been the most vociferous in

---

[1] *Débats,* X/67, No. 93, p. 40.

calling for the progressive development and strengthening of the Communities, and for the eventual creation of a federal state. The Socialists have also been most active in exercising the Parliament's supervisory powers *vis-a-vis* the other organs, and calling for democratic control. They have, for example, made by far the most use of the written question. Except in the years 1958–59 and 1963–64 they have asked half (1959–60), or more than half the total number of written questions put by the Parliament each year, and in 1965–66 no less than 68 per cent.[1] (They have been assisted in this task by the indefatigable Dutch Socialist interrogator M Vredeling.) It has been the Socialist Group, too, which has come nearest to introducing a motion of censure against the High Authority (in 1956, and again in 1963).

These two lines of policy, one favouring further integration and the other favouring greater democratic control, are to some extent at variance. By sternly calling to account the executives of the Communities, the Socialists are in a sense 'holding up' the most powerful supranational force in the European Communities. In the Common Assembly the Socialists followed single-mindedly the path of control and scrutiny and, as a result, became to some extent the 'opposition' party within the Assembly; the Christian Democrats and Liberals tending to side with the High Authority against them. In the European Parliament, there has been no such crystallization, and the dilemma which the Socialists' dual policy creates is real. It has been expressed by the present Leader of the Socialists, Mr Vals: 'We have struggled too long for Europe to lose faith in the European idea under the pretext that the roads which lead to a democratic United States of Europe are sown with obstacles. But we have also struggled too long for democracy to sacrifice the parliamentary regime to the European idea.'[2]

At the 1962 Conference of the Socialist Group and the various affiliated national parties a 'Common Action Programme for the Socialist Parties of the European Community' was drawn up; an

[1] H. A. H. Andretsch, 'Les Questions Écrites au Parlement Européen. Quelques Statistiques', *Revue du Marché Commun*, No. 105, September 1967, *passim*.
[2] Francis Vals, speech on the occasion of the Tenth Anniversary of the signing of the Rome Treaty, March 23, 1967, printed in the *Courrier Socialiste Européen*, No. 6, 1967, p. 26.

undertaking which none of the other party groups have attempted. This programme enunciated a number of the policies described above, calling notably for a federal and democratic Europe, moderate economic planning at the European level and a tough restrictive practices policy. It does not seem to have affected the policies of the national parties, and although it probably gave the group a greater feeling of ideological unity it has rarely been referred to as a guide for action.

Looking at the national tendencies within the Socialist Group, it is difficult to make categorical distinctions. One member of the group told the author that the Dutch Socialists were the most vociferously in favour of 'popular control of government', whilst the Belgians were keenest on policies favouring the working class. This would seem to be reflected in many debates, for the two Walloon Socialists Toubeau and Troclet actively seek a more vigorous Community welfare policy, while the Dutch are frequently demanding more democratic control in the Community. However, the line of division is not fixed. The German Socialists are most concerned with the group's economic policy, notably the emphasis on effective rules of competition and planning of a carefully non-directive nature.

There is no rigid line separating Socialist and Christian Democrat policies in the Parliament. The Christian Democrats also favour, but in a less extreme manner, the progressive development of European unification and the democratization of the Communities. On several issues of economic policy, there is much overlapping. Some members of the Christian Democrat Group, notably Italian members such as Sabatini and Rubinacci, who have had links with the Trade Union movement, are as emphatically in favour of vigorous Community welfare measures and 'programmation' as any member of the Socialist Group. In the field of energy policy there are several members of the Christian Democrat Group, particularly those from mining constituencies, who are as much in favour of intervention to help the coal industry as the Socialists. Perhaps the two main features of the Christian Democrat Group which distinguish them from the Socialists are, first, that they contain a large number of members, supporting a high level of protection for the Community farmer, and thus high food prices; and secondly, they contain some members, notably the German

CDU member Dichgans, who strongly favour a market economy and are suspicious of measures such as 'programmation', incomes policies, protective subsidies and so on, which might paralyse such an economy. These two trends separate the Christian Democrats from the Socialists and, in combination with the 'left-wing' trend mentioned above, make it much more difficult for the former to agree amongst themselves on a positive and consistent economic policy.

One interesting area in which the Christian Democrats (and the Liberals) differ from the Socialists relates to nuclear armaments. In a debate held in March 1967 on the effects of the proposed Non-proliferation Treaty on Euratom, Dr Hallstein (himself a Christian Democrat), the Christian Democrats, and the Liberals all saw the Treaty as a threat to the extension of European integration to military and nuclear matters. The Socialists did not see such a threat and clearly did not envisage an extension of integration to the military sphere.

The Group of Liberals and *apparentés* is much more loose-knit than either the Socialists or the Christian Democrats, and is drawn from a much larger number of national parties. This is largely because the traditional liberal party of France, the Radical Party, has split into a number of separate groups in the French Senate and Assembly, or in other words because a heterogeneous collection of French political groups, who are uncertain of their international allegiances, find it convenient to sit with the Liberals. The situation is further confused by the presence in the group, alongside the Italian Liberal Party, of representatives from the Italian Social Movement, and the Italian Monarchist Party, both of which belong to the extreme right. The Benelux countries and Germany are all represented by one party only. It is difficult to describe precisely the group's view-point, but one can certainly question Van Oudenhove's assertion that they 'remain the champions of freedom in all its forms'.[1] The representatives of the traditional Liberal parties may certainly see themselves, and vote in this light, but the others do not give many signs of doing so. The most prominent theme of Liberal statements in debates concerns the need to give European farmers a reasonable income. It is the members of the French Independent and Peasant parties

---

[1] Guy Van Oudenhove, *The Political Parties in the European Parliament*, Sijthoff, Leyden, 1965, p. 233.

who are usually the most vocal in presenting this theme. In M Blondelle and M Boscary-Monsservin, both French farmers, the Liberal Group in fact possesses two of the Parliament's most articulate and old-established speakers on agricultural policy, and the Liberals have significantly held the chairmanship of the Agricultural Committee since the Parliament was established. Another theme of the Liberals is the need for a positive Community regional policy, which can be understood from the fact that many members of the group come from backward or depressed areas of the Community—the present President, for example, M Pleven, is a deputy from Brittany. Apart from these two themes, it may be said that the Liberal Group supports the further development of European integration; that it possesses one or two individual speakers of considerable ability, notably M Pleven and (until recently) M Maurice Faure; that its MSI members, notably M Ferretti who was a former minister of Mussolini's, can on occasion make political statements of an extremely right-wing nature; and that some of its members, e.g. M Armengaud, have spoken in favour of highly dirigist economic policies.

The European Democratic Union (UDE), being composed entirely of French Gaullists, is not unnaturally more cohesive than any other group except the Socialists. It differs from all the other groups in its views on the nature and goal of European integration itself, and in this field it performs the vital role of providing an 'opposition'. This could be seen most clearly during the year 1965, the year of the 'constitutional crisis', when debates in the Parliament were dominated by very lively and heated exchanges between the UDE and all the other groups on the form and nature of future integration. There is no need to describe in detail the UDE's views on this subject, for they are identical with those of General de Gaulle. The group would like to see Europe develop a common foreign and defence policy; it wishes Europe to be as independent as possible of the United States; it favours integration by inter-governmental methods, and is critical of measures to increase the powers of such supra-national bodies as the European Commission. On issues other than these, for example agricultural policy, the group supports those measures which seem most in accordance with French interests. It often votes in the same way as the Christian Democrats and Liberals.

It would be a mistake to deduce from this brief survey of the standpoints of the four party groups that each debate in the Parliament is marked by a sharp interparty dispute. Partisan battles emerge in some debates and disappear totally from others, in a way that is almost unpredictable. Nor, as van Oudenhove has shown, has there been a steady increase in the number and intensity of these battles;[1] they seem to have shown roughly the same frequency throughout the existence of the Parliament and its predecessor. (This can, of course, be contrasted with the steady increase in the group's influence over the Parliament's organization and procedure.) If the party groups play a significant role in the Parliament's debates there are clearly other forces which also play an important part. The national delegations will often vote together, usually with the party that most favours their national interest, but sometimes forming a separate voting bloc of their own. As Table II shows, the Dutch and Italians demonstrate the greatest voting cohesion. Dutch cohesion can be readily understood. The Dutch feel most strongly in favour of an increase in the Parliament's powers. This could be seen vividly in the hectic debate of May 1965 when the Dutch formed their own group and expressed a unanimous view on this subject. Dutch food prices are also the lowest in the Community, and the Dutch, therefore, tend to vote *en bloc* with the Socialists against the fixing of high Community prices. The Dutch transport system is the only one in the Community which works effectively according to market principles, and the Dutch, therefore, tend to express a common view on this. Finally, the Dutch are not beset by the problems of a declining coal industry, and therefore tend to see energy policy in a different light from many of their colleagues.

The strength of Italian cohesion is less easily explained but there are certain factors which help one to understand it. Italy, like Holland, does not face the problem of a large declining coal industry. Italy also, unlike most other Community countries, imports a large quantity of oil from behind the Iron Curtain. The Italians, therefore, tend to speak with one voice on the problems of energy policy. Similarly, there are certain agricultural products—rice and olive oil for example—in which Italy has, with France, special interests. Close Italian cohesion when these matters are discussed is again understandable.

[1] Guy Van Oudenhove, *op. cit.*, p. 124.

Interest-group cohesion is another factor cutting across the party spectrum. By interest group is meant, here, purely the sharing by certain individuals in the Parliament of the same interests regarding a particular issue. The only important group of this sort in the Parliament is the agricultural one. This does not mean that the members of the Parliament who are farmers and/or members of farming organizations always speak with the same voice; there is often a significant cleavage between the grain-producing and the grain-consuming farmers. Nevertheless, the farmers show a cohesion which manifests itself in debates and voting on agricultural issues. They are also strongly entrenched in the Parliament's Agricultural Committee. Of the 28 effective members of this Committee in 1967, 16 were farmers and/or members of agricultural interest groups. Occasionally, one has glimpses of other transnational interest groups—for example, a group of those members who come from regionally backward constituencies—but these are so transitory as to be scarcely worth the title of group.

The day-long debate of July 19, 1967, is illustrative of the inter-action between national, party, and pressure-group views which is characteristic of many debates in the European Parliament. On this occasion the Parliament had been asked for its opinion on the EEC Commission's proposal for fixing the future Community price level for grains, beef, and pigmeat.[1]

The debate opened with the presentation of the views of the Parliament's Agricultural Committee, by the *rapporteur*, M Dupont, who is himself vice-president of the Community farming organization ASSILEC (the Association for the Community Milk Industry). The Committee wanted the EEC Commission to raise its proposed price-level for soft wheat by 5 per cent and to raise the price of feeding grains to correspond to this new level. This view, it became clear later, was also that of COPA, the biggest of the Community's farming associations (Committee of Professional Agricultural Organizations). The Agricultural Committee further wanted the EEC Commission to introduce its proposed price increase for beef one year earlier than was envisaged. Over pigmeat prices, the Committee had split in two: half wanted the Commission's proposed prices to be raised sharply; and half agreed with the Commission. The Committee, therefore,

---

[1] For a full account, cf. *Débats*, X/67, No. 93.

adopted a compromise position. It is interesting that the *rapporteur* expressly stated that he had recently had numerous contacts with both individual farmers and farm organizations.

In the debate which followed the official spokesman of the Socialist Group attacked the price rises proposed by the Agricultural Committee and supported instead the EEC Commission's original proposals. A splinter group of Socialists actually wanted a reduction in the price level for cereals proposed by the EEC Commission. Attempts by the Socialists, however, to amend the Agricultural Committee's proposals failed.

The spokesman of the Gaullist Group, the UDE, and other members of this body, spoke out strongly in favour of the Agricultural Committee's proposals, and also called for an uncompromising increase in the price of pigmeat since, as the spokesman said, 'this is an extremely important problem for France'. Numerous French members of the Liberal Group also spoke in this vein, and stressed that farmers, in particular those from the more depressed areas of France, might lose interest in the EEC if prices did not go up. If farming was not given an equal rank with industry, one of them remarked, 'the revulsion of European farmers will be as violent as their adhesion to the European idea has been sincere'. Italian Christian Democrats and Liberals expressed the same point of view as the French right, emphasizing the special needs of certain backward areas of Italy. The UDE, and some French, Belgian, and Italian Liberals and Christian Democrats sponsored a successful amendment calling for a sharp increase in the price of pigmeat. The German Christian Democrats, on the other hand, were divided. One, a farmer, favoured higher prices. Two others, who were not farmers, criticized the economic irrationality of merely increasing subsidies. The two Dutch speakers, one Christian Democrat and one Liberal, were both farmers, but they spoke out strongly *against* a general increase in grain prices. Such a rise would merely increase the costs of production in the 'transformation sector' of agriculture, however much it might help other farmers.

This brief sketch illustrates the cross-cutting of national, party political, and interest-group opinions in the European Parliament when agriculture is discussed. In the end, the national and farming interests which were in favour of higher prices won; the opposition, consisting of the Socialist Group, the Dutch, and some of the

German Christian Democrats, were not strong enough to withstand them. It should be added that the Parliament's final views, like those of some of the powerful farm organizations, were not endorsed when the Council of Ministers took its decisions.

FACTORS PREVENTING THE EMERGENCE OF STRONG EUROPEAN PARTY GROUPS

This chapter has examined the emergence of transnational party groups in some European assemblies. It has shown that they have emerged in those assemblies which have been designed as independent, quasi-parliamentary bodies in their own right, and that they have developed furthest in the European Parliament. Party groups completely dominate the organization and procedure of the latter body and they play a significant role in its debates and voting patterns. Nevertheless, they lack the cohesion and discipline of parties, for example, in the House of Commons or the *Bundestag*. Morevoer, the debates in the European Parliament often lack the partisanship of debates in national parliaments. Some of the reasons why party groups have not developed any further in the Parliament will now be considered.

The first and most obvious reason why the party groups lack much of the vigour of their national counterparts is that they have no following or organization outside the Parliament. There is no electorate to be wooed and there are no elections to be won. The groups are, to use the German term, *Fraktionen*, not full-blooded parties. If debates in many national legislatures are given point and vigour through being 'continuous general elections' then those in the European Parliament are clearly not. It is this absence of a struggle for power through a fight for votes that often gives the debates in the Parliament the appearance merely of Platonic shadows of the 'real thing' which takes place in national parliaments. This absence of struggle also makes party programmes of the sort drafted by the Socialist Group in 1962 seem largely irrelevant, and probably explains why there have been no further attempts in this direction.

A further factor which has made the development of party programmes seem unrealistic is that the parties do not and cannot determine in advance the subjects which substantiate the Parliament's debates. These subjects are 'fed' to the Parliament, as the

Community develops, by the Executive and Council but neither of these bodies is related in any close manner to the party groups. It is partly for this reason that the groups have considered it wiser to treat each issue as it comes, rather than to lay down prior principles which may prove to have no application.

It is true that most members of the Executive—not only the old triple Executive but the new joint Commission—have meetings with the party groups with which they sympathize. This applies not only to those members who have followed political careers, but also to some, for example Hans von der Groeben, who have had careers in the civil service. Party political considerations also play at least some part in the deliberations of the Executive. However, the over-riding consideration of the Executive in deciding policy issues is that of finding a formula which will be acceptable to the six national governments. It is, therefore, against the interest of the Executive to tie itself too closely to either the Parliament or its party groups. Similarly, efforts made by the Executive to formulate a programme for the future—such as the Action Programme of 1962—are more expressions of hope than of any ability to fulfil them.

The Council is, of course, composed of leading members of national political parties. Their main concern, however, is to ensure that their own nation's interest is adequately safeguarded when a Community policy is being decided. They, therefore, have little reason to link themselves closely with the Parliament or its groups; it is the views of the national electorate and parliaments which primarily command their attention. Nor is it easy for the Council to indicate its future line of action, at the moment it only provides the Parliament with reports of action already taken.

Yet one more reason why interparty strife is not as marked in the European Parliament as in national parliaments, is that whereas the latter are assured of their place in the governmental process (except possibly the French Assembly) the Parliament's status and authority are not assured. It lies at the periphery of the Community's decision-making process, and is in constant danger of having its views and opinions ignored completely. There is therefore strong pressure on the three main party groups to come together and speak with one voice in order to give greater authority to the Parliament's views; a pressure which runs counter to the desire to act as a real debating chamber in which partisan views can flourish. Linked with this is the fact that the bulk of the parliamentarians are keen 'Europeans' who wish to push the work of integration as far and as fast as possible. The extent of the three main parties' desire both to promote integration and to increase the powers of the Parliament can be seen, with particular clarity, during the course of the debates of 1965, when they frequently spoke with one voice on these matters. But even on lesser issues than those presented during 1965, the three main parties do not disagree on the need to give as much power as possible to the supranational organs in the Community and to interpret the Treaties' stipulations as widely as possible.

Thus from one point of view the European Parliament is a huge pressure group; a pressure group for faster European integration and for more power to the Parliament. This runs counter to its position as a debating chamber in which all sides of a problem can be stated; for a pressure group requires unanimity and closed ranks, whereas a debating chamber requires precisely the opposite. However much the three main party groups may have disliked the UDE's point of view during 1965, it cannot be denied that (ironically) it was the UDE, by its staunch opposition to the idea of increasing both the Commission's and the Parliament's budgetary powers, which preserved the parliamentary nature of the Parliament's debates and prevented them from declining into a mere chant in favour of European integration.

An institutional feature of the Parliament itself which serves to diminish interparty strife is the committee system. It has been mentioned earlier that the Parliament's standing committees play a highly important role in the work of the Parliament. They meet very frequently between sessions, and will often question members of the executives on their policies and actions. They discuss all matters which come before the Parliament prior to any discussion in the plenary assembly and committee *rapporteurs* always speak first in debates. They will often draft resolutions on their own initiative for discussion by the Parliament, indeed it has been the sheer quantity of reports emanating from the committees which has led the Parliament, in recent years, to reduce the number of committees. The committees, in effect, have a life of their own alongside and within the Parliament.

The way in which the position of the committees affects the work of the political groups has been described by Neunreither, part of whose analysis was mentioned earlier. When a matter is sent to committee, which has been the subject of previous discussions by the Parliament, it is clear that the representatives of the party groups in the committee will generally know what line of policy to adopt. However, when the subject in question is a new one 'work in committee frequently goes ahead rapidly and even finishes before the political groups have been able to decide their policy. When one realizes that integration continually expands into new areas where the political groups have not defined their policy, then the discussions in committee take on a much greater importance than in the national parliaments. It may be added that the political groups are hindered in their work by the fact that they only organize a few study sessions each year and that the meetings they hold during the Strasbourg sittings are almost exclusively dedicated to problems which already appear on the day's agenda. To remedy this situation in some measure the Christian Democrats and Socialist members of a particular committee will sometimes caucus before the official meeting for a brief exchange of views, though this hardly permits a real confrontation of opinions.'[1]

A final factor which tends to lessen the vigour of party political debate in the Parliament is the technicality of much of the subject-matter which comes up for discussion. Despite the efforts of the party groups to 'politicize' these technical subjects, many of them—colouring matter in foodstuffs, for example—obstinately refuse to be 'politicized'. It is interesting that, largely as a result of Socialist pressure, the Parliament has now started to devote an occasional debate to issues of world politics not directly concerned with integration. Whether these debates will bring national view-points to the fore in lieu of party political ones remains to be seen.

There remains one relevant aspect of the work of the Parliament which has not yet been discussed: when the European Parliamentarians return to their national parliaments do they combine to act together either within their own party groups or in the parliaments as a whole? This is a subject on which several of the other chapters in this book have touched. It is clear that not only is there very little co-ordinated action by European parliamentarians in their national parliaments, but that there is, surprisingly, little effort made by the

---

[1] Neunreither, *op. cit.*, p. 7.

latter to debate, discuss and control the decisions which are being made in the Common Market. More is done in the *Bundestag* and the Dutch Second Chamber to discuss European problems than is done in the other parliaments, but even here the action does not seem very significant. The reason given by A. Spinelli for the 'strange negligence which prevails among the parliamentarians as soon as they leave Strasbourg' would seem to be convincing. 'When they return to their capitals', he writes, 'they are caught up in the discipline of their parties, both inside and outside of parliament, in other words, by the logic of the internal struggle for power. As European parliamentarians in their countries they would count only if they were protagonists in an incipient power struggle in Strasbourg, in which their party were involved and for which it would ask their support.'[1]

[1] Altiero Spinelli, *The Eurocrats, Conflict and Crisis in the European Community*, Johns Hopkins Press, 1966, p. 171.

CHAPTER 13

CONCLUSION

The late 1960s have not been an easy time for compiling an anthology on European Political Parties. Central to the consideration of each country's parties has been the suggestion that the future could in certain features be strikingly different from the past. The explosions in France in May 1968 even made some wonder if the historian of the future would regard the period in somewhat the same light as we now look back on 1848. In France, in particular, it is by no means clear what constitutes the party system: the traditional political formations, and some of the new ones, are alike in a state of total disarray, whilst the dominant Gaullists have an uncertain future now their hero has ceased to be President. In Germany, the apparent evolution towards a two-party system faces an insidious challenge from the growth of a neo-Nazi group. Belgium has almost split apart under the pressure of ethnic and linguistic divisions. The traditional pattern of Dutch politics has been eroded. In Italy, the political frustrations, partly created by a system which does so much to check them, have the potential for explosion. Even Northern Europe has not been immune to change. Political changes account for the overthrow of the Social Democrat dominated governments of Denmark and Norway, but if the new constellations acquire any permanence, they must in turn affect the systems in which they operate. In the United Kingdom, the possible threat to the traditional pattern arises from the Scottish and Welsh Nationalist movements. Finally, in Austria the end of the big coalition has ushered in a period of relative uncertainty, whilst even Switzerland has evinced discontent with the ruling coalition at the most recent election.

One should not be mesmerized by present discontents. A state of flux is a fairly natural state of affairs in politics, and crisis can even, as in the French Fourth Republic, be institutionalized. However, this last chapter is setting out on the ambitious task of gauging the patterns and trends in the evolution of political parties in Western Europe. Of necessity, this must be based on what has happened so far, with little account taken of speculations about sudden and decisive changes.

The starting point must be the democratic nature of government in these 15 countries. Freedom of political organization and the possibility of peaceful change are enshrined into the political system. It follows that such a system imposes certain roles on the parties, whose existence indeed it predicates. Whilst political power must inevitably be divided in any complex pluralistic society, the parties play a prime role in its allocation. Their actions ensure that peaceful change is a practical as well as theoretical possibility. A common type of representative government can be discerned in at least 13 of the 15 countries. The first step in the allocation of formal political power is the election of a parliamentary assembly. The government emerges because it can control majority support in the assembly. In theory the assembly always remains the power base for the government which is its formal institutional subordinate.

The two exceptions are France and Switzerland. In France, a Head of State is also directly elected and he has the formal power of designating a Prime Minister. Clearly, the latter needs to control majority support in the assembly, but his formal power base remains the President. The crucial stabilizing factor revolves around the fact that the President needs the support of a majority in the assembly. Should the evolution of French politics deprive him of this, the alternatives are the collapse of the constitution, or the replacement of the President by the Prime Minister as the real head of government. That such a development has not yet occurred arises from the unique contribution made by the UNR-UDR to French political life in providing for the first time a firm parliamentary base for government, albeit in a system which is part presidential.

In Switzerland, strong elements of direct democracy co-exist with a curious type of depoliticization of the political process. The parties' contest for political power is muted by a tacit agreement to allocate seats on the ruling Federal Executive to the major parties in a formula which the detailed results of individual elections for the National Council are unlikely to change.

The party systems here analysed can be classified in a variety of ways. For such an exercise to be possible, it must group together

501

certain countries between which there will be some dissimilarities. The justification for the classification here adopted is that it makes for greater understanding of European party systems: within each category the similarities are more significant than the differences.

Generally speaking the country-by-country chapters have indicated a threefold classification between bipolar, unipolar and multipolar party systems.[1] In bipolar systems the legislature and government are dominated by two parties. Neither can dominate to the exclusion of the other, although one may enjoy long periods of being the governing party. Nonetheless government will be dominated either by the two parties singly with at least the possibility of alternation, or by both together in a 'big coalition'. In a unipolar system, on the other hand, there is one large party which can be considered dominant. Occasionally, all its smaller rivals may coalesce to produce a temporary alternative government. However, the norm is for one party to be easily the largest legislative group and to dominate the executive. In multipolar systems, neither one nor two parties are dominant even to the extent of always emerging the strongest from succeeding elections. The legislature will contain more than two sizeable parties, with at least the mathematical possibility of a number of different government combinations.

Following the arguments of earlier chapters, it seems that the United Kingdom, Austria, Germany and Luxembourg should be considered bipolar. In Britain each party, and in Germany and Austria the largest party, has been able on occasion to rule alone. In Austria and Germany, too, the dominant parties have alternatively resorted to the 'big coalition' to dominate political

---

[1] The authors apologize for the term 'multipolar' which is strictly a contradiction in terms. 'Multipartism' would be more appropriate, but it was thought better to preserve linguistic symmetry between the three classifications. Professor Blondel in a paper entitled *Party Systems and Patterns of Government in Western Democracies*, presented at the 1967 Congress of the International Political Science Association, produces an additional category—the two-and-a-half party system. He argues that a three-party system is inherently unstable, and in his special category he places Germany, Belgium and Ireland. His major argument is that in these three countries the difference between the two major parties over a long period is much greater than the difference in Austria or the United Kingdom. The weakness of this classification seems to be that the third party in Germany is little stronger than its British counterpart. Developments in Belgium since the paper was written have, of course, strengthened the 'half' party. Perhaps the classification is most suitable for Ireland.

power. Finally, on past patterns it is possible in Austria, and even in Germany, for the lesser of the two parties to aspire one day to form a government alone.

The category of unipolar countries is at present the largest, including Norway, Sweden, Denmark, Iceland, Italy and possibly Fifth Republic France. Developments in Scandinavia could affect several countries in this category. The decline of the Social Democrats in Denmark could ultimately shift that country to the multipolar group, whilst any real coalescence by the bourgeois parties in Norway might even one day bring about the beginning of a two-party system. The inclusion of Iceland in this category at all is also open to some controversy. However, in all six cases one party is always easily the largest in the legislature and is always, or nearly always, in office alone or with some smaller partners. Successful combinations of the other parties against the dominant one are possible but only on a temporary basis. If they threaten to become more than temporary, then the leading party can hardly be considered dominant and its minor rivals would be acting as one block: the unipolar classification would require to be moderated.

Ireland fits neatly into neither of the categories already discussed. In many cases Irish politics are maverick to Western Europe and this is no exception. There are two large and dominant parties, but one is always very considerably the bigger. Interestingly, as in Britain the 'big coalition' is not a favoured expedient.

The four remaining countries—Belgium, the Netherlands, Switzerland and Finland—emerge as multipolar, although during the 1950s the first two showed certain bipolar trends. Into the multipolar category would also fit Fourth Republic France.

So far this has mostly been generalization. However, some characteristics can be found for the identification of these different systems. In the bipolar systems, the two major parties normally win at least 80 per cent of the popular vote and take 85 per cent of the parliamentary seats.[1] Neither party can consistently win more than 50 per cent of the popular vote and each always wins a minimum of 35 per cent. In a unipolar system, the dominant party normally

---

[1] Luxembourg seems properly to fall in the bipolar category, although on average the two largest parties do not attain quite the degree of dominance here indicated. There seems to be a trend to multipolarity at every second general election with a move back at the others.

holds about 40 per cent of votes and seats whilst no other can aspire to even 30 per cent. It follows that the two largest parties together are unable to win 70 per cent of votes and seats. Finally, multipolar systems are characterized by the fact that no party can regularly hold more than one-third of votes and seats. A certain tendency may also be discerned for the three largest parties to be roughly equal in size.[1] To balance these considerations, it might also be considered useful to attempt the establishment of further criteria with relation to participation in government. The difficulty of this task emerges quite clearly from the work of Professor Blondel,[2] who has constructed an ingenious index of party representation in government. Two distorting factors are immediately apparent and they make it impossible to draw conclusions about systems from this kind of index alone. In the first place, in a two-party system one may always be the government. There is no contradiction between this state of affairs and the earlier assertion that a condition for a two-party system is that both can aspire to control the government. Thus since 1950 Australia, clearly a two-party system, has been governed by the Liberal and Country Party (correctly looked on as one party) solely and constantly. In no West European unipolar system has the dominant party such a governmental record. Again, since 1957 Germany has appeared bipolar from almost every point of view and certainly party strengths in the legislature reflect this. However, using a Blondel-type index brought up-to-date, the Christian Democrats have a 67 per cent participation in government over this period, against 12 per cent for the Social Democrats, whilst the Free Democrats also have 12 per cent. The other distorting factor arises in a multipolar system where it is deemed desirable to keep certain parties out of office. Thus in Fourth Republic France the Communists were usually the largest party in the legislature, but their total participation in government was only 2 per cent.

It follows that generalizations about participation in government designed to help in the recognition of the party system operating in a particular country would be dangerous. In considering these countries, the electoral strengths of the parties can be regarded

[1] In the Netherlands, this kind of symmetry might also appear if there were only one Protestant party.

[2] Blondel, *op. cit.* All those working in this field should be grateful for this pioneering work.

as criteria for the systems; government participation can be cited only as illustration.

About the bipolar category there is least doubt. The United Kingdom and Austria are virtually perfect examples. In the UK the two major parties have at the last three elections taken 87 per cent of the votes and 98 per cent of the seats. In Austria the comparable statistics are 89 per cent and 95 per cent. In no case in either country has a major party won more than 50 per cent of the popular vote or fallen below 42 per cent. On the governmental side, the UK is divided practically equally since the war between the two major parties. In Austria a 'big coalition' divided government participation equally until 1966, since when there has been single party rule.

Germany is a less perfect example of bipolarization and some would not even include it in this category. However, the share of votes taken by the two largest parties has continually increased and in the last three elections they have taken over 80 per cent of the vote and 85 per cent of the seats. One party has always been the bigger, once even taking an overall majority of votes. However, the share going to the smaller of the two has increased steadily to 39 per cent. Until 1966 the Social Democrats were excluded from government, and participation since then has been through a 'big coalition'. Germany's party system has clearly been in a state of continuing development. Its citation as bipolar can be challenged not so much on arguments about the real meaning of what has happened, but rather through speculation about the future.

In none of the six countries labelled unipolar can the two largest parties jointly aspire to win 70 per cent of votes and seats—in contrast to the figures in excess of 80 per cent recorded for the three major bipolar countries. One-party domination emerges most clearly, in the statistical sense, in Sweden and Norway. In Sweden the Social Democrats regularly hold over 46 per cent of votes and seats with no other party ever able to exceed 25 per cent in either category. They have never been excluded from the government since the war and for all but six years have monopolized all positions. The Norwegian Labour Party achieved even more until 1965, with total monopoly of the government over this period. Since then, the other parties have aligned to keep it for the present out of office. However, it remains dominant, always holding at least 43 per cent of the votes and 45 per cent of the seats. In 1965 its nearest rival barely exceeded 20 per cent in the two categories.

The position in the other two Scandinavian countries labelled unipolar is rather different. In Denmark the dominant Social Democrats seem to be in decline. At the last three elections their average of votes and seats has been only a fraction under 40 per cent but on the most recent occasion they were well below this figure. A further erosion in support would shift Denmark to the multipolar category. The Social Democrats have still been far and away the leading government party, only excluded for three years in the early 1950s and since the 1967 election. Interestingly their record of participation is just a little better than that of the Christian Democrats in Germany. In Iceland, by way of contrast, the position and strength of the dominant Independence Party remain stable, although at a lower level than the leading parties in Sweden and Norway. It averages marginally less than 40 per cent of votes and seats, whilst the next party tends to take about 28 per cent of votes and 30 per cent of seats. It is almost permanently in the government, but has not normally taken the same share of seats as Scandinavia's other dominant parties.

The remaining two countries in this group are Italy and, during the Fifth Republic, France. The Italian Christian Democrats' electoral record is virtually identical to that of the Icelandic Independence Party, averaging about 40 per cent of votes and seats, whilst their Communist rivals take about 28 per cent of votes and 30 per cent of seats. However, the tacit agreement since 1947 by all the other parties to exclude the Communists from government has inevitably meant that the Christian Democrats have a participation record only exceeded by the dominant parties in Sweden and Norway. In view of the change in French politics since the beginning of the Fifth Republic, it is justifiable to consider separately France's two postwar political regimes. The electoral system since 1958 has produced more distortions in the pattern of representation than has been the case in any other country. However, even on the criterion of popular vote, the Gaullists can claim to be dominant. Averages may be a little misleading in view of the state of flux in the system and few conclusions about the future can be drawn. At the 1968 general election the Gaullists took 43 per cent of the first ballot vote and 70 per cent of the seats. The Communists took 23 per cent of the first ballot vote, whilst the second biggest parliamentary force, the Federation of the Left, holds only 15 per cent of the seats.[1] In governmental terms, there are difficulties of classification partly because deputies cannot be ministers and some of the latter come directly from the civil service. In general terms, the Gaullists gave a small share of government participation to some of the old parties until 1962 since when their monopoly has been virtually complete.

It has already been suggested that Ireland cannot be fitted into either of these two categories and electoral statistics justify this assertion. Fianna Fail always wins well over 40 per cent of votes and seats, but the second party is normally in the range 30–35 per cent. The largest party thus has a more serious rival than any dominant party in avowedly unipolar systems. On the other hand, unlike the situation in Germany the second party is not increasing in size, whilst the traditional third party is very gradually increasing.[2] In terms of government, Fianna Fail has enjoyed a complete monopoly since the war for all but six years when a combination of all other groups excluded it. Their record as a result is almost the same as that of the Italian Christian Democrats.

One of the countries presently multipolar—Belgium—showed many signs during the 1950s of moving towards bipolarism. During three general elections in that period, the two major parties averaged 80 per cent of votes and 87 per cent of seats. Recent developments have weakened the internal cohesion of the major parties and helped to erode their support in favour of the Liberal, Flemish and Franco-phone parties. In size the Liberals are now almost as important as the major parties. In terms of governmental participation the Christian Social Party has been easily the most important. Since 1947, the Liberals opted only once for the Socialist coalition to exclude the other major party. The political results, not least for the Liberals, made it improbable that the experiment would be repeated very soon. In the Netherlands, also, two parties have been con-sistently considerably larger than any rival. A unified Protestant

[1] The Giscardiens are here included with the Gaullists, although this is perhaps not strictly accurate. Taken separately they are the second largest parliamentary force.

[2] Fine Gael's best postwar result was 34 per cent in 1969, and Labour's 17 per cent.

Party might, though, have brought about changes. Neither of the major parties could win more than 35 per cent of votes and seats and recent developments, particularly the formation of new parties, have changed the position. In 1967 the two biggest parties won only about 25 per cent each of the votes and seats. Three medium-sized parties took over three-quarters of the rest, but since at least three other groups won some representation, the Netherlands could claim now to have more significant parties than any other of these countries. Participation in government fairly accurately reflects general political strength, save for a certain amount of 'ganging up' against the Labour Party.

It is appropriate though to talk of three-party domination in the other multipolar countries—Switzerland and Finland. These two countries have always fallen clearly into this category: in each case three parties take about one-quarter of votes and seats apiece, whilst the fourth largest takes rather more than half of the remainder. Participation in government is organized in Switzerland through an inter-party pact, although the details can occasionally be modified. In fact, of the three major parties, the Socialists have had a little less than an equal share in participation in government owing to their exclusion by agreement between the other three important parties during the period 1953–59. Since then the agreement has resulted in a share of government participation between the four chief parties which reflects their political strength virtually exactly. The minor parties are of course totally excluded under this arrangement. In Finland, the Agrarian Party, through their pivotal position, have played the leading role in government, rather as did the Radicals in the French Third Republic. The Communists, who are the fourth largest party, have for most of the postwar period been excluded from government, whilst over the whole period the Socialists have taken second position for government participation.

Finally, it is worth recalling that during the Fourth Republic, France, too, was multipolar and there is a possibility of reversion to this state post-de Gaulle. During the Fourth Republic, no party ever won 30 per cent of votes or seats. At the last election in 1956 the Communists took just over 25 per cent of the votes whilst three other groups each won about 15 per cent. As mentioned earlier, the Communists were normally the largest party, but played virtually no role in government. The biggest roles were taken by the Radicals, Independents and MRP.[1]

It is sometimes erroneously supposed that uni- and multipolar systems are bound to be unstable in comparison with countries in the bipolar category. Much must depend on the establishment of broadly acceptable criteria for measuring stability. Blondel argues that in general 'stability cannot be measured directly in the context of Western democracies'.[2] Later on, he considers the question of the duration of governments and tends to equate this with stability. He considers as one government, any administration 'headed by the same Prime Minister' and 'relying on the support of the same party or parties in the Chamber'. This is a fairly traditional Anglo-Saxon approach, and may give an artificial picture. It can be argued that Macmillan's 1962 purge represented as sweeping a change for Britain as the replacement of Pleven by Faure in France in 1952. However, in neither case did the party composition of the government alter. There seems some justification then for constructing an index of stability based on the number of changes in the party composition of government. Operational yardsticks of change seem to necessitate that one or more major parties are either brought into, or excluded from, the government. However, it is clearly a major stabilizing factor when one party plays a dominant role in government, both before and after the change. Table 1 is an attempt to establish a highly impressionistic, and even subjective, rank order of stability.[3] Table 1 has no scientific pretensions. Sometimes it is not clear when a party change has taken place. This was often the case in Fourth Republic France.[4] However, the table does enable

---

[1] MRP had, perhaps, marginally the greatest participation. Blondel's table, *op. cit.*, is misleading, since this party was excluded from the Mendès-France government.

[2] Blondel, *op. cit.*

[3] This has been done initially by plotting the position of each country on a graph. One point is given for each change in government, as defined above, but where one party holds more than 60 per cent of government posts before and after the change, only one half point is given.

[4] If one is considering stability as the absence of real change in the political constellation of government, then the factors of pure chaos in the French system like the following should perhaps strictly be ignored: for ten days in July 1950 a French government existed without the SFIO for the first time since the war; then the Socialists returned. If this were counted as two changes of government for the purpose of Table I, then the position of the Fourth Republic would be rather less stable, but the rank order would be unchanged.

TABLE I

Types of Party system measured against composition of government stability in party, 1949–68

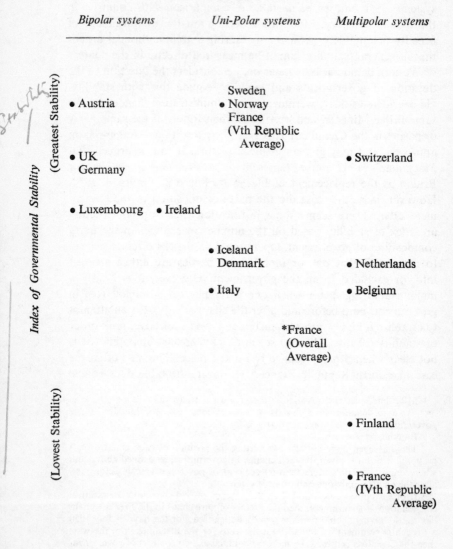

	Bipolar systems	Uni-Polar systems	Multipolar systems
(Greatest Stability)	● Austria	Sweden ● Norway France (Vth Republic Average)	
	● UK Germany		● Switzerland
	● Luxembourg ● Ireland		
		● Iceland Denmark	● Netherlands
		● Italy	● Belgium
		*France (Overall Average)	
			● Finland
(Lowest Stability)			● France (IVth Republic Average)

Index of Governmental Stability

510

useful comparisons to be made between the sixteen countries listed.[1]

Six groupings can be discerned, and it may be immediately noted that only one bipolar system features in the most stable of these. Unipolar systems feature amongst the most and least stable. Multipolar systems are not necessarily always the least stable. Certainly, amongst multipolar systems, Switzerland is exceptional through its continued use of a collegiate system. It may be worth pointing out that the problems facing Belgium in the future may be not dissimilar from those which Switzerland has been able to overcome in part at least through the use of such a system. It may not be too fanciful to detect in the most recent Belgian governmental compromise a slight move in this direction.

Amongst bipolar countries, stability will also be conditioned by the keenness of the battle for supremacy between the two major parties. Certain unipolar countries, in effect, operate in a similar way, for the only alternative to the dominant party is a coalition of all the others. This is possible only if the dominant party is on one side of the political spectrum as in Scandinavia and possibly the Fifth Republic. In Italy the Christian Democrats are the central party in the political spectrum and could hardly be excluded from office. They have a wide choice of political allies, and this fact conditions the number of changes. However, use of this refined gauge for stability takes into account the continuing governmental role of the Christian Democrats.[2]

Before leaving these considerations two further points should be noted. This kind of gauge of stability clearly cannot take full account of major political crises as in Belgium and France in 1968 which leave the constellation of government virtually unchanged. Finally, stability is not necessarily always a virtue. Lack of change can

[1] France is listed twice because of the total change in political system resulting from the change in Republic. This could give a misleading impression since the periods are thus very short. In the period since 1959, Iceland has been even more stable than the Fifth Republic.

[2] It is interesting to compare the rank order of countries on this gauge of stability with a rank order in the Blondel sense of duration of government. The latter table ranks Austria sixth, whilst the former takes full account of her total political ossification until 1966. The average duration of Italian governments is about the same as in Finland. This gauge of stability takes full account of the continuing dominating role of one party.

produce political frustration. This may be so where one party always dominates or where multipolarity prevents real change by constantly producing relatively broad coalitions. This may be an advantage for bipolarity where it is working sufficiently well to produce alternation in government by the two major parties.

A major factor in the foregoing which has not yet been analysed relates to the electoral system. In all countries, a crucial function of parties is to catalyse and reflect public opinion. The manner in which this task is carried out will be conditioned by the electoral system. De Gaulle's complaint that the Assembly resembled France as in a cracked mirror led to his advocacy of the referendum and direct election of the President. At the same time, some in France have admired the British electoral system which, they feel, ensures a bipolarism and one-party government[1]. Of necessity the electoral system cannot be considered the only factor influencing this. Indeed, the electoral system is as much the product as the cause of the party system.

Three crucial variables delineate the electoral systems operated in these countries. The first concerns the size of constituency. The United Kingdom, Germany and France alone make use of single-member constituencies. The other countries all have multi-member constituencies. The second variable concerns the degree of proportionality in the electoral system. In the 12 countries operating multi-member constituencies, the seats within that unit will be distributed by one or other of the proportional methods. This is in contrast to the technique adopted in some French local elections where the winning list takes all the seats. However, proportionality may not mean very much where the units are small. One suggestion is that there must be at least five members per constituency for proportionality to work, i.e. to ensure that the distribution of seats on a national basis reflects accurately the distribution of votes. Several Swiss cantons are so small that they only have one or two members, so that proportional representation is a little artificial. The technique of making the whole country one constituency to return all the members would ensure perfect proportionality. Outside Europe, this has been adopted in Israel. The nearest European echo is in Germany where a second category of Assembly membership

---

[1] These admirers include certain political scientists like Professor Duverger.

allocates seats to ensure that the overall result is in conformity with the distribution of the popular vote. This system of 'remainder seats' has also been adopted, if not quite so sweepingly, in Austria, Belgium, Iceland, Italy, and the Netherlands, whilst Denmark distributes such seats on a regional rather than national basis. Interestingly, all these countries save Iceland also use certain rules for distributing these non-constituency seats to safeguard against the proliferation of small parties and groups.

The third variable relates to the degree of choice given to the electorate to choose the candidate. At one extreme, in the United Kingdom and Germany, party control is complete. The parties designate candidates for the constituencies and control the national list in Germany. There are no preferential votes. In all the other countries save France and Ireland, the parties compile lists for use in multi-member constituencies and electors may have certain, if limited, rights to change the order of candidates. In France and Ireland a different principle is introduced—that of preference. By different mechanisms, the voter is given an opportunity of giving his second choice of representative on the assumption that his first choice cannot win. This deals with the problem of wasted votes in a rather different manner to that embodied in the proportional principle. In Ireland the single transferable vote and in France the second ballot alike give the voter a chance to indicate his second choice. In Ireland, though, the voter also gives his third, fourth and fifth choice. The mixture of proportionality and preference voting on the Irish pattern ensures that only a very small number of votes do not help to elect a representative whose name and identity may be clearly known within his constituency. Table II attempts to tabulate the various systems.

Relations between electoral and party systems emerge as rather less close and definite than is sometimes thought to be the case. The proportional method is usually considered likely to co-exist with multipolar or unipolar systems. However, two of the bipolar countries employ electoral systems with a considerable degree of proportionality. Ireland has moved a long way towards bipolarity, employing a proportional and preferential system. It can be argued, of course, that both Austria and Germany discriminate against the smaller parties in the allocation of 'remainder' seats. Too much should not be concluded from this. Denmark discriminates against small groups in a much milder way. If that country adopted the more stringent German rules, then, other things being equal, it would still have five parliamentary parties. In any event, the institution of 'remainder' seats by helping smaller parties not to waste votes might seem to make for a certain amount of fractionization. However, amongst countries using multimember constituencies inside which the seats are distributed proportionally, the average number of parties is between five and six, whether or not a system of 'remainder' seats is used. Of the two countries which make no concessions to proportionality, the United Kingdom is bipolar, but no more so than

TABLE II

Nature of European Electoral Systems

	Single-member constituency Without preferential voting	*Single-member constituency Two ballots*	*Multi-member constituency Limited or no preferential voting*	*Multi-member constituency Full preferential voting*
Non-proportional	UK	France (Fifth Republic)		
Proportionality inside constituencies			Finland Sweden Norway Switzerland France (Fourth Republic) Luxembourg	Ireland
Use of remainder seats to achieve overall proportionality	Germany		Austria Belgium Denmark Iceland Italy Netherlands *	

* A constitutional reform will place Sweden in this category after 1971.

Austria. The French two ballot system gives preferentiality which may under certain circumstances have similar results to proportionality. Clearly, this has not been the case in the Fifth Republic. However, the political realignment seems to owe little to the system of Assembly election, which was used for much of the Third Republic when there was a multipolar party system. One can probably only conclude that there is no acceptable proof of a close and necessary relationship between party and electoral system. Each is the result of the configuration and history of politics.

Another set of considerations link the electoral system to the nature of the parties operating within its context. Whilst the individual chapters of this book have revealed certain differences between parties in different countries, political culture rather than the electoral system seems to be the cause of both the strength and the nature of party organization.[1]

It now seems appropriate to turn to the individual parties, first to classify them and then to try to establish certain characteristics which have emerged as being peculiarly important. Some parties are small and others ephemeral. The French Poujadists, after polling well in 1956, sank without trace. The independent Left in France—neither Communist nor Socialist—has a continuing existence, and probably an importance disproportionate to the number of its supporters. The Swiss *Landesring* remains a protest party, but is clearly not simply ephemeral. Democrats 66 in the Netherlands are difficult to classify and are, at this stage, unpredictable. Welsh and Scottish Nationalism in the United Kingdom have not, as yet, been able to prove substantial strength at a general election, although many expect them to do this in 1970 or 1971. Another set of problems relates to parties emerging as a result of alliances or splits. In the case of mergers, should the new alliance or the constituent units or both be counted? These considerations apply particularly strongly in France and also in Italy.

Table III is based on the earlier chapters and should be treated as a general guide to the classification of parties. It lists parties which obtained a minimum of 3 per cent popular support at the most recent national election. An indication is also given in the case of

[1] Professor Duverger in *Political Parties*, 2nd English Edition, Methuen, London, 1959, delves extensively into all questions regarding relationship of electoral system to the political parties.

TABLE III: *Classification of Political Parties*

	Communist	Left Socialist	Social Democrat	Liberal	Agrarian	Christian	Conservative	Protest	Ethnic minority	Extreme Right
U.K.			Labour	Liberal			Conservative			
Austria			Socialist	Free			People's			
Germany			Social Democrats	Free Democrats			Christian Democrats			
Ireland			Labour		Fianna Fáil?		Fine Gael?			
Norway		Socialist People's	Labour	Left	Centre	Christian People	Right			
Sweden	Communist		Social Democrat	Liberal	Centre		Right			
Iceland	People's		Social Democrat		Progressives		Independence Party			
Denmark		Socialist People's	Social Democrat	Radical Left Liberal	Left		Conservative People's			
Italy	Communist	Independent Socialist	United Socialist			Christian Democrat				Social Movement
France Pre-1962			Socialist	Radical*	Peasants ←→	Christian Democrats ←→	Gaullists →Independents			
France 1968	Communist	Unified Socialist	Federation of the Left		Democratic Centre	Democratic Centre	Gaullists and Independent Republicans			
Finland	Communist		Social Democrat	Liberal	Centre		Conservative		Swedish People	
Belgium	Communist		Socialist	Liberty		Social Christian			French Front Flemish People	
Netherlands	Communist	Pacifist Socialist	Labour	Freedom	Farmers	Catholic Anti-Revolutionary Christian Historical Catholic		Democrats 66		
Switzerland			Social Democrat	Radical	Peasant			Landesring		
Luxembourg	Communist		Socialist	Liberal		Christian Social				

←→ Signifies parties in alliance,   * Some of the 1962 Radicals joined the Federation of the Left and some the Democratic Centre.

France, of the traditional formations before the current process of realignment.

One variety of party exists in a clearly recognizable, and very broadly similar, form in all countries: the Social Democratic. The party is dominant in Denmark, Norway and Sweden. In these countries and also in Austria and the United Kingdom it can normally count on the support of two-fifths of the electorate. In Germany the figure is rather below this. The Social Democratic party is one of the two leading parties in eleven countries—the six already mentioned, plus Finland, Switzerland, Belgium, Luxembourg and the Netherlands where its support varies between one-quarter and one-third of the electorate. The four weakest Social Democratic parties are in Italy, France, Iceland and Ireland. Significantly, three of these are amongst the six countries where there are other strong left wing parties. Communist parties appear on this table in seven countries, but in Sweden, Belgium and the Netherlands they have little strength. The result is an inverse and almost exact correlation between Communist strength and Social Democratic weakness. Left-wing Socialist parties, independent of Communists and Social Democrats alike, have achieved little success, even in Denmark and Norway where there is no formal competition from the Communists. Only in Italy has a norm of three sizeable Socialist parties been established. Until the recent realignment the Social Democrat group was easily the weakest. Now the new left-wing Socialists have a strength about that of the former Social Democrats and Nenni's united Socialists (here considered as the Social Democratic party) are about the equal of his former left-wing party. In France, the PSU has still not really established itself as a strong political force and any assessment of the strength of social democracy is clouded by confusion as to the future of the Federation of the Left and the part actually played in it by the Radicals.

The majority of Social Democratic parties owe some part of their origin to Socialist, although not necessarily always or exclusively Marxist, ideology. The most rigid parties in doctrinaire terms were once the German and Austrian Social Democrats, whilst the French and North Europeans could draw on their own native traditions and thinkers. In some cases Communist movements split away from the Social Democrats, but this did not always have an immediate impact on the latter in terms of making them less ideological and

517

more pragmatic. This latter development seems to have taken place simultaneously with the possibility of acquiring or sharing political power. Today, patterns of behaviour amongst Social Democratic parties in the 14 countries do not vary greatly and most have openly eschewed outright Socialism. Not all of them even pay the lip service of the British Labour Party to nationalization of the means of production. In principle, Social Democratic parties favour economic planning without possessing any clear monopoly in its advocacy. Extension of social services and a certain amount of income redistribution seem also to be characteristic. In foreign policy some criticism of alignment with the United States may be voiced by Social Democratic parties. In Germany, the Social Democrats have taken the lead in overtures to the East. On the other hand, the French SFIO has been left well behind by the Gaullists in detente policies. The Social Democratic parties of the EEC countries have also, after a hesitant start in Germany, played an important role in furthering integration. These parties often consider themselves as particular champions of the extension of the European idea, through some kind of political community as well as the admission of further members to the existing community.

West European Communist parties are theoretically bound to Marxist ideology, without a strategy of revolution to achieve it. The events of May 1968 made this clear in France and it is arguable that the most burning ambition of the French and Italian Communist parties is to be awarded a share of political power. Since these parties represent the working class in a manner similar to that of Social Democratic parties in other countries, they naturally advocate extension of workers' rights and other planks of traditional Socialist policy. The striking difference from the Social Democrats is perhaps in the sphere of foreign policy. Despite destalinization, there remains a tendency in West European Communist parties to echo fairly faithfully the Moscow line in international matters. The first major exception to this was the refusal by all except the Luxembourg party to endorse the invasion of Czechoslovakia.

Table III seems to suggest that another category of party—the Liberal—is also practically universal. Whilst, however, parties calling themselves 'Liberal' or claiming to follow that tradition exist everywhere save in Ireland, there is not the same comparability as among the Social Democrats. Outside Scandinavia and the United

Kingdom, Liberal parties frequently developed as a riposte to Church influence. Free enterprise played some part in these parties' thinking, and lately they came to be rather anti-Socialist. In Germany, Italy and Austria, these parties are the home of the anti-dirigiste Right. In France, and to a limited extent in Switzerland, the anti-clerical tradition of the Radicals continues, hence the claim to be on the left of the political spectrum. Only in the UK and sometimes in Scandinavia have Liberal parties fought for progressive policies whilst differing from the Social Democrats in being less tied to the aspirations of Trade Unions. Few of these parties can count on much popular support, although sometimes they acquire extra influence through being in a pivotal position in the political spectrum. In Switzerland, the Radicals are one of the three major parties, whilst the Swedish Liberals actually rank a rather poor second to the Social Democrats. Elsewhere only the Belgian and Dutch Liberals and the Danish Radical Left can count on more than 10 per cent support.

Save in the United Kingdom and Denmark, Liberal parties seem to find it more natural to align with parties other than Socialist parties. Despite their historic importance, however, Liberal parties, as has been shown, have rarely been able to establish themselves as the leading non-Socialist group. Obviously the terms 'right' and 'left' wing beg certain questions, but with reservations they can be used as a help to understanding the political contest in most of these countries. Apart from the Liberals, the moderate right wing in West European countries seems to be made up of broadly three types of party: Agrarian, Christian and General Conservative. Lack of unity may be indicated by the fact that whilst the Social Democrats have virtually monopolized the Socialist vote in ten countries, only five countries have just one moderate right-wing party and even they face competition from Liberal parties. Four countries have three sizeable moderate right-wing groups.

Unity has been preserved in the UK, Austria, Germany, Italy, Luxembourg and, so far, in Belgium. With all save the British Conservatives, the Christian origin is clearly recognized. The Italian Christian Democrats have stuck most closely to their clerical origin and, in one of Europe's most intensely Catholic countries, this has been no bar to their mobilization of the bulk of the non-Socialist vote. With almost equal inevitability in a country divided between Catholics

519

and Protestants, the German Christian Democrats have moved furthest to becoming a more general Conservative party. In any case, in these five countries the moderate right wing party is normally the biggest, and, save recently in Belgium, usually wins over 40 per cent support. The other equally powerful party is the French UDR. Although this party still has rivals on the moderate right, in the 1968 Election it mobilized the bulk of this electorate, uniting former supporters of the Christian Democrats, the Independents and the Peasants. But the continued existence of the latter groups in a new alignment and the emergence of the Giscardiens cast doubts over the future unity of the moderate right when it no longer has a charismatic leader.

Agrarian parties seem to be a particularly Scandinavian phenomenon, although they exist also in Switzerland and still perhaps in France. In Scandinavia these parties, representing farming interests, have specially close links with the Liberal centre, espousing independence of both Trade Unions and big business. In Finland, Iceland and Denmark the party ranks second.

Religious based parties seem to be more normal in Catholic than Protestant countries. Protestant parties exist only in the Netherlands, Norway and, tenuously, in Sweden. Apart from those already mentioned, the Swiss Catholics are one of the big three, whilst the Dutch Catholics are usually narrowly the largest party. The Netherlands is another country religiously divided, but the emergence of any single Christian Democratic party can hardly be foreseen: there are still two Protestant parties. Finally, the Scandinavian countries have general Conservative parties, with, unlike their British counterpart, no monopoly of the moderate right wing. This leaves only the Irish parties which are not really classifiable, although Fianna Fail seem nearer to the Agrarian pattern and Fine Gael to the Conservative.

It is harder to deal with the philosophy and ideology of such a disparate set of parties than it is with the Social Democrats. Some indication has already been given of the position of Agrarian groups, so that the outstanding question relates to the difference between Conservative and Christian Democrat groups. In each case the party in question is likely to preserve links with the business community, who see them as a bastion against Socialism. However, planning has been espoused by several of the Christian Democrat parties, with the Germans perhaps the main exception. The continuation, though, of Christian parties seems normally to accompany continuing controversy over the role of the Church and normally the existence of an anti-clerical group. Since Radical anti-clericalism was inherited by many Socialist parties, political battle-lines obviously take account of the Church question, and this remains a source of support for non-Socialist parties.

The most unifying ideological factor for all these parties remains anti-Communism, and this has been a crucial factor in their espousal of European integration. The Gaullists substitute alignment for integration, but the more important difference is that this group is strongly anti-American and would like to re-align Europe as a third force, perhaps ultimately with the political power to persuade the Russians to withdraw their military presence from Eastern Europe.

The extreme right-wing category is very small. Attempts to base a party on this section in France have failed, whilst the German NPD have yet to prove themselves at a general election. The Italian Neo-Fascists maintain a tenuous existence.

Europe's other parties can be divided into two categories: those representing an ethnic minority, or the extreme wing of an ethnic majority, and those embodying general protest. In the former category are the two parties representing the ethnic communities of Belgium—the Volksunie and the Francophone parties—and also the Swedish People's party of Finland and the Scottish and Welsh Nationalists. The two protest parties currently figuring in the table are the Landesring and Democrats 66. Through the former the Swiss have even managed to institutionalize protest, but the future of the latter, as already mentioned, remains obscure.

Before an attempt is made to speculate on the possible alignment of political parties if a united Europe ultimately emerges, it would first be appropriate to look a little more closely at some points of organizational detail. It is probably true to say that the West European political party has gradually evolved something approaching a common structure. All parties today make some provision for a mass membership paying a more or less nominal subscription for the privilege of belonging, although the importance placed on this varies. Social Democratic parties are in form, and usually origin, mass parties. The membership are the party, and they control it through various representative forms which theoretically take the major policy and administrative decisions. In practice, though, much of this is more apparent than real. In several of the preceding chapters it has been indicated that where a party constitution reserves the prime role for a Congress, this is only one factor conditioning the power structure. This is perhaps particularly the case where non-Socialist parties have imitated the characteristic organization of the left: Italian and German Christian Democrats and most Scandinavian parties. Amongst Social Democratic parties, representative organs seem to play a more prominent role in Scandinavia than elsewhere. On the other hand, Congress seems to be a more important power base inside the French SFIO than it is in the British Labour Party.

At one time old-fashioned parties of the caucus type, with leadership from a collection of notables, was more characteristic of the right wing in politics. This was always the case with French Conservatism, whilst their British counterparts have evolved a mixed system. The British party has a separate mass membership section, autonomous in its own affairs but with no formal control over the whole party. The UDR in France has placed hardly any emphasis on a mass membership and linked the caucus tradition to the personality of an almost Biblical leader. The rules of the Dutch Catholic Party too make it quite clear that Congress has no decision-making power and may only discuss party policy.

Where democracy is the form of government, parties play a prime role as the agents for political discourse. They are the means by which many people not closely bound up with the machinery of government can feel they are helping to shape political events. The requirements of the system probably force all parties to pay a certain amount of attention to internal structure and to the needs of members, as well as party workers. However, in very few parties indeed can the members be said to control what is being done in their name.

Some parties endeavour to be much more than machines for winning elections. They appear to aim at attempting to make of themselves a way of life for members: a 'world' in the Belgian term. Activities connected with the party would ideally fill all the life of the member and this, in turn, would help to stratify the pattern of politics and society. This was a traditional pattern in both Germany and Austria—the fact that the conflicts thus engendered helped in each case to weaken the first republic shows the dangers of this 'lager' mentality. Today, the phenomenon persists in a milder form in Austria, Italy, the Netherlands and Belgium, and also in certain areas and parties in Germany and Switzerland. Generally Socialist and religious parties have made greater use of this than Liberal and other right-wing groups. Trade Unions and the church act as re-inforcements to the tendency.

A dominant theme throughout the individual chapters has centered on the relations between parliamentary and party leaders. Arrangements to lessen the tension and friction have usually led to the parliamentary leadership coming to dominate the party, or at least being able to do as it pleases. There is a certain inevitability to this trend when parliamentary leaders are placed in a much better position to exploit the mass media than will be the relatively obscure secretary or chairman of a party organization who has to eschew the limelight. Perhaps it is a realization of the potency of the mass media which has led Communist leaders to enter parliament even though these parties have been those most fully to maintain the subordinate status of the parliamentary group. If one had to generalize, it would probably be broadly accurate to say that the further right one moves in the political spectrum, the greater the concentration of power in the parliamentary wing. This is, however, only a rough guide. The power relationship is peculiarly difficult to assess when, as is frequently the case in Scandinavia, the parliamentary and party leadership is formally amalgamated. On the one hand the Belgian Social Christian Party has a divided leadership, and the outside party has occasionally been able to dictate to the parliamentary group on the tactics it ought to follow. On the other hand in the British Labour Party the parliamentary group is formally subservient but in practice the most powerful wing of the party.

Evidently, more than one question must be considered—there is the relationship of parliamentary to non-parliamentary leaders, and also the relationship of rank and file members to all categories of leaders. Certainly, it cannot be said of any major party that its members control it save in the most vague and general sense that the leaders must engender some support amongst their followers. It is not, though, easy to generalize about the degree of oligarchy which exists in political parties today. A crucial aspect relates to the ease with which the party machine can control who enters parliament.

This links back to a question already posed. Clearly, the party machine gains in strength where there are few political parties which together wield a near monopoly of political power. Oligarchical tendencies are, not surprisingly, evident in the UK and, perhaps even more so, in Germany. The Dutch Catholic Party has traditionally operated in the same kind of way, but recently changed political circumstances have weakened organizational authority. In France, the SFIO's rules about the length of party service before possible adoption as a candidate are an attempt at party control, but the general political environment does not work in this direction. Not surprisingly, Communist parties are the most oligarchic of all with virtually complete control by the machine. The French RPF operated for some time in a similar way.

Party leaderships are concerned not only with problems of the power of sections of their own organization and the relationship of parliamentary to mass wings of the group. Many parties have close links with outside groups who supply funds and support. In Continental Liberal parties and the British Conservative Party, business interests play an important role. This is probably almost equally true with the German Christian Democrats. The Church continues to play some role in the more formally Catholic parties, whilst Trade Union influence and authority are considerable in the various Social Democrat parties. The attitudes of big union leaders are certainly more important to the British Labour leadership than the outcome of a particular vote at a party conference. Even with Communist parties, pressures from outside cannot be ignored. The relationship between the French Communist Party and the CGT certainly does not work in only one direction.

Turning to finance, there are country and party differences. Three countries—Germany, Finland, and Sweden—give state subsidies to parties proportionally according to political strength. At a local level, Austria is moving somewhat hesitantly in the same direction, and the idea is being considered in Norway. Other countries grant parties a modicum of help through such devices as free radio and television time. In France, though, the government machine has undoubtedly tended to be, to a large extent, at the disposal of the parties in power. This tendency has been much exacerbated, although not created, by the Fifth Republic. At the same time, the demarcation between legitimate trading and commercial interests of parties and

524

outright corruption may be tenuous, particularly in Italy where patronage at local and national level is more blatant than in the other countries.

Outside these channels, regular sources of political funds are four-fold. As just indicated, trading and commercial interests are an important source in Italy and also in Austria and Germany. All mass membership parties have a system of subscription and this tends to be most significant for the Social Democrats. In Austria and Germany these parties have a bigger income from this source than do their chief rivals, but this is not the case in Norway. The German Social Democrats have adopted the device of grading subscription according to personal income. Social Democrat parties in Sweden, Norway, Ireland and the United Kingdom also benefit from direct Trade Union affiliation, whilst the same source helps these parties in other countries. The French MRP used to be able to count on some support from its Trade Union as well.[1] By way of contrast, non-Socialist parties are more secretive about their financial sources. Clearly, they tend to rely fairly heavily on business and individual donations. Whilst this may make them less secure, it sometimes makes them richer, as in Britain.

Some conclusions can be drawn about comparative membership. Perhaps the most valid international standard of comparison is that used in the Scandinavian chapter which relates membership to the number of votes obtained by a party at elections. Since complete and accurate information cannot be obtained for all countries, the following offers only a rough comparative guide to the organizational strength of Western Europe's political parties.

Organizational strength almost certainly varies more between countries than between parties. The overall West European average of membership strength to votes at elections appears to be rather over 10 per cent, but this conceals too many variations to be really meaningful. One crucial factor is whether or not to take account of trade union affiliated members. This makes a massive difference in the case of the British Labour Party, who can boast of 60 per cent if all categories of member are included, but less than 10 per cent

[1] In none of the 15 countries are Trade Union funds available to openly anti-Socialist parties. No country has adopted the Israeli system where trade union political funds are distributed to the parties in proportion to the actual political allegiance of union members.

only including individual membership. Finland can perhaps boast the greatest politicization with an overall average of 30 per cent, not artificially boosted by trade union affiliation. The Finnish Agrarian Centre has enrolled half its voters as members. Counting affiliations, Sweden and the United Kingdom also reach about 30 per cent. The two major parties in Austria average about 28 per cent, placing that country just ahead of Norway. The Danish average is about 15 per cent, whilst the average for Italy's three largest parties is very similar. In the Netherlands the average is about 10 per cent, whilst in Belgium it is rather lower. Germany, Ireland and France are considerably under 10 per cent.

Little correlation can be found between organizational strength and either position in the political spectrum or political power itself. Amongst dominant parties, the French Gaullists do not bother with members, the Swedish Social Democrats score 40 per cent, but the Italian Christian Democrats only 15 per cent. Whilst in Sweden and Austria the Social Democrats do better than their rivals, in the Netherlands the Catholics lead the way. The Norwegian Labour Party, despite its huge political strength, fares relatively badly with only 20 per cent. The Italian Unified Socialist Party, politically weak, also fares badly with only 10 per cent. The two major Communist Parties—in Italy and France—lead the way in their two countries. In Italy the figure is 20 per cent, whilst in France it is probably about 14 per cent.

Finally, it may be appropriate to consider the question of future alignments of parties within a more unified Europe. Sections on the existing Assemblies show the extent of the co-operation already achieved. Despite the different histories and traditions of many national parties, it has not been difficult for them to establish a working relationship. Similarity of language and ideology have enabled the Social Democrats to function particularly effectively as a supranational grouping. The importance of these developments has been indicated already in the Introduction—parties have a special role to fulfil in the integration process, not altogether dissimilar to the one they fulfil through catalyzing political opinion within an existing nation state. The alternative courses of development for political parties operating in the 'European' context are to form confederations or even federations of existing parties, or the continued existence of large numbers of national parties, preserving their own independence. In the case of the latter, the parties will hardly fulfil their role in promoting integration. Lessons can perhaps be drawn from the Belgian experience of 1968. Then splits in national parties nearly caused a complete constitutional breakdown.

Existing parties, moulded through differing and often out-dated historical circumstances, may need first to modify themselves before unity can be achieved between them. On the other hand, pressures of international unity may impose domestic realignments. Thus the emergence of a single Christian Democrat Party in the Netherlands could be brought nearer by the fact that the three existing religious parties are in the same group in the European Parliament.

Alignments within the context of the Six are already relatively clear, with the only real question mark hanging over the future of the Gaullist group. What emerges from the French right-wing post-de Gaulle seems quite likely to be one or even two general Conservative parties which will be appealing also to the French Catholic tradition. For this reason, such parties might very well find themselves more at home with the Christian Democrat group rather than with the Liberal group of which they were once members. Another set of speculations relates to the question of the enlargement of the Community. If all 15 countries discussed in this book were eventually members or associates, then there would be great pressures for close inter-party links. For the Social Democrats and even for Western Europe's small number of Communist parties, co-operation should be relatively easy along obviously marked out routes. With the bourgeois parties, the likely links seem more problematic. British and Scandinavian Conservatives feel certain obstacles to working with avowedly Catholic parties. The Italian Christian Democrats claim to be unwilling to link with what they consider the right-wing economics of the British Conservatives. In practice the latter are much less anti-planning than the German Christian Democrats, so Church politics may be involved. However, it does seem that gradually Europe's religious based parties are attempting to broaden their support to appeal to all the bourgeois, whilst not losing all working class links. Again the future course of French political developments is crucial. If post-de Gaulle France had one general conservative party which was not particularly religiously oriented, then the Italian Christian Democrats might be more out of line with current trends than the British Conservatives. In any case, the political position of these parties within the context of their national systems does not seem to differ all that much. There is no intrinsic reason why bourgeois parties cannot work together in a European framework and one powerful political reason why they may be forced to. Given the espousal by the Social Democrats of the extension of integration to the political sphere and also the ease with which they are able to work together, these parties are likely to lead the way in supranational groupings. The dynamics of the situation could mean that this unity will force the bourgeois parties to act in a similar way.

More of a question mark hangs over the future of the existing Liberal group. The realignment post-de Gaulle in France may again give them additional allies but cannot resolve the contradiction involved in any effort ultimately to link British and Scandinavian Liberal and Agrarian Parties to groups such as the Austria Freedom Party and the Italian Liberals. These inner contradictions must overcome the feeling that unity means strength, since the group will anyway be relatively small. In an enlarged Europe the more radical brand of Liberalism could group together as a non-Socialist progressive force, with the other parties ultimately coming to terms with the main body of the right wing.

This is a time of flux for both Western Europe's political parties and also for the 'European' idea. The completion of the customs union amongst the six-member EEC throws into clearer perspective the ultimate goal of political unity and the difficulty in reaching it. Certainly West European countries are now more closely linked in all senses than ever before, and these processes seem likely to continue, involving political parties as both subject and object.

THE INTERNATIONAL LINKS OF EUROPE'S POLITICAL PARTIES

In addition to their specifically European links, most of the major political parties are also grouped into ostensible world-wide organizations or Internationals. Four such groupings can be discerned, although that of the Communists probably falls rather beyond the scope of this book. In fact since the dissolution of the Comintern in the 1950s, the International Communist movement has lacked formal organization. For various reasons there have been few attempts to hold congresses of all the world's Communist parties. Those of Western Europe have continued to have close bilateral relations with the Soviet Union, although there has been some loosening. The admission of Italian Communists to the European Parliament and attempts by the French party to attain a new respectability could ultimately lead to much closer co-operation between those Communist parties operating within multi-party systems.

The three most common types of party to be found in Western Europe—Social Democratic, Christian Democrat and Liberal—are each grouped into Internationals. Since the type for each party is essentially European, it is not surprising to find that all three Internationals possess a heavy European bias.

The Socialist International has, in fact, developed the most world-wide organization. It considers itself the direct heir of the First International founded by Karl Marx in 1864. Once the essential continuity between the First International and the Second (founded in 1879) is established, the claim has a certain substance, although the split with the Communists and two world wars have resulted in several lacunae in activity. For present purposes, a convenient starting point is the First Post-war Congress held in Frankfurt in 1951. The declaration then adopted—'Aims and Tasks of Democratic Socialism'—remains the manifesto of the International. Reading at times like a nineteenth-century declaration of the rights of man, and replete with references to the class struggle as well as colonial exploitation, this document defines the essential characteristics of the International Socialist movement—opposition to both capitalism and communism, and dedication to democracy.

As an organization, the International does not claim to be directly involved in the struggle for the attainment of democratic socialism. Its purposes are less ambitious—to strengthen relations between affiliated parties, to try by consent to co-ordinate their political attitudes and to extend relations with other progressive democratic parties. The latter object would have been quite inconceivable for either the First or Second International.

Given these relatively modest objectives, the Socialist International can claim to have achieved some success from its small headquarters in London. Its three classes of members embrace fifty-two parties in forty-nine countries. Half the parties are non-European with representation in every continent. It is to be noted that only national parties can affiliate. There is no possibility, as with the Christian Democrat and Liberal Internationals, of affiliation by a national group specifically established for the purpose. The difference between the number of parties and countries is to be accounted for by the inclusion of two from Japan and two parties which are international in character—the Jewish Labour Bund and the Labour Zionist Movement. On the other hand, the influence of British Labour in the International should not be underestimated. The International boasts that its member parties have more than fifteen million members. British Labour contributes 40 per cent of this total, and constituent parties in Australia, Venezuela, Sweden, Madagascar, Austria and Germany together make up a further 40 per cent. On the other hand the seventy plus million votes gained by these parties at the most recent elections are a little more evenly spread, although Britain, Germany, Japan (Socialist party) and India (Praja Socialists) make up 60 per cent of this total. In fact ten of the parties represent groups in exile from Spain and Eastern Europe, whilst six more have little real importance. However, thirty-four parties playing a significant role in their country's political affairs makes the Socialist International a more important grouping than either rival.

The structure of the International comprises four organs—Congress, Council, Bureau and Secretariat. The first two represent all constituent parties, although Congress is the larger and meets only once in three years. To it are reserved powers of admitting and expelling members and changing the statutes. In other respects the Council, meeting annually, has full powers. The Bureau is a smaller body with only eighteen members. It meets several times a year and is responsible for the day-to-day running of the International. It thus controls the Secretariat which is permanently based in London.

The chief concern of the International is liaison between member parties. It constitutes another international talking centre, but due to its wide range of participants it can claim to be more successful than some. International controversies are discussed, and even if policies are not determined, postures are adopted. The International has thus given general support to Britain's bid to join the European Communities and was felt to be broadly sympathetic towards Israel at the time of the 1967 war. A regular newsletter is produced in addition to occasional research documents.

Various other bodies operate within the aegis of the Socialist International. The most important is the least formal—the occasional meetings of Socialist International Leaders. A recent meeting was in England in 1967. In addition to officers of the International, 15 parties were represented. Partly for reasons of distance, many important non-European parties were not represented. Of the 15, only Canada, Israel and Mauritius were from outside Europe. Another organization is the Latin American Liaison Bureau, but its work is hampered by the fact that Socialist as distinct from left wing populist parties are weak throughout the continent. The International Union of Socialist Youth has some significance. Like the youth movements of the other Internationals it has attained a degree of penetration around the world which exceeds that of the parent body. IUSY can claim 116 organizations in 74 countries. That the organization has actually campaigned on various issues, relating, for example, to Spain and Southern Africa, suggests both a greater degree of ideological homogeneity and more youthful vigour than are possessed by the parent body. Finally, the Socialist International has acquired, somewhat belatedly, a regular liaison with the Internal Confederation of Free Trade Unions.

The Socialist International has spread outwards from Europe, which is still a centre. However, it has a genuine claim to being considered a world-wide organization. Whilst its work probably makes little impact on rank and file members of affiliated parties, useful contacts have been established between both the leadership of these parties and their own functionaries. Some educative effect in making these groups more internationally conscious can be discerned. On the other hand the day is long since gone when the Social Democratic parties could, or even wanted to, consider themselves as part of a world-wide movement, as can the Communist parties to some extent even today. When the French Socialist Party adopted the name French Section of the Workers International seventy years ago it was not entirely propagating myth. Today, the continued use of such a name is an historic absurdity.

In comparison with the Socialists, co-operation between Christian Democratic parties is young, as indeed are many of the parties, and frequently rudimentary. Liaison before the Second World War was fragmentary—the Italian and German parties were successively submerged by fascist regimes. During the war the idea of co-operation between these parties was kept alive by Don Luigi Sturzo and other refugees in England. After the war, only the Swiss Catholic party had survived in recognizable form and it played a leading role as host in the early meetings. The emergence of strong Christian Democratic parties in Italy, Germany and France gave a new vigour to the urge to co-operate, resulting in the emergence of Nouvelles Equipes Internationales—the international movement for Christian Democracy deliberately eschewing the word Christian in its title for fear of confusing the religious with the political field. It has been described as 'a hybrid organization situated halfway between the

European Movement and the organized party.'[1] The first conference in Belgium in 1947 had representatives from all Western European countries and also Czechoslovakia. The basis of affiliation to NEI tended to vary, so that the nature of the organization is hard to define. Where a country had more than one Christian party, as in Holland, an 'equipe' or group could be founded for the purposes of affiliation. Groups were also established, not altogether successfully in countries without a party like Britain. NEI itself remained a European body, with exile parties representing Eastern Europe and the dominant influence inevitably being the countries of the European Community. In 1964 it became the European Union of Christian Democrats. This successor body has been more outward looking. It has strengthened links with the Christian Democrat movement in Latin America, and also admitted to membership the governing Nationalist party of Malta. A study and documentation centre has been established with the secretariat in Paris, whilst leading members of individual parties have been taking a much greater interest in the International.

The basic difficulty with establishing extra-European links has been the lack of comparable parties. In the Western European context some kind of common ideological origin can be found for these parties, as well as a similar political purpose. Points of contact with non-European parties are likely to be much more tenuous. Certainly there is no world-wide common ideological origin as is the case with the Socialists. In fact the only region outside Europe with Christian Democrat parties is Latin America. In the decade after the war these parties, existing in some form in practically every country, established their own links and international organization— the Organization of Christian Democrats in America. It was natural for NEI to look towards the OCDA for extra-European links. After an initial joint conference in Paris in 1956, such meetings have been held every two or three years, and in 1961 a World Union of Christian Democrats was established with a three-fold structure—Congress, meeting alternately in the two continents; a twelve-member executive committee with a considerably closer liaison; and a Secretariat situated in Rome. Efforts have been made to establish links with parties in other areas of the world, but they have met with little success. The Indonesian Catholic Party joined in 1967 and the Pakindo (Indonesian Protestant Party) is now considering following the same course. In Latin America strength is heavily concentrated on a small number of countries, especially Chile and Venezuela.

In the circumstances, it would be unreasonable to expect the emergence of common policies; the World Union is hardly more than an organization for the exchange of information. On the other hand, in the European context the Christian Democrats have been able to evolve a broadly

[1] D. Karl heinz Neuenreither, 'Le Role du Parlement dans la Formation de Décision des Communautés Européennes', paper presented to the Colloque on 'La Décision dans les organisations Européennes', Lyons, November 1966, p. 10.

common outlook on international issues—characterized by forthright opposition to Communism and, therefore, support for the Atlantic alliance. They have also played a most important role in the movement for European integration. During the period in which the idea of a European Community was a subject of controversy, the Christian Democrats could pose as its principal champions.

Of associated organizations, two are worthy of mention. There is a permanent conference of Presidents and General Secretaries of European Christian Democratic parties. This meets at irregular intervals to discuss urgent problems and a clue to its orientation may be given by the fact that Christian Democrat members of the Commission of the European Communities are invited. There is also an International Union of Young Christian Democrats with European and Latin American sections. It too is based in Rome.

It would be unwise to give too much prominence to these organizations and links. The Christian Democrat parties discussed in the rest of this book are a peculiarly European phenomenon and similarity with parties elsewhere is dubious. It can reasonably be concluded that almost inevitably the Christian Democrat International has little significance in its world-wide manifestations. On the other hand, inside Europe it is beginning to establish a degree of liaison to rival that of the Social Democrats.

The Liberal International (or World Liberal Union) is even more European oriented. It was founded at Oxford in 1947 and has no real link with the tenuous contacts built up before the war. Despite its intentions it has never been able to build up a world-wide membership. Outside Europe it has a member party in Israel and a group in India; otherwise a few scattered contacts. There are various exile organizations from Eastern Europe but their influence has declined, so that predominantly the organization is West European. Its membership includes all those parties categorized as Liberal except the Austrian in the table on p. 516 together with the Danish Agrarian Party and the Swiss Liberals. There is no member organization in Iceland or Ireland; and the French Radical party has drifted out of touch. In Austria, the neo-Nazi origins of many FPO leaders resulted in its exclusion; instead an independent group has been admitted.

Ignoring the exile organizations, the International is thus represented in fifteen countries, of which thirteen are in Western Europe. In some respects it is strange that the Liberals have been even less successful than the Christian Democrats in establishing non-European links. Ostensibly, their ideology and political purpose might seem to have a wider application than those of the Christian Democrats. On the other hand, even within the European context, Liberalism often seems to be an historic, essentially nineteenth-century force. There is a basic split between the parties of Southern Europe, which are right wing in economic matters but possess an historic left-wing *raison d'être* in their anti-clericalism, and those of

Northern Europe which can be considered as progressive non-Socialists. This split has meant that the International has never acquired any ideological homogeneity, although the dominant stream has probably been the Southern with support from the exile organizations. This split probably prevents a basis being established for extension outside Europe of the International. In fact the right-wing anti-clerical brand of Liberalism is intrinsically unlikely to have a world appeal. The relatively suppressed left-wing tendency could potentially find links with populist parties especially in Latin America, and this may account for the success of the International's youth organization.

Two types of base organization have been employed. Either the national Liberal party concerned joins directly or some kind of Liberal International Group is established. Although such groups have a certain identity with the parties, save in the special cases of Austria and France, they have the extra advantage of bringing together those particularly interested in international activities. The constitution of the International resembles its rivals, although the smaller number of members means that all parties or groups are represented on the executive committee, whilst the Congress meets annually. The Secretariat is in London and the General Secretary has always been British.

Each annual congress has concentrated on a particular theme and has been the occasion for attempts to work out common attitudes to problems. For reasons already made clear there have been obvious difficulties. Emphasis has been placed on the over-riding need for freedom in all its aspects, whilst only a limited degree of economic planning and social security is acceptable. In international affairs, the extreme anti-Communism of the early days has tended to be moderated, whilst all factions have been able to agree on support for the European Communities (the International includes the most pro-EEC parties in Britain, Sweden and Denmark). As with the other Internationals there is provision for a leaders' meeting, although this is a recent innovation.

The most important associated organization is the World Federation of Liberal and Radical Youth. With virtually no participation from France, Switzerland or Austria and a very left-wing membership from Germany and the Netherlands the WFLRY has a very different centre of gravity from the parent body. It is in fact dominated by Britain and Scandinavia, with a result that its economic and social policy visualizes a much greater role for the state. It also places considerable emphasis on anti-colonialism and has opposed the American position in Vietnam. Membership is entirely through youth and student organizations, and recently some expansion into Latin America has taken place.

The Liberal International emerges as much the more European oriented of the three. Given the dominance of the EEC parties, it can almost be looked on at times as an appendage of the Liberal group there with the uneasy participation of the Northern Europeans.

534

BIBLIOGRAPHY

GENERAL

Alford, R. *Party and Society*, New York, Rand McNally, 1963, London, Murray, 1964.

Beloff, M. *The Party System*, London, Pheonix House, 1958.

Dahl, R. *Political Oppositions in Western Democracies*, New Haven, Yale University Press, 1966.

Duverger, M. *Political Parties: their Organization and Activity in the Modern State*, 2nd rev. ed. London, Methuen; New York, Wiley, 1962.

Einaudi, M. *Communism in Western Europe*, Ithaca, New York, Cornell University Press, 1951.

Epstein, L. D. *Political Parties in Western Democracies*, London, Pall Mall, 1967.

Fogarty, M. P. *Christian Democracy in Western Europe, 1820–1953*, London, Routledge and Kegan Paul, 1957.

Jupp, J. *Political Parties*, London, Routledge and Kegan Paul, 1968.

Kornhauser, W. *The Politics of Mass Society*, Glencoe, Illinois, Free Press, Macmillan, 1959.

La Polambara, J. and Weiner, M. (eds) *Political Parties and Political Development*, Princeton University Press; Oxford University Press, 1966.

Lavau, G. F. *Partis politiques et réalités sociales; contribution à une étude réaliste des partis politiques*, Paris, Colin, 1953.

Lazitch, B. *Les partis communistes d'Europe 1919/1958*, Paris, Les isles d'or, 1956.

Leiserson, A. *Parties and Politics; an institutional and behavioral approach*, New York, Knopf, 1958.

Lipset, S. M. (ed.) *Party Systems and Voter Alignments: Cross-national Perspectives*, New York, Free Press, 1967.

Mackenzie, W. *Free Elections*, London, Allen & Unwin, 1958.

McDonald, N. A. *The Study of Political Parties*, Garden City, Random House, 1955.

Macridis, R. C., and Ward, R. E. (eds) *Modern Political Systems: Europe*, Englewood Cliffs, Prentice–Hall, 2nd ed., 1967.

Michels, R. *Political Parties: A Sociological Study of the Oligarchical Tendencies of Modern Democracy*, London, Dover; New York, Collier Books, 1962 (re-issue).

Neumann, S. (ed.) *Modern Political Parties*, rev. ed., University of Chicago Press, 1965.

Ostrogorski, M. Y. *Democracy and the Organization of Political Parties*, New York and London, Macmillan, 1962 (re-issue).

Spiro, Herbert J. *The German Political System*, in Beer, S. and Ulam, A. eds., *Patterns of Government*, New York, Random House, 1962.

GERMANY

Bibliographical Sources:

Schumann, H.-G.   *Die politischen Parteien Deutschlands nach 1945. Ein bibliographisch-systematischer Versuch*, Frankfurt on Main, Bernard und Graefe, 1967.

General Background and History:

Balfour, M.   *West Germany*, London, Benn Bros., 1968.

Boelling, K.   *Republic in Suspense: Politics, Parties, and Personalities in Postwar Germany, a Short Political Guide*, London, Pall Mall Press, 1964.

Braunthal, G.   'West Germany', in Christoph, J. B. (ed.) *Cases in Comparative Politics*, Boston, Little, Brown, 1965.

Deutsch, K. W., and Breitling, R.   'The German Federal Republic', in Macridis, R. C., and Ward, R. E. (eds). *Modern Political Systems: Europe*, Englewood Cliffs, Prentice–Hall, 1963.

Grosser, A.   *The Federal Republic of Germany*, Praeger, 1964, Chapter IV; see also A. Grosser, *Die Bundesrepublik Deutschland*, Tübingen, Wunderlich Verlag, 1967.

Heidenheimer, A. J.   *The Governments of Germany*, 2nd ed. London, Methuen, 1966.

Kaiser, K.   *German Foreign Policy in Transition*, London, OUP for RIIA, 1968.

Manon, A., and Marcou, L.   *La République Fédérale Allemande: évolution politique, économique, et sociale de sa creation à nos jours*, Paris, Fayard, 1967.

Mommsen, W.   *Deutsche Parteiprogramme*, Isar Verlag, Munich, 1954.

Pollack, J. K., and others   *German Democracy at Work*, Ann Arbor, University of Michigan Press, 1955.

The Party System:

Barzel, R.   *Die Deutschen Parteien*, Geldern, Schaffrath, 1952.

Bauer, H.   *Die Fraktionszwang*, Mainz, 1956.

Bergsträsser, L.   *Geschichte der politischen Parteien in Deutschland*, 11th ed., Munich, Isar Verlag, 1965.

Dübber, U.   *Parteifinanzierung in Deutschland*, Cologne, Westelestschen Verlag, 1962.

Ellwein, T.   *Das Regierungssystem der Bundesrepublik Deutschland*, rev. ed. Cologne and Opladen, Westdeutscher Verlag, 1965.

Engels, K. G.   *Die Auflösung politischer Parteien*, Münster and Wesphalia, M. Kramer, 1958.

Eschenburg, T.   *Zur politischen Praxis in der Bundesrepublik. Kritische Betrachtungen, 1957–1961*, Munich, Piper, 1964.

Flechtheim, O. K.   *Dokumente zur parteipolitischen Entwicklung in Deutschland seit 1945*, 5 vols, Berlin, Dokumenten-Verlag, 1962–66.

Heidenheimer, A. J.   *Adenauer and the CDU*, The Hague, Nijhoff, 1960.

Heynitz, W. von *Die verfassungsrechtliche Stellung der politischen Parteien*, Munich, 1954.

Horn, M. von *Weisst du, was Bonn wirklich will? Die Parteien im Bundestag*, Wuppertal, H. Putty, 1956.

Institut für Politische Wissenschaft *Parteien in der Bundesrepublik*, Schriften B.6, Stuttgart and Düsseldorf, Ring–Verlag, 1955.

Kaack, H. *Die Parteien in der Verfassungswirklichkeit der Bundesrepublik*, Kiel, Der Landesbeauftragte für Staatsbürgerliche Bildung in Schleswig–Holstein, 1963.

Lane, J. C., and Pollock, J. K. *Source Material on the Government and Politics of Germany*, Ann Arbor, Wahrs Publishing, 1964.

Loewenberg, G. *Parliament in the German Political System*, Ithaca, New York, Cornell University Press, 1966.

Markman, H. *Das Abstimmungsverhalten der Parteifraktionen in deutschen Parlamenten*, Meisenheim on Glan, A. Hain, 1955.

Mueller, U. *Die demokratische Willensbildung in den politischen Parteien*, Mainz, Hase and Koehler, 1967.

Neumann, R. G. *The Government of the German Federal Republic*, New York, Harper and Row, 1966.

Newman, S. *Die Parteien der Weimarer Republik*, Munich, Kohlhammer, 1965.

Olzog, G. *Die politischen Parteien*, 3rd ed. Munich and Vienna, Olzog, 1967.

Sternberger, A. *Lebende Verfassung: Studien über Koalition und Opposition*, Meisenheim on Glan, A. Hain, 1956.

Sund, O. *Die Parteien der Bundesrepublik als Volksparteien*, Hannover, Landesarbeitsgemeinschaft Arbeit und Leben, Niedersachsen, 1965.

Treue, W. *Die deutschen Parteien*, Weisbaden, F. Steiner, 1962.

Verkade, W. *Democratic Parties in the Low Countries and Germany*, Leiden, Universitaire Pers, 1965.

Wallraf, R. *Parteien, Wähler, und Programme*, Cologne, Deutsche Industrie Verlag, 1965.

Wasser, H. *Die politischen Parteien*, Lübeck and Hamburg, Mathiesen, 1966.

Wildenman, R. *Partei und Fraktion: ein Beitrag z. Analyse der politischen Willensbildung und des Parteiensystems in der Bundesrepublik*, Meisenheim on Glan, Westkulturverlag, 1954.

Wittkamper, G. W. *Die verfassungsrechtliche Stellung der Interessenverbände nach dem Grundgesetz*, Cologne, Westdeutscher Verlag, 1963.

Individual Parties and their Ideologies:

Bessel-Lorck, L., and others *National oder Radikal? der Rechtsradikalismus in der Bundesrepublik Deutschland*, Mainz, Hase und Köhler, 1966.

Booms, H. *Die deutschkonservative Partei; preussischer Charakter, Reichsauffassung, Nationalbegriff*, Düsseldorf, Droste–Verlag, 1954.

Buchheim, K. *Geschichte der christischen Parteien in Deutschland*, Munich, Kösel–Verlag, 1953.

Chalmers, D. A. *The Social Democratic Party of Germany: from Working Class Movement to Modern Political Party*, New Haven, Yale University Press, 1964.

Childs, D. *From Schumacher to Brandt*, Oxford, Pergamon Press, 1966.

Erler, F. *Politik für Deutschland: eine Dokumentation*, Stuttgart, Seewald, 1968.

Gutscher, J. M. *Die Entwicklung der F(reien) D(emokratischen) P(artei) von ihren Anfängen bis 1961*, Meisenheim on Glan, Hain, 1967.

Jenke, M. *Die nationalen Rechte: Parteien, Politiker, Publizisten*, Berlin, Colloquium, 1967.

Kutscher, H. *Die deutschen Parteien der Gegenwart und ihre Programme*, Gerabronn (Würt.), W. Rothe, 1953.

Pirker, T. *Die SPD nach Hitler*, Munich, Rütten und Loening, 1965.

Sozialdemokratische Partei Deutschlands. *The Social Democratic Party of Germany*, Bonn, 1953.

Political Sociology:

Noelle, E. *Auskunft über die Parteien; Ergebnisse der Umfrage Forschung in Deutschland*, Allensbach on Bodensee, Verlag für Domoskopie, 1955.

Narr, W.-D. *C.D.U./S.P.D. Programm und Praxis seit 1945*, Stuttgart and Berlin, Kohlhammer, 1966.

Unkelbach, H. *Wähler, Parteien, Parlament; Bedingungen und Funktionen der Wahl*, Frankfort on Main, Athenäum Verlag, 1965.

Electoral Studies:

Kaasl, M. *Wechsel von Parteipräferenzen: eine Analyse am Beispiel der Bundestagswahl*, Meisenheim on Glan, A. Hain, 1967.

Kitzinger, U. *German Electoral Politics* (A Study of the 1957 campaign) Oxford University Press, 1960.

Periodicals containing relevant articles:

Frankfurter Hefte
Der Monat
Das Parlament
Politische Vierteljahrsschrift
Die Zeit
Zeitschrift für Politik

BELGIUM

General Background and History:

Höjer, C. H. *La régime Parlementaire Belge de 1918 à 1940*, Uppsala and Stockholm, Almquist and Wiksell, 1946.

Pierson, M. A. *Histoire du socialisme en Belgique*, Brussels, Institut Emil Vandervelde, 1953.

Simon, C. A. *Le parti Catholique Belge, 1830–1945*, Brussels, Renaissance du Livre, 1958.

The Party System:

Impe, H. van *Le rôle de la majorité parlementaire dans la vie politique belge*, Brussels, Bruylant, 1966.

Liebman, M. 'The Crisis of Belgian Social Democracy', in Miliband, R., and Saville, J. *The Socialist Register*, London, Merlin Press, 1966.

Lorwin, V. R. 'Belgium: Religion, Class and Language in National Politics', in Dahl, R. A. *Political Oppositions in Western Democracies*, New Haven, Yale University Press, 1966.

Meynaud, J. (ed.) *La décision politique: le pouvoir et les groupes*, Paris, Colin, 1965.

Philippart, A. 'Language and Class Oppositions', in *Government and Opposition*, Vol. 2, London, Weidenfeld and Nicolson, 1967.

Verkade, W. *Democratic Parties in the Low Countries and Germany*, Leiden, Universitaire Pers, 1965.

Individual Parties and their Ideologies:

Georis-Reitshop, M. *L'extrême droite et le néo-fascisme en Belgique*, Brussels, P. de Meyere, 1962.

Electoral Studies:

Deguelle, C., and others *Les élections législatives belges du 1er juin 1958*, Brussels, Les Editions de la Librarie encyclopédique, 1959.

De Smet, R-E., Evalenko, R., and Fraeys, W. *Atlas des élections belges, 1919–1954*, Brussels, Institut de Sociologie Solvay, 1958.

Fraeys, W. 'Les résultats des élections du 26 mars 1961', *Res Publica*, Vol. 3, 1961.

Fraeys, W. 'Les résultats des élections législatives du 23 mai 1965', *Res Publica*, Vol. 8, 1966.

Periodicals:

Courriers Hebdomadaires (Centre de Recherche et d'Information Socio-Politiques, Brussels).

Res Publica (Institut Belge de Science Politique). See particularly Vol. 8, No. 3, 1967.

La Revue Nouvelle, Tournai.

La Revue Politique, 1945–1955. See particularly 'La vie politique belge,' Numero spécial 1, Dec. 1955. Brussels, 1955.

FRANCE

General Background and History

Avril, P. *Le régime politique du Cinquième République*, Paris, Pichon, 1965.

Avril, P. *Politics in France*, London, Penguin, 1969.

Bosworth, W. *Catholicism and Crisis in Modern France*, Princeton University Press, 1962.

Duverger, M. *French Political System*, Chicago University Press, 1958.

Duverger, M. *La Cinquième République*, Paris, Presses Universitaires, 4th ed. 1968.

Duverger, M. *La VIe République et la régime presidential*, Paris, Fayard, 1960.

Duverger, M. *Les institutions françaises*, Paris, P.U.F. 8th ed. 1965.

Ehrmann, S. *Politics in France*, Boston, Mass., Little Brown, 1969.

Fauvet, J. *La IV République*, Paris, Fayard, 1959.

Goguel, F. *France under the Fourth Republic*, Ithaca, New York, Cornell University Press, 1952.

Macridis, R. C., and Brown, B. E. *The De Gaulle Republic*, Homewood Illinois, Dorsey Press, 1960.

Macridis, R. C., and Brown, B. E. *Supplement to The De Gaulle Republic*, Homewood, Illinois, Dorsey Press, 1963.

Pickles, D. *The Fifth French Republic*, 3rd ed. London, Methuen, 1965.

Pickles, D. *The Fourth French Republic*, 2nd ed. London, Methuen, 1958.

Thomson, D. *Democracy in France Since 1870*, Oxford University Press, 4th ed. 1964.

Wahl, N. 'The French Political System', in Beer, S., and Ulam, A., *Patterns of Government*, New York, Random House, ed. 1962.

Werth, A. *France 1940–1955*, London, Robert Hale, 1956.

Williams, P. M., and Harrison, M. *De Gaulle's Republic*, London, Longmans, Green, 1960.

Wright, G. *Rural Revolution in France*, Oxford University Press, 1964.

The Party System:

Barron, R. W. *Parties and Politics in Modern France*, Washington, D.C., Public Affairs Press, 1959.

Chapsal, J. *La vie politique et les partis en France depuis 1940*, Paris, Cours de Droit, 1961.

Duverger, M. *Party politiques et classes sociales en France*, Paris, Colin, 1955.

Faucher, J. A. *Les clubs politiques en France*, Paris, J. Didier, 1965.

Fauvet, J. *Les forces politiques en France*, Paris, Edition Le Monde, 1951.

Garas, F. *Charles de Gaulle seul contre les pouvoirs*, Paris, René Julliard, 1957.

Laponce, J. *The Government of the Fifth Republic; French Political Parties and the Constitution*, Berkeley, University of California Press, 1961.

Leites, N. *On the Game of Politics in France*, Stanford, Stanford University Press, 1959.

MacRau, D. *Parliament, Parties and Society in France 1946–58*, London and New York, Macmillan 1967.

Malterr, J., and Benoist, P. *Les partis politiques français*, Paris, Editions Temoignage Chrétien, 1957.

Maze, J. *Le système* (1943/1951), Paris, Ségur, 1951.

Meynaud, J. *Nouvelles études sur les groupes de presion en France*, Paris, Colin, 1962.

Taylor, O. R. *The Fourth Republic of France, Constitution, Political Parties*, London, Royal Institute of International Affairs, 1951.

Williams, P. M. *Crisis and Compromise, Politics in the Fourth Republic*, London, Longmans, 1964.

Individual Parties and their Ideologies:

Bardonnet, D. *Evolution de la structure du parti radical*, Thesis, University of Paris, 1960.

Barrillon, R. *La Gauche française en Mouvement*, Paris, 1968.

Biton, L. *La demokratie Chretienne dans la politique française, sa grandeur, ses servitudes*, Angers, H. Siraudeau, 1954.

Brayance, A. *Anatomie du parti communiste français*, Paris, Denoel, 1952.

Capelle, R. B. *The M.R.P. and French Foreign Policy*, New York, Praeger, 1963.

Charlot, J. *L'Union pour la Nouvelle République: étude du pouvoir au sein d'un parti politique*, Paris, Colin, 1967.

Club Jean Moulin, *Un Parti pour la Gauche*, Paris, Editions du Seuil, 1965.

De Tarr, F. *The French Radical Party, from Herriot to Mendès-France*, London, Oxford University Press, 1964.

Domenack, J. M. 'The French Communist Party', in Einaudi, M. *Communism in Western Europe*, Ithaca, New York, Cornell University Press, 1951.

Fauvet, J. *Histoire du parti communiste français*, Paris, Fayard, 1964.

Fauvet, J., and Medras, H. *Les Paysans et la politique dans la France contemporaine*, Paris, Colin, 1958.

Fejtö, F. *The French Communist Party and the Crisis of International Communism*, Cambridge, Mass., MIT Press, 1967.

Goguel, F. 'Christian Democracy in France', in Einaudi, M., and Goguel, F., *Christian Democracy in Italy and France*, Notre Dame, Indiana, University of Indiana Press, 1952.

Hoffman, S., et al. *Le Mouvement Poujade*, Paris, Colin, 1956.

Ligou, D. *Histoire de Socialisme en France, 1871–1961*, Paris, Presses Universitaires de France, 1962.

Micaud, C. A. *Communism and the French Left*, London, Weidenfeld and Nicolson, 1963.

Mollet, G. *Bilan et perspectives socialistes*, Paris, Plon, 1958.

Nicolet, C. . . . *Le radicalisme*, Paris, Presses Universitaires de France, 1957.

Perrot, M. *Le socialisme français et le pouvoir*, Paris, Etudes et Documentation Internationale, 1966.

Phillip, A. *Les socialistes*, Paris, Editions du Seuil, 1967.

Remond, R.   *The Rightwing in France from 1815 to de Gaulle*, Philadelphia, University of Pennsylvania, 1966

Schwartzenberg, R.   *La Campagne Presidentielle de 1965*, Paris, Presses Universitaires de France, 1967.

Political Sociology:

Association Française de Science Politique, *Partis politiques et classes sociales en France*, Paris, Colin, 1955.

Dogan, M., and Narbonne, J.   *Les françaises face à la politique—comportement politique et condition sociale*, Paris (Cahiers de la Fondation Nationale des Sciences Politiques, No. 72), Colin.

Fauvet, J., and Medras, H. (eds)   *Les paysans et la politique dans la France contemporaine*, Paris, Colin, 1958.

Periodicals:

Revue Juridique et Politique de l'Union Française.
Revue Française de Science Politique.
Année Politique.

Electoral studies

Campbell, P.   *French Electoral Systems and Elections since 1789*, London, Faber, 2nd ed., 1965.

Gogoel   *Geographies des elections françaises de 1870 a 1951*, Paris, Colin, 1951.

The above was published by Armand Colin on behalf of the Fondation National des Sciences Politiques. Subsequently in the same series there have been individual studies of each election and each referendum. These have been written by individual authors; the Association Française de Science Politique; or the Centre d'Etude de la Vie Politique Française.

ITALY

The literature in Italian is immense and largely ephemeral. For this reason, the bibliography which follows is largely confined to works in English and French as being more accessible to the average English reader. The Italian titles are considered fundamental.

Bibliographical sources:

Meyriat, J.   'Problèmes politiques de la république italienne, état des travaux', *Revue française de Science Politique*, Vol. XII, No. 1, March 1962.

Sivini, G.   *Il comportamento elettorale*, Quaderni dell'Istituto Carlo Cattaneo, Bologna, Il Mulino, 1967.

Vitto, F.   (ed.) *Gli studi politici in Italia: saggio bibliografico*, Milan, Societa Editrici, Vita e Pensiero, 1964.

Reports

The Acts and Documents, Congress Reports, etc., are published by the leading parties, publishing houses (Editori Reuniti (PCI), Cinque Lune (DC), Edizioni dell'Avanti e dell Gallo (PSI-PSIUP) etc). *Annuario Politico Italiano*, prepared by the Italian Centre of Research and Documentation (CIRD), 1963–present, is a further source of serious information.

General Background and History:

Grindrod, M. *The Rebuilding of Italy. Politics and Economics, 1945–1955*, London, RIIA, 1955.

Hildebrande, G. H. *Growth and Structure in the Economy of Modern Italy*, Cambridge, Mass., Harvard University Press 1965.

Kogan, N. *A Political History of Postwar Italy*, London, Pall Mall Press, 1966.

Mack-Smith, D. *Italy, A Modern History*, Ann Arbor, University of Michigan Press, 1959.

Mammarella, G. *Italy after Fascism*, Notre Dame University Press, 1965.

Nichols, P. *The Politics of the Vatican*, London, Pall Mall Press, 1968.

Schacter, G. *The Italian South. Economic Development in Mediterranean Europe*, New York, Random House, 1965.

Webb, L. C. *Church and State in Italy, 1947–1957*, Melbourne, Melbourne University Press, 1958.

The Political System:

Adams, J. C. and Barile, P. *The Government of Republican Italy*, 2nd. ed. Boston, Houghton Mifflin, London, Allen and Unwin, 1962.

Fried, R. C. *The Italian Prefects. A Study in Administrative Politics*, New Haven, Yale University Press, 1963.

Germino, D. C. and Passigli, S. *The Government and Politics of Contemporary Italy*, New York, Harper and Row, 1968.

Galli, G. *Il Bipartismo imperfetto*, Bologna, Il Mulino, 1966.

Kogan, N. *The Politics of Italian Foreign Policy*, London, Pall Mall, 1963.

La Palombara J. *Interest Groups in Italian Politics*, Princeton, Princeton University Press, 1964.

La Palombara J. *Italy: The Politics of Planning*, Syracuse, Syracuse University Press, 1966.

La Palombara J. 'Political Party Systems and Crisis Government: Italian and French Contrasts', *Midwest Journal of Political Science*, Vol. 5, February 1961.

Meynaud, J. *Rapport sur la classe dirigeante italienne*, Lausanne, Etudes des Sciences Politiques, 1964.

Meynaud, J. *Les partis politiques en Italie*, Paris, Presses Universitaires de France, 1965.

Posner, M. V. and Woolf, S. *Italian Public Enterprise*, London, Duckworth, 1967.

Sartori, G.   'European Political Parties: The case of Polarised Pluralism' in La Palombara J. and Weiner, M., *Political Parties and Political Development*, Princeton, Princeton University Press, 1966.

Tosi, S.   'Italy: Anti-system Opposition within the System' in *Government and Opposition*, Vol. 2, No. 1, Oct.–Jan. 1967.

Individual Parties and their Ideologies

Barnes, S. H.   *Party Democracy: Politics in an Italian Socialist Federation*, New Haven, Yale University Press, 1967.

Bibes, G.   *Etat des travaux sur le communisme en Italie*, mimeographed paper presented to the Colloque in *Le communisme en France et en Italie*, Paris, 1968.

Blackmer, D. L. M.   *Unity in Diversity. Italian Communism and the Communist World*, Cambridge, Mass., MIT Press, 1968.

Chasseriaud, J. P.   *Le parti democrat chrétien en Italie*, Paris, Colin, 1965.

Einaudi, M.   'Christian Democracy in Italy', in Einaudi M. and Goguel, F. *Christian Democracy in Italy and France*, University of Notre Dame Press, 1952.

Evans, R. H.   *Coexistence: Communism and its Practice in Bologna, 1945–1965*, University of Notre Dame Press, 1967.

Foa, V.   *Italian Democracy, Yesterday and Today*, Reading, Occasional Paper, University of Reading, 1968.

Gramsci, A.   *The Modern Prince and Other Writings*, London, Lawrence and Wishart, 1957.

Galli, G. and Facchi, P.   *La Sinistra Democristiana: storia e ideologia*, Milan, Feltrinelli, 1962.

Garosci, A.   'The Italian Communist Party' in Einaudi, M. and others, *Communism in Western Europe*, Ithaca, New York, Cornell University Press, 1951.

Godechot, T. *Le parti democrat chrétien italien*, Paris, Librairie Droz.

Hilton-Young, W.   *The Italian Left, a Short History of Political Socialism*, London, Longmans, Green, 1949.

Halliday, J.   'Structural Reform in Italy: Theory and Practice', *New Left Review*, No. 50, July–August, 1968.

Magri, F.   *La Democrazia Cristiana in Italia*, 2 vols, Milan, Editrice la Fiaccola, 1954–5.

Tarrow, S.   *Peasant Communism in Southern Italy*, New Haven, Yale University Press, 1967.

Togliatti, P.   *Le parti communiste italien*, Paris, Maspero, 1961.

Webster, R. A.   *Christian Democracy in Italy, 1860–1960*, London, Hollis and Carter, 1961.

Zariski, R.   'The Italian Socialist Party: a Case Study in Factional Conflict', *American Political Science Review*, Vol. LVI, No. 2, June, 1962.

Zariski, R.   'Intra-party Conflict in a Dominant Party: the Experience of Italian Christian Democracy', *Journal of Politics*, Vol. 27, No. 1, February 1965.

Political Sociology:

Cantril, H.   *The Politics of Despair*, New York, 1958, Collier Books, 1962.

Dogan, M.   'Le comportement politique des italiens', *Revue française de sciences politiques*, Vol. IX, No. 2, June 1959.

Dogan, M.   '*Comportement politique et condition sociale en Italie*' *Revue Française de Sociologie*, Vol. VII, 1966.

Dogan, M. and Petrarca, O. M.   *Partiti politici e strutture sociali in Italia*, Milan, Comunità, 1968.

Edelman, N.   'Sources of Popular Support for the Italian Christian Democrat Party' in the Postwar Decade, *Midwest Journal of Political Science*, Vol. 2, May 1958.

Edelman, N.   'Causes of Fluctuations in the Popular Support for the Italian Communist Party', *Journal of Politics*, Vol. 20, No. 3, August 1958.

Fried, R. C.   'Urbanisation and Italian Politics', *Journal of Politics*, Vol. 29, No. 3, August 1967.

Istituto Carlo Cattaneo, *L'Attività di Partito*, Bologna, Il Mulino, 1967.

Istituto Carlo Cattaneo, *L'Organizzazione partitica del PCI e della DC*, Bologna, Il Mulino, 1969.

La Palombara, J.   'Italy, Fragmentation, Isolation and Alienation', in Pye, L. W. and Verba, S. (eds.), *Political Culture and Political Development*, Princeton, Princeton University Press, 1964.

La Palombara, J.   'Left-wing Trade Unionism: the Matrix of Communist Power in Italy', *Western Political Quarterly*, June 1954.

La Palombara, J. and Walters, J. B.   'Values, Expectations and Political Predispositions of Italian Youth', *Mid-west Journal of Political Science*, Vol. 5, February 1961.

Passigli, S.   'Italy', *Comparative Political Finance: a Symposium*, Special Number of *Journal of Politics*, edited by Heidenheimer, A. J. and Rose, R., Vol. 25, No. 3, August 1963.

Poggi, G. F.   *Le preferenze politiche degli italiani*, Quaderni dell'Istituto Carlo Cattaneo, Bologna, Il Mulino, 1968.

Sartori, G., and others   *Il Parlamento Italiano*, 1946–1963, Naples, ESI, 1963.

Electoral Studies:

Allum, P. A.   'The Italian Elections of 1963' *Political Studies*, Vol. XIII, No. 3, October 1965.

Carey, J. P. C., and C. A. G.   'The Italian Elections of 1958—Unstable Stability in an Unstable World', *Political Science Quarterly*, Vol. 73, December 1958.

Istituto Carlo Cattaneo, *Il comportamento elettorale in Italia, 1946–1963*, Bologna, Il Mulino, 1968.

La Palombara, J.   'The Italian Elections and the Problem of Representation', *American Political Science Review*, Vol. XLVII, No. 3, September 1953.

La Palombara, J., and Spreafico, A. *Elezioni e comportamento politico in Italia*, Milan, Comunità, 1963.

Pryce, R. *The Italian Local Elections of 1956. A Nuffield College Electoral Survey*, London, Chatto and Windus, 1957.

NETHERLANDS

General Background and History:

Berg, J. van den *De Anatomie van Nederland*, Vol. 1, Amsterdam, De Bezige Bij, 1967.

Daalder, H. 'The Netherlands', in Lindsay, K. (ed.), *European Assemblies*, London and New York, Stevens, 1960.

The Party System:

Bone, R. C. 'The Dynamics of Dutch Politics', *The Journal of Politics*, Vol. XXIV, 1962.

Couwenberg, S. W. *Het Nederlandse partijstelsel in toekomstperspectief*, The Hague, Pax, 1960.

Daalder, H. 'De kleine politieke partijen-een voorlopige poging tot inventarisatie', *Acta Politica*, Vol. I, 1965–66.

Daalder, H. 'The Netherlands: Opposition in a Segmented Society', in Dahl, R. A. (ed.), *Political Oppositions in Western Democracies*, New Haven, Yale University Press, 1966.

Daalder, H. 'Parties and Politics in the Netherlands', *Political Studies*, Vol. III, No. 1, Feb. 1955.

Daudt, H. 'Party System and Voters' Influence in the Netherlands', Mimeographed paper presented at the Third International Conference on Comparative Sociology, Berlin, Jan. 16–20, 1968.

Geismann, G. *Politische Struktur und Regierungssystem in den Niederlanden*, Frankfort on Main and Bonn, Athenäum Verlag, 1964.

Leih, H. *Kaart van politiek Nederland*, Kampen, J. H. Kok, 1962.

Lipschits, I. 'De organisatorische structuur der Nederlandse politieke partijen', *Acta Politica*, Vol. II, 1966–67.

Lipschits, I. 'Partijbestuur en fractie', *Acta Politica*, Vol. I, 1965–66.

Lipschits, I. 'De politieke partijen en de selectie van candidaten', *Sociologische Gids*, Vol. X, No. 5, Sept.–Oct. 1963.

Lijphart, A. *The Politics of Accommodation: Pluralism and Democracy in the Netherlands*, Berkeley and Los Angeles, University of California Press, 1968.

Schaper, B. W. 'Religious Groups and Political Parties in Contemporary Holland', in Oxford–Netherlands Historical Conference, Oxford, 1959, Britain and the Netherlands, 1960.

Stichting Nederlands Politiek Jongeren Contact Raad *Politieke Partijen. Functies, geschiedenis en toekomst*, The Hague, 1968.

Verkade, W. *Democratic Parties in the Low Countries and Germany*, Leiden, Universitaire Pers, 1965.

Individual Parties and their Ideologies:

Eekeren, W. A. M. van *The Catholic People's Party in the Netherlands*, Unpublished Ph.D. dissertation, Georgetown University, Washington, D.C., 1956.

Ruitenbeek, H. M. *Het Onstaan van de Partij van de Arbeid* (with a summary 'The Rise and Development of the Dutch Labour Party'), Amsterdam, De Arbeiderspers, 1955.

Political Sociology:

Dam, M. R. A. van, and Beishuizen, J. *Kijk op de kiezer: feiten, cijfers en perspectieven op basis van het Utrechtse kiezeronderzoek van 15 februari 1967*, Amsterdam, Het Parool, 1967.

Goudsblom, J. *Dutch Society*, New York, Random House, 1967.

De Nederlandse Kiezer: een onderzoek naar zijn Gedragingen en opvattingen, The Hague, Staatsdrukkerij-en Uitgeverijbedrijf, 1956.

Electoral Studies:

Kiezer en Verkiezing: verslag van een onderzoek met betrekking tot de verkiezingen van 1956 in Nieuwer Amstel voor de Tweede Kamer der Staten Generaal, Amsterdam, mimeographed paper, 1963.

De Nederlandse Kiezers in 1967, rapport van de afdeling politicologie van het Sociaal-wetenschappelijk Instituut der Vrije Universiteit, Amsterdam, Agon Elsevier, 1967.

AUSTRIA

General Background and History:

Benedirkt, H. (ed.) *Geschichte der Republik Österreich*, Munich, R. Oldenbourg, 1954.

Gorbach, A. *Gedanken zur Politik*, 2nd ed., Vienna, Frick, 1962.

Hiscocks, R. *The Rebirth of Austria*, Oxford University Press, 1953.

Renner, K. *Österreich von der ersten zur zweiten Republik*, Vienna, Wiener Volksbuchhandlung, 1953.

Schärf, A. *Österreichs Wiederaufrichtung in Jahre 1945*, Vienna, Wiener Volksbuchhandlung, 1960.

Schärf, A. *Österreichs Erneuerung, 1945–1955, Das erste Jahrzehnt der zweiten Republik*, rev. ed. Vienna, Wiener Volksbuchhandlung, 1960.

Schorske, C. E. 'Politics in a New Key: Schönerer', in Krieger, L., and Stern, F. R. (eds), *The Responsibility of Power: Historical Essays in Honor of Hajo Holborn*, New York, Doubleday, 1968.

The Party System:

Berchtold, K. (ed.) *Österreichische Parteiprogramme 1868–1966*, Vienna, Verlag für Geschichte und Politik, 1967.

547

Diamant, A. 'The Group Basis of Austrian Politics', *Journal of Central European Affairs*, Vol. XVIII, July 1958.

Engelmann, F. C. 'Austria', in Dahl, R. A. (ed.), *Political Oppositions in Western Democracies*, New Haven, Yale University Press, 1966.

Engelmann, F. C. 'Haggling for the Equilibrium. The Renegotiation of the Austrian Coalition, 1959', *American Political Science Review*, Vol. LVI, Sept. 1962.

Hackl, V. 'The Public Service in Austria', *Revue Internationale des Sciences Administratives*, Vol. XXVIII, No. 2, 1962.

Kafka, G. E. 'Die verfassungsrechtliche Stellung der politischen Parteien im modernen Staat', *Veröffentlichungen der Vereinigung der deutschen Staatsrechtslehrer*, Vol. XVII, Berlin, 1959.

Karisch, A., Korinek, K., and Pelinka, A. 'Parteien und Verbände in Österreich', *Politische Studien*, July–Aug. 1966.

Kirchheimer, O. 'The Waning of Oppositions in Parliamentary Regimes', *Social Research*, Vol. XXIV, Summer 1957.

Lunzer, M. *Die Entstehung der österreichischen Parteien und ihre Presse*, Hrsg. von der Arbeitsgemeinschaft Zeitung und Forschung, Vienna, 1954.

Magenschab, H. *Die zweite Republik zwischen Kirche und Parteien*, Vienna, Herold, 1968.

Marcic, R., and others (eds) *Dokumentation zur Reform der österreichischen Innenpolitik*, Vol. II, Vienna, Europa Verlag, 1968.

Marwick, D., and others *Wahlen und Parteien in Österreich. Österreichisches Wahlhandbuch*, Vienna, Österreichischer Bundesverlag, 1966.

Pittermann, B (ed.) *Mensch und Staat: Handbuch der österreichischen Politik*, Vienna, Danubia Verlag, 1962.

Powelson, L. *The Political Parties of Austria, 1945–1951*, New Haven, Yale University Press, 1953.

Sartori, G. 'Political Development and Political Engineering', *Public Policy*, XVII. Cambridge, Massachusetts, Harvard Graduate School of Public Administration, 1968.

Secher, H. P. 'Coalition Government: The Case of the Second Austrian Republic', *American Political Science Review*, Vol. LVII, Sept. 1958.

Secher, H. P. 'Representative Democracy' or 'Chamber State'. The Ambiguous Role of Interest Groups in Austrian Politics', *Western Political Quarterly*, Vol. XIII, Dec. 1960.

Simon, W. B. *The Political Parties of Austria*, Ann Arbor, University Microfilms, 1957.

Vodopivec, A. *Wer regiert in Österreich? Die Ära Gorbach–Pittermann.* 2nd. ed., Vienna, Verlag für Geschichte und Politik, 1962.

Vodopivec, A. *Die Balkanisierung Österreichs. Die grosse Koalition und ihr Ende*, Vienna and Munich, Molden, 1966.

Individual Parties and their Ideologies:

Buttinger, J. *In the Twilight of Socialism. A History of the Revolutionary Socialists of Austria*, New York, Praeger, 1953.

Diamant, A. *Austrian Catholics and the First Republic*, Princeton, Princeton University Press, 1960.

Figl, L. *Reden für Österreich*, Vienna, Europa Verlag, 1965.

Hannak, J. *Vier Jahre Zweiter Republik: ein Rechenschaftsbericht der Sozialistichen Partei*, Vienna, Wiener Volksbuchhandlung, 1949.

Heindl, G. *1945–1960 Wie wir wurden, der Weg der österreichischen Volkspartei*, Vienna, Bundesparteileitung der Österreichischen Volkspartei, 1961.

Pittermann, B. *Das Zeitalter der Zusammenarbeit. Reden aus zwei Jahrzehnten*, Vienna, Wiener Volksbuchhandlung, 1966.

Shell, K. L. *The Transformation of Austrian Socialism*, Albany, State University of New York, 1962.

Skalnik, K. *Republikanische Mitte: Überlegungen und Überzeugungen*, Vienna, Europa Verlag, 1966.

Whiteside, A. G. 'Austria', in Rogger, H., and Weber, E. (eds), *The European Right. A Historical Profile*, Berkeley and Los Angeles, University of California Press, 1965.

Political Sociology:

Blecha, K., Gmoser, R., and Kienzl, H. *Der durchleuchtete Wähler. Beiträge zur politischen Soziologie in Österreich*, Vienna, Europa Verlag, 1964.

Blecha, K., and Kienzl, H. 'Österreichs Wähler sind in Bewegung', *Die Zukunft*, H.8/9, May 1966.

Bodzenta, E. *Die Katholiken in Österreich. Ein religionssoziologischer Überblick*, Vienna, Herder, 1962.

Lackinger, O. 'Die gesellschaftspolitischen Aussagen des 6. März', *Österreichische Monatshefte*, Vol. XXII, No. 4–5, April–May 1966.

Lackinger, O. *Die regionale Verteilung der Wahlberechtigten. Eine Analyse zur Bevölkerungsentwicklung in Österreich, 1949 bis 1965*, Beiträge zu aktuellen Fragen der Raumordnung 1, Vienna, Österreichisches Institut für Raumplanung, 1966.

Liepelt, K. 'Une typologie des électeurs allemands et autrichiens', *Revue française de sociologie*, Vol. IX, No. 1, January–March 1968.

Electoral Studies:

Kitzinger, U. W. 'The Austrian Election of 1959', *Political Studies*, Vol. IX, June 1961.

Kitzinger, U. W. 'The Austrian Electoral System', *Parliamentary Affairs*, Vol. XII, Summer 1959.

Periodicals:
Die Furche.
Die Zukunft.
Neues Forum.
Österreichische Monatshefte.
Österreichische Zeitschrift für Aussenpolitik.
Wiener politische Blätter.

SCANDINAVIA

General Background and History:

Heckscher, G. *Democratie Efficace*, Paris, Presses universitaires de France, 1957.

Nissen, B. A. *Political Parties in Norway: an Introduction to their History and Ideology*, Oslo, Kongelige Norske Frederiks-Universitet, 1949.

Storing, J. A. *Norwegian Democracy*, Oslo, Universitetsforlag, 1963.

The Party System:

Andrén, N. *Government and Politics in the Nordic Countries*, Stockholm, Almquist and Wiksell, 1964.

Andrén, N. *Modern Swedish Government*, 2nd ed., Stockholm, Almquist and Wiksell, 1968.

Finnish Political Science Association *Democracy in Finland—Studies in Politics and Government*, Helsinki, 1960. (See particularly Bonsdorff, G. von, *The Party Situation in Finland*; Nousiainen, J., *The Structure of the Finnish Political Parties*.)

Hancock, M. D. *Sweden: a Multiparty System in Transition?* University of Denver Press, 1968.

Molin, B. 'Swedish Party Politics: A Case Study', *Scandinavian Political Studies*, No. 1, Helsinki, Göteborg: Akad. förl./Gumpert, 1966.

Nilson, S. S. 'The Political Parties', in Lauwery, J. A. (ed.), *Scandinavian Democracy*, London, Danish Inst., Bailey Bros, 1958.

Pedersen, M. N. 'Consensus and Conflict in the Danish Folketing 1945–1965', *Scandinavian Political Studies*, No. 2, Helsinki, Göteborg: Akad. förl./Gumpert, 1967.

Pedersen, M. N. 'Preferential Voting in Denmark: The Voters' influence on the Election of Folketing Candidates', *Scandinavian Political Studies*, No. 1, Helsinki, Göteborg: Akad. förl./Gumpert, 1966.

Rantala, O. 'The Political Regions of Finland', *Scandinavian Political Studies*, No. 2, Helsinki, Göteborg: Akad. förl./Gumpert, 1967.

Rokkan, S. 'Norway: Numerical Democracy and Corporate Pluralism' in Dahl, R.A. *Political Oppositions in Western Democracies*, New Haven and London, Yale University Press, 1966.

Rokkan, S., and Valen, H. *Parties, Elections, and Political Behavior in the Northern Countries: a Review of Recent Research*, reprinted from Stammer, O. (ed.), *Politische Forschung, Beiträge zum zehnjahrigen Bestehen des Instituts für politische Wissenschaft*, Cologne, Westdeutscher Verlag, 1960.

Rustow, D. A. 'Scandinavia: Working Multiparty Systems', in Neumann, S., *Modern Political Parties*, University of Chicago Press, 1965.

Sjöblom, G. 'Analysis of Party Behavior', *Scandinavian Political Studies*, No. 2, Helsinki, Göteborg: Akad. förl./Gumpert, 1967.

Stjernquist, N. 'Sweden: Stability or Deadlock?' in Dahl, R.A. *Political Oppositions in Western Democracies*, New Haven and London, Yale University Press, 1966.

Further titles in the P.E.P. Series

EUROPEAN UNITY

'Having so much information in one volume is not only useful, but serves as a reminder of the vast complex of levels in which European Governments are in touch with each other. It deserves to be widely read and consulted.'—*Public Administration*

'P.E.P. excels in the objective presentation of facts and the elucidation of complex issues.'—*Times Literary Supplement*

ECONOMIC PLANNING AND POLICIES IN BRITAIN, FRANCE AND GERMANY

'It is extremely valuable to have this comprehensive P.E.P. survey of the experience of planning and economic policies in Britain, France and Germany over the last two decades prepared by specialists on the three countries.'—*New Society*

EUROPEAN ADVANCED TECHNOLOGY

CHRISTOPHER LAYTON

The challenge posed to Europe by American technology has been well publicized in terms of generalities. This book expounds a programme of action for Europe's response.

'Mr Layton's detailed and thoughtful book. Certainly it should be compulsory reading for governments, for civil servants, for industrialists, and for lecturers on European affairs.'—*Times Educational Supplement*

POLITICS AND BUREAUCRACY IN THE EUROPEAN COMMUNITY

DAVID COOMBES

The key institution in the European Common Market is its Commission, and a critical assessment of its role raises new and crucial issues about the basic principles on which the Common Market is based. This book, which is a definitive study of the Commission, is therefore most opportune, especially now that the question of Britain's entry into the European Communities is becoming so vital.

LONDON: GEORGE ALLEN AND UNWIN LTD

GEORGE ALLEN & UNWIN LTD

Head Office
40 Museum Street, London W.C.1
Telephone: 01–405 8577

Sales, Distribution and Accounts Departments
Park Lane, Hemel Hempstead, Herts.
Telephone: 0442 3244

Athens: 34 Panepistimious Street
Auckland: P.O. Box 36013, Northcote Central N.4
Barbados: P.O. Box 222, Bridgetown
Beirut: Deeb Building, Jeanne d'Arc Street
Bombay: 103/5 Fort Street, Bombay 1
Calcutta: 285J Bepin Behari Ganguli Street, Calcutta 12
Cape Town: 68 Shortmarket Street
Hong Kong: 105 Wing On Mansion, 26 Hancow Road, Kowloon
Ibadan: P.O. Box 62
Karachi: Karachi Chambers, McLeod Road
Madras: 2/18 Mount Road, Madras
Mexico: Villalongin 32, Mexico 5, D.F.
Nairobi: P.O. Box 30583
Philippines: P.O. Box 157, Quezon City D–502
Rio de Janeiro: Caixa Postal 2537–Zc–00
Singapore: 36c Prinsep Street, Singapore 7
Sydney N.S.W.: Bradbury House, 55 York Street
Tokyo: C.P.O. Box 1728, Tokyo 100–91
Toronto: 81 Curlew Drive, Don Mills

Valen, H., and Katz, D. *Political Parties in Norway*, London, Tavistock Publications, 1964.

Verney, D. *Parliamentary Reform in Sweden*, Oxford University Press, 1957.

Individual Parties and their Ideologies:

Berg, O. 'Basic Dimensions of Finnish Party Ideologies. A Factor Analytical Study', *Scandinavian Political Studies*, No. 1, Helsinki, Göteborg: Akad. förl./Gumpert, 1966.

Fusilier, R. *Le Parti Socialiste suedois: son organisation*, Paris, Les Editions ouvrières, 1954.

Political Sociology:

Särlvik, B. 'Political Stability and Change in the Swedish Electorate', *Scandinavian Political Studies*, No. 1, Helsinki, Göteborg: Akad. förl./Gumpert, 1966.

Särlvik, B. 'Party Politics and Electoral Opinion Formation: A Study of Issues in Swedish Politics 1956–1960', *Scandinavian Political Studies*, No. 2, Helsinki, Göteborg, Akad. forl./Gumpert, 1967.

Valen, H. 'The Recruitment of Parliamentary Nominees in Norway', *Scandinavian Political Studies*, No. 1, Helsinki, Göteborg: Akad. förl./Gumpert, 1966.

SWITZERLAND

(In view of the extreme shortage of material on Swiss political parties, a slightly different form of presentation has been adopted.)

General Background:

Hughes, C. J. *The Parliament of Switzerland*, London, Cassell for the Hansard Society, 1962, (this covers the whole structure of representation at federal level).

Gruner, E., Frey, K., etc. *Die Schweizerische Bundesversammlung*, 1848–1920, Berne, Francke, 1966, (this is essential as a work of reference for information on the parties pre–1919).

Meynaud, J., and Korff, A. *Les organizations professionelles en Suisse*, Lausanne, 1963, (this deals with the influence of vocational pressure groups).

The Party System:

Gruner, E. *Die Parteien in der Schweiz*, Bern, 1969, (the first full length study of political parties, but published too late to be taken account of in the preparation of this book. It does, though, contain a full bibliography).

Lachenal, F. *Le parti politique, sa fonction en droit publique*, Basle, Helbing et Lichtenhahn, 1944, (a challenging study heavily influenced by Michels).

Individual Parties:

Masnata, F. *Le Parti Socialiste et la tradition democratique en Suisse*, Neuchâtel, Editions de la Baconnière, 1963.

Meynaud, J., and Korff, A. *La Migros et la Politique, L'Alliance des Indépendants*, Lausanne, 1965, (this deals with the Landesring).

Writers who have contributed important articles to learned journals on Swiss political parties include: Erich Gruner, Roger Girod (especially in *Cahiers internationaux de sociologie*, July–December 1965), Jean Meynaud, M. Rosenberg (on the Catholic Party, in *Politische Studien*, July–August 1964). The most thorough method of scavenging information is through the bibliographical notes contained in the *Annuaires suisses de science politique* (Roland Ruffieux).

Elections

The Federal Statistical Bureau in Berne publishes an analysis after each National Council Election. This contains data on for example the extent to which voters for one party list select isolated candidates from other lists. Cruder statistics are to be found in the *Annuaire Statistique Suisse*.

UNITED KINGDOM

Reports:

Conservative Party *Campaign Guide, 1966*
Conservative Political Centre reports.
Labour Party, *Annual Conference Report*.
Labour Party *Twelve Wasted Years*.
Liberal Party *Annual Report*.

Also publications by Bow Group and Fabian Society.

General Background and History:

Blondel, J. *Voters, Parties and Leaders; The Social Fabric of British Politics*, London, Penguin, 1963.

Cole, G. D. H. *A History of the Labour Party from 1914*, London, Routledge, 1948.

MacFarlane, C. J. *The Communist Party: Its Origin and Development until 1929*, London, MacGibbon and Kee, 1966.

Miliband, R. *Parliamentary Socialism*, London, Allen and Unwin, 1961.

Pelling, H. M. *A Short History of the Labour Party*, 3rd ed., London, Macmillan, 1968.

Poirier, P. *The Advent of the Labour Party*, London, Allen and Unwin, 1958.

Pulzer, P. *Political Representation and Elections in Britain*, London, Allen and Unwin, 1967.

Tracey, H. *The British Labour Party: its History, Growth, Policy, and Leaders*, London, Caxton Publishing Co., 1948.

The Party System:

Bailey, S. (ed.)   *The British Party System: a Symposium,* 2nd ed., London, Hansard Society, 1953.

Bailey, R. (ed.)   *The Practice of Politics,* rev. ed., London, Conservative Political Centre, 1952.

Beer, S. H.   *Modern British Politics: a Study of Parties and Pressure Groups,* London, Faber, 1965.

Bow Group   *The Conservative Opportunity,* London, Batsford, 1965.

Britten, S.   *Left or Right; the Bogus Dilemma,* London, Secker and Warburg, 1968.

Budge and Urwin   *Scottish Political Behaviour,* London, Longmans, Green, 1966.

Bulmer-Thomas, I.   *The Growth of the British Party System,* 2 vols, 2nd ed., London, John Baker, 1967.

Derry, J. W.   *Political Parties,* London, Macmillan, 1968.

Jennings, I.   *Party Politics,* 3 vols, Cambridge University Press, 1960–62.

Maynos, S.   *The Churches and the Labour Movement,* London, Independent Press, 1967.

McKenzie, R. T.   *British Political Parties,* 2nd ed., London, Heinemann, 1964.

Pritt, D. N.   *The Labour Government, 1945–51,* London, Lawrence and Wishart, 1963.

Rose, R.   ed. *Studies in British Politics,* London, Macmillan, 1966.

Individual Parties and their Ideologies:

Brand, C. F.   *The British Labour Party,* Stanford University Press, 1965.

Crosland, C. A. R.   *The Future of Socialism,* London, Jonathan Cape, 1956.

Dowse, R. E.   'The Parliamentary Labour Party in Opposition', *Parliamentary Affairs,* Vol. 13 (4), Autumn 1960.

Harrison, M.   *Trade Unions and the Labour Party since 1945,* London, Allen and Unwin, 1960.

Hoffman, J. D.   *The Conservative Party in Opposition, 1945–1951,* London, MacGibbon and Key, 1964.

Janosik, E.   *Constituency Labour Politics in Britain,* London, Pall Mall, 1968.

Rasmussen, J. S.   *The Liberal Party—A Study of Retrenchment and Revival,* London, Constable, 1965.

Thayer, G.   *The British Political Fringe: a Profile,* London, Anthony Blond, 1965.

Watkins, A.   *The Liberal Dilemma,* London, MacGibbon and Key, 1966.

White, R. J. (ed.)   *The Conservative Tradition,* London, Black, 1950.

Political Sociology:

Bealey, F. *et. al.*   *Constituency Politics—A Study of Newcastle under Lyme,* London, Faber and Faber, 1965.

Goldthorpe, *et al.*   *The Affluent Worker: Political Attitudes and Behaviour,* Cambridge University Press, 1968.

Guttsman, W. *The British Political Elite*, London, MacGibbon and Kee, 1965.

McKenzie, R. T. *Angels in Marble: Working-class Conservatives in Urban England*, University of Chicago Press, 1968.

Nordlinger, E. A. *The Working-class Tories: Authority, Deference, and Stable Democracy*, London, MacGibbon and Kee, 1967.

Rose, R. *Influencing Voters*, London, Faber, 1967.

Electoral Studies:

McCallum, R., and Readman, A. *The British General Election of 1945*, Oxford University Press, 1947.

Nicholas, H. *The British General Election of 1950*, London, Macmillan, 1951.

Butler, D. *The British General Election of 1951*, London, Macmillan, 1952.

Butler, D. *The British General Election of 1955*, London, Macmillan, 1955. (Reprinted by Cass.)

Butler, D., and Rose, R. *The British General Election of 1959*, London, Macmillan, 1960.

Butler, D., and King, A. *The British General Election of 1964*, London, Macmillan, 1965.

Butler, D., and King, A. *The British General Election of 1966*, London, Macmillan, 1966.

Butler, D. *The Electoral System in Britain since 1918*, Oxford University Press, 2nd ed., 1963.

Periodicals:
The Political Quarterly.
Political Studies.

Other Sources and Statistics:

Butler, D. E., and Freeman, J. *British Political Facts, 1900–67*, London, Macmillan, 1968.

The Times *Guide to the House of Commons* (revised edition after each General Election).

Mckenzie, R. T. *British Political Parties, op. cit.*, and Pulzer, P. *Political Representation and Elections in Britain, op. cit.*, both contain exhaustive bibliographies.

IRELAND

Chubb, B. (ed.) *A Source Book of Irish Government*, Dublin, Institute of Public Administration, 1964.

Coogan, T. P. *Ireland since the Rising*, London, Pall Mall Press, 1966.

McCracken, J. L. *Representative Government in Ireland*, Oxford University Press, 1959.

Moss, W. *Political Parties in the Irish Free State*, New York, Columbia University Press; London, P. S. King and Sons, 1933.

Rumpf, E. *Nationalismus und Sozialismus in Irland*, Meisenheim am Glan, A. Hain, 1959.

Thornley, D. A. 'Development of the Irish Labour Movement', in *Christus Rex*, Vol. 18, 1964.

EUROPEAN PARLIAMENTARY INSTITUTIONS

Political Groups in European Assemblies:

Anderson, S. V. *The Nordic Council, A Study of Scandinavian Regionalism*, Seattle, University of Washington Press, 1967.

Haas, E. B. *Consensus Formation in the Council of Europe*, London, Stevens, 1960.

Haas, E. B., and Merkl, P. 'Parliamentarians against Ministers: The Case of Western European Union', *International Organization*, Vol. XIV, 1960.

Hovey, J. A. *The Superparliaments*, New York, Praeger, 1966.

Krämer, H. *Die Stellung der politischen Parteien in der Völkerkammer eines künftigen Europa-Parlaments*, (Thesis), Mainz, 1957.

Lindsay, K. *European Assemblies: The Experimental Period, 1949–1959*, London, Stevens, 1960.

Merkl, P. H. 'European Assembly Parties and National Delegations', *Journal of Conflict Resolution*, Vol. VIII, 1964.

Neunreither, K. *Le rôle du Parlement dans la formation de décision des communautés européenes*, Paper presented to the Colloque on 'La décision dans les organisations européenes', Lyons, 1960. A German version to be found in *Europa-Archiv*, 1966, No. 22.

Political and Economic Planning. *European Unity. A Survey of the European Organizations*, M. Palmer and others, London, Allen and Unwin, 1968.

Political and Economic Planning. *The Parliament of the European Communities*, M. Forsyth, P.E.P. Vol. XXX, No. 478, London, 1964.

Robertson, A. H. *Constitutional Developments in the Council of Europe*, Brussels, Universitaire Libre de Bruxelles, 1964.

Robertson, A. H. *European Institutions, Co-operation, Integration, Unification*, London, Stevens, 1966.

Spinelli, A. *The Eurocrats. Conflict and Crisis in the European Community*, Baltimore, Johns Hopkins Press, 1966.

Stein, E. 'The European Parliamentary Assembly: Techniques of Emerging Political Control', *International Organization*, Vol. 13, 1959.

Van Oudenhove, G. *The Political Parties in the European Parliament*, Leiden, Sijthoff, 1965.

Zellentin, G. 'Form and Function of the Opposition in the European Communities', *Government and Opposition*, Vol. 2, No. 2, April 1967.

INDEX

INDEX

Nenni, Pietro, 215–17, 223, 224, 242, 523
Netherlands 256–81
  background 258–64
  bibliography, 546–7
  Catholic party , 260–1
  characteristics of the party system, 268–81
  Democrats 66, 266–7
  election results, 262
  Farmers' party, 265
  Liberals, 261–3
  multipolarity, 507–8
  party finance, 271–2
  party membership, 271
  Protestant parties, 259–60
  recent political developments, 264–8
  Socialists, 263–4
Neumann, S., 27n, 45n
Neunreither, Dr Karl-Heinz, 484, 485, 497, 498n, 503n
Nicholson, Nigel, 416–17
Nicols, P., 253n
  background, 258–64
Nordic Council, 467–9, 475
Norway, 320–64
  election results, 342–3
  government composition, 343–4
  unipolarity, 505–6
  see also Scandinavia
Nouvelles Equipes Internationales, see European Union of Christian Democrats

Olah, Franz, 299, 308, 310
Ollenhauer, Erich, 35, 40, 41, 60, 65

Pajetta, 210
Papen, Franz von, 28
Parri, 228
Passigli, S., 212n, 213n, 223n, 234
Paul VI, 253n
Pavolini, P., 219n, 224n
Peel, Sir Robert, 431
Pelinka, A., 295n, 299n
Pella, Giuseppe, 232
Pétain, Henri Philippe, 101
Peter, Friedrich, 298
Petitpierre ,382
Pêtre, R., 91
Pfleiderer, Karl, 62
Pickles, Dorothy, 119n

Pinay, Antoine, 120, 131
Pinson, Koppel S., 25n
Pirker, Theo, 35n
Pittermann, Dr Bruno, 293, 316, 318
Pizzorno, A., 198n, 199, 204n, 247n
Pleven, Réné, 115, 185, 491, 515
Poher, Alain, 161, 484
Pohlmann, Siegfried, 58
Pompidou, Georges, 123, 130, 131, 145, 146, 153, 154, 170, 318
Posner, M. V., 198n
Poujade, Pierre, 106
Pulzer, P. G. J., 284n

Queuille, Henri, 114

Raab, Julius, 296, 308, 310
Radoux, 482
Reale, 210
Reimann, Viktor, 297, 298
Reinthaller, Anton, 298
Remer, Major Otto, 56
Remond, R., 180
Renner, Karl, 285, 304
Republic of Ireland, 447–64
  background, 449–52
  bibliography, 554–5
  election results, 463–4
  Fianna Fail, 452–3, 459
  Fine Gael, 453
  international relations of parties, 460–3
  Labour party, 454, 459
  party finance, 458–9
  party membership, 456–7
  party system, 507
  political system, 447–8
Reuter, Professor Ernst, 38, 39
Robertson, A. H., 467n, 470n, 473n
Rocard, Michel, 170
Rose, Professor Richard, 212n, 406n, 410n, 416n, 426, 427, 434, 443n
Rutschke, 62

Salisbury, Lord, 388
Salomone, W. A., 194n
Samuel, Lord, 202
Santoro, C., 250n
Saragat, Giuseppe, 213, 216, 224, 245n
Scandinavia, 320–64
  attitudes towards Europe, 362–4
  bibliography, 550–1
  Communist parties, 324

563